# VIDEO GAMES
# AND GAMING CULTURE

T0144439

# VIDEO GAMES AND GAMING CULTURE

Critical Concepts in Media and Cultural Studies

*Edited by*
*Mark J. P. Wolf*

**Volume III**
**Play and Players**

Routledge
Taylor & Francis Group
LONDON AND NEW YORK

First published 2016
by Routledge
2 Park Square, Milton Park, Abingdon, Oxon OX14 4RN

and by Routledge
711 Third Avenue, New York, NY 10017

*Routledge is an imprint of the Taylor & Francis Group, an informa business*

*British Library Cataloguing in Publication Data*
A catalogue record for this book is available from the British Library

*Library of Congress Cataloging in Publication Data*
A catalog record for this book has been requested

ISBN: 978-1-138-81125-6 (Set)
ISBN: 978-1-138-81130-0 (Volume III)

Typeset in Times New Roman
by Book Now Ltd, London

**Publisher's Note**
References within each chapter are as they appear in the original complete work

# CONTENTS

CONTENTS

vii

# ACKNOWLEDGEMENTS

The Publishers would like to thank the following for permission to reprint their material:

Routledge for permission to reprint Torben Grodal, 'Stories for Eye, Ear, and Muscles: Video Games, Media, and Embodied Experiences', in Mark J. P. Wolf and Bernard Perron (eds), *The Video Game Theory Reader* (New York, NY: Routledge, 2003), pp. 129–155.

Routledge for permission to reprint Andreas Gregersen and Torben Grodal, 'Embodiment and Interface', in Bernard Perron and Mark J. P. Wolf (eds), *The Video Game Theory Reader 2* (New York, NY: Routledge, 2008), pp. 65–83.

James Newman, 'The Myth of the Ergodic Videogame: Some Thoughts on Player-character Relationships in Videogames', *Game Studies: The International Journal of Computer Game Research*, 2(1), July 2002, available at http://www. gamestudies.org/0102/newman/.

Routledge for permission to reprint Bob Rehak, 'Playing at Being: Psychoanalysis and the Avatar', in Mark J. P. Wolf and Bernard Perron (eds), *The Video Game Theory Reader* (New York, NY: Routledge, 2003), pp. 103–127.

Helen W. Kennedy, 'Lara Croft: Feminist Icon or Cyberbimbo? On the Limits of Textual Analysis', *Game Studies: The International Journal of Computer Game Research*, 2(2), December 2002, available at http://www.gamestudies.org/0202/ kennedy/.

*Eludamos: Journal for Computer Game Culture* for permission to reprint Jennifer Jenson and Suzanne de Castell, 'Theorizing Gender and Digital Gameplay: Oversights, Accidents and Surprises', *Eludamos: Journal for Computer Game Culture*, 2(1), 2008, 15–25.

Anna Everett, 'Serious Play: Playing with Race in Contemporary Gaming Culture', in Joost Raessens and Jeffrey Goldstein (eds), *Handbook of Computer Game Studies* (Cambridge, MA: The MIT Press, 2005), pp. 311–325.

Anna Everett and S. Craig Watkins, 'The Power of Play: The Portrayal and Performance of Race in Video Games', in Katie Salen (ed.), *The Ecology of Games: Connecting Youth, Games, and Learning* (Cambridge, MA: The MIT Press, 2008), pp. 141–164.

Anna Everett, 'Race', in Mark J. P. Wolf and Bernard Perron (eds), *The Routledge Companion to Video Game Studies* (New York, NY: Routledge, 2014), pp. 396–406.

Sage for permission to reprint T. L. Taylor, 'The Assemblage of Play', *Games and Culture*, 4(4), 2009, 331–339.

Bernard Perron, 'Coming to Play at Frightening Yourself: Welcome to the World of Horror Video Games', *Aesthetics of Play: A Conference on Computer Game Aesthetics*, Norway, University of Bergen, 2005, available at http://www. aestheticsofplay.org/perron.php.

Digital Games Research Association for permission to reprint Espen Aarseth, 'I Fought the Law: Transgressive Play and the Implied Player', *Situated Play: Proceedings of DiGRA 2007 Conference*, Digital Games Research Association (DiGRA), Japan, The University of Tokyo, 2007, pp. 130–133.

Taylor & Francis for permission to reprint Torben Grodal, 'Video Games and the Pleasures of Control', in Dolf Zillmann and Peter Vorderer (eds), *Media Entertainment: The Psychology of its Appeal* (Mahwah, NJ: Lawrence Erlbaum Associates Publishers, 2000), pp. 197–213.

Radical Philosophy for permission to reprint Alexander R. Galloway, 'Allegories of Control', *Gaming: Essays on Algorithmic Culture* (Minneapolis, MN: University of Minnesota Press, 2006), pp. 85–106.

Katie Salen and Eric Zimmerman, 'The Magic Circle', *Rules of Play: Game Design Fundamentals* (Cambridge, MA: The MIT Press, 2003), pp. 93–99.

Sage for permission to reprint Mia Consalvo, 'There is No Magic Circle', *Games and Culture*, 4(4), 2009, 408–417.

The author for permission to reprint Eric Zimmerman, 'Jerked Around by the Magic Circle – Clearing the Air Ten Years Later', *Gamasutra.com*, 2012, available at http://www.gamasutra.com/view/feature/135063/jerked_around_by_the_ magic_circle_.php.

Laura Ermi and Frans Mäyrä, 'Fundamental Components of the Gameplay Experience: Analysing Immersion', in Stephan Günzel, Michael Liebe, and Dieter Mersch (eds), *DIGAREC Keynote-Lectures 2009/10* (Potsdam: Potsdam University Press, 2011), pp. 88–113, available at http://pub.ub.uni-potsdam.de/ volltexte/2011/4983/ [urn:nbn:de:kobv:512-opus-49831].

Piotr Kubiński, 'Immersion vs. Emersive Effects in Videogames', in Dawn Stobbart and Monica Evans (eds), *Engaging with Videogames: Play, Theory and Practice* (Oxford, England: Inter-Disciplinary Press, 2014), pp. 133-14 [e-book].

Julian Dibbell, 'A Rape in Cyberspace: How an Evil Clown, a Haitian Trickster Spirit, Two Wizards, and a Cast of Dozens Turned a Database into a Society', *The Village Voice*, December 23, 1993, 36–42.

The author for permission to reprint Gonzalo Frasca, 'Ephemeral Games: Is It Barbaric to Design Videogames after Auschwitz?', *Cybertext Yearbook 2000* (Saarijärvi, Finland: University of Jyväskayla, 2000), pp. 172–182.

American Psychological Association for permission to reprint Craig A. Anderson and Karen E. Dill, 'Video Games and Aggressive Thoughts, Feelings, and Behavior in the Laboratory and in Life', *Journal of Personality and Social Psychology*, 78(4), April 2000, 772–790.

Craig A. Anderson and Brad J. Bushman, 'Effects of Violent Video Games on Aggressive Behavior, Aggressive Cognition, Aggressive Affect, Physiological Arousal, and Prosocial Behavior: A Meta-Analytic Review of the Scientific Literature', *Psychological Science*, 12(5), September 2001, 353–359.

American Psychological Association for permission to reprint Craig A. Anderson, Akiko Shibuya, Nobuko Ihori, Edward L. Swing, Brad J. Bushman, Akira Sakamoto, Hannah R. Rothstein, and Muniba Saleem, 'Violent Video Game Effects on Aggression, Empathy, and Prosocial Behavior in Eastern and Western Countries: A Meta-Analytic Review', *Psychological Bulletin*, 136(2), 2010, 151–173.

Bernard Perron, 'Sign of a Threat: The Effects of Warning Systems in Survival Horror Games', *COSIGN 2004 Proceedings*, Art Academy, University of Split (Croatia), 2004, pp. 132–141.

Sage for permission to reprint Andrew K. Przybylski, Richard M. Ryan, and C. Scott Rigby, 'The Motivating Role of Violence in Video Games', *Personality and Social Psychology Bulletin*, 35(2), February 2009, 243–259.

## Disclaimer

# INTRODUCTION TO VOLUME III

*Mark J. P. Wolf*

## Part 6: Embodiment and identity

Video games bridge the gap from physical to digital, and from the real world to secondary worlds; so it is only natural that one of the topics that appears repeatedly in video game studies is that of embodiment, since the player controls (some might even say "inhabits") the avatar on-screen, forging a relationship between the two which is different than that of a spectator and a character in a movie. At the same time, identity is also still functioning, and in multiplayer games, especially those like MMORPGs, the player-character's identity and the player's identity are closely connected, even though they are inevitably different. The first essay of the section, Torben Grodal's "Stories for Eye, Ear, and Muscles: Video Games, Media, and Embodied Experiences" (2003), applies cognitive psychology to video games and looks at how they provide experiences which are simulations of basic modes of real-life experiences, and more than simply audiovisual ones. He suggests that such an approach is more fruitful than a merely semiotic one, an idea that has even more relevancy now that gestural controllers have come into use. Writing five years later, Grodal and Andreas Gregersen advance some of these ideas further in their essay, "Embodiment and Interface" (2008), looking at how play is rooted in biological embodiment. Embodiment connects us to the environment, allowing us to influence it as well as become influenced by it. Gregersen and Grodal note how different types of interfaces and game worlds affect players' embodied experiences.

Embodiment is also related to identity, and Bob Rehak's essay, "Playing at Being: Psychoanalysis and the Avatar" (2003), traces the evolution of avatars, revealing ongoing concerns with the player-character's capabilities and vulnerabilities, as well as its relationship to player corporeality. His essay shows how point of view in first-person shooting games constitutes a powerful interpellative system in which players take on the avatar's perspective as their own, using psychoanalytic concepts to explore this aspect of avatarial operations. James Newman's essay, "The Myth of the Ergodic Videogame: Some Thoughts on Player-character Relationships in Videogames" (2002), takes the stance that "primary-player-character relationship is one of vehicular embodiment" and examines just how ergodic video games really are, when cut-scenes, informational screens, and other

1

interruptions of game action are taken into account and also how these affect the identity of the player-character.

Identity is closely connected to embodiment, since bodies are such an integral part of identity. The next two essays explore issues of gender and identity in video games and the theorizing of it as well. The first essay, Helen W. Kennedy's "Lara Croft: Feminist Icon or Cyberbimbo? On the Limits of Textual Analysis" (2002), takes a look at the ambivalent reception given to Lara Croft of *Tomb Raider* (1996) and the difficulty of positioning her as a cultural icon, and the fact that she is a video game character controlled by the player complicates things even further than if she were merely a character in a film. The second essay, "Theorizing Gender and Digital Gameplay: Oversights, Accidents and Surprises" (2008) by Jennifer Jenson and Suzanne de Castell, "is an attempt to rethink the assumptions and presumptions of work on gender and gameplay in an effort to demarcate more clearly how those are not only implicated in our analyses to date, but also misleading and misdirecting what we could 'find' and what might well be present if we had a different framework for viewing." Ever conscious of their own methodology, the authors raise engaging questions for researchers of games and gender.

Race is another aspect of identity which has been investigated in video games. In the last three essays in this section, race studies scholar Anna Everett writes about race in video games. The first essay, "Serious Play: Playing with Race in Contemporary Gaming Culture" (2005), examines the role of race not only in video games and their characters but also in paratexts such as video game user manuals, strategy guides, computer game magazines, and other such materials in gaming culture. Written with S. Craig Watkins, Everett's second essay, "The Power of Play: The Portrayal and Performance of Race in Video Games" (2007), looks at the influence of the depiction of race in games and asks what younger players' interactions with video games teach them about race and race-related issues. Finally, Everett's third essay is the "Race" entry in *The Routledge Companion to Video Game Studies* (2014), which provides an up-to-date general overview of the topic of race in video games in a succinct but detailed survey.

## Part 7: Play, control, and the magic circle

Crucial to the study of games is the study of play, which, as Huizinga has shown, is older than culture itself. One aspect of play—control (and perhaps lack of control as well)—is central to such an examination and particularly in video games where the machine controls the game yet allows a certain amount of player control as well. Control of the game world also leads to Huizinga's concept of "the magic circle", the space of the game world where the game's rules apply which is set off from the rest of the world and the concept of immersion. Writings on all of these issues appear in this section.

The first essay, T. L. Taylor's "The Assemblage of Play" (2009), applies the idea of assemblage to game studies and proposes a methodological approach to games and play, looking at mods (user-created modifications of games) in *World of Warcraft* (2004) and discussing the relationship between technology, the gaming experience, and the actors involved. The next essay, Bernard Perron's "Coming to Play at Frightening Yourself: Welcome to the World of Horror Games" (2005), looks at a very particular type of play, that of being frightened. He notes how the horror genre itself has always been gamelike and discusses its adaptation into games. Espen Aarseth's essay, "I Fought the Law: Transgressive Play and the Implied Player" (2007), discusses the notion of the implied player and its relationship with transgressive play.

Torben Grodal's essay, "Video Games and the Pleasures of Control" (2000), is an early look at the role of control in video games, and Grodal argues that danger and violence in video games can serve cognitive and emotional learning processes. He compares emotions and their contexts in real life, in film, and in video games and how they differ. Alexander R. Galloway's essay, "Allegories of Control" from his book *Gaming: Essays on Algorithmic Culture* (2006), looks at video games as algorithmic objects that represent systems of control and display those systems in ways unlike film, television, and other media and without sublimating them. He argues that video games are "at their structural core, in direct synchronization with the political realities of the informatic age" and initimately tied to contemporary experiences.

The notion of the magic circle is discussed by Katie Salen and Eric Zimmerman in "The Magic Circle" from their book *Rules of Play: Game Design Fundamentals* (2003), while Mia Consalvo's essay, "There is No Magic Circle" (2009), critiques the very notion and existence of the magic circle. Finally, Eric Zimmerman's "Jerked around by the Magic Circle—Clearing the Air 10 Years Later" (2012), examines the use of the magic circle concept in game studies, the attitudes toward it, and the value that it has.

Immersion is the topic of the section's last two essays. Laura Ermi and Franz Mäyrä's essay, "Fundamental Components of Gameplay Experience: Analysing Immersion" (2011), examines the role of immersion in games and proposes a gameplay experience model. Writing about the reverse process which is rarely discussed, Piotr Kubiński's essay, "Emersion as an element of gaming experience" (2014), explores the idea of *emersion*, the experience of players coming out of a game, something which occurs inadvertently but which also can be the result of a game designer's deliberate design. All these essays, taken together, provide a wide range of views regarding the game player's experience.

## Part 8: Threat, aggression, and violence

Since their earliest days, questions about representations of violent acts, ethics within virtual settings, aggression, and desensitization of the viewer and player toward violence seen on screen have been raised and discussed. While the ontology of video game worlds and characters is clearly different from that of the real world, the connections and overlap between the two, as well as the ways play in the former affects what players do in the latter, are still the subject of debate. The first essay in this section, Julian Dibbell's often-cited essay, "A Rape in Cyberspace: How an Evil Clown, a Haitian Trickster Spirit, Two Wizards, and a Cast of Dozens Turned a Database into a Society" (1993), is a real-world case study of online violence and its effects and consequences among the players of the online community in which it occurred. Next, Gonzalo Frasca's essay, "Ephemeral Games: Is It Barbaric to Design Videogames after Auschwitz?" (2000), argues that "that current computer game design conventions have structural characteristics which prevent them from dealing with 'serious' content" and considers what kind of limitations video games face when they attempt to deal with certain topics.

The next three essays look at the role of aggression in video game play and the study of violence in video games. Craig A. Anderson and Karen E. Dill's well-known study, "Video Games and Aggressive Thoughts, Feelings, and Behavior in the Laboratory and in Life" (2000), demonstrates links between aggressive behavior and video games, using quantitative methods and the General Affective Aggression Model (GAAM). The next two essays, "Effects of Violent Video Games on Aggressive Behavior, Aggressive Cognition, Aggressive Affect, Physiological Arousal, and Prosocial Behavior: A Meta-Analytic Review of the Scientific Literature" (2001) by Craig A. Anderson and Brad J. Bushman, and "Violent Video Game Effects on Aggression, Empathy, and Prosocial Behavior in Eastern and Western Countries: A Meta-Analytic Review" (2010) by Craig A. Anderson, Akiko Shibuya, Nobuko Ihori, Edward L. Swing, Brad J. Bushman, Akira Sakamoto, Hannah R. Rothstein, and Muniba Saleem, are both meta-analyses which compile the data from a variety of studies for an overall look at the work that has been done on the effects of video games associated with aggression and violent behavior, with interesting results.

The last two essays in this section examine particular aspects of violence in video games. Bernard Perron's essay, "Sign of a Threat: The Effects of Warning Systems in Survival Horror Games" (2004), looks at how horror games use player expectations and anticipation of violence to heighten the gaming experience, making comparisons between video games and movies. Finally, "The Motivating Role of Violence in Video Games" (2009) by Andrew K. Przybylski, Richard M. Ryan, and C. Scott Rigby demonstrates that violence adds little or no motivation or enjoyment to video game play, once the need for autonomy and competence have been satisfied, showing that the presence of the latter two aspects is of much greater importance to the average gamer.

# Part 6

# EMBODIMENT AND IDENTITY

# 45

# STORIES FOR EYE, EAR, AND MUSCLES

## Video games, media, and embodied experiences

*Torben Grodal*

Source: Mark J. P. Wolf and Bernard Perron (eds), *The Video Game Theory Reader* (New York, NY: Routledge, 2003), pp. 129–155.

### Video games, media, stories, and the embodied brain

A common way of describing representational structures is by way of media. Central problems such as "narrative" or "point of view" are explained by referring to those media forms in which we ordinarily find manifestations of such structures. Some researchers, for example, define narratives by referring to literary works, others, like Brenda Laurel,[1] describe video games and other computer applications by reference to theatre and theatrical structures. Such descriptions have some advantages, but also problematic consequences, because phenomena such as "story" or "narrative" are then only defined in relation to their media realizations, not by their relation to unmediated real-life experiences and those mental structures that support such experiences. This raises special problems for describing mediated activities such as virtual reality and video games because these activities are in several dimensions simulations of real-life activities. Media representations are better described as different realizations of basic real-life experiences. As early as 1916, the Harvard psychologist Hugo Münsterberg[2] showed how the film experience might be described as a cued simulation of central mental and bodily functions. Such an approach provides many advantages for describing video games, because, as I will argue in detail in the following, videogames and other types of interactive virtual reality are simulations of basic modes of real-life experiences. This also means that cognitive psychology provides many advantages as a tool for describing video games compared with a semiotic approach; even if games may be provided with some symbolic signs, most of the game activity consist in seeing, hearing and doing in a simulation of a real-world interaction.

Before proceeding further, let me provide a definition of "story":[3] a story is a sequence of events focused by one (a few) living being(s); the events are based on simulations of experiences in which there is a constant interaction of perceptions, emotions, cognitions and actions. An example: Harry sees the dragon coming, he is upset, thinks that he needs to grasp his sword, he does that, and he kills the dragon. The experience of stories is based on central embodied mental mechanisms. The primary story-regulating brain structures are probably located in amygdala-hippocampus, the left peri-Sylvian region, the frontal cortices and their subcortical connections,[4] but these structures rely on many other cognitive and emotional mechanisms.[5] Our experience of stories exist as representation of exterior worlds and they may be described as such, but at the same time they are body-brain-internal processes that need to follow the innate specification of that platform.

The story-mechanisms in the brain provide the superior framework for our experience of events by integrating perceptions, emotions, cognitions and actions. When going to the supermarket, for instance, a micro story in our mind tells us that we have left home because we desired to buy vegetables, that we are now at the entrance of the mall and tells us our ideas of how to find the grocery store. The micro story thus orients us in space, describes our desires and projects and thus guides our motor actions. Damage to some brain structures important for "narrative" may lead to confusion: where am I and why, where shall I go, and so on. The story includes a quest and its motivation. The story also can be a medium-sized one: I met Linda, we had some lovely days in San Diego, she disappeared, but I want to find her again. The story can furthermore be a macro story of my life up till now, including how the past set up some agendas for my future.[6] In such stories there are actors and settings, actions and happenings, but not because such elements exists in mediated representations, like novels dramas or video games, but because such things are important for my experience of, navigation in, and interaction with the world. Stories are based on innate mental functions that match the ecological niche of humans, they are not just social constructions or media constructions. Even if the basic story structure (agency, setting, actions, etc.) is based on functions shaped in our embodied brain by evolution, we may of course fill in real as well as invented material in our stories, and learning mediated stories may enhance our ability to structure nonmediated events.

Human motivations exist in a nested hierarchy. There are high-order goals, like those folktale motives of being married or becoming a king, or high-order existential goals such as survival, as in horror fiction. High-order goals may presuppose lower goals, like courting or fighting dragons; the last may presuppose getting a good weapon, a magic sword, or laser gun. Such goals presuppose that you sleep and eat. At a basic level, you may have simple muscular activations and very basic perceptions. The representation may focus on high-order goals and motivations, because such goals are emotionally very activating, and may to a varying extent recruit nested activities. Some scholars may think that such high-order "dramatic" events are essential to a definition of stories. However, realism or modern high art narratives may focus on low-level events, like kitchen sink realism, stream- of-consciousness, and Sarraute's *tropisms*. Video games may have some high-order motivations, but for a series of reasons games will often also have a strong focus on the execution of low-level (sub)goals like simple navigation and handling processes. An intro to the game may provide the superior motivation, say, to crush an evil empire, and this will provide motivation for the lower-order processes.

My characterization of "story" accords with state-of-the-art psychological descriptions and has the advantage in comparison to those definitions that define narrative as "cognitive-logical" patterns in that it makes explicit how many story events that are described as "logical" consist of emotional-motivational reaction patterns. In *Moving Pictures*,[7] I have shown how film experience may be described by a flow model: the fundamental narrative flow is based on the way in which incoming perceptual (story) information relevant for some vital protagonist concern cues emotional activation linked to the protagonist's preferences. The emotional activation of body and brain informs the problem-solving activity of the protagonist and motivates motor actions that are relevant for the concerns and preferences. The basic story experience consists of a continuous interaction between perceptions (I see a monster approaching), emotions (I feel fear, because I know or feel that monsters are dangerous), cognitions (I think that I better shoot the monster), and an action (the actual motor act of shooting that changes the motivational emotion fear into relaxation). The flow model also explains a series of experiential consequences that may be caused by blocking the canonical flow in different ways and at different stages of the perceptual-emotional-cognitive-enactional processing. Narrative forms based on auto-nomic reactions, like sorrow or laughter, are based on blocking the motor outlet. Associative forms are made conscious by a block of the flow in an earlier stage of the processing; and experiences based on "pure" perception, such as perception of abstract forms, only activate the first stage of the flow.Narrative models, such as those of the French structuralists that dominate narrative theory, do not concern themselves with the brain implementation of narratives and cannot account for the intimate relation between perception, emotion, and action in narrative structures.

The story experience need not have any verbal representation, as the ability to "hold" the story in consciousness (including ideas of future possibilities) that is important for prolonged action patterns can take place on a nonverbal perception-emotion-motor-level. Thus, the neurologist Antonio Damasio describes core consciousness as a wordless storytelling:

> Movies are the closest external representation of the prevailing storytelling that goes on in our minds. What goes on within each shot, the different framing of a subject that the movement of the camera can accomplish, what goes on in the transition of shots achieved by editing, and what goes on in the narrative constructed by a particular juxtaposition of shot is comparable in some respects to what goes on in the mind, thanks to the machinery in charge of making visual and auditory images, and to devices such as the many levels of attention and working memory.[8]

This mental film is of course not a silent one, it is only lacking that possible "constant voice-over" of doubling the experiences with a phonological stream of words, that is, an inner monologue. As a verbal "voice-over," an inner monologue may strongly enhance our cognitive analysis of our experience and make it easier to manipulate the experience, for example, to compare it with other experiences or to imagine possible consequences. But the "inner monologue" may also mask part of the salience of the perceptual-motor experience.[9]

Damasio could have pointed out that in several respects video games of the 3-D kind typical, for instance, for first-person shoot-'em-up games or some types of virtual reality are even closer to our core consciousness, because not only are we able to see and feel, we are even able to act upon what we see in light of our concerns, our (inter)active motor capabilities allows us to so shoot at what frightens us or approach what activates our curiosity. Thus, video games and some types of virtual reality are the supreme media for the full simulation of our basic first-person "story" experience because they allow "the full experiential flow" by linking perceptions, cognitions, and emotions with first-person actions. Motor cortex and muscles focus the audiovisual attention, and provide "muscular" reality and immersion to the perceptions. Even visually crude video games such as *Pac-Man* (1980) might provide a strong immersion because of their activation of basic visuo-motor links.

An embodied brain-approach to story experience allows us to characterize the way in which verbal storytelling is a media-specific variant of the story experience. Many language-based story-descriptions have derailed descriptions of video games (and films) because they ignore the fact that semantic meaning is based on concrete perceptions and motor patterns, not on some abstract "semantics," kept in place by verbal signifiers. Humans have probably only acquired language within the last one hundred thousand to two hundred thousand years, whereas the basic story mechanisms may have existed for several million years. Some researchers have even argued that the use of language only took place sixty to seventy thousand years ago.[10] Language has certainly been important for communicating such story experiences and has been a superior tool for the retrieval of and the complex manipulation of the basic experiences.[11] But a purely linguistic model may seriously impede descriptions of those media like video games that rely on a series of nonverbal skills.

Stories are not the only way that we may experience the world. We may perform analytical reasoning similar to that in an essay, we may have thematic-categorical principles of organization or principles based on a network of lyrical associations.[12] Novels, films, or video games may be full of nonnarrative material, like philosophical reflections, descriptions unrelated to the narrative core, or lyrical segments.

## Video games in the perspective of media history

The basic story format is the one called the "canonical story,"[13] that is, a story with one (or a few) focusing characters that unfolds itself in a linear, progressive time, from beginning through middle to end, as Aristotle noticed. A canonical representation does not only accord with the way in which we experience unmediated reality as a series of events in a progressing time, it is also the one that is easiest to remember and represent.[14] People will tend to reproduce a story in a canonical fashion even if they have heard it "uncanonically," that is, heard it with temporal rearrangements. Thus, our innate mental machinery seems to take the canonical story format as its baseline. It is important to point out that the basic story experience must be described as taking place in the present, the experiencer is situated in a "now" that is anchored in the memory of a past that causes and informs the cognitions, emotions, and actions directed toward the future. Furthermore, the nucleus of the story experience is the first-person experience, because third-person perspectives are—from an evolutionary point of view—expansions of a first-person point of view[15] even down to the level of motor activation. We infer how other people experience things by extrapolation from our own experiences, using for instance the so-called mirror neurons.[16] In the following, I will show why media representations of experiences have lead many theoreticians into making misleading descriptions of stories. Theoreticians have focused on story mediation and left out those aspects of stories that the French structuralists called *l'enoncé*, the story as such, in order to define "story" as a discursive phenomenon *(l'énonciatiorn)*. They have further tended to define stories as being based on a "retelling" or "representation," not as an experience that takes place in a progressing present.

The first media representation of the brain's story experiences took place when language was invented. This has lead to several changes and additions to narratives. Linguistic representations stabilize the experiences and make them easier to recall and to manipulate. Furthermore, a central purpose of language is to provide stories with an intersubjective form and this refocuses the story experience from a mainly first-person to a mainly third-person perspective (that of the listener), although a basic story experience also includes perceiving others from a third-person perspective. Verbal representations enhance the already-existing possibility of providing a third-person perspective to stories, because even if the story is one of one's own experience, language enhances the possibility of reliving past experiences out of their direct perceptual context. Even a first-person "autobiographical" narrative is made by the storyteller from a distanced position to the previous on-line experiences. The distance is also possibly a temporal one, because retelling enhances the ability to mentally represent past experiences as past by means of linguistic tense markers.

The stable, intersubjective representation by language provides a symbolic filter (in the Peircian sense of symbolic) between the perceptions, emotions, and actions, and their communicative existence. Language enhances the possibility of describing fictitious events, because even if a central function of imagining a "story" is linked to those mechanisms that make it possible to imagine different possible future actions, language has removed all constraints on the veracity of stories by removing on-line indexicality. Vision (before paintings, film, and television) represented what existed and thus had strong indexical links, but in language (or even in paintings) it is just as easy to lie or fantasize as to "tell the facts."[17] This has lead many into making a link between "story" and "fiction," although story structures do not have a fixed reality status, they may have all kinds of truth values.

Oral narratives were and are predominantly canonical, because, due to memory constraints and cognitive constraints, radical changes in the temporal order raised and raise difficulties.[18] Thus, even for oral stories, the distinction between story and discourse is of limited value, because one of the main practical uses of the story-discourse distinction has been as a tool for describing texts with a scrambled temporal order and to compare several versions of the "same" story. But if there is no scrambled temporal order and no other versions, the degree of story compression and focus on important events seems to be the only use that one can make of the story/discourse distinction. Oral narratives enhance that aspect of stories that many find to be an important story-defining feature, namely, that a story mainly represents very salient events (love, fight, death, etc.) and leaves out trivial events. But to define "story" by a compression that focuses on high-order experiences, and thus to define story as the opposite of representations of trivial events, is problematic.

Prelinguistic "mental" narratives probably made a strong selection among those aspects that existed prominently in the ongoing "story": some aspects of the experience were probably more important than others in a nonverbalized story-experience. Thus, to compress and focus the story on salient events is an aspect of how the mind works by making priorities for access to a limited working memory space. Joseph Anderson has provided a description of how superior structures are important for the comprehension of detail.[19] Compression may thus be described as a "proto-discursive" phenomenon, because it is not really possible to distinguish between a story as "it really happened" and the presentation. But what is compressed in a given story depends on its purpose: if the purpose is also practical, it may focus on certain details and leave out a detailed description of the superior motivation. Thus, video games often focus on the "how" questions of a story.

The verbal form of narratives until the beginning of the twentieth century has led theoreticians, for instance Marie-Laure Ryan,[20] into thinking that the story phenomenon is centrally a verbal phenomenon, because they conflate the story experience with the verbal retelling. In principle, Ryan follows Jakobson's very prudent semiotic definition of stories as something that can be manifested in many forms and that is not defined in relation to one medium,[21] and her general description of narrative avoids a series of "linguistic" traps. Nevertheless, the verbal form seems to be the central one for her. She thus thinks that video games "embody a virtualised, or potential dramatic narrativity," because games provide some experiences that might be retold by means of language, although these virtual stories may ever be told, that is, provided a verbal form. But this conception is paradoxical, because by these criteria we would never experience any "stories" unless they got a linguistic form; even films would only become stories when we made a verbal resumé of a film.

The way in which verbal representations enhance the possibilities for taking a third-person perspective on stories also greatly enhances the experience of stories that rely on certain third-person emotions, like empathy. The most fundamental emotions like love, hate, jealousy, curiosity, sorrow, and fear rely on a first-person perspective for a full experience of these emotions.[22] But emotions also maybe simulated in a third-person perspective in which these emotions are modulated by empathy, like pitying the tragic hero or admiring the superhuman hero. First-person emotions are dynamic action-motivating emotions, whereas third-person emotions like pity or admiration may motivate action, but also more static dispositions. Some theoreticians think that empathic emotions are more valuable than first-person emotions (especially those connected with active coping) and more typical of stories. Thus, Marie-Laure Ryan[23] uses such an emotional valorization as an argument against video game stories and possible VR stories because such stories are better at presenting first-person emotions than, for instance, novels that excel in evoking empathic involvement. It is, however, problematic to make empathic emotions a criterion for whether something is centrally a story or not. In an evolutionary perspective, first-person emotions like the urge for exploring, fighting (based on sympathetic reactions), or emotions linked to sex, food, and laughter (linked to parasym-pathetic reactions) are more fundamentally linked to stories than empathic emotions. But Ryan is right in her criticism of Janet Murray's claim[24] of the unimportance of media for the story experience, and in pointing out that video games better support some emotions than others. The centrality of motor control in video games makes emotions supported by sympathetic reactions based on coping more probable than emotions supported by parasympathetic reactions based on acceptance and relaxation,[25] and first-person emotions more probable than third-person emotions. A game that presupposed an active striving for causing the death of a nice game character would be perverse and not even attractive for players with suicidal tendencies. But those emotions that are centrally afforded in video games are sufficient for providing holodeck-like experiences as described by Murray.[26]

The invention of dramatic representations provided yet another expansion of the story experience. The dramatic form (re)infuses online perceptual qualities to story-representations. The actors are physically present and some dramatic representations rely on sets and props. The representation is perceived in a third-person perspective (the distanced position in the theatre seat as well as the phenomenological "outside" views on actors), although spectators might mentally identify with some of the protagonists. The physical constraints on dramatic performances made some stories more suitable for dramatic presentation than other stories. Verbal narratives have no cost in providing representations of movement through vast spaces, of handling complicated props and performing complicated actions, or to represent a quick temporal progression. Drama is much more confined to some limited spaces, and to representations of a few contiguous temporal scenes. But it is well suited to represent personal interaction based on strongly emotion-evoking events, from courting to tragic death. Theater has prompted a series of ancillary techniques, from the art of making sets to the art of structuring events and characters. Nevertheless, it is difficult to understand why Brenda Laurel[27] uses the theater as a special metaphor for computers. Those Aristotelian elements that she uses as reasons for describing the computer as theater, namely action, character, thought, language, melody, and spectacle are a list of human capabilities that are neither exhaustive nor exclusive to theater. The reference to theater only provides a starting point for breaking down computer features into some functions that also could be derived from other domains.

Dramatic representations are mostly done in the present tense, and thus challenge the belief that the core element of stories in general is their pastness (that is evident in the experiential basis of story comprehension). There are good emotional reasons that make a present tense experience the core story mode. The activation of the central action-motivating or curiosity motivating emotions demands that a given point in the story is simulated with an open, undecided future. If the hero with certainty is going to fall in the pit there is no reason to feel fear or to simulate active coping in order to avoid the danger, but just to feel a distanced pity. If we are totally certain that the hero will get the heroine there is not much suspense. Even if folktales are told in the past tense, the listener will take that past point in time as the focus of "presentness" and construct an open future. The problem with some types of strongly narrative video games is that it is difficult to simulate such stories in a dynamic real time and this will deprive the player of a strong sense of experiencing the story in the present tense.

The dominant present tense of drama may be somewhat blurred by the fact that some dramas, for instance, the most famous Greek tragedies, are based on stories that are well-known on beforehand, so that the viewer may know what happens and only asks how it happens. Tragedies and melodramas are however a variant of stories because they rely on passive emotions and/or third-person emotions. For such stories, pastness, decidedness, and fatality is important in order to block a present-tense experience that would make the passive acceptance of the inevitable and painful more difficult,[28] that is, make the transformation from first-person to third-person emotions more difficult. Comedies do not ordinarily need nor presuppose such a pastness.

The invention of written story representations surpassed some of the memory constraints of oral stories. The written medium affords complex narratives, including discursive rearrangements. The written form may emphasize the pastness of the experience, and at the same time it enhances the experience of the "fixity" of the story, because beginning, middle and end of the story exists physically in a fixed form. That does not exclude that stories are read in a simulated present and that the reader may tend to experience a given narrative future as "undecided," just that the medium emphasizes the fixity of the story (and often the third-person perspective). In the twentieth century, film and television became the prime vehicles for basic storytelling, whereas high-art literature increasingly emphasized the discursive dimensions by a series of complex narrative strategies (or by filling in nonnarrative material such as philosophical reflections).

14

The invention of film created a new medium for the simulation of basic story experiences. Like theater, film makes it possible to present events in a direct perceptual form. In some respects the screen does not have the same intense physical "presence" of space and characters as theatre. But in other respects film affords a story-presentation that is free of some of the constraints of theater. Films make it possible to move freely through time and space. Films make it possible to cue and simulate an experience that is close to a first-person perception (either directly by subjective shots, POV-shots) or from positions close to the persons, contrary to the fixed and distant perspective in the theater.[29] The focusing and framing of persons, objects and events simulate and cue the working of our attention. The representation can furthermore represent various aspects of reality with photographic verisimilitude. As an audiovisual media, the dominant temporal dimension is the present tense; we directly witness the events. To present them "in the past tense" is possible but is not the norm, as it is in written stories. The medium more easily affords story development that focuses on a "now" with an undecided future that has to be constructed by the actions of the hero. Furthermore, there are also strong emotional reasons for a present tense presentation because this supports experiences based on emotions linked to active coping (hate, fear, love, desire), although the medium is also excellent for presenting passive emotions.[30]

The dominant mode of representation is a canonical one, because film viewing often works under strong time constraints that strain the viewer's cognitive capacities.[31] In mainstream cinema, mental capacity constraints impede narrative complexity. This does not mean that films—like written narratives—often use more complex forms of representation. They may use explicit narrators and discursive rearrangements, but in mainstream cinema such devices mostly serve special functions (explicit narrators are thus most typical for creating passive effects), and discursive rearrangements mostly serve to provide subjective dimensions (e.g., flashbacks to childhood experiences).

## Video games, story experience, and game playing

The computer is the newest medium for story simulation. By providing an "interactive" motor dimension to story experience the computer adds a powerful new dimension to the possibility of simulating first-person experiences. The motor link is still primitive compared to our capabilities to physically interact with a real-life environment (speech is in this respect also a motor act). However, eye and ear will not only be linked to an activation of the premotor cortex (as in previous media) but also to a full motor cortex and muscle activation. Like cinema, the video game screen predominantly simulates perceptions of spaces and objects that are present to the senses, but they can be influenced by actions. In several respects, then, video games are, as mentioned, the medium that is closest to the basic embodied story experience.

The interactive capability also raises a series of new problems that were absent in the earlier media, but are similar to those raised by interacting with real-life phenomena on a first-person basis. The reader/viewer of "traditional" mediated stories needs only to activate some general cognitive skills, including the ability to have some expectations. The story will proceed even without such expectations. The computer story, in contrast, is only developed by the player's active participation, and the player needs to possess a series of specific skills to "develop" the story, from concrete motor skills and routines to a series of planning skills. Therefore, the new activations also increase the capacity problems, and the increased demand on working memory space also increases immersion.

In earlier media, story progression is controlled by the author/director. To follow protagonists through space only demands rather vague mental models (for instance, to imagine that a character somehow gets from his apartment in Berkeley to Golden Gate Bridge), not detailed cognitive maps and hand-eye coordination. Watching John Wayne shooting an opponent only demands crude models for actions, not precise motor programs for grasping the gun and aiming precisely. But in video games such activities often demand rather detailed cognitive maps and motor skills, and playing therefore often requires extensive training of necessary skills. One of the reasons why video games are called *games* is precisely because the repetitive training of coping skills is an important element in many of those activities covered by the term "games."

However, the term "game" is very loosely-defined, and Wittgenstein used the term as a prime example of a category based on "family resemblance" and Lakoff used "family resemblance" to describe categorizations based on prototypes.[32] There are no necessary and sufficient conditions for belonging to or not belonging to the category "games," only a loose network of interconnected resemblances. Several video game researchers have used Roger Caillois's[33] categorization of games as a tool for characterizing video games in contrast to narratives. Caillois divides games into four types, *agôn* (competition), *alea* (chance), *mimicry* (simulation), and *ilinx* (vertigo). But a comparison between video games and Callois's categories creates more problems than it solves. Mimicry may be used when playing, but is also central in film and theatre. Ilinx is a central element in many action films. Agôn is central in many action films, alea is prominent in lotteries, and so on, but neither typical of fiction nor of video games, although of course most events in this world may possess an element of chance.

It is more rewarding to take the point of departure for describing games in a more general definition of "play" and then describe games and fictions as special forms of play. The ability to play is a very general innate feature that characterizes all mammals.[34] To play means to perform an activity for pleasure, not out of a necessity, although the survival value of playing may be to train important skills, from motor skills to imagination and hypothesis-formation. Cats may play "fighting" or "hunting" and even if their playing may enhance their skills for real-life fighting or hunting, the play situation is not carried out with full real-life intentions, their claws are withdrawn. Humans may play cops and robbers, perform an act, play soccer or Monopoly, but it is only play as long as it is not carried out with real-life intentions, where the players kill each other or risk their fortunes. Thus, a central element in the concept of "play" is linked to what kind of reality status is manifested in a given play activity.

In some fictions (for instance, realist fictions) the fictive "playfulness" of the activity is only a general prescript that prevents the viewer (or actor) from confusing the fiction with reality, but they are in several respects consumed as if they were real. Other fictions are overtly playful. The fictions may be fantasy stories that activate the spectators' or readers' joy by seeing a series of laws of reality violated. But they may also be fictions that cue the spectators into seeing the events as playful, as it is often the case in comedies. Thus, when *The Cosby Show* is called a show and not just a film or comedy, the name clearly indicates that these are some "artist performances" that the characters do in order to please the audience, enhanced by the laugh track. Thus, the more the "fourth wall" of the "theater" is negated, the more the actors are not only communicating to other people in the diegetic world, but also to the spectators, the more we will think that the activity is "a performance," a "game." Such comic shows will never produce any final results, because in the next sit-com, all the activities will start again, just as we know that Laurel and Hardy will never develop, but repeat the same stupidities.

A central element in those playful activities that we call games is therefore their repetitiveness, because somehow repetitive (reversible) activities are felt as less serious, less "real" than activities like tragic stories that represent irreversible processes. A sophisticated viewer of, say, a tragic western might however see that film as a "game" and thus as something more formal (less real) that could be repeated in another western. Thus we might define games as a special kind of playfulness that is characterized by a virtual or actual element of repetitiveness, linked to a conscious feeling that the activity consists of exploring some pattern-bound, rule-bound possibilities (narrative schemas, comic schemas, etc.). The repetitiveness may diminish the felt seriousness. Although some activities may afford playfulness better than other, playfulness depends on subjective attitudes and skills as well as on object affordances. Just as we may either enjoy a western as a "serious" simulation of reality, but also as a "game" with some patterns, so we may also play a video game in a serious-realist mode, but also in a "playful mode." The ease with which we can start a new game certainly supports playfulness, but there is a tradeoff between depth of involvement and degree of playfulness.[35] The lack of depth of involvement may, however, be an advantage if the purpose is to try out roles that conflict with our normal set of identity-defining roles, and the playfulness may then function as an excuse (e.g., for playing monsters, killer-drivers, angels, or devils).

Mediated fictions are mostly enjoyed from a "perceptual" third-person perspective that eventually is simulated mentally from a first-person perspective, whereas many types of playing are enjoyed from a first-person perspective even in its motor dimensions, although many people also watch soccer games, and so on. Fictions are about the concerns of anthropomorphic beings, whereas some kinds of playing, like solitaire, lack an anthropomorphic dimension. And furthermore, most kinds of playing when experienced from a first-person perspective are repetitive in nature, although competition may change playing into distinct events. Thus, big professional soccer games may be experienced in a mode similar to a drama, and more so from the perspective of the spectators than the players. The question of repetitiveness versus unique events is based on subjective, experiential evaluations: players of all kinds of games or consumers of stories may experience a game or a story on the superior level of pattern repetition or focus on the unique variations of a genre or a game-world (or, in structuralist terminology, a system-based vs. a manifestation-based experience).

Stories and games are prototypical categories (or, in Wittgenstein's terminology, categories based on family resemblance). They bleed into each other and cannot sharply be delimited from yet other categorizations. Thus, the central prototype of stories are similar to those games that, like action, shoot-'em-up, and adventure video games, are based on intelligent agencies that act in space-time, whereas other games—like *Tetris*—have weaker links to stories.

## Linearity, non-linearity, and interactivity as agency

I noted that, contrary to the reader/viewer of mediated stories (and texts), the player of video games (and related phenomena such as hypertexts) needs to actively develop the story. This development is often described by means of some "hyped" terms like "interactivity" and "nonlinearity," especially when those terms are used in a semiotic context. My definition of "inter-activity" in relation to computer application is simple: Interactivity means that the user/player is able to change the visual appearance of a computer screen (and/or sounds from speakers) by some motor action via an interface. The more this motor interaction takes place in a world that simulates being an agent in a world that simulates aspects of a possible real world the greater experience of interactivity. This definition is in accordance with our everyday experience of interaction (in contrast to mental processing). To describe an active reader or viewer of texts as interactive is confusing in relation to ordinary language. The definition furthermore focuses on the experience of the user/player (performing motor acts) and thus avoids those metaphysical speculations of whether the user/player is "really" in control or not. The media theoreticians Bordewijk and Kaam have tried to make an objectivist typology of different types of communication.[36] Traditional one-way media like television are "transmissions." Information that is produced by a "center" and distribution is controlled by the user (like a database or video games) are characterized as "consultation." The true interactive forms are telephone, e-mail, and chat groups, and so on, because only those media formats enable the user to produce and distribute information. But such a description clearly violates normal language. We do not "consult" *Doom* in order to find out what information the producers of that game have provided, we play the game in order to get an experience that is a simulation of the way in which we might act in a hypothetical world. Our primary model is the way in which we experience interaction in a real world.

In a real world as well as in simulated worlds our influence is limited by the general design of that world: we follow roads, tunnels or career tracks, and obey rules, but within a given framework we may alter some elements, take different roads, build houses, and so on. The only necessary condition for experiencing "agency" and interactivity is that our actions make a difference. Ryan (2001) provides a distinction between four kinds of interactivity, made up of two pairs internal/external (roughly equivalent to first-person/third-person) and exploratory/ ontological. The last pair distinguishes between those games in which the player moves around the database but is unable to alter the plot and the virtual world, and those games in which the player can influence that world and consequently influence the possible stories. When exemplified, however, it becomes obvious that this distinction is difficult to maintain, because there is no clear distinction between exploring and altering. The reason for this is that the key element in agency and thus in the feeling of interactivity is the ability to change the player's experience. In real life, I may feel agency by changing my experiences by going to Italy, and this might be described as "exploring" the "database Italy" and that does not change much in the world. The "database Italy" is pretty much the same after my visit, but nevertheless I experience agency by my power to change my mental states by my "navigation." But I also may experience agency by building a house or making a table. Is the first experience just exploratory whereas the last is ontological? When I wander around in a mystery, adventure or a shoot-'em-up game, I cannot change the fundamental layout of the game-world just as I cannot change Italy by my visit, but nevertheless I control my navigation, my ability to shoot monsters, and so on, and create many different stories. Thus, interactivity is not centrally about changing a world; on the contrary, it is about changing the mental states of the player, whether that takes place by changing some objects in the world or by changing one's point of view.

Ryan describes some adventure and mystery games as (internal) exploratory whereas other adventure games are characterized as (internal) ontological. However, the difference between *Myst* and *Quake* is not one between a game in which the story is "predetermined" and one in which the player creates the story. In *Quake*, the player also needs to do certain things that are inscribed in the game by the producer of the game, to shoot certain adversaries and find certain paths, for instance. The main difference is the salience of the experience of the player's game alter ego in different games. In contemporary shoot-'em-up games the player more often navigates in a real-time 3-D world, the player may "die" or "crash" his or her plane, or whatever, whereas a problem in a mystery game would be more "external," some headache caused by game problems but projected out in the game world. Thus, even if both worlds are equally free or controlled by some built-in functions and trajectories, the surface of some games are more inviting for experiencing first-person involvement (including the speed of events). The slow and totally player-determined time in *Myst* may lead players into feeling that the "game-resistance" to agency, for instance, troubles with finding out the mysteries, is caused by "narration." However, the "game-resistance" to agency caused by troubles with steering an airplane through a tunnel or keeping a car on a racetrack in real time may be experienced as a personal failure to cope. The distinction between "exploratory" and "ontological" is very much created by an implicit "hype" that thinks that the essence of interactivity consists of free, demiurgic powers for world-making, instead seeing interactivity as the creation of experiences that appears to flow from one's own actions.

A description of the game experience cannot only be "objective" but must take its point of departure in a psychological description. Brenda Laurel has pointed out[37] that the computer experience is a first-person activity and that it is most activating if the proper sensory modalities are stimulated. Vividness of the sensory and motor interface provides salience to the experience of agency irrespective of objective control. The "subjective" aspect of the experience of agency can be observed in the difference in experience between film sequences in film and the same or similar "film"-sequences in a video game, that is, sequences that temporarily block interaction. Because such sequences in a video game are experienced in a context of interaction, they are experienced as more "dead," less "vivid" than in a film context.

Our experience of our interactive capabilities are, however, not constant over time. When beginning a new behavior and/or learning a new environment, we may feel that we have many options that depend on our own choices. However, as we learn those behaviors and environments, we may increasingly get a clear "map" of our options, and we may even feel that we are just alienated robots that follow the commands of society or our own fixed compulsions. To play video games provides a similar variation in our experience of interactivity. When starting a new game we may follow different routes and have an experience of controlling many options. But when we gain mastery we may not only experience the game as a series of routes that we may follow but also create a total "map" of the game and realize that we have a set of limited options. In this stage, the game is more likely to be experienced as a "message" from the game producers because we get insight into their game design. Experienced players may get to that stage sooner and shift more often between experiencing the game as an interactive world and reasoning about the possible intentions laid down by the producers. But it spoils some of the fun to see fictions and games as communication, although it creates other connoisseur pleasures. You may ask yourself the question, will Hitchcock kill this woman? instead of simulating her destiny as a real-life event. Similarly, some pleasures of game playing are linked to the simulation of an experiential flow, although other pleasures consist in getting insight into the intentions of the creators. Our experience of basic mimesis is one of "naturalness," "it has to be so." However, our experience of "art" is based on our insight into the way in which a given creator realizes specific intentions that are only fully understandable as a choice selected among several possible options, and this demands expertise. The metaphors "game as an experiential route" versus "game as a map and as a system" sum up the two poles in the game experience (novice to master), and may perhaps also cover the way in which "texts" may be either experienced as mimesis or as art.

The term "nonlinearity" is closely related to the question of interactivity, because for many scholars within the humanities, the idea of total interactivity and supreme agency is linked to that term. The term is heavily loaded with associations provided by different strands of postmodernist-deconstructionist thinking, for example, those derived from Derrida. According to their philosophy, linearity is a product of a Western, metaphysical logos-thinking (e.g., causality), enhanced by the linearity of alphabetical writing. These ideas are often linked to rather patronizing ideas that consist in implicitly claiming that non-Western people should be more illogical than Western people. The computer "hype" version of nonlinearity consists in claiming that the computer media possibly emancipates one from these metaphysical and ideological constraints.

However, linearity is not a product of Western metaphysics but based on very fundamental features of the world, of action, and of consciousness. An experiential flow is—unless totally unfocused—a linear process in time. At the same time, linearity is a mental representation of the essential features of the world; that it exists in time, and that time is experienced as linked to irreversible processes. Such processes are represented mentally by concepts like cause and effect. The sun begins to shine and then the snow melts. The arrow pierced the heart, and then the person or animal died. The man entered the tunnel, went through and came out on the other side of the mountain, and so on. Lakoff[38] has shown how such causal links are universally represented by source-path-goal-schemas. By playing a film backward, it becomes obvious that our whole conceptual machinery is based on such linear processes, based on concepts of causality that we share even with animals. The role of linearity and causality in science is only a sophisticated version of innate mental mechanisms that have been developed because of their survival value. Actions are causes that make a difference of effect, and therefore it would be difficult to make a story that was not based on some kind of linearity and causality, because the actions of the story would otherwise make no difference.

A given effect may have different causes: the street may be wet because of rain or because a city water wagon has passed. We may construct video games that consist of different paths that cross each other at some points. In one of the storylines we may arrive to a given space after having followed a path that simulated rain, in another storyline we may arrive to the same space by another path after having witnessed how a water wagon made the street wet. Thus by providing several linear trajectories to the same point we may create ambiguity (seen from a "system" point of view: one effect, several possible causes, as in the deliberations of possible motives and causes in crime fiction, including representations of alternative possible scenarios). It is, however, evident that because a given effect cannot have an unlimited amount of different causes, there can only be a limited amount of such causally motivated crossing paths.[39] A hypertext-like computer story in which all the scenes of the game story were connected by a complex web of links, would have to be a fairly primitive one, or one with insignificant effects. It would be impossible to figure out hundreds of different paths crossing in hundreds of different scene-nodes that provided significant processes and actions irrespective of what concrete trajectory was taken in the web of links. Thus such "a-linear" hypertext web structures afford association-like phenomena (similar to those of dictionary cross-reference links, lyrical associations, literary allusions, etc.) that get their significance by the accumulation of associations. But complex hypertext-like networks do not afford those narrative actions well that rely on causality, a certain time direction, and some irreversibility. Networks of (lyrical) associations versus linear (narrative) trajectories are linked to two different types of emotions, the unfocused emotions that I have called "saturated"[40] and those "tense" emotions like aggression that motivate action, and that need a "linear-causal" setting. Media cannot change our innate cognitive and emotional architecture, only invent products that may activate and enhance the innate specifications.

The reason for wanting multiple choices and multiple possible storylines is the desire to simulate the feeling of a (relative) freedom of choice that we may have in real life, or an utopian-romantic wish for a virtual world that liberates from the restrictions of the real world. Seen from this point of view the creation of several alternative routes simulates freedom. We may, for instance, follow one path to the princess on which we need to kill a dragon in order to proceed to the princess, whereas the other path to the princess has a trial that consists in solving riddles. But choices based on path bifurcation and path separation also imply some constraints on "significance," because if one path implied that the hero lost an eye, and the other one did not, they could not meet. If the choice is "only" created by combining several alternative paths leading to different goals they are collections of linear stories. They just make something explicit which is implicit in other story forms; namely that our story comprehension is based on the fact that the story is a series of "forks" (of alternatives, as pointed out by Bremond[41]). We may go left or right, the hero may win or lose the battle, and so on. Normally, the options in stories are only virtual, even in the second reading or viewing, whereas a computer story may be constructed in such a way that what was virtual in the first playing is chosen and actualized in the second playing.

Thus, we may conclude that stories are essentially linear in their realization: (1) all texts and experiences are linear as experiential processes, because even when "reading" a hypertext the experiential flow would always be linear as it would be revealed if we taped our hypertext activity, our netsurfing, or our consultation of an electronic dictionary with links between articles and terms; (2) the story as a sequence of significant events is linear because a significant story relies on causality, on irreversible processes, and of choice of a trajectory of action. Freedom is the transient feeling that precedes a choice. This insight may be blurred by the fact that a given story world may support different stories, different choices of paths (and in computer stories different player performances). However, we need to distinguish between story experience and story world affordance, because a given story world or game world may afford one or several story experiences.[42] The experience of the way in which a game/story world affords one or several story experiences is however not an a-linear experience, but an insight into the difference between an "experiential route" and a game world as a "map," that is, a system of multiple linear routes. Described in psychological and experiential terms we might say that our visual perception is a two- or three-dimensional field that is supported by a multidimensional a-temporal web of associations, but our actions are based on linearity and time.

## The aesthetics of video games

Several theoreticians have pointed out that at least at present most video games have a less complicated story than films or novels. Thus, Jesper Juul compares some films with their game versions[43] (e.g., *Star Wars* and *Tomb Raider*). He points out that the game versions are much simpler than the film versions and uses this as one of his arguments for thinking that video games are not a storytelling media. The problem with this argument is that it is normative. That some stories are rather simple in some dimensions is not a reason for depriving them of their status as stories. There is obviously a tradeoff between control and some dimensions of complexity. Films based on novels may often in some dimensions be simpler than the novels because the richness of the perceptual presentation and the pressure of experiential time are in conflict with other dimensions of complexity that may characterize the printed medium. Similarly, the complexity of the active control of story development in video games is in conflict with other dimensions of complexity. Playing video games demands a detailed richness and specificity in cognitive maps of spaces and opposing agents, of causal inferences that do not only have to be vague premonitions as in films or novels in which the author/ director is in control, but precise ideas in order to work. The perceptions have to be fast and precise, the motor control coordinated with the perceptions, and thus the computer story demands the acquisition of a series of procedural schemas. From another point of view, therefore, video games are not imploded stories, but on the contrary the full, basic story that the retelling has to omit, including its perceptual and muscular realization. Video games are based on learning processes and rehearsals and are therefore stories *in the making*, sketches of different stories, different coping strategies. In our first-person experience of a series of events the actual physical manipulation may be intriguing: how to dress oneself, how to control a car, how to deal with a given piece of machinery. All those procedures may be vital elements in our first-person experience. However, such "procedural" experiences are often not very interesting for other people, they do not like to hear about all those "low level" procedures and learning processes, but only to get the bottom line, whereas video games communicate such procedural knowledge. In retelling, there is often a conflict between the teller who wants to provide all the salient details and the listener who wants the big picture. Video games activate a first-person perspective and furthermore often possess a time-frame of many days that allow for a story that is realized on a procedural micro level as well as on a macro level. Films provide a rich access to those perceptual experiences that ground the basic story experience, whereas video games provide the full agency-dimensions of story experience.

23

In several respects, video games provide an *aesthetic of repetition*, similar to that of everyday life. A film is mostly experienced as a unique sequence of events, and we do not learn the physical outlay of a given simulated world very well, we are carried from space to space. In everyday life, however, we repeat the same actions over and over in order to gain mastery. When we arrive to a new city or a new building we slowly learn how to move around, and if we want to learn to drive or bike, we exercise those skills until we have acquired the necessary procedural skills. The video game experience is very much similar to such an everyday experience of learning and controlling by repetitive rehearsal. We often tell our everyday experiences to others, but often learn that all those details that we find intriguing may be boring for other people.

The video game experience consists of different phases. The first time a game is played, it is experienced with a certain unfamiliarity; the world is new and salient and poses challenges and mystery. By playing the game numerous times, the game world will become increasingly familiar. The peak result of such a learning process may be a trancelike immersion in the virtual world, because of the strong neuronal links that are forged between perceptions, emotions, and actions. But the end result of the learning process is what the Russian Formalists called *automation*, and what psychologists might call *desentization by habituation*. The virtual world becomes predictable, it loses its visual and acoustic salience, and the player will probably stop playing the game at this stage. Thus, this aesthetics of repetition is based on the sequence: first *unfamiliarity and challenge*, then *mastery*, and finally *automation*. The experience is thus in some respects similar to the way in which we enjoy music—musical appreciation is also strongly based on repeating the listening process until it has reached a stage of automation.

The repetitive and interactive nature of video games leads to changes in the function of central devices in the emotional experience of "narratives," namely *curiosity, surprise,* and *suspense*. In a film, the curiosity that is cued by secrets of the narrative world is a passive one, and mainly linked to first-time viewing. The viewer will activate a passive curiosity that supports the viewer's attention. In a video game, however, curiosity takes the form of *explorative coping*. The game only develops if the player performs a series of explorative actions. This self-controlled exertion of active agency is a central fascination in one type of game segment. However, other segments, especially in shoot-'em-up games, are based on the experience of personal agency as being *dynamic coping* by interacting with other *dynamic agencies*, from monsters to gravity, in a simulated *real time*. Explorative coping and dynamic coping provides two distinct experiences of agency as control and agency as playful interaction with other dynamic agencies.

In films, surprising events are mainly emotionally activating in the first viewing. But in video games, what was surprising in the first playing of the game is transformed into a suspenselike coping anticipation in subsequent playings. When the player advances toward the space in which the "surprising" event previously has occurred, for example, the sudden appearance of a fierce antagonist, it will induce an increased arousal. The arousal will diminish over time as the player

24

learns some coping mechanisms, for instance, fast routines for shooting the monster despite the surprising speed or the surprising location of the monster.

A film will create arousal related to the viewer's expectations of what will happen to the central protagonists. This combination of arousal and expectation is what is ordinarily called *suspense*, and it is mainly linked to first-time viewing. Video games also evoke suspense related to the outcome of local sequences as well as related to the final outcome of the game. But suspense in video games is interwoven with the interactive and repetitive nature of the game. The outcome in a given game is in principle just as uncertain the second time through as it is the first time. The player might, in the first playing, by chance shoot an important antagonist or by chance solve a problem, make a perceptual or motor mistake, or forget a step. The time factor in games characterized by dynamic interaction will often create differences in performance from one playing to another. Only by training will the player achieve such an expertise that the game will lose its suspense, and thereby its ability to arouse and stimulate the player. Suspense in video games is partly linked to explorative and dynamic coping, because, contrary to film suspense, video game suspense supports coping, not passive expectations.

I mentioned that the playing of a video game could be divided in three phases: challenge, mastery and automation. The player may have a strong experience of agency and free will in the first two phases. However, the way in which the game is controlled by the designer, and is therefore a "noninteractive" experience, may surface in the third, automated stage. In order to experience our exertion of agency and free will, we need to feel that we are not enacting some stimulus-response patterns. Not only do we need to have a choice between a series of different options, we also need to "feel" that they are real options. But even if a given game world has a series of different paths and options at a given moment, not all these options are equally valid. Often a game will have rather few optimal strategies. The final stage in playing a given game therefore consists in explicitly or intuitively learning these constraints and the optimal strategies of a given game world, just as our everyday may become a dull routine that carries out some automated optimal strategies that rule out a series of alternatives. This further underlines the fact that the experience of interactivity and agency is a subjective one that varies over time, not something that is a static feature of a given game. The experience of interactive agency demands a certain degree of unpredictability in order to guarantee challenge and salience, but also a certain degree of predictability in order to support active coping.

That video games are based on repetitive playing and on interaction has important consequences for the emotional experience in comparison with films. The player's emotional experience is a personalized one. When a viewer is observing, say, how a monster is approaching a character, the possible arousal in the form of fear is not linked to the personal coping potential of the viewer, the viewer has to vicariously identify with the coping potentials of the endangered film character. The viewer cannot personally come up with specific coping strategies; like the rest of the audience, the viewer can only hope for a positive outcome and eventually make some more personal predictions. But a player of a video game is personally responsible for the outcome of such a confrontation. It is the player's evaluation of his own coping potential that determines whether the confrontation with a monster will be experienced as fear (if the evaluation of his coping potential is moderate), despair (if he feels that he has no coping potentials), or triumphant aggression (if he feels that he is amply equipped for the challenge). This entails that the emotional experience will vary over time, because of the learning processes leading to a change in coping potentials. The first-time player of a game may feel despair, the more experienced player may feel a little fear, whereas the master will feel triumphant aggression. Furthermore, different players will have different emotional experiences, linked to their different expertise, although such devices, like options for playing the game on different levels of difficulty, make it easier for the unskilled player to get some of the emotional experiences of the more skilled. There is no such thing as pre-programmed levels of difficulty in film viewing, because the basic assumption in film viewing is that viewing is not an individualized experience, although some films may possess symbolic and enigmatic elements that are not accessible to everybody.

The interactive, output-directed nature of video games puts some constraints on the types of emotions that can be elicited by video games compared with films that are mainly input-driven, driven by the powerful screen representations that viewers passively receive. By its emphasis on motor control it is obvious that video games are mostly able to evoke those emotions that are supported by the sympathetic nervous system (fight and flight-related emotions). The typical emotions evoked by video games are related to active coping. The film experience is basically a passive one, although simulation of character actions can provide a strong active dimension to film. But many films are centrally aimed at evoking strong passive emotions, for instance, melodramas. The input-driven nature of film makes it easy to cue strong passive emotions, including experiences of fate, and they may evoke a strong autonomic outlet, like crying. In contrast, video games are based on acting out the emotions, and the games may therefore even create some kind of catharsis.[44]

Murray's vision of holodeck-like video stories implies stories that would also appeal to our active social skills and social emotions, like establishing friendship, exerting care, feeling jealousy, falling in love, and so on. Such stories would be more attractive to women, and the success of the doll-house game *The Sims* shows the market potentials for games that take some steps toward modelling the non-aggressive social world. There are, however, important technical problems that have to be solved before video games can have holodeck-like or filmlike stories. Some problems, like making programs that could make flexible, individualized, and context-dependent facial expressions and body language for the protagonists that could create empathy, love, or jealousy in the player, might be solved. But to make fully autonomous agents that function like real human beings presupposes a full AI model of humans.

Some video games also excel in evoking lyrical-associative experiences, closer to emotions supported by the parasympathetic nervous system. Games such as *Myst* and *Riven* and other adventure games are experientially based on series of audiovisual freeze-frames and pauses that the player can explore and seek out one by one. Part of the pleasure of such games is therefore not active control of the type exerted in dynamic interpersonal and inter-agency relations (like the control exerted in shoot-'em-up games in which the player in dynamic real time is confronted with monsters, etc.). On the contrary, the pleasure of such *Myst*-type adventure and mystery games is partly a series of associative and contemplative situations and feelings, in which the associative processing of the perceptual input is just as important as the motor output. Such static associations cue feelings, that is, general emotional states without specific objects or specific action tendencies, not emotions. Such "passive" feelings of a mismatch between grandiose input and blocked output[45] were called "sublime feelings" by the preromantic and romantic poets, and the quest for sublime feelings is one of the main parasympathetic reactions cued by video games, as an alternative to the dominant aesthetics of sympathetic control.

Because the story development in video games is driven by the player's motor action, its central story format is linked to a first-person perspective of the basic story experience. Video games may also be used as a vehicle for third-person stories, driven by curiosity. But third-person stories in the computer have some difficulties in synthesizing the function of player control and player agency, with the "passive" simulation of third-person actions, cued by visual stimuli. In films and novels (third) persons are infused with the life and agency by authors and characters, and most readers and viewers will attribute that life to the characters, not to the "storyteller." In the video game, it is the job of the player to create "life" in the third person, and failure to do so will create feelings of a mechanical lifelessness, eventually perceived as due to the designer and his or her system or as a feeling of insufficiency.

## Conclusion

The basic narrative format is a way of arranging perceptions, emotions, cognitions, and motor actions (pecma), based on innate brain modules and with or without a linguistic representation. Narrative mechanisms predate language and even the linguistic forms are (also) cues for reactivations of the pecma-structures. The mental mechanisms are geared to the ecological niche of humans. Narratives presuppose living agents that act and experience in space-time, contrary to other formats of representations, like associative forms, prepositional forms, and so on, that are often linked to an "interior" mental niche. Features of the narrative first-person experience may be represented in different media that each have their specific affordances. In general, media representations (including language) afford discursive rearrangements and deviations from canonical forms. Film and video games afford first-person perceptions, video games afford motor interaction, written stories afford complicated deviations from canonical representations, and so on. The media forms are therefore not only representations but also forms that afford new activities (from circumventing internal memory constraints to enhancing the possibility already latent in fantasy of creating virtual actions and scenarios). Media forms also greatly enhance the possibilities of choosing different levels of representation, from ten-minute representations of the history of the universe to fine-grained visuo-motor simulations of actions. It may be difficult to make a lower limit to the phenomenon "narrative," although most would think that learning quite basic action patterns like those found in *Tetris* (which lacks an agent-in-time-space dimension) fall below the category of narrative.

The basic narrative format is linked to a living agent in a natural environment, and therefore does not presuppose any storyteller except the experiencing agent. Mediated representations may be experienced as "untold," as a simulation of an experiential sequence, but also as "told," as a communicative text. The last point of view also implies that the text may be understood as "art," as a specific communicative strategy among several possible strategies. The basic narrative format is linked to linearity, because significant actions and processes are based on linearity and irreversibility. The linear narrative forms are different from some "paratelic"[46] phenomena like dancing in which there is reversibility and in which there is no source-path-goal-schema, and different from associative structures as found in hypertexts with dense nonlinear links. Although a given instantiation of a video game is linear, a given game "world" affords many different instantiations. We may thus distinguish between a given game sequence that is linearly narrative and the affordances of the game world (and its representation in the player's mind) that might be called "meta-narrative" because the player envisions the individual game from a meta-perspective of possibly all the different options and trajectories within the game world. This meta-narrative stance is similar to art appreciation, because art appreciation is based on comparing a given choice of representation with other possible choices.

Video games provide personalized experiences that are based on playing (that is: pleasurable *repetitive learning* processes), backed up by emotions that change over time not only because of the events but also due to the development of the learning processes. The subjective experience of nonlinear choice is strongly enhanced by the repetitive nature of games that allow different lines of actions in different playings of the same game, contrary to film, which chooses one line of action and one narrative out of the virtual options. The experience of agency may over time be constrained by learning the way in which the game world is a designer construct, and thus provide an experience of automation or provide an experience of interacting with designer intentions.

Video games are furthermore mainly based on sympathetic, aversive emotions, due to their output-driven setup, contrary to films which are input-driven, and thus able to simulate parasympathetic emotions, but also to a certain extent able to simulate output-driven narratives, thus cueing sympathetic emotions.

# Notes

1 Brenda Laurel, *Computers as Theatre* (Reading, MA: Addison-Wesley, 1993).
2 Hugo Münsterberg, *The Film: A Psychological Study* (New York: Dover, [1916] 1970).
3 See Torben Grodal, *Moving Pictures: A New Theory of Film Genre, Feelings, and Cognition* (Oxford: Clarendon/Oxford University Press, 1997).
4 See Kay Young and Jeffrey L. Saver, "The Neurology of Narrative," *SubStance* 30, Nos. 1–2 (2001): 72–84.
5 See Antonio R. Damasio, *The Feeling of What Happens: Body and Emotion in the Making of Consciousness* (New York: Harcourt Brace, 1999).
6 Torben Grodal, "Art Film, the Transient Body and the Permanent Soul," *Aura* VI, No. 3 (2000).
7 See Grodal, *Moving Pictures*.
8 See Damasio, *The Feeling of What Happens*, 188, passim.
9 A description of the prelinguistic basis of experiences and thinking may also be found in Gilles Fauconnier and Mark Turner, *The Way We Think: Conceptual Blending and the Mind* (New York: Basic Books, 2002).
10 See Ian Tattersall, *The Monkey in the Mirror* (New York: Harcourt Brace, 2001), and also Fauconnier and Turner, *The Way We Think*.
11 See Michael C. Corballis, *The Lopsided Ape: Evolution of the Generative Mind* (New York: Oxford University Press, 1991), Antonio R. Damasio, "Brain and Language," in *Mind and Brain: Readings from Scientific American Magazine* (New York: Freeman, 1993), and Fauconnier and Turner, *The Way We Think*.
12 See David Bordwell and Kristin Thompson, *Film as Art*, 6th ed. (New York: McGraw-Hill, 2001) and Grodal, *Moving Pictures*.
13 See David Bordwell, *Narration in the Fiction Film* (London: Methuen, 1986) and Grodal, *Moving Pictures*.
14 See Jean M. Mandler, *Stories, Scripts and Scenes: Aspects of Schema Theory* (Hillsdale, NJ: Lawrence Erlbaum, 1984).
15 See Torben Grodal, "Film, Character Simulation, and Emotion," in *Nicht allein das Laufbild af der Leinwand* . . . , ed. Friss, Hartmann and Muller (Berlin: VISTAS, 2001).
16 See Grodal, "Film, Character Simulation, and Emotion."
17 See Fauconnier and Turner, *The Way We Think*, esp. chapter 11.
18 See Mandler, *Stories, Scripts and Scenes*.
19 See Joseph Anderson, *The Reality of Illusion: An Ecological Approach to Cognitive Film Theory* (Carbondale: Southern Illinois University Press, 1996).
20 Marie-Laure Ryan, "Beyond Myth and Metaphor—The Case of Narrative in Digital Media," *Game Studies* 1, No. 1 (July 2001). Available online at <http://www.gamestudies.org/0101/ryan/>.
21 See Roman Jakobson, "Linguistics and Poetics," in *Style in Language*, ed. Sebeok (Cambridge, MA: MIT Press, 1960).
22 See Grodal, *Moving Pictures* and "Film, Character Simulation, and Emotion."
23 For instance Marie-Laure Ryan, "Beyond Myth and Metaphor."
24 Janet Murray, *Hamlet on the Holodeck* (Cambridge, MA: MIT Press, 1997).
25 See Torben Grodal, "Video Games and the Pleasures of Control," in *Media Entertainment: The Psychology of its Appeal*, ed. Zillman and Vorderer (Mahwah, NJ: Lawrence Erlbaum, 2000).
26 Murray, *Hamlet on the Holodeck*.
27 Laurel, *Computers as Theatre*.
28 See Grodal, *Moving Pictures* and Torben Grodal, "Die Elemente des Gefühls. Kognitive Filmtheorie und Lars von Trier," in *Montage/av 9/1/00*:63–98.
29 Bela Balazs, *Theory of the Film* (New York: Dover, 1970).
30 See Grodal, *Moving Pictures*.

31  Bordwell, *Narration in the Fiction Film*.
32  George Lakoff, *Women, Fire, and Dangerous Things: What Categories Reveal about the Mind* (Chicago: Chicago University Press, 1997).
33  Roger Callois, *Les jeux et les hommes* (Paris: Gallimard, 1958).
34  See Paul D. MacLean, "Ictal Symptoms Relating to the Nature of Affects and Their Cerebral Substrate," in *Emotion: Theory, Research and Experience*, Vol. 3, ed. R. Plutchik and H. Kellerman (New York: Academic Press, 1986), 61–90.
35  In the article "Film Futures," published in *Substance* 31, No. 1 (2002), David Bordwell has described a group of films that try out different options and different futures, thus telling stories that wind back to a possible point of bifurcation. The experience of such films may however often change from a mimetic to a playful mode. The first version of the narrative is experienced in a more serious, "existential" mood by the viewers than the following versions, because the viewer feels the playful intentions of the addresser in version two and three (see Tom Tykwer, *Lola Rennt)*. However, if the film's use of multiple futures is based on some supernatural premises, as in Harold Ramis's *Groundhog Day* or James Cameron's *Terminator II*, the viewer may accept alternative versions with the same kind of existential involvement, because they are not playful repetitions any more but consequences of supernatural laws.
36  J. L. Bordewijk and B. van Kaam, "Towards a new classification of TeleInforation Services," *Inter-Media* 14, No. 1 (1986).
37  Laurel, *Computers as Theatre*.
38  Lakoff, *Women, Fire, and Dangerous Things*.
39  See Ryan, "Beyond Myth and Metaphor."
40  Grodal, *Moving Pictures*.
41  Claude Bremond, "Le message narratif," *Communications 4* (1964): 4–32.
42  See David Bordwell, "Film Futures."
43  Jesper Juul, "Games Telling Stories?," *Game Studies* 1, No. 1 (July 2001). Available online at <http://www.gamestudies.org/0101/juul-gts/>.
44  See Grodal, "Video Games and the Pleasures of Control."
45  See Torben Grodal, "Subjectivity, Realism and Narrative Structures in Film," in *Moving Images, Culture and the Mind*, ed. I. Bondebjerg (Luton: University of Luton Press, 2000), 87–104.
46  See Grodal, *Moving Pictures*.

## Bibliography

Anderson, Joseph. *The Reality of Illusion: An Ecological Approach to Cognitive Film Theory*. Carbondale: Southern Illinois University Press, 1996.

Balazs, Bela. *Theory of the Film*. New York: Dover, 1970.

Bordwell, David. "Film Futures." *Substance* 31, No. 1 (2002).

——. *Narration in the Fiction Film*. Madison: University of Wisconsin Press, 1985. Other edition: London: Methuen, 1986.

Bordwell, David, and Kristin Thompson. *Film as Art*. 6th Edition. New York: McGraw-Hill, 2001.

Bordewijk J. L., and B. van Kaam. "Towards a new classification of TeleInforation Services." *Inter-Media* 14, No. 1 (1986): 16–21.

Bremond, Claude. "Le message narratif." *Communications 4* (1964): 4–32.

Caillois, Roger. *Les jeux et les hommes. Le masque et le vertige*. Paris: Nrf Gallimard, 1958. Other editions: Paris: Gallimard, 1967; *Man, Play, and Games*. Translated by Meyer Barash. New York: Schocken Books, 1979. *Polish edition: Gry i ludzie*. Translated by Anna Tatarkiewicz and Maria Zurowska. Warszawa: Volumen, 1997.

Corballis, Michael C. *The Lopsided Ape: Evolution of the Generative Mind.* New York: Oxford University Press, 1991.

Damasio, Antonio R. *The Feeling of What Happens: Body and Emotion in the Making of Consciousness.* New York: Harcourt Brace, 1999.

———. "Brain and Language." In *Mind and Brain. Readings from Scientific American Magazine.* New York: Freeman, 1993.

Fauconnier, Gilles, and Mark Turner. *The Way We Think: Conceptual Blending and the Mind.* New York: Basic Books, 2002.

Grodal, Torben. "Film, Character Simulation, and Emotion." In *Nicht allein das Laufbild af der Leinwand . . .* , edited by Friss, Hartmann and Müller. Berlin: VISTAS, 2001.

———. "Art film, the Transient Body and the Permanent Soul." *Aura* VI, No. 3 (2000).

———. "Video games and the pleasures of control." In *Media Entertainment: The Psychology of its Appeal*, edited by Zillman and Vorderer. Mahwah, New Jersey: Lawrence Erlbaum, 2000.

———. "Subjectivity, Realism and Narrative Structures in Film." In *Moving Images, Culture & the Mind*, edited by I. Bondebjerg, 87–104. Luton: University of Luton Press, 2000.

———. "Die Elemente des Gefühls. Kognitive Filmtheorie und Lars von Trier." *Montage/av 9/1/00*, 63–98.

———. *Moving Pictures: A New Theory of Film Genre, Feelings, and Cognition.* Oxford: Clarendon/Oxford University Press, 1997.

Jakobson, Roman. "Linguistics and Poetics." In *Style in Language*, edited by Sebeok. Cambridge, MA: MIT Press, 1960.

Juul, Jesper."Games Telling Stories?" *Game Studies* 1, No. 1 (July 2001). Available online at <http://www.gamestudies.org/0101/juul-gts/>.

Lakoff, George. *Women, Fire, and Dangerous Things: What Categories Reveal about the Mind.* Chicago: Chicago University Press, 1997.

Laurel, Brenda. *Computers as Theater.* London: Addison Wesley, 1993.

MacLean, Paul D. "Ictal Symptoms Relating to the Nature of Affects and Their Cerebral Substrate." In *Emotion: Theory, Research and Experience*, Vol. 3, edited by R. Plutchik and H. Kellerman, 61–90. New York: Academic Press, 1986.

Mandler, Jean M. *Stories, Scripts and Scenes: Aspects of Schema Theory.* Hillsdale, New Jersey: Lawrence Erlbaum, 1984.

Münsterberg, Hugo. *The Film: A Psychological Study.* New York: Dover, [1916] 1970.

Mürray, Janet H. *Hamlet on the Holodeck: The Future of Narrative in Cyberspace.* MIT Press, 1997. [Other editions: NewYork: Free Press, 1997; and Cambridge, MA: MIT Press, 1998.]

Ryan, Marie-Laure. "Beyond Myth and Metaphor—The Case of Narrative in Digital Media." *Game Studies* 1, No. 1 (July 2001). Available online at <http://www.gamestudies.org/0101/ryan/>.

Tattersall, Ian. *The Monkey in the Mirror.* NewYork: Harcourt Brace, 2001.

Young, Kay and Jeffrey L. Saver. "The Neurology of Narrative." *SubStance* 30, Nos. 1–2 (2001), 72–84.

# 46

# EMBODIMENT AND INTERFACE

## Andreas Gregersen and Torben Grodal

Source: Bernard Perron and Mark J. P. Wolf (eds), *The Video Game Theory Reader 2* (New York, NY: Routledge, 2008), pp. 65–83.

Our biological embodiment is one of the most fundamental conditions that govern our experience of the world. The basic features of our biological embodiment have evolved to interact with a natural, non-mediated world and are a conglomerate of different capabilities. Besides having senses to monitor the world, body surface and body interior, we are agents that influence the world, and we may also be patients, that is: objects of other agents' actions or events unfolding around us. Interactive media activates aspects of this embodiment: audiovisual data stimulates eyes and ears to simulate a time-space—a simulated world (SW)—and a series of interfaces map actions in order to integrate the player with a SW in an interactive feedback loop, with resulting emotions that reflect the interaction. The interfaces provide motor links to a SW and may, to a limited extent, provide tactile aspects of interaction (in its active, but not in its passive patient, aspect). This essay will discuss how different types of interfaces and different game worlds mold players' embodied experiences, and centrally how player actions fuse with the audiovisual information.

We will refer to embodiment in two somewhat different, but related ways. One entails conceptualizing the human body as a physically-existing, biologically-evolved entity. The other entails *our experience of ourselves as embodied beings* and our mindful experiences of the world due to our embodiment. These two are obviously related, and since we work within a modern cognitive science framework incorporating questions of embodiment,[1] we assume that there is a set of rather tight connections between the two—to paraphrase an oft-quoted slogan of cognitive neuroscience, "the embodied mind is what the organism does". We will apply this idea of the embodied mind to examples of body-mapping within the realm of video games that map specific aspects of our physical actions to a virtual body in a virtual environment: different control schemes map different aspects of action onto different virtual bodies—all of them take our specific physical embodiment into account in order to produce specific experiences of embodiment.

## Agency and ownership, body schema, and image

When it comes to questions of agency and embodiment, a fruitful distinction has been proposed by philosopher Shaun Gallagher (Gallagher, *Body*), when he distinguishes between sense of agency and sense of body ownership as separable aspects of our embodiment. In normal embodied interaction with the environment, these two aspects are fused and operate pre-reflexively: We experience ourselves as instigating agents and we feel that the acting body is our own. Ownership of our bodies, but not of agency, is also in place when we are patients rather than agents—we know, for example, that it is *our* body that is being pushed down the stairs, even though we do not feel any ownership of action. We can thus distinguish between ownership of action (agency) and ownership of body. In relation to agency, the question of self-efficacy[2] is central: We may very well have an acute sense of body ownership and still have a distinct non-agentive feel if we believe that we lack the ability to influence states around us.

Although our physical embodiment ultimately determines the extent of our potential experiences, our experience of ourselves cannot be *reduced* to the actual, physical body as a thing among other things: one need only to consider the many instances where we literally feel the pain or joy of other people or represented avatar-agents as we observe them while linking aspects of our body image to that of the avatar. A person may literally wince as he scratches the red paint on his new car during a failed attempt at parking, because aspects of his body surface image and body experience have been projected to the car's surface to make a temporarily extended body image.

The "lived body" in Merleau-Ponty's[3] terms is thus not independent of the physical body, but it certainly is not reducible to it, either. This distinction raises a series of interpretational problems; we will follow Gallagher in making a basic and somewhat rough distinction between *body image* and *body schema:*

> A *body image* consists of a system of perceptions, attitudes and beliefs pertaining to one's own body. In contrast, a *body schema* is a system of sensory-motor capacities that function without awareness or the necessity of perceptual monitoring.
>
> (Gallagher, *Body*, 24)

Among the information systems used by the body schema processes are the visual, somatosensory, and proprioceptive systems. Visual systems yield information about the body as seen from the outside, while somatosensory systems give information related to touch and temperature of the skin and proprioceptive systems about body posture including muscle and joint position. Gallagher (*Body*, 24) further argues that the distinction between image and schema "is related respectively to the difference between having a perception of (or a belief about) something and having a capacity to move (or *an ability to do something*)" [emphasis added]. Gallagher also argues that although perceptual feedback

33

both contributes to a sense of body ownership and is important for our sense of agency, a primary cause of agency experiences seems to be processes tied to the actual intention to perform an action. In a summary of neurological studies related to agency and ownership, Gallagher and Zahavi[4] conclude that a sense of agency depends upon both higher-order intentions to perform an action, the motor commands issued, and proprioceptive feedback. Psychologist Daniel Wegner and others have argued that a sense of agency has a tendency to increase body ownership.[5]

Following this, we would argue that interacting with video games may lead to a sense of extended embodiment and sense of agency that lies somewhere between the two poles of schema and image—it is *an embodied awareness in the moment of action*, a kind of *body image in action*—where one experiences both agency and ownership of virtual entities. This process is a fusion of player's intentions, perceptions, and actions. Once the player stops acting in relation to the game system and pays conscious attention to his or her own embodiment, this effect subsides in favor of a more regular body image.

Interactive interfaces and game systems may selectively target and activate the auditory, visual, somatosensory, and proprioceptive systems. The extent to which an embodied sense of agency, ownership, and personal efficacy is fostered by games is very much a question of overall design including interface design.

## Possible actions

Merleau-Ponty writes that the body is "a system of possible actions". This is a strong claim, and it seems rather obvious that even though we encounter many different action opportunities throughout our lives, our physical body does not change in many of these. As already mentioned, however, anecdotal evidence suggests that even though the actual body does not change, different situations change *the experience of our embodiment*. For instance, we feel a range of situations in an almost somatosensory modality, even though the nerve endings of the somatosensory system are not being stimulated. And it is, of course, not the case that people feel actual pain when they scratch paint off beloved artifacts or when they watch others feel pain—but we do *feel* something distinctly body-related in these situations.

In embodied experiences related to video games incorporating virtual environments, there seems to be two related but different issues involved each of them due to different neurological structures. The first is the oft-noted flexibility of our embodiment; we are easily able to include parts of our environment into our intentional projects as clothes, canes, and even automobiles may become integrated parts of our embodied activity (Merleau-Ponty). Neuroscientists have identified specific structures that are plausibly responsible for this flexibility of the body schema to incorporate tools and other objects, including those virtually represented.[6] Bimodal neurons, that normally keep track of both somatosensory areas of hands or shoulders together with the visual field close to these areas, apparently enlarge their visual field to include tools while keeping this visual field tied to the body parts in question. This bimodal integration of visual information with somatosensory information provides a partly sub-personal but very real and efficacious feeling of an incorporated and augmented embodiment when we use tools for manipulating: we feel a clear sense of both agency and ownership with tool extensions that we are thoroughly familiar with.

The other issue is the well-known fact that observing other agents who perform bodily actions tends to activate parts of one's own motor system—and if the observing person also performs a motor action herself, the movements may be congruent or incongruent; the latter phenomenon is usually called motor interference.[7] For example, when people observe hand movements, those areas that prepare hand movements in their own nervous systems are activated, and a person instructed to perform movements in one direction while watching another person performing an action that is directionally opposed (for instance, up vs. down) suffers slight performance degradation.[8] The idea that perception and action is intricately linked is a main tenet of both classic phenomenology and modern cognitive science, and it has gained further support through the hotly-debated mirror systems or resonance systems tied to the motor systems. The basic idea is that many of the perceptually-driven motor activation and interference effects are due to specific mirror neurons (especially in the prefrontal motor cortex) that fire both when the subject observes an action and when she performs one herself; that is, they fire when a person plans and performs an act of grasping, but also when that person watches other people grasp. Such "shared circuits"-approaches[9] argue that we are fundamentally intersubjectively attuned to the movements of other bodies. Thus, modulations in our embodied experiences may come in several interacting streams from the body (somatosensory and proprioceptive) and (audio)visual information related to motor pattern stimuli from outside that activates mirror neurons. Both of these systems may come into play when experiencing embodiment effects in relation to virtual environments. One allows us to feel our own body extending into the virtual environment through a kind of virtual tool-use, the other activates our own motor system as a response to observed motor patterns.

## Mappings and interfaces

We have just mentioned that flexible embodiment is fundamental to our acting in the world, and we would hold that this includes the virtual worlds and synthetic environments presented by many video games. One of the fundamental conditions that govern our interactions with video game virtual environments is that our actions are mapped[10] onto the game system by various technological means, since we cannot physically manipulate the virtual entities directly. Such physical input devices (hereafter referred to as physical control interfaces) can take the form of keyboards, mice, joysticks, gamepads, motion-sensing devices such as the Wii-remote, steering wheels, trackballs, paddles, flight yokes, and, less often, dancing mats, plastic guitars, and other custom devices. All of these interfaces are designed to provide a more or less straightforward coupling with the constraints inherent in the biological human body, and as such they provide affordances, such as lifting, grasping, and pushing.[11] When coupled to a properly programmed game system, however, they also provide a mapping functionality that allows us to perform a wide range of actions in relation to that game system and its virtual environment. Importantly, this means that the combination of controller and game system provides both *physical affordances* and *intentional affordances*,[12] the latter often designed to yield a sense of augmented embodiment.

In what follows, we will discuss how actions are mapped through different physical control interfaces, and pay special attention to the recent mainstream adoption of the Nintendo Wii-remote control interface—an interface that prioritizes input related to hand movement in ways that have clear connections with the proprioceptive system. We will distinguish between primitive actions meaning actual body movements and on the other hand actions in the wider sense: moving the index finger (to pull a trigger) is a primitive action, whereas discharging a firearm is an action.[13] For the present purposes, a primitive action (P-action) is thus defined as merely a movement of the body. A given P-action may be part of many different actions, and an action may be constituted by different P-actions—there are many ways to skin a cat, as the saying goes. P-actions are usually performed to do something else by that movement: A break-down of many action descriptions is thus possible by using the formula "she performed the action *by* performing a P-action".[14] Applied to gaming, we perform a wide variety of game actions *by* performing P-actions in relation to control interfaces: The resulting state changes in the controller are mapped to the virtual environment.

We may grade P-actions in relation to different interfaces on a scale from the minimal action of moving a thumb or index finger to the maximal action such as a full swing of the arm. There is an arbitrary relation between P-action, the mapping, and its effects as relayed by the audiovisual feedback. In *Halo 3*, a move of the index finger will blow up a nuclear reactor, and in *Wii Tennis* a full swing of the arm will merely return a tennis serve. Thus some video games and their requisite control schemes emphasize motor activation and encourage players to perform maximal P-actions, while others prioritize the audiovisual effects resulting from the P-actions without emphasizing the latter. One end of the spectrum prioritizes contact senses and muscle sense input for its effects and emotional impact, while the other prioritizes the distal systems of visual and auditory perception.

We will return to the relationship between P-actions and their audio-visual consequences later in this essay, but we will note here that the typical action adventure game orchestrates virtual action opportunities that are positively grandiose and spectacular,[15] while actual body movements are limited to button pushes and joystick manipulation, and as such they rely very much on the *consequences of actions* relayed through audiovisual feedback for their embodied effects. With regard to this, several studies suggest that the area of visual field as a result of display size, together with spatio-temporal resolution, matters in terms of viewer arousal, perceived realism and emotional response—all else being equal, of course.[16]

Another important aspect of the mapping relation is the fact that our P-actions are very often—but not always—mapped to a representation of a body on screen, in such a way that when we perform a P-action, it causes changes to this body representation. Body representations in games may be more or less detailed and stylized to various degrees, and we shall not attempt a general typology of avatar embodiment here, but rather proceed by analyzing some cases in which a full or partial body representation on screen is visibly influenced as a result of mapped P-actions, since we find this relationship to be general enough to warrant investigation across cases which may exhibit differences (and undeniably significantly so) in avatar representations. We will very briefly introduce some general aspects of control schemes and then devote more attention to the games *Wii Sports* (Nintendo, 2006), *Eyetoy: Kinetic* (SCEA, 2005), and *ICO* (SCE, 2001), focusing on how the body and player actions are mapped onto or into video game spaces by analyzing the relationship between P-action and control interface.

## Different control schemes

The most widespread control relation in console gaming is what one could call the mainstream controller scheme, where minimal P-actions are performed on a standardized physical game controller. These P-actions are minimal and the necessary repertoire of P-actions is also rather small; all one needs to do is press buttons and move thumbsticks with the fingers—though precision and timing may be an issue. The mapping is most often both arbitrary and natural in the terms of psychologist and design theorist Don Norman (Norman, *Design*). Action mappings are often arbitrary in that you push buttons with your thumb to virtually jump or swing your arms—as opposed to any real jumping or swinging of arms or hands in physical space—but they can be said to provide a minimum of natural mapping in so far that the application of force in P-action may correspond to application of force in the virtual environment. Thumbsticks allow for a slightly greater degree of *motor isomorphism* and this is often exploited: forward locomotion of an avatar will almost invariably be mapped from a forward movement of the stick, and so on. This makes for motor congruence in the case of both avatar and virtual object movement. One might also note that certain domains of virtual action may make this correspondence even more direct, as in the case with games that include operating virtual firearms fired by index triggers—light guns, of course, take this principle to its logical conclusion.

The standard interface for PC gaming is the keyboard and mouse combination. The button presses on the individual keys are similar to buttons on the controller, although the keyboard makes possible a much wider range of discrete button mappings. Most game controllers are setup to be used by index and thumb on both hands, whereas the de facto standard of so called WASD key-mapping for locomotion (W=forward, S=backwards, A=left, D=right) in combination with

37

mouse movements for orientation uses three or four fingers for operation of the keys on the left side of the keyboard and the whole hand plus two fingers for the mouse. P-actions are quite minimal, and mouse movement may be isomorphic and naturally mapped in 2-D game spaces and cursor-operated 3-D games, and often semi-natural in the case of 3-D games with avatar embodiment. The WASD movement keys corresponds to movement changes in congruent directions, but in actual control, the key-operating fingers are usually not moved in any direction but down, and a forward movement of the mouse does usually not make the avatar move forward, but rather changes the virtual camera orientation—on a game controller this usually done via a thumbstick.

It is matter of debate how the motivation for the standard camera control scheme is understood best. One explanation could be that an image-schematic model of an object that can be tilted up or down replaces our natural perceptual actions: moving the mouse is equal to tilting the vehicle of our perceptual embodiment up or down. The flexibility of such a model may explain why some people need to reverse the camera controls in games—the dynamic will depend upon the imaged shape of the object in combination with the point of force application in relation to the axis of tilt or pan. A related aspect of this is that some games allow switching between first- and third-person viewpoints. In first person the default mode is usually "move mouse or thumbstick left to look left" whereas the third-person camera is often tethered behind the avatar and thus needs to move virtually to the right in order for the player to "look left". A potential complication here is whether the control relation is actually the avatar's orientation with a yoked camera position or the camera is independent of the avatar. These design decisions in combination with different image-schematizations of the relationship may result in different control preferences.

The Wii-remote departs from other standard game industry interfaces in that it combines the elements of the standard controller (discrete button presses and joystick movements), with something much less discrete, namely, the seeming ability to take actual body movement as input. In reality, and just like standard controllers, the Wii-remote does not actually map actions or actual body movement, but rather a set of state changes in the control system. The technology consist of accelerometers inside the Wii-remote together with an infrared positioning system using a sensor bar outside the controller coupled to an infrared camera in the controller. This enables the Wii-remote to be used to point toward the screen if one does not move outside the field of the infrared reception area, and it can also register controller movement in three-dimensional space since the accelerometers register changes on three axes (up-down, left-right, up-down)—one directional axis more than the standard joystick. An almost completely unified design intention seemed to be behind many of the launch games using this new type of controller, namely that of *isomorphic relations between an existing (and non-minimal) P-action motor domain and a virtual one*, with a direct mapping of real movements to virtual movements: a tennis stroke executed in the living becomes a tennis stroke on the virtual tennis court, and so forth. This control scheme enables the player to experience his own embodied interaction through both postural and, to a lesser extent, somatosensory input. The aim seems to be immersion in game actions through motor activation, motor isomorphism, and related ease of use. This is a design strategy, however, and one could argue that the issue of maximal and highly isomorphic P-action is primarily relevant in the cases where the player actively pursues similarity to an already well-known motor activity domain. Since the Wii-remote reacts to movements, not body acts per se, it is usually possible to use "medium-sized" or smaller P-actions instead of maximal swinging and so on. In other words, the desire for high motor congruence may or may not be present in the player, even though the game system setup offers it.

### Wii Tennis

Nintendo game designer and celebrity Shigeru Miyamoto introduced *Wii Tennis* in 2006 with the following words "Control is simple and intuitive. Even your mom can play." The game is as the name implies; a tennis game of the casual variety, since it only maps the control of one particular aspect of a tennis player's actions, namely the swinging of the racket, whereas positioning the avatar is taken care of by the AI in the game. Using *Wii Tennis* as an example of the aforementioned immediate-immersion-through-isomorphism strategy, it can be argued that such a strategy poses certain problems for games aiming for immersion in virtual environments, in that it may lead to a somewhat harmful bifurcation between actual and virtual space. In a nutshell, the dilemma is that if one prioritizes the actual physical control interface (PCI) and P-actions performed in relation to this, the phenomenal action space might switch from virtual space to actual space; available add-ons in the shape of mock tennis rackets that may be attached to the Wii-remote play up the physical reality of the PCI even more. This latter strategy might lead to trouble. One might accept this or not, based on one's own experience of Wii-remote functionality, and though one could argue that there is no sharp boundary between the screen space and the physical space experientially speaking, neuroscientific evidence suggests a slightly different picture.

In the comprehensive study of visual perception in relation to visually-guided behavior, it has become commonplace to distinguish between two separate brain systems that use visual information for different purposes: the dorsal and the ventral system. Originally, this was proposed by neuroscientists Ungerleider and Mishkin as the "where" and the "what" systems, respectively, the idea being, very briefly, that one system in the brain deals with spatial location ("where") whereas others deal with properties such as form and color ("what"). Another pair of neuroscientists, namely Milner and Goodale,[17] have later proposed that the actual distinction is better understood as that between "how" and "what". They argue that the dorsal system delivers "vision for action" and operates outside consciousness, while the ventral system deals with "vision for perception", the latter being a more traditional perceptive system delivering consciously-accessible perceptual information. So, a common scenario in which one wants to pick up a ball with one hand runs like this: the "vision for perception" system allows you to consciously see the ball and plan the actual action, but it is "vision for action" that sub-consciously controls the ongoing visual guidance of the actual hand movement. As such, the "vision of action" feeds directly into the motor system, or so the theory holds. This is by no means an uncontroversial thesis, especially not when applied to agency, perception, and awareness in general,[18] but the evidence seems pretty robust in favor of at least some functional division between these two systems.

Applied to *Wii Tennis* however, this seems to spell trouble: we see the ball on screen, not in our peripersonal space close to our own hand or to its extension, the Wii-remote. Despite the previously-mentioned results proposing body schema flexibility in relation to tools, other studies suggests otherwise; "vision for action" uses an exclusively egocentric frame of reference and coordinates this with actual body structure such as grip aperture of the hand, and this makes for incongruence when facing a screen that presents data in an allocentric—that is, an object-centered—representation scheme. The "vision for action" system simply is not built for relative size projections situated in virtual space.[19] A closer look at *Wii Tennis* in comparison with the actual motor domain of real tennis shows that the extent of such problems might depend on the task-interface structure at hand. As a casual analysis of real tennis suggests, the speed of the ball makes it difficult for visual guidance and online monitoring and correction of action by "vision for action". Studies support this intuition: in fact, a tennis pro needs to calculate, prepare, and execute motor movements that position himself and the racket properly *before the ball is served* in order to successfully return it, and much the same holds for baseball.[20] One of the primary cues used to select the proper motor plan seems to be the posture of the serving or pitching agent before and during the serve. Thus, a salient cue besides ball movement in a realistic tennis simulation would be the spatio-temporal biological motion pattern exhibited by the virtual serving agent prior to the actual serve and *Wii Tennis*, obviously, does not try to simulate this cognitive-perceptual challenge. Furthermore, the movement of the player getting into striking position—a key component in serve returns in real tennis that demands almost explosive body activation—is in any event computer-controlled: the key problem and requisite motor domain here is solely when and how to return the virtual ball by moving the Wii-remote, and the ball moves slowly enough to cue action in regard to this task.

On the one hand, the Wii-remote coupled to a screen display may lead to trouble if the games put too much emphasis on P-actions performed in the peripersonal space and on the actual controller in combination with virtual cues in screen space that do not correspond with the "vision for action"-space: players may spend cognitive and emotional resources inhibiting visually-guided action potentials that work with cues in relation to the hand and controller, not the virtual space—less efficacy of agency and less ownership of the virtual body may be the result. On the other hand, it is obvious that *Wii Tennis* works pretty well in terms of immediate control and the establishment of agency and ownership of actions—the 3-year old son of one of the authors needed only two swings in order to tacitly understand the mapping involved, and he had never seen or tried the system before—and this is probably largely due to the motor isomorphism facilitating ownership of agency and both bodies (real and virtual) to some extent. So, even although relatively slow and visually-guided actions may not be possible through "vision for action" in relation to virtual environments displayed on screen, the actual ease of control in such games as *Wii Tennis* and *Wii Baseball* makes it highly plausible that other systems, possibly tied to vision for perception, are perfectly able to execute a kind of visually-guided action based on allocentric, distal cues outside the peripersonal space. Furthermore, if the Wii-remote—or other input devices using similar, but more advanced technology—could be made to deliver a more nuanced action individuation and map these accordingly, interesting and quite complex artificial conflict patterns might be the result. The task-structure may profitably exploit perceptual-cognitive learning of the anticipatory variety, present its visual cues saliently on screen and make use of motor congruence, but designers should not bank on our otherwise amazing abilities to act effectively in peri-personal space, since this may be the work of motor schemas served by "vision for action", that is, structures that demand egocentric data for their proper functioning. Otherwise, problems with both agency and ownership may be the result.

*Swinging, hitting and grasping forcefully*

Another problem with the Wii-remote—and one that we find potentially more problematic for the technology's ability to produce a robust sense of agency and ownership—has to do with both the touch systems' and the proprioceptive systems' role in action. Physical force and force dynamics are central to our understanding of the physical world and thus, to a wide extent, our engagement with the world. A basic problem with the Wii-remote and many other game controllers is that true force feedback is impossible to implement in controllers of this kind, and in a nutshell, this yields a dissociation of sensory experience: in the games launched with the console, the actions depicted were, among others, using a racket to hit a tennis ball, using a sword to kill gangsters or smite mythological enemies, using a fishing rod to catch fish, and using fists to hit another agent in the face during a boxing match. Once again, the aim seems to be immersion through isomorphic movement patterns, and in most of the examples, the Wii-remote becomes a stand-in for a virtual tool that is grasped and handled in similar ways to the physical counterparts. But, this makes for some tradeoffs in the different kinds of information delivered by the perceptual systems. While the Wii-remote and the audiovisual feedback can manage a certain range of modal information, the force feedback is necessarily missing. When one swings a real weapon, the weight and length is easily felt by body schema processes, and if one hits something with the weapon as a consequence of a full swing, the impact can be literally stunning for the somatosensory system and muscles and joints. When one operates a real fishing rod, the interplay between such variables as weight, length and elasticity

41

of the rod, the elasticity of the line and the angle as a result of fish position, and, of course, the dynamic movements of a hooked fish will all translate into easily felt force dynamics. Part of these dynamical patterns will be felt through the posture and touch system, but one of the primary variables here seems to be the sheer amount of muscle tension involved in reeling in a fish. All of these crucial sensory inputs will be missing from the P-action performed in physical space. It seems obvious that in the absence of force feedback, the game will have to deliver through other input channels, but the question remains what exactly is gained by allowing one aspect of the action to be directly isomorphic while a very important aspect is completely missing. While the standard controller schemes couple minimal P-action with maximal audiovisual feedback, the Wii-setup makes for a kind of *incongruent motor realism*—the sense of ownership of the real body is high because body schema processes are activated, but both the sense of agency and transfer of ownership to the virtual space may be hampered severely, since what you feel and what you see does not add up. Less motor activation means less incongruence in these cases, which suggests a "less is more" strategy might be more useful. Another factor involved here is of course that force *is actually necessary* in the real world, but may not be in the games: In real tennis, you need a fast, powerful swing to make the ball move, but *Wii tennis* does not actually track a movement pattern in real space, just simple accelerator changes inside the controller. *Wii tennis* is thus essentially a game of timing, not of strength, and since it is much easier to time a quick flick of the wrist than a full swing, this quickly becomes the preferred strategy if one is interested in winning a match.

The problems of missing force dynamics is also quite pronounced in the boxing game included in *Wii Sports*. Here, the player can throw punches by making punching motions while grasping the Wii remote and the Nun-chuck and block punches by holding these controllers in front of the face. An actual punch may be more or less accurately mapped visually and thus quite isomorphic and congruent, but the feeling of landing a punch is, of course, sorely missing in terms of proprioception and somatosensory stimulation—thus minimal agency and efficacy might be the result of such *ghost physics*.[21] Blocking punches is also a semi-embodied affair since the action of holding up both hands will be mapped to a blocking movement, but once again the P-action and the visuals do not match up with the expected impact on the physical body. This shows the problematic dichotomy between acting upon other agents and being acted upon—the active and tense acts of hitting someone virtually benefits to some extent from the ability to actually make punching motions, but the patient-relations involved in the boxing match must be left to the audiovisual feedback—and since this is comparatively sparse when hitting or blocking in *Wii Boxing*, the game does not do a very good job of fostering ownership of the virtual body in that situation. Being hit, however, results in a very simple "explosion" effect, which is surprisingly effective on a large screen display. We would argue that the ownership effect here is tied as much to the real body as to the virtual one, which makes this particular aspect of the game somewhat successful in producing a patient effect in actual, not virtual, space.

Once again, we are of course not claiming that players are consciously expecting the boxer on screen to land a physical blow that can be physically felt—we are rather arguing that sub-personal expectations may lead to less than ideal feelings of being an embodied agent responsible for the actions portrayed on screen since the input is often incongruent over several channels of sensory input.

## *EyeToy and agency*

For a short comparative example of how game systems can map P-actions to virtual bodies and allow these to influence virtual entities, consider the EyeToy peripheral for the PlayStation 2 as used in the game *EyeToy: Kinetic* (2005). The game does not use a physical control interface; rather, the EyeToy camera captures video of the space in front of the camera and displays this as live video on screen—whatever P-action you perform, you will see on-screen as in a mirror (with a slight delay and potential size variation due to screen size). Typically, graphical objects are then rendered on top of this image, and the player is then prompted to perform actions in relation to the objects on screen, such as hitting or avoiding balls, etc. *Eye Toy: Kinetic* seems to rely solely on a primitive motion detection algorithm in order to calculate proximity and eventual collision between the screen body and virtual objects, and this combination of a moving visual image together with a very sparse underlying structural model of the displayed body makes for a potential asymmetry of inputs in relation to player body awareness, as could be seen during two *EyeToy: Kinetic* sessions. In one instance, the player's objective is to avoid a bouncing object, but when the player accidentally remained completely still, the virtual object "passed directly through" the body on screen, making the screen body a "ghost". In another situation, the player's objective is to hit a large object in the lower left corner of the screen, but several attempts to hit the object were rendered unsuccessful, although the on-screen body seemed to connect quite well. This turned out to be a matter of visual obstruction, since the back of an office chair obstructed the camera's field of view in the outermost left corner. In both instances, the algorithm could not cope with mapping the actual P-action to virtual action and the resulting discrepancy between body schema processes and visual feedback from the screen yielded distinct problems of both agency and ownership of the screen body.

## *Interface aesthetics in ICO*

One could also apply considerations of interface choice to the problem of theme in games—a kind of interface aesthetics with regard to the connection between embodiment, interface, and thematic content: How well would a different interface and its physical affordances serve the intentional affordances of a given game? As a very brief example of how this may play out, consider the highly regarded *ICO* (2001) for PlayStation 2, a game rightfully considered a modern classic. One of the main game mechanics is that the player avatar Ico has to protect the young girl Yorda from various demons or monsters. These monsters exhibit the kind of ghost-physics mentioned earlier: they seem to be like smoke or fog when it comes

43

to substance, but they have the power to physically affect their surroundings, as when they knock Ico over or grab Yorda. One way of repelling these ghost-like monsters is to repeatedly swat them with a wooden stick or sword, and this (somewhat curiously, given their apparent body composition) will drive them off eventually. If one were to use a control scheme utilizing motion sensing for this game action (as seen in *Red Steel* (Ubisoft, 2006) and *The Legend of Zelda: Twilight Princess* (Nintendo, 2006) on the Wii), it would fit the bill neatly in terms of force dynamics, since the thematically-motivated ghost physics and resulting absence of resistance should make for direct isomorphism of the movement kinematics and the expected feedback resulting from force dynamics. Transfer of agency and ownership should be high. The bouts of fighting are intricately tied to another central mechanic, namely the holding of Yorda's hand by pushing one of the shoulder (also called trigger) buttons operated by the index finger when gripping the controller. This is an important action in the game world, since the demons constantly try to carry Yorda away, and if they succeed the game ends prematurely. The P-action is of course a kind of grasping in force-dynamic terms, but neither the somatosensory dynamics of gripping a hand nor the tug of holding another person's hand can be simulated adequately by any of the standard controllers. Agency may be somewhat intact, but ownership might be hampered.

*ICO* is not a game that flaunts its own status as an artifact of audiovisual and ludic fiction—there is no Head Up Display showing score points, health, etc., no in-game map, and there are no postmodern pointers to the world of the player, not even the widespread conflation of interface relations and game world ("press 'X' to hit the demons") found in many other games.[22] One could nonetheless argue that, considering the importance of the emotional themes of solitude, bonding, and attachment, some of the constraints inherent in the game system setup serve the game quite well aesthetically. There is no question that Ico is just as much a character as he is an avatar, and the highly arbitrary mapping nature of the PS2 controller makes sure that the actions of player and avatar stay detached as far as P-actions go. Moreover, the game thrives on our interest in and empathy with the couple's predicament, and one might argue that Ico is doubly abandoned: both by his tribe and, albeit to a lesser extent, by the player who is forever situated outside Ico's action space. The minimal interface relations thus helps keep the player suitably detached from both the girl and the boy in the virtual space. So, if one were to translate *ICO*'s control scheme into motion sensing, one might gain immersion in one game mechanic, but at the same time it may alter the game as a whole in a direction adverse to the overall cognitive and emotional theme of the work as it stands on the PS2.

## Agency as experiencing the actions of others

This leads us to more fundamental considerations regarding the nature of mapping in relation to agency and some of the related fundamental emotional complexes.

It seems that interface relations in general support primarily the "positive performance" side of agency,[23] while leaving out those situations in which we might want to remain passive or invite actions of other agents and/or events to influence us, also physically. A wide range of actions facilitated by standard control schemes may be termed either kinaesthetically involving and/or agonistic; the most common game action in the action-oriented game is to attack something either with a projectile or a melee weapon. By their very nature, such actions usually involve an agonistic intention and a muscular tone best characterized as tense. Being a human agent, however, is also a matter of letting oneself be acted upon. The dyadic character of certain interaction patterns seem to involve a kind of turn-taking, and this phenomenon is well known from most agonistic games where it might be implemented directly (in turn-based games) or rather emerge from gameplay mechanics (virtual resources, fixed time delays after using a virtual skill, etc.). But this is only the abstract structure of letting others act—the actual embodied experience of being acted upon is still missing: the class of actions which are not exactly actions but rather "receptions" are still only evoked audiovisually and, with what one could only call minimal somatosensory stimulation, such as "rumble" motors inside controllers. It may be a banal observation that video game characters cannot touch us in a purely somatosensory way, but when one considers some of the design intentions behind motion sensing and body mapping, it becomes clear that interfaces facilitate certain isomorphisms related to agency but not others. As motion sensing and other technologies increasingly allows body schematics to be isomorphically mapped to a game space, we take another step in making embodied interaction *fundamentally asymmetric:* dishing out blows, blowing kisses, and petting one's virtual dog becomes eminently possible when one opens up this other channel of input with regards to the system, but the reciprocity in these actions is not facilitated by the interface setup: input to the system may be in the tactile modality, but system output serving as input to the player may not.

The above goes some way in showing that there are certain domains of actions that lend themselves less well to the interface relations of today, and among these are many of the action-emotion complexes involved in nurturing and bonding relations. We are not arguing that one cannot communicate, say, love through a letter, a telephone line, or any other technological medium. The visual feedback of doggish gratitude and playfulness that we get when petting a virtual Dalmatian in *Nintendogs* (Nintendo, 2005), for example, may, via synaesthetic networks, activate emotions and even low-level tactile sensations.[24] However, if one thinks that the actual body matters and subsequently privileges the actions of the actual, physical body in interface design in a given computer game, there are still certain constraints including a technological bias in favor of positive performance. In other words, players can dance, swordfight, and fish the nights away in the comfort of their living room, but they still get no hugs or kisses.

## Conclusion

Video games are computer-and-monitor-supported activities that select a small basketful out of all the possible ways that embodied brains may relate to worlds and other agents. A given real life event will also demand or emphasize a specific subset of the total set of possible ways such interactions may exist, also because the embodied brain is a pragmatic set of different functions evolved to perform different tasks.[25] This is even truer in relation to video games; there may (or may not) be core elements in play and games as a general category (Juul), but surely no total theory of video games is possible: Some games emphasize visually salient and/or association-rich audiovisual worlds and emotionally engaging characters, while others are highly abstract, some employ cognitively or emotionally intriguing challenges, while others prioritize physical action; some games are strongly goal-oriented and telic—others are paratelic, process-oriented, and so on. We have argued that embodied interface interaction is general enough to warrant attention, and the continuing work on making new interfaces points to the problem of how to activate the basic experiences of agency, efficacy, and ownership leading to immersion in relation to the player's embodied interaction with the screen-and-speaker world, partly by providing salient somatosensory and proprioceptive support for the feeling of embodied presence in the game world. The existing interfaces primarily support agency, and thus possibly feelings of active ownership and efficacy in relation to avatars and tools. In contrast, experiences of being patients, being objects of embodied actions deriving from game worlds, are presently not supported by existing interface technology.

## Notes

1 For examples, see Andy Clark, *Being There. Putting Brain, Body, and World Together Again* (Cambridge, MA: MIT Press, 1997); Shaun Gallagher, *How the Body Shapes the Mind* (Oxford: Clarendon, 2005), hereafter cited as Gallagher, *Body;* Raymond W. Gibbs, *Embodiment and Cognitive Science* (New York: Cambridge University Press, 2006); Torben Grodal, *Moving Pictures. A New Theory of Film Genres, Feelings and Cognition* (Oxford: Clarendon Press, 1997); Torben Grodal, "Video Games and the Pleasures of Control," in *Media Entertainment: The Psychology of Its Appeal*, eds. Dolf Zillmann and Peter Vorderer (Mahwah, NJ: Lawrence Erlbaum Associates, 2000), 197–213; Torben Grodal, "Stories for Eye, Ear, and Muscles: Video Games, Media, and Embodied Experiences," in *The Video Game Theory Reader*, eds. Mark J. P. Wolf and Bernard Perron (New York: Routledge, 2003), 129–155; Torben Grodal, *Embodied Visions* (New York: Oxford University Press, forthcoming); Alva Noë, *Action in Perception* (Cambridge, MA: MIT Press, 2004); and Edward E. Smith and Stephen M. Kosslyn, *Cognitive Psychology: Mind and Brain*. 1. (Upper Saddle River, NJ: Pearson/ Prentice Hall, 2007), hereafter cited as Smith and Kosslyn.

2 Albert Bandura, *Self-Efficacy: The Exercise of Control* (New York: W. H. Freeman, 1997), and Albert Bandura, "Toward a Psychology of Human Agency," *Perspectives on Psychological Science* 1, no. 2 (2006): 164–180.

3 Maurice Merleau-Ponty, *Phenomenology of Perception* (London: Routledge & Kegan Paul, 1962); hereafter cited as Merleau-Ponty.

4 Shaun Gallagher and Dan Zahavi, *The Phenomenological Mind. An Introduction to Philosophy of Mind and Cognitive Science* (Oxon: Routledge, 2008).

5 Jonathan Cole, Oliver Sacks and Ian Waterman, "On the Immunity Principle: A View from a Robot," *Trends in Cognitive Sciences* 4, no. 5 (2000): 167; Daniel M. Wegner, *The Illusion of Conscious Will* (Cambridge, MA: MIT Press, 2002); and Daniel M. Wegner and Betsy Sparrow, "Authorship Processing," in *The Cognitive Neurosciences, Third Edition*, ed. Michael S. Gazzaniga (Cambridge, MA: MIT Press, 2004), 1201–1209.

6 Angelo Maravita and Atsushi Iriki, "Tools for the Body (Schema)," *Trends in Cognitive Sciences* 8, no. 2 (2004): 79–86.

7 For an introduction, see G. Rizzolatti, L. Fogassi, and V. Gallese, "Mirrors in the Mind," *Scientific American* (November 2006); and Smith and Kosslyn.

8 James Kilner, Antonia F. de C. Hamilton, and Sarah-Jayne Blakemore, "Interference Effect of Observed Human Movement on Action is Due to Velocity Profile of Biological Motion," *Social Neuroscience* 2, no. 3 (2007): 158–166; and J. M. Kilner, Y. Paulignan, and S. J. Blakemore, "An Interference Effect of Observed Biological Movement on Action," *Current Biology* 13, no. 6 (2003): 522–525. Some of these effects extend even to language processing. See Daniel C. Richardson, Michael J. Spivey, Lawrence W. Barsalou, and Ken McRae, "Spatial Representations Activated During Real-Time Comprehension of Verbs," *Cognitive Science* 27, no. 5 (2003): 767–780.

9 Susan Hurley, "Active Perception and Perceiving Action: The Shared Circuits Model," in *Perceptual Experience*, eds. Tamar Szabó Gendler and John Hawthorne (Oxford: Oxford University Press, 2006), 205–259. See also Gallagher, *Body*, Ch. 9.

10 Donald A. Norman, *The Design of Everyday Things* (New York: Basic Books, 2002); hereafter cited as Norman, *Design*.

11 James J. Gibson, *The Ecological Approach to Visual Perception* (Boston: Houghton Mifflin, 1979).

12 Michael Tomasello, *The Cultural Origins of Human Cognition* (Cambridge, MA: Harvard University Press, 1999).

13 As implied in Donald Davidson, *Essays on Actions and Events* (Oxford: Oxford University Press, 1980); hereafter cited as Davidson.

14 Following Davidson; Georg Henrik von Wright, *Explanation and Understanding* (Ithaca, IL: Cornell University Press, 1971); and Jennifer Hornsby, *Actions, International Library of Philosophy* (London: Routledge & Kegan Paul, 1980).

15 Geoff King, *Spectacular Narratives: Hollywood in the Age of the Blockbuster* (London: I. B. Tauris, 2000); and Geoff King and Tanya Krzywinska, *Tomb Raiders and Space Invaders: Videogame Forms and Contexts* (London: I. B. Tauris, 2006).

16 See Matthew Lombard and Theresa Ditton, "At the Heart of It All: The Concept of Presence," *Journal of Computer-Mediated Communication*, no. 2 (1997); and Byron Reeves and Clifford Nass, *The Media Equation: How People Treat Computers, Television, and New Media Like Real People and Places* (Stanford: CSLI Publications, 1996).

17 Arthur David Milner and Melvyn A. Goodale, *The Visual Brain in Action, Oxford Psychology Series*, no. 27 (Oxford: Oxford University Press, 1996), hereafter cited as Milner and Goodale.

18 See Pierre Jacob and Marc Jeannerod, *Ways of Seeing. The Scope and Limits of Visual Cognition* (Oxford: Oxford University Press, 2003); and Johannes Roessler and Naomi Eilan, eds. *Agency and Self-Awareness. Issues in Philosophy and Psychology* (Oxford: Oxford University Press, 2003).

19 Milner and Goodale; see also Y. Hu and M. A. Goodale, "Grasping after a Delay Shifts Size-Scaling from Absolute to Relative Metrics," *Journal of Cognitive Neuroscience* 12, no. 5 (2000): 856–868.

20 Nicola J. Hodges, Janet L. Starkes, and Clare MacMahon, "Expert Performance in Sport: A Cognitive Perspective," in *The Cambridge Handbook of Expertise and Expert Performance*, eds. K. Anders Ericsson, Neil Charness, Paul J. Feltovich and Robert R. Hoffman (Cambridge: Cambridge University Press, 2006), 471–488.

21 Pascal Boyer, "Cognitive Constraints on Cultural Representations: Natural Ontologies and Religious Ideas," in *Mapping the Mind: Domain Specificity in Cognition and Culture*, eds. Lawrence A. Hirschfeld and Susan A. Gelman (Cambridge: Cambridge University Press, 1994), 391–411.

22 See Jesper Juul, *Half-Real: Video Games between Real Rules and Fictional Worlds* (Cambridge, MA: MIT, 2005), hereafter cited as Juul.

23 Jennifer Hornsby, "Agency and Actions," in *Agency and Action*, eds. John Hyman and Helen Steward (Cambridge: Cambridge University Press, 2004), 1–23.

24 For an overview of synaesthesia, see Simon Baron-Cohen and John E. Harrison, eds. *Synaesthesia* (Cambridge, MA: Blackwell, 1997).

25 Lawrence A. Hirschfeld and Susan A. Gelman, eds. *Mapping the Mind: Domain Specificity in Cognition and Culture* (Cambridge: Cambridge University Press, 1994); Elizabeth S. Spelke, "Core Knowledge," *American Psychologist* 55, no. 11 (2000): 1230–1233; and Elizabeth S. Spelke and Katherine D. Kinzler, "Core Knowledge," *Developmental Science* 10, no. 1 (2007): 89–96.

# THE MYTH OF THE ERGODIC VIDEOGAME

## Some thoughts on player-character relationships in videogames

*James Newman*

Source: *Game Studies: The International Journal of Computer Game Research*, 2(1), July 2002, available at http://www.gamestudies.org/0102/newman/.

### Introduction

One of the most common misconceptions about videogames is that they are an interactive medium. By this, I do not mean to draw attention to the problematic and ideologically charged notion of "interactivity" (see Aarseth, 1997 for example) or even to the difficulty in conceiving videogames as a medium as Friedman (forthcoming) has noted. Rather, the misconception reveals a more fundamental misunderstanding of videogames and the experience of play. Quite simply, video-games are not interactive, or even ergodic. While they may contain interactive or ergodic elements, it is a mistake to consider that they present only one type of experience and foster only one type of engagement. Videogames present highly structured and, importantly, highly segmented experiences. Play sequences, from where the idea of the interactivity or ergodicity of videogames derives, are framed and punctuated by movie sequences, map screens, score or lap-time feedback screens and so on.

Moreover, by examining the contexts in which videogames are actually used, it is possible to suggest that play need not be simply equated with control or active input. The pleasures of videogames are frequently enjoyed by those that commonsense might encourage us to consider as non-players—"onlookers" that exert no direct control via the game controls. In this article, I want to suggest that videogame players need not actually touch a joypad, mouse or keyboard and that our definition needs to accommodate these non-controlling roles. The pleasure of videogame play does not simply flow through the lead of a joystick.

I want also to suggest that the interplay of sequences requiring greater or lesser degrees of control, coupled with the variety of "controlling" and "non-controlling" or "primary" and "secondary" roles has significant implications for the ways in which videogame characters are understood, composed and related to. I want to suggest that, for the controlling player during gameplay sequences, the notion of "character" is inappropriate. Here, the "character" is better considered as a suite of characteristics or equipment utilised and embodied by the controlling player. The primary-player-character relationship is one of vehicular embodiment. In suggesting this model, I seek to challenge the notion of identification and empathy in the primary-player-character relationship and, consequently, the privileging of the visual and of representation-oriented approaches. Moreover, I want to show how the porting of videogame characters into other media further illuminates the complexity and multiplicity of character existences.

Expanding on Friedman's work on *SimCity* and *Civilization* (1995, forthcoming), it is possible to go further and suggest that the very notion of the primary-player relating to a single character in the gameworld may be flawed. Rather than "becoming" a particular character in the gameworld, seeing the world through their eyes, the player encounters the game by relating to everything within the gameworld simultaneously. Perhaps the manner in which the *Super Mario* player learns to think is better conceived as an irreducible complex of locations, scenarios and types of action. Certainly, it is difficult to dislocate Mario the "character" from Mario World, with its interconnecting pipes, or from running, jumping, and puzzling, or even from the enemies, adversaries and opponents encountered in Dinosaur Island. In this way, perhaps the very notion of player-character relationships, and characters in locations performing actions and encountering other non-player-characters, still betrays an insensitivity to the experience of videogame play.

## Beyond visualism

Last year, at the UK's first academic videogames conference, I took the opportunity to present a deliberately provocative paper that suggested that when playing videogames, appearances do not matter. Subsequently, I have tried this idea on groups of undergraduate media students and they, like many of the delegates at Game Cultures, look at me as if I've gone completely mad. Why expend so much effort on lavish visuals, CGI intros, cut-scenes, graphics engines, texturing systems, lighting models and so on, if these things aren't important? Videogames and systems are sold on the basis of their graphical prowess. Before long, in grappling with the apparent idiocy of such a blinkered view, discussion turns to the *L-word* . . . Lara. Can you seriously expect me to believe that if Lara Croft looked like Vibri from *Vib Ribbon* that *Tomb Raider* would have sold so well? Well no, I'm not quite saying that. In fact, in terms of the way the game sells or rather, has been sold, I'm not saying that at all. When I say that appearances don't matter, I am certainly not talking about advertising and marketing games. What I am saying is that the pleasures of videogame *play* are not principally visual, but rather are kinaesthetic. In this way, the appearance of Lara or Vibri is not crucial to the primary-player during play. The way it feels to be in the *Tomb*

*Raider* or *Vib Ribbon* gameworld is, however, of paramount importance. Many a great game has poor visuals—an entire generation of players grew up with blips of light, @ signs and even text-only games—but there are few good games with bad controls. Few good games feel bad. What I am suggesting is that, by better understanding the particular types of engagement that occur between players and on-screen characters during play, we may begin to arrive at a point where we don't have to think about Lara in playable game sequences in terms of representation—we don't have to think about her in terms of representational traits and appearance—we don't even have to think about "her" at all.

## Ergodic videogames?

Aarseth (1997) has rightly pointed out the redundancy of the concept of "interactivity". The use of the term in a variety of contexts as qualitatively and experientially diverse as videogames and DVD scene access menus has rendered it meaningless and of use only to the marketer. While the concept of ergodicity, being grounded in a concrete definition, is immeasurably favourable, it is important to note that its application to videogames is by no means simple. It is useful to start by asking a seemingly simple but frequently overlooked and critical question: How ergodic are videogames?

We have all asked and have been asked questions along this line, and we are most used to thinking in comparative terms. So, we tend to ask whether games are more or less ergodic than television, or film or the web? However, such responses mask the true complexity of videogame ergodicity. A more fruitful way of conceiving the question is to consider how much time we spend actually in non-trivial action when "playing" a videogame. Unfortunately, the answer is not as simple as the question and rather depends on the specific game, but importantly, the answer in (I think) all cases, is "not all the time."

If we look at a game like *StarFox 64* (renamed *Lylat Wars* in Europe), we begin to get some idea as to the amount of "non-ergodicity" in videogames. Turn on your N64 and you will be treated to nearly two minutes of intro movie before you get to the PRESS START BUTTON "title screen". Even then, you receive nearly three minutes of further contextualising/intro movies before you can start flying your Arwing spaceship. Importantly then, videogames do not present a singularly ergodic experience. They are highly structured and comprise episodes of intense ergodic engagement. However, these sequences are punctuated and usually framed by periods of far more limited ergodicity and very often, apparently none at all. Even once you have stepped into your Arwing and begun flying, the experience is not one of continuous play. Most videogames are portioned and packaged into discrete if interconnected sequences. These may take the form of levels (*StarFox*), laps (*Gran Turismo*), bouts (*Virtua Fighter*), or zones, stages, matches etc. This is not to say that you are staring at a blank screen waiting for the next level to load. These "non-ergodic" sections are integral parts of the game. They might, perhaps, give us some sense of progression through a world and explain how the levels fit together as in *StarFox*. They may offer breaks between levels informing us of our performance (*Super Mario Kart*) allowing us to gauge our progress, compare lap-times, bask in our glory or chide ourselves for the way we took that last corner. They might present cut-scenes that advance the game's framing narrative (if one is present) as in the *Metal Gear Solid, Final Fantasy* or *Tomb Raider* series, or they may simply reflect the technical limitations of the host game system with its limited RAM and comparatively slow media access times. Regardless of their specific function or the reason for their existence, it is vital to note that videogames are not uniformly ergodic.

## On-Line/Off-Line

In my previous research, I have proposed a model based around the identification of two fundamental states of engagement with videogames that I have termed "On-Line" and "Off-Line". Broadly, On-Line refers to the state of ergodic participation that we would, in a commonsense manner, think of as "playing the game". So, I'm On-Line when I'm actually playing *Metal Gear Solid*—when I'm Mario in *Super Mario 64*; when I'm hurtling round a track in a souped-up Skyline in *Gran Turismo 3*. Off-Line engagement, could be seen as equating with non-ergodicity, and while it is important we do not allow ourselves to confuse this with passivity for reasons shall explain below. Off-Line describes periods where no registered input control is received from the player. In this terminology, I refer to players' On-Line or Off-Line engagement with games and also On-Line or Off-Line sequences or sections within games.

The demarcation between On-Line and Off-Line sections need not be as blunt as simple switch from cut-scene to play sequence and a number of techniques are used that more subtly manage the segue. Perhaps the most obvious example would be a race game like *wipEout* in which the player is treated to a pre-race pan over the starting grid, before being deposited in the driving seat of their vehicle—waiting for the green light . . . During this section, the game is out of the player's hands . . . However, rather than simply handing over control when the green light shows, the player gets to rev their engine. This doesn't sound too impressive but it serves a number of purposes. Most importantly, as in games like *Super Mario Kart* and *wipEout*, you can try and elicit an extra fast Turbo Start. Consequently, boundary between Off-Line and On-Line sections and engagement is effectively blurred. Similar techniques can be seen in the most recent incarnations of the *Final Fantasy* series (e.g. *FFVII* and *IX*), for example, where attempts are made to more seamlessly integrate pre-rendered Off-Line and On-Line sequences. In games like *Shenmue*, for example, this boundary blurring helps generate a sense of experiential cohesion in which the player does not feel any wrench as they move from ergodic play to movie sequence. Similarly, as is the case with some of *Shenmue*'s QTEs (Quick Time Events), ergodic punctuations can interrupt and break up otherwise Off-Line sections and effectively lend the whole scenario a sense of enhanced participatory involvement as attention is maintained more solidly to guard against the potential for surprise attacks.

We can begin to see that the binarism of On-Line and Off-Line is insufficient to capture the variety of states of engagement. For this reason, On-Line and Off-Line engagement should be thought of as the polar extremes of an experiential or ergodic continuum. In this way, we can better account for states such as the acutely attentive watching and readiness as in the *Shenmue* QTE example above, where, despite the primary-player's lack of control input, they seem more involved than when watching the opening intro sequence (or any other non-ergodic media form). *Shenmue*'s QTE device, like *wipEout* revving, imbues these sequences with an ergodic *potential* that demands and fosters a greater degree of player engagement than a standard cut-scene or introduction.

Moreover, an ergodic continuum of On-Line/Off-Line engagement allows us to account for roles such as the "non-controlling navigator'. As Jessen (1995, 1996, 1998) has noted, videogames are not exclusively solitary experiences, regardless of what popular discourses might suggest about their inherent aso-ciality. Even ostensibly single-player games like *Tomb Raider* are often played by "teams"—with the primary-player performing the traditional task of control while others (secondary players)—interested, engaged with the action, but not actually exerting direct control through the interface, perform tasks like map-reading, puzzle-solving and looking out for all the things that the principal player doesn't have time for. Here then, we note a level of ergodicity in non-controlling players. In fact, judging by their reactions, the level of secondary-players' par-ticipative engagement during play sequences can be seen to be greater than in the primary-player during standard cut-scenes. While cut-scenes provide primary and secondary-players a chance to relax between sequences of frenetic, high velocity and volume play, play sequences maintain interest and attention with frequent and often frantic suggestions, advice and warnings coming from secondary-players.

The secondary-player role is frequently taken by players who like the idea of games but find them too hard and is just one example of the ways players appropriate videogame experience in manners often not intended by producers (or observed by researchers). A number of players I have worked with love the idea of the *Legend of Zelda* series but get frustrated as their attempts lead to a few minutes of joystick mashing and then death. So they play together. Furthermore, adopting a "co-pilot" role allows one to notice aspects of the game that are missed in the role of primary player. Thus one can perfect one's own skills Off-Line through the adoption of the secondary-player role.

A realisation of these often unacknowledged roles goes some way to address-ing my students' natural concerns as to the seeming waste of effort that is repre-sented in the continuing battle for increased visual richness in videogames. Why bother painstakingly animating Lara's ponytail if it is of no consequence to the player? Lara's ponytail, like the gorgeous reflections in *Gran Turismo 3*, and the water effects in *Wave Race: Blue Storm* exist for a number of reasons. Firstly, it is incredibly difficult to sell "interactivity" through non-participative advertising channels (TV, print etc) or even in a retail environment as controls take time to master making throughput is poor, while the initial period of frustration encountered in most games is hardly conducive to sales. Selling games on the basis of their visual richness is much easier—non-playable demo sequences on videowalls, screen shots on packaging, TV and print ads . . . Secondly, the audio-visual richness of the gameworld potentially serves the secondary-player. In addition to map making and reading, pre-empting danger and puzzle solving, being able to scrutinise the gameworld, marvelling at the reflections, discerning graphical nuances and even spotting glitches, amplify and heighten the experience of the non-controlling, secondary player. Off-Line ergodicity can be characterised by this combination of activity contributing to the attainment of the game objective and the pleasure of the audio-visual.

## Playing games

The On-Line relationship between primary-player and system/gameworld is not one of clear subject and object. Rather, the interface is a continuous feedback loop where the player must be seen as both implied by, and implicated in, the construction and composition of the experience. Locked into this feedback loop at the level of interface or controls (hence the significance of the feel of the game), the player experiences at the level of first-hand participation and can then sustain and decode multiple and apparently contradictory presentations of the self. So, in a CoinOp driving game, for example, it is possible to be, at once, seated in a mock-up car chassis, grasping a steering wheel with pedals beneath one's feet, staring at a screen (presumably the windscreen), through which we view a remote, clearly mediated vision of ourselves as relayed by a camera in a trailing helicopter. The view is replete with the trappings of explicit camera mediation such as lens flare. Yet the experience is reported as one of first-hand, being, doing and participation. Nintendo's GameCube *Wave Race: Blue Storm* not only includes lens-flare but also shows raindrops and spray from the player's jetski hitting the screen, yet first-hand participation is not diminished and the game does not take on the feeling of remote control. However, many game designers, critics and commentators, suggest that it should. Bob Bates' (2001: 48) view is typical.

> First-person games tend to be faster paced and more immersive. There is a great sense of being "in the world" as the player sees and hears along with his character. Third-person games allow the player to see his character in action. They are less immersive but help the player build up a stronger sense of identification with the character he is playing

However, if we see first-hand participation as being derived from an interface-level control loop we can disentangle viewpoint from reported feelings of immersion, engagement and *being-in-the-gameworld*. What Bob Bates seems to be better describing is the secondary-player who does scrutinise the gameworld and derives pleasure from taking in the sights and sounds. For the secondary-player, it may well be more accurate to discuss the greater degree of identification that comes with third-person viewpoint. For the primary-player, however, viewpoint is important only in so far as it impacts upon the game. Primary-players are often given dynamic control of viewpoint with the ability to switch between a number of preset viewtypes as in Sega's *Virtua Racing/Daytona* series, or full "360°" manipulative control as in *Super Mario 64*. Nintendo's GameCube joypad has a dedicated "C" stick nominally set aside for in-game camera control.

It is because the sense of being-in-the-gameworld derives from an interface-level connection rather than being a product of viewpoint that games such as *Super Mario World* that present their gameworld in a third-person viewpoint can be just as engaging as (pseudo-) first-person viewpoint games like *Quake* or even second (or dynamically shifting-) person games like *Super Mario 64*. During On-Line play, videogames are experienced by the primary-player first hand regardless of the mode of their presentation or content mediation. In recollection of their play, players talk not of playing or controlling but of "being". The concentration on viewpoint (often erroneously referred to as "perspective") reveals an over-reliance on representational models and mechanisms of player/viewer connectivity. It is my assertion here that the degree of participative involvement and engagement with any specific game is not contingent upon the mode of representation. While to the non-participating observer, or even secondary-player, gameworlds frequently present themselves in forms which deconstruct into "fake" or "unrealistic" or demonstrate flaws or bugs undermining the authenticity of the presentation (e.g. polygon shearing, tearing, z-buffering errors or polygonal "blocking in", see Psygnosis' *wipEout*), to the actively engaged, implicated On-Line player, such limitations lose their immediate significance and the same gameworlds gel with an experiential coherence that renders them both believable and perhaps even "real".

The On-Line/Off-Line continuum reflects the significance of player involvement and implication in the generation and functioning of the experience, the need to move beyond detached and disintegrated analysis of "systems", "output stimuli" and "interfaces" (as in much classical HCI research, e.g. Benyon and Murray, 1988), and incorporate a recognition of the difference between controlling and non-controlling, primary and secondary player appreciation of, and engagement with, videogames.

## There's only one Mario?

In her discussion of the Oedipalised narrative of videogames, Kinder (1993) identifies each of the four player-selectable characters in *Super Mario Bros.2* with a target audience of players, thereby justifying and explaining the existence of each discrete appearance as a means to foster connectivity with each player-group. For Kinder, males 7–14 have "Mario" and "Luigi", pre-schoolers have "Toad", whilst females have "Princess Toadstool". (Incidentally, "Toad" is an anthropomorphised toadstool although Kinder omits to mention this fact. Perhaps there is no age or gender coding in fungal representation?) In fact, Kinder, herself, goes some way to highlighting the problem with this apparently neat classification by pointing out that:

> ... despite her inferior jumping and carrying power [Princess] has the unique ability of floating for 1.5 seconds—a functional difference that frequently leads my son and his buddies to choose her over the others, even at the risk of transgender identification
>
> (Kinder, 1993: 107)

Quite rightly, Jenkins has pointed to the potential inadequacy of the traditional approaches of identification that are implied in Kinder's account

> Does this not suggest that traditional accounts of character identification may be inadequate descriptions for the children's relationships to these figures?
>
> (Jenkins, 1993: 68)

Perhaps the apparent willingness of these boys to select a female character in certain circumstances "even at the risk of transgender identification" is suggestive of a process of character selection based not on empathetic identification or even representation at all. However, it is not just that at the character selection stage players rationally select the best character for the task at hand (although this does happen, especially when players gain expert knowledge of a gameworld and the demands placed upon them in specific environments, at specific times, or even by other players/NPCs in combative games, for example). Far more significant is the realisation that the character-selection process described by Kinder reveals a relationship with these characters that disregards representational traits in favour of the constitution of character as sets of capabilities, potentials and techniques offered to the player. The player utilises and embodies the character in the gameworld. While it may retain significance on the box, in adverts, even in cut scenes and introductions within the game, during On-Line engagement, the appearance of the player's character is of little or no consequence. By this, I mean to suggest that the level of engagement, immersion or presence experienced by the player—the degree to which the player considers themselves to "be" the character—is not contingent upon representation. On-Line, "character" is conceived as capacity—as a set of characteristics.

The On-Line/Off-Line distinction provides a useful framework within which to further examine these multiple existence. Sonic the Hedgehog in a cel-animation cartoon is a very different character than in an On-Line section of a videogame. In the cartoon, Sonic has an autonomy and an independence. In short, he has a character (limited, perhaps, but a character nonetheless, while Off-Line there is no "he"). It only makes sense to talk of Sonic as "he" in this world beyond the On-Line videogame. In the videogames, "Sonic" becomes the ability to run fast, loop-the-loop, collect rings . . . . In Lucozade adverts, Lara walks and talks, she shoots and runs. Importantly, she does all these things without a player. In the On-Line sections of *Tomb Raider*, without a player, "Lara" just stands there. In the *Tomb Raider* movie, I can go to sleep or walk out and Lara will still save the day. But the game needs me. Lara doesn't need me in the introductions and cut scenes but *Tomb Raider* needs a player On-Line. The game is nothing without a player. The characters are nothing without a player. On-Line, the individuality and autonomy of character that we see Off-Line whether in films, adverts, cut-scenes or even on the packaging the game comes in, is subsumed and gives way to game-specific techniques and capabilities that the player uses, and more importantly, embodies within the gameworld. We can see that as characters move between mediums they both gain and lose traits as the particular form demands. Jenkins notes the way in which, upon making the transition to the video game-world, cartoon characters are stripped of many of their identifying traits rendering them " . . . little more than a cursor which mediates the players' relationship to the story world" (1995: 61).

Thus, On-Line "character" in the sense we understand it in non-ergodic media, dissolves. Characters On-Line are embodied as sets of available capabilities and capacities. They are equipment to be utilised in the gameworld by the player. They are vehicles. This is easier to come to terms with when we think of a racing game like *Gran Turismo* where we drive a literal vehicle, but I am suggesting that, despite their representational traits, we can think of all videogame characters in this manner. On-Line, Lara Croft is defined less by appearance than by the fact that "she" allows the player to jump distance $x$, while the ravine in front of us is larger than that, so we better start thinking of a new way round . . .

The videogame production process reveals much about the (in)significance of representation and characterisation in the "traditional" sense. *Pilotwings64* is illustrative.

> [character designs] just turned up one day and we immediately started to implement them in the [partially complete] game. There's no story built around the characters as such, but they are very visible in the game and possess different characteristics, the strong burly guy obviously requires a lot more lift but can turn the hang glider faster
>
> (Gatchell, 1995: 64)

Again, characters here are defined around gameplay-affecting characteristics. It doesn't matter that it's a burly guy—or even a guy—or even perhaps a human. That the hang glider can turn faster is a big deal; this affects the way the game plays. This affects my chances of getting a good score.

The television advertising campaign for Ubisoft's *Rayman 2* for Nintendo64 is similarly illustrative of the dominance of capability and experiential opportunity in the appeal of the videogame. "Rayman" is defined not by his appearance or any traits of individuality or autonomy but by his ability (to allow the player) to run, jump, swim . . .

> No arms, no legs . . . True, but Rayman can do anything (or almost!):
> jump, swim, loop de loop, climb, scale walls, slide and fly using his hair
> as a helicopter . . . Rayman will evolve throughout the game and will be
> given some temporary powers by his friends such as flying helicopter
> mode, or grabbing onto Purple Lumz, and even progressively increasing
> the power of his shot!
>
> (Ubisoft (US) website, 2001)

Hideo Kojima, producer of the phenomenally successful *Metal Gear Solid* series
(for PlayStation and PlayStation2), lauded for its filmic qualities, is similarly
revealing,

> We tried not to give him [Snake] too much character because we want
> players to be able to take on his role. Snake isn't like a movie star. He's
> not someone you watch, he's someone you can step into the shoes of.
> Playing Snake gives gamers the chance to be a hero
>
> (Kojima, 1998: 43)

The "characterisation", individuality and distinctiveness of Snake comes not from
his appearance On-Line (where "he" is embodied by the player as a set of available
techniques and capacities) but rather in the Off-Line cut-scenes and contextualis-
ing narratives of the introductory sequences. On-Line, there is no Snake.

## Thinking like a computer

The discussion thus far has centred on reconceiving player-character relationships. In doing so, I have distinguished between primary and secondary players
and have suggested that, to the primary player at least, the appearance of the character both in terms of their representational traits and the mode of presentation,
is comparatively insignificance during play sequences. Following from Friedman
(e.g. 1995), I want to suggest an even more radical way to conceive this relationship. On-Line, the "character" is a complex of all the action contained within the
gameworld. By which I mean that On-Line, "being" Lara is as much about being
presented with puzzles as it is having the techniques and resources to solve them.
It's as much about being in dark, dank caverns and being attacked by wolves as
it is having the equipment to combat them. The situation and action within the
gameworld are inexorably bound into the players' conception of the experience of
being within that gameworld. Player accounts are structured around action, around
environment, around activity. In this way, any model of connection based around
identification with a single entity in the gameworld is perhaps oversimplified. It
is important to note that, while my examples have focused upon videogames in
which a clearly defined player-controlled "character" may be identified (whether
that be man, woman, car, spaceship, fungus), this principle can be seen at work
in games where there is no apparent mediating "character" or even abstract

58

"cursor", in Jenkins' terms. As one of my PhD field research participants boldly but insightfully proclaimed, "when I play *Tetris*, I am a tetraminoe." In exploring these issues more thoroughly, they suggested that they didn't consider themselves to be a single Tetris block so much as every Tetris block whether falling, fallen or yet to fall. Clearly, this demands a totally new framework within which to understand the relationship between player and gameworld. Even the notion of On-Line character as an identifiable and singular entity embodied by the player may be an oversimplification indicative of an implicit reliance on existent models of audience. As I have indicated, my previous and current research exploring the On-Line relationship between player and gameworld suggests that this linkage is best considered as an experiential whole that synthesises, action, location, scenario, and not merely as a bond between subject and object within a world . . . On-Line, the player is both the goal and the act of attaining it. Here, Friedman's notion of "thinking like a computer" seems particularly pertinent.

> When you play a simulation game like *Civilization II*, your perspective—the eyes through which you learn to see the game—is not that of any character or set of characters, be they Kings, Presidents, or even God. The style in which you learn to think doesn't correspond to the way any person usually makes sense of the world. Rather, the pleasures of a simulation game come from inhabiting an unfamiliar, alien mental state: from learning to think like a computer.
>
> (Friedman, forthcoming: 2)

It is possible to suggest that Friedman's concept has currency beyond the "simulation" games he focuses on (*Civilization* and *SimCity*), and may be applicable in games where an apparent player-character is identifiable. In games like *Tomb Raider* or *Super Mario*, just as in Friedman's *Civilization*, the primary-player may not see themselves as any one particular character on the screen, but rather as the sum of every force and influence that comprises the game.

## References

Aarseth, E. (1997) *Cybertext: Perspectives on ergodic literature* Baltimore, Md. London: Johns Hopkins University Press

Bates, B. (2001) *Game Design: The art and business of creating games* California: Prima Tech (division of Prima Press)

Benyon, D. & Murray, D. (1988) "Experience and Adaptive Interfaces" *The Computer Journal* 31 (5): 465–473

Emes, CE. (1997) "Is Mr Pac Man Eating Our Children? A Review of the Effect of Video Games on Children" *Canadian Journal of Psychiatry*, 42, (4): 409–414

Friedman, T. (1999) "Civilization and its discontents: Simulation, Subjectivity and Space" in *Discovering Discs: Transforming Space and Genre on CD-ROM*, edited by Greg Smith (New York University Press). Available at http://www.duke.edu/~tlove/writing.htm

Fuller, M. & Jenkins, H. (1995) "Nintendo® And New World Travel Writing: A Dialogue" in Jones, SG. (ed) *Cybersociety: Computer-Mediated Communication and Community* Sage Publications

Gatchell, D. (1996) "Nintendo's Ultramen", *Edge* (UK Edition), (29), February: 50–64

Graybill, D., Kirsch, JR. & Esselman, ED (1985) "Effects of Playing Violent Versus Nonviolent Video Games on the Aggressive Ideation of Aggressive and Nonaggressive Children" *Child Study Journal*, 15 (3), 1985: 199–205

Graybill, D., Strawniak, M., Hunter, T. & O'Leary, M. (1987) "Effects of Playing Versus Observing Violent Versus Nonviolent Videogame on Children's Aggression" *Psychology*, 24 (3), 1987: 1–8

Jenkins, H. (1993) "x Logic": Repositioning Nintendo in Children's Lives" *Quarterly Review of Film and Video*, 14 (4), 1993: 55–70

Jessen, C. (1995) Children's Computer Culture in *Children's Computer Culture: Three Essays on Children and Computers* available at http://www.hum.sdu.dk/center/kultur/buE/articles.html consulted January 2002

——. (1996) Girls, Boys and the Computer in the Kindergarten: When the Computer is turned into a Toy in *Children's Computer Culture: Three Essays on Children and Computers* available at http://www.hum.sdu.dk/center/kultur/buE/articles.html consulted January 2002

——. (1998) Interpretive Communities: The Reception of Computer Games by Children and the Young in *Children's Computer Culture: Three Essays on Children and Computers* available at http://www.hum.sdu.dk/center/kultur/buE/articles.html consulted January 2002

Kinder, M. (1993) *Playing with Power in Movies, Television and Videogames: From Muppet Babies to Teenage Mutant Ninja Turtles* London: University of California Press

Kojima, H. (1998) "Hideo Kojima Profile' *Arcade* 1 (1) December: 42–43

Newman, J. (2001) *Reconfiguring the videogame player* Paper presented at Game Cultures international computer and videogame conference, Bristol, 29 June-1 July

Segal, K. & Dietz, W. (1991) "Physiological Responses to Playing a Video Game" *American Journal of Diseases of Children*, 145 (9): 1034–1036

Ubisoft (US) website, URL (consulted July 2001): http://www.ubisoft.com/usa/rayman2/index.html

# 48

# PLAYING AT BEING

## Psychoanalysis and the avatar

### *Bob Rehak*

Source: Mark J. P. Wolf and Bernard Perron (eds), *The Video Game Theory Reader* (New York, NY: Routledge, 2003), pp. 103–127.

Christian Metz, writing of the psychodynamic effects at work in cinema reception, observes that film is like the "primordial mirror"—the original instance in which subjects are constituted through identification with their own image—in every way but one. Although on the cinema screen "everything may come to be projected, there is one thing and one thing only that is never reflected in it: the spectator's own body."[1] Because processes of identification are clearly involved in film viewing, and yet the cinema screen fails to "offer the spectator its *own* body with which to identify as an object,"[2] Metz is forced to distinguish between primary (ongoing) and secondary (intermittent) identifications with, respectively, the camera that records a given scene and the human actors that appear within the field of vision.

But the application of psychoanalytic theory to technological mediations of identity is surely both simplified—in one obvious sense—and complicated in unexpected ways when it comes to figures that appear on screen in place of, indeed as direct *extensions* of the spectator: sites of continuous identification within a diegesis.[3] The video game avatar, presented as a human player's double, merges spectatorship and participation in ways that fundamentally transform both activities. Yet film theory, particularly the psychoanalytic turn popularized by the journal *Screen* in the 1970s, offers one productive way to understand the processes of subjectivization from which video games derive their considerable hold on our eyes, thumbs, and wallets.

The recourse to film theory also seems logical given the accelerating convergence between video games and certain movie genres—science fiction, action, and horror—notably in the registers of thematics (similar storylines and dramatic exigencies), aesthetics (lighting, camera angles, and conventions of mise-en-scène, as well as the use of narrative space and nondiegetic music), and visual traces of the cinematic apparatus itself (the simulation of lens flares and motion blur, for example). Video games *remediate* cinema; that is, they demonstrate the propensity of emerging media forms to pattern themselves on the characteristic behaviors and tendencies of their predecessors.[4] That video games are starting to resemble movies more than they do "real life" suggests that games, as a cultural form, are produced and consumed in phenomenological accord with preexisting technologies of representation. At the same time, video games plainly rework the formulas of cinema—and spectatorship—in ways that demand addressing.

The traditional first-person shooter (FPS) organizes its user interface around a software-simulated "camera" that, in the game's representational system, serves double duty as a body situated within the diegesis. The avatar's navigation of "contested spaces"[5] and its often violent interactions with other avatars (either human- or computer-controlled) generate the narrative- strategic pleasures of the video game experience. But the crucial relationship in many games—both contemporary standards like the *Quake* series (1996–1999) and its ancestors from the 1960s and 1970s such as *Spacewar!*, *Space Invaders*, and *Battlezone*—is not between avatar and environment or even between protagonist and antagonist, but between the human player and the image of him- or herself encountered onscreen.

Often collapsed in discussions of virtual reality (VR) to a transparent, one-to-one correspondence, players actually exist with their avatars in an unstable dialectic whose essential heterogeneity should not be elided. Players experience games through the exclusive intermediary of another—the avatar—the "eyes," "ears," and "body" of which are components of a complex technological and psychological apparatus. Just as one does not unproblematically equate a glove with the hand inside it, we should not presume the subjectivity produced by video games or other implementations of VR to transparently correspond to, and thus substitute for, the player's own (although it is precisely this presumption that appears necessary to secure and maintain a sense of immersion in "cyberspace"). To blur the distinction between players and their game-generated subjectivities is to bypass pressing questions of ideological mystification and positioning inherent to interactive technologies of the imaginary.[6]

Jacques Lacan's account of the mirror stage constitutes an entry point to this investigation of the ways in which video games "reflect" players back to themselves. Whereas first-person shooters remain the clearest example of the suturing effects of interactive technologies, it is helpful to consider how avatars first came into being as a defining component of such technologies, long before the advent of hardware and software required for the simulation of embodiment in three-dimensional spaces. This abbreviated history therefore touches on key moments of avatarial "evolution" (in games such as *Spacewar!*, *Space Invaders*, *Pac-Man*, *Battlezone*, *Myst*, and *Quake*) in order to build a case that models of identification and discursive address derived from film theory sharpen our understanding of video games as powerful interpellative systems with profound implications for subjects—and subjectivity—in densely mediated societies.

As described by Lacan[7] and elaborated by Samuel Weber,[8] the mirror stage occurs in human infants between the ages of six and eighteen months, when they first encounter and respond to their own reflection as an aspect of themselves.

Unlike other animals, which rapidly lose interest in mirrored surfaces, the human infant seems engrossed, and commences a kind of gleeful experimentation:

> A series of gestures . . . in which he experiences in play the relation between the movements assumed in the image and the reflected environment, and between this virtual complex and the reality it reduplicates—the child's own body, and the persons or things, around him.[9]

Lacan stresses two important aspects of this "jubilant assumption" of the image. First, it precipitates the "I" or ego within a symbolic matrix, producing for the child a perception of itself as observing individual and sign in a differential series of signs. Second, it is a *taking-place* (in that phrase's full meaning) in which the infant, at that point mostly helpless and unable to control its body, responds to the attraction of unity, wholeness, and power promised by the reflected form. For Lacan, this move is at heart a mistake or misrecognition, permanently dividing one from oneself as sign and referent are divided:

> The important point is that this form situates the agency of the ego, before its social determination, in a fictional direction, which will always remain irreducible for the individual alone, or rather, which will only rejoin the coming-into-being (le *devenir*) of the subject asymptotically, whatever the success of the dialectical syntheses by which he must resolve as *I* his discordance with his own reality.[10]

The ego formed through identification with a reflection or representation of itself is thus forever split, rendered incomplete by the very distinction that enables self-recognition. The subject that comes into being stands in sharp contrast to the Renaissance category of the unitary self: a stable, autonomous individual, capable of accessing all truth through reason and possessing "a human essence that remains untouched by historical or cultural circumstances."[11] Indeed, the split subject goes through life alienated from itself and its needs, endlessly seeking in external resources the "lost object" (*objet petit a*) from which it was initially severed—an object that "derives its value from its identification with some missing component of the subject's self, whether that loss is seen as primordial, as the result of a bodily organization, or as the consequence of some other division."[12]

In his reading of Lacan, Weber emphasizes the fundamentally *aggressive* nature of the child's assumption of the image: "The ego comes to be by taking the place of the imaginary other."[13] The roles of *self* and *other* take on a paradoxical or mutually contradictory quality; each contests its counterpart's privileged wholeness even as it depends on the counterpart to confirm those qualities. The reflected image must be recognizably related to the physical body in order to maintain the image's fascination—a requirement that may necessitate willful misrecognition. "The ego is thus initially constituted through the child's identification with an image whose otherness is precisely overlooked in the observation of similarity."[14]

Yet in order for the image to function as a projective ideal, it must ultimately resist or thwart that similarity: "Despite the effort to ignore it . . . such alterity can never be entirely effaced, since it is what permits the identification to take place."[15]

The formation of identity through dialectical synthesis, then, conceives subjectivity as a tense, oscillatory motion toward and away from the other: a process in which irst originating consciousness and then idealized reflection are alternately embraced and rejected. Furthermore, this "fictional" aspect of the ego is not just an originary instance—the installation of an "I" remaining stable thereafter—but a gesture of maintenance, opening notes of a discordant melody that will play throughout the subject's life.

> The *stade du miroir* is thereby defined not primarily as a genetic moment, but rather as a *phase* and as a turning-point or trope, destined to be repeated incessantly, in accordance with a schema whose moments are inadequacy, anticipation, and defensive armoring, and whose result is an identity that is not so much *alienated* as *alienating*, caught up in "the inexhaustible squaring of its own vicious circle of ego-confirmations."[16]

The video game avatar would seem to meet the criteria of Lacan's *objet petit a*. Appearing on screen in place of the player, the avatar does double duty as self and other, symbol and index. As *self*, its behavior is tied to the player's through an interface (keyboard, mouse, joystick): its literal motion, as well as its figurative triumphs and defeats, result from the player's actions. At the same time, avatars are unequivocally *other*. Both limited and freed by difference from the player, they can accomplish more than the player alone; they are supernatural ambassadors of agency.

But most significant (and often overlooked thanks to the event's ubiquity), avatars differ from us through their ability to *live, die, and live again*. Their bodies dissolve in radioactive slime or explode into a mist of blood and bone fragments, only to reappear, unscathed, at the click of a mouse. In terms of extradiegetic frame—the apparatus of software, operating system, and computer hardware—avatars are "killed" and "resurrected" with the flick of a power switch or the selection of a QUIT command on the File menu.[17] Rapid-fire representations of violence and death in video games, and the formal mechanisms by which avatars can be paused, erased, or restarted, are necessary moments in a cycle of symbolic rebirth: a staging, *within* technology, of the player's own "vicious circle of ego-confirmation."

In a specifically agential sense, avatars reduplicate and render in visible form their players' actions—they complete an arc of desire. This relationship is evident from the outset of video games in the linkage of players with avatars of spaceships, tanks, even ping-pong paddles. The emergence in recent games of simulated first-person perspectives, graphically sophisticated bodies, and camera movement suggesting corporeal presence underscores an obsessive concern with the avatar's function as acting stand-in for the player.

But the long history of video games also makes clear that there is no per-fectly "reflective" avatar, that is, one that resembles the player visually and (in the fashion of a real mirror) seems to gaze back on him or her.[18] If the avatar is a reflection, its correspondence to embodied reality consists of a mapping not of *appearance* but of *control*. Somewhat in the manner of a customer in an appliance store, who, catching sight of himself on a wall of monitors, waves his arms— "a series of gestures . . . in which he experiences in play the relation between the movements assumed in the image and the reflected environment"[19]—players pleasurably experiment with the surprising, often counterintuitive articulation between their manipulation of the interface and the avatar's obedient responses. If anything, such pleasures seem amplified by the uncanny difference between reality and reflection: an alterity enabling players both to embrace the avatar as an ideal and to reject it as an inferior other.

The avatar is not simply a means of access to desired outcomes, but an end in itself—a desired and resented lost object, existing in endless cycles of renuncia-tion and reclamation. Willingly inverting self-other distinctions, players invest an acted-on object with the characteristics of an acting subject. That status is then rescinded in moments of avatarial rupture to prove the object's fundamen-tal alterity and confirm, through contrast, the player's (fictive) ego unity. The contradictions opened up by this figure enhance, not detract, from game play, which consists—at least in part—of a toying with unstable categories of identity, presence, and subjectivity.

Contradictions in self-image opened by the avatar must be reconciled as part of the game's process. This reconciliation—the collapse of belief structures necessary to the assumption of an idealized other—takes the symptomatic form of the avatar's destruction: its fragmentation by shotgun blast or consumption by zombie. Graphic portrayals of dismemberment and death, the wounded bod-ies notoriously common to video games, are a mandatory punctuation to the out-of-body experience. The animated *grand guignol* shores up players' whole-ness, working out in technological form our aggressive response to our reflected images, our constitutive others.[20]

## Refining our reflections: an avatarial history

If the release in 1992 of the first-person shooter *Wolfenstein 3D*—a game that popularized the genre's signature over-the-gun viewpoint—marked the moment at which avatarial operations matured into a formal system, the roots of avatarial fascination extend back more than forty years, to early experiments in recrea-tional computer programming. Before we turn to an examination of the sutur-ing and misrecognition that subtend interactive technologies of the imaginary, it may be helpful to consider how the onscreen "other" has developed over time, for avatars are shaped as much by players' psychological needs as by advances in computer hardware and software. Our search for and rejection of digital ego ideals—a search that, like desire itself, is without end—has worked in combination with technological, economic, and aesthetic factors to refine avatarial look and behavior, embroidering a diversity of game "surfaces" atop a fundamental relationship of reflection and rejection.

This very diversity renders any taxonomy of the avatar provisional at best. Therefore, my intent in delving into history is neither to recapitulate video games' development in detailed sequence, nor to represent every genre. The games discussed later in this essay mark significant junctures in avatarial operations: the first appearance, in *Spacewar!*, of avatars in the form of player-controlled icons; the shift during the dominant years of the arcade from avatars coded as mechanical to avatars coded as organic; and the ultimate emergence, with the FPS and its relatives, of realistic human(oid) avatars whose troubled relationship to players' bodies becomes the game's primary concern—and primary source of pleasure. Crucial to this evolution is the avatar's gradual but relentless acquisition of "liveliness." In appearance, movement, and character, avatars have ever more clearly come to mimic their players, developing personality, individuality, and an ability to act within the (virtual) world—as must any infant on its way to maturity.

It is also important to note the increasing *subjectivization* of video games: a move from the God's-eye perspective utilized in early games to perspectival rendering that simulates three-dimensionality, first as static scenery, then as fluidly navigable space. Avatarial operations flow from two elements that interdepend in various ways. First is the foregrounding of an onscreen body, visible in whole or in part. Second is the conceit of an offscreen but assumed body constituted through the gaze of a mobile, player-controlled camera. Differing articulations between camera-body and avatar-body lead to different, though related, modes of play and subject effects. In every case, the intent—to produce a sense of diegetic embodiment—announces itself from the dawn of video game history.

In May 1962, at the annual MIT Open House, the hackers fed the paper tape with twenty-seven pages worth of PDP-1 assembly language code into the machine, set up an extra display screen—actually a giant oscilloscope—and ran *Spacewar!* all day to a public that drifted in and could not believe what they saw. The sight of it—a science-fiction game written by students and controlled by a computer—was so much on the verge of fantasy that no one dared predict that an entire genre of entertainment would be spawned from it.[21]

Retold with little variation across many different folk histories of the computer, the creation of *Spacewar!* has come to be viewed with a reverence befitting the Book of Genesis. Indeed, the first video game was seminal in several respects. As a "hack" of unprecedented popularity—a program whose original code, written by Steve Russell, J. M. Graetz, and others, was distributed to and modified by students and faculty at the Massachusetts Institute of Technology—*Spacewar!* exemplifies the steps by which avatarial operations—and the narrative-strategic context on which they depend—first came into being and continue to operate today. Russell, along with Alan Kotok, AI theorist Marvin Minsky, and other pro-grammers, had developed numerous display hacks: elegant or visually impressive graphics routines. Russell, however, envisioned a more active role and rewards for the user. Building on his love of the pulp space operas published by E. E. "Doc" Smith,[22] he wanted *Spacewar!* to absorb the user in an *experiential* simulation. Russell "let his imagination construct the thrill of roaring across space in a white rocket ship . . . and wondered if that same excitement could be captured while sitting behind the console of the PDP-1."[23] Russell produced what amounted to the first avatar: an onscreen blip subject to user control, accelerating and chang-ing direction based on toggle-switch settings. Eventually these points of light would evolve into icons of rocket ships, which, set against a starry background, engaged in warfare. Suggestive of a human ensconced within a mechanical shell, the rocket-ship imagery of the first avatars harkened to the external reality of the player seated at the terminal, hands on the controls.

*Spacewar!* established a set of elements vital to avatarial operations in most video games that followed:

1   Player identification with an onscreen avatar.
2   Player control of avatar through a physical interface.
3   Player-avatar's engagement with narrative-strategic constraints organizing the onscreen diegesis in terms of its (simulated) physical laws and semiotic content—the "meaning" of the game's sounds and imagery—that constitute rules or conditions of possibility governing play.
4   Imposition of extradiegetic constraints further shaping play (for example, timer, music, scorekeeping and other elements perceptible to the player but presumably not by the entity represented by the avatar; an instance of this in the relatively austere *Spacewar!* would be the software function that ended a game when one player "died").
5   Frequent breakdown and reestablishment of avatarial identification through destruction of avatar, starting or ending of individual games and tournaments, and ultimately the act of leaving or returning to the physical apparatus of the computer.

This final trait, at once the most common and least discussed dynamic of game-play, is central to the *repetition* from which video games, perhaps more than any other medium, take their structure. Systematic rupture of the agential and identifi-catory linkage between players and avatars is a defining characteristic, suggesting that the mirror-image's *loss* is as vital as its acquisition. As I will discuss later in this essay, repetition is central to another aspect of psychoanalytic theory: the game of *fort/da* in which an object that "stands in" for a lost and desired other is repeat-edly tossed away, retrieved, and tossed again. Sigmund Freud[24] observed that his grandson, disconsolate at being left alone by his mother, used *fort/da* to substitute an arbitrary object—a spool—for his absent caregiver, and to bring that caregiver under (symbolic) control. But this mastery, as Silverman points out, is ambiguous:

The game through which he masters the trauma of her departures, however, proves the vehicle through which that trauma returns, now in a guise which will prove much more significant for his future history. The child puts himself in an active relation to his mother's disappearances by throwing away and then recovering the toy which is her symbolic representative, while uttering the words "*fort*" ("gone") and "*da*" ("there"). In so doing, he employs language for the first time as a differential system, and so stages the trauma of his own disappearance. His ostensible mastery is consequently based upon a radical self-loss, and upon his subordination to the order of discourse.[25]

Repetition aside, the other elements listed above characterize (with minor modifications) our engagement with computer operating systems as standardized in the WIMP (Windows-Icon-Menu-Pointer) interface developed at Xerox PARC and adopted by Apple Macintosh and Microsoft Windows. As real-time processes, video games demand continuous involvement. Players' hands are always at the joystick, mouse, or keyboard, performing actions immediately reflected in the on screen behaviour of avatarial forms. This behavior in turn creates new exigencies to which players respond. Video games from their birth depended on a particularly *reactive* programming paradigm, one that updated screen content moment to moment in response to user input.

This mode of activity, where "what happens on a computer matches the frame of reference in which human beings are actually working,"[26] inaugurated a different way of thinking the human-computer agential circuit, and influenced future development of both hardware (toward processing power for improved graphic responsiveness) and software (toward icon-based operating systems and applications organized by visual and spatial metaphor). *Spacewar!* was the first of many games that

> repurposed the mainframe and the mini[computer] as well as the desktop computer, with an implicit suggestion that gaming, or at least an immediately responsive, graphical interface, is what computing should really be about . . . . There was a vast difference between this graphic behavior and the operations of a traditional computer, which manipulated symbols and presented its results only in rows of alphanumeric characters on the screen or on perforated printer paper. The game suggested new formal and cultural purposes for digital technology.[27]

Through gaming, then, the concepts of *avatar* and *interface* became linked; part of what users seek from computers is continual response to their own actions—a *reflection* of personal agency made available onscreen for reclamation as surplus pleasure. Russell and the other *Spacewar!* programmers were among the first to bind human agency to discrete graphical bodies on the computer screen. Furthermore, the situation of those bodies within a systematic context

68

limited, and thus helped define, their activity and purpose.[28] As an early avatarial mirror, *Spacewar!* shared with its descendants—video games as well as nonrecreational applications such as word processors and web browsers—an apparatus that directed user agency and subjectivity, creating a spectatorial/participatory relationship with onscreen traces of self.

Although rendered in text, Will Crowther and Don Wood's *Adventure* (1972–1977) marks an important movement toward the immersive mechanisms of later video games. Its themes of puzzle-solving, treasure-hunting, and interaction with fictional characters within a rule-bound otherworldly environment—as well as its branching structure of decision nodes navigated by the player—set the model for contemporary games such as *Myst* (1993) and *Half-Life* (1998). *Adventure's* interface invited players to imagine themselves as the observing/participating "I" in an unfolding narrative and brought to gameplay a sensation of first-person experience. Produced through textual collaboration between player and program, *Adventure's* hybrid player-avatar epitomized the simultaneous splitting/suturing at the heart of video games.

*Adventure* powerfully conveyed a sense of depth generated by players' exploration of fictive territory—a territory populated by creatures and objects that could be interacted with and manipulated systematically. *Adventure's* diegesis was described in textual passages, to which the player responded with typed commands.[29]

Computer: YOU ARE STANDING AT THE END OF A ROAD BEFORE A SMALL BRICK BUILDING. AROUND YOU IS A FOREST. A SMALL STREAM FLOWS OUT OF THE BUILDING AND DOWN A GULLY.
Player (typing): GO SOUTH.
Computer: YOU ARE IN A VALLEY IN THE FOREST BESIDE A STREAM TUMBLING ALONG A ROCKY BED.[30]

The sense of embodiment produced *by Adventure's* exchanges prompts the question of who and where the player "is" within the diegesis. While screen output was usually phrased in second person ("YOU ARE IN A MAZE OF TWISTY PASSAGES, ALL ALIKE"), the grammar of the interface required imperative interjections from the player (GO EAST, EXAMINE CARPET, and so on), commands presumably addressed to an implied intermediary body: a textual avatar. In one sense, this differs only slightly from the procedure that vision-based games use to map players' positions. For example, a subroutine might generate the sign-of-the-player at a particular set of screen coordinates ("YOU ARE OUTSIDE A HOUSE"); the player then nudges the joystick ("GO EAST"); a subroutine reads the signal from the input device and redraws the sign-of-the-player an inch to the left ("YOU ARE INSIDE A HOUSE").

This breakdown reveals a shared workload between player and computer: a halved (or doubled) agency undercutting the apparent unity that encourages imaginary investment in avatarial bodies and perspectives. As I will argue later, the discursive gaps opened in *Adventure's* interface—and, by extension, any interface—seem to beckon us as unique individuals. Imagining ourselves as the addressee of the computer screen's discourse, the "I" misrecognizing itself in the computer's "YOU," is part of video games' lure, as programmer Roberta Williams discovered in her first encounter with *Adventure* more than a decade after the game appeared:

> From the moment [she] tentatively poked GO EAST she was totally and irrevocably hooked . . . . She would be up until four in the morning, trying to figure out how to get around the damn snake to get to the giant clams. And then she would sit up in bed thinking, *What didn't I do? What else could I have done? Why couldn't I open that stupid clam? What's in it?*[31]

In his analysis of the sim (simulation) game genre, Ted Friedman locates within the human-machine collaboration a cybernetic circuit "in which the line demarcating the end of the player's consciousness and the beginning of the computer's world blurs."[32] This blurring constitutes an effacement of self, in that agency is simultaneously diluted by being transferred to a mechanical other, and amplified in resulting onscreen behavior. Construction of an office building, slaying of a monster, casting a magic spell: these achievements are only experientially possible (for the meager price of a mouse click) within the game diegesis. Friedman labels this "strange sense of self-dissolution"[33] both a denial of one's own material existence and a seductive generator of new perspectives: effectively a cyborg consciousness that identifies with the computer.[34]

The 1970s saw the rise of arcades as popular entertainment venues in the United States and Japan. During a decade that began with the placement of the first dedicated cabinet or arcade machines in bars and pinball parlors and the subsequent founding of Atari by Nolan Bushnell in 1972, video games and the social contexts in which they were played underwent rapid change, with corresponding alterations of both diegetic and avatarial content. *PONG* (a hit when released in 1972) sold players brief sessions of head-to-head combat for a quarter a turn. Because of limitations of integrated-circuit technology—the first game to use a dedicated microprocessor, Midway's *Gun Fight*, didn't appear until 1975—single-player games were rare; technology and aesthetic trends had yet to reach the point where a "machine enemy" could take on individuals.

One exception was *Breakout*, an Atari product designed for solo play. *Breakout* was essentially *PONG* turned on its side; a paddle at the bottom of the screen deflected a bouncing ball into rows of bricks hovering above. Like *PONG*, *Breakout* offered little in the way of embodiment; yet its rudimentary interface held a certain fascination, as David Sudnow attests:

> The *Breakout* hand doesn't move a paddle freely among all facets of bodily space and surroundings. It encircles the knob, to be sure, but

all actions transmit back and forth between the mere surface of things. I look down and watch my fingers quickly adjusting the control, the shot made to happen with superrapid, flexible-looking motion. But it's as if the fullness of things, and of myself, has been strangely halved. I could even say that I wasn't so much interfaced on screen as I was "interpictured" there.[35]

The lack of a computer-controlled other changed in 1978, when Midway unveiled its version of Taito's *Space Invaders*. Refashioning the bricks of *Breakout* into rows of insectoid or skull-like aliens ("invaders" of a formerly safe recreational "space"), the game imbued computer-controlled avatars with militaristic malevolence. Players steered a gun platform—an armed version of *PONG*'s paddle—from side to side, firing up at the descending aliens. It is difficult to say whether the gun's blunt utility as a representation of self, the leering faces of the invaders, or some combination of both, were responsible for the game's hold on the public imagination, but something certainly spoke to audiences; only a year after its introduction, there were 350,000 *SpaceInvaders* cabinets worldwide, 55,000 in the United States alone.[36] In addition, the game's popularity spurred sales of Atari's VCS 2600, a console system designed to be hooked to a television, bringing *Space Invaders* into the home—a second invasion, this time of domestic, and to that point uncomputerized, space.

The game's aliens, with their oversized heads, small legs, and disproportionately large faces, were, for the player, plainly "not-I," but in another sense they were the player-avatar inverted—in the spatial coordinates of the screen as well as the flipped ethical map of their destructive agency. *Space Invaders* introduction of nonhuman others restructured screen identity, disarticulating avatarial forms from material bodies and shifting the mode of consumption from two-player dyads to solitary space. Although the aliens always began the game moving in collective lockstep, each was potentially capable of surviving as an individual to the end, racing across the screen and dropping bombs. This implacable purposefulness modeled for players an ideally tireless, ever accelerating style of play—which the computer, of course, always finally won. At the same time, there was pleasure in defeat by *Space Invaders* and similar games structured around ever-faster enemies: surrender to the inevitable as opposing forces finally reached overwhelming intensity. *Missile Command* (1980), an Atari game in which players defended cities against nuclear assault, was capable of prompting euphoria as the mushroom clouds bloomed.[37]

You knew that you were gonna die, that you were within seconds of everything going black . . . . You're dying. You're dead. And then you get to watch all the pretty explosions. And after the fireworks display, you get to press the restart button, and you're alive again, until the next collision with your own mortality. You're not just playing with colored light. You're playing with the concept of death.[38]

71

This aspect of gameplay—the simulated experience of death and resurrection—is a key function of the avatar, one that would become more explicit as avatarial forms metamorphosed from the crosshairs, spaceships, and missile bases of the late 1970s to the "living" bodies of the early 1980s.

The commercial space of the arcade—whose darkened interiors were raucous with robotic sounds and strobe-lit by video explosions—was like a large-scale, physical analog of video games themselves. Indeed, many games that appeared between 1978 and 1984 shared thematic elements that could be taken as ironic commentary on the arcade environment: *Asteroids, Defender, Centipede, Missile Command, Galaxian, Star Castle, Tempest, Qix*, and *Zaxxon* all featured claustrophobic diegeses filled with deadly obstacles in constant motion. Player-avatars had to maneuver safely through this maze of shifting spatial relationships, a task not unlike that faced by individuals in a crowded arcade.

The threat in most of these games was impersonal, often automated assault. In *Asteroids*, the danger was posed by a colliding field of rocks, though flying saucers intermittently appeared to fire upon the player. *Centipedes* eponymous peril was a segmented insect that, vivisected by the player's weapon, would merely continue its attack on separate fronts. Against such tireless synthetic threats, a player was only as good as his or her gun; indeed, collapsed by avatarial synecdoche, a player-avatar *was* the gun.

This began to change with the arrival of Namco's *Pac-Man* (1980),which dispensed with mechanistic signs of gun and spaceship, embodying players instead as a round yellow "voracious dot."[39] The avatar's organic status was marked by its color as well as by its only feature, a gaping mouth whose obvious function was as consumptive orifice. Rather than spitting dots, Pac-Man—the game's title designated the avatarial protagonist rather than the villain to be defeated—endlessly absorbed them, a reversal in thematic focus from anal expulsion to oral incorporation.

> Before this epoch-making game, the player controlled spaceships, gun turrets, or other mechanical devices. Suddenly, though, the player of *Pac-Man* controlled a *being:* an animated, eating thing. The game's designer, Toru Iwatani, says that he got the idea for Pac-Man's form after eating a slice of pizza, and seeing the shape that was left.[40]

The Pac-Man avatar semiotically collapsed *subject* (a thing that eats) with *object* (a thing that is eaten) to constitute a closed circuit of desire. Equally important, the body acquired its signification through a missing part ("the shape that was left"); Pac-Man was recognizable *as* Pac-Man because of what was excluded from its form. This pie-slice absence also structured Pac-Man's agency within the game, its ceaseless voracity. Like the player for whom it stood in, Pac-Man was never at rest within its infinite progression of mazes, consuming dots—his own *objects a*, frail reflections, perhaps, of an eternally missing slice.

Atari's *Battlezone* (1980), while not the first video game to shift camera position from an elevated, omniscient viewpoint to a gaze located at eye level—sports and racing games had experimented with this throughout the 1970s—did originate first-person perspective. *Battlezone* situated the player behind the controls of a tank capable of movement, allowing players to change their perspective at will by driving through an environment rendered in green vector wireframes. The game thus created a dual sense of enclosure: immersing players not only in an artificial world (a desert patrolled by enemy tanks and hunter-killer satellites), but in an artificial vehicle capable of free navigation.

*Battlezone's* graphic conceit would be repeatedly copied, adapted, and refined by its descendants, culminating in the FPS. By locating players at the still center of a world that seems to pirouette around them, subjective-viewpoint displays blend enclosure and embodiment, implying the existence of a body—logically and physiologically associated with the presence of eyes and ears at a specific set of coordinates—as it simultaneously feeds players sensory imagery of created environments. The shift *Battlezone* signaled is like the introduction of perspective in post-Renaissance painting, which gave

> landscapes their formal focus in the human figures in them. The paired techniques involve the creation of a dreamscape, and the provision of figures for identification that call the viewer to enter fictive space, changing with their movements, inviting their co-authorship. They are fundamentally navigable.[41]

An *Adventure-like* meander over deserted islands in multiple "ages," *Myst* (1993) substituted ray-traced scenes of near-photographic quality for the descriptive textual passages of its predecessor. Yet, *Myst* emulated *Adventure* in fundamental ways, including a puzzle format, absence of explicit instructions, and an emphasis on spatial exploration over linear plot development. In addition to the still frames that parceled out the island topography, *Myst* used ambient sound effects to deepen the player's sense of immersion: wind whistling through trees, waves washing up on shore, and mechanical objects that whirred and clicked. The game also made use of nondiegetic music, the equivalent of a movie soundtrack, to build suspense or indicate proximity to clues.[42]

Just as *Myst* formally combined old and new media—"three-dimensional, static graphics with text, digital video, and sound to refashion illusionistic painting, film, and, somewhat surprisingly, the book as well"[43]—its diegesis involved the superimposition of two sets of events. The first, an Oedipal struggle[44] between a father and two sons, was over before the game even began: buried in the past, this conflict drove the second, contemporary sequence of the player's point-and-click search for clues, the successful assembly of which rendered the fragmented back story comprehensible, solving the mystery. The subject position offered to players was that of private detective in a "whodunit,"[45] ironically gesturing toward the subjective point-of-view (POV) experiments of *film noir* that presented the detective as scientist/voyeur.[46]

Most striking to many was the eerie sense of stillness and solitude produced by *Myst's* interface, which lacked visible avatarial forms. Players moved through the diegesis as though watching a slide show, clicking at the borders of each image to choose where they would go next. The only mark of this control onscreen was a cursor in the shape of a pointing hand. Omitting representations of the body in favor of a single, stylized point of control, *Myst*'s interface epitomized the "tourist mouse" aesthetic[47] in which access to the computer's imaginary takes the form of a restless search for "an impossibly pristine discovery"[48]—the pursuit of an object to fill an essential lack.

> The cursor as perpetual tourist meanders through a landscape which is always foreign, in which it seeks perpetually a home that it will recognize less by identification than by an impossible welcome which its denizens will give it . . . . The impossibility of this quest derives from the tourist's fate: always to be seeking to arrive, not "here," but "there."[49]

For some, *Myst*'s appeal was less in its puzzles than in its ability to transport players to a detailed environment; the game was "a grand exercise in virtual tourism."[50] At the same time, technological limitations made both an onscreen body and fluid navigation unfeasible; other subjective-viewpoint games of the period, like *Wolfenstein 3D* (1992), could not approach the rich level of detail offered by *Myst*. The avatarial point of presence consisted of *Myst*'s relatively inflexible camera, an apparatus that produced a corresponding sense of ghostliness for the player. Able to observe with relative freedom and work small-scale effects on the environment—opening books, turning knobs, pressing buttons—players were nonetheless barred from the (illusory) corporeality afforded by avatars in later games. The result was a diegesis in which the player could not die and was at risk of little more than frustration.

Id Software, responsible for the archetypal "shoot-'em-up"s *Wolfenstein 3D* and *Doom*, refined the FPS formula further with the launch of the *Quake* series in 1996. Incorporating both a single-player mode and multiplayer or deathmatch scenarios, *Quake* emphasized the avatar's physical boundaries and tolerances, subjecting it to near-continuous assault from environmental forces. The multiple diegeses of *Quake*—a game now in its third official iteration, not including expansion packages or countless player-created levels—have successively stripped away the trappings of narrative, leaving only a plot based on the protection and loss of bodily integrity. *Quake III: Arena* (1999) was geared solely around deathmatch battles, with an option for solo players to train against bots: artificially intelligent avatars.

The *Quake* avatar, represented on screen by a gun-holding hand, could be customized through the use of "skins" to have different appearances in the virtual environment of networked play. Players cloaked themselves as men, women, cyborgs, demons, and cartoon characters, and other guises, suggesting that, in the contemporary FPS, visibility is the first order of interaction. Avatars both *see* and are *seen;* as seer, players are called on to conduct an ongoing surveillance. They are assigned explicitly or implicitly the role of security guards, whose simple task is to shoot anything that appears threatening. Because the ultimate threat is that the enemy will destroy the equilibrium of the system and eventually halt the game by destroying the player himself, the player must constantly scan the visual field and direct his fire appropriately.[51]

An inverse logic, of course, applies to the body as *seen*—the avatarial extension that enables player's presence within the game also places them at the focus of the other's destructive surveillance. Constituted through a routinized, ceaseless hunt with violence an inevitable endpoint, the player-avatar bears authority's gaze even as he or she is disciplined by it.

Yet, in *Quake* and its ilk, the avatar's visual attributes were overshadowed by its somatic character, a "material" vulnerability conveyed through multiple codes of representation. Players heard their own avatars' footfalls and breathing. Collision detection bounced avatars off walls and forced them into crouching or crawling positions to enter tight spaces. Forces of gravity prevented avatars from jumping too high, and made falls from a sufficient distance lethal. Impact wounds were signaled by a shaking of the camera coupled with the sound effect of a groan or gasp, and a corresponding loss of health points (replenished by running over "medkits," white crates iconically labeled with a red cross). As avatarial damage mounted, players watched their own blood spray; "death" was signified by a toppling of the avatarial camera,which laymotionless—but still feeding visual and auditory information to the screen—until reborn with a mouse click.

As this brief survey shows, video games have evolved toward ever more complex simulations of corporeal immersion, subsuming economic, social, and technological determinants under an overarching goal: to confront players with detailed and lifelike "doubles." As the avatar took on character, history, and presence within increasingly detailed story worlds, the coded representation of sensory immersion epitomized by the FPS brought video games into dialogue with the dominant representational system of Hollywood filmmaking. In multiple ways—from the simulation of first-person perspective to the illusory wholeness that editing conventions offer the spectator—video games and movies invite comparison.

## The speaking mirror: video games and cinema

If the pleasures of the video game stem as much from avatarial "reflection" as from narrative and strategic engagement with its diegesis, then spectatorship is clearly central to the form. As we play we also watch ourselves play; video games are by turns, and even simultaneously, participatory and spectatorial. Thus it is more accurate, or at least more inclusive, to speak of the *avatarial relation:* a "structure of seeing" in which the subject, acting on its desire to see itself as other, pursues its reflection in the imaginary like a cat chasing its tail.

The study of cinema has been informed in multiple ways by psychoanalytic insight into the role played by vision—looking as well as being looked at—in the inscription of sexual difference and power.[52] In addition, much attention has been given to the ways in which the material apparatus of camera/projector and stylistic devices of editing and narrative operate, with varying degrees of effectiveness, to produce a coherent space of reception for the viewing subject.[53] In order to analyze related effects on subjectivity in video games, I touch on two aspects of film theory. First, the use of subjective POV to create a newly participatory role for the spectator; and second, the concept of interpellation and its function, within discourse, in constructing apparently unified subject positions.

In any application to one medium of theory developed for another, care must be taken to distinguish the codes organizing each. The FPS borrows certain aspects of cinematic storytelling, most explicitly the tracking POV shot, but makes little use, at least while players are controlling the avatar, of editing or montage in a traditional sense.[54] Rarely, for example, do conventional video games rely extensively on shot-reverse-shot constructions, which counterpose two images— a viewed object, person, or scene and a corresponding image of a viewing subject—to create for spectators the illusion of a contiguous space which they inhabit as an invisible presence. Crucial to the account of suture advanced by Jean-Pierre Oudart and Daniel Dayan,[55] the subject position created through shot-reverse-shot is replaced in the FPS by a camera simulated through software rendering of three-dimensional spaces. Individual control over this camera's behavior—its ability to tilt, pan, track, even climb ladders and descend staircases at the behest of the player—literalizes the conceit of an embodied diegetic participant that cinema, because of its material technologies, can only imply. The FPS's direct (visual) address, updated in real time, presents one ongoing and unbroken half of the shot-reverse-shot construction, enabling a snug fit between the player and his or her game-produced subjectivity.

As an example of film's failure to convincingly assert the embodiment that avatars routinely generate, it is instructive to consider Robert Montgomery's *film noir* experiment *Lady in the Lake* (1947), which exemplifies the costs of truly subjective narration. *Lady in the Lake* takes as its narrative and formal task the construction of a seamless subjective and embodied POV. As private eye Philip Marlowe, actor-director Robert Montgomery makes only desultory appearances on screen, directly addressing the audience to introduce the story and provide updates on its progress, or appearing as a reflection in the many mirrors sprinkled throughout the film's locations. The majority of his role, however, is "performed" by a camera whose diegetically situated look we are meant to adopt as at once Marlowe's and our own.

What follows is an experience that audiences and critics found more exasperating than engrossing. Some rejected the story as "an insipid anecdote that would not have required any innovation to be developed adequately,"[56] but most criticized the subjective camera itself as an awkward gimmick, the technological limitations of which nullified its ability to substitute for a novelistic "I."

There is therefore a misinterpretation here which fails to understand that it is not at the place of the subject that the camera operates, but at the place of the Other . . . . We cannot identify with someone whose face is always hidden from us. And if we cannot identify ourselves, we cannot share the anxieties of the character. In a thriller this can become rather annoying.[57]

Underlying many reactions of the time, however, is an acknowledgment that subjective narration through the simulation of first-person presence is a desirable goal, even a workable one if the technique were appropriately modified— by taking into account, for example, that the human eye discards extraneous detail when looking at an image, or that our attentiveness to scenic elements is determined as much by affective interest as by optical properties. This suggests an implicit endorsement of narrative immersion and embodiment as a pleasurable frontier for the spectator; indeed, some critical rhetoric prefigures the current hyperbole surrounding video games and other interactive technologies of the imaginary:

> The subjective camera can explore subtleties of experience hitherto unimaginable as film content. As the new technique can clearly express almost any facet of everyday human experience, its development should presage a new type of psychological film in which the camera will reveal the human mind, not superficially, but honestly in terms of image and sound . . . permitting the audience to see a human being both as others see him and as he sees himself.[58]

Hyperbolic dreams of "psychological film" aside, Montgomery's failed attempt to subjectivize cinema bears examining, for it points the way toward a broader agenda of particularized embodiment realized more than forty years later in the FPS. While *Lady in the Lake's* first-person camera amounted to little more than tiresome artifice, its later mobilization in video games attests to the technique's effectiveness when transferred to a medium offering greater interactivity.

According to Lacan, the ego produced through identification with an image attains its entry into language and meaning at the price of determination/domination by the governing symbolic order. Social theorists, notably Louis Althusser,[59] have linked this alienation and the psychic misrecognition on which it is based to ideological forces that reproduce themselves through naturalization in discourse and self-image. For Althusser, subjectivity is shaped, even generated, by social institutions and processes, acting through systems of signification that supply individuals with their identifications.

In the 1970s, cinema came under investigation as one of the social technologies included in Althusser's account of the ideological state apparatus (ISA). This critique studied cinema as a signifying system that produces specific ideological effects by positioning its spectators as the understood subjects of screen discourse.

The constructed quality of this discourse, in turn, is made invisible through the same effects—for example, shot-reverse- shot constructions, discussed above, are central to the suture by which spectators are "stitched into" the signifying chain through edits that articulate a plenitude of observed space to an observing character. This onscreen figure, presented as author/owner of the gaze, serves also as identificatory site for the spectator willing

> to become absent to itself by permitting a fictional character to "stand in" for it, or by allowing a particular point of view to define what it sees. The operation of suture is successful at the moment that the viewing subject says, "Yes, that's me," or "That's what I see."[60]

Suture's coercive effects consist precisely in "persuading the viewer to accept certain cinematic images as an accurate reflection of his or her subjectivity . . . it does this *transparently* (i.e. it conceals the apparatuses of enunciation)."[61]

While the frustrations of extended first-person POV in cinema have been noted, fewer pitfalls occur in video games that operate according to a similar code of signification. The game apparatus—a software engine that renders three-dimensional spaces from an embodied perspective, directed in real time by players through a physical interface—achieves what the cinematic apparatus cannot: a sense of literal presence, and a newly participatory role, for the viewer. Yet the question of ideological positioning is as pertinent to this new medium as it is to cinema. More so, in fact, because of video games' amplified effect on subjectivity and corresponding elision of authorship. The film spectator's role as an implied observer of narrative events—an "absent one" flickering ghostlike through the diegesis, positioned anew from shot to shot—is concretized in the video game imaginary through the figure of the avatar, a "present one" standing in for the player, who chooses the path of the camera-body with apparent freedom. The disavowal necessary to gameplay is like the "Yes, that's what I see" of successful cinematic suture, but goes further: it is "Yes, that's what I *do*."

Interfaces, then, are ideological. They work to remove themselves from awareness, seeking transparency—or at least unobtrusiveness—as they channel agency into new forms. Whatever the aesthetic by which a given interface has been designed, the computer's interactive address produces an additional, *anesthetic* effect, threatening mystification for the user. Moreover, interfaces are discursive, in that their signifying elements are organized around a continuous hailing of the human beings who use them—a beckoning spatial representation marked by the cursor, the startup beep, the avatarial gun. This is the uncanny power of what we might call *speaking technologies:* the perception, produced even through mundane interaction, that we are the subject of their address, that we have been recognized. Joseph Weizenbaum's ELIZA (1966), written to simulate psychotherapeutic discourse by parroting back typed input in interrogative form, also provoked enthusiastic responses from its users:

Weizenbaum thought that ELIZA's easily identifiable limitations would discourage people from wanting to engage with it. But he was wrong. Even people who knew and understood that ELIZA could not know or understand wanted to confide in the program. Some even wanted to be alone with it.[62]

Recognition-by-interface situates the user within a software-driven signifying chain, a discourse full of gaps that invite participation. To sit at a computer and handle mouse and keyboard is to be physically positioned; to misrecognize one-self as the addressee of the screen's discourse is to be interpellated as a subject. Under this model, the FPS becomes an extreme form of subject positioning, a scenario of continuous suture.

But the model described above runs a risk in postulating a completely deter-ministic system, the smooth functioning of which precludes any space of negotia-tion. This does not square with most people's experience of computers in general or video games in particular. Interactions with computers are complicated by the interruptions of everyday life, hardware and software failure, and an affective user response ranging from joyful transport to seething rage. In addition, the discourse of the screen is itself a collage of different hails that compete for recognition and attention: multitasking operating systems "window" applications so that users move jarringly among word-processing documents, games of Solitaire, and the World Wide Web. In this sense, the computer screen is more closely related to television than to movies.[63]

Subjective-viewpoint video games, however, *do* resemble cinematic address, in the specialized ways described above. Where, then, is the space of resistance in the video game? The answer is in the relationship between player and avatar—a relationship that, because of the intersubjective mechanisms on which it is pre-dicated, is an always-already "contested space." In addition to games' preferred meanings, players derive pleasure from avatarial instability. On the most basic level, avatars enable players to think through questions of agency and existence, exploring in fantasy form aspects of their own materiality.

If the mirror stage initiates a lifelong split between self-as-observer and self-as-observed, and the video game exploits this structure, then, in one sense, we already exist in an avatarial relation to ourselves. Our experience of the world itself is based on equal parts participation and spectatorship; we are certainly here, acting, but we do so in a constant tension between the illusory unity of self that our observing consciousness delivers to us, and the fragmented multiplicity of a self riddled with unbridgeable gaps. Egos are founded on the assumption of wholeness, a wholeness misperceived in the form of a symbolic other. The other that functions retroactively to bestow authenticity on the self could be described as a living avatar.

Movement back and forth across the border separating self from other might therefore be considered a kind of liminal play: an attempt to isolate and capture (fleetingly) the oscillatory motion of consciousness by which we are sutured into this reality. As argued above, video games seem to enact the *fort/da* game. If our unity is itself a misrecognition, then the video game, for all its chaotic cartoon-ishness, may constitute a small square of contemplative space: a laboratory, quiet and orderly by comparison with the complexity of the real world, in which we toy with subjectivity, play with being.

As small-scale implementations of VR and other interactive technologies of the imaginary, video games seem to offer the potential for profound redefini-tions of body, mind, and spirit. In theory, avatars need not be hampered by any semblance of physicality—not even a unitary, ground-level perspective. They need not pretend to tire as they struggle uphill, need never "die." Yet, the avatar's structuring metaphor, source of its believability and, perhaps, its fascination for users, is the very vulnerability that attends embodied existence. We create avatars to leave our bodies behind, yet take the body with us in the form of codes and assumptions about what does and does not constitute a legitimate interface with reality—virtual or otherwise.

Why should experiential simulations be limited in this way? Why should any tics of corporeality, any perverse obsessions or "slips of the tongue," interrupt the carefully engineered flow of virtual fantasy? The answer, I have argued, can be found in the origin of subjectivity itself—in the moment of mistaken recognition that ties self-consciousness to an idealized representation of self and launches a lifelong struggle for guarantees of authenticity. If, as Lacan argues, we win our experience of wholeness through the establishment early in life of a permanent divide, then our extension through technological networks becomes both possible yet restrictively conditional. If we already understand our bodies to be in some sense "escapable," then the magical projections of telephone line, movie screen, and computer generated battlefield flower before us as spaces into which we can nimbly step—then step back as suddenly, without suffering any consequences save, perhaps, the memories left by a vivid dream.

But if our extension through various media is predicated on the body as root metaphor, then the body becomes an inescapable aspect of fantasized experience. Images of self demand recognition through identification. Yet, once established, this identification must be demolished, so that players can remember where and who they "really" are—and the cycle can begin again.

That the total control promised by the avatar has not been fully exploited is a positive sign: an indication that engagement with interactive technologies of the imaginary will be limited in ways specific to embodied human existence and dis-cursively determined subjectivity. It suggests further that the ideological potential of immersive interfaces is doomed to operate in contention, forever breaking its own flow by violating the seamless suture between its technologically produced perspective and our own. The ambivalence that marks our experience of ourselves will continue to manifest itself in the rules, images, and interactions produced through technologies of the imaginary. The worlds we create—and the avatarial bodies through which we experience them—seem destined to mirror not only our wholeness, but our lack of it.

# Notes

1 Christian Metz, *The Imaginary Signifier: Psychoanalysis and the Cinema*, trans. Celia Britton, Annwyl Williams, Ben Brewster, and Alfred Guzzetti (Bloomington: Indiana University Press, 1982), 45.

2 Elizabeth Cowie, *Representing the Woman: Cinema and Psychoanalysis* (Minneapolis: University of Minneapolis Press, 1997), 99.

3 *Diegesis*, from the Greek term for "recounted story," is conventionally employed in film theory to refer to the "total world of the story action" (David Bordwell and Kristin Thompson, *Film Art*, 6th ed., New York: McGraw-Hill, 2001, 61). I use it here to designate the narrative-strategic space of any given video game—a virtual environment determined by unique rules, limits, goals, and "history," and additionally designed for the staging and display of agency and identity.

4 In introducing the concept of remediation, Bolter and Grusin emphasize the hybrid, dialectical nature of media appropriation:

> The new medium can remediate by trying to absorb the older medium entirely, so that the discontinuities between the two are minimized. The very act of remediation, however, ensures that the older medium cannot be entirely effaced; the new medium remains dependent on the older one in acknowledged or unacknowledged ways (Jay David Bolter and Richard Grusin, *Remediation: Understanding New Media* [Cambridge, MA: MIT Press, 2000], 47).

5 Arguing that video games are as much about architectural, sculptural, and other "spatial" properties as they are about narrative or cinematic pleasures, Jenkins and Squire remind us that if games tell stories, they do so by organizing spatial features. If games stage combat, then players learn to scan their environments for competitive advantages. Game designers create immersive worlds and relationships among objects that enable dynamic experiences (HenryJenkins and Kurt Squire, "The Art of Contested Spaces," in *Game On: The History and Culture of Video Games*, ed. Lucien King [New York: Universe, 2002], 65).

6 Here and throughout, I use the term "imaginary" in the Lacanian sense, to denote the realm of subjective experiences formed and maintained through identification, dualism, and equality. In Kaja Silverman's words, the imaginary order precedes the symbolic order, which introduces the subject to language and Oedipal triangulation, but continues to coexist with it afterward. The two registers complement each other, the symbolic establishing the differences which are such an essential part of cultural existence, and the imaginary making it possible to discover correspondences and homologies (Kaja Silverman, *The Subject of Semiotics* [NewYork: Oxford University Press, 1983], 157).

7 Jacques Lacan, "The Mirror Stage as Formative of the Function of the I as Revealed in Psychoanalytic Experience," in *Ecrits*, trans. Alan Sheridan (New York: W.W. Norton, 1977), 1–7.

8 Samuel Weber, *Return to Freud: Jacques Lacan's Dislocation of Psychoanalysis*, trans. Michael Levine New York, NY. Cambridge University Press, 1991).

9 Lacan, "The Mirror Stage," 1.

10 Lacan, "The Mirror Stage," 2.

11 Silverman, The Subject of Semiotics, 126.

12 Discussing the ways in which external entities—the mother's breast, the feces, the gaze of another—take on erotic significance for the developing child, Silverman observes that "[t]here will be many such objects in the life of the subject. Lacan refers to them as '*objets petit a*,' which is an abbreviation for the more complete formula '*objets petit autre*.' This rubric designates objects which are not clearly distinguished from the self and which are not fully grasped as other *(autre)*." Silverman, *The Subject of Semiotics*, 156.

13  Weber, Return to Freud, 14.

14  Weber, Return to Freud, 14.

15  Weber, Return to Freud, 14.

16  Weber, Return to Freud, 14.

17  Another version of this occurs when loading a saved game, which, in effect, obliterates the current avatar in order to substitute an earlier version.

18  One way to consider such "reflective relationships" in third-person games such as the *Tomb Raider* series (1996–present), in which a "chase camera" follows the avatar but rarely reveals its face, is by analogy to a two-mirror system. Positioning a hand mirror so that its reflection is visible in a larger mirror, I can, for example, glimpse the back of my own head: the image is still recognizable as me, yet I do not return my own gaze.

19  Lacan, "The Mirror Stage," 1.

20  In her analysis of historical trauma and the death drive, Silverman identifies the subject's repetitive (symbolic) staging of its own destruction as a particularly *male* syndrome; one that, furthermore, even the father of psychoanalysis could not bring himself to confront:

> Masculinity is particularly vulnerable to the unbinding effects of the death drive because of its ideological alignment with mastery. The normative male ego is necessarily fortified against any knowledge of the void upon which it rests, and— as its insistence upon an unimpaired bodily "envelope" would suggest—fiercely protective of its coherence. Yet the repetition through which psychic mastery is established exists in such an intimate relation with the repetition through which it is jeopardized that Freud shows himself unable to distinguish clearly between them . . . . Disintegration constantly haunts the subject's attempts to effect a psychic synthesis." (Kaja Silverman, *Male Subjectivity at the Margins* [New York: Routledge, 1992], 61.)

21  Steven Levy, *Hackers: Heroes of the Computer Revolution* (NewYork: Anchor, 1984), 52.

22  Levy, *Hackers*, 46.

23  Levy, *Hackers*, 47.

24  Sigmund Freud, *Beyond the Pleasure Principle* (New York: Bantam Books, 1959).

25  Silverman, Male Subjectivity at the Margins, 61–62.

26  Levy, *Hackers*, 61.

27  Bolter and Grusin, *Remediation*, 90.

28  The *Spacewar!* diegesis—derived from the preexisting media form of printed science fiction—also foreshadowed the metaphoric borrowings of WIMP operating systems, which take their shape from preexisting material technologies of desktops, folders, trash cans, and so on.

29  Levy equates this line-by-line exploration of a fantasy world with programming itself, suggesting that the original players were able to achieve partial metaphorical contiguity between their actual lives and their experiences as avatarial presences within the domain of *Adventure*. A similar parallel might be drawn between *Spacewar!'s* battling vessels and its hacker combatants, whose social and professional lives were characterized by highly competitive struggles to demonstrate flamboyant programming abilities.

30  Quoted in Levy, *Hackers*, 132.

31  Quoted in Levy, *Hackers*, 295.

32  Ted Friedman, *"Civilization* and Its Discontents: Simulation, Subjectivity, and Space," in *On a Silver Platter: CD-ROMS and the Promises of a New Technology*, ed. Greg M. Smith (New York:New York University Press, 1999), 137.

33  Friedman, *"Civilization* and Its Discontents," 136.

34  Friedman, *"Civilization* and Its Discontents," 138.

35  David Sudnow, *Pilgrim in the Microworld* (New York: Warner, 1983), 66.

36  Scott Cohen, *Zap: The Rise and Fall of Atari* (New York: McGraw, 1984), 78.

37  *Missile Command* had its start in a Rand Corporation simulation of ICBM air-defense management, the goal of which was to determine how quickly human controllers would be overwhelmed (J. C. Herz, *Joystick Nation: How Video Games Ate Our Quarters, Won Our Hearts, and Rewired Our Minds* [Boston: Little, Brown, 1997], 216).

38  J. C. Herz, *Joystick Nation: How Video Games Ate Our Quarters, Won Our Hearts, and Rewired Our Minds*, 64.

39  Marsha Kinder, *Playing with Power in Movies, Television, and Video Games: From Muppet Babies to Teenage Mutant Ninja Turtles* (Berkeley: University of California Press, 1991), 106.

40  Steven Poole, *Trigger Happy: Videogames and the Entertainment Revolution* (New York: Arcade, 2000), 148.

41  Sean Cubitt, *Digital Aesthetics* (London: Sage, 1998), 75.

42  Janet H. Murray, *Hamlet on the Holodeck: The Future of Narrative in Cyberspace* (Cambridge, MA: MIT Press, 1997), 53.

43  Bolter and Grusin, *Remediation*, 94.

44  Kinder notes in video games a tendency toward Oedipal narratives "in which male heroes have traditionally grown into manhood and replaced father figures, and on myths . . . in which little guys beat giants" (Kinder, *Playing With Power,* 105); she sees this as a uses-and gratifications strategy whereby "the games can help boys deal with their rebellious anger against patriarchal authority" (Kinder, *Playing With Power,* 104).

45  Herz, Joystick Nation, 150.

46  "*Myst* is an interactive detective film in which the player is cast in the role of detective. It is also a film 'shot' entirely in the first person, in itself a remediation of the Hollywood style . . . like many of the other role-playing games, *Myst* is in effect claiming that it can succeed where *film noir* failed: that it can constitute the player as an active participant in the visual scene" (Bolter and Grusin, *Remediation*, 97).

47  Cubitt, *Digital Aesthetics*, 85.

48  Cubitt, *Digital Aesthetics*, 90.

49  Cubitt, *Digital Aesthetics*, 90.

50  Herz, Joystick Nation, 151.

51  Bolter and Grusin, *Remediation*, 93.

52  The touchstone in this body of work remains Laura Mulvey's "Visual Pleasure and Narrative Cinema" (*Visual and Other Pleasures* [Bloomington: Indiana University Press, 1989], 14–26), which first articulated the connection between cinematic representation and the phallocentric imaginary.

53  See, for example, Jean-Louis Baudry, "Ideological Effects of the Basic Cinematic Apparatus," 531–542, and Jean-Luc Comolli and Jean Narboni, "Cinema/Ideology/ Criticism," 22–30, both in *Movies and Methods*, Vol. 2, ed. Bill Nichols (Berkeley: University of California Press, 1985).

54  By contrast, video games often insert "cut-scenes" intended for viewing, not playing. At these moments, the game cues players (typically by shifting to a "letterboxed" mode with black bars at screen top and bottom) to remove their hands from the controls and simply watch information that advances the game's narrative. During cut-scenes, conventional codes of cinema reassert themselves; viewing competencies developed through movies (and, arguably, television and graphic novels) guide players in the proper interpretation of "unembodied" visual grammar such as shot-reverse-shot, dissolves, zooms, fade-ins and fade-outs, and so on.

55  Daniel Dayan, "The Tutor-Code of Classical Cinema," in *Movies and Methods*, Vol. 1, ed. Bill Nichols [Berkeley: University of California Press, 1976], 438–450. See also

David Bordwell, *Narration in the Fiction Film* (Madison: University of Wisconsin Press, 1985), 110.

56  Julio L. Moreno, "Subjective Cinema: And the Problem of Film in the First Person," *Quarterly of Film, Radio, and Television* 7 (1953): 349

57  Pascal Bonitzer, "Partial Vision: Film and the Labyrinth." Trans. Fabrice Ziolkowski. *Wide Angle* 4, No. 4 (1981): 58.

58  Joseph P. Brinton III, "Subjective Camera or Subjective Audience?" *Hollywood Quarterly* 2(1947): 365.

59  Louis Althusser, "Ideology and Ideological State Apparatuses (Notes toward an Investigation)," in *Mapping Ideology*, ed. Slavoj Žižek (London: Verso, 1994), 100–140.

60  Silverman, *The Subject of Semiotics*, 205.

61  Silverman, *The Subject of Semiotics*, 215.

62  Sherry Turkle, *Life on the Screen: Identity in the Age of the Internet* (New York: Simon and Schuster, 1995), 105.

63  Computers share with television a technological base—the CRT display—as well as domestic and professional spaces of consumption that stand in sharp contrast to the collective, uninterrupted viewing environment of theater-based cinema.

# Bibliography

Althusser, Louis. "Ideology and Ideological State Apparatuses (Notes toward an Investigation)." In *Mapping Ideology*, edited by Slavoj Žižek, 100–140. London: Verso, 1994.

Baudry, Jean-Louis. "Ideological Effects of the Basic Cinematic Apparatus." In *Movies and Methods*, Vol. 2, edited by Bill Nichols, 531–542. Berkeley: University of California Press, 1985.

Bolter, Jay David, and Richard Grusin. *Remediation: Understanding New Media*. Cambridge, MA: MIT Press, [1999] 2000.

Bonitzer, Pascal. "Partial Vision: Film and the Labyrinth." Translated by Fabrice Ziolkowski. *Wide Angle* 4, No. 4 (1981): 56–63.

Bordwell, David. *Narration in the Fiction Film*. Madison: University of Wisconsin Press, 1985. Other edition: London: Methuen, 1986.

Bordwell, David, and Kristin Thompson. *Film Art*. 6th Edition. New York: McGraw-Hill, 2001.

Brinton III, Joseph P. "Subjective Camera or Subjective Audience?" *Hollywood Quarterly* 2 (1947): 359–366.

Cohen, Scott. *Zap: The Rise and Fall of Atari*. New York: McGraw, 1984.

Comolli, Jean-Luc, and Jean Narboni. "Cinema/Ideology/Criticism." In *Movies and Methods*, vol. 1, edited by Bill Nichols, 22–30. Berkeley: University of California Press, 1976.

Cowie, Elizabeth. *Representing the Woman: Cinema and Psychoanalysis*. Minneapolis: University of Minneapolis Press, 1997.

Cubitt, Sean. *Digital Aesthetics*. London: Sage, 1998.

Dayan, Daniel. "The Tutor-Code of Classical Cinema." In *Movies and Methods*, Vol. 1, edited by Bill Nichols, 438–450. Berkeley: University of California Press, 1976.

Friedman, Ted. *"Civilization* and Its Discontents: Simulation, Subjectivity, and Space." In *On a Silver Platter: CD-ROMS and the Promises of a New Technology*, edited by Greg M. Smith, 132–150. New York: New York University Press, 1999.

Herz, J. C. *Joystick Nation: How Video Games Ate Our Quarters, Won Our Hearts, and Rewired Our Minds*. Boston: Little, Brown, 1997.

Jenkins, Henry, and Kurt Squire. "The Art of Contested Spaces." In *Game on: The History and Culture of Video Games*, edited by Lucien King, 64–75. New York: Universe, 2002.

Kinder, Marsha. *Playing with Power in Movies, Television, and Video Games: From Muppet Babies to Teenage Mutant Ninja Turtles.* Berkeley: University of California Press, 1991.

Lacan, Jacques. "The Mirror Stage as Formative of the Function of the I as Revealed in Psychoanalytic Experience." *Écrits.* Translated by Alan Sheridan, 1–7. New York: W.W. Norton, 1977.

Levy, Steven. *Hackers: Heroes of the Computer Revolution.* New York: Anchor, 1984.

Metz, Christian. *The Imaginary Signifier: Psychoanalysis and the Cinema.* Translated by Celia Britton, Annwyl Williams, Ben Brewster, and Alfred Guzzetti. Bloomington: Indiana University Press, 1982.

Moreno, Julio L. "Subjective Cinema: And the Problem of Film in the First Person." *Quarterly of Film, Radio, and Television* 7 (1953), 341–358.

Mulvey, Laura. "Visual Pleasure and Narrative Cinema." In *Visual and Other Pleasures.* Bloomington: Indiana University Press, 1989. Originally published in *Screen* 16, No. 3 (1975), 6–18.

Murray, Janet H. *Hamlet on the Holodeck: The Future of Narrative in Cyberspace.* MIT Press, 1997. [Other editions: New York: Free Press, 1997; and Cambridge, MA: MIT Press, 1998.]

Poole, Steven. *Trigger Happy: Videogames and the Entertainment Revolution.* New York: Arcade, 2000. Other edition: *Trigger Happy: The Inner Life of Video Games.* London: Fourth Estate, 2000.

Silverman, Kaja. *Male Subjectivity at the Margins.* New York: Routledge, 1992.

———. *The Subject of Semiotics.* New York: Oxford University Press, 1983.

Sudnow, David. *Pilgrim in the Microworld.* New York: Warner, 1983.

Turkle, Sherry. *Life on the Screen: Identity in the Age of the Internet.* New York: Simon and Schuster, 1995.

Weber, Samuel. *Return to Freud: Jacques Lacan's Dislocation of Psychoanalysis.* Translated by Michael Levine. New York, NY: Cambridge University Press, 1991.

# 49

# LARA CROFT: FEMINIST ICON OR CYBERBIMBO?

## On the limits of textual analysis

*Helen W. Kennedy*

Source: *Game Studies: The International Journal of Computer Game Research*, 2(2), December 2002, available at http://www.gamestudies.org/0202/kennedy/.

As the title suggests, the feminist reception of Lara Croft as a game character has been ambivalent to say the least. The question itself presupposes an either/ or answer, thereby neatly expressing the polarities around which most popular media and academic discussions of Lara Croft tend to revolve. It is a question that is often reduced to trying to decide whether she is a positive role model for young girls or just that perfect combination of eye and thumb candy for the boys. It is also increasingly difficult to distinguish between Lara Croft the character in *Tomb Raider* and Lara Croft the ubiquitous virtual commodity used to sell products as diverse as the hardware to play the game itself, Lucozade or Seat cars. What follows then is an analysis of the efficacy and limitations of existing feminist frameworks through which an understanding of the kinds of gendered pleasures offered by Lara Croft as games character and cultural icon can be reached. I will begin by analyzing Lara primarily as an object of representation—a visual spectacle—and then move on, considering the ways in which the act of playing *Tomb Raider* as Lara disrupts the relationship between spectator and "spectacle."

There is no doubt that *Tomb Raider* marked a significant departure from the typical role of women within popular computer games. Although a number of fighting games offer the option of a female character, the hero is traditionally male with females largely cast in a supporting role. In this respect alone Lara was a welcome novelty for experienced female game players. "There was something refreshing about looking at the screen and seeing myself as a woman. Even if I was performing tasks that were a bit unrealistic . . . I still felt like, Hey, this is a representation of me, as myself, as a woman. In a game. How long have we waited for that?" (Nikki Douglas in Cassell and Jenkins 1999).

When *Tomb Raider* hit the games market, it did so with a good degree of corporate muscle behind it: indeed the game was launched as a significant part of the Sony Playstation offensive. It was a game which deployed the latest in technical advances in games design. Featuring a navigable three-dimensional game space, a simple but atmospheric soundtrack and a level of cinematic realism previously unattainable.[1] The game also made use of a familiar and popular adventure-based narrative format. A great deal has been said already about the extent to which *Tomb Raider* pillages the *Indiana Jones* movies for its narrative structure and setting. The success of the game is arguably attributable to this synchronicity between new techniques, a highly immersive and involving game space and game narrative and the controversial (and opportunistic) use of a female lead. Lara is provided with a narrative past appropriate to her status as an adventurer and an aristocratic English accent–a greater degree of characterization than the norm. Certainly, fans and critics suggest that none of these factors alone can explain the world beating success of the first game and its many sequels. "Lara's phenomenal success wasn't just about a cracking adventure, other games had that too. Lara had something that hooked the gamers like nothing has before. At the center of *Tomb Raider* was a fantasy female figure. Each of her provocative curves was as much part of the game as the tombs she raided. She had a secret weapon in the world of gaming, well . . . actually two of them" (Lethal & Loaded, 8.7.01). For this fan, judging from the tone, it seems that Lara herself is *at least* as significant as the story or gameplay. This comment also signals Lara's status as an object of sexual desire, a factor which the marketing/advertising of *Tomb Raider* was keen to reinforce.

It is clear that the producers of Lara wanted to market her as a character *potentially* appealing to women; her arrival on the game scene dovetailed nicely with the 90's "girlpower" zeitgeist and could potentially have hit a positive chord with the emergent "laddette" culture which very much centred around playing "lads" at their own game(s). In *Killing Monsters* Gerard Jones locates Lara amongst a number of feisty and highly sexualized female characters that rose to prominence in the 90s—including *Buffy the Vampire Slayer* (2002). These characters have a strong "bimodal" appeal in that they manage to engage a large following of both young men and women. The console games market has traditionally been very explicit in their exclusive address to a male audience. In the late 80s and early 90s both Nintendo and Sega made it very clear that to attempt to market games for girls would threaten their real market—boys and young men. Sony's? Playstation, by addressing youth culture in general, broke with this tradition.[2] The featuring of Lara Croft as girl power icon and cover girl for *The Face* magazine (1997)—where she is compared to both Yoda and Pamela Anderson–demonstrated the success of the marketing campaigns and signaled her penetration within a wider cultural landscape: people who had never played *Tomb Raider* could not help but have some awareness of Lara the character/icon.

## Lara Croft as action heroine

The obvious connection between *Tomb Raider* and film narrative conventions and the way in which the game deploys themes and tropes from other popular cultural forms means that a feminist critique at the level of the politics of representation is somewhat inevitable. One such possible feminist approach might be to welcome the appearance of active female heroines within traditionally male or masculine genres. Lara Croft is by no means the first gun-toting action heroine and the iconography of her representation conforms to conventions deployed from *Annie Get Your Gun* onwards, but also has forerunners in comic book heroines such as *Tank Girl*. If, for example, we were to compare her to the representations within the female buddy-movie *Thelma and Louise* we can find many key commonalities. *Tomb Raider* also reworks a male-dominated genre and features a female central character: Lara totes a gun as she navigates a hostile landscape fraught with danger. Consider also the ending of *Thelma and Louise*—they die within the story yet the white screen and the snapshots of them during the credits offer other possible, more positive, endings; with Lara this process becomes even more elaborated as she is resolutely immortal—with each death there is the possibility to replay the level over and over until it comes out right. The popular media and feminist response to *Thelma & Louise* was also similarly polarized around the issue of their representation–did the fact that they wielded guns guarantee or undermine the film's status as feminist?[3] The juxtaposition of physical prowess and sexuality continues to produce a great deal of ambivalence amongst feminist and non-feminist commentators.

Thelma and Louise, and other action heroines such as Trinity in *The Matrix*, can also be considered as what Mary Russo describes as "stunting bodies" (1994): Female figures which, through their performance of extraordinary feats, undermine conventional understandings of the female body. Thelma and Louise, Trinity and Lara explosively take up space within a particularly masculinized landscape—the desert, dark urban landscapes, caves and tombs—and in doing so offer a powerful image of the absolute otherness of femininity within this space. The action genre is typically masculine so this type of characterization is often celebrated as at least offering some compensation for the ubiquity of oppressive representations of women and the preponderance of masculine hard bodies. The general absence of such characters is part of the reasons why fans become so invested in these characters and helps to explain why the popular, critical and academic response is often so polarized. The transgressive stunting body of the action heroine is replicated in the figure of Lara. Her occupation of a traditionally masculine world, her rejection of particular patriarchal values and the norms of femininity and the physical spaces that she traverses are all in direct contradiction of the typical location of femininity within the private or domestic space. If women do appear within these masculine spaces their role is usually that of love interest (often in need of rescuing) or victim. Lara's presence within, and familiarity with, a particularly masculine space is in and of itself transgressive. By being there she disturbs the natural symbolism of masculine culture.

The absence of any romantic or sexual intrigue within the game narrative potentially leaves her sexuality open to conjectural appropriation on the part of the players. The fact that little evidence can be found of lesbian readings of Lara does not in itself prove that this does not or cannot happen. The ubiquity of the heterosexual readings and re-encodings of Lara leaves little space or legitimacy for this form of identification and desire. Within the masculine culture that pervades gaming practice/discussion and dissemination it is unlikely that female gamers will feel adequately empowered to make such a position explicit. However, the fact that a number of the female fan drawings/images of Lara are ones which portray her in sexually coded poses at least hints at this possibility. (For examples of this artwork see http://www.ctimes.net, http://www.eidos.co.uk; http://network. ctimes.net/volcl). So within this particular feminist framework there is some cause for celebration of Lara's presence as marking a significant breakthrough in the representation of women within the game space itself.

## Lara as fatal *femme*

There is another feminist film studies approach that is much less inclined to celebrate the presence of masculinized female bodies. Psychoanalytically informed approaches which have developed from the insights offered by Laura Mulvey's landmark essay (1975) on the function of women within film narrative have a very different take on the tropes of this type of image. Two key insights which appear relevant to Lara are Mulvey's argument that the female body oper-ates as an eroticized object of the male gaze and the fetishistic and scopophilic pleasures which this provides for the male viewer. The second argument was that "active" or "strong" female characters signify a potential threat to the masculine order. This is a more complex argument, dependent as it is on a psychoanalytic reading of unconscious processes. Within this narrative the female body is a cas-trated body and as such it represents the threat of castration itself. This threat, it is argued, is disavowed or rendered safe by the phallicization of the female body. It could be argued that Lara's femininity, and thus her castratedness, are disavowed through the heavy layering of fetishistic signifiers such as her glasses, her guns, the holster/garter belts, her long swinging hair.

What is certainly apparent is the voyeuristic appeal of Lara. This is clearly expressed in the critical analysis of Lara by Mike Ward. In a discussion of the relationship between the male player and Lara, he describes his initial discomfort when faced with a photograph of the latest model posing as Lara for marketing purposes (Lara Weller). What disturbs Ward about this image is that Lara is look-ing directly out at the viewer of the photograph, a look he interprets as signal-ing her awareness of herself as the object of the gaze. This is something which never happens in the game–voyeuristic pleasure depends upon being empowered to look without being seen. For Ward this appears to betray the contract between the player and Lara. In his view "If Lara never returns the ever-present look, she demonstrates her awareness of the player in other ways: her only spoken word is a terse, slightly impatient, "no" if you try to make her perform a move that isn't possible. To the novice player at an impasse, there seems to be a frustrated potentiality in the way she stands and breathes, the user's ineptitude holding all her agility and *lethality* at bay"(Ward 2000, my emphasis).

By looking back, Lara disrupts the "circle" of desire which he describes: "And even if she incorporates my banality, my ordinariness, still, she's beautiful. The player's gaze is a strange closed circle of the desiring look and the beautiful, powerful exhibition. In fact, the look and the exhibition are one and the same, bound into a single, narcissistic contract safer and more symmetrical than anything Leopold von Sacher-Masoch was ever able to dream up" (Ward 2000). What is curious about this article by Ward is both his apparent awareness of the complex range of scopophilic pleasures which Lara affords and his utter acceptance of, if not abandonment to, these pleasures. In his reference to Sacher-Masoch he also signals an awareness of their potentially sadistic nature. It has been argued that the internal spaces of game worlds stand in for the mysterious and unknowable interior of the female body; deploying Lara's *lethality* to navigate and master this space could be argued to enhance these pleasures. Ward does acknowledge that Lara is not real, yet his investment in her and the pleasure he derives from looking at her appear to be very real. Lara is the perfect "object" of desire in what he describes as the equivalence between his look and her performance: she is unwittingly consumed and incorporated through this look. This pleasure is only disrupted when she is made flesh in the form of Lara Weller who *can* look back, and though this can express a subjectivity outside of this phantasmic circle. The discussion of Lara as a male fantasy object can, however, foreclose any discussion of how she might equally be available for female fantasy. The encapsulation of both butch (her guns/athletic prowess) and femme (exaggerated breast size, tiny waist, large eyes, large mouth) modes of representation makes Lara open to potentially queer identification and desire.

There are also limits to the applicability of this theory to a games character who is simultaneously the hero (active) and the heroine (to be looked at). Lara is closer to Mulvey's later work on the Pandora myth which she explores in *Fetishism and Curiosity* (1996). Lara too has "a beautiful surface that is appealing and charming to man [which] masks either an "interior" that is mechanical or an "outside" that is deceitful" (1996). Mulvey argues that "Pandora prefigures mechanical, erotic female androids, all of whom personify the combination of female beauty with mechanical artifice." (1996) Whilst relating Pandora to the femme fatale Mulvey finds this productive of a more interesting reading when discussing an active female protagonist.

"Pandora's gesture of looking into the forbidden space, the literal figuration of curiosity as looking in, becomes a figure for the desire to know rather than the desire to see, an epistemophilia" (1996). Mulvey's conceptualization allows us to move from considering "activity" as masculine within the dynamics of the spectacle. Within this framework Lara's active negotiation of these hostile landscapes can be conceptualized as a feminine coded "desire to know"—a curiosity which enables us to sidestep the "rather too neat binary opposition between the spectator's gaze, constructed as active and voyeuristic, implicitly coded as masculine, and the female image on the screen passive and exhibitionist." (1996) Whilst this is a useful framework which allows for a more positive reading of

Lara it cannot account for how the processes of identification and desire may be enhanced or subverted through playing the game. By focusing on Lara as an agent and a spectacle there is little here that would differ from a reading of the film version of *Tomb Raider* (2001), and this does not account for the specificity of the *experience* of playing as Lara.

## But playing as Lara . . . what then?

What difference does it make to the argument if we focus on Lara as a character within a game and not a film? One response is to suggest that there may be something of interest in the fact that it is typically a male player who, at least for the duration of the game, is interacting with the game space as a female body. In the game it is the player who determines the actions, so the involvement is potentially that much greater than with other media forms—"the computer "functions as a projection of certain parts of the mind . . . producing the uncanny effect of the computer as a second self" (Sofia 1999). Thus, interaction with, and immersion in the game "affords users the narcissistic satisfaction of relating to a technological second self," in this case a *female* second self (Sofia 1999). The relationship between male player and Lara when playing the game could be seen as analogous to the relationship between Case and Molly in Gibson's *Neuromancer* (1984). Case is a "console cowboy" who is able to "jack-in" to Molly's sensorium and experience her actions and sensations—she becomes an extension of his nervous system. "Between self and other, subject and object, [the interface] permits quasi-tactile manipulation of computational objects that exist on the boundary between the physical and the abstract" (Sofia 1999). This collapse offers a promise of a utopian subjectivity which is free from the constraints of fixed gender boundaries.

Thus, in this complex relationship between *subject* and *object* it could be argued that through having to play *Tomb Raider* as Lara, a male player is transgendered: the distinctions between the player and the game character are blurred. One potential way of exploring this transgendering is to consider the fusion of player and game character as a kind of queer embodiment, the merger of the flesh of the (male) player with Lara's elaborated feminine body of pure information. This new queer identity potentially subverts stable distinctions between identification and desire and also by extension the secure and heavily defended polarities of masculine and feminine subjectivity. Through this transgendering process, the Lara/player interface is open to two possible queer readings. One is that she is a female body in male drag—a performance of masculinity that undermines its reliance upon a real male body and highlights the instability of masculinity as an identity. Or conversely, Lara could be considered a female drag performer in that the bodily signifiers of femininity are grossly exaggerated to the extent where they threaten to collapse. "What drag exposes . . . is the "normal" constitution of gender presentation in which the gender performed is in many ways constituted by a set of disavowed attachments or identifications" (Butler 1993). However, this transgendering process can only be argued through if we agree that Lara is in fact a feminine subject in any real sense. Lara's femininity is only secured through these key exaggerated signifiers (or perhaps just the two). This femininity is immediately and irrefutably countered by other phallic signifiers.

Furthermore, the potential transgendering function of playing as Lara does not appear to have any real consequences in the gaming culture sustained by the male players. If anything, any kind of identification with Lara is disavowed through the production of stories and art that tends to want to securely fix Lara as an object of sexual desire and fantasy. The fact that Lara has no sexual or romantic encounters within the game also suggests that the male players and, of course, the designers might feel uncomfortable with identifying her as the object of male desire. It also means that Lara has no sexual identity or subjectivity. To date there are no male-authored fan sites which deal with the question of "how it feels to play as a woman" and it is hard to imagine that there ever could be. Instead, you have a proliferation of sexualized imagery dominating the official and unofficial websites. Alongside these images, there exist rumours and discussions about game patches which enable the player to play with a nude Lara—the legendary "Nude Raider" game patch, or to get her to perform a strip tease. These appear to be more grounded in fantasy than reality, although there are nude images of Lara available on the web. There are also a number of web pages which offer "fragging" opportunities for female gamers to "set fire to" these nude images (see for example http://www.grrlgamer.com/fraggednude.htm). It is the presence of both the official and unofficial highly sexualized images of Lara which is often the focus of critical discussion.

It seems much more likely that the pleasures of playing as Lara are more concerned with mastery and control of a body coded as female within a safe and unthreatening context. The language and imagery remains resolutely sexist and adolescent. However, Jones (2002) argues that "indirectly, these boys are accommodating shifting gender roles, building confidence that they can find even strong, challenging women attractive and that they wont be overwhelmed by their own fears as they deal with real girls." Jones sees these sexy and powerful female characters as providing complex resources for both fantasy and identification as stable gender roles are eroded. Playing as Lara, enables engagement with an active female fantasy figure, providing opportunities for exploration of alternative versions of themselves. He argues that although "these kids may approach their bad girls as objects at first, as the game or movie or the tv show begins to unfold, they are clearly identifying with them" (2002). Even the apparent use of sexist imagery within the fan culture does not necessarily foreclose a feminist reading of playing as Lara. Jones goes on to argue that young men often choose to play games as a female character (when provided the choice or given the opportunity to design their own) as it enables them to experience a greater range of emotional complexity. For Jones, the popularity of these games and the female characters is a positive sign of greater gender flexibility and a general license to experiment with alternative identities. (2002).

But we are still some way from a full analysis of the game/player interaction. It may be that the relationship between player and game character advances in phases as the player becomes increasingly proficient at working the controls. As this proficiency or expertise develops the game character may become an extension of the player herself and Lara's separateness as a female body is eventually obliterated. "Engagement is what happens when we are able to give ourselves over to a representational action, comfortably and unambiguously. It involves a kind of complicity, we agree to think and feel in terms of both the content and conventions of a mimetic context. In return, we gain a plethora of new possibilities and a kind of emotional guarantee" (Laurel 1993). Thus the technology (including Lara) becomes a mask which signals our participation in an artificial and immersive reality and simultaneously "signals that we are role-playing rather than acting as ourselves' (Murray 1997). As a liminal space the game world allows a transgression of social and cultural norms—as an act of play we recognize the time spent playing as separate to other forms of interaction and unbound by conventional rules of behaviour. When what Murray describes as "the symbolic drama" reaches a level of intensity we become compelled to complete the game, often neglecting other activities in order to do so. The sense of presence we experience within the game world means that it can be hard to "jack out" of the game sensorium and attend to mundane matters. Thus, potentially, the fact that the polygons within the game are arranged in such a way as to denote a female body adds becomes an extra dimension in developing an understanding of the game playing experience.

For the female game player, these complex and visceral experiences may provide further opportunities for the gratification of fantasies of omnipotence and may allow for empathic experience of the pleasures of exploration and adventure which are absent in the real world. This may even be enhanced by the possibilities of identification with the game character—"empathy is subject to the same emotional safety net as engagement—we experience the characters" emotions as if they were our own, but not quite; the elements of "real" fear and pain are absent" (Laurel 1993).[4] From this we might also speculate that some of the desperate re-encoding of Lara as "sex object"—on the part of male players—may arise from an anxiety over the fact that these experiences *are* mediated by a female character and thus signify an attempt to deny any empathy/identification with Lara.

## Virtual Lara: cyborg embodiment

*Don't look at the Idoru's face. She is not flesh; she is information. She is the tip of an iceberg, no an Antarctica, of information . . . she was some unthinkable volume of information. She induced the nodal vision in some unprecedented way; she induced it as narrative.*

(Gibson 1996)

In 1996, Kyoko Date—another virtual character—released a single in Japan. She was created by the Visual Science Lab in Japan and was promoted through a successful talent agency Hori Pro. Kyoko's personality and performance were scripted and controlled in exactly the same way as Stock, Aitken and Waterman managed and controlled the identity and image of Kylie Minogue or Jason Donovan. As virtual commodities invested with a specifically human backstory and personality it could be argued that Date & Lara destabilize the reality of more human idols. It could be argued that Madonna is no more real or approachable than Lara or Date. In a sense, Lara the game character is no more virtual than the images of real movie or pop stars: they too are representations which are carefully managed. Gibson's *Idoru*, published in 1996 at the same time as the launch of *Tomb Raider* and Date, pivots around the romance between a real rock star and Idoru herself, a virtual performer/artist.

The Idoru appears omniscient within this story. She is able to reflect and respond to whoever she communicates with—each encounter with her is particular to the interlocutor and Idoru herself demonstrates no central subjective coherence–she is as depthless as a mirror. The same is true of Lara, who will perform differently (and reflect differently) depending on the skill and proficiency of the player. These virtual "babes" are ludic postmodern signifiers par excellence (Morton 1999), endlessly available for resignification, and providing multiple possibilities for narcissistic pleasure. When the game is mastered the player experiences Lara's mobility, agility and athleticism as his or her own. The creation and maintenance of a fairly complex backstory for Lara is an attempt to secure control of her virtual identity—she is a commercial product after all. Providing Lara with a (fairly) plausible history gives her some ontological coherence and helps to enhance the immersion of the player in the *Tomb Raider* world, and abets the identification with Lara. What Idoru, Lara and Date all highlight is the willingness on the part of real humans to invest erotically in fictional characters. It could potentially be argued that this is in no way a new insight—people have always invested emotionally in literary, film and television characters. This could also be seen to underline the fact that male sexual desire and fantasy are always bound up in an image of femininity which is virtual (in the sense that it is not *real*). Femininity is thus finally exposed as an empty signifier, a sign without a referent.

These occasions for both virtual embodiment and "erotic interfacing"(Springer 1999) need to be more fully understood as complex experiences in their own right.

"The phantasmic mobility of virtual bodies not only satisfies our infantile desires for omnipotence and omnipresence, but can provide hallucinatory satisfaction to those whose real body's mobility is impaired in some way" (Sofia 1999). This celebration of virtuality is also premised on an understanding that "computers are machines for producing postmodern forms of subjectivity" (Sofia 1999) and that these may help to bring about the collapse of other more oppressive subjectivities. As with the examples above, these more celebratory readings remain somewhat utopian in the face of the extent of the proliferation of virtual female bodies which are mere "objects". "Lara Croft is the monstrous offspring of science, an idealized eternally young female automaton, a malleable, well-trained technopuppet created by and for the male gaze" (Schleiner 2000). Technology becomes a means of extending or transcending the body as the final site of the monstrous feminine other, as well as providing opportunities for the playing out of fantasies of conquest and control of this "other." These hypersexualized versions of virtual femininity are strategies of containment which need to be understood as such. The trenchant encoding of the technological imaginary as a masculine preserve and the positioning of femininity as an aesthetic rather than agentic (i.e. the player is the agent) presence within this landscape serves to maintain the exclusion of girls and women from the pleasures of the interface, erotic or otherwise.

These virtual "babes" are *not* welcomed by some feminists. Elaine Showalter argues that "since the computerized cover girls are patched together from the best features of real models and stars no real woman can ever hope to equal them; but their popularity . . . nonetheless is part of the millennial taste, for elaborate feminine artifice, especially an artifice shrewdly designed to look natural" (*Sunday Times*, 10 June 2001:6). Like the earlier discussion around transgendering, this *elaborate artifice* could serve to underline the very constructedness of conventional ideals of femininity. However, Showalter and others fear that we will have a generation of young girls who grow up even more dissatisfied with their own bodies and who are willing to make more and more drastic interventions in order to recraft their bodies in line with these impossible images, there is a sad irony in the idea that real women are more and more likely to use technology in order to become more like virtual women who fundamentally *are* just technology. "More generally, Croft and the cybermodels epitomize the era of power grooming. No longer can women depend on a dab of powder and lipstick before they face the public" (Showalter 2001).

In the end it is impossible to securely locate Lara within existing feminist frameworks, nor is it entirely possible to just dismiss her significance entirely. These readings demonstrate the range of potential subversive readings, but there exists no real "extra-textual" evidence to back this up–hence the focus on the text itself, which is on its own inadequate to explore the range of pleasures available from playing as Lara—we can only conjecture. The girl gaming community which communicates via the internet has its own highly critical discourse about the imagery and content within computer games. They not only complain about the degree of sexist portrayals of women but also bemoan the stupidity of many female games characters and lack of strong female leaders in role playing games.[5] This critique must be acknowledged and addressed by designers and producers of games if they intend to attract and retain this audience.

> Where are the game companies that say its okay to be girl who doesn't think like one? . . . I refuse to be charted like a map, and confined to several "common" characteristics. I am uncommon. Make games for me.
>
> (Douglas 1998)

If we are going to encourage more girls into the gaming culture then we need to encourage the production of a broader range of representations of femininity than those currently being offered. We also need to offer a critique of the entire discourse around gaming which serves to create the illusion that it is a masculine preserve. Feminist film criticism has had an impact (albeit only to a limited extent) on the representation of women in cinema. This critique has inspired many writers and directors, both within and outside the Hollywood system, to increase the range of possible subject positions offered to women. It is similarly vital that in the construction of a critical discourse about games we encourage and stimulate innovative and alternative images of men and women that do not simply reinstate doggedly rigid gender stereotypes.

In this article, I have tried to be attentive to what might be different about the relationship between representations within the game world and the experience of playing the game. It is clear that games *are* an increasingly sophisticated representational and experiential medium and that we need analytical tools which are precise enough to capture both the similarities *and* the differences to other forms of leisure consumption. Simultaneously, it is becoming more and more evident that the interactive and immersive modes of engagement so central to gameplay are the model driving other forms of computer mediated consumption. This means that feminist theory cannot afford to ignore the games paradigm. By the same token, the politics of representation—and here I would extend this to racist and homophobic as well as sexist modes—is a vital issue which the games industry should not ignore.

## Notes

1 Sony are alleged to have invested $500 million in the hardware behind the Playstation and a further $500 million in the software. These figures are quoted in *The Face* (1997) but also in Poole (2001).
2 See Poole (2001), Herz (1997) but ample evidence for this address to a male audience is provided in early marketing campaigns and was certainly a factor in the *Tomb Raider* adverts. This is most particularly evident in the "Where the Boys Are" advertising campaign for *Tomb Raider II*.
3 For an overview of the complex debates around *Thelma & Louise* see Read, Jacinda (1999), "Popular Film/Popular Feminism: The Critical Reception of the Rape-Revenge Film" 29.11.99. in *Scope Online Journal* www.nottingham.ac.uk/film/journal/articles/popular_feminism.htm
4 The degree to which fear and pain are *not* experienced by the player is debatable. I know that my heart rate rockets, my palms sweat, I leap out of my chair and develop callouses on my thumbs. The experience of playing *Tomb Raider* has often left me shaken and exhausted.
5 For some fairly typical examples of this discourse see www.grrlgamer.com & www.chiq.net

## References

Balsamo, Ann (1995) "Forms of Technological Embodiment: Reading the Body in Contemporary Culture", *Body & Society* 1 (3–4):215–237.
Bell, David (2001) *An Introduction to Cybercultures*, London: Routledge.
Butler, Judith (1993) *Bodies That Matter: On the Discursive Limits of "Sex"*, London: Routledge.
Cassell J and Jenkins H (1999) *From Barbie to Mortal Kombat: Gender and Computer Games*. MIT Press.
Demaria, Cristina & Mascio Antonella, *Little Women Grow Up: A Typology of Lara Croft's Sisters* http://www.women.it/4thfemconf/workshops/laracroft5/demariamascio.htm. Accessed 21.06.2001.

Douglas, Nikki (1998) "Uncommon Me" *Grrl Gamer* http://www.grrlgamer.com/gamergrrl04.htm. Accessed 05.02.2002

Gamman, L and Marshment, M. (Eds) (1988) *The Female Gaze: Women as Viewers of Popular Culture*. London: The Women's Press Ltd.

Gibson, William (1997) *Idoru*, Penguin Books.

Gibson, William (1984) *Neuromancer*, Penguin Books.

Hayles, N. Katherine (1999) *How We Became Posthuman: Virtual Bodies in Cybernetics, Literature, and Informatics*, University of Chicago Press.

Herz, J.C. (1997) *Joystick Nation: How Videogames Gobbled Our Money, Won Our Hearts and Rewired our Minds*, Abacus Books.

Jones, Gerard (2002) *Killing Monsters: Why Children Need Fantasy, Super Heroes and Make Believe Violence*. NY: Basic Books.

Laurel, Brenda (1993) *Computers as Theatre*, Addison Wesley Longman Ltd.

*Lethal & Loaded*, Documentary Channel 5, 8th July, 2001.

Mitchell, Juliet (1987) *Psychoanalysis and Feminism: A Radical Reassessment of Freudian Psychoanalysis*, Penguin Books.

Morton, Donald (1999) "Birth of the Cyberqueer", pp. 295–313 in J. Wolmark (ed) *Cybersexualities: A Reader on Feminist Theory, Cyborgs and Cyborgs*. Edinburgh University Press.

Mulvey, Laura (1975) "Visual Pleasure and Narrative Cinema", *Screen* 16 (3):6–18.

Mulvey, Laura (1996) *Fetishism & Curiosity*, London: BFI.

Murray, Janet (1997) *Hamlet on the Holodeck: The Future of Narrative in Cyberspace* Mass: MIT Press.

Oliver, Kelly (1997) *The Portable Kristeva*, Columbia University Press.

Poole, Steven (2000) *Trigger Happy: The Inner Life of Videogames*, Fourth Estate Ltd.

Read, Jacinda (1999), "Popular Film/Popular Feminism: The Critical Reception of the Rape-Revenge Film" 29.11.99. in *Scope Online Journal* www.nottingham.ac.uk/film/journal/articles/popular_feminism.htm

Russo, Mary (1994) *Female Grotesque: Risk, Excess and Modernity*, NY: Routledge.

Sawicki, Jana (1991) *Disciplining Foucault: Feminism, Power and the Body*, Routledge.

Sawyer, Miranda (1997) "Lara Croft: The Ultimate Byte Girl", *The Face*.

Schleiner, Anne Marie (2000) "Does Lara Croft Ware Fake Polygons: Gender Analysis of the "1st person shooter/adventure game with female heroine' and Gender Role Subversion and Production in the Game Patch" available Switch: Electronic Gender: Art at the Interstice at http://switch.sjsu.edu/web/v4n1/annmarie.html. Accessed 19/06/01

Showalter, Elaine (10th June, 2001) *The Sunday Times*.

Shulusky, Edward *In Love with Lara: Reflections on an Interactive It-Girl*, http://www.tombraiders.com/lara_croft/Essays/Edward_Shulusky/default.htm accessed 19/06/01

Sobchack, Vivian (1987) *Screening Space: The American Science Fiction Film*. NY: Ungar.

Sofia, Zoe (1999) "Virtual Corporeality: A Feminist View", pp.55–68 in J. Wolmark (ed) *Cybersexualities: A Reader on Feminist Theory, Cyborgs and Cyberspace*. Edinburgh University Press.

Springer, Claudia (1999) "The Pleasure of the Interface", pp. 34–54 in J. Wolmark (ed) *Cybersexualities: A Reader on Feminist Theory, Cyborgs and Cyberspace*. Edinburgh University Press.

*The Matrix*, (1999) The Wachowski Brothers.

*Thelma & Louise* (1991) Ridley Scott

Turkle, Sherry (1984) *The Second Self: Computers and the Human Spirit*. NY: Simon & Schuster.

Ward Gailey, Christine (1994) "Mediate Messages: Gender, Class, and Cosmos in Home Video Games", *Journal of Popular Culture* 27 (4): 81–97.

Ward, Mike, 14 January 2000, "Being Lara Croft, or, We are All Sci Fi", *Pop Matters*. Available at http://popmatters.com/features/000114-ward.html. Accessed 19/06/01

Woolley, Benjamin (1993) *Virtual Worlds: A Journey in Hype and Hyperreality*, Penguin Books.

# 50

# THEORIZING GENDER AND DIGITAL GAMEPLAY

## Oversights, accidents and surprises

*Jennifer Jenson and Suzanne de Castell*

Source: *Eludamos: Journal for Computer Game Culture*, 2(1), 2008, 15–25.

> If someone returns from work one night and announces he has accidentally run over a cat on the way home, that's one thing. If he comes home night after night having accidentally run over one cat after another, its reasonable to question his affection for cats, and to dispute the extent to which this can be rightly called an 'accident' anymore.
>
> —D.W. Hamlyn (class notes, c. 1977)

This paper is about an apparent inability so frequent as to appear no longer "accidental," in current work on gender and gameplay: an apparent inability to theorize, analyze or interpret gender research in which "equity" takes center stage. This is a question that has been stewing for us for quite a long time. Some years ago, similarly baffled at the apparent inability of otherwise well informed, theoretically sophisticated educational researchers and scholars working on a "gender equity" committee to muster any but the most outdated and soundly-critiqued conceptions of gender equity as "equal numbers of males and females in all subjects," it began to dawn on us that something was going persistently and systematically wrong with work on this issue (Bryson and de Castell, 1993). Now to be clear, it's not that there is no theoretically insightful, radical, intellectually exciting ground being broken in gender studies more generally: for example, brilliant work in queer theory from the likes of Eve Sedgewick, Judith Butler, Michel Foucault, and Donna Haraway amply testifies to the advances in conceptualization that can be and have been made: our puzzlement is about what happens in the move from theory to application, whether in sociology, in gender-based design practices, in gender-based research, in gender equity policy, in women in game studies or in any other arena of "progressive" gender-centric practice.

In this paper, we mobilize some of that insightful and innovative theoretical work to interrogate the apparent "mistakes" of contemporary work on gender and digital gameplay as a means to re-consider deficiencies as Efficiencies, as deeply-rooted forms of productive "bio-power" (Foucault, 1990) which induce a perception of the constructed and artificial as "natural" and essential, in such a way as to render any kind of profound inquiry inconceivable and, in this way, systematically to disable critical inquiry. In other words, this paper is an attempt to rethink the assumptions and presumptions of work on gender and gameplay in an effort to demarcate more clearly how those are not only implicated in our analyses to date, but also misleading and misdirecting what we could "find" and what might well be present if we had a different framework for viewing. In some sense, this is, as Iris Marion Young (among many others) has pointed out, a struggle over language, that is over the very words we use to describe events, to encode practices, to grammatically shape and give design to the stories we tell as researchers (Young, 1998/2005). In this attempt to rethink persistent and repetitive "accidents" of theory, we will touch briefly on a longitudinal study (three years) of gender and digital gameplay whose subjects were over 100 girls and boys aged 12–15 (for a fuller description of the study see: Jenson and de Castell, 2007) in order to show more fully the workings of some of these all too familiar discursive "traps."

A useful beginning in nearly all work now on gender is with Butler's analysis of gender performativity, which invites us to distinguish between what appears to be an essential, authentic or inner "truth" of gender from daily performances of gender conventions that, through their repeated embodiment in actions and self-representations, make those conventions, that artifice, appear both necessary and natural. Echoing earlier arguments by feminist sociologist Dorothy Smith that explanations invoking "womens' *roles*" are in actuality ideological "moves" which reify conventions and impose upon women expectations and obligations which a feminist sociology ought instead to be critically exposing, Butler writes that "gender cannot be understood as a role which either expresses or disguises an interior 'self,' whether that 'self' is conceived as sexed or not. As performance which is performative, gender is an 'act,' broadly construed, which constructs the social fiction of its own psychological interiority" (Butler, 1990).

On this view, what the repetition of conventional gender performances accomplishes is hegemony. So seen, this repetition is far indeed from being a "mistake," an unhappy "accident" of scholarship gone wrong: rather, from this perspective what we are looking at are the deepest epistemic roots of scholarly inquiry in a culturally extremely important area. This would be a different vision altogether, a vision of something working very well indeed, working so well, in fact, that even experienced and accomplished researchers find themselves, ourselves, steering to aporia, mesmerized. What repetition signals, then, at least perhaps in this field, is not an accident, but something quite purposeful, a deeply structured process which naturalizes convention and makes it impossible to see or hear anything other than an 'inner truth' of gender that little seems capable of dislodging when discussions move from the esoteric domains of high theory into applied areas like social, technological, and educational research, design, policy, and practice.

In this next section we begin by enumerating some of the conventions and "norms" that are often repeated when writing and talking about women/girls and playing digital games and then show how those "norms" are often misinterpreted, indeed mis-labeled as "evidence" for a stable "fact" about gender. As Butler reminds us, "Whether gender or sex is fixed or free is a function of a discourse which seeks to set certain limits to analysis or safeguard certain tenets of humanism as presuppositional to any analysis of gender" (Butler, 1999, p.12). Here we examine those limits and presuppositions that delimit gender analysis in relation to digital games.

## Cooperation vs. competition: is Florence Joyner competitive? Or is she not a "woman?"

It has become a timeworn orthodoxy in discussions of "girl-friendly" game design that girls like to cooperate in their gameplay, whereas boys like to compete (Cassells and Jenkins, 1998). What is far less clear is what "competition" and "cooperation" mean? Whose conceptualizations of these alternatives are running this show? In the work we have done observing and interviewing girls about how they play, and what they like and dislike in video and computer gameplay, it soon becomes clear that the *very idea* of "competition," for example, is both gendered and contestable. If we think we know what competition means, then we probably have not observed, analyzed, or talked to very many girls playing games. It's commonplace that many female athletes, for example, are highly competitive, so why would we not expect girls who play computer games to be "competitive"? It's time we expended some intellectual effort de-coding competition, before going blithely on to invoke the term as a marker of gendered play preferences.

The point we are trying to make here is that there seems to be a systematic need to theorize the axiomatic concepts within which research is attempting to study gender and digital gameplay. Theoretical work, for example, on "competition" demonstrates its "essentially contested" character (M. Fielding, 1976, after W.B. Gallie, 1956); it's meaning is neither transparent nor persistent, so it's important to sort out what "competition" means. We obviously do not refer by this term to the structure of the games played, since many of the games girls like and choose to play are "competitive" in their structure. In *Super Monkey Ball*, for example, you have to fly more accurately, race faster, rollover more bananas and so on, than your fellow players. Even if you are playing solo, you are challenged by the game itself to get the highest score, even if it's only relative to your own last highest score. Wherever there is scoring, there is competition of at least this kind. Is there any videogame that doesn't have some form of competition inbuilt?

In fact, of course, many girls do like, even "love" competitive gameplay. Many girls we interviewed (over 80) said that they enjoy the same kinds of competitive gameplay boys do: fighting, beating, racing against one another, building higher, faster, deeper, longer, accumulating the most points, knocking out opponents, all that. Many other girls seem to love to play with others, but their competition takes a rather different, not necessarily gender-specific, form—what one of our research assistants designated "benevolent competition." When girls in our study played in this benevolently competitive way, they are still very much "competing," however, they are also supporting, encouraging and even helping their playmates to succeed in the game. The point is that they *are* competing. They are playing competitively in the ways enabled and supported for girls. That means only that these girls, and girls like them, are competing in ways socially regulated as appropriate to and acceptable for them "as girls." If their competition took the same form as that of their brothers, this might be cause for trouble on all sides. What this account doesn't do—and unless we already attain equality of access and experience, never can do—is tell us about "gender differences in girl-friendly game design" (Graner-Ray, 2004). If the very terms of our calculations, our axiomatic concepts and foundational practices, embody and express and re-cite hegemonic rules, we will continue to define for women and girls, activities, dispositions, aspirations and accomplishments in the terms of what these are and mean for boys and men. The problem is one of terms and turf. If we define the matter from the outset in terms that describe only what happens on male turf, we are unlikely to illuminate much about the situation as it is possible for women. As Butler elsewhere explained, the state accords rights to those that it then goes on to represent. This is "always already" a hegemonic performance, however worthy or "progressive" our intentions. So our first interpretation of "benevolent competition", was in some sense, already predefined and put in binary opposition to how the boys were playing, and led to us mistakenly trying to attribute something about how "girls play" to our repertoire of "findings".

An example of research intended to challenge and invert the usual way that work on gender and gameplay has been reported on is the work of Valerie Walkerdine, which strongly argues:

> many games are the site for the production of contemporary masculinity because they both demand and appear to ensure performances such as heroism, killing, winning, competition and action, combined with technological skill and rationality. In relation to girls, this constitutes a problem because contemporary femininity demands practices and performances which bring together heroics, rationality, etc. with the need to maintain a femininity that displays care, co-operation, concern and sensitivity to others. (2007, p. 48)

It is one thing to acknowledge and work with the recognition of the gender constructions within which children in our studies play games. But to theorize our own findings from this standpoint is another thing, and it demands that we take into serious account how the gender imperatives we are acknowledging work also within and against our analytical and interpretive efforts. It's inscribed in both our *concepts* (e.g. an unproblematically gendered conception of "competition" which is then, necessarily, not "found" in girls' play), and in our *methods*, which misconstrue normatively constrained gendered performances as "data" from which we might literally "read off" truths about what girls like, what they can do, what they are interested in, and how they play. If researchers are prepared to acknowledge that the boys in their studies come into the research situation with more experience and greater gender-investment in performing gaming interest and ability—and, with that, "competitiveness"—they surely *must* also acknowledge that it's necessary to bring girls to a comparable experience/investment level in order to entertain any conclusions about gender-based differences in digital game play. Experience and investment are not "variables" to be acknowledged and then summarily dismissed from consideration. All that can leave us with is re-citation and re-inscription: boys necessarily always already perform masculinity and girls perform and practice femininity. This is likely part of why it is that gender and gameplay studies have told us little in the past 10 years that we had not already "discovered" in the first-gen gender research.

So when we say above, that girls are "playing competitively in the ways enabled and supported for girls" what we are trying to say is not that girls are thereby channeling some kind of hardwired femininity, but instead, clumsily, we are trying to draw attention to the irrefutable importance of *context and knowledge* to their play performances. It is absolutely significant, for example, that in each of the years we studied girls' play that in the first weeks of the club, there is much more "helping" dialogue occurring than direct competition as they familiarize themselves with the games. Later on, for most players who attend regularly, this dialogue drops off and they begin taking up positions as "experts" in particular games. Instead of reading this as "help vs. competition" we see it more as moving from more novice to expert roles, a factor which commentary on competition versus cooperation in gameplay often overlooks.

The approach we propose to this kind of research instead is one that takes the careful work of theorists like Butler, Foucault and Smith into account and begins with a very different premise: given that games have been and continue to be a popular cultural site for play, especially for men and boys, who and what supports their play and under what conditions, and when, how, with whom and under what conditions do girls and women play games? This might shake loose and put into question some of those limiting binary readings of masculinity and femininity that past studies have replicated (c.f. Walkerdine, 1998, 2007: Graner Ray. 2004).

## From novice to expert:
## another account of gendered "differences"

In our own work on gender and gameplay, taking differences in experience and investment seriously into account has radically altered our own perceptions of our subjects, our data, and our methods.

Observing youth between 12 and 13 for over three years as they learn and play console games, we saw a wide *range* of performances: from hypermasculinity to hyperfemininity from *both* girls and boys. So we came to see games less as a site for the production of "contemporary masculinity" than as a leisure site in which, given time and permission, girls were as eager to spend time as boys. Performance, under these conditions was very much regulated by technological skill: the better the player, the less "performance" *per se*.

For example, in the final year the girls decided to hold a game tournament and compete directly with one another over a period of a few months (interestingly, the boys did not want the option of competing either among themselves or, later, with experienced girl-players) to see who could achieve the highest overall score. One of the games chosen for the tournament was *Guitar Hero (GH)*, which they played on the Playstation 2 using a plastic guitar as a controller. For those not familiar with the game, the goal of GH is to accurately press the keys on the guitar in time with the music; the more accurately a song is played, the higher the score.

Observing the girls play, we noted that initially (that is the first one to three times they played) there was a *lot* of chatter: how to hold the guitar, how to play, encouragement from onlookers, exclamations when missing notes, and quite a lot of self-effacing commentary like "I suck/I can't do this/This is too hard". Not too much later, as the girls began (en masse) to master the game, the chatter died away, and we observed many play sessions with very little talk, other than "I missed/Oh Crap/That Sucked". All of the self-deprecating talk had nearly vanished, and the girls eagerly checked their final scores to see who had won in "head to head" competition. Interestingly, because GH was a game that none of the boys had at home (at least to begin with, although after the first few weeks, 3 of the boys had acquired GH for their homes; none of the girls were purchased GH) we observed the exact same cycle in their play as we did with the girls—a cycle that we had not fully recognized before as being related so directly to game familiarity. We had, in years past, commented on how little the boys spoke to one another in many of the play sessions, unless it was to show off and brag about their skills, put down another player or ask for or receive help. We attributed some of this behaviour as "unique" to the groups of boys playing, however, it could just as easily be attributed to the *difference between experienced gameplayers and novices*. In other words, the more skilled the players, the less collaboration, less talk, less self-deprecating commentary, less help offered, all performances which could be (and have been) attributed to girls playing games. So what we've been (mis)reading as research about girls and gameplay as we've said before, could in actuality be research about *novices* and gameplay. In fact, Dianne Carr's work on gender and play preferences maps neatly onto the work we document here. Hers was a study of a girls game club in an all girls' school in which she examined the "relationships between taste, content, context and competence, in order to explore the multiple factors that feed into users' choices and contribute to the formation of gaming preferences" (Carr, 2005, p. 466). She concludes, not with a reinscription of gendered gameplay preferences (e.g. what games the girls in her study most preferred to play), but instead by acknowledging that while it is possible to "map patterns" for play preferences, to do that assumes they are stable instead of preferences being "an assemblage, made up of past access and positive experiences and subject to situation and context" (p. 479). Finally, and importantly, Carr states that "What did become apparent was that the girls' increasing gaming competencies enabled them to identify and access the different potential play experiences offered by specific games, and to selectively actualize these potentials according to circumstance and prerogative. This indicates that forms of competency underlie and inform our gaming preferences—whatever our gender" (p.478). It might well be, then, that competency has been too often misrecognized as some factual attribute for gender. In the next section, we attempt to give examples of how research in this area is to used re-entrench gender "norms".

## Re-citing gender research

That research "data" no less embody naturalized hegemonic conventions about gender should of course come as no surprise. So why does it? If pressed, even the most entrenched gender essentialist of girl-game theorists would acknowledge that this must of course be the case, since research is itself a socially situated practice, so must therefore be the "data" it elicits. In the face of this intransigent fact, what have we done in practice to take acknowledged epistemic bias into account in such a way that we might make it possible for our research to "surprise" us (Jenson and de Castell, 2005; Smith, 1989)? In *Tricks of the Trade*, research methodologist Anselm Strauss argues persuasively for the usefulness of having richer "*contra*-factual possibilities" inbuilt in our very research design, from contexts to characters to questions (Becker 1998). So how is it that we appear to "forget," for example, the need to *substantively* control for greater investment and prior experience in studies of what games "girls like best," (Carr, 2005; Walkerdine, Thomas and Studdert, 1998; Walkerdine, 1998) or most typically choose to create (Denner, J., Werner, Bean, and Campe, 2005; Kafai, 1995).

It is by now surely well-understood that the responses people give to questions about what and how they like to play best, necessarily vary as a function of the situation they are occurrently in, what they take the intent of these questions to be, who is asking them—all of these things reconstitute and reconfigure what the question "is" for informants', and shape the range and nature of the responses they will give in the moment. One telling respondent early in the study commented, for example that:

> If a guy asks another guy, "do you play video games?" he'll pretty much always say yes, because guys know video games are about competing with other guys, and about winning. But if a girl asks a guy if he plays, he'll say no, so she doesn't think he's a social misfit who only likes to stare at a computer screen.

And yet when we asked over 80 respondents, almost all the girls replied they played with brothers or male relatives, even though none of the boys reported that they played with sisters or female relatives. These discrepancies only make sense if we presume that what we have are not informative answers to our questions, but informative performances of gender-normativity—unless we alter the conditions so as to make something other than that response possible and visible, that is to say, make it possible for us as researchers to be "surprised" by our own findings. This common enough realization has had a hard time impacting upon gender-focused research, however. A thorough application of Bakhtin's insightful analysis of "addressivity" and "dialogicality" would go a long way towards redressing the studied naiveté of what remain resiliently stereotypical research "findings" about girls and gaming. But improving the intellectual quality of gender-focused research is only a part, and perhaps the lesser part, of what is at stake here.

It has often been the case, for example, when we interviewed girls about their gameplaying that most of them name a few titles, sometimes not accurately, and then indicate that they "play" but they do not always get to choose the game. Interestingly, in one focus group interview, after going round the table and naming games, one girl asked if computer games "counted" and the researcher responded "Yes" to which everyone replied by talking at once and naming off their favorite, free, online games. So, in one way, we had initially asked the wrong question, or they had perceived it as a question simply about console gameplay. A similar incident is reported in Walkerdine (2007), but she interprets the question as being "too difficult" for the respondent to answer, instead of speculating on why that question might have produced an awkward silence on the part of the female participant (the question was "what are your favorite game characters"). The interpretation that seems most direct in both these situations is that what girls like best are, for the most part, "girl games" like the Sims or broadly, "racing games" but those stock answers miss out the surprising fact that by and large the games that these girls are playing are puzzle, online, free games when they have computer time, while their brothers and cousins and male peers are playing console games that cost money, and to which their sisters often do *not* enjoy equal access.

## Re-citing stereotypical practice: other discourses?

One way out of this stranglehold might be to enlist a different methodological approach than has been previously taken, one that was present both in our study and Carr's (though not explicitly stated), which is to take context, actors, and tools into consideration. Actor network theory (ANT), a conceptual framework which investigates human agency as always already "networked" across an intersecting landscape of affordances, both human and non-human, of context, tools, symbols, plants, and animals, is of particular interest to digital games researchers, for whom ANT offers a full "voice" so to speak, to artificial intelligence in its varied forms and functions. Seth Giddings (2007) explains why actor network theory appears particularly well suited to digital games studies, and promising as a standpoint from which to carry out studies in a field new and under construction. He argues that digital gameplay "transgresses" the boundaries between subject and object through its conflation of game, machine, and player, in particular that: "a full understanding of both the playing of digital games, and the wider technocultural context of this play, is only possible through a recognition and theorization of the reality of technological agency" (p. 115). Employing ANT as a theoretical lens makes this possible, as it "claims both the agency of non-humans and, moreover, the *symmetry* of agency between humans and non-humans in any network (p.118).

It is our contention that ANT seems as well a highly suitable approach to studying gender and gameplay. Take, for example, the description earlier in the paper of the girls playing *Guitar Hero*: there we reported that a shift in controllers actually contributed to an overall gain in competence on the part of the girls. In other words, the change in controllers (e.g. change in technology) actually *enabled* for those particular girls a way in to one of the "cultures" of gameplay. ANT seems as well a highly suitable approach to studying changes in technology design, in this case, new forms of game controllers, affordances that are restructuring users' interaction with digital gameplay. We argue that the *way* this restructuring of interactivity is happening suggests considerable changes for both theories and practices of "serious play," and invites major shifts in the design of games for education and training. By contrast with the intense interest and attention (and fan base!) that has been devoted to game design and designers across all sectors of game culture, the 'things' players directly interact with, the "objects" they use to play, and, in particular, the end user's hardware, has not enjoyed comparable airtime. It's an understandable human failing to accord primacy of place to human agents in explaining innovation, though it may in fact be user interface design that turns out to be far more significant for advancing new audiences, inviting new players, and thereby affording new possibilities to those previously marginalized.

The "trouble" with studies of gender and gameplay has most frequently been the static attribution of gender norms and characteristics to actors, contexts and artifacts that are always in flux. It is not that previous research has been inadequate or "wrong" it is simply that in the telling of those stories (Visweswaran, 1994), in the recounting of "findings" that researchers have "fixed" gender in order to stabilize the network of interactions and the possibilities for troubling gender shifts. Carr's work resists this fixing: she does not enumerate a list of games that girls "preferred," nor does she attempt to label "what girls like best", but there is a whole other stream of work that has been popularized and is recounted again and again at academic game conferences as well as at commercial games conferences in which Freud's old question of "what women want" has somehow become the holy grail of how to "make more money" in the industry. While money is less an object on the academic side of the question, it gets no less a contested response as at the recent DiGRA 2007 conference, in Tokyo a prominent European academic sitting in the audience following a panel on women in games in which the panelists had detailed the gender stereotypes that keep women out of the lucrative games industry asked pointedly: "Don't you want to try to present your stuff in a way that doesn't burn bridges?" Moving past the decidedly retro discourse of his response, what we think he was really asking was, "If you think that it is a problem that more women and girls don't play games and aren't in the industry, can't you just play nice and tell us we are doing a good job?"

Gender is and has been for some time a contested site: it is "at play" and "in play" in radically different ways, given different contexts, actors and tools/technologies. What we are calling for here is a way of holding tight to that complexity, to in some sense, "live in the eye of the storm" in a way that opens up possibilities for telling stories in ways that are more faithful to action and interaction. Identity recast in such a way, taking in earnest Butler's (1999) claim that "Gender is a complexity whose totality is permanently deferred, never fully what it is at any given juncture in time" (p. 151) might begin to loosen the noose that heteronormative sentiment has had on gender and gameplay research for some time.

The main problem with flawed research is that it can drive flawed practice. Going back to the catastrophic driver earlier introduced, neither better night-vision lenses, nor new and improved headlights, nor any other intervention directed at improving his ability to see cats on the road could prove effective if the real problem was a bad "tic" about cats and a deep-seated desire to rid the world of their kind. In a not—dissimilar way, when "girl-friendly" principles derived from research which forgets itself as gender-performance and mis-reads itself as an "inner truth" of gender, drive "girl- friendly" intervention efforts to engage girls with game play, or with game design, or with games as a route to computer programming, those interventions will themselves structurally re-cite and re-entrench the very inequities they seek to remediate. And we should not be surprised if "gender equity interventions" of that persistently if unwittingly conservative kind are those most highly and prestigiously funded. We cannot look to practical work, no matter how well supported, whose very foundations are flawed, to remediate problems that remain undetected and therefore unacknowledged from the start. A good first step would be to resuscitate *interpretation* as an indispensable tool for gender research in game studies, to unlearn the stereotypical assumptions, and challenge covertly stereotyped concepts (such as "competition") that have thus far driven gender research in this field, and, by these simple means, to begin to make it possible to discover something *other* than that which we always already "know" about girls and video gameplay, and to be *surprised* about "what girls like best".

## Acknowledgements

We gratefully acknowledge the work of research assistants Jeff Zweifl, Claire Fletcher, Sheryl Vasser and Stephanie Fisher on this project as well as funding from the Social Sciences and Humanities Research Council (SSHRC) of Canada, and the SAGE Network (http://www.sageforlearning.ca/). An earlier draft of this paper is to be found in the Digital Games Research Association (DiGRA 2007) conference proceedings.

# References

Becker, H.S. (1998) *Tricks of the Trade: How to Think About Your Research While You're Doing It.* Chicago: University of Chicago Press.

Bryson, M., and de Castell, S. (1993). En/Gendering equity. *Educational Theory*, 43(4), pp. 341–355.

Butler, J. (1990) Performative Acts and Gender Constitution: An Essay in Phenomenology and Feminist Theory. In S. Case (Ed.), *Performing Feminisms: Feminist Critical Theory and Theatre.* Baltimore: Johns Hopkins UP.

Butler, J. (1999) *Gender Trouble: Feminism and the Subversion of Identity.* Routledge: New York.

Cassells, J. and Jenkins, H. (Eds.) (1998). *From Barbie to Mortal Kombat.* Boston: The MIT Press.

Carr, D. (2005) Context, Gaming Pleasures and Gendered Preferences. *Simulation and Gaming*, 36(4), p. 464–482.

Denner, J., Werner, L., Bean, S., and Campe, S. (2005) The Girls Creating Games Program: Strategies for engaging middle school girls in information technology. *Frontiers: A Journal of Women's Studies.* Special Issue on Gender and IT, 26, pp. 90–98.

Fielding, M. (1976) Against Competition: In Praise of Malleable Analysis and the Subversion of Philosophy. *Journal of Philosophy of Education, 10(1)*, pp. 124–146.

Foucault, M. (1990) *The History of Sexuality, An Introduction: Volume I.* New York: Vintage.

Gallie, W.B. (1956) Essentially Contested Concepts, *Proceedings of the Aristotelian Society, 56*, pp.167–198.

Giddings, S. (2007) Playing with Non-Humans: Digital Games as Technocultural Form. In S. de Castell and J. Jenson (Eds.), *Worlds in Play: International Perspectives on Digital Games Research.* New York: Peter Lang, pp. 115–128.

Graner Ray, S. G. (2004) *Gender Inclusive Game Design: Expanding the Market.* Hingham, Massachusetts: Charles River Media, Inc.

Jenson, J. and de Castell, S. (June 2005) Her Own Boss: Gender and the Pursuit of Incompetent Play. Paper presented at the International DiGRA conference, Vancouver, Canada.

Jenson, J. and de Castell, S. (2007) Girls Playing Games: Rethinking Stereotypes. Proceedings of Futureplay 2007 (Toronto, Canada, 14–18 November 2007).

Kafai, Y. B. (1995) *Minds in Play: Computer Game Design As a Context for Children's Learning.* Hillsdale, NJ: Lawrence Erlbaum Associates.

Smith, D. E. (1989) *The Everyday World as Problematic.* Lebanon, NH: Northeastern University Press.

Walkerdine, V., Thomas A. and Studdert, D. (1998) Young Children and Video Games: Dangerous Pleasures and Pleasurable Danger. Available at http://creativetechnology.salford.ac.uk/fuchs/projects/downloads/young_children_and_videogames.htm. Last accessed April 10, 2007.

Walkerdine, V. (1998) Children in Cyberspace, in K. Lesnik-Oberstein (Ed.). *Children in Culture.* London: Macmillan.

Walkerdine, V. (2007) *Children, Gender, Video Games: Towards a Relational Approach to Multimedia.* New York: Palgrave Macmillan.

Visweswaran, K. (1994) *Fictions of Feminist Ethnography.* Minneapolis: University of Minnesota Press.

Young, M. I. (1998/2005) Five Faces of Oppression. In Ann E. Cudd & Robin O. Andreasen (Eds.) *Feminist Theory: A Philosophical Anthology.* Malden, MA: Blackwell Publishing.

51

# SERIOUS PLAY

## Playing with race in contemporary gaming culture

*Anna Everett*

Source: Joost Raessens and Jeffrey Goldstein (eds), *Handbook of Computer Game Studies* (Cambridge, MA: The MIT Press, 2005), pp. 311–325.

> [W]ho would have predicted that young black and Latino males would spend enough time in Times Square video arcades during the late seventies to make those games the million-dollar industry that they are?
>
> —*Greg Tate*

> In the 80s and 90s you never saw black characters. If there were any black ones, they would get beat up, really whumped so fast, before they had time to get into character.
>
> —*Orpheus Hanley*

> I hacked another game and created a game called *Blacklash* . . . . I was fed up with companies making black games that have got no relation to black people whatsoever. You'll have someone make a game, and one of their characters got dreadlocks—and it's like someone put a mop on his head.[1]
>
> —*Richard-Pierre Davis*

> Machines have the morality of their inventors.
>
> —*Amiri Baraka*

When my preteen niece challenged me to a game of *Super Mario Brothers* during a family Christmas gathering a decade ago, it was my reintroduction to video game play since my casual initiation during the *Pac-Man* and *Ms. Pac-Man* computer game craze of the mid 1980s. I was unprepared for the seductive and addicting qualities of this second generation of video games due, in part, to the striking evolution of gaming hardware and software packages, narrativity, and character designs from blocky, one-dimensional geometric renderings to the more technically accomplished Disneyesque animation standards featuring fully individuated cartoon character types. I am thinking here of Mario and Luigi, popular characters

110

of the *Super Mario Brothers* game franchise, which has been described as "one of the best selling games ever."[2] At the time, I found the hand-eye coordination demands of interactive play (predicated on mastering the action keys of Nintendo's control pads) a welcome distraction from and counterbalance to the cerebral demands of my graduate school course of study. From that moment on, I became a fan of video game entertainment, unaware of how this seemingly innocuous diversionary play would become an important part of my later scholarship and research interests.

Exhilarated by my easy mastery of relatively complex controller key commands and minimal "story" advancement demands, using intuition instead of manual instruction (although my niece talked me through the basics), I rushed out and bought my own Nintendo console and *Super Mario Brothers* game. Looking back on that pleasurably fateful Christmas break, I suspect the lure of video game play for me (an African American woman graduate student) was only differentiated from that of more traditional players to the extent that my pleasure inhered in a displacement of the high-stakes, immersive intellectual work of graduate study, temporarily, onto the no-stakes "immersive play" of the game. Of course this is not to suggest that traditional players are not highly educated. My point is to stress the surprising fetish object gameplay had become for me as my weekends increasingly became structured around this alternative mode of intellectual engagement and interactivity. The work/play dialectic of intellectual growth at school and digital dexterity (fingers in this case) at home effected a balanced scale of my "transmedia"[3] mastery during the ensuing decade, which happened to coincide with the gaming industry's own development of interactive play designs.[4]

However, as the current research progressed, my efforts to dissociate my objective study of race in video games from my subjective experiences with and frustrations about enjoying gaming, despite its encrusted discourses of racial difference and otherness, seemed less crucial. After all, Hayden White reminds us that hoary, or "outmoded conceptions of objectivity" do little to conceal the subjective nature of evidence and facts "constructed by the kinds of questions which the investigator asks of the phenomena before him"[5] (White, 1978, p. 43). Moreover, I am convinced that White's observations about objectivity in discourse production in the field of history remain pertinent. About writing histories of History, White argues, "It is difficult to get an objective history of a scholarly discipline, because if the historian is himself a practitioner of it, he is likely to be a devotee of one or another of its sects and hence biased; and if he is not a practitioner, he is unlikely to have the expertise necessary to distinguish between the significant and the insignificant events of the field's development" (p. 81). As a practitioner and historian of popular culture, and a longstanding fan and foe of video game texts, I share White's estimation, and easily recognize its applicability to my concern with examining race matters in the short history of video games.

Until late 1999, most public concern about video games focused on presumed dangerous behavioral consequences for minors and impressionable teens due to excessively violent content[6] and, to a lesser extent, on gender bias.[7]

Race was the structured absence in this latest iteration of generation-gap politics between parent and youth cultures. The present discussion addresses this all-too-familiar lacuna by interpolating race matters into the fracas. I situate my critique of gaming culture within a discursive ambit that includes select game titles, video game journalism, personal interviews, and formal and informal survey data that specifically engage matters of race in video and computer games. Finally, I reference methodological approaches and precedents from influential and emerging scholarship on cultural theory, gaming, and other modes of contemporary popular culture as hermeneutic touchstones, or useful conceptual models in this interrogation.

## Game boys remaster orientalist and high-tech blackface metanarratives

Because the video game industry privileges "boys in their pre- and early teen" years (Bolter & Grusin, 2000, p. 91), I am acutely aware that my mature, black, and female body is marked and thus marginalized as a shadow consumer in the gaming industry's multibillion dollar marketplace. Moreover, my informal surveys of video game cover art and game descriptions, print and online game reviews, manufacturer strategy guides, and popular media coverage of expert gamers uncover not only an essential and privileged male gaming subject, but one who is "universalized" under the sign of whiteness. For me, this distinct racial discourse in gaming culture's dramatic movement from its second- to third- generation of sophisticated 3D character designs, with various racial types in tow, begged the question, "When and where does the racial problematic enter in contemporary culture's moral panics about gaming's potential dangers?"

Society's vocal moral outrage over gaming culture's gender troubles (to borrow Judith Butler's fecund phrase), especially its sexist and misogynistic constructs of women and girls, did not find a parallel in terms of race. Nonetheless, racially offensive depictions of minority groups, namely blacks, Asians, and Jews, appear to demand similar scrutiny and just concern. To be sure, I am not suggesting returns to outmoded logics of behavioral and media effects determinism because we know the communication process is more complex and nuanced than that. And, Stuart Hall reminds us that dominant discourses, such as Orientalism, do not constitute a closed system of meaning in the sender-message-receiver feedback loop, because audience-receivers' interpretive processes are subject to distortions (Hall, 1986, p. 134–135). Yet we must not underestimate the lure and "textual erotics" that certain representational possibilities promise over others. In other words, although it certainly is the case that readers/audiences and, of course, gamers can and do actively resist and often misread dominant plot structures, Peter Brooks's assertion that "the reading of plot [is] a form of desire that carries us forward, onward, and through the text" (Brooks, 1984, p. 37) is instructive. Thus we see that part of the pleasure *is* reading the plot "correctly" and as intended, which Brooks's notion of "textual erotics" illuminates. In this way, gaming plot structures that posit an occidental *self* in conflict with an oriental *other* structure in a narrative pleasure principle predicated upon Orientalism's binary logics.

After all, as Marsha Kinder warns in *Playing with Power*, the danger in gaming's "cultural reinscriptions" is that "within particular social and economic contexts, the recognition of specific allusions makes certain inter-textual relations payoff—especially at the point of purchase" (Kinder, 1991, p. 45). The payoff in these games' intertextual relations is their reinforcement of dominant culture's racist hegemony, and their redeployment and reification of specious racial difference for new generations and their new media culture industries. In his study of Asian American representations in American televisual discourses, Darrell Hamamoto stresses the fact that we must recognize how race is a fundamental organizing principle of America's pluralist society, and that we cannot afford to ignore the real consequences of this reality for nonwhite Americans (Hamamoto, 1994, p. x). We know that popular culture texts are effective conduits for the transmission, if not preferred reception, of privileged socio-cultural-political messages and ideas. However, we should not presume some *a priori* value neutrality when narratives find novel expressive apparatuses, such as with computer games.

Clearly, encryption message senders presume decryption message receivers, otherwise the attempted communication exchange process is futile, and more importantly, cost-ineffective. Given the importance of the profit motive in the gaming industry, we likewise can presume a correlative if not a cause-effect dynamic at work here. Even taking into account contemporary media theories of the polysemous nature of signs and signification, privileged cultural ideologies (i.e., race and gender differences) remain "transcendent signifiers" or primary cultural reference points. It is in such racialized and orientalizing discourses that Roland Barthes's assertion that there is no "zero degree of meaning" gains some material force. As Barthes cogently puts it, "discourse scrupulously keeps within a circle of solidarities . . . in which 'everything holds together'" (Barthes, 1974, p. 156), for gaming's readerly participants. In other words, we are confronted with the resilience and tenacity of ideology and its stranglehold on a particular circuit of cultural meaning. Terry Eagleton further clarifies the solidarities of how ideology holds together: "It is one of the functions of ideology to 'naturalize' social reality, to make it seem as innocent and unchangeable as Nature itself. Ideology seeks to convert culture into Nature, and the 'natural' sign is one of its weapons" (Eagleton, 1983, p. 117). These analyses remind us that resistance to what Wolfgang Iser calls an "ideal meaning" and its corollary the "ideal reader" are predicated upon, in this case, an understanding of encrypted (or encoded) meanings that represent desirable gaming heroes naturally as predominantly white, and victims and antagonists naturally as nonwhite "others".

What, then, are the means by which we can effectively explore this racialized meaning-encryption-decryption feedback loop in popular and alternative computer games? To the extent that gaming's readerly and writerly narrative structures draw upon and are imbricated in such traditional meaning-making media as print, theater, film, and television, insights gained from influential and emerging work on ideologies and theories of race become especially productive. Indeed, poststructuralist, postcolonial, and critical race theories, whiteness studies, and cultural studies provide effective epistemological lenses for critiquing the racial discourse in gaming's parallel and support industries: the computer magazines and specific game tie-ins—the strategy guides.

## "Reading race" in video game user manuals and strategy guide texts

Because videogame magazines and strategy guides increasingly constitute a significant element of gaming culture's specific narrative dispositions and logics of mastery, how they engage the racial problematic becomes a key concern in this study. Any excursion into computer superstores, or perusals of retail store magazine aisles and magazine stands conveys well the sophisticated nature of these specialized texts' visual appeal. To compete in an oversaturated marketplace, gaming magazines, like the others, attract their readers with splashy and visually sumptuous cover art, usually featuring recognizable game characters in striking and vibrant photorealistic renderings. Other visceral lures in cover art feature celebrity images and interviews, film or TV show tie-ins to games, samples of "free games," scantily clad, buxom young women, and most important, text promising "cheat" keys to mastering gameplay such as "the latest tricks, tips, and game shark codes,"[8] or "how to unlock each character."[9]

Although the gaming magazine and strategy guides' cover art warrant detailed analyses of their own, we are most concerned with the textual discourses and meaning assumptions between the covers. To investigate the racial discourse of these specialized texts, I have selected as exemplars *Next Generation* (October 1996), *Computer Player* (October 1996), *Playstation Magazine* (October 1999), *Incite* (2000, both Video and PC Gaming editions), and *Prima's Official Strategy Guide* (2000, both their *Ready 2 Rumble Boxing: Round Two*, and *Tekken Tag Tournament* editions) (Figures 1, 2).

That there are specific generic, ideological, and representational coherences unifying these different texts is granted and thus not at issue. However, it is the photographic confirmation of an unbearable whiteness of being underpinning the editorial hierarchies and advertising copy of these magazines that suggested this particular line of inquiry. For instance, the investigative journalism in Michael Marriott's *New York Times* article "Blood, Gore, Sex and Now Race: Are Game Makers Creating Convincing New Characters or 'High-Tech Blackface'?" and Anthima Chansanchai's *Village Voice* article "Yellow Perils: Online 'Coolies' Rile Asian Americans foregrounds the dominance of white males in video game design and production. But it was the above mentioned gaming magazines' own practices of including photos or drawings of their editorial teams, ad copy featuring young white males as ideal consumers, and the strategy guides' rhetorical privileging of white game characters that struck me. And although *Incite's* "PC Gaming" magazine features photos of its lone black and two Asian males, and one white woman,

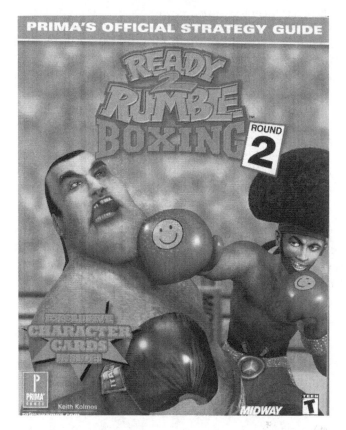

*Figure 1* Prima's Official Strategy Guide for Midway's game sequel *Ready 2 Rumble: Round 2*

among its nine-member editorial team, I would argue that this racial inclusiveness, though important, does little to balance the magazine s overriding narrative ecology of whiteness.

Another ideological touchstone informing our concern with the intersections of race, representation, and gaming interactivity is the matter of new media commercialization. Along this critical axis, the editors of one *Next Generation (NG)* article sum up the limitations of the gaming industry's ability to break out of dominant culture's discursive formations because of their commercial imperatives. In its special feature article "Money Makes the Games Go Round," the *NG* editors admit that:

> From Silicon Graphics to 3DO, the world of gaming comes with strings attached, held in the hands of a coterie of venture capitalists . . . . You might think that the game business is driven by creativity, which it is to

a greater degree, but the barriers to entry get higher every day . . . . The cost of distribution, marketing, and of course, development for games are reaching Hollywood proportions . . . .You end up paying the stores all kinds of marketing money to get them to put your product on the shelf. On top of all this, you have to make sure that people know your software is out there. Now, what developer can afford to do all that?[10]

The answer, of course, is that gaming magazines are tapped to share the financial burden of marketing games to this very lucrative target market. Unquestionably, then, our analysis must encompass this commodification of gaming narrativity and iconographical representations, which we know from other media texts are difficult to disaggregate from dominant cultures' institutional racism, or what Aldon Lynn Nielsen discusses as the "frozen metaphors within American speech" (Nielsen, 1988, p. 3).

In Nielsen's analysis of how poetic language often constructs representational blackness within a "white discourse as a set of self-confirming propositions," we find a useful approach for avoiding essentializing positions in this look at gaming discourse. As he correctly points out:

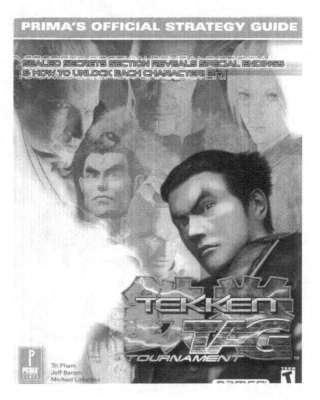

*Figure 2*  Nameco's *Tekken Tag Tournament*

Through the power of white hegemony, the signifiers of that system have been placed into circulation within society such that they are distributed fairly evenly across the population. It is thus not necessary that the full discourse appear each time that its operations are to be manifested. It is required, as [Hans Robert] Jauss has pointed out, only that one element of the system be presented . . . . Only one small portion of the imaging system, only a suggestion of blackness need appear for the entire structure to be articulated. (p. 6)

This is an important point because it reminds us that rarely is language as transparent or clear-cut as once imagined. Instead, as part of a cultural as well as linguistic syntax and structure, words are often sedimented with troubling ideologies of race. For example, in designing the game *Daikatana*, John Romero of *Doom* and *Quake* fame created "a well muscled African American" [character named] Superfly Johnson. As imagined by Romero, this character was crafted to be a "large menacing character" (quoted in Chansanchai, 1997, p. 25) who achieves his narrative and gameplay impact through an intertextual reference to American society's reified imagery of the criminalized black male brute icon of historic films and television news. This is in addition to the character's easily understood Blaxploitation film moniker *Superfly*. If we have learned anything from semiotics, structuralism, and poststructuralism's influential critical demystifications of linguistic and imagistic signifying functions, as Nielsen illustrates, it is that cultural inscriptions acquire meaning only as part of intact language systems that more or less rely on readers' varying fluency in diverse media literacies.

To reiterate a previous point, this presumptive media literacy thesis does not foreclose what cultural studies' proponents advocate as readers' negotiated and oppositional reading practices against such ideal meaning—reception structures. So, despite the fact that gamers might read against, say *Prima's Official Guide's* penchant for privileging *Ready 2 Rumble: Round 2*'s white characters against the game's nonwhite characters in the mode of address and descriptions of racialized characters, we can not ignore the political economy served by the games' and game magazine editors' abilities to draw upon only a small portion of racial difference signifiers to naturalize their strategic positioning of white characters to maximize game points.

The focus here on some rhetorical contours of gaming magazines' and strategy guides' racial discourses reveals a binary address to ideal players according to a racialized "You" versus "Them" conflict structure that is rapidly becoming a standard and understood functional motif. The problem is that such standardization practices increasingly reify or naturalize nonwhite characters as objectified third-person Others whose alterity[11] is so irremediably different that ideal players would have little to no incentive to adopt them as avatars or skins. Indeed, the welcome diversification of game characters is significantly delegitimated when minority characters function primarily as objects of oppression, derision, or as narrative obstacles to be overcome or mastered.

117

Another structured form of gameplay based on racialized characters is crafted by designers of the role play game *Imperialism: The Fine Art of Conquering the World*. This particular game conveys explicitly gaming's colonialist remythologizing aspects along the lines of what Abdul R. JanMohamed terms "The Economy of Manichean Allegory. *Imperialism* is a neo-colonialist strategy-sim game that bears out the racist logic of colonialist power relations that postcolonial theorist Abdul R. JanMohamed describes: "The colonialist's military superiority ensures a complete projection of his self on the Other: exercising his assumed superiority, he destroys without any significant qualms the effectiveness of indigenous economic, social, political, legal moral systems and imposes his own versions of these structures on the Other" (JanMohamed, 1995, p. 20).

JanMohamed goes on to highlight colonialism's representational economies in terms of an Manichean allegory that are useful for us when thinking about games, their manuals, guides, and iconographies. For him,

> the imperialist is not fixated on specific images or stereotypes of the Other but rather on the affective benefits proffered by the manichean allegory, which generates the various stereotypes . . . . The fetishizing strategy and the allegorical mechanism not only permit a rapid exchange of denigrating images which can be used to maintain a sense of moral difference; they also allow the writer to transform social and historical dissimilarities into universal, metaphysical differences . . . . African natives can be collapsed into African Animals and mystified still further as some magical essence of the continent. (p. 21–22)

In the game manual's section called "Imperialism Basics," the countries in *Imperialism* articulate not only how certain racialized characters are programmed at a strategic disadvantage, but how the game structures-in biased advantages. As if a complete confirmation of JanMohamed's charge, the manual states:

> In *Imperialism* there are two types of countries. The first type, Great Powers, are actors in the game, each ruled by a human or by a wily computer foe. The second type, *Minor Nations, serve as regions for exploitation and battle by the Great Powers*. A Minor Nation in *Imperialism cannot* develop into a Great Power, *nor can it win the game* . . . . In *Imperialism*, colonization refers to a *"peaceful"* takeover. *(Imperialism* manual, 1997, p. 13 [emphases added])

It is telling enough that *Imperialism* programs a nineteenth-century colonialist military ethos into contemporary gameplay, as it states, "modeled on the real world of the nineteenth century" (p. 1), yet recasting colonialism as "peaceful." But coupled with the game's striking cover art displaying an illuminated white-skin hand grasping a globe (Figure 3), such representational economies advance a worrisome, yet unrepentant ideology of neo-colonialist Eurocentrism that

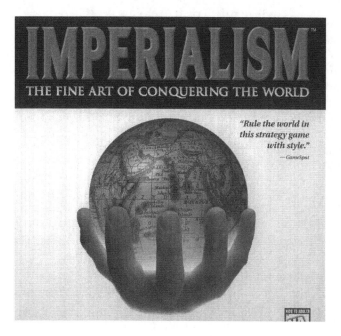

*Figure 3* Imperialism's game box cover design

posits imperialism as spreading the necessary light of western civilization. And given this game's obvious Eurocentrism, it might be reasonable to presume its relative lack of appeal for nonwhite gamers interested in mastering strategy-sim games.

However, one gamer informed me that this particular genre does not necessarily foreclose participation, pleasure, and mastery from those gamers other than the ideal or targeted end user. In his article "Black Spectatorship: Problems of Identification and Resistance," Manthia Diawara problematizes what he calls the "impossible position" of black spectators, which bears similarly on black gamers. Following feminist filmmaker and theorist Laura Mulvey's ideas of gendered spectatorship, Diawara notes that black film spectators' pleasure in film and TV texts are obtained via transgender and transracial identification with white male characters as heroic ideals (Diawara, 1993, p. 211–214) or by resisting this narrative hegemony altogether through "active criticism" and oppositional film-making (p. 219). I have argued elsewhere and in a related context that black spectators attenuate their visual displeasure by deliberately misreading "explicit antiblack character types so as to recode and reinvest such images with transcendent meanings to suit their own visual imaginings" (Everett, 2001, p. 309). Such approaches certainly seem pertinent to and applicable strategies for black gamers.

## Civilize this! Or in geek-speak: RTFM!

Despite game designs' restraint on users according to what Jean Francois Lyotard suggests is the tyranny of the computer bit (the basic unit of information regulated and circumscribed by the programmer) (Lyotard, 1991, p. 34), one black geek lets us in on some subversive tactics and strategies to avoid such gaming circumscription and frustration. This geek, University of California, Santa Cruz doctoral candidate Rebecca Hall, informed me that the first rule of geekiness is to *RTFM (read the freaking manual)*, and for gamers it is essential for circumventing the game's prescriptions, understanding its Byzantine rules, and mastering the gameplay of any genre. Hall finds it important to read closely and thoroughly any game's manual before attempting to play because she hates having an information deficit when her goal is to overcome some games' discursive tyranny. Hall became a video game fan in the mid 1980s. A favorite game was Avalon Hill's *Civilization*, a precursor to such strategy-sims as *Imperialism*. What is interesting about Hall's approach to *Civilization* and what makes it pertinent to our study is her example of how people actually play these games. In addition, her deployment of a stealth essentialism strategy that allows her to win games by playing against the norm speaks volumes about gamers, willingness to re-fuse and reject games privileged narratives while still finding hours of challenging and pleasurable play. Hall's own description of her gameplay makes the point convincingly. It is important, however, to note that *Civilization* is not a wargame (wargames do not generally appeal to female gamers), but according to one website, FunagainGames, "The object of the game is to gain a level of overall advancement to which cultural, economic, and political factors are important. The winner is the player who maintains the best balance between activities of nomads, farmers, citizens, merchants and adventurers."[12]

Hall's gameplay is a novel enactment of this ideal scenario, and how she describes her stealth essentialism approach is revealing. The game begins with the dawning of civilizations somewhere between 4000–8000 B.C. to 250 B.C. What Hall appreciates most about the game is that game players set the condition for winning, whether it is through world conquest, being the first to launch a successful spaceship from earth, spiritual transcendence, or heading a world-class government. Where some of her acquaintances who play the game opt for traditional European civilizations as game avatars, she also notes that the game presents other options as well.[13] As she puts it:

> There are ten-fifteen different peoples that you can pick, and they have different characteristics, like the Zulu, who are militaristic and expansionistic. This means you go into the game with certain technologies and certain advantages (military). And in this way it is coded. The Egyptians are spiritual and commercial, the Americans (I don't know why there are Americans and Abe Lincoln in 4000 B.C. right?) . . . And there's the Sioux and the Chinese . . . . They all have strengths and weaknesses, and anyone of them can win.[14]

As for Hall, it is important to play and win as an African civilization, which the game essentializes as Chaka Zulu (although sometimes she renames the character after an actually existing seventeenth-century African queen of Angola, named Nzenga). Hall continues:

> When I play the Zulu . . . [with rules establishing that] you know how to build stone walls and you have the wheel. And then you've got to dedicate certain of your resources to research. So over time you learn more and more technology. If you pick a culture that is scientific you start up ahead of the game. But the Zulu are not scientific. So what I do (and this is where the resistance part comes in) is, I take the military advantage that is there, but then I focus more of the resources on the scientific. By the time I get to 1000 B.C. they are both the strongest militarily and the strongest scientifically, which positions them in a way that is stronger than the other groups . . . . There is also a telos . . . . After you've done enough research you go into different ages, like the Barbarian Age, the Premodern, the Enlightenment, whatever. And by the time you get to the 1800s, and the way I play it, the Zulus have the railroad by 1000 A.D. You see Chaka in a suit, with the bone piercing in the ear—you know. So, its got the Western telos— right, but, it's a little bit subversive, and it is racially coded [according to white norms] . . . . I wonder how much I am deluding myself, but this game is different.[15]

Hall is not alone in her appreciation of *Civilization*'s various interactive modes wherein militarism is merely one of its many strategic foci. Other gamers, some hailing from Germany, England, and so on, who reviewed the game *Civilization* for the website FunagainGames, also find its nonwargame emphasis particularly appealing. As Lane Taylor from London writes to the website, *"Civilization* is NOT a war game . . . or is it? The great thing about this game is that it can be different things to different people. If you want to play it as a war game, you can; if you want to play as a trading game, you can; if you want to play as a building game, you can." For Hall, it was finally a chance to "pick the Zulu and kick everybodies' asses" both militarily and scientifically in a popular videogame not designed for that purpose. And no matter how opaque, incomplete, and generally incompetent the technical writing of the manuals, Hall's example reminds us of the necessity to RTFM before one can effectively resist or transgress programmers' tyranny of the bit!

## Playing the "skin" game

Where the strategy-sims marginalize the Other, both qualitatively and quantitatively, gaming's sports and fighting genres, by contrast, foreground the Other in their interactive fictions. Still, first-person games such as Nameco's *Tekken Tag Tournament* and Midway's *Ready 2 Rumble: Round 2*, for example, are in little danger of contributing to what Uma Narayan and Sandra Harding call "decentering the center." It is difficult to discern any progress between sports and fighting games, overrepresentation of racial minorities and strategy-sims, underrepresentation of these groups when white male characters (especially Americans) are continually privileged. For example, as in real life (RL) sports, all of the characters in *Ready 2 Rumble Boxing: Round 2 (R2R-2)* bear colorful names and nicknames that enliven and amplify their stereotypical "personalities," and delimited skills (Figure 4). The problem is that such charged enunciations appearing in strategy guides and manuals either fire or dull users' imaginations as they "select" or choose to play as these highly racialized game "skins." Writing for *Prima's Official Strategy Guide to R2R-2*, Keith Kolmos and his team reinforce heroic and sympathetic stereotypes of white game characters, while redeploying ridiculous and pernicious ones for black and other Others.

Afro Thunder and his cousin G. C. Thunder as "arch rivals" not only evoke the discourse of black-on-black violence, but because the former "went Hollywood for a while" (Kolmos, 2000, p. 22) and the latter uses "boxing as a vehicle for opening a chain of hair facilities" (p. 62), and because each is "more of a performer than a boxer," these black skins are silly, malevolent, and trivialized dissimulations of black boxers' RL dominance of the sport. Furthermore, black skin Butcher Brown's King Kong look, "much-needed mental stability" and "banned . . . deadly knock-out punch" complete the familiar rhetoric of black male criminality and brawn over brains image. (Interestingly, these characters "special moves," and "combo moves" were programmed with too many skill deficits to be purely coincidental or insignificant.)

Again, high-tech blackface and black "skins" are not the only representational casualties of the "joystick nation," to borrow J. C. Herz's terminology. As surprised as I was to discover Maori, Brazilian, Hawaiian, Taiwanese, Mexican, and Thailand "skins" also among Midway's *R2R-2* pugilistic ensemble, I was less surprised by the rhetoric and rendering that constructed them. Like the black American "skins," these other racialized Others also were marked by such rhetorical differences as "Beast from the East," "Maori fighting ways are savage," "400-pounder . . . short on ring experience but long in the tooth," "lacking confidence," and so on. These are not exactly the skill levels that lure most users. These avatars are even more undesirable when white, ethnic "skins" representing Italy, Croatia, England, Canada, and America are described sympathetically, powerfully, and affirmatively: "high tolerance for pain," "dedicated to boxing," "story is enough to bring a tear to your eye, "out to prove to the world that he'll be able to beat the best with just one hand," "although he's laid back, Brock gets pretty serious when he hits the canvas," "improved on his formerly rudimentary boxing skills," "refined skills and superior knowledge of the sweet science" (Kolmos, 2000, p. 34– 73). With such visual and narrative inducements, and at costs ranging from five to more than fourteen dollars an issue, these texts and their alluring codifications of whiteness should not be underestimated. After all, stories of the comic book's strong influence on directors of films, music videos, and television shows are legion and legendary. To some extent, these guides seem more potent as

*Figure 4* (a) B-Brown. (b) Illustration shows Selene Strike. (c) Jet-Chin. (d) Mama-Tua. (e) Wild Stubby

imagistic ideals for the computer literate Internet generation. And their discourses of racial difference can be subtle and disarming.

## Conclusion: *Ethnic Cleansing*—the game

[*Ethnic Cleansing* is] the most politically incorrect video game made. Run through the ghetto blasting away various blacks and spics in a attempt to gain entrance to the subway system, where the jews have hidden to avoid the carnage. Then, if YOU'RE lucky . . . you can blow away jews as they scream "Oy Vey!," on your way to their command center. The Race war has begun. Your skin is your uniform in this battle for the survival of your kind.—*Ethnic Cleansing*[16]

In February 2002, analysts of the U.S. videogame industry announced record shattering retail sales of interactive game units in 2001 that topped out at $9.4 billion.[17] That same month, cybersleuth H.A. alerted our virtual community on the Afrofuturism listserv to the existence of an alarming, tour de force racist

123

computer game called *Ethnic Cleansing* by simply posting its URL, or web address, under the subject "Ethnic Cleansing: The Game!" Despite H.A.'s uncharacteristic lack of commentary in that initial post, the following few days were abuzz in thoughtfully passionate, detached, enraged, and engaged responses. For some, the question concerned whether or not black people should use the same "powerful open source game engine, Genesis 3D," used to create the racist *Ethnic Cleansing* game, to create games of retaliation or overdue reparations for centuries of oppression and legalized injustice against African Americans. Others, especially L.d.J., were unconvinced that the Internet could be "the great equalizer," given troubling developments in gaming culture as reported by the Anti Defamation League (ADL). L.d. J. posted information from the ADL on hate groups' "manipulation of available technology to create violently racist and anti-Semitic versions of popular video games . . . with titles such as *Ethnic Cleansing* and *Shoot the Blacks*."[18]

Clearly such use of the Internet for recruiting youths to the ideology of hate does not exactly embody the progressive revolutionary imperative of the temporary autonomous zone (TAZ) that Hakim Bey imagined when he spoke of data-piracy and other forms of leeching off the Internet itself for "reality hacking" and "the free flow of ideas" (Bey, 1991, p. 108). But the fact remains that manipulated games began proliferating on the Internet to be "previewed, purchased or downloaded on the websites of the nation's most dangerous hate groups" including "neo-Nazis, white supremacist and Holocaust deniers."[19] The ADL reports that "In 'Ethnic Cleansing'", the player kills Blacks and Hispanics (the game uses pejorative terms) before entering a subway . . . sound effects, described as 'Realistic Negro Sounds, 'turn out to be 'monkey and ape sounds' that play when dark-skinned characters are killed in the game's first level."[20] What struck me about this particular egregiousness was its eerie resonance with Lester A. Walton's 1909 essay about "The Degeneracy of the Moving Picture Theater," where Walton describes his encounter with the early cinema's profiteering on black pain and suffering. Walton writes incredulously: "Several days ago, the writer was surprised to see a sign prominently displayed in front of the place bearing the following large print 'JOHN SMITH OF PARIS, TEXAS, BURNED AT THE STAKE. HEAR HIS MOANS AND GROANS. PRICE ONE CENT' "! (Walton, 1909, p. 6). Most salient here is Walton's admonition that our failure to protest vigorously against such racist commodification of black victimhood would engender worse images in the future. As Walton put it, "If we do not start now to put an end to this insult to the race, expect to see more shocking pictures with the Negro as subject in the near future" (p. 6). Certainly there has been a steady historical progression of pernicious representations of blackness in many film and television texts that bear out Walton's prescience. Unfortunately, video games such as *Ethnic Cleansing* only exacerbate the situation.

Exactly one month after H.A. posted *Ethnic Cleansing*'s URL to the Afrofuturism list, ABC's *World News Tonight* ran a segment on the game and its intergenerational group of hatemongers, revealing that the game's January 20, 2002 launch was planned to coincide with the nation's official Martin Luther King, Jr. holiday.

This is not the only time television has addressed gaming issues. On July 10, 2002, ABC's news show *Nightline* aired a program entitled "Just a Game: Playing *Grand Theft Auto* 3" *(GTA3)* that interrogates this game's excessive violence, incredible photorealism, amazing popularity, and staggering financial success. Certainly, I am interested in *Nightline*'s disclosure that *GTA3* has sold three and a half million copies at $50 each, and concerns about the game's "stunning realism" taking interactive gaming to a new level.[21] However, I am more interested in how the discourse of race and gaming gets played out in *Nightline*'s latest moral panic and traditional versus new media rivalry episode couched as news. *Nightline* points out the fact that the games graphic violence has attracted both detractors and loyal consumers, that the U.S. congress has denounced the game, and that *GTA3* has been outlawed in Australia, with other countries considering bans. The program also highlights the debate about whether or not *GTA3*'s high-tech make-believe and ferocity might be considered cathartic, whereas others ask if *GTA3* and others of its ilk should be called games at all.[22]

Obviously this timely show has a general relevance for this essay because it concerns video games and social values. However, certain aspects are especially pertinent as these issues intersect with race matters. First of all, *Nightline*'s in-studio panel of four, including host Ted Koppel, consists only of white males. And despite the show's packaged introductory piece featuring African American reporter Michele Norris, the all-white male panel assembled to discuss the issue displays the still unbearable whiteness of being in mainstream media's future vision and current conceptualizations of new media technologies and gaming cultures' increasing cultural power and much-lamented societal influences. Secondly, I was struck by the fact that the only representations of "minority" (particularly black) characters in *Nightline*'s select video clips of *GTA3* were victims of the game's narrative violence meted out quite gratuitously by the game's white male protagonist. At this point it is important to state that *Nightline*'s all- white and all-male panel is not the biggest problem here. The biggest problem is that *Nightline* anchor Ted Koppel and his fellow white male guests, D.C. police officer Sergeant Gerald Neill, seventeen-year-old *GTA3* player Steve Crenshaw, and Cornel University instructor James Garbarino, find a way to evoke black criminality despite the obvious absence of blacks as gamers or participant agents in this story. Moreover, this panel constructs a narrative of normative suburban whiteness capable of neutralizing and policing video games' violent influences that, noticeably, hinges on conflating real life street-level violence in urban areas with the game's virtual urban violence.

Now, what angered me about this hyperbolic discussion of video game violence and the show in general was the fact that the show began with exculpatory rhetoric surrounding a white, seemingly middle- to upper-class female parent who purchased *GTA3* for her underaged, thirteen-year-old son and two of his same-aged white friends to enjoy and master, despite the game's clearly labeled warning of unsuitability for children. *Nightline* continued in this vein by using seventeen-year-old Steve Crenshaw as a privileged *GTA3* native informant who could serve double duty. First, he signified an older, more age appropriate and mature white teenaged boy fan of *GTA3* (obviously one experienced with earlier iterations of the *Grand Theft Auto* game). And second, Crenshaw's apparent normalcy and reiteration of the thirteen-year-old's statement that gamers understood the difference between real life and video game fantasy functioned to absolve the thirteen-year-old *GTA3* player, his irresponsible mother, and his two friends of blame. And, as I have been arguing throughout this essay, a significant transposition is effected around race, but in this instance *Nightline*'s Koppel, the police officer, and the elite university instructor effectively displace *GTA3*'s social menace onto urban— read black—communities. Even though *Nightline*'s television viewers are shown powerful images of *GTA3*'s white male protagonist's unprovoked shootings of police officers and prostitutes (with graphic displays of blood spurting from their wounded digital bodies), and his hit and run vehicular massacres of black and other characters for extra game points, still Koppel, Sergeant Neill, and instructor Garbarino unproblematically inculpate blackness, or more accurately urban people, as the problem.

The consensus of the panelists is that *GTA3*'s narrative fantasy becomes a dangerous step toward reality for those who desire to act out the game's violent scenarios. *Nightline*'s experts do concede that most kids won't go out and kill. However, when Koppel, asks Sergeant Neill to use his twenty-plus years of police experience to ascertain where *GTA3* might rank in comparison to "poverty, drugs, gang warfare, as a societal threat, he betrays a racist assumption about which groups are susceptible to gaming's putative corruptions, especially with such racially charged signifiers of urban decay and blight. Sergeant Neill's response is equally telling. He states: "This is a game. But it is a violent game. There is a thing called *urban terror*. There are some parts that are controlled by *armed youths who are urban terrorists*, and this game isn't a part of that for the average person. But for someone who lives in *that* neighbourhood, *his reality is different from Steve's*"[23] [emphasis added]. Again, the implicit racial opposition being constructed here cannot be denied. For young Steve Crenshaw not only functions in this rhetoric as the responsible, white face of *GTA3* fandom, but the sergeant is clearly positioning him as an average person in opposition to youthful urban terrorists that most *Nightline* viewers would presume to be poor black and other minority youths. Once again, the hegemony of white supremacy is interpolated here and it only undermines sober and fair discussion about gaming culture and its uses and abuses.

Returning briefly to the Afrofuturism list's engagement with the racist videogame *Ethnic Cleansing*, a few points should be made. Significantly, responses to the game were varied, cogent, passionate, thoughtful, and quite provocative. The discussion thread ranged from ideas about the creation of black owned and operated video game businesses, including establishing of manufacturing factories in Africa;[24] the development of black games and game consoles with the goal of replicating a movement much like "what the black comic book industry did in the early 90's."[25] Still others saw the issue in much broader global terms, and within a post-September 11 ideological context. For example, regarding historical racism in gaming, g-tech writes:

> In fact, if you really want to be technical about it games like this have existed for, oh . . .maybe fifteen years or so since the first iteration of DOOM to be exact. Nothing new here. What has changed is the ability of propaganda pieces like this to garner attention, thus giving them a bit of legitimacy and free press . . . . In essence, we are doing the work for them . . . . The gaming community isn't dumb, they aren't mindless drones who are being brainwashed or hypnotized. They are people like you, me, the guy across the street, etc. who are probably getting a bigger kick out of the competition of winning rather than the look of the toons (toons are the characters for you non-gamers). In fact, the subject of cheating is much more of a problem than racism.[26]

For g-tech it is important not to buy into the alarmist hype surrounding *Ethnic Cleansing*, especially when the game is decontextualized and removed from larger geopolitical factors. G-tech continues:

> In fact the most popular shooters are the patriotic ones. Take a look at the sales of *Soldier of Fortune, Rainbow Six, Counterstrike, Operation Flashpoint, Delta Force Land Warrior, Return to Castle Wolfenstein, Medal of Honor* and others if you want to see some really scary stuff. Teaching kids that it's OK for America to send covert operatives into foreign countries and assassinating or killing [leaders of] other cultures and getting points or rewards for it is probably the biggest problem we may face in the future. On their own the games are harmless, but coupled with a real war where you can mimic the actions of the real soldiers in a virtual environment, a President who supports these shadow wars and a patriotic state of mind in the country and you have a recipe for trouble. I can't begin to count how many "Get Bin Laden" scenarios are popping up all over the net.[27]

Although I selected this particular post to highlight, some Afrofuturists participating in the *Ethnic Cleansing* discussion thread were not convinced by the arguments presented here, and presented convincing counter-arguments that I cannot elaborate in this space. However, one is particularly pertinent and makes a great concluding point because it addresses several issues at the heart of this essay. One of Mr. B's numerous responses to g-tech's commentary that is pertinent for us is his respectful yet counter response to g-tech's remark that "on their own the games are harmless". Mr. B. replies: "I would never consider anything that structures the way people spend their time among a wide variety of options 'harmless'. They [games] might not be causal or deterministic, they are definitely not neutral, and as a result, not harmless in my opinion . . . . Let's keep this discussion going.

I don't think we're at odds here, but we do need to refine exactly what we are talking about."[28]

We have been talking about the need to pay attention to how video and computer games, like other forms of popular entertainment, might be considered in relation to issues of identity politics, reproduction of racist ideologies and hegemonies despite gaming's novel expressive hardware apparatuses. At issue here has been the concern over the politics of representation regarding race, and the question about gaming culture's ability to replicate or challenge existing portrayals of specific groups in films, TV shows, and print media. We are talking about the ascendancy of a very powerful and technically evolving medium, and we want be sure that race does not remain the structured absence or specious virtual presence in our concern about where the future of gaming is headed.

## Acknowledgement

This article is excerpted from Anna Everett's book manuscript, *Digital Diaspora: A Race for Cyberspace* (in progress).

## Notes

1  Richard Pierre Davis is a UK-based community activist and technology worker who teaches information technology to disadvantaged groups around the globe. (Interview by author, tape recording, London, England, July 9, 2001.)
2  For almost everything you ever wanted to know about the *Super Mario Brothers* games, go to the online *Super Mario Brothers* Headquarters at http://www.smbhq.com\who.htm.
3  I follow Marsha Kinder's usage of this term in her important book *Playing with Power in Movies, Television and Video Games*, p. 3.
4  Henry Jenkins treats the subject of immersive play and interactivity in computer games more thoroughly in "'Complete Freedom of Movement': Video Games as Gendered Play Spaces," in *From Barbie to Mortal Kombat: Gender and Computer Games*.
5  Hayden White has been very influential in advancing the critical project of writing revisionist historiographies. See his essay "The Burden of History," in *Tropics of Discourse: Essays in Cultural Criticism*.
6  See for example, Carey Goldberg's article "Children and Violent Video Games: A Warning," *New York Times*, December 15, 1998, A14, which begins "It's almost Christmas. Do you know what your children are playing? Might they perhaps be ripping out the spines of their enemies, perpetrating massacres of marching bands and splatting their screens with sprays and spurts of pixelated blood?"; see also, John M. Glionna, "Computer Culture Breeds Ambivalence," *Los Angeles Times* November 19, 2000, A30; a Routers wire story on video game violence picked up by the *Philadelphia Enquirer* newspaper. The story was entitled "Study Questions Video-Game Ratings," *Philadelphia Enquirer* August 1, 2001, A3; and for a less- condemnatory perspective see, Steve Lohr's "The Virtues of Addictive Games: Computer Pastimes No Longer Viewed as Brain Poison, "*New York Times*, December 22, 1997, C1+; Austin Bunn's article "Video Games Are Good for You: Blood, Guts, and Leadership Skills?" *Village Voice*, September 21, 1999, 31; and Ted C. Fishman's "The Play's the Thing: The Video-Game Industry, Already a Juggernaut, Plans to Swallow Even More of Children's Time. So Who's Complaining," *New York Times* Magazine, June 10, 2001, 27.

7  For important scholarly discussions of gender bias in video gaming that address the subject of girl's problematic positionings within gaming culture, see Marsha Kinder, *Playing With Power in Movies, Television, and Video Games*, Yasmin B. Kafai, "Video Game Designs by Girls and Boys: Variability and Consistency of Gender Differences," *Kid's Media Culture*, ed. Marsha Kinder (Durham: Duke University Press; 1999), and in the same anthology, Heather Gilmour, "What Girls Want: The Intersections of Leisure and Power in Female Computer Gameplay."

8  See the March 2000 cover of *Incite* magazine's "Video Gaming." *Incite* also published a "PC Gaming" magazine version.

9  *Prima's Official Strategy Guide* made this boast on the cover of its special 2000 *Tekken Tag Tournament* issue.

10  "Money Makes the Games Go Round," *Next Generation*, October 1996, 59–63.

11  I borrow this phrasing from Abdul R. JanMohamed, "The Economy of the Manichean Allegory," p. 18.

12  See a game description and several reviews of *Civilization* at the website called FunagainGames, at www.funagain.com.

13  I conducted this interview on gaming culture with former lawyer, now Ph.D. candidate, Hall on May 5, 2002, in Santa Barbara, California.

14  Hall interview.

15  Hall interview.

16  The game *Ethnic Cleansing* could be found during the first months of 2002 at http://www.resistance.com/ethniccleansing/catalog.htm.

17  The NPD Group, who conducted the study, noted that video game accessories also posted record-breaking sales. The top selling PC games were *The Sims* by Electronic Arts. See the full online report, "NPD Reports Annual 2001 U.S. Interactive Entertainment Sales Shatter Industry Record," 7 February 2002, http://www.npd.com/corp/content/news/releases/press_020207. htm.

18  These quotes are excerpted from H. Allen, *"Ethnic Cleansing*: The Game!" AfroFuturism, February 20, 2002, and L. Johnson, "Racist video games target youth," February 25, 2002, both at http://afrofuturism.net.

19  L. Johnson, "Racist video games target youth," February 25, 2002.

20  Ibid.

21  Michele Norris and Ted Koppel, "Just a Game," ABC's *Nightline*, June 10, 2002. This show explores the popularity of the first-person sim game *Grand Theft Auto 3*.

22  "Just a Game," *Nightline, June* 10, 2002.

23  Sergeant Gerald Neill, comments made on *Nightline*, June 10, 2002.

24  Mr. B, "Re: —Racist video games target youth—," Internet, Afrofuturism list, February 26, 2002.

25  C_splash, "Re: —Racist video games target youth—," Internet, Afrofuturism list, February 26, 2002.

26  G-tech, "Re: —Racist video games target youth—," Internet, Afrofuturism list, February 26, 2002.

27  Ibid.

28  Mr. B. "Re: —Racist video games target youth—," Internet, Afrofuturism list, February 26, 2002.

# References

Baraka, A. (1971). Technology & ethos: Vol. 2, book of life. *Raise race rays raze: Essays since 1965*. New York: Random House.

Barthes, R. (1974). *S/Z: An Essay*, translated by Richard Miller. New York: Hill and Wang.

Bey, H. (1991). *The temporary autonomous zone: Ontological anarchy, poetic terrorism.* Brooklyn: Autonomedia.

Bolter, J. D., & Grusin, R. (2001). *Remediation: Understanding new media.* Cambridge, MA: MIT Press.

Brooks, P. (1984). *Reading for the plot.* Cambridge, MA: Harvard University Press.

Butler, J. (1999). *Gender trouble: Feminism and the subversion of identity.* New York: Routledge.

C_splash. (2002). Re: —Racist video games target youth—. Internet, Afrofuturism list, February 26.

Chansanchai, A. (1997). Yellow Perils: Online "Coolies" Rile Asian Americans. *Village Voice.* 7 October, p. 25.

Dery, M. (Ed.). (1995). "Black to the future: Interviews with Samuel A. Delany, Greg Tate, and Tricia Rose." In *Flame Wars* (pp. 179–222). Durham: Duke University Press.

Diawara, M. (1993). "Black spectatorship: Problems of identification and resistance." In M. Diawara, *Black American cinema.* New York: Routledge, pp. 211–220.

Eagleton, T. (1983). *Literary theory: An introduction.* Minneapolis: University of Minnesota Press.

Everett, A. (2001). *Returning the gaze: A genealogy of black film criticism, 1909–1949.* Durham: Duke University Press.

G-tech. (2002). Re: —Racist video games target youth—. Internet, Afrofuturism list, February 26.

Gilmour, H. (1999). What girls want: The intersections of leisure and power in female computer gameplay. In Ed. M. Kinder, *Kid s media culture.* Durham: Duke University Press.

Goldberg, C. (1998). Children and violent video games: A warning. In *New York Times* December 15, A14.

Hall, S. (1986). Encoding/decoding. In *Culture, media language, working papers in cultural studies, 1972–1979.* London: Hutchinson & Co., p. 128–138.

Hamamoto, D. Y. (1994). *Monitored peril: Asian Americans and the politics of TV representation.* Minneapolis: University of Minnesota Press.

Herz, J. C. (1997). *Joystick nation: How videogames ate our quarters, won our hearts, and rewired our minds.* Boston: Little, Brown and Company.

*Imperialism: The fine art of conquering the world: A user manual.* (1997). Sunnyvale, California: Strategic Simulations.

JanMohamed, A. R. (1995). The economy of the Manichean allegory. In B. Ashcroft, G. Griffiths, & H. Tiffin (Eds.), *The post-colonial studies reader.* New York: Routledge, pp. 18–23.

Jenkins, H. (1999). Complete freedom of movement: Video games as gendered play spaces. In J. Cassell & H. Jenkins (Eds.), *From Barbie to Mortal Kombat: Gender and computer games* (pp. 262–297). Cambridge, MA: MIT Press.

Kafai, Y. B. (1999). Video game designs by girls and boys: Variability and consistency of gender differences. In Ed. M. Kinder, *Kid s media culture.* Durham: Duke University Press.

Kinder, M. (1991). *Playing with power in movies, television and video games.* Berkeley: University of California Press.

Kolmos, K. (2000). *Prima's official strategy guide: Ready 2 rumble boxing, round 2.* Roseville, CA: Prima Communications; Inc.

Lyotard, J. F. (1991). *The inhuman: Reflections on time.* Stanford: Stanford University Press.

Marriott, M. (1999). Blood, gore, sex and now: Race: Are game makers creating convincing new characters or "high-tech blackface"? *New York Times* October 21, D7.

Mr. B. (2002). Re: —Racist video games target youth—. Internet, Afrofuturism list, February 26.

Narayan, U., & Harding, S. (2000). *Decentering the center: Philosophy for a multicultural, postcolonial, and feminist world.* Bloomington: Indiana University Press.

Nielsen, A. L. (1988). *Reading race: White American poets and the racial discourse in the twentieth century.* Athens: University of Georgia Press.

Taylor, L. Not a War Game? Funagain Games. http:// www.kumquat.com/cig-kumquat/ funagain/04253.

White, H. (1978). *Tropics of discourse: Essays in cultural criticism.* Baltimore: Johns Hopkins University Press.

Walton, L. A. (1909). The degeneracy of the moving picture. *New York Age*, August 5, p. 6.

## 52

# THE POWER OF PLAY

## The portrayal and performance of race in video games

*Anna Everett and S. Craig Watkins*

Source: Katie Salen (ed.), *The Ecology of Games: Connecting Youth, Games, and Learning* (Cambridge, MA: The MIT Press, 2008), pp. 141–164.

### Introduction: young people, games, and learning

The growing presence of games in the lives of young people creates perils and possibilities. Games have been a constant source of criticism and alarm among parents, researchers, child advocacy groups, and elected officials. The potential harmful effects of gaming have been linked to society's understandable concerns about the increasingly sedentary lifestyles of youth and childhood obesity, addiction, gender socialization, poor academic performance, and aggressive behavior.[1] An area of growing concern is the role of games in the learning experiences and environments of youth.[2]

While there is growing consensus that learning takes place in games, the question we ask is: "What kinds of learning?" in this chapter we shift the focus on youth, learning, and video games generally to consider the extremely significant but often overlooked matter of race. Specifically, we address the following question: In what ways do young people's interactions with video games influence how and what they learn about race? We present a critical framework for thinking about how popular game titles and the professionals who design them reflect, influence, reproduce, and thereby teach dominant ideas about race in America. Engaging with an assortment of media—books, animation, television, home video, video games, and the Internet—children as young as three years old develop schemas and scripts for negotiating perceived racial differences.[3] Research suggests that by the time children are five years old they have already started to develop strong ideas about race and difference. Historically, the popular media examined in this context have been television.[4]

In their discussion of the role television plays in the multicultural awareness and racial attitudes of children and adolescents, Gordon L. Berry and Joy Keiko Asamen write that "fact or fiction, real or unreal, television programs create cognitive and affective environments that describe and portray people, places, and things that carry profound general and specific cross-cultural learning experiences" for young people growing up in a media-saturated culture.[5] As digital media forms like video games compete with television for the time and attention of young media users, researchers must examine rigorously how the shift to digital and more interactive forms of media influences how and what young people learn about race.

We, therefore, direct these questions and issues toward video games to increase our understanding of the rapidly evolving ways in which young people are exposed to and learn racial narratives, representations, and belief systems. Parents and critics readily discuss the potential negative social outcomes associated with exposing young people to violent or sexual content in video games. But, as Anna Everett has asked elsewhere, "'When and where does the racial problematic enter in contemporary culture's moral panics about gaming's potential dangers?' Society's moral outrage over video game culture's gender troubles (to borrow Judith Butler's fecund phrase), especially its sexist and misogynistic constructs of women and girls, has not found a parallel in terms of race." This leads us to ask, "What are the consequences of exposing youth to content that renders racist representations, beliefs, and attitudes playable and pleasurable?"[6]

The chapter sets out to demarcate some of the specific ways in which race resonates throughout the culture and industry of video games. We begin by examining the design of one of the most heavily marketed categories in the video games marketplace, what we call "urban/street" games. Specifically, we consider how these games, and the richly detailed and textured urban landscapes they present, establish powerful learning environments that help situate how young gamers understand, perform, and reproduce race and ethnicity. Next, we focus on the aesthetic and narrative properties of one of the most controversial yet successful video games franchises in America, *Grand Theft Anto* (*GTA*). More precisely, we consider how *GTA* teaches dominant attitudes and assumptions about race and racial otherness through what we term "racialized pedagogical zones" (RPZs). In other words, these games draw heavily from racist discourses already circulating in popular and mainstream culture and arguably intensify these messages and lessons of racial difference through the power and allure of interactive gameplay. Essentially, we argue that by striving to locate players in what are often promoted as graphically real and culturally "authentic" environments, urban/street games produce some of the most powerful, persistent, and problematic lessons about race in American culture.

In the final section of the chapter, we shift from discussing race as representation, simulation, and pedagogy to considering race as an important dimension in the ongoing but steadily evolving public conversation regarding the digital divide. Here, we advocate expanding the discussion of race and video games to include concerns about access to and participation in digital media culture, communities, and user-generated content.

133

## Learning race

Recent theories on digital games and learning argue that games represent a dynamic learning environment.[7] Marc Prensky has argued that games encourage learning and challenge the established conventions in more formal spaces of learning, such as in schools. He notes, for instance, that games demand parallel versus linear processing. Additionally, Prensky maintains that games promote problem solving in the form of play versus work.

Similarly, James Paul Gee believes that games offer good learning principles. For Gee the genius of games is their ability to balance the delivery of overt information and guidance (think of the manual that offers instructions for a game) with "immersion in actual context of practice" (think of the process of trial and error that is involved in mastering a game Games, unlike conventional schooling, effectively combine "telling and doing." Good videogames, Gee notes, require gamers to "learn from the bottom up" and master the technical and logical aspects of games.[8] This, he argues, is accomplished via experimentation, exploration, and engagement. What games ultimately accomplish, according to both Prensky and Gee, is the creation of environments in which active (doing) rather than passive (telling) learning takes place. It is this aspect of video gaming—the act of doing—and its implication for both learning and performing race that we address here.

Still, while advocates of video games as learning spaces argue that they provide a new means to engage young people by producing rich educational experiences, we would like to caution that not all forms of learning that take place in the immersive world of video and computer games are socially productive. Thus, we ask a slightly different set of questions regarding video games as learning tools, namely, "Can video games facilitate learning that is anti-social?" Put another way, "Do the entertainment and interactive aspects of video gaming reproduce common-sense ideas about race and gender?" Ideas, that is, which can enliven long-standing and problematic notions of racial difference and deviance.

## Portraying race

At least some of the absence of discussions of race in public and policy dialogues about video games can be attributed to the fact that the use of racially marked characters, themes, and environments, historically speaking, is a relatively recent development in video games. That is not to say that video games, even during the earliest periods of development, were necessarily race neutral but rather that efforts to build explicitly raced characters and worlds were limited by the styles of games being produced, screen resolution (4-, 8-, and 16-bit), and processing speeds. Indeed, as Steven Poole maintains, the early attempt to design characters for video games was limited by technology.[9] "In the early days of video games," Poole writes, "technological considerations more or less forced designers into exactly the same style."[10] That style typically led to one-dimensional blocky characters such as *PacMan* that lacked few, if any, truly distinguishing features or marks.

The first, and most famous, humanoid character in a video game was the moustached hero, Mario. Poole notes that because of the low resolution offered at the time, character designers had a limited number of pixels to play with. That period, described by Japanese game designer Shigeru Miyamoto as the days of "immature technology," imposed certain technological constraints on both game design and representation.[11] But as the rendering power of video game engines evolved, artists and designers benefited from the ability to produce characters who were more lifelike in appearance and motion. Whereas the ethnically marked features of Mario, the Italian plumber, were limited primarily to relatively innocuous phrases like, "it's-a me, Mario" or, later, his love of pasta and pizza, games like *GTA: Vice City*, and *Godfather: The Game* benefit from enhanced technology and software that portrays the markers of race and ethnicity—skin color, gestures, voice, music, and setting—in a much more explicit and powerful manner.

Though technological changes have opened the way for upgraded representational depictions, and a more diverse range of themes and characters, the portrayal of race in video games remains remarkably narrow. In an examination of racial diversity in the top-selling console and computer games, an important study by the Children Now organization concluded that black and Latino characters were often restricted to athletic, violent, and victim roles, or rendered entirely invisible.[12] Since that report, the state of race in games has, paradoxically, changed and stayed the same due, in part, to the rise of "urban/street" games. The arrival of this generic category has led to a discernible growth in the number of black and Latino-based characters and themes in some of the most heavily marketed games. But urban/street games also reproduce many of the representational problems identified by Children Now.

Games within the urban/street category cut across a variety of genres: for example, third- person action/shooter games like hip-hop star *50 Cent's Bulletproof*, action/adventure titles like *Saints Row*, sports games like *NFL Street* 3 and *NBA Ballers: Phenom*, fighter games like *Def Jam: The Fight for NY*, and racing games like *Midnight Club 3: Dub Edition Remix*. Despite the range of genres represented, the games tend to share similar types of characters, narratives, environments, and gameplay elements. For instance, earning street credibility or respect is a recurrent theme across these games as is the emphasis on building and playing hyper-masculine characters who use street slang and aggressive behavior to navigate the urban world boldly and effectively. More importantly, they demonstrate the degree to which game developers are moving toward recreating culturally specific and racialized environments that are packaged and marketed as authentic expressions of the social world. Significantly, these games, and particularly their questionable claims of authenticity, establish compelling learning environments that help facilitate how young gamers develop their knowledge of and familiarity with popular views of race and urban culture.

## Can you feel it? Simulating blackness

The successful development and marketing of urban/street games is based on the idea that these titles represent culturally authentic spaces. Claims of authenticity in the sphere of cultural production are, of course, always fraught with tensions. As we explain in great detail below, the aspects of urban/street gaming that are often presented as authentic—the characters, environments, music, and language, just to name a few—are, in reality, deliberately selected symbolic materials that draw much of their appeal and believability from representations of urban life in other popular media cultures.

Like the gaming landscape in general, the evolution of urban/street games is shaped by an increasing emphasis on photorealistic environmental designs, recognizable stories/plots, compelling character ensembles, and dramatic action sequences that work to achieve greater verisimilitude in overall gameplay design and presentation. Geoff King and Tanya Krzywinska maintain that "the history of video games is one that has been dominated, on one level, by investments in increasing realism, at the level of graphical representation and allied effects."[13]

But the commitment to designing games that are more realistic points to the need not only to capture more honest character portrayals, human motion, and environments, but also and perhaps more importantly, to capture the cultural sensibilities of a particular racial or ethnic group's world experience. This aspect of a video game's design is a constant selling point in the marketing positions staked out by some of the video game industry's most prominent players. For instance, in its promise to offer sports game enthusiasts a powerful and engaging gameplay experience, Electronic Arts' (EA) tagline asks, "Can You Feel It?" Likewise, Microsoft's Xbox 360 invites gamers to "jump in" to their online gaming world. And Sony PlayStation encourages gamers to "live in your world, play in ours." in games studies, the idea of creating a world that feels real is referred to as "presence" or a "sense of being there."[14] This represents the degree to which developers strive to create gaming environments that deepen the sense of engagement in the game world through simulation, leading to what some argue is a richer sensory experience.

Part of achieving a believable simulation includes maintaining fidelity to what we already know or expect from a specific world and those who are likely to people it. Consequently, the design of gaming environments that look, sound, and feel real is critical in order to achieve high degrees of "perceptual" and "social" realism. The former refers to how closely the characters, environments, objects, and other in-game elements match popular perceptions of urban street life and culture. The latter refers to the extent to which the events and activities in a video game resonate with those in the real world. The quest by the designers of urban/street games to immerse gamers in culturally specific or authentic spaces also offers insight into the ways in which these games become powerful learning environments that construct informal yet effective spaces for teaching, or in many instances, reproducing particular ideas about race, ethnicity, and difference. More significantly, if video games portraying urban life and culture are perceived as authentic, then they become effective and, in many cases, uncontested devices for transmitting certain kinds of ideas about race, geography, and culture. For example, Children Now asks game developers to "think about the messages they deliver to youth when characters of color often are found at the business end of a fist, club, or gun or competing in a sports arena." [15]

What makes urban/street games feel "authentic?" More precisely, what is it about these titles that enables gamers to experience presence, a sense of urban culture? First, many of the titles in this category feature a rarity in entertainment games: visually recognizable black lead characters. Children Now's analysis of the ten top-selling games for each of the six video game consoles available in the United States found that the characters populating the virtual world of video games at the time were predominantly white. [16] White males, for example, represented 52 percent of the male player-controlled characters compared to 37 percent for black males and 5 percent and 3 percent, respectively, for Latinos and Asians. According to the report, when black and Latino characters did appear in video games, it was often as supporting rather than lead characters and oftentimes in stereotypical roles (i.e., athletes, urban outlaws, violent offenders, etc.). Unlike the bulk of commercial video games, black and Latino characters appear throughout urban/ street games both as primary and secondary characters, thus establishing the genre as a gaming space distinct in its representational focus.

In his discussion of *True Crime: Streets of LA*, Chan notes that while the game offers a first in a North American designed game—a Chinese antagonist—the game's digital cast of characters and setting reinscribe popular notions of racial otherness and exotica. [17] In addition to the representation of racially marked spaces like Chinatown, Chan notes that the game's Asian American central character and the use of neo-Orientalist motifs demonstrate "how racial difference may be simultaneously fetishized and demonized, and how hegemonic whiteness is positioned as the taken for granted racial norm in game-world environments." [18]

In addition to the hypervisibility of black and Latino characters, the environments in urban/street games are marked as racially specific story-worlds. Above, we suggested that the first humanoid character, Mario, did not bear many explicitly recognizable racial markers besides white skin. This also holds true for the game environment in the first game in which Mario appeared, *Donkey Kong*. Gameplay typically took place in brightly lit fun spaces, or an occasional dimly lit place that signified heightened danger. Rarely, however, did these game environments evoke racial and/or culturally specific spaces like an urban ghetto *Saint's Row* or an elite boarding school as in *Bully*. As designers strive for greater cultural authenticity, the spatial environment itself, where the characters live, play, fight, and compete, also becomes a culturally specific location that animates ideas about race, class, and gender.

The elaborately textured environments in urban/street games feature a wide range of objects associated with socially and economically marginalized communities. *NBA Street Volume 2*, for example, uses digitized photos from many urban playgrounds around the country, including Harlem's legendary Rucker Park and Oakland's Mosswood. In Mark Ecko's *Getting Up: Contents Under Pressure*, several of the game's key action sequences take place in dark underground subways where graffiti artists once "tagged" their way to local fame. Other objects typically appearing in these video games include graffiti-covered buildings, dilapidated housing, trash-filled streets, candy-painted low riders (customized cars), and background characters engaged in petty crimes, drug deals, and prostitution. The selection of these objects works ideologically to invigorate dominant ideas that construct poor urban communities as deviant, different, and dangerous.

EA hired urban street artist Bua as a consultant and artist for *NFL Street*. His work, along with the work of other hand-selected street artists, was incorporated not only to give the game an "urban feel," but also to provide credibility among young gamers as an authentic engagement with urban culture. The environments in urban/street games are not only racially coded as black and brown spaces, they are also built to simulate dangerous and exotic spaces. Many of these video games take players into the center of illegal street activities, drug-infested neighbourhoods, street gangs, and rampant gun violence. In instances like these, game design labors to simulate an authentic environment in order to deliver a more compelling gaming experience.

Along with immersing players in a world that *looks* urban, designers of urban/street games also strive to immerse players in a world that *sounds* urban. In many urban/street action and shooter games, police and emergency vehicle sirens, rounds of gunfire, and screeching tires from drive-by shootings, and other ambient noises, establish—via sound design—a place and mood. As the games have grown more cinematic in tone and style, developers have also employed carefully selected voice actors. The makers of *Saint's Row* worked with street gang members to help script dialogue and gang-related slang. Hip-hop-based sound tracks are pervasive, and it has become common practice among developers to hire hip-hop producers and performers to select music that evokes the ethos and energy of urban ghetto life. In many ways, the rise of urban/street games illustrates how hip-hop has influenced young people's media and cultural environment by projecting meticulously packaged images of "urban realism" into a media mix that includes video games, film, music, and other sources of entertainment.

The design of urban/games is a vital aspect of how learning takes place. But equally important are the repertoires of cultural knowledge that players bring to their gaming experiences. In other words, whatever forms of learning that take place in video games happens not only because of meticulous game design elements, but also because of the social schemas, scripts, and beliefs players develop from the larger cultural and ideological environment.

## Learning to reproduce race

Learning in urban/street games is based on multiple competencies—technical and cultural. In his argument explaining what games can teach us about learning, Gee emphasizes the technical aspects of the learning process in games. The technical aspects involve learning how to navigate and, eventually, master the challenges and obstacles that structure the gameplay experience. Indeed, the open mode design of many urban/street games demands that players progressively build their technical mastery by "adapting and transferring earlier experiences to solve new problems."[19] But mastery of urban/street games also requires a great degree of cultural competency and knowledge. In this case, we are referring to the familiarity with certain racial themes, logics, and commonsense ideologies that make urban/street gaming a resonant, entertaining, and, ultimately, powerful learning experience. Part of the payoff in urban/street gaming, that sense of accomplishment and immediate reward gaming provides, is understanding, though not necessarily subscribing to, the racial cues, assumptions, and sensibilities embedded in these games. For instance, if urban/street-gamers are already predisposed to believe that "authentic" poor urban neighborhoods are violent and drug-infested, then these games go a long way in confirming those views.

The selling and marketing of urban culture is premised on notions of difference that, ultimately, reproduce rather than contest racial hierarchies. Discussing this very fact, S. Craig Watkins writes that "certain types of representations of blackness are more likely to be merchandised, not because they are necessarily real but rather because they fit neatly with the prevailing commonsense characterizations of black life."[20] Thus, hip-hop-oriented video games, like other hip-hop-oriented media, establish the ideas, values, and behavioral scripts that facilitate how young media users make sense of blackness.

Urban/street games rely on subject matter and gameplay elements that construct authentic urban culture as ultraviolent, hypersexual, exotic, and a repository of dangerous and illegal activity. The content descriptors for urban/street games support this representation. *Def-Jam: Fight for NY* and *True Crime: New York City* carry descriptors like "blood and gore," "realistic violence," and "suggestive themes." *Def Jam Vendetta*, a game rated T for teenagers, contains "strong language," "strong lyrics," and "suggestive themes." Mature (M) rated titles, *GTA: San Andreas* and *Saint's Row*, add descriptors like "strong sexual content" and "use of drugs and alcohol." These descriptors not only describe games; they also illuminate the narrative and thematic conditions under which black and brown bodies, cultures, spaces, and styles are simulated and rendered visible in the world of video games.

These narrative and thematic conditions are visible in sports-themed video games that also simulate black urban bodies, culture, spaces, and styles. Titles like *NFL Street 3* and *NBA Ballers Phenom* bring urban/street gaming to the sports category in video games. According to the Entertainment Software Association (ESA), sports titles (17 percent) were second only to action games (30 percent) in terms of market share in 2005. Overall, seven of the twenty top-selling games belonged in the sports genre. In 2000, a new generation of sports games entered this highly competitive niche with EA release of *NBA Street*. The publishing giant marketed *NBA Street* as an extreme sports game complete with state-of-the-art graphics, over-the-top character animation, and street-tough attitude. Shortly after developing *NBA Street*, EA released *NFL Street*, a football video game that looked to create characters, sounds, and environments that simulated an urban culture that was familiar to young media audiences.

Unlike previous sports titles, however, this new generation of video games had little interest in simulating the strategic and tactical aspects of basketball and football. Rather, like many of the urban/street games discussed previously, the cultural and lifestyle aspects of the modern sports world came to the fore. *NBA Ballers*, for example, represents a digital articulation of the classic "hoop dream" phenomenon that teaches many poor and working-class black boys that athletic celebrity, despite impossible odds, is an attainable goal.[21] One of the primary incentives for mastering the different challenges and sequences in *NBA Ballers* is to acquire status conferring symbols that include, among other things, palatial homes, luxurious cars, expensive jewelry, designer clothing, and, most problematically, women. The pursuit of these goals establishes a seductive learning environment, one that enlivens hegemonic notions of black masculinity and urban social mobility. For many young black males the power and pervasiveness of these representations can often skew their values and thus profoundly influence the lifestyle choices and behaviours that impact their life chances.

In addition to privileging hegemonic ideas about race, urban/street games privilege hegemonic ideas about gender. In their analysis of the top-sixty selling console and computer games, Children Now's gender results are instructive. Not surprisingly, they found that video games are an overwhelmingly male-dominated universe. Of the 1,716 characters identified in the study, 64 percent were male, 19 percent nonhuman, and 17 percent female. The racial dimensions of the gender patterns are equally revealing. More than two-thirds of the female player-controlled characters, 78 percent, were white. African Americans made up 10 percent of the female player-controlled characters, whereas Asian and Native American women constituted 7 percent and 1 percent, respectively. Not one of the 874 player-controlled characters in the study was identified as Latina. The characterization of women in urban/street games is also consistent with another Children Now's finding. "African American females," Children Now reports "were far more likely than any other group to be victims of violence."[22] Many titles from the urban/street category resist some of the notable changes that have labored to make the video games industry more receptive to women.

Whereas the industry, historically, has relegated women to the periphery, there has been a movement to make games much more gender-inclusive.[23] But whereas recent game protagonists like Lara Croft and Jade (*Beyond Good and Evil*) break away from some of the strict gender norms of games, the heavily marketed urban/street games in which black women and Latinas are likely to appear are much more restrictive.

In games like *GTA: San Andreas*, *Def Jam Vendetta*, and *Saint's Row*, women remain marginal and generally figure as props, bystanders, eye candy, and prizes to be won by the male protagonists. Like other background visual elements—street signs, graffiti art, cars, buildings—women are presented as accessories and used to enhance the presentation of the environment, not the core action. The fact that black women and Latinas are also portrayed quite casually as sexually available bystanders in fighter games like *Def Jam Vendetta* and as street-walking prostitutes in action/adventure/shooter games like *GTA: Vice City* reinforces lessons about race and sexuality, especially the sexual mores, appetites, and behaviors of women marginalized by race and ethnicity.

What makes these elements in urban/street games prominent sites and sources of learning? First, urban/street games represent the first concerted effort by developers of entertainment- based video games to create characters and worlds that presumably draw from black American life. Moreover, the developers of these games hire artists, music producers and performers, voice actors, and highly skilled designers to build worlds that resonate with popular perceptions of urban culture. Ultimately, these video games bring the popular notions of blackness circulating in the cultural environment to the world of video games and interactive media. This enables young game players not only to experience powerfully rendered representations of urban culture but also to immerse themselves in environments that encourage active ways of playing with and learning about race. Urban/street gaming does more than present urban life in photorealistic ways or immerse gamers in racially designed environments. These titles also establish dynamic environments for performing race and gender.

## Digital minstrelsy: doing and learning race in the urban game world

In his assessment of urban/street games, Adam Clayton Powell III characterizes them as "high-tech blackface."[24] David J. Leonard has also explored the notion of digital minstrelsy in games.[25] The idea that games constitute a form of minstrelsy compels us to think carefully about how learning about race takes place in video games. Powell and Leonard note that the articulation of the minstrel tradition, for example, is visible in the digitally manipulated black caricatures that populate urban/street themed games—distorted body types and facial features, clothing, voice acting, and over-the-top behaviors and movements that reflect a design ethos that mobilizes certain notions of blackness for popular consumption.

As we have seen, in the action/shooter variety of urban/street gaming, blacks and Latinos are portrayed as brutally violent, casually criminal, and sexually promiscuous. Blacks are typically characterized as verbally aggressive[26] and extraordinarily muscular and athletic[27] in sports action games. Minstrelsy, from this perspective, refers to how blackness is configured as a racialized body (albeit virtual) and commodity. Our focus, however, is on gameplay and what we believe is another manifestation of minstrelsy in gaming—performance. How, we ask, do urban/street games establish a powerful learning environment for not only *portraying* but also *performing* race in the form of blackface?

Many historians of minstrelsy allude to the complex social and psychological aspects of the tradition, the fact that it embodied whites' fear of and fascination with black bodies, what Eric Lott calls racial insult and racial envy.[28] At its most basic level, historians note, minstrelsy became a means for white men to occupy and play out fantasized notions of black masculinity, but in ways that were entertaining, nonthreatening, and committed to sustaining racial hierarchies. The same dynamics, in many respects, are at play in the case of urban/street gaming.

In this context of play and entertainment, distorted notions of blackness are rendered consumable and desirable, playable and accessible for young gamers. Referring to the growing inventory of urban/street-based sports titles, Leonard writes, "the desire to 'be black' because of the stereotypical visions of strength, athleticism, power and sexual potency all play out within the virtual reality of sports games."[29] In the immersive environment of urban/street gaming, young people not only interact with photorealistic environments, they also have the opportunity to interact with and perform fantasy-driven notions of black masculinity. Hence, when we talk about young people and video games marketed as authentic depictions of urban culture, the performative and interactive aspects of video games facilitate learning race by "doing" race. Video games represent another distinct development in young people's rapidly evolving media environment: the movement of racial image production into the terrain of "new media."

While the term *new media* should be used cautiously, it is often deployed to refer to technologically mediated conditions like interactivity, convergence, genre hybridity, and nonlinearity.[30] Take, for example, the shift from portraying blackness on television (the equivalent of telling about race) to performing blackness in video games (the equivalent of doing race). Historically, critical media scholars have examined how television projects racial imagery and narratives. In one of the most productive analyses of race, representation, and television, Herman Gray carefully explores how the textual, narrative, and aesthetic properties of television facilitate how we "watch race."[31]

Video games, however, have a way of allowing players not only to watch the action, but to participate in and drive the action. Consequently, in the context of video games, players are not only watching race; they are also performing and, as a result, (re)producing socially prescribed and technologically mediated notions of race. The rise of digital media culture demands that we modify "old media" derived terms like audience and text.[32] Audience, for instance, conjures up the image of someone who is positioned primarily to receive a one-way source of narrative/information transmission passively. But in video games, *players* supplant audiences and imply a much more dynamic engagement with media. Similarly, text can suggest that narrative and representational forms are static, fixed, and redundant. The scenes in a favorite television program or classic film never change. But in video games, the process of narration and representation is dynamic, contingent, and variable. Video games respond to player choice; as a result, it is possible—and even likely—to have a different experience with a game each time you play it.

No title epitomizes urban/street gaming more spectacularly or problematically than the *GTA* franchise. Like many of the urban/street games, this franchise is populated by a host of black and Latino characters, located in culturally specific and photorealistic environments, and purports to immerse gamers in authentic black and brown urban spaces. The bold and imaginative gameplay elements in *GTA: San Andreas*, for example, greatly expanded the technical and representational parameters for urban/street gaming, as well as the means by which blackness and Latinoness are rendered playable, pleasurable, and knowable in the burgeoning world of video games.

## Understanding race and ethnicity in games' racialized pedagogical zones (RPZs)

Haitians have been protesting *GTA*, calling it racist. Funny, but I thought Haitians were a nationality, not a race. Besides, the game portrays everyone negatively regardless of race, ethnicity, and so forth. I mean, "ELLO, ITS CALLED GRAND THEFT AUTO!!!"

—Paul Gonza

Please bear in mind that I'm a huge fan . . . Sure the game portrays everyone negatively. But Haitians are the only nationality being explicitly referred to in the game . . . The statement . . . "Kill all the Haitians"—could be replaced with, say the name of that Haitian gang, in which case probably no one would have raised an eyebrow . . . There is a big difference between reading about killing members of a group or culture, or watching a movie portraying slaughter of said group, and actually doing the slaughtering in a game.

—Nickelplate

To explore the racial discourse in the *GTA* game franchise, we want to propose a consideration of what we term the games' racialized pedagogical zones. RPZs refer to the way that video games *teach* not only entrenched ideologies of race and racism, but also how gameplay's pleasure principles of mastery, winning, and skills development are often inextricably tied to and defined by familiar racial and ethnic stereotypes. In working through these ideas, Katie Salen and Eric Zimmerman's[33] influential work on the rules and subsequent meanings of gameplay is quite instructive, especially their fitting return to Johan Huizinga's[34] key metaphors of childhood play: the "playground" and the "magic circle." Following Salen and Zimmerman, we see Huizinga's powerful metaphors of childhood play and rules as productive for analyzing ways that contemporary game designers and players/users often reflect, rehearse, reenact, and reaffirm culturally familiar and highly problematic discourses of race in gaming space. It is Salen and Zimmerman's own articulation of games' "framing systems" that addresses more precisely the present discussion. On the matter of games' cultural connotations, and formal systems of play, and utilizing the game of *Chess* as one exemplar, they write:

> [T]he system of play is embedded in the cultural framing of the game . . . . For example, answering a cultural question, regarding the politics of racial representation would have to include an understanding of the formal way the core rules of the game reference color. What does it mean that white always moves first? Similarly, when you are designing a game you are not designing just a set of rules, but a set of rules that will *always* be experienced as play within a cultural context. As a result, you will *never* have the luxury of completely forgetting about context when you are focusing on experience, or on experience and culture when you're focusing on the game's formal structure . . . . it is important to remember that a game's formal, experiential, and cultural qualities *always* exist as integrated phenomena [emphasis added].[35]

The cultural framing of the *GTA* games within hegemonic or dominant structures of race and class systems is exactly what this study evaluates through a formulation of the *GTA* trilogy's RPZs. More specifically, *GTA* game designers and players understand, expect, and desire these games' formal structures to participate in our culture's "integrated phenomena" of urban crime literature, films, and TV shows, hip-hop and other musical idioms, street fashion/costuming, slang and profane speech/dialogue, and hyperviolent as well as hypersexual activities. Rather than bracketing the real world's racist logics or subverting them through the artificial construct of the game world, "[for] better or for worse, kids use video and computer games as a filter through which to understand their lives" and the role of race therein.[36]

## Mapping RPZs in *GTA* games

This interrogation of race in the production and consumption of gaming poses a challenge to our collective understanding of video games as powerful, next-generation learning tools increasingly celebrated for being easy and pleasurable lead-ins to computer literacy and advanced placement in colleges and universities.[37] This analysis is about seeing how they also can be equally pleasurable tools for teaching racism and other modes of social intolerance. In mapping some pertinent contours of RPZs in the *GTA* games, we easily recognize familiar discourses of race and racial stereotypes from print, film, TV, radio, music, and other cultural productions at play within *GTA's* video game spaces.

We have seen that the portrayal of race is embodied in many aspects of a video game's design, from its visual and audio stylings to the world space, narrative context, and play mechanics. Similarly, RPZs emerge from a range of intersecting features. In the *GTA* series, for example, RPZs are established through (a) its hyperviolent genre norms—a hybrid first-person shooter and adventure game;

(b) its aesthetics and formal structures—realism, cinematic look, and function (especially the cut scenes)—and its hip-hop music and other youth culture influences; (c) its narrative structures: open-ended and mission driven; (d) its settings: urban locales, ghetto environments; (e) its dialogue: street and ethnic slang, thug and gangster-speak; (f) its star discourses: racially and ethnically diverse celebrities from the film, TV, and music industries; and (g) its marketing iconographies online and in print.

The significance of this tentative schematic is to locate precisely where we can expect to encounter, interact with, and indeed learn the RPZs in the *GTA* trilogy's carefully crafted and "incredibly immersive" game worlds. As Marc Prensky points out, a most effective game technique for transmitting contextual information is immersion. "It seems that the more one feels one is actually 'in' a culture," he elaborates further, "the more one learns from it—especially nonconsciously . . . Kids will learn whatever messages are in the game."[38] The veracity of this observation will be supported by some gamers' postings to online game fora, excerpted below.

We should note briefly several obvious film and TV crime genre markers that contextualize and render race in the series meaningful and intelligible: for example, the 1970s and 1980s Italian mafia films—*Scarface*, *Goodfellas*, and the *Godfather* series; the 1990s black 'hood films—*Menace II Society*, *Straight Out of Brooklyn*, *New Jack City*, among others; and the 1980s-era procedural crime dramas par excellence the *Miami Vice* TV series. Each became the standard after which the *GTA* games were modeled. In terms of aesthetics, we call attention to the games' interactive functions that mimic cinema's moving camera perspectives, mise-en-scéne constructions, gangster and other underworld costumes, pervasive assault weapons, drug and alcohol paraphernalia, and voyeuristic strip club settings. All this coupled with the games' reliance on recognizable celebrities who are cast as the central character voices in the *GTA* games. Indeed, the actual voices of film and music stars Ray Liotta, Samuel Jackson, Dennis Hopper, Burt Reynolds, Phillip Michael Thomas, Deborah Harry, James Woods, Ice-T, George Clinton, Louis Guzman, and others enliven the dialogue in the games' crucial mini-filmlike scripted sections or "cut scenes" as they are more familiarly known. It is within the games' effective and affective remediation of these already meaningful cinematic and televisual conventions that we find *GTA*'s RPZs.[39]

## RPZs in *GTA: San Andreas* and *Bully*, toward a discourse analysis

It is telling that as the controversy surrounding Rockstar Games' "Hot Coffee" bonus segment (an encrypted pornographic cut scene in the *GTA: San Andreas* game) waned, the company released a sort of mea-culpa game entitled *Bully* in late October 2006. *New York Times* Columnist Seth Schiesel described the game as "a whimsical boarding-school romp."[40] Based on screen grabs from Rockstar Games' *Bully* Web site (in advance of the game's release, the game trailers, the preliminary game description, and other information provided by Schiesel, and gameplay observations prior to and shortly after the game's release), this game represents an important corollary to our consideration of RPZs in the *GTA* series.[41] As a result of *Bully*'s setting in an upscale environment denoting white privilege and nonlethal juvenile pranks, the game arguably provides certain counternarratives and iconic visuals representing racial difference and otherness unavailable in the highly controversial *GTA* games. For example, *GTA* games seem to reproduce dominant messages about the rampant dangers of black urban/street life, and *Bully* simultaneously contests and affirms social ideas about race and ethnicity through its rendering of abusive teen life in an affluent school not restricted to an urban setting. Although it is interesting that some of *Bully*'s outdoor settings suggest an urban feel, its sprinkling of black and white athlete characters, who are bullies, complicate somewhat notions of the two games' essential racial discourses.

Comparing the representational economies of race and difference in *GTA: San Andreas* and in *Bully*, it becomes clear that meaningful play in these games is predicated on Rockstar Games' appropriation of mainstream cinematic and television taxonomies of contemporary youth cultures and their specific environmental dangers. The urban 'hood versus the upscale prep school setting clearly demarcates relative zones of danger triggered by gamers racialized points of reference, real-life experiences, peer group composition, and degrees of actual interracial contact and interaction on all sides of the racial–ethnic divides. Coupled with these powerful, photorealistic digital renderings of socially constructed environmental spaces and neighborhood dangers are equally compelling representations of dangerous game characters, and racially situated narratives or gameplay missions.

While a one-to-one comparison of RPZs in *Bully* and *GTA* games is beyond the scope of this study several screen shots provide useful—if limited—points of contrast between the varied depictions of violence in black and white contexts as imaged by the company's game designers. Regardless of the company's rationale and timing for introducing *Bully* (on the heels of the June 14, 2006, Senate hearings on sexuality and violence in *GTA: San Andreas*), the fact remains that these comparable constructions of masculine power and action convey incomparable messages about the game characters' use of their powerful actions. Both games present an antihero lead character playing through a series of missions. For gamers playing as Carl "CJ" Johnson.

GTA: *San Andreas* provides big guns and bigger firepower to effect drive-bys and targeted shootings in the 'hood. Conversely, for gamers playing as Jimmy Hopkins, *Bully* provides big $CO_2$ canisters to extinguish even bigger fires in the school. Nothing about these two RPZs contests dominant culture's socially constructed messages/lessons about race, masculinity, and class in America. Instead, everything about CJ, *GTA*'s black protagonist, conforms to America's hyperviolent and superpredator black male stereotypes, and the racially codified violence that defines success in the gameplay missions undertaken throughout the virtual ghetto environment. Similarly, Jimmy Hopkins, *Bully*'s white protagonist,

146

comports with our stereotypical expectations about white males' moral superiority and demonstrations of social responsibility even though "he's been expelled from every school he's ever attended, left to fend for himself after his mother abandons him at Bullworth to go on her fifth honeymoon."[42]

One professional review of *Bully* posted on YouTube characterizes the game's narrative departure from the *GTA* games rather adeptly. According to RockstarAl:

> The story is nowhere near as raunchy as any of the *Grand Theft Auto* games and ends up playing out like a slightly scandalous Nickelodeon cartoon. There is little to no swearing and the violence only adds up to a few black eyes here and there. But there's still plenty of laughs to be had from the conniving and emotionally imbalanced characters Rockstar writes so well.[43]

Contrast *Bully*'s rather benign story description to its *GTA* counterpart, also on YouTube. In a review entitled "The History of *Grand Theft Auto*," the game world and gameplay are defined as amoral and forbidden digital spaces of danger and hyperviolent performance:

> These missions would take you all over the city and varied from simple taxi jobs to assassinations and even car theft rings. A big part of the fun was exploring each city and finding the secret missions to do, or just causing general mayhem while eluding the police and using weapons like machine guns, rocket launchers, and flame throwers ("The History of Grand Theft Auto").[44]

As these game reviews make clear, on the one hand, *GTA: San Andreas* positions CJ as a digital simulation trading on the cinematic tropes of the endangered, as well as dangerous, black male protagonists delineated in John Singleton's 1991 film *Boyz N the Hood* and the 1993 Hughes brothers' film *Menace II Society* (outlined above), or the *de rigueur* menacing black youths who dominate newspaper headlines, TV and radio news shows, and other mainstream media texts. On the other hand, Jimmy Hopkins is Rockstar Games' innovative digital persona simulating a troubled-yet-heroic white teenager verging on juvenile delinquency, whose cinematic alter ego could easily have been expelled from the privileged schoolyard of the wildly popular *Harry Potter* films, or TV's charmingly angst-driven coming-of-age narratives found in *The Wonder Years* and *Boy Meets World* shows, for example.

What many video game theorists and critics agree upon, and what matters most to our inquiry, is the fact that video games teach—they are pedagogical—and that "what we're learning from them bears no resemblance whatsoever to what we think we're learning."[45] It is precisely the learning "about life" in America with its entrenched racial problems that is at issue here. As the foregoing examples demonstrate, and as Ian Bogost points out elsewhere in this volume, it is difficult, if not impossible, for games not to have a pedagogical function. Given the increasing number of hours youths today spend playing—fourth-grade boys spend about nine hours per week playing and eighth-grade boys log nearly five hours per week at play[46]—young people are spending a great deal of time immersed in the kinds of RPZs discussed here.

## Reception and fandom contexts

Any foray into the online fan culture of the *GTA* games quickly reveals an alarming reality; the video game playground on- and offline too often replicates racist attitudes, values, and assumptions found in larger social structures. As contested a site as actual children's playgrounds often are, some online fora are notorious zones of contestation and violent speech acts when race and issues of diversity surface.[47] In evidence was the racial diversity of the online gamers, whose debates about race often bordered on flame wars. The majority of gamer-respondents freely self-identified along racial lines. They were African American, Asian, Arab, black, Mexican, Jewish, white, or racially mixed. Overwhelmingly male, these gamers used screen names and expressed sentiments, which ranged from racial inclusion (or color blindness) to outright racist rants, with some featuring both. Exchanges also ranged from a sort-of free-speech, Habermassian public sphere ideal to condemnations of the system administrator for permitting such a topic to appear on the forum at all. In some instances, posts to the threads were censored or replaced with a note that read, "This message was deleted at the request of a moderator or administrator."[48]

The rhetorical rough-and-tumble in these discussion threads began largely with assertions that many white gamers boycotted *GTA: San Andreas* because the lead character, CJ, was black and the game protagonist's digital skin could not be modified to present as a white avatar. Reviewing the emotional content on various user fora dedicated to the *GTA* games and their fan bases reveals much about the complexity of gamers' racial attitudes and belief systems, at least those posting to the sites under consideration here. While these sites are worthy of more detailed analysis than time or space permits here, a few select quotes can illustrate quite convincingly the need to think seriously about the lessons video games teach and how we can fairly, honestly, and effectively address and assess games' potentially harmful—as well as beneficial—RPZs.

In his recent historical analysis of modern boy culture in formation, E. Anthony Rotundo's insights are useful for framing the selected quotes. According to Rotundo, "Rivalry, division, and conflict were vital elements in the structure of boy culture." He added that "the boys world was endlessly divided and subdivided" and split into groups by residence, ethnicity, and social status, with daring and bravado as a "ritual expression in boy's games."[49] We culled the following quotes from three separate discussion threads. The first set of quotes are direct responses to a discussion entitled "What the hell is everyones [*sic*] problem?" The fracas in this discussion concerns a new video game (not identified in this thread, but likely the game is *GTA4*). The postings concern gamers' attitudes about the possibility of another black protagonist in this next *GTA* game.

#1: The thing is that in *SA* [*GTA: San Andreas*] you played someone who dealt drugs and is in a gang . . . you know your average black guy. Now you have someone who upholds the law and is black???? people need to realize that this game is in no way trying to emulate reality like *SA* was. I believe it is cel-shaded so people won't lose themselves in it and believe it's happening in the real world."[50]

#2: ^^^^^ Oh ****!!!! Wait. Your average black guy???? Okay, obviously you live under a rock in a small hik [*sic*] town because the average black in Houston, TX or at least my friends are in college. I have braids but I've never been in a gang and neither has my family or friends. Just because 50 Cent raps about detailed stories that he fabricates, America thinks ALL black guys are gangsters. Your ignorance is hilarious because 50 used his proceeds from his album to make a sports mineral water and cheaper version of Apple computers. People like you should not be allowed to reproduce.[51]

#3: Well one of my big gripes with *GTA* and one of the main reasons why I don't [*sic*] play the francise, except at friends houses is because they don't let you customize your character. In mexican and I have yet to see a mexican protagonist in a game, except that stereotypical under the border game. I just want to be able to make the character look like me, or how I want.[52]

Discussion thread number two is entitled "Is the main character black again?"

# 1: BobbyQt [a pseudonym] is right!!! I don't wanna play as a black character. Ever since the 8 bit era, the characters have been white, why change all that. I'm pretty sure black people don't mind playing as white characters. There are already enough games with black characters, NBA live, Madden, Fifa and San Andreas of course isn't that enough?!?![53]

#2: Well that was pretty interesting why aren't you ok with playing as A character (oh and by the way I am capitalized [*sic*] 'A' because that is exactly what game characters are, simple, not specifically white, male, american, 18–34). It does matter what they look like they are a character I think its great that there are different ethnicities in games but I think that shouldn't turn a logical person away from a game because of an individuals race or gender. If you have a problem playing with an african american character then you have a problem with people in general not just video game persona's. END[54]

The third and final discussion topic is "So, what minority character should the new character be?"

#1: I don't care what the character is, but I wouldn't mind a Hispanic character or another White character. Maybe a Jew. Like me ☺

#2: with the current situation in the states [*sic*] Im leaning towards the mestizo character also, granted I am a White bigot but I wouldn't mind playing as a salvadoran or mexican killer, those dudes are ruthless, plus they sound cooler than ol cj

#3: Are you for real?

#2: Me? Yeh im "for real" flame me all you like I really don't care if your gonna say something homophobic its your own problem

#4: I'd like a white or Italian guy. I'm black but for some reason, I don't like playing video games as black people. Playing as a white guy makes the game feel more normal. And Italian guy makes it more mafia like and mafia=good.

#5: asian. so I can finally connect with a character in *GTA*.[55]

The expressions here range from blatant racism to racial tolerance or inclusion, and provide an interesting feedback loop for some of the concerns outlined above. We wanted to juxtapose some feedback from *GTA* gamers themselves to comments of these games' designers and industry critics, to balance out our own considerations of industry practices and player response. While this study is not arguing that *GTA* fandom represents a racist community, it does suggest, however, that there is much food for thought here.

It is our aim to explore and better understand how usefully and effectively to study young people's increasing interaction with discourses of race in video gaming culture. This formulation of RPZs sketches out directly, if not fully, gamers' readings and likely enactments of game scenarios such as those found in *GTA*. These are scenarios told in racial terms and in alluring role-playing game structures, where gamers are said to have more choice and freedom in producing, as well as consuming, the video games' narratives or story lines.[56] Our inclusion of such frameworks is intended to encourage the monitoring of how these games' various missions depend upon the mastery of established mainstream codes of meaningful play bound by racially suspect cultural scripts.[57]

The significance of this project is contextualized quite convincingly by Salen and Zimmerman's reminder of Huizinga's truism, that "all play means something."[58] It is also important to recognize one of gaming's welcome unintended consequences—how it alters the familiar descriptive trifecta of nonwhite youths as poor, minority, and illiterate. For one thing, as the above quotes from *GTA* gamers bear out, these video games require a certain amount of computer and other cultural literacies simply to play the games well. After all, there are manuals, onscreen instructions, and community fora devoted to improved gameplay and social networking that require basic-to-exceptional literacy competencies.

## Want to play? Some final thoughts on race and games

Our focus in this chapter on the simulation and representation of urban culture in video games, and the consequences for learning, does not intend to be exhaustive in the effort to illuminate the rising significance of race and ethnicity in the ecology of games. In the final section of this chapter, we move away from discussions of representation, game design, and pedagogical zones to identify and cautiously map what we believe are additional, yet underexplored matters related to race, video games, learning, and young people. As we stated in the opening, public dialogue about race and video games has been marginal at best. In addition to the issues addressed above, we want to identify some other ways in which race matters in the video game world. Specifically, we consider video games in the context of a rapidly evolving digital media environment.

Any analysis of the relationship between video games, young people, and learning must also seek to understand the larger context in which these issues began to take on their complex shape. One of the more notable transformations taking place in the rapidly evolving digital media landscape is the extent to which young people have gained access to tools and skills that enable them to produce as well as consume cultural content. According to the Pew Internet & American Life Project (2005), more than half, 57 percent, of the teens aged 12–15 create and share content online.[59] Many scholars celebrate the sense of freedom and empowerment that young people gain from "participatory culture."[60] Salen and Zimmerman argue that a Do-It-Yourself (DIY) approach to cultural resistance, most notably reskinning and modding, has made video games a form of culturally transformative play.[61] Moreover, the brave new world of digital media culture— modding, world-building, user-generated content, and file sharing—has the potential not only to build new learning environments and modes of digital literacy, but equally importantly to empower young people to cultivate actively practices that resist the once-taken-for-granted hegemony of corporate produced and preprogrammed media into their lives.

Young people are not passive consumers of media and cultural content. Increasingly, they are producing and sharing content with their peers, thus altering their media and cultural environment in unprecedented ways.[62] Video games, for example, can no longer be viewed as merely a source of leisure and entertainment, but also as a site of cultural resistance and empowerment.[63]

However, as we begin to understand more thoroughly the lively ways in which digital media enables young people to assert greater control over their cultural environments, we must also be mindful of the fact that this does not hold true for all young people. We ask then, what are the consequences for young people whose access to digital technology is either limited (i.e., accessed at school or the local library) or essentially nonexistent? As video games evolve into a dynamic form of cultural production, personal expression, and social capital, we see, once again, how the divide between the "technology haves" and "technology have-nots" continues to matter. Elite gaming communities usually, though not always, involve a high degree of involvement in online digital publics that cultivate very specialized bodies of knowledge and expertise. Deep participation in elite video gaming also demands more than casual or occasional access to digital media, that is, the ability to access gaming environments from wired homes, offices, college dormitories, and public spaces—environments that are not universally available to all. In this case, we draw attention to multiple forms of access—physical access to the hardware and broadband connections, as well as access to the mentors and learning environments that cultivate digital forms of literacy, skills, and social capital.

Poor and working-class youth play video games, but primarily on consoles rather than on the personal computers, that foster more transformative gaming practices like modding and world-building. According to Roberts et al. black and Latino youth are *more likely* than their white counterparts to live in homes that own a television or video game console.[64] Additionally, black and Latino youth are *less likely* than their white counterparts to live in a household with a personal computer. And while computer ownership among the poor and working class continues to increase, these households are still unlikely to have access to high-speed Internet connections.[65] Young people who have limited access to advanced computing technology are less likely than their more affluent counterparts to participate in digital media culture as producers and distributors of content.

In addition, overcoming the barriers regarding content creation in games poses tough challenges. In his analysis of how Asian Americans are portrayed in games, Dean Chan urges scholars and cultural critics to "remain steadfast in the call for more diverse and equitable representations in commercial games." [66] However, before game content becomes more diverse, the industry will have to cultivate greater racial and cultural diversity in its workforce. This is especially important given that video games which simulate culturally specific environments require designers to be not only technically literate, but socially and culturally literate as well.

So, what do we know about the makeup of the video game development community? In a 2005 published report titled "Game Developer Demographics: An Exploration of Workforce Diversity," the International Game Developers Association (IGDA) set out to answer one question: "who makes games?" Whereas the Children Now report found that the overwhelming majority of player-controlled characters in games are white, the IGDA found that an overwhelming majority of the personnel creating games is also white. According to the IGDA, the "typical" game development professional can be described as white, male, young (median age 31), and college educated. if high degrees of learning and education are essential for gaining meaningful employment in the video games industry, the future prospects of black and Latino talent finding a secure place among programmers, design artists, writers, and designers seem limited.

One interesting avenue of intervention involves the creation of digital learning environments that work to close the participation gap. As debates about the digital divide have been refined, technology activists note that successful intervention requires more than providing the technology-poor access to hardware. The technology-poor also need access to mentors and environments that enable them to cultivate the skills that lead to greater forms of agency. Addressing the participation gap, researchers claim, is the next great challenge in closing the digital divide. Nichole Pinkard, principal investigator of the Center for Urban School Improvement, writes, "the new divide will not be caused by access to technology but rather by lack of access to mentors, environments, and activities where the use of digital media is the language of communication."[67] Community technology centers like this one are not only making technology accessible to poor and working class youth but also, as Pinkard notes, developing programs that "enable urban youth to become discerning new media consumers and fluent media producers."

In short, we believe that future discussions about race and games should be twofold. First, we must continue to document and analyze what the racial content, themes, and design elements in video games teach young people about race. Second, we believe that future discussions about race and video games should engage broader debates about the rise and diffusion of digital media technologies and the educational pathways that lead to greater forms of new media literacy and participation in the digital media sphere, particularly as they pertain to race and ethnicity. Empowering young people on the social and economic margins to create content not only diversifies what content they consume; it also holds the promise of expanding how they learn and reproduce race for public consumption for generations to come.

## Notes

1 Elizabeth A. Vandewater, Shim Mi-Suk, and Allison G. Caplovitz, Linking Obesity and Activity Level with Children's Television and Video Game Use, *Journal of Adolescence* 27 (2004): 71–85; Carol A. Phillips, Susan Rolls, Andrew Rouse, and Mark D. Griffiths, Home Video Game Playing in School Children: A Study of Incidence and Patterns of Play, *Journal of Adolescence* 18 (1995): 687–91; K. Roe and D. Muijs, Children and Computer Games: A Profile of Heavy Users, *European Journal of Communication* 13 (1998): 181–200; and Jeanne B. Funk and Debra D. Bachman, Playing Violent Video and Computer Games and Adolescent Self-Concept, *Journal of Communication* 46 (1996): 19–32.
2 James Paul Gee, *What Video Games Have to Teach Us About Learning and Literacy* (New York: Palgrave Macmillan, 2003).
3 Gordon L. Berry and C. Mitchell-Kernan, eds., *Television and the Socialization of the Minority Child* (New York: Academic, 1982).
4 Gordon L. Berry and Joy Keiko Asamen, Television, Children, and Multicultural Awareness: Comprehending the Medium in a Complex Multimedia Society, in *Handbook of Children and the Media*, eds. Dorothy G. Singer and Jerome L. Singer (London: Sage, 2001).
5 Ibid.

6 Anna Everett, Serious Play: Playing with Race in Contemporary Gaming Culture, in *Handbook of Computer Game Studies*, eds. Joost Raessens and Jeffrey Goldstein (Cambridge, MA: The MIT Press, 2005), 311–26.
7 Marc Prensky, *Digital Game-Based Learning* (New York: McGraw-Hill, 2001); and Gee, *What Video Games Have to Teach Us*, 136–37.
8 Gee, *What Video Games Have to Teach Us*.
9 Steven Poole, *Trigger Happy: The Inner Life of Video Games* (London: Fourth Estate, 2000).
10 Ibid, 152.
11 Poole, *Trigger Happy*.
12 Children Now, *Fair Play? Violence, Gender and Race in Video Games* (Oakland, CA: Children Now, 2001).
13 Geoff King and Tanya Krzywinska, *Tomb Raiders and Space Invaders: Video Game Forms and Contexts* (New York: 1. B. Palgrave Macmillan, 2006).
14 Alison McMahan, Immersion, Engagement, and Presence: A Method for Analyzing 3-D Video Games, in *The Video Game Theory Reader*, eds. Mark J. P. Wolf and Bernard Perron (New York: Routledge, 2003).
15 Children Now, *FairPlay*, 23.
16 The six consoles included in the study were Dreamcast, Game Boy Advance, Game Boy Color, Nintendo 64, PlayStation, and PlayStation 2.
17 Dean Chan, Playing with Race: The Ethics of Racialized Representations in E-Games, *International Review of Information Ethics* 4 (2005): 24–30.
18 Ibid.
19 Gee, *What Video Games Have to Teach Us*, 127.
20 S. Craig Watkins, *Representing: Hip Hop Culture and the Production of Black Cinema* (Chicago: The University of Chicago Press, 1998), 228; see also S. Craig Watkins, *Hip Hop Matters: Politics, Pop Culture and the Struggle for the Soul of a Movement* (Boston: Beacon Press, 2005).
21 Richard Lapchick, *Five Minutes to Midnight: Race and Sport in the 1990s* (Lanham, MD: Madison Books, 1991).
22 Children Now, *Fair Play*, 23.
23 Justine Cassell and Henry Jenkins, eds., *From Barbie to Mortal Kombat: Gender and Computer Games* (Cambridge, MA: The MIT Press, 2000); and Diane Carr, Games and Gender, in *Computer Games: Text, Narrative and Play*, eds. Diane Carr, David Buckingham, Andrew Burn, and Gareth Schott (London: Polity, 2006).
24 Michel Marriott, The Color of Mayhem in a Wave of "Urban" Games, *New York Times*, August 12, 2004.
25 David J. Leonard, High Tech Blackface: Race, Sports Video Games and Becoming the Other, *Intelligent Agent* 4 (2004): 1–5.
26 Children Now, *Fair Play*.
27 Leonard, High Tech Blackface.
28 Eric Lott, *Love and Theft: Blackface Minstrelsy and the American Working Class* (New York: Oxford University Press, 1993).
29 Leonard, High Tech Blackface, 2.
30 Sonia M. Livingstone, *Young People and New Media: Childhood and the Changing Media Environment* (London: Sage, 2002).
31 Herman Gray, *Watching Race: Television and the Struggle for Blackness* (Minneapolis, MN: University of Minnesota Press, 1995).
32 Martin Lister, Jon Dovey, Seth Giddings, Iain Grant, and Kieran Kelly, *New Media: A Critical Introduction* (New York: Routledge, 2003).
33 Katie Salen and Eric Zimmerman, Game Design and Meaningful Play, in *Handbook of Computer Game Studies*, eds. Joost Raessens and Jeffrey Goldstein (Cambridge, MA: The MIT Press, 2005), 59–80.

34  Johan Huizinga, *Homo Ludens: A Study of the Play Element in Culture* (Boston: Beacon Press, 1955).

35  Ibid., 68–9.

36  Marc Prensky, Computer Games and Learning: Digital Game-Based Learning, in *Handbook of Computer Game Studies*, eds. Joost Raessens and Jeffrey Goldstein (Cambridge, MA: The MIT Press, 2005), 106.

37  Henry Jenkins, "Complete Freedom of Movement": Video Games as Gendered Play Spaces, in *From Barbie to Mortal Kombat: Gender and Computer Games*, eds. Justine Cassell and Henry Jenkins (Cambridge, MA: The MIT Press, 1998), 262–97; and Aphra Kerr, Non-Entertainment Uses of Digital Games, in *The Business and Culture of Digital Games* (London: Sage, 2006).

38  Prensky, Computer Games and Learning, 107.

39  While this comparative media framework does provide useful parallels to understanding and mastering gaming's racialized *meaningful play*, to borrow Katie Salen and Eric Zimmerman's term, it is not a reductive exercise that fails to recognize the raging debate in game studies between theories of narratology and ludology, with other emergent critical paradigms in the offing. Narratologist Janet Murray correctly cautions that "one cannot use old standards to judge the new formats," while acknowledging that "games are always stories," with a specific type of interactivity unique to games' cyber-dramas Jant Murray quoted in Kerr, Non-Entertainment Uses of Video Games, 24). Ludologists, mainly building upon the seminal works of Johan Huizinga and Espen Aarseth, to name two, posit the necessity for moving games studies "away from representation towards simulation semiotics or 'semiotics.'" Moreover, their largely formalist critiques pivot on the "shift from narrative to ludic engagement with texts and from interpretation to configuration," as Stuart Moulthrop sees it (quoted in Kerr, Non-Entertainment Uses of Video Games, 33–4). And while such ground-clearing critical approaches to game studies constitute a necessary move forward for the nascent field, they do recall the infamous realism versus formalism debates of classical film theory that remain generative and productive to established cinema and TV studies even today. And for our purposes, Aphra Kerr is on target with the observation that "[g]iven both the diversity of narrative theories and the diversity of games, some of which are clearly more narrative driven than others, it would be unwise to dismiss narrative theory outright" (ibid., 26). When we contextualize the RPZ idea within the *GTA* metanarratives and interactive modes of engagement, we feel the need to retain narratology and embrace ludology, though not always in equal measure. After all, game theorists correctly emphasize that games position players as the spectator and protagonist simultaneously (Kerr, Non-Entertainment Uses of Video Games, 38; and Mark J. P. Wolf, Genre and the Video Game, in *Handbook of Computer Games Studies*, eds. Joost Raessens and Jeffrey Goldstein [Cambridge, MA: The MIT Press, 2005], 193). Thus, it seems that we can benefit from both critical approaches.

40  Seth Schiesel, Welcome to the New Dollhouse, *New York Times*, May 7, 2006, Sec. 2: 1f.

41  Anna Everett acknowledges the superb assistance she received from her graduate students at UCSB, Noah Lopez and Dan Reynolds, especially, and the entire group of students enrolled in her New Media Theory seminar in 2006. Noah Lopez was her summer research assistant with whom she spent numerous thrilling hours playing *GTA: Vice City* and *GTA: San Andreas*, and the *Sims 2* games. They embarked upon an odyssey of exploration into these games' depictions of race, gender, and class politics, and specific treatments of the game genres and other aesthetic features. She thanks Lopez for helping to lower the learning curve of *GTA's* mission structures and logics. Dan Reynolds was instrumental in presenting some of *Bully's* game details immediately after that game's release. Reynolds played (actually finished) the game within a few weeks and discussed many of its racial dimensions with her during the course of their New Media Theory seminar that focused particularly on games theory and practice. She

hopes to revisit the wealth of information they provided as avid gamers and critically aware graduate students of film and media study.

42 Rockstar Games, *Bully*: "Overview." http:/www.rockstargames.com/bully/home. Accessed October 20, 2006.

43 Rockstar Al, *"Bully* Gametrailers Review." YouTube. http://www.youtube.com/watch?v= 9ioKpSb6AEO. Accessed October 20, 2006.

44 While the production date of this video review of *GTA* ran initially on GameSpot.com, a user posted the review to YouTube on May 6, 2006.

45 Ralph Koster, quoted in Jane Avrich, Steven Johnson, Ralph Koster, and Thomas de Zengotita, Grand Theft Education: Literacy in the Age of Video Games, *Harper's Magazine* 313 (2006): 31–40.

46 Sandra Calvert, Cognitive Effects of Video Games, in *Handbook of Computer Game Studies*, eds. Joost Raessens and Jeffrey Goldstein (Cambridge, MA: The MIT Press, 2005), 125–32.

47 In a sampling of representative gamers' thoughts on race in the gaming firmament, the forum at GameSpot.com proved to be one of the most popular, prolific, and useful, followed by the user fora at the IGDA Web site and at Gameology.org.

48 Is the Main Character Black Again? *Gamespot.com*, Forums, 2006. http://www.gamespot.com/ebox360/action/crackdown/show-msgs.php?topic_id=1-31063566&pid—930144&page=0. Accessed October 20, 2006.

49 E. Anthony Rotundo, Boy Culture, in *The Children's Culture Reader*, ed. Henry Jenkins (New York: New York University Press, 1998), 337–62.

50 "What the hell is everyones [*sic*] problem?" http://www.gamespot.com/xbox360/act3on/crackdown/show-msgs.php?topic_id=m-l-31063566&pid=930144&page=0.

51 Ibid.

52 Ibid.

53 Is the Main Character Black Again?

54 Ibid.

55 So What Minority Should the New Character Be? *Gamespot.com*, Forums, May 18, 2006. http:www.gamespot.com/pse/action/grandtheftauto4/show_msgs.php. Accessed May 18, 2006.

56 Avrich, Grand Theft Education, 31–40.

57 Anna Everett, P.C. Youth Violence: What's the Internet or Video Gaming Got to Do with It? *Denver University Law Review* 77, no. 4 (2000): 689–698.

58 Katie Salen and Eric Zimmerman, Game Design and Meaningful Play, in *Handbook of Computer Game Studies*, eds. Joost Raessens and Jeffrey Goldstein (Cambridge, MA: The MIT Press, 2005), 59–80.

59 Pew Internet & American Life Project, *Teen Content Creators and Consumers* (Washington, DC: Pew Research Center, 2005).

60 Henry Jenkins, *Fans, Bloggers, and Gamers: Exploring Participatory Culture* (New York: New York University Press, 2006).

61 Salen and Zimmerman, Game Design and Meaningful Play.

62 Pew Internet & American Life Project, *Teen Content Creators and Consumers*.

63 Salen and Zimmerman, Game Design and Meaningful Play.

64 Donald Roberts, Ulla G. Foehr, Victoria J. Rideout, and Mollyanne Brodie, *Kids and Media in America* (Cambridge, UK: Cambridge University Press, 2004).

65 U.S. Department of Commerce, *Computer and Internet Use in the United States: October* (Washington, DC: U.S. Census Bureau, 2003).

66 Chan, Playing with Race.

67 Nichole Pinkard, Developing_opportunities for Urban Youth to Become Digital, 2006. http://spotlight.macfound.org/main/entry/nichole_pinkard_developing_opportunities_for_urban_youth_to_become_digital/. Accessed June 16, 2007.

# 53

# RACE

*Anna Everett*

Source: Mark J. P. Wolf and Bernard Perron (eds), *The Routledge Companion to Video Game Studies* (New York, NY: Routledge, 2014), pp. 396–406.

When we consider the matter of race in contemporary gaming culture, a few important contextual frameworks come to mind to situate our knowledge of the topic. First, there is the heightened racial framework of American civil society still adjusting to having elected the nation's first bi-racial Commander-in-Chief, President Barack H. Obama who self-identifies, proudly, as black or African American. Second, there is the industry framework driven by the enlarged roles of global audiences and market shares to which game developers cater with strategies and tactics unparalleled even during the golden age of the industry's expansion in the Bushnell and Miyamoto eras of the mid- to late 1970s through the mid-1980s. (Though it is important to add that Miyamoto still reigns as a gaming deity to this day.) Third, there is the digitized race and ethnicity framework promulgated by Rockstar Games's *Grand Theft Auto* franchise that introduced mainstream gaming's most high-profile, if not first-ever, central black protagonist Carl "CJ" Johnson as a must-play character (MPC). Fourth, there is the gender framework following the girl games movement that gave rise to the highly successful Lara Croft game brand at the end of the twentieth century. Fifth, and last for our purposes, there is gaming's networked online framework that has taken the industry by storm and to new heights of social, cultural, global, and financial influence and significance. A throughline transecting each of these frameworks is the often disavowed problematic of racial otherness in gaming's historic march to cultural relevance and power, particularly its masterful arbitration and commodification of contemporary identity politics as play. Put simply, we can ascertain key aspects of gamers' and developers' racial attitudes and assumptions via gaming journalism, blogs, social media platforms (Facebook, Twitter, Instagram, Tumblr), and other online fora.

## Race and games in the age of Obama?

> Just as narratives, computer games are expressions that, among other things, play a function in the formation of our identity . . . [W]e could say that the (computer) games we play are nothing but a remote imitation of the infinite play of the world.
>
> (De Mul, 2005, p. 260)

Without a doubt, much has changed even as too much remains the same in the years since journalist Michael Marriott's 1999 clarion call in the *New York Times* for interrogating the limits of the video games industry's treatment of race and ethnicity, and the need for doing something about it. Nothing signals the depth of change in our national mindset and political economy than the remarkable 2008 election and subsequent 2012 re-election of President Obama against formidable odds. Consequently, discourses of race and identity politics in the country frequently toggle back and forth between often naive, well-intentioned rhetorics of color-blindness or race neutrality and emboldened racist rhetorics trading on covert and overt logics of racial animus and entrenched white supremacy.

Clearly, it is not a radical move to situate this interrogation of the gaming industry's meaningful play structures within the crucial sense-making frameworks of racial intelligibility and identification. However, it remains a radical act when game industry observers, critics, fans, designers, and developers resist, call out, and reject the tired, familiar, and damaging racist cultural scripts routinely cloaked in gaming's newfangled technological wizardry and today's powerfully immersive multicultural narrative-quests. More radical yet are those gamer/designer communities of practice who modify and recode our racist cultural scripts to effect antiracist sandbox experiences either in wildly successful game design or pleasurable gameplay, or both. I have in mind here technological innovations in character designs that promise infinitely customizable avatars and gameworlds more attuned to the lived realities and expectations of post-Civil Rights era Millennials, or "Generation C" (for *connect*) as trend watchers for the Nielsen corporation dubs today's "most digitally connected" 18-to-34-year-olds (Fox, 2012). Moreover, these youths' habitual digital connectivity is matched in intensity and ubiquity only by their willing attachments to so-called "addictive" mobile games on smartphones tablets and other toting technologies. Whether or not we are considering the Millennials or gamers more broadly, with respect to categories of epistemic games, serious games, casual games, retro games, and cute games, we understand that none is impervious to the sense-making contexts of volatile and shifting cultural frameworks. Again, these include the winds of historical and contemporary racism or conversely the countervailing winds of antiracist activist practices. For example, the decisive electoral victory of President Obama manifests a transformation of race relations and realpolitik in the US despite a palpable uptick in racist attacks prior to, during, and in the aftermath of the historic 2008 election. In his intelligence report for the Southern Poverty Law Center entitled "Racist Backlash Greets President Barack Obama," Larry Keller (2009) recounts a number of chilling incidents across the country, ranging from official hate crimes to offensive pranks and protests, and most disappointing many involving youths, "students from grade school to college":

A life-sized likeness of Obama was found hanging from a noose in a tree at the University of Kentucky. The co-owner of a Palm Beach, Fla., restaurant wrote "White Power" on staff memos taped to the eatery's kitchen walls. She told her black employees they would be fired if they voted for Obama . . . A black Muslim teenager in Staten Island, N.Y., said he was assaulted by four white men who yelled "Obama." That same restaurant owner in Palm Beach wrote "KKK" on employee timecards . . . In Snellville, Ga., a boy on a school bus told a 9-year-old girl that he hoped Obama would be assassinated. That night, also in Snellville, a vandalized Obama sign and two pizza boxes filled with human feces were left on a black family's lawn. Small black effigies were found hanging from nooses in trees in two Maine towns. In Midland, Mich., a pistol-packing member of the Knights of the Ku Klux Klan wore his Klan uniform and carried an American flag on a city sidewalk.

The point of quoting this stark reminder of persistent racism in US society and culture is to underscore the point that deeply problematic attitudes about race and identity politics continually surface with damaging and dangerous consequences even in the twentyfirst century, in the age of President Obama, and in regions all across the nation. It is hardly surprising, then, that cultural narratives about race most familiarly transmitted via theater, print, film, radio, television, as gaming industry precursors of video games in arcade, console, and online formats, become nearly impossible to dislodge. And games, like these cultural modalities before them, help render and standardize historic racial myths as it does myths and discourses of the body, as "Judith Butler speaks of [with her term] 'bodily intelligibility'" (quoted in Richard and Zaremba, 2005, p. 293).

Having emerged now as a media industry giant and a potent cultural force, the video/computer games industry and the narrative texts it creates, promote, sell, and profit from both racist and antiracist cultural values. The significance of gaming discourses of race is, as Jos de Mul points out (2005, p. 262), that

> computer games are not "just games" but play a constitutive role in our cognitive development and in the construction of our identity . . . You have to do more than identify with a character on the screen. You must act for it.

"Identification through action," de Mul continues, "has a special kind of hold" (2005, p. 262). This special hold is at the crux of our concern with race in games' arguably heightened identification affect over traditional discursive forms such as print and film. Identification with games "might be more intense than in the case of narratives," de Mul suggests (2005, p. 262). And if we accept gaming's growing influence on identity formation and normative racial discourses in society, and especially on Generation C, our investigation into the twinning of gaming and race takes on a particular urgency.

Furthermore, confused public discourses about video games more broadly undergird contradictory logics about the medium's newly embraced beneficial roles in society, including its ability to spur pre-science, technology, engineering, and math (STEM) learning in youths, and to improve physical and cognitive skills in elderly populations (Castillo, 2013; Nauert, 2012). In addition, public discourses about video games also maintain a heightened scrutiny and condemnation of sexist and misogynist content in gaming narratives, play structures, and their "procedural rhetorics," to use Ian Bogost's (2008, p. 125) terms. Concern about the problematic nature of gaming's gender dynamics is ongoing in academia and more so in the blogosphere. Now, the racial problematic in gaming is finally garnering some of the scholarly and popular attention or scrutiny it has long deserved.

## A proliferation of racially diverse MPCs

It is true that numerous successful game titles and franchises featuring racially diverse MPCs and optional-playable characters (OPCs) have become widely available. Some of the most racially-inclusive mainstream/popular games developed over the decades and in recent years are: *Final Fantasy* (Square Enix, 1987–2013), *Prince of Persia* (Brøderbund, TLC, Mattel, Ubisoft, SCEJ, 1989–2010), *Madden NFL* (Electronic Arts, 1992–2013), *FIFA International Soccer* (EA Sports, 1993–2012), *Resident Evil* (Capcom, 1996–2012), *Half-Life* (Valve Corporation, 1998–2007), *Tiger Woods PGA Tour* (Electronic Arts, 1999–2013), *Blade* (Activision, 2000), *Halo* (Bungie, Ensemble Studios, 343 Entertainment, 2001–2012), *Grand Theft Auto* (Rockstar Games, 2002–2013), *Battlefield* (Electronic Arts, 2002–2013), *Call of Duty* (Activision, 2003–2012), *Men of Valor* (Vivendi Universal, 2004), *NBA Ballers* (Midway, 2004), *NFL Street* (Electronic Arts, 2004), *Afro Samurai* (Seven Seas Entertainment, 2009), *Prey* (2K Games, 2006), *Gears of War* (Microsoft Game Studios, 2006–2011), *Saints Row* (THQ, 2006), *Mass Effect* (Bioware, 2007–2012), *Left 4 Dead* (Valve Corporation, 2008), *Prototype* (Activision, 2009–2012), and *StarHawk* (Sony Computer Entertainment, 2012).

Now, *Assassins' Creed 3:Liberation* (Ubisoft, 2012) is a special title in the franchise produced exclusively for the PlayStation Vita handheld gaming device and it marks a unique offering that fuses both race and gender in one powerful action-adventure character design (more about this later).

For some time, as the abovementioned titles suggest, games companies have targeted African Americans, Latino/a Americans, Asians Americans, Native Americans, Arabs, and other Others (though not in equal measure) as a deliberate business model of product expansion. After all, as Erica Saylor (2012) observes in "Latinos Drive Video Game Sales," the gaming industry is well aware that this gamer demographic considers video games as a primary source of entertainment by 32 percent more than others. "According to Microsoft XBox sales," she writes, "Hispanic gamers contributed to 23% [industry] growth while non-Hispanic gamers grew [by] a sheer 10%." Referencing *Call of Duty: Black Ops II* (Activision, 2012), Saylor alerts us to the game's Latino MPC named Raul Menendez, a political activist or narco-terrorist hailing from Nicaragua ("Latinos Drive"). Despite crafting a lead Latino playable character (PC) in one of the world's most popular and lucrative franchises, *Call of Duty: Black Ops II* is not likely to spur an industry rush or avalanche of Latino/a themed games or heroic Latino/a protagonists to satisfy one of its largest and most loyal fan bases.

Frederick Luis Aldama (2012) posits a possible rationale. He contends that a plethora of Latino OPCs and MPCs can be found in successful genres, which serve to mollify if not fully satisfy this gamer clientele. Acceptable archetypes such as footballers, gangsters, matador-style warriors, and other underworld stereotypes dominate several games in the *Grand Theft Auto, Tekken, Madden, FIFA*, military combat, and first-person shooter game franchises. Furthermore, some niche and mainstream games provide dialogue/audio in Spanish (Aldama, 2012, p. 359). That said, Saylor and Aldama emphasize that gaming's representation of underrepresented racial and ethnic groups (especially Latinos) remains woefully incommensurate with their demographic percentages in society, and within the industry's own market shares.

Still, a key part of gaming's steady rise as a media industry powerhouse and formidable rival to motion pictures and other big entertainment media corporations is its ability to keep pace with changes in social and cultural norms. This means game narratives, genres, worlds, and characters necessarily have evolved. New and established game titles and franchises now feature MPCs and PCs that are racially and ethnically diverse.

I have argued elsewhere that *Grand Theft Auto: San Andreas*'s African-American character Carl "CJ" Johnson (the gang-member protagonist) and *Grand Theft Auto: Vice City*'s Italian American character Tommy Vercetti (the mafia protagonist) provided the preeminent racial MPCs outside of gaming's privileged masculine archetypes of heroic whiteness (Everett, 2005). In fact, Rockstar Games's creation of CJ and Tommy as bankable gaming stars foregrounding race, masculinity, and ethnicity was the precondition that made it possible for other racially and ethnically defined MPC and PC types. These include *Mass Effect*'s black soldier Commander John Shepard, *Men of Valor*'s black Vietnam veteran Dean Shephard, *Starhawk*'s black gunslinger Emmet Graves, and *Resident Evil 5*'s black African woman bioterrorism fighter Sheva Alomar, and many, many more.

## At last, black women are PCs

I play, therefore I am.

(Jason Callina et al., 2011)

As we have been observing, there is an interesting and obvious shift occurring in gaming's engagement with race. A striking case in point is the industry's discovery of black heroines as badass action-adventure types on the order of Lara Croft (*Tomb Raider*) and D'arci Stern (*Urban Chaos*). Now, black women, as well as other women of color, are feasible as MPCs and PCs in popular game series and franchises unlike in previous eras, except for Zelda, the enduring fantasy-adventure genre character. Among the dominant game companies leading in this practice are Capcom with its 2008 release of *Resident Evil 5* that features one kickass woman

MPC of African descent, Sheva Alomar, and Ubisoft, most recently, with its 2012 release of *Assassin's Creed* 3 (*AC3*)*: Liberation* featuring kickass black heroine number 2, Avenline de Grandpre, an African-French avenging assassin rampaging through a historic antebellum gameworld set in eighteenth-century New Orleans.

And though these powerful characters foreground race less stereotypically in some respects, online debates about the confluence of race and gender in popular gaming underscore aspects of these character formulations that redeploy stereotypical racial tropes and persistent reifications of black and other women/girls of color as gaming's ultimate outsiders, players, and characters alike. Nonetheless, it is important to acknowledge Sheva Alomar's and Avenline de Grandpre's departures from black female characters largely overrepresented as non-playable victims of gaming violence. As recent narrative agents in action-adventure, open-world, and first-person and third-person shooter genres in mainstream, casual, and online gaming spaces (including networked gaming such as Xbox Live), gaming's women of color characters are redefining the gaming experience in general, and in terms of twenty-first-century multicultural, multiracial, heroic character ideals in particular.

Alerting us to one particular instance of black women redefining their gaming experience is Kishonna L. Gray (2013) who investigates sexist and homophobic taunts and other oppressive gameplay practices within Xbox Live's various gaming communities. Centering on networked *Gears of War* I and *II*, and *Call of Duty* 4: *Modern Warfare* games, she considers how black and Puerto Rican women clans and guilds intentionally harass, disrupt, and interrupt normal gameplay progression through an oppositional play strategy Gray calls "collective resistance griefing." Their resistance occurs once male players in the session initiate racist and sexist social interactions, usually triggered by calling the women players "bitches," "spics," and "niggers" or by commenting derogatorily on their citizenship status.

Favored griefing tactics for the women are activating the *hardcore* play mode in *Call of Duty*, which permits the women to engage defensively in deliberate friendly-fire kills of as many of their own offending teammates as possible; to create lag and glitches; to enact virtual sit-ins, essentially doing nothing in-game beyond moving the cursor to avoid being booted off the network for inactivity (Gray, 2013). For these heterogeneous black women gamers (English and Spanish speaking, lesbian and straight), collective resistance griefing serves as a means of indulging their fangirl gaming pleasures while opposing oppressive interactions encountered on Xbox Live that Microsoft admins apparently failed to address, at least to their satisfaction. In fact, instead of the male perpetrators being suspended, they report that the complaining women were. Because the membership fees for Xbox Live are significant, the male majority gamers on the network were very upset with these women's acts of "resistance griefing," which was the point precisely. Offline, the women continued their protests and activism by creating websites and blogs to publicize the racial and sexual discrimination they routinely experienced on Xbox Live (Gray, 2013).

Another game engendering new modes of play with race and identity is *Sims 2* (Electronic Arts, 2004). Whereas *Sims* games permit sophisticated racial identity experimentation and commodification or racial tourism, to use Lisa Nakamura's (2000) terms, the game's expansion packs help fuel new creative expressions involving race through the wildly popular practice of machinima. One interesting conflict develops when we consider Cassandra Jones's critique of a 2008 *Sims 2*machinima text entitled "Run DMC *King of Rock* (*Sims 2*)" created by Rain Arenas. Produced in January 2008, it casts the African American rap artists Run DMC as white. Describing the text on YouTube (Figure 1), Arenas writes:

> It's hard to tell in the video, but all of the Sims are composed of Elvis Presley (which I had downloaded from www.modthesims2.com). *King of Rock* was and still is one of my favorite jams from RUN DMC, and the inspiration for this machinima music video.
>
> (Arenas, 2008)

Neither Arenas nor any of her viewers or subscribers was troubled by the racial swap. On the contrary, most assertions were "Love it!!" or "Cool." Returning to context, Cassandra Jones troubles this colorblind representational strategy by reminding us of an historical racial problematic attending this machinima modding approach and others of the ilk. It should not be forgotten that such representational economies participate in longstanding appropriations, subversions, and rip-offs of black artistry and cultural productions by white individuals and non-black business interests (Jones, 2011).

Race, as we have been considering, is a complex vector in contemporary gaming structures, narratives, and ludic practices. Coupled with the advent of new

*Figure 1* Whitening Run DMC: Rain Arenas' *Sims 2King of Rock* machinima

digital tools, racial affect engenders powerful participatory cultures of play and critique (Callina et al., 2011; Saylor, 2012; Midori237, n.d.). Leveraging the power of the web, gamers readily talk back to designers and programmers about their own takes on the phenomenon of new racial scripts in the gaming firmament. Most famous in this regard early on were the vociferous commentaries and condemnations that ensued when Capcom unveiled its *Resident Evil 5* game trailer at the 2007 E3 convention. That Capcom was unprepared for the controversy and reaction against its latest iteration of the lucrative *Resident Evil* franchise is telling.

A self-styled "American Geek," calling himself moviebob, like many others, rejected the company's unconvincing rationale of pitting its scantily clad, *one good black babe* heroine as a sufficient counterbalance to the horde of bad black Majini (evil spirit) boyz in the jungle conflict-narrative driving this game (moviebob, 2009). Also of interest here is how contemporary game designers, as well as and fans, engage charges of endemic sexism intertwined with both virulent and genteel or "cloaked" racism, to borrow Jesse Daniels's (2008) apt usage, in the gaming industry especially following the public relations debacle of Capcom's *Resident Evil 5* rollout.

Although moviebob is not alone in taking his condemning assessment of *Resident Evil 5* to the digital public sphere, not all commentary revolving around Capcom's black bombshell, Sheva Alomar (Figure 2), was derisive. One young black woman found the character a welcome contribution. Writing under the pseudonym Midori (from a video game character of the old PSX game *Evil Zone* (Titus Software, 1999)), Midori, a self-identified 22-year-old African-American woman was ecstatic after learning of the character's creation and narrative centrality to the game. She writes:

*Figure 2 Resident Evil 5*'s Sheva Alomar

Screen shot courtesy of http://electricblueskies.com.

[I] decided to click on *Resident Evil 5* . . . And omg one of the main characters is a BLACK WOMAN!!! I know this might not seem exciting to some but being a black woman myself, and a big fan of videogames I'm just stoked! We get no representation.

(Midori237, n.d.)

As stoked as Midori was, she had not abandoned all critical thinking regarding the representational economies at work in this character construct. She continues:

Anyway[,] her name is Sheva Alomar and she's absolutely gorgeous. I believe she's supposed to be from West Africa (she works for in an organization in West Africa) and she even has a tattoo on her arm that says "soldier" in Swahili. (Nevermind that Swahili is spoken in East Africa, not West) where she's supposed to be from. lol It's possible though and I guess we can't expect too much. lol. The symbol part of the tattoo is from West Africa, one of my friends has that tattooed on his arm. See the tattoo in the last image . . . it means "soldier." Isn't she stunning? It's about time a black woman is one of the leads in a videogame. First Obama, now Sheva . . . I don't know what to do with myself!:☺ lol

(Midori237, n.d.)

What is useful about Midori's 2009 post to her website (now defunct) that she calls "The Diary of Midori" is its tally of clearly-delineated black women PCs in video games that totaled approximately five to seven at that point. In addition to Sheva Alomar, the others she identifies are precursors including: Darci Stern from the *Urban Chaos* (Eidos Interactive, 1999) action game, with Stern imagined as a rival to Lara Croft in 1999 for the original PlayStation; Lisa Hamilton aka La Mariposa from the fighter game *Dead or Alive* (Tecmo, 1996); Fran, the non-human character, from *Final Fantasy VII* (Square, 1997); and Tanya from the *Mortal Kombat* brand. Like others online who interrogate the abysmal number of heroic black women characters in gaming, prolific vlogger, Essence of Truth is particularly compelling. Her YouTube channel is devoted to gaming, and she has produced upwards of 160 videos on her channel.

While Essence of Truth and Midori, among other black women social media creators, are serious about their online cultural activism and fan participation in gaming's networked cultures, business practices, and influential cultural capital, they do not seem to take themselves too seriously as their affective labor, and pleasure in being part of a web of social media communities of practice (Wenger, 2006) expresses unequivocally. Moreover, they are not in lockstep, and it is not clear if their social networks and collectives are intertwined at all.

What is clear about gaming's online participatory sectors is the emergence of savvy, passionate DIY citizen journalists who embrace new media's digital toolkits and open-source programs to enact some code breaking and compelling code-shifting (in the linguistic sense) in a process I am calling "gaming race." They clearly understand and master gaming's meaningful play structures and proceduralities (Salen and Zimmerman, 2005; Bogost, 2008), while subverting or refusing some of the suspect racial and downright racist interpellations or identifications many games encode. Issuing public correctives of and challenges to erroneous character designs is one such instance, as Midori demonstrates above by calling out Sheva Alomar's tattoo symbol in *Resident Evil 5*. Gaming race also occurs between gamers who face-off on Twitter and other fora when hotly contested views about race erupt and disrupt self-serving boasts of performance mastery usually concerned with cheat codes, disclosing secret powerups and Easter eggs, etc. in the no-longer homogeneous spaces comprising today's digital sandbox.

As troubling as the often virulent racist rants and intolerant speech are that inundate videogame fora, websites, and other media outlets that dare address the persistence and unacceptability of misogynist and racist representations and cultures in gaming, interesting examples of resistance and pushback are occurring. Moreover, it is important to stress that some of the conversations around race in gaming fora have become more nuanced and thoughtful since 2008.

### CJ's global progeny: *Assassin's Creed*'s black girl avenger, Orientalism 2.0, and *Grand Theft Auto V*

The phenomenal success of the *Grand Theft Auto* franchise (Figure 3) across racial and ethnic demographics has tracked closely with changing societal attitudes about race and difference for better and worse especially post-9/11, among other seismic cultural changes. For one thing, the rise of networked gaming and its stratified communities of practice have generated the good, the bad, and the ugly of online interactivity and participatory cultures. Whereas the good sees the instantiation of powerful people of color MPCs as exemplified by *AC3: Liberation*'s Avenline de Grandpre, whose narrative power and agency is somewhat curtailed by her temporal displacement to antebellum, pre-Revolutionary New Orleans. And, when considered in tandem with Sheva's strong playable buddy-role in *Resident Evil 5*, Aveline's solo heroic role marks a crucial turn in gaming's address to race.

Still, Ubisoft has moved gaming's multicultural, mixed-race, and transgender play options forward as evidenced in its guide to *AC3: Liberation* players. In its "Game Overview," Ubisoft writes: "No matter the persona you choose, you are Aveline. Wielding a machete, poison-dart blowpipe, and dueling pistols, you'll master all new ways to hunt down and eliminate your enemies-fighting for your beliefs, your people and your freedom." Returning to our consideration of context, it is not unreasonable to situate Aveline's mixed French and African heritage within a larger discursive ecology of socially-acceptable mixed-race populations in the US following President Obama's public embrace of his own mixed-race lineage, and the burgeoning academic study of mixed-race identity politics. Now,

*Figure 3  Grand Theft Auto V*

males of all racial and ethnic groups confess online to enjoying gameplay as a powerful black female MPC.

Be that as it may, Ubisoft is not alone in its push beyond the racial boundaries of normative whiteness in building its gameworld temporalities. This brings us to the bad in gaming. We have discussed already, for instance, a potent example of *bad* gaming practices and cultures experienced by women gamers of color playing *Call of Duty* on Xbox Live's online network (Gray, 2013). In our post-9/11 political environments, games companies are discovering Asian as well as Arab, Muslim, and other youths in the Middle East as new market and demographic shares and business opportunities to cultivate. Vit Sisler (2008) notes that digital Orientalism has long been a feature of fantasy and adventure games. But since 9/11 the complexity of Arab nations, the Islamic religion, and Muslim countries have been flattened out essentially into gaming's favored terrorist and Islamic extremist caricatures.

Game developers in the Middle East, Sisler (2008) explains, have in recent years begun to resist and counter such anti-Arab games such as *War in the Gulf* (Empire, 1993), *Delta Force* (NovaLogic, 1998), *Conflict: Desert Storm* (SCi Games, 2002), *Full Spectrum Warrior* (THQ, 2004), *Kuma/War* (Kuma Reality Games, 2004), and *Conflict: Global Terror* (SCi Games, 2005). To re-capture the hearts and minds of young Arabic and Muslim gamers from western media influences, Syrian and Lebanese game developers created *Special Force* (Solution, 2003), *Under Ash* (Dar al-Fikr, 2002), and *Under Siege* (Afkar Media, 2005), military games from their own national and ideological points of view. As Sisler (2008) puts it, "*Special Force* and *Under Ash* can be considered as the first attempts to participate in video games' construction of Arab and Muslim selfrepresentation [*sic*]."

Alternatively, games developer Mahmoud Khasawneh (2011) argues that Western game companies need to partner with Middle Eastern games companies to tap into this potentially highly lucrative market. With a region of more than 400 million people speaking a single language, Arabic, and with half of some populations under age 25, and highly tech-savvy, Khasawneh (2011) believes the

> Middle Eastern gaming industry is likely worth somewhere between $1 billion and $2.6 billion in terms of revenue across software and hardware. Western developers and publishers have the chance to successfully enter and influence a very green and receptive market, ready to be engaged and monetized.

Time will tell if gaming's address to race will move beyond some of the promising steps it has taken to attract larger and more racially, ethnically, gendered, and other diverse populations in the West and across the globe, as discussed here. Any cursory look at online fora devoted to these new racially-inclusive games reveals enthusiastic gamers embracing novel approaches to race and difference, as well as, unfortunately, persistent racial stereotypes. With Rockstar Games's long-awaited *Grand Theft Auto V* nearing release at the end of 2013, it will be interesting to see what CJ's progeny will portend for race and games in digital times.

## References

Aldama, F. L. (2012). Latinos and Video Games. In M. Wolf (Ed.), *The Encyclopedia of Video Games: The Culture, Technology and Art of Gaming* (pp. 356–360). Santa Barbara, CA: Greenwood.

Arenas, R. (2008). Run DMC *King of Rock* (*Sims* 2). YouTube, January 23. Retrieved April 13, 2013, from www.youtube.com/watch?v=ZvWdPi4vEf8.

Bogost, I. (2008). The Rhetoric of Video Games. In K. Salen (Ed.), *The Ecology of Games: Connecting Youth, Games, and Learning* (pp. 117–139). Cambridge, MA: The MIT Press.

Callina, J. D., Y. Wohn, H. Kim et al. (2011). Finally, a Black Female Protagonist in a Game. Play as Life. Digital Games as a Form of Play. Play as a Part of Life. Retrieved March 29, 2013, from www.playaslife.com.

Castillo, M. (2013). Video Games May Help Seniors Stay Healthier Emotionally, Physically. Retrieved March 14, 2013, from www.cbsnews.com.

Daniels, J. (2008) Race, Civil Rights, and Hate Speech in the Digital Era. In A. Everett (Ed.), *Learning Race and Ethnicity: Youth and Digital Media* (pp. 129–154). Cambridge, MA: The MIT Press.

De Mul, J. (2005). The Game of Life: Narrative and Ludic Identity Formation in Computer Games. In J. Raessens and J. Goldstein (Eds.), *Handbook of Computer Game Studies* (pp. 251–266). Cambridge, MA: The MIT Press.

Everett, A. (2005). Serious Play: Playing with Race in Contemporary Gaming Culture. In J. Raessens and J. Goldstein (Eds.), *Handbook of Computer Game Studies* (pp. 311–326). Cambridge, MA: The MIT Press.

Fox, Z. (2012). Forget Generation Y: 18- to 34-Year Olds Are Now "Generation C." Retrieved March 15, 2013, from www.mashable.com.

Gray, K. L. (2013) Collective Organizing, Individual Resistance, or Asshole Griefers? An Ethnographic Analysis of Women of Color in Xbox Live. *Ada: A Journal of Gender, New Media, & Technology*, Issue 2: Feminist Game Studies, June.

Jones, C. (2011). Collapsing/Eliding of Otherness in *Sims 2*Machinima. From Digital/ Media, Race, Affect and Labor Conference, Bowling Green State University, OH.

Keller, L. (2009). Racist Backlash Greets President Barack Obama. Southern Poverty Law Center, Spring 2009 (33). Retrieved March 22, 2013, from www.splcenter.org.

Khasawneh, M. (2011). Untapped Opportunity: Exploring the Arab Video Game Notice. Retrieved April 30, 2013, from www.mashable.com/2011/03/04/arab-world-video-games/.

Marriott, M. (1999, October 21). Blood, Gore, Sex and Now, Race: Are Game Makers Creating Convincing New Characters or "High-Tech Blackface"? *New York Times*, pp. D7.

Midori237. (n.d.) "My Opinion" and "The Diary of Midori." Retrieved April 13, 2013, from www.wordpress.com.

Moviebob. (2009). Gameoverthinker V23. Retrieved August 8, 2011, from www.youtube. com/watch?v=DhopxZqQrmo.

Nakamura, L. (2000). Where Do You Want to Go Today? Cybernetic Tourism, the Internet, and Transnationality. In B. Kolko and L. Nakamura, and G.B. Rodman (Eds.), *Race in Cyberspace* (pp. 15–26). New York: Routledge.

Nauert, R. (2012). Video Games Hold Promise for Healthy Aging. Retrieved February 19, 2013, from http://psychcentral.com/.

Richard, B. and J. Zaremba. (2005). Gaming With Girls: Looking for Sheroes in Computer Games. In J. Raessens and J. Goldstein (Eds.), *Handbook of Computer Game Studies* (pp. 283–300). Cambridge, MA: The MIT Press.

Salen, K. and E. Zimmerman. (2005). Game Design and Meaningful Play. In J. Raessens and J. Goldstein (Eds.), *Handbook of Computer Game Studies* (pp. 59–80). Cambridge, MA: MIT Press.

Saylor, E. (2012). Latinos Drive Video Game Sales. Retrieved February 19, 2013, from http://blogviacom.com.

Sisler, V. (2008). Digital Arabs: Representation in Video Games. Retrieved April 30, 2013, from www. digitalislam.eu/article.do?articleId=1704.

Wenger, E. (2006). Communities of Practice: A Brief Introduction. Retrieved June 25, 2013, from www.ewenger.com/theory.

# Part 7

# PLAY, CONTROL, AND THE MAGIC CIRCLE

# 54

# THE ASSEMBLAGE OF PLAY

## T. L. Taylor

Source: *Games and Culture*, 4(4), 2009, 331–339.

### Abstract

This article explores the notion of assemblage for computer game studies. Drawing on this framework, the author proposes a multi-faceted methodological approach to the study of games and the play experience. Drawing on user-created mods (modifications) in the game *World of Warcraft* and an analysis of a raid encounter there, a discussion is undertaken about the relationship between technological artifacts, game experience, and sociality. Primary to the consideration is an argument for the centralizing the *interrelation* of a variety of actors and nodes when analyzing lived play in computer games.

The field of computer games research has undergone dramatic growth and expansion since some of those first explorations into the specificities of digital play early scholars tackled (Aarseth, 1997; Jenkins & Fuller, 1995; Murray, 1998; Turkle, 1984). There are certainly many ways to tell this early history. One familiar approach is to emphasize the ways games were taken seriously as systems and analyzed as artifacts in their own right. Rules, mechanics, and the deep structure of the game were finally given precise analytic attention. And of course, there is the oft-seen counterposing stance to try and understand games as narrative structures, story worlds to be inhabited and explored. This debate itself has been now unpacked, undone, and revisited (Copier, 2003; Frasca, 2003). Rather than tread into that thicket (it probably deserves a rest), I want to propose another branch of computer game studies history we would be remiss to forget, if for no other reason that it seems to so strongly inform the field at this moment. Running nearly parallel to the familiar track of the classic narratology/ludology framing has been scholarship that sought to understand actual players and their everyday practices, as well as research that considered broader structural contexts and histories at work in the construction of play (to name only just a few see, e.g., Burke, 2002; Carr, 2005; Humphreys, 2003; Jakobsson & Taylor, 2003; Kennedy, 2006; Malaby, 2007; Mortensen, 2000; Postigo, 2003; Simon, 2005; Steinkuehler, 2006; Sun, Lin, & Ho, 2003; Williams, Caplan, & Xiong, 2007; Yee, 2002). Without dredging up a new fault line, or trying to crudely glue together system, narrative, and player, might we find a framework to not only include these parts but also makes way for others and their interrelations?

The notion of assemblage is one way to help us understand the range of actors (system, technologies, player, body, community, company, legal structures, etc.), concepts, practices, and relations that make up the play moment.[1] Games, and their play, are constituted by the interrelations between (to name just a few) technological systems and software (including the imagined player embedded in them), the material world (including our bodies at the keyboard), the online space of the game (if any), game genre, and its histories, the social worlds that infuse the game and situate us outside of it, the emergent practices of communities, our interior lives, personal histories, and aesthetic experience, institutional structures that shape the game and our activity as players, legal structures, and indeed the broader culture around us with its conceptual frames and tropes. While looking at a game as it is presented as a boxed product may tell us something about the given structure of the artifact or its imagined player, understanding it as a lived object— as a playful artifact—comes via an attention to the assemblage that constructs our actual games and play.

Certainly this is an ambitious framework as it calls the researcher to pay attention to a number of parts interwoven in complex ways at particular historical moments. Indeed as Rabinow (2003) notes regarding assemblages, "They are not yet an experimental system in which controlled variation can be produced, measured, and observed. They are comparatively effervescent, disappearing in years or decades rather than centuries" (p. 56). While in the field assemblages can seem as if they are always somewhat eluding us, giving us glimpses of the whole but often leaving us feeling like we never fully capture it, the conceptual orientation this turn provides is invaluable. Centrally important is the embedded notion of the *interrelation* of the agents and processes that emerge through them. As Seth Giddings (2006) argues in his very interesting work on the subject, "We are no longer looking at just a 'technology' and its 'users' but the event of their relationships, of their reciprocal configuration" (p. 160). In the space of interrelations lie the dynamic processes of play. Thinking about games as assemblage, wherein many varying actors and unfolding processes make up the site and action, allows us to get into the nooks where fascinating work occurs; the flows between system and player, between emergent play and developer revisions, between practices and player produced software modifications, between local (guild) communities and broader (server) cultures, between legal codes, designer intentions, and everyday use practices, between contested forms of play, between expectation and contextualization.

However, rather than force a cataloguing at the outset the constituents of an assemblage that should be then tracked down for any given analysis, we might fruitfully pull from the artistic instantiation of the technique and weave it with an ethnographic sensibility which seeks out "found objects" from everyday life. This notion of assemblage is then deeply interwoven with the contextual analysis of games and play, one which situates them within their specific interrelations and practices. While we may have hunches or gut feelings about lines to follow, we very often do not know in advance of our arrival in the field (however defined) what we might find, what actors are present, what practices we will encounter, what meaning systems will be in operation. One of the tasks of the games researcher interested in the contextual nature of play—in its assemblage—is in exploring the everyday, the mundane, the "found objects" that construct it.

In arguing for such an approach, we can see then that computer games are not simply the packaged products that come off the shelf (or tucked neatly into the downloaded executable) but artifacts that traverse multiple communities of practice and can hold multiple, often contested, meanings. Bowker and Star (1999) have written about boundary objects, suggesting that they "are both plastic enough to adapt to local needs and constraints of the several parties emptying them, but robust enough to maintain a common identity across sites" (p. 297). I find this a useful starting hook in thinking about what a computer game is. They (and here I mean both their underlying mechanics and often their technology) are extended and altered by a range of actors, from designers, marketing departments, publishers, legal teams, and players and indeed traverse a variety of communities of practice. What makes the notion of boundary objects so useful for game studies is that we are then able to look at a particular object (be it an MMOG or console game) and analyze then the ways provisional agreements, or at the minimum imagined communities, form around specific artifacts simultaneous to the varying understandings and practices with the object (sometimes ones that are quite contested, for example, in the case of MMOG account sharers and legal teams of game publishers). This approach evokes something along the lines of what Bowker and Star (1999) call an "ecological understanding" of phenomena which I would argue resonates with assemblage.

There are many ways to think about entering into this conceptual framework and I will only focus on one in particular here. An angle that might prompt us to resist a simple system-user/game-player notion and adopt such an approach is a consideration of how we are interwoven with our technologies and how they may at times come to act as a kind of independent agent we play alongside (Giddings, 2007; Kennedy & Giddings, 2008). I was struck by this most directly through my time raiding in Blizzard's massively multiplayer online game (MMOG) *World of Warcraft* and watching the ways player-produced modifications (mods) were deployed. One in particular, CTRaidAssist (CTRA) enacted a wide range of functionality in managing raid and boss monster encounters.[2] WoW's user interface (UI) mods do not simply add polish to the interface but can radically reconfigure play (for more on this see Taylor, 2006). They can stand in and do work for us, monitoring our play, automating actions, providing key information, and in general facilitating a range of both mundane and complex action. Sometimes, however, they also seem to escape our grasp and I would argue that it is in this experience with such mods and that we can find a node that not only tells us something about how a particular game works but highlights a larger conceptual intervention around how play is constituted in computer games.

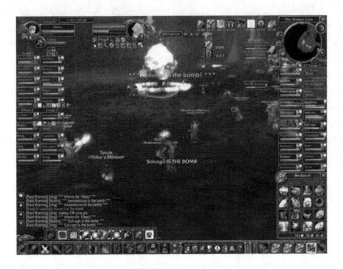

*Figure 1* Screenshot of the Baron Geddon event with modded UI.

One powerful example of this is watching how CTRA works in the Baron Geddon encounter in Molten Core.[3] During the event, a player is, in essence, turned into a bomb which will detonate, injuring them and anyone around. When this happens, the person needs to move away from others so as to minimize the impact on the group. Normally the player will see a single text message in their chat window when they are transformed but CTRA develops this in a fascinating way. It broadcasts to everyone using the mod (which is often a mandatory requirement for participation[4]) an urgent warning in the center of the game screen [see Figure 1].

On one hand, the mod is simply translating information buried in a player's own UI and representing it. However experientially, this is a moment in which the mod comes to stand as a kind of autonomous agent, the 41st member of the raid. The collective use of the mod seems to evoke a new member to the group. CTRA calls out to the party valuable information—indeed if you are the bomb, it shouts (textually) to you directly, "You are the bomb!".[5] Certainly, the first time you see it in action it can be thrilling and a bit of a surprise—indeed you may not have even known what this technology you are using was going to do in advance.[6] Without the mod, it is common for a member of the raid to do the work of typing out the information in a chat channel or speaking it over a voice server, but here the mod takes over, it stands alongside the players—sometimes simply facilitating their actions, sometimes acting as a kind of additional member to the group. A "distribution of competences between humans and nonhumans" (Latour, 1992, p. 233) is at work here, not only between an individual member and their mods but among the competencies of the group as a whole and their collective use of various software.

This software actor is a somewhat ambiguous member, of course. If one looks at the chat window it is a designated player (typically the raid leader) that calls out the information, though they are actually typing nothing themselves. Their machine, channeling the mod, has taken over that action. If one looks at the rest of the screen, however, the words appear almost out of thin air. There is an always present double nature to the mod's autonomy. Indeed all raid commands in CTRA are like this, anchored to a human actor in the chat channel but in the other part of the screen spoken as if from this 41st member. And there is no necessary privilege to the "voice" of the "real" player in the chat channel. Indeed in heavy action intensive moments, it is not uncommon for players to totally miss what is happening in that part of the screen, which is at least part of the reason mods like CTRA pipe information to other places in the visual field, typically making them more prominent (and sometimes accompanied by sound). In those moments, the raid leader's commands in the chat channel may go unheeded until "spoken" by the mod.

The setup for the system is, however, not perfect, not necessarily totalizing. Someone might participate without the mod and to them,[7] in their experience of the game world, there is no extra nonhuman member tagging along, assisting play, and issuing commands to them in the center of their screen. Experientially the player without CTRA will be not only outside of the technological system at work for the other players, they will also be outside of a *social system* in operation. This has profound implications not only for our analysis of a game and a play moment, but how we more generally understand the objects of our inquiry.

It is also the case that our fellow nonhuman actors can be unreliable at times, breaking down at inopportune moments. It is not uncommon for a mod to not broadcast what it is supposed to, for it to be improperly synched to an event (thereby giving misleading information), for some players to be using an older version that no longer "talks" to either the game or newer versions of itself (and thus by extension other players). In such moments, players often have to sort out the glitches in the various instantiations of game experience that may be happening simultaneously. Decisions are made if the gaps are so important that action needs to be taken (sometimes everyone has to log off and get an update of the mod) or if human players can simply step in and, in a poignant full-circle move, take over the now-failed action of the nonhuman (mod) actor (as when a raid leader will start calling out instructions for running, removing a curse, switching targets).

Frameworks that divide up the gaming moment into structure (or narrative) and player seem to me incapable of fully dealing with the kind of delegation or translation work (Latour, 1992) we see in these simple examples. It is not simply a technological issue (or failure). We can see a complex set of relationships between not only the player and their software, but the *collective* use of software and the production of *group practices*. And though I will not delve into it here in detail, there is a corresponding reverse move in the ways we at times act as translation devices, as delegates, for our computer games (Giddings, 2007; Kennedy & Giddings, 2008). We do not simply play but are played. We do not simply configure but are configured (Akrich, 1995; Woolgar, 1991). In the long run, this is not meant to be a one way descriptive street but instead an approach that suggests a circuit of relations that runs across a number of actors, human and non, conceptual and material. Here, we begin to get at another useful notion, that of the ways nonhuman actors—and I am not simply talking about nonplayer characters (NPC) which is where we might normally begin, and end, with such a notion—help constitute the "missing mass" that orders the play experience (Latour, 1992). I would argue that contextual, assemblage-based, approaches that take into account this range of agents (human, nonhuman, social, institutional) and their interrelations will better equip us for our analyses of computer games.

Finally, while the notion of assemblage may open up productive terrain for understanding our various field sites, we might also reflect on how it can fold back upon us in complex ways. In the same moments the players and games we study are situated in a complex matrix of actors, as a researcher-player we also become configured by these technologies and practices. They shape our experience of the space and our data. As we embody ourselves digitally, participate in modding our own UIs, inhabit specific server communities—all the grainy specificity of our work—we are ourselves embedded in a particular assemblage of play. We do not stand outside of it. This is not to call for trying to methodologically construct some "pure" space for us to occupy, but more clear-eyed acknowledgement and discussion about our location within this matrix and the ways game players, mechanics, and technologies are our co-conspirators—or resistant interlocutors—in the field.

## Acknowledgement

The authors thank Anne Beaulieu, Tim Burke, and Thomas Malaby for helpful feedback and pointers.

## Declaration of conflicting interests

The author declare that they do not have any conflict of interest.

## Funding

The author received no financial support for the research and/or authorship of this article.

## Notes

1  I am very loosely using the term assemblage—sometimes anchored in the work of science technology scholars, sometimes tied to the work of Deleuze and Guattari (1987), sometimes grounded in a particular form of artistic practice—to prompt an alternate heuristic for analysis. For an excellent broader discussion of this approach and a more general application of Actor Network Theory to game studies, see Giddings, 2006.
2  CTRA is actually much less used now than when I first undertook this research. There are a growing number of mods regularly used now that do very similar (and additional) work including oRA, BigWigs, X-Perl, and Omen Threat Meter.

3 At the time of my research on this subject, it was a 40-person raid event so I will speak of it here as such. For an excellent description of a guild's experience with raiding Molten Core, see Mark Chen's article "Cooperation, Coordination, and Camaraderie in *World of Warcraft*" in *Games and Culture* (Chen, in press).

4 As Latour (1992) notes of cars and their mandatory seatbelts, "It has become logically— no, it has become sociologically—impossible to drive without wearing a belt. I cannot be bad anymore. I, plus the car, plus the dozens of patented engineers, plus the police are making me be moral" (p. 226). Indeed it is regularly through mods that not only is an idealized player (and set of practices) is constructed but that not using them is nearly unthinkable to many raiders.

5 One cannot help but be reminded of Latour's car commanding him to buckle his seatbelt.

6 What is striking is how often players install things that they may not fully anticipate the ramifications of. In this regard, I have written elsewhere (Taylor, 2006) about this mod and its surveillant qualities.

7 You can generally tell who has the mod installed and who does not (that ability is built in and is part and parcel of its surveillant character). Aside the instances in which the mod triggers something in a general common channel, the nonmodded player would have no direct experience of the additional layer at work.

# References

Aarseth, E. (1997). Cybertext: Perspectives on Ergodic Literature. Baltimore, MD: The Johns Hopkins University Press.

Akrich, M. (1995). User representations: Practices, methods and sociology. In A. Rip, T. J. Misa & J. Schot (Eds.), *Managing technology in society: The approach of constructive technology assessment*. London: Pinter Publishers.

Bowker, G. C. and Star, S. L. (1999). Sorting Things Out: Classification and Its Consequences. Cambridge, MA: The MIT Press.

Burke, T. (2002). Rubicite breastplate priced to move, cheap: How virtual economies become real simulations. Game culture conference, University of West England, Bristol.

Carr, D. (2005). Contexts, gaming pleasures, and gendered preferences. *Simulation & Gaming, 36*, 464–482.

Chen, M. (2009). Cooperation, coordination, and camaraderie in *World of Warcraft. Games and Culture, 4(1)*, 47–73.

Copier, M. (2003). *The other game researcher, Digital games research association conference proceedings*. Utrecht, The Netherlands.

Deleuze, G., & Guattari, F. (1987). *A thousand plateaus: Capitalism and schizophrenia*. (B. Massumi Trans.). Minneapolis: University of Minnesota Press.

Frasca, G. (2003). *Ludologists love stories too: Notes from a debate that never took place*. Digital games research association conference proceedings, Utrecht, The Netherlands.

Giddings, S. (2006). *Walkthrough: Videogames and technocultural form*. PhD dissertation, University of the West of England, Bristol.

Giddings, S. (2007). Dionysiac machines: Videogames and the triumph of the simulacra. *Convergence, 13*, 417–431.

Humphreys, S. (2003). Online multi-user games: Playing for real. *Australian journal of communication, 30*, 79–91.

Jakobsson, M., & Taylor, T. L. (2003). *The Sopranos meets EverQuest: Socialization processes in massively multiuser games*. Digital arts and culture conference, Melbourne, Australia.

Jenkins, H., & Fuller, M. (1995). Nintendo and new world travel writing: A dialogue. In S. G. Jones (Ed.), *Cybersociety: Computer-mediated communication and community.* Thousand Oaks: SAGE Publications.

Kennedy, H. (2006). Illegitimate, monstrous and out there: Female *Quake* players and inappropriate pleasures. In J. Hollows & R. Moseley (Eds.), *Feminism in popular culture.* London: Berg.

Kennedy, H., & Giddings, S. (2008). Little Jesuses & fuck-off robots: Aesthetics, cybernetics, and not being very good at Lego *Star Wars.* In M. Swalwell & J. Wilson (Eds.), *The pleasures of computer gaming: Essays on cultural history, theory and aesthetics.* Jefferson, NC: McFarland.

Latour, B. (1992). Where are the missing masses? The sociology of a few mundane artifacts. In W. E. Bijker & J. Law (Eds.), *Shaping technology/building society.* Cambridge, MA: The MIT Press.

Malaby, T. (2007). Beyond play: A new approach to games. *Games and Culture, 2,* 95–113.

Mortensen, T. (2000). *Playing with players: Creative participation in online games.* Digital arts and culture conference, Bergen, Norway.

Murray, J. (1998). *Hamlet on the holodeck: The future of narrative in cyberspace.* Cambridge, MA: The MIT Press.

Postigo, H. (2003). From *Pong* to *Planet Quake*: Post-industrial transitions from leisure to work. *Information, Communication & Society, 6,* 593–607.

Rabinow, P. (2003). *Anthropos today: Reflections on modern equipment.* Princeton University Press.

Simon, B. (2005). *The gamer and the case mod: Socio-material play and expression in the LAN Party.* Digital games research association conference proceedings, Vancouver, Canada.

Steinkuehler, C. (2006). The mangle of play. *Games and Culture, 1,* 199–213.

Sun, C. -T., Lin, L., & Ho, C. -H. (2003). *Game tips as gifts: Social interactions and rational calculations in computer gaming.* Digital games research association conference proceedings, Utrecht, The Netherlands.

Taylor, T. L. (2006). Does *WoW* change everything? How a PvP Server, multinational player-base, and surveillance mod scene caused me pause. *Games and Culture, 1,* 1–20.

Turkle, S. (1984). *The second self: Computers and the human spirit.* New York: Simon and Schuster.

Williams, D., Caplan, S., & Xiong, L. (2007). Can you hear me now? The impact of voice in an online gaming community. *Human Communication Research, 33,* 427–449.

Woolgar, S. (1991). Configuring the user: The case of usability trials. In J. Law (Ed.), *A sociology of monsters: Essays on power, technology and domination.* London: Routledge.

Yee, N. (2002). *The Daedalus project.* http://www.nickyee.com/index-daedalus.html. Retrieved 27 July 2009.

# 55

# COMING TO PLAY AT
# FRIGHTENING YOURSELF

## Welcome to the world of horror video games

### *Bernard Perron*

Source: *Aesthetics of Play: A Conference on Computer Game Aesthetics* (Norway: University of Bergen, 2005), available at http://www.aestheticsofplay.org/perron.php.

In response to critics of supernatural horror tales, H.P. Lovecraft commenced his now famous work of literature with this incisive reply:

> The appeal of the spectrally macabre is generally narrow because it demands from the reader a certain degree of imagination and a capacity for detachment from everyday life. Relatively few are free enough from the spell of the daily routine to respond to tappings from outside, and tales of ordinary feelings and events, or of common sentimental distortions of such feelings and events, will always take first place in the taste of the majority . . . ([1927] 1973: 12).

Reformulated nowadays, Lovecraft might as easily have suggested that the appeal of the spectrally macabre demands that one plays its game. Because, while it is true that all genres are characterized by a set of pre-established conventions that generate a certain number of more or less precise expectations stimulating a certain reflexive game of guesswork and recognition, the horror genre might be the one that has been most often compared to a game. Dealing with the industrialization of fear, Ruth Amossy has notably stated that the «art to frighten» is openly presented as a ludic activity, its stereotypes being direction signs that «announce at the entry and at critical points of the fictional terror: "All those that enter here accept to surrender to the dizziness of fear"» (Amossy, 1991: 142, freely translated). Many film scholars have made references to a game analogy in order to explain contemporary horror cinema. Vera Dika has shown in *Games of Terror* how the Stalker film formula of the 80's placed the spectator in a condition «less like watching a tennis match, for example, than like playing a video game» because it involves an interaction with both the narrative and the formal elements (1990: 22). In *Planks of Reason: Essays on the Horror Film*, Morris Dickstein emphasized that «the main

181

point of a horror film is to frighten us or rather to play on our fears (1984: 65, underlined by the author), whereas Dennis Giles explained that certain «viewers displace themselves from the fiction by laughter, intentionally misreading the emotional cues of the text, refusing to play by the rules of its game» (1984: 41).

Insofar as the contemporary horror film was already playful and "interactive", it was then just a short step to remediate cinematic conventions and effects, and to make horror video games. Looking at it from this perspective, the survival horror genre might be the game genre most often compared to film. From *Resident Evil* (Capcom/Capcom, 1996) to *Resident Evil 4* (Capcom/Capcom, 2005), the «challenging cinematic gameplay» (*RE1*) and the «game's movielike feel» (*RE4*) have been for example underlined by the Gamespot.com's reviewers. It is as a «cinematic horror experience» (box sets of *SH1*, 1999 and *SH2*, 2001) that the *Silent Hill* series (Konami/Konami) has been advertised. Speaking of these two series, Steven Poole reasoned:

> Why is it particularly the horror genre, and to a lesser extent science-fiction, that largely provides the aesthetic compost for supposedly "filmlike" videogames? ( . . . . ) The answer is that horror genre can easily do away with character and plot; it is the detail of the monster, the rhythm of the tension and shocks that matter. Plot and characters are things videogames find very difficult to deal with (2000: 79).

Indeed, the connection between horror film and game remains obvious. It's for this reason that one has to acknowledge yet again their similarities and differences to better expose the specificity of the video game which, to agree with Tanya Krzywinska's contention, «is organised to intensify and extend the types of emotional and affective experiences offered by the horror film» (2002: 207).

It's worth stating from the outset that in spite of the detail of its monsters, its tension and its shocks, horror video games do not have much to do with "horror" itself. In fact, like Steven Jay Schneider rather relevantly observed in «Toward an Aesthetics of Cinematic Horror», a small number of contemporary films (post-1960) actually succeeded in horrifying entire audiences. Schneider quotes philosopher Robert C. Solomon explaining that «horror "is an extremely unpleasant and even traumatizing emotional experience which renders the subject/victim helpless and violates his or her most rudimentary expectations about the world"» (2004: 135). Horror, as opposed to fear, is a spectator emotion that sees one aghast.[1] Although extreme graphic violence does not guarantee to qualify images as horrifying, it remains true that the 3-D design of games lacks the photorealism of cinema. It lacks the *that-has-been* (*ça-a-été*) which is the essence of photography for Barthes (1980) and which would place us in a pure spectator position.[2] Even the few interactive horror movies have never reached this essence as their video pixilation and/or the actors in front of obviously rendered backgrounds were creating a certain distanciation, distanciation manifest in current 3-D imagery. There might be some revolting moments, such as a woman's slaughter by means of a spade to the mouth in Chapter Four of *Phantasmagoria* (Sierra/Sierra, 1995) [Figure 1], but not horrifying ones.[3]

What horror video games—labelled survival or not—actually offer is similar to what the mainstream contemporary horror cinema proffers. To refer to the well-known expression of Isabel Pinedo, it's a «bounded experience of fear» (1996: 25 and 2004: 106). This bounded dimension explains in part the famous paradox of horror. According to Pinedo: Horror is an exercise in recreational terror, a simulation of danger not unlike a roller coaster ride. Like the latter, people in a confined space are kept off-balance through the use of suspense and precipitous surprises achieved by alternating between seeing what lies ahead and being in the dark (for instance, tunnels and other shadowy regions, closed and shielded eyes). Throughout, the element of control, the conviction that there is nothing to be afraid of, turns stress/arousal (beating heart, dry mouth, panic grip) into a pleasure sensation. Fear and pleasure commingle (2004: 106).

Pinedo further notes that although the violation and death of the body is only experienced partially, although the danger fails to materialize, we fear the threat of physical danger. «The experience of terror is bounded by the tension between proximity and distance, reality and illusion» (2004: 107). In Caillois's ludic terms, we would say that we are aware of the second reality and freely devote ourselves to it. In Murray's terms, we would emphasize that we are actively creating beliefs. For instance, we've all seen a horror movie scene like the one at the beginning of *The Grudge* (Takashi Shimizu, 2004): in a house that suddenly gives you the creeps, a young and innocent nurse hears odd sounds coming from the dark attic. Even if she is on her own, in a place she does not know and only has a lighter to guide her later on, the nurse decides to go investigating. If we are questioning why she chooses not to flee, then we displace ourselves from the fiction, and the effects of the scene will be lost. But as horror spectators we are willing to properly read the emotional

*Figure 1  Phantasmagoria* (Sierra/Sierra, 1995)

cues of the text. Even if we are seated in a theatre, feeling safety in numbers, we choose to go along with the character – who is going to move forward in any case (we are in a ride!) – and become scared. A similar scene will not play on our fears in the same way as in the case of a single player game where we are sitting playing alone in the dark. Since we are in control of our avatar (or point of view), the analogy with the old haunted house that one has to walk-through – as opposed to those where we are seated in a doom buggy – obviously better suits the horror video game than the relentless forward ride of a roller coaster.[4] Even if we follow a path, we are made to feel that we are actively exploring a place. We could choose to make a bolt for it, but that would not bring us far in the game and sometimes it's not even an option, sometimes there is no escape, for example when the avatar is locked in a room with no obvious way out. Although we might judge the film character's curiosity, in playing the game we are required to be inquisitive, in so far as there might be a key, an item or a door where the odd sound is emanating from.[5] That's what's happening continuously in the *Silent Hill* series which is filled with eerie, growling and shrieking sounds that make us hesitate before moving forward. But we remain aware that we are in a game, actively playing it. That is why it is essential to nuance the reflection in the March 2005 issue of the *Edge* magazine about «Scare Tactics»:

> Games that want to capitalise on their ability to hurt you in the real world can only do it by threatening loss of progress and repetition, and that repetition invariability dulls the fright of the horror that the game has in store for you. It's an issue that undermines many of the most successful frighteners ever made. *Fatal Frame 2*, from the moment the first ghost hand slips on to Mio's shoulder, does a master job of creating a sickening, threatening world. But the moment you become more concerned about finding a save point than finding your sister, all that atmospheric effort becomes irrelevant. Replaying sections of *Doom 3* has all the terror of a fairground duck shoot as you wait for zombies to shamble into place. All too often, the interactivity of games can undermine their scariness, rather than enhance it (Editorial team, 2005: 70).

*Ringu*-evil-killer-types of videotape, we must acknowledge, exists only in fiction. If danger was to actually materialise, there would certainly be less gamers of the night. Nevertheless, the playmood is labile in its very nature (Huizinga). A game can bore us or frustrate us. We can perceive it only as a map or a system, and only think about «gameplay consequences». Pure repetition or discovered algorithms indeed destroy the frightening moments, not even transforming surprise into suspense. But again, more than any other genre, horror is an experiential route[6] best lived in the course of its first walk-through. Besides, horror video games are mainly story-driven ones. As long as we're caught up in the experience, it does not really change anything to find as in *Clock Tower 3* (Sunsoft/Capcom, 2003) a place to hide from a stalker [Figure 2], a place that will enable us to overpower or distract the aforementioned monster in order to escape from it [Figure 3], or a point to save our game (or to refill the bottle of Holy Water) [Figure 4].

184

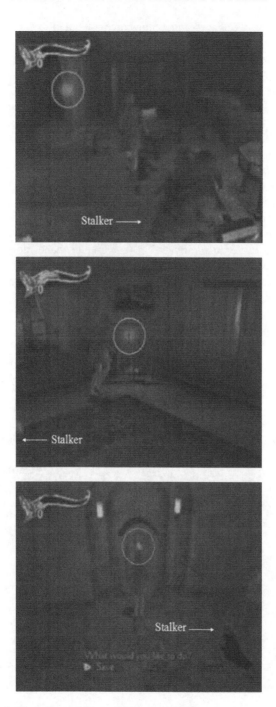

*Figures 2 – 3 – 4  Clock Tower 3* (Sunsoft/Capcom, 2003)

While the first two places and actions are associated to the second reality of the game-world (intradiegetic) and the third one more related to the first reality of playing a game (extradiegetic), they all bring a great relief upon our nightmarish journey.[7]

The paradox of horror also depends upon the fact that ludic fright elicits real fear. We will startle, as we've all experienced, upon a sudden burst whether it be in real life, in a film or in a game. Everyone who has played *Resident Evil* (1996) remembers the effect of the dogs bursting through windows while we are crossing a corridor at the beginning of the game. In addition, like Scissorman's sudden blow to the security guard just before the heroine Jennifer Simpson goes back into the university research building [Figure 5], few cinematics of *Clock Tower* (Human Corporation/ASCII Entertainment, 1997) are still very effective today.

However that may be, our real reactions are not merely automatic responses. As far as cognition and emotion work together, fear and its physiological responses (changes in heart rate, respiration, skin temperature, hand moistness, muscular tension, etc.) depend on the ways a real or a fictive situation is appraised. Noël Carroll has quite pertinently shown in his famous thought theory of emotional responses to fiction how those responses do «not require the beliefs that the things that move us be actual. We can be moved by prospects that we imagine» (1990: 88). We are returning here to Lovecraft's opening quotation. Fear is broadly conceived as a negative emotion related to the perception of a threat. When we become aware of a danger, we are knocked off-balance. We start to anticipate what could happen next and to begin to dread that the threat might materialize itself. It might finally be when we are afraid that we are telling ourselves the greatest short scary stories. At the moment we hear odd sounds coming from the attic at the beginning of *The Grudge*, we start to imagine what might happen to the young nurse. Our fear is rooted in the fictional world and is linked to the nurse's behaviour.

*Figure 5 Clock Tower* (Human Corporation/ASCII Entertainment, 1997)

But as I have explained elsewhere (Perron, 2005), the emotional experience of games does not revolve around those kinds of fiction and witness emotions. We are playing games for *gameplay emotions*, emotions arising from our actions in the game-world and the consequent reactions of the game(-world). Fear is in that sense a very suitable gameplay emotion.

Emotions are action tendencies. They prompt us to establish, maintain, or disrupt a relationship with the environment. To refer once more to Solomon as quoted by Schneider, fear is not the same thing as horror. Fear has an action-orienting quality that the latter spectator emotion is missing. While the "gawking impulse" of horror leads us to contemplation or fixation, there is an inherent urge to act when we are scared (Schneider, 2004: 140). Fear is by and large manifested by the impulse to move, to run away. On the one hand, fear has a strong action tendency because it is clearly object-oriented. We might not agree with the overall relevance of Carroll's art-horror definition since it does not deem fear as central to the horror genre, but it is easy to accept his focus in regards to horror video games. Because, from encounters with «giant hairy tarantulas, vampire bats and menacing ghost» (Atari's *Haunted House* box set) to battles with «Host of Evil Ghouls and Terrifying Spirits» (*Clock Tower 3* box set) or with «creatures that defy the laws of nature» (*Resident Evil 4* box set) [Figure 6], from the «more ghastly apparitions to vanquish» (*Fatal Frame 2* box set) [Figure 7] to the not to be ignored boss confrontations, the figure of the monster is at the core of the videoludic experience of fright.

Designed as disgusting entities, the monsters of horror video games are dangerous. On the action level, they are physically threatening because they are lethal and have the power to maim and to kill. On the narrative level, they become psychological, moral or social menaces by their attempt to destroy one's identity and moral order. Horror video games ask for cognitive engagement, in order to, in

*Figure 6 Resident Evil 4* (Capcom/Capcom, 2005)

*Figure 7* Fatal *Frame 2* (Tecmo/Tecmo, 2003)

Carroll's terms, discover those impure, disgusting and scary monsters, and imaginative engagement to speculate about what they might be like and how they might be managed and destroyed.[8] On the other hand, fear is goal-oriented. Afraid, we want to disrupt the relationship with the monsters. In that sense, horror video games can be seen as a mutated form of recreational terror, a form where the simulation of danger, stressed by Pinedo, has evolved so as to become increasingly genuine. We do not feel fear by empathizing with a character as we do in film, and as we did in interactive horror movies. Once we've pointed-and-clicked on the haunted bed in the first chapter of *Phantasmagoria* for example, we couldn't try to make Adrienne escape the hands that were suddenly grabbing her. We could only watch until the end of the sequence. But if we could have been in command of our avatar, we would have experienced the action on a personal level as we do with game real-time controls. Games are simulation, not representation. Following Frasca: «Simulation does not simply retain the – generally audiovisual – characteristics of the object but it also includes a model of its behaviours. This model reacts to certain stimuli (input data, pushing buttons, joystick movements), according to a set of conditions» (Frasca, 2003: 223). Regarding behaviours, horror video games draw upon the psychology of fear:

> [L]imiting ourselves to the most general statement possible, we may say that a frightened animal is most likely to try one of the three F's – freezing (keeping absolutely still and silent), flight, or fight – when he is faced with a punishment or the threat of a punishment; or he may learn something quite new which will terminate the danger to keep him out of the dangerous situation in the future. That most interesting of the animals, Man, behaves in much the same way (Gray, 1971: 10).

We are indeed likely to try the three F's in games. The most important thing is that we have a choice. It's our perception of the threat and our coping potentials that determine the intensity of our fear and how we'll respond. That's why videogames «simulate emotions in a form that is closer to typical real life experiences than film» (Grodal, 2000: 201). Depending upon the weapons we have at hand, on the supply of ammunition or the amount of health in reserve, and on the game controls (for instance, we can shoot and run at the same time in *The Suffering*, but not in *Resident Evil 4*), we may flee in a zigzag to avoid being attacked, stand still to let the danger pass, slowly bypass unnecessary confrontations, charge the enemies or circle around them while fighting, etc.

If the horror film is as much an exercise in terror as «an exercise in mastery, in which controlled loss substitutes for loss of control» (Pinedo, 1996: 26), this latter exercise takes a practical dimension in games. It leads to yet another paradox: the paradox of control. Following Csikszentmihalyi's flow theory, Salen and Zimmerman describe it this way: «In an optimal experience, the participant is able to exercise control without completely being in control of the situation» (2004: 337). For instance, *Clock Tower 3* and *Eternal Darkness: Sanity's Requiem* (Silicon Knights/Nintendo, 2002) have explicitly incorporated this dialectic in their gameplay. In the former, there is a Panic Meter visible at the upper left corner of the screen.[9] When Alyssa is getting scared, this meter rises and Alyssa begins to act more and more erratically. Running in every direction or stumbling around, she becomes hard to control. It even comes to a point where she is not responding to our commands anymore, freezing for example in fright in front of the lethal monster [Figure 8].

It's by hiding and by escaping from the monster that Alyssa will calm down. *Clock Tower 3* puts into play – *met en jeu* – the off-balance of fear. It shows how it is not easy to master our (avatar's) loss of control. *Eternal Darkness: Sanity's Requiem* is known as «the first example of a game that plays the player» (*Gamespot.com*). In that sense, the game stands at the limit of the temporary world it creates and the ordinary world where it is played. It possesses a Sanity Meter visible on the inventory screen. This meter decreases every time we encounter a monster. Once it falls very low, it makes weird things happened to our avatars,

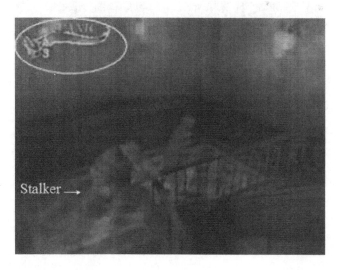

*Figure 8  Clock Tower 3* (Sunsoft/Capcom, 2003)

game-world, television set and console (i.e.: sounds of someone being tortured in another room, room where we enter is upsidedown, our avatar turns into a zombie, we have a "disk error", etc.). It is effectively quite scary – especially in the middle of the night – to see that while we are saving our progress after many hours of play, our operation leads to the erasing of our saved games, and not the inverse. Personally, during "A Journey into Darkness", I wondered for moment – even after the end of my game session – if I had made Edwin Lindsey shoot directly at the screen accidentally, leaving buckshot holes, or if it was really an insanity effect triggered by the game system as the result of my action. I was made to lose control of myself [Figure 9].

As I have shown, studying the effects of forewarning systems in the survival horror genre and the way the tension of suspense was as central to the experience as the shock of surprise (Perron, 2004), horror video games make great use of the notion of uncertainty, a key component of games. With its creepy atmosphere creating a fearful mood that encourages and prepares us to experience fright, the horror video game once again refines the effects of what Pascal Bonitzer has called "blind space" (1982). The screen being a mask, our vision remains partial. If the vision is partial, «the enemy is virtually everywhere» (1982: 96). While cinema «implicates that which is happening in the contiguity of the off-screen space, it has as much importance, from a dramatic point of view – and sometimes even more – than what is happening inside the frame» (Bonitzer, 1984: 97, freely translated), the entire visual field of the video game is much more dramatised because we can and have to walk-through this off-screen space. Indeed, the videoludic art of fright revolves in great part around the blind space. Everyone remembers the first long fanged monster breaking through the window on a sudden music chord

*Figure 9  Eternal Darkness: Sanity's Requiem* (Silicon Knights/Nintendo, 2002)

in order to attack us in the attic at the beginning of *Alone in the Dark* (I-Motion Inc. & Infogrames/Interplay, 1992). But there is a more effective and representative scene of the genre to come once we go downstairs to the room where we find Hartwood's diary about Decerto's malediction. If we walk into the room and go directly to the diary, a long fanged monster suddenly enters by the left side of the frame and attacks us [Figure 10]. But if we further penetrate into the room when we walk in – bringing a new camera angle – and investigate the window, we hear a scary growl behind the curtain, but nothing will happen [Figure 11].

It is only when we return to the first frame of the diary that we'll be attacked. The monster is meant to be lurking in the blind space, sometimes very close for a surprising attack. The cinematic fixed camera angles of the *Alone in the Dark*

*Figures 10–11 Alone in the Dark* (I-Motion Inc. & Infogrames/Interplay, 1992)

series which have been exploited in the *Resident Evil* series – and in many other games – obstructs us intentionally from seeing what danger lies ahead. Although *Resident Evil 4* is introducing moving camera view and is enabling us to adjust the angle, the zoom view behind Leon's shoulder when he is aiming and shooting reduces our field of vision and makes us less aware of what's around. Much more clever than zombies, the enemies are actually coming from everywhere in the game-world and it is hard to "disrupt the relationship". This is the case for instance in our first visit to Pueblo in Chapter One or during the enemies' assault in the barricade cabin of Chapter Two. It is terrifying and panic-inducing to realize that the foes keep coming at us. But at least, we are not in complete darkness. Because, as fear of the dark is one of our primary frights, horror video games also render our vision partial inside the frame by playing with lighting. Atari's *Haunted House* (1981) gave the adventure its first pitch-black representation. The reddish diamond-form view representing the lighting of matches around the pair of eyes – our avatar – made the search for three pieces of a magic urn and the master key more difficult and the bumping into monsters less inevitable. Working differently as a FPS, *Doom 3* (id Software/Activision, 2004) dramatizes its 3-D navigable by asking us to choose between a flashlight and a gun. Its Mars research facility is a labyrinth among others, full of dark corners that might at first glance be taken for walls, but from which monsters can spring [Figure 12].

Therefore, holding the flashlight enables us to spot the corners but leaves us defenceless, while gripping the gun gives us protection but allows for less or even no time for response – from which the numerous startle effects. However, it is certainly the *Silent Hill* and the *Fatal Frame* series that have best exploited the relation between darkness and blind space. In *Fatal Frame*, the notion of space is itself altered since the ghosts we fight with our camera are translucent incorporeal entities that can pass through walls and closed doors. While *Fatal Frame* also draws upon the device, *Silent Hill* might offer the best use of the flashlight. Since we can almost only see what we light in the first three games of the series, we have to be more careful, because monsters can not only be waiting beyond the limits of the frame, but also just outside the realtime light halo [Figure 13].

What's more, monsters are even scarier with their appearances greatly increased by their big and distorted body silhouetted on the floors and walls [Figure 14].

*Figure 12 Doom 3* (id Software/Activision, 2004)

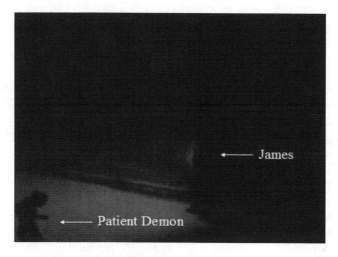

*Figure 13  Silent Hill 2* (Konami/Konami, 2001)

*Silent Hill* has also a great forewarning system in the pocket radio that transmits only white noise when there are enemies nearby. Just as good scary film relies a lot on the audio, one should not forget that the visual blind space is couple with a hearing space, perhaps less partial but very variable and much more imprecise.[10] Not knowing exactly from where the threat will come from and what it will be like as the static grows louder, we imagine the worst and stay on our guard until we encounter or escape the source of the emission.

*Figure 14  Silent Hill 3* (Konami/Konami, 2003)

Morris Dickstein wrote in «The Aesthetics of Fright»: «Getting caught up emotionally, walking out drained and satisfied, waking up relieved to deal with workaday problems – this is the secret of horror films (1984: 77). Well, the video game has also found this secret, making our «bounded experience of fear» more intense. Horror video games, and I made this comment about the *Silent Hill* series, are fiendishly designed to scare us. But in so far as the horror genre asks for imagination, that fear depends on our perception of a threat and our coping potentials, and that the simulation of danger draws on the psychology of the aforementioned emotion, horror video games are nothing else than Haunted Houses, playgrounds where we come to play at frightening ourselves.

## Acknowledgements

I wish to thank Shanly Dixon for her proofreading and suggestions and Eugenie Shinkle for sending *Edge* magazine's articles.

## Notes

1 Just think of how terrorist acts reported and/or shown live in the news leave us aghast, horrified.
2 The *has-been-there* might be the whole point of snuff movies.
3 Quite apart from the fact that the gamer could have played a censured version.
4 Besides, from Atari's *Haunted House* (1981) to *The Suffering* (Surreal Software/ Midway, 2004), mansions, prisons, schools, hospitals, villages or cities visited by ghosts, evil spirits and dangerous creatures are common places in the video game.
5 Like Krzywinska underlines: «Unlike that of the horror films, the operation of the moral occult in videogames is rarely oriented around the punishment of curiosity. ( . . . ) In games, therefore, space is something to be actively, physically, investigated if the player is to beat the game. ( . . . ) What is "punished" in videogames is not so much curiosity, as in the horror film, but the failure to make it to the next scene» (2002: 217).
6 I'm making reference here to Grodal's distinction between the «game as an experiential route» and the «game as a map and as a system». But one does not need to see those poles as totally opposite as they both can bring their own pleasures (2003: 144).
7 As the rest of my argument will show, this assertion of the *Edge* magazine is also to be questioned: «Just what it is that shoots through you when Yoshi loses hold of Mario in *Yoshi's Island*? It makes your heart pound and your palms flash with sweat, no question. Mario's desperate bleats assault your ears as all your skills desert you in your desperate flounderings to recover him. But just what is it you're feeling? Panic? Certainly. Anxiety? Sure. Guilt? A little bit. But fear? Not really. Face off with a boss in *Devil May Cry* and you're likely to swallow a gulp. You're daunted by his size, nervous about your performance, dread-filled at the prospect of repeated defeats. Scared? Not so's you'd notice» (Editorial team, 2005: 71). Well, *Mario Bros.* games are not horror games and are not meant to be scary. *Mario Bros.* is not *Castelvania*. Then, isn't it odd to think that we could feel regret for Mario as regret is an emotion elicited when one cannot redo something, and not be scared in the underworld of *Devil May Cry* where the object of fear and the goal are patent?
8 The cognitive engagement refers to Noël Carroll's curiosity theory about horror and the imaginative engagement to the critic of the work of Carroll by Mark Vorobej in «Monsters and the Paradox of Horror» (1997).

9  There was also a Panic Mode in the first two *Clock Tower* games, but it was less effective in those point-and-click adventure games. This device is also used in *Haunting Ground* (Capcom/Capcom, 2005).

10 As my colleague Serge Cardinal, a film sound specialist, pointed out to me, the horror genre modulates sound to a great extend according to its sources: invisible-silent/ invisible-sound, or visible-silent/visible-sound. This allows for the creation of surprise or of suspense.

# References

Amossy, Ruth (1991). «L'industrialisation de la peur», *Les Idées reçues. Sémiologie du stéréotype*, Paris: Nathan, p. 121–142.

Barthes, Roland (1980). *La chambre claire. Note sur la photographie*, Paris: Cahiers du cinéma, Gallimard and Seuil.

Bonitzer, Pascal (1982). *Le champ aveugle. Essais sur le cinéma*, Paris: Cahiers du cinéma and Gallimard.

Caillois, Roger ([1958] 1961). *Man, Play, and Games*. Translated by Meyer Barash. New York: The Free Press of Glencoe.

Carroll, Noël (1990). *The Philosophy of Horror or Paradoxes of the Heart*, New York: Routledge.

Dickstein, Morris (1984). «The Aesthetics of Fright», in Barry Keith Grant (ed.), *Planks of Reason: Essays on the Horror Film*, Metuchen, N.J.: Scarecrow Press, p. 65–78.

Dika, Vera (1990). *Games of Terror. Halloween, Friday the 13th, and the Films of the Stalker Cycle*, Rutherford, New York: Fairleigh Dickson University Press.

Editorial Team (2005). «Scare Tactics. Exploring the Bloody Battleground Between Fear and Frustration», *Edge* (UK), No 149 (March), p. 69–73.

Frasca, Gonzalo (2003). «Simulation versus Narrative. Introduction to Ludology», in Mark J.P Wolf and Bernard Perron (eds.), *The Video Game Theory Reader*, New York: Routledge, p. 221–235.

Giles, Dennis (1984). «The Conditions of Pleasure in Horror Cinema», in Barry Keith Grant (ed.), *Planks of Reason: Essays on the Horror Film*, Metuchen, N.J.: Scarecrow Press, p. 38–54. Gray, Jeffrey A. (1971). *The Psychology of Fear and Stress*, New York: McGraw-Hill Book Company.

Grodal, Torben (2003). «Stories for Eye, Ear, and Muscles: Video Games, Media, and Embodied Experiences», in Mark J.P Wolf and Bernard Perron (eds.), *The Video Game Theory Reader*, New York: Routledge, p. 129–155.

Grodal, Torben (2000). «Video Games and the Pleasure of Control», in D. Zillmann and P. Vorderer (eds.), *Media Entertainment: The Psychology of Its Appeal*, Mahwah, N.J.: Lawrence Erlbaum Associates, p. 197–213.

Huizinga, Johan ([1938] 1955). *Homo Ludens. A Study of the Play Element in Culture*. Boston: The Beacon Press.

Krzywinska, Tanya (2002). «Hands-on Horror», in Geoff King and Tanya Krzywinska (eds.), *ScreenPlay. Cinema/videogames/interfaces*, London: Wallflower, p. 206–223.

Lovecraft, Howard Phillips ([1927] 1973). *Supernatural Horror in Literature*, New York: Dover Publications.

Murray, Janet H. (1997). *Hamlet on the Holodeck: The Future of Narrative in Cyberspace*, New York: The Free Press.

Perron, Bernard (2005). «A Cognitive Psychological Approach to Gameplay Emotions», *DIGRA 2005 International Conference Proceedings*, available online: <http://www.gamesconference.org/digra2005/papers/86d8ad01c953fad695c3549ac644.doc>.

Perron, Bernard (2004). «Sign of a Threat: The Effects of Warning Systems in Survival Horror Games», *COSIGN 2004 Proceedings*, Art Academy, University of Split, 2004, p. 132–141, available online: <http://www.cosignconference.org/cosign2004/papers/Perron.pdf>.

Pinedo, Isabel Cristina (2004). «Postmodern Elements of the Contemporary Horror Film», in Stephen Prince (ed.), *The Horror Film*, New Brunswick: Rutgers University Press, p. 85– 117.

Pinedo, Isabel (1996). «Recreational Terror: Postmodern Elements of the Contemporary Horror Film», *Journal of Film and Video*, Vol 44, No 1–2 (Spring-Summer), p. 17–31.

Poole, Steven (2000). *Trigger Happy: The Inner Life of Video Games*. London: Fourth Estate. Salen, Katie and Eric Zimmerman (2004), *Rules of Play. Game Design Fundamentals*, Cambridge, MA: MIT Press.

Schbeider, Steven Jay (2004). «Toward an Aesthetics of Cinematic Horror», in Stephen Prince (ed.), *The Horror Film*, New Brunswick: Rutgers University Press, p. 131–149.

Vorobej, Mark (1997). «Monsters and the Paradox of Horror», *Dialogue*, No 24, p. 219–249.

# 56

# I FOUGHT THE LAW

## Transgressive play and the implied player

### *Espen Aarseth*

Source: *Situated Play: Proceedings of DiGRA 2007 Conference*, Digital Games Research Association (DiGRA) (Japan: The University of Tokyo, 2007), pp. 130–133, available at http://www.digra.org/dl/db/07313.03489.pdf.

### Abstract

This paper is an attempt to understand Game Studies through the contested notion of the "player" both inside and outside "the game object" – that is the object that game users perceive and respond to when they play. Building on Hans-Georg Gadamer's notion of games as a subject that "masters the players", the paper will go beyond the traditional split between the social sciences' real players and the aesthetics/humanities critical author-as-player, and present a theory of the player and player studies that incorporates the complex tensions between the real, historical player and the game's human components. Since games are both aesthetic and social phenomena, a theory of the player must combine both social and aesthetic perspectives to be successful. The tension between the humanities and the social sciences over who controls the idea of the player can be found mirrored also in the struggle between the player as individual and the "player function" of the game. Transgressive play, the struggle against the game's ideal player, far from being a marginal, romanticized phenomenon, is the core expression of this struggle.

## Introduction: who is the player?

" . . . the game masters the players. [ . . . ] The real subject of the game [ . . . ] is not the players but the game itself" –Gadamer,

*Truth and Method, p.106*

What is a player? In what sense does a player exist? *When* does a player exist? Can there be a player, if there is no game? Before there is a game? Clearly, players cannot exist with out a game they are players *of*. A generic *player* is an unthinkable, not merely a historical, figure. Games, on the other hand, can

197

exist without actual, current players, as material and conceptual game objects ("texts"). While the game-without-a-player is a limited perspective, it does denote a hierarchical relationship: the historical player cannot exist without a game, but the game, at some point in its existence (e.g. before the first play-testing session in a development cycle), can exist without players, and always without one particular, historical player.

The potential player, before becoming an actual player, must receive some instructions, either from the game itself, or from a guide or accompanying material. Thus, the player is created, by these instructions, and by his or her initial learning experience. In many cases, this experience is social, and the player learns from other, more experienced players. But this is far from always the case, especially with singleplayer games. While it is important to acknowledge that even single-play can be perfectly social (eg. when two players cooperate or in a group discuss the intricacies of a singleplayer game) it is perhaps just as important not to forget the solitary player, exploring by herself, Bartelian-explorer style, and discovering esoteric aspects that socially conformed, player-oriented gamers may never find.

In *Truth and Method* [4], Hans-Georg Gadamer argues that games are the real subject in play, not the players:

> . . . all playing is a being-played. The attraction of a game, the fascination it exerts, consists precisely in the fact that the game masters the players. [. . .] Whoever "tries" is in fact the one who is tried. The real subject of the game (this is shown in precisely those experiences where there is only a single player) is not the player but instead the game itself. What holds the player in its spell, draws him into play, and keeps him there is the game itself (106).

By accepting to play, the player subjects herself to the rules and structures of the game and this defines the player: a person subjected to a rule-based system; no longer a complete, free subject with the power to decide what to do next.

At this point, a working definition of *game* is in order. This is not the place to discuss previous definitions of games, so instead I will simply present my own, which should be relevant for the issue at hand: *Games are facilitators that structure player behavior, and whose main purpose is enjoyment.* Hence, a theory of games, whether ontological, aesthetic, or socially oriented, must focus on player behavior. This definition is intentionally wide open; it will encompass toy-like games such as *The Sims* and *GTA3* as well as social online worlds (MMOGs) such as *Eve* and *Second Life*, and thus serve the goal of the paper, which is to discuss the notion of the player in the broadest possible sense.

## The two players

In his recent PhD dissertation, Jonas Heide Smith [6] gives an excellent overview over the way game research literature has dealt with the player. Smith outlines four main approaches: 1) the susceptible player model (from effects research), the Selective Player Model (from media studies), 3) the active player model (from computer game studies) and 4) the Rational player model (from game design and economic game theory). He then goes on to focus his dissertation on the fourth model, which he finds most fruitful. To give Smith the attention he deserves would unfortunately bring us outside the scope of this paper. Instead, a single point will be engaged with here: the notion that Game Studies harbors a dominant player model, the "active player": "actively engaged with the game or gamespace in ways often not prescribed or predicted by the game designers" (p.24). Citing a number of studies, Smith notes that Game Studies researchers seem to prefer the type of player behavior that is active, creative and subversive, and going against the designs of the game makers. Although Smith here carefully avoids overt criticism of the "Active player" perspective as naïve, celebratory, misguided and romantic, such a criticism can easily be made following his observation, especially given the clear bias such a view represents in favor of the statistically marginal subversive or truly innovative play styles. Most players simply follow the directions and play to win, so why put the focus on those few who don't? Are game studies research- ers really unaware of what typical players actually do, or are they just bored by it, and look for more colorful examples to liven their writing?

While Smith has pointed to a trend in Game Studies that clearly invites some self-critical rethinking and academic soul-searching, I would here like to argue that innovative, subversive and transgressive play, while perhaps statistically unrepresentative, is nevertheless a crucial aspect of, and the key to understanding all kinds of play and game culture; and therefore one that deserves the (critical) attention we can give it. Also, Smith puts little weight on the fairly visible divide in game studies between "player" studies and "text" studies, that is, the potential conflict between the humanist and the social sciences camp. These two camps, one focused on understanding games through playing them, and one focused on observing actual players, represent two quite separate paradigms in terms of their player perspective, and two that are not always living happily side by side.

On the one hand, there is the critical player-theorist, whose empirical target is the game as an aesthetic object, just like any other (films, music, visual art) but with the added challenge of gameplay. This researcher considers her own play- ing experience as a valid basis for doing theory, and is interested in the game as a cultural, expressive object. The fact that she is studying an object that at the time of study is a process partly instigated by her, and not necessarily shared by any other player, is seldom a topic for discussion, but bracketed by experience of play.

On the other hand, there is the ethnographic player-observer, whose empiri- cal focus is the other players, their habits, actions, values and relationships. This researcher is careful to extract or neutralize her own experience, to the extent that it is possible. Self-play is here potentially suspect, since it is subjective and quite likely unrepresentative. While her own experience of the game might be used as back- ground information to better understand the observed players, the data samples are a presumably representative and hopefully diverse group of real, historical players.

A tension exists between these two researcher types, caused partly by the lack of realization that the object they study is not the same. For the humanist, the player is a function of the game, a slot in a game machine that can be filled by any rational, critical, informed person – a model reader, in Umberto Eco's terms [3]. For the sociologist or ethnographer, the player is an actual, historical person, or better, persons.

However, there is another tension at work, which is just as important: the methodological divide between formal and informal methods. (In the social sciences, between quantitative and qualitative, and in the humanities, between structuralism/"theory" and close reading). In other words, we can divide the field of gameplay studies in four, along empirical and methodological lines:

|  | Social sciences | The Humanities |
|---|---|---|
| Case studies | Field work | Close playing (reading) |
| Formal methods | Statistics | Game ontologies |

While the Humanities and the Social sciences both have formal and informal methods, it is in their empirical object that they differ most clearly: their conception of the player. For the social scientist, whether doing qualitative or quantitative research, the player is historical, situated, flesh and blood. For the humanist game scholar, whether engaged in close playing analysis of a single game, or trying to make sense of games as a complex, multifaceted medium with a huge repertoire of genres, the player is a necessary but uncontrollable part of the process of creating ludic meaning, a function that is created by the gameplay as well as cocreator of it. Given the origin of the text-oriented humanities as a discipline for the study of biblical meaning (exegesis), this abstracting of the reader should not be seen as a disregard for social reality, but as a means to govern interpretation. By positioning the ideal reader as a function of the text, the humanist is trying to exclude himself from the interpretation, while acknowledging that this is impossible. Thus, far from being ignored or glossed over, the problem of reading and interpretation is the central one in textual studies.

## The implied player

To solve the problem of textual meaning, the 20th century literary theorist Wolfgang Iser [5] came up with a model termed "the implied reader". Iser argues that a literary text addresses an ideal reader, which "embodies all those predispositions necessary for a literary work to exercise its effect – predispositions laid down, not by an empirical outside reality, but by the text itself. Consequently, the implied reader as a concept has his roots firmly planted in the structure of the text; he is a construct and in no way to be identified with any real reader."

The notion of the implied reader has been applied to the field of games before; e.g. [1], p. 127, where I talk of the "implied user" in my discussion of adventure games. The implied player, then, can be seen as a role made for the player by the game, a set of expectations that the player must fulfill for the game to "exercise its effect". Following [1], we can come up with the following three-level model:

| Implied Player | |
|---|---|
| Interface addressee | The real, historical player |
| Avatar/vehicle (if any) | |

The game houses expectations for a player's behavior, which is supported by an interface, and represented in-game by an avatar (but not the latter in all games). Even more than the implied reader, the implied player has a concrete, material existence, because the game will not be realized unless some mechanism allows player input.

If we also link the notion of the implied player to Gadamer's notion of the unfree player subject, we can start to see the implied player as a boundary imposed on the player-subject by the game, a limitation to the playing person's freedom of movement and choice.

## You found a secret area: the transgressive player

While the implied player model is sufficient to understand the expectations laid down by the game for the player, it is not enough to explain real player behavior. Games are machines that sometimes allow their players to do unexpected things, often just because these actions are not explicitly forbidden. In other words, they are not part of the game's intended repertoire, and would in most cases have been rendered impossible if the game designers could have predicted them.

These moments of game transgression are nevertheless highly important to players, and in many cases celebrated as important events, or vilified as problematic and destructive. A list of such cases might include the famous heist in *Eve Online*, where a covert "assassin guild" killed the leader of a major in-game cooperation and stole its assets, worth many thousand dollars of real money. Another event is the death of Lord British in the beta trial version of *Ultima Online* in 1996: Rainz, a common player, managed, implausibly, to kill the game designer's supposedly immortal avatar, by using a fire spell that worked in a way it should not have. In *Halo*, a method called warthog jumping was discovered to propel player avatars high into the air, and thereby access unintended parts of the landscape.

All these moments, whether celebrated or derided as cheating, represents a transgression of the implied player. Transgressive play is a symbolic gesture of rebellion against the tyranny of the game, a (perhaps illusory) way for the played subject to regain their sense of identity and uniqueness through the mechanisms of the game itself.

## Breaking the law in Cryodiil: wondrous Oblivion

*The Elder Scrolls IV: Oblivion* (2006) is a particularly relevant but also challenging game to use in an analysis of player participation. Oblivion combines an open and persistent world, Cryodiil, with a fairly linear main quest: the player is invited, but not forced, to fight the evil spreading in the gameworld by closing a number of "Oblivion gates" – doorways to Hell. The world is geographically continuous and eminently detailed, consisting of one large level sprinkled with a large number of dungeons and caves, as well as towns, shops, inns, and treasures and hundreds of named non-playing characters (NPCs) and monsters of all kinds. The leveling and customization possibilities are overwhelming: New potions and weapons can be made by combining materials and spells, and the world can be explored for months of playing time. Given the complexity of both the world simulation and the sheer number of combinable elements in it, the possibility for unlikely and curious events are a great source of player entertainment. This potential for player creativity is supplemented by the usual exploitable bugs that inevitably plague such complex software projects.

At one time of playing, I was exploring the hills northwest of the central city, when I came across two foresters of the imperial army who were engaged in a bow and arrow duel, to the death. They simply kept firing, no explanation given, until one of them was killed. I have no idea what could have caused this animosity, and I had no way to find out.

There was no indication that this was a scripted event, and probably some small coincidence, such as one of them hitting the other by mistake while trying to kill a wild animal, had caused the fight to break out, but who knows. Later, as I

*Figure 1* Melons in Oblivion; the item duplication trick [2]

was climbing a steep hillside to get into a mine, a wolf charged me jumping from above, but missed, hit some rocks further down, and died.

One of the more memorable exploits in the game is the item duplication trick, which allows players to create hundreds of copies of an item in-game. A movie posted to google [2] (Figure 1) shows an avatar on a rooftop preparing to fire an arrow, stopping and changing the arrow to a large watermelon in the inventory screen and as the arrow/melon is then fired, it turns into several hundred watermelons, filling up the nearby area. This ridiculous spectacle is then made even more absurd by an NPC that comes walking by, completely ignoring the flow of melons, while greeting the avatar with a calm "Oh, Hello".

My own most hilarious moment in the game was when I got into a fight with the annoying and arrogant Captain of the City Watch, Hieronymus Lex. He is an imposing figure, in silver armor and a huge silver sword. I had finally managed to enter the Arcane University as part of the mage quest line, and consequently the mage scholars there became my friends and allies.

Also patrolling the area are the battle mages, a different faction employed as peacekeepers by the City. Somehow, while trespassing I managed to draw their unfriendly attention and so I was attacked by a small group of them in the Arcane University grounds. Hieronymus Lex was also there, and joined the fight with his usual cold persistence. My friends the mage scholars, however, are not cowards when it comes to defending their own. A wild battle broke out, and I managed to stay alive while the spells and swords flashed and bodies started to litter the ground. Even Lex got his comeuppance, and was knocked out by the sturdy scholars. Seizing my chance, I grabbed his sword lying on the ground beside him. In Oblivion, important NPCs can't be killed before they are supposed to, so Captain Lex was not dead, only unconscious. After a few moments he got up, picked up a little green magic dagger from one of my dead friends, and continued the fight. Luckily, the scholars carried the day, leaving me with some very nice loot, including the sword that I later sold to my fence in the Thieves Guild. I also paid a bribe to get me off the Cryodiil's-most-wanted list. Now, whenever I happen to meet Captain Lex in the street, I get a huge kick out of seeing him prancing around, fiercely ignoring my presence, while carrying a little green dagger.

## Conclusion

These anecdotes, while not typical of the events a player will encounter in a game like *Oblivion*, nor representative of my own play experience in that game, are nevertheless among the most important aspects of play and gaming. The unexpected happening, the lucky shot, the brilliant move, the last-minute goal, the 99.99% unlikely drop of an epic item, the completely ridiculous situation produced by a software bug, are not incidental to gaming, but a vital part of the play experience. They may not happen all that often, but they are necessary as a counterweight to the implied player position, the prison-house of regulated play. If we look beyond normal, everyday computer gameplay, and take a look at sports, competitive gaming of all kinds, and phenomena like gambling, it is the unique event, the brilliant innovative player, the exceptional team among so many, that is celebrated and remembered by our culture. The unique, against-all-odds play event is what players live for, as they carry out their rather meaningless, repetitive tasks in the service of the game. While it is important to be aware of what players actually do, we cannot ignore this marginal phenomenon when trying to explain why they do it.

The games rule us. We as players are only half-ourselves when we play, the rest of us is temporarily possessed by the implied player. These marginal events and occurrences, these wondrous acts of transgression, are absolutely vital because they give us hope, true or false; they remind us that it is possible to regain control, however briefly, to dominate that which dominates us so completely.

# References

[1] Aarseth, Espen 1997. *Cybertext: Perspectives on Ergodic Literature*. Baltimore and London: Johns Hopkins University Press.

[2] Bethesda Softworks 2006. Oblivion: Melons. http://video.google.com/videoplay?do cid=8960256445634741451

[3] Eco, Umberto 1979. *The Role of the Reader: Explorations in the Semiotics of Texts*. Bloomington: Indiana University Press.

[4] Gadamer, Hans-Georg 1989 [1960]. *Truth and Method*. London: Sheed & Ward.

[5] Iser, Wolfgang 1974. *The Implied Reader: Patterns of Communication in Prose Fiction from Bunyan to Beckett*. Baltimore and London: Johns Hopkins University Press.

[6] Smith, Jonas Heide 2006. *Plans And Purposes: How Videogame Goals Shape Player Behaviour*. PhD dissertation. IT University of Copenhagen. http://jonassmith.dk/weblog/wp-content/dissertation1-0.pdf

# 57

# VIDEO GAMES AND
# THE PLEASURES OF CONTROL

## *Torben Grodal*

Source: Dolf Zillmann and Peter Vorderer (eds), *Media Entertainment: The Psychology of its Appeal* (Mahwah, NJ: Lawrence Erlbaum Associates, 2000), pp. 197–213.

Video games are remarkable new forms of entertainment. Video games import and customize many different forms of entertainment, from games related to jigsaw puzzles and chess simulations to games related to novels or to action films. Video games provide simulations of a series of aspects of reality, like racing, flying, or playing soccer, or simulations of complex social developments, from urban development to the evolution of civilization. The hallmark of most video games is that they transform these traditional forms of entertainment into an interactive form that enables the player actively to participate in shaping the games. Films or videos enable their viewers to interact only passively, by following the narrative and predicting possible outcomes, whereas video games provide the Player with interactive means to change the course of the narrative. The interaction with such possible audiovisual worlds provides the player with an experience of being immersed in a "virtual reality," because our experience of reality is linked not only to the possible salience of what we see and hear, but is also centrally linked to whether we are able to interact with such perceptions. A key to explaining why video games have become very popular forms of entertainment is to explore those gratifications that are linked to the interactive form.

Most scholarly studies of video games have focused on the possible negative effects of video games, especially of the violent "shoot-'em-up" games. The perceptual salience of such games is very much inferior to that of, for instance, a gory movie played in a wide-screen THX-sound movie theater. However, the argument has been that the interactivity of the video games would make the player personally responsible for the atrocious acts and implicate the player in the morally dubious actions. In this chapter I supplement some of the findings of studies aimed at measuring possible negative effects of video games with an analysis of a series of gratifications derived from the interactivity of the video games in comparison with film (as a term covering film, TV, and video fiction).

This chapter concentrates on games that provide *narrative simulations*, that is, fictitious actions. The narrative games can be subdivided into two groups.

205

One subgroup within narrative video games could be called adventure-mystery games. These games tend increasingly to emulate the more complex world of films in respect to themes, character complexity, and so on. In order to do so, some experiences are provided by inserting non-interactive film sequences. However, the time is often player-generated; that is, time progresses only when the player makes a move, and the game narration is often partly shown from an exterior, third-person point of view. The other subgroup consists of action games, centered on interactive realism, often shown in a three-dimensional world and by point of view. Games like *Wolfenstein, Mortal Kombat,* and *Quake* belong to this subgroup. They elicit strong arousal because of their combination of violent images, strong aggressive player reactions, and point-of-view editing. I use those games as material for my analysis, because they are the best matches to an interactive simulation of an "online" reality, and because those games have caused most public concern, due to their portrayal of violence. My prototype for the analysis will be *Quake.*

## The impact of violence on film and in video games

The public debate about the possible impact of violent video games has had a precursor in the heated debate of similar features in film. Those in favor of violent or sexual films have used different arguments. One line of defense is the catharsis argument: Fictions serve as safety valves for aggression or sexual urges. A variant of this theory is an equilibrium theory, which claims that people use films in order to control their level of arousal, a position that could be explained by uses-and-gratification theories (Rubin, 1994). Another theory is that the fictional nature dissociates the film experience from real-life experiences. Those concerned by violent or sexually explicit films have other arguments. One is the desensitizing argument: Exposure to violence or strong sex will accustom viewers to such phenomena. Another argument is that such exposure provides social learning: People will learn violent behavior from films and copy the violent behavior in real life (Bandura, 1994). A variant of this argument is a priming argument: Violence activates and strengthens violence-related associations and emotional charges. A third argument is the arousal argument: Violent films raise the level of arousal and will therefore provide a basis for violent acts if they are put into a violent context.

Contrary to studies of the impact of film violence, several studies of video games have found either catharsis effects, equilibrium effects, or lack of any significant increase in aggressive tendencies (e.g., Calvert & Tan, 1994; Graybill, Strawniak, Hunter, & O'Leary, 1987; Kerstenbaum & Weinstein, 1985). Graybill, Kirsch, and Esselman (1985) found that children who played the violent video game showed fewer defensive fantasies and tended to show more assertive or need-persistent fantasies than did children who played the nonviolent game. Other studies have found aggression, arousal effects, and social learning induced by playing violent video games more similar to those found in film and television studies (Ballard & Wiest, 1996; Hoffman, 1995; Shutte, Malouf, Post-Gorden, &

Rodasta, 1988; Silvern & Williamson, 1987). No studies have proven any long-term effects.

A series of studies have addressed computer games from the point of view of cognitive and perceptual development. This is, for instance, the case with two studies by Loftus and Loftus (1983) and Greenfield (1984). They each analyzed how video games enhanced perception, attention, spatial skills, memory, and motor performance. In a more recent collection of studies *(Journal of Applied Developmental Psychology, 15,* 1994) Greenfield and associates have come up with additional experimental evidence for the role of video games as part of learning processes.

However, most studies do not consider any positive gratifications from playing violent video games. Although most children and adolescents use a lot of time playing such games, this only causes concern, not any interest in the fascination. A reason for this lack of interest is that the fascination is regarded as one focused on violence and aggression per se. It might, however, be argued that the fascination consists of many different elements. A central fascination with violent games is linked to the strong arousal caused by the dangerous situations portrayed. The playful simulation of dangerous situations is often gratifying because such simulations allow the player to cope with strong aversive sympathetic reactions. Coping with situations linked to strong aversive arousal is not only linked to criminal behavior; firefighters, drivers, rescue workers, or victims of violence will often experience dangerous situations. Daily life is based not only on empathy, cooperation, and compromise, but also on aversive situations that demand assertiveness. Respectable forms of entertainment like chess or fairy tales are often centered on confrontation and aversion.

The arousal motivates a series of cognitive and motor responses, some of which are violent. Many of these responses are defensive, other responses are linked to violent reactions to fantasy creatures, yet other responses are directed at humans, although even games like *Mortal Kombat* portray the possible victims of violence in a rather exotic, stylized manner, very different from the realist portrayal of victims in, for instance, splatter films. It is reasonable to be concerned that strong video game violence may be harmful for players disposed toward violence by other factors. However, there is no conclusive evidence for the impact on normal players.

There are some clearly immoral games, like the car game *Carmageddon*, in which the player gets points for killing innocent pedestrians. Such games raise problems similar to those raised by comic fictions in which the pain and abuse of clowns and other comic figures cue pleasurable viewer reactions. The ability to get comic pleasure out of such reversals of normal empathic relations between viewers (or players) and fictitious characters is based on innate dispositions. Comic reversals presuppose some kind of moral maturity that prevents viewers and players from experiencing such reversals as normal interpersonal relations. The limits to such comic reversals clearly depend on moral evaluations of the limits for what kinds of themes are acceptable, and on commonsense assessments of to what extent some reversals may lead to moral confusion.

In general we may assert that we possess aggressive potential, which we have inherited because aggression had a clear survival value for our ancestors. Many reactions supported by such inherited mechanisms are clearly harmful in our present environment (murder and other violent acts). However, it is not clear whether other types of "aggressive" behavior that does not lead to physical abuse of other people serve possible beneficial mental mechanisms; for instance, assertiveness, need-persistence, and emotional control in confrontation with aversive stimuli. It is not obvious that the media society only supports lack of empathy due to an overload of violence; on the contrary, more people than ever are deeply concerned with the well-being of other people, and empathic concerns are increasingly also directed at animals and lower life-forms. Intuitively this seems partly to be an effect of the way in which modern audiovisual media increasingly make it possible to empathize with other beings. In this larger context the aggression displayed in some types of media products and the comic reversal of empathy might partly be explained as negotiations and regulations of the level of empathy.

In the rest of this chapter I explore the hypothesis that danger and violence in video games serve as part of cognitive and emotional learning processes. I will analyze some reasons why the interactivity of video games supports emotional control by linking the experience of strong emotion-eliciting stimuli to cognitive and physical interaction with the game world. I further analyze some of the gratifications that are elicited by the playful simulations of "live" interactive processes.

## Emotions in real life, on film and in video games

In order to provide a framework for understanding possible differences between the emotional impact of film and interactive video games I recapitulate some fundamentals in emotion theory (cf. Grodal, 1997) and relate these to film and video games. A precondition for eliciting strong emotions is to present some stimuli that are central concerns of living beings, for instance threats on life or health. Such stimuli will elicit physical arousal. Arousal is a very general physiological process, and, as argued by cognitive labeling theorists of human emotions, in order to create emotions out of arousal you need cognitively to specify, to contextualize the arousal, in order to elicit emotions. The situational context cues a dominant action tendency by means of a cognitive analysis of the situation, resulting in a cognitive labeling of the arousal. As described, for instance, by the Dutch psychologist Frijda, emotions are "modes of relational action readiness, either in the form of tendencies to establish, maintain, or disrupt a relationship with the environment or in the form of mode of relational readiness as such" (1986, p.71).

A simple example: If you suddenly meet a lion on a savannah it would create arousal. The context will determine how the arousal is molded into an emotion. If you are armed, you may feel aggression and shoot the lion, but if unarmed you might feel fright and look for escape, or you might feel that you are unable to cope with the situation and feel despair. If you are safely placed in a photo safari jeep, the arousal is transformed into delight. These emotions are phasic, that is, there is an eliciting cause of arousal, followed by an appreciation of what to do, which then leads to actions that will eventually transform the emotion by removing or transforming the causes of the emotions. The emotional experience will therefore consist of phases: a cause, an arousal, a cognitive appreciation and a labeling, followed by some actions that remove the cause of arousal. In order to elicit phasic emotions in relation to fiction we need a focusing character, because without such a character we cannot specify any coping strategies.

The emotional experience of a given situation will consequently be different according to whether it is cued by a film or by a video game. When viewing a film the labeling of the emotions felt is determined by the viewer's passive appreciation of the film character's coping potentials. But when the situation is part of a video game, it is the player's assessment of his own coping potentials that determines the emotional experience. The unskilled player may feel despair when confronted with the lion, but the skilled player will fuel the arousal into a series of courageous actions. Video games therefore simulate emotions in a form that is closer to typical real-life experiences than film: Emotions are motivators for actions and are labeled according to the player's active coping potentials.

## The input-output problem and the game player's virtual reality simulation

A film viewer has no control over the direction of his or her perceptions and no control over possible reactions to possible arousing events. However, the viewer can bridge the gap between perceptions and actions by several cognitive and affective strategies. The viewer can think up several coping strategies and hope for given outcomes. The terms *interest* and *suspense* often cover these passive viewer expectations. Films shown in the cinema are especially, so to speak, input-driven: the salience and magnitude of the screen in combination with engrossing events ensure a strong input, and often whole genres like melodrama are constructed in order to overwhelm the viewer, eventually by cuing strongly passive emotional responses like crying or great fear. The viewer may thus experience the film from a third-person position of being a witness to events (Carroll, 1990). The passive third-person aspects of film viewing are often partly masked by providing close links between the point-of-view presentation of emotion-eliciting elements and the protagonist's concerns and possible or effected actions. If there are a close knit and fast-paced relation between these three factors, the viewer is led into simulating such sequences of perceptions, concerns and actions as if they were performed actively by the viewer (Grodal, 1997; Smith, 1995). However, the coping potentials of the viewer are mostly very general and are linked to mental simulations.

Compared with cinema films and even with TV screen-transmitted fictions, video games have a less salient input, although sound and graphics have improved significantly. But the games make up for this by providing more sophisticated devices for processing the input in relation to output. A video game provides an interactive interface, which enables the player to control actions and often also perceptions by an ability to control the point of view, that is, to control the point from which, and the direction by which, the game world is represented. This leads to several dramatic changes compared to film viewing:

- The player needs to use attention in order to control perception, including the point of view.
- The player needs to make mental maps of the game-space as if it were a real three-dimensional world. He or she needs to notice landmarks, significant causal relations, and so on.
- The player needs to actively coordinate visual attention and motor actions (by mouse, joystick, or keyboard). The feedback from the activation of these procedural schemata will create additional arousal. The activation and coordination of the different mental functions and representations will compete with limited capacity in working memory and possibly cause mental overload.
- The emotional significance and labeling of a certain event-induced arousal are linked to the player's own ability to cope with a given problem. It will therefore vary over time (and vary from player to player).
- The player will get a continuous satisfaction from his performance. Therefore, the pleasure is derived not only from the global performance, but also from a series of local achievements, local sequences of arousal leading into coping actions.
- The game processes are driven by the player's motivation for performing, and success and failure is partly attributed to the player, not to the game-world. The length of the home video game relates to the player's own motivation.

All these characteristics emphasize that video games are much more focused on the relation between input and output, the relation between perception, attention, emotion, and motor control, than films (Kubey & Larson, 1990). Therefore the arousal is not only derived from input but also experienced in relation to processing the input in a more profound way than just guessing the probable outcome. The player participates in a virtual reality simulation of a possible real world. When a player accepts to play a given character in a game, it is done from the inside as a temporal fusion with a given world, with some game-defined perception capabilities and action capabilities. It is well documented that the interactions between persons and computers and with computers as platforms for video games are experienced as an involvement on a first-person level (Reeves & Nass, 1996; Shapiro & McDonald, 1992; Turkle, 1984). These studies emphasize that a naturalistic conception of the interaction with media, and especially with computer media, is the typical attitude.

The computer media experience underlines that actions and interactions are very strong components in our experience of reality. The fascination many players felt with the (by modern standards) often crude visual interfaces of the first video games of the early 1970s showed that the salience of the perceptual input was powerfully enhanced by feedback from the interactive output capabilities.

## Types of interaction in video games

Our experience of our relations to reality may have three main forms. The first form consists of being a passive, perceptual witness to spaces, actions, and processes, as when we are viewing a film. Some video games have inserted such film-type sequences with which the player cannot interact. Because such sequences do not afford interaction, they are experienced as subjective (Grodal, 1997). The second form is based on an active exploration of spaces, actions, and processes that are fully self-controlled, as when we take a walk, whether this walk is taken in real life or in a virtual reality. Mystery games like *Myst* typically possess such a player-generated time, in which processes take off when the player performs some actions and stop when the player stops. Action-centered video games like *Quake* also have some sequences in which the player is in total control over the actions and processes. The third form is not only active, but also centrally interactive, because the player is confronted with other processes and agencies that are only partly under the control of the experiencing agency. The player has to perform actions at a certain pace, because otherwise he or she will "die," for instance, because he or she cannot prevent his or her vehicle from crashing. Furthermore, in centrally interactive sequences, it is not only the player who can seek out events, other agencies like monsters can seek out the player (or the player's character). The player has to cope with antagonistic forces and processes according to some game-world time. The sense of realism is enhanced because the player's control is not absolute, but relative to his skills.

Video sequences that are based on player-generated time support exploratory gratifications; for instance, curiosity and cognitive problem solving. The game proceeds at a speed that suits the player's sense of control. When a player has solved a problem, he can proceed to the next set of stimuli, the next problem. Game-world–generated time provides other gratifications because it evokes much stronger emotions. The problems need to be solved under severe time constraints similar to those in emotional peak situations in real life. The player has to integrate perceptions, cognitions, emotions, and actions fast in order to survive and is provided with a strong feeling of interaction. The closer a game experience gets to the player's optimal mental and motor capacity the less capacity is available for being conscious about the game being just a game: the game provides total immersion.

Such strong interaction will, however, also cause fatigue and eventually a sense of lack of control. Most action video games are therefore constructed in such a way that they provide the player with choices between playing in a player generated and a game-world–generated time. Some spaces in the game-world are defined as player-controlled. In such spaces (zones) the player may "rest," perform strategic thinking, or carry out exploratory actions, by which he can control motion, and point of view, or explore objects. Other zones, other spaces, are defined as having game-world–defined times and processes; here the monsters can seek out the player-character and here the processes cannot be stopped, only mastered by some actions. If, for instance, the player falls into a pool of slime, he needs to get out "before he is out of air."

To control all the different activities of playing video games presupposes training by repetitive playing. Training will enable the player to transfer some of the activities from conscious control into a control by nonconscious procedures. The perfect mastering of such tasks will lead to the experience of mental flow, as described by Turkle (1984). The player who has perfectly learned all the different complex procedures can play in a highly active, but semiconscious, state. The performance demands total concentration in order to integrate a series of automated and nonconscious processes within a conscious framework. By having learned a series of procedural schemata the player will gain the necessary capacity for effortless voluntary control.

Thus video games are structured according to a principle of uses and gratifications similar to that of real life: We can seek out stimulating spaces when bored and take shelter in some other spaces when overstimulated and in need of rest. The video game enables the player to control his or her perceptual, emotional, and enactional activation. The feeling of being able to customize one's control over the relation between challenge and personal control is further enhanced by three additional features of most video games: the existence of a pause button, the possibility of saving intermediate results, and the existence of different levels of difficulty. Thus the player can choose the level of difficulty in relation to skill that the player considers to be optimal.

## Repetitive game-playing, curiosity, surprise, and suspense

The typical film is viewed one time only, whereas the typical video game is played many times, and the cognitive and emotional differences between these two modes of reception accounts for central differences in the experience of the two media.

In a film there is a big difference between the first viewing and the following viewing(s) (Brewer, 1996). For most viewers the first viewing is the central film experience. The first-time viewing of a narrative takes place with an uncertain narrative future. This cues curiosity, surprise, and suspense. As the narrative proceeds, the film will make the narrative factual. When the film viewing is finished, the viewer has received the final and irreversible version of the narrative. Our cognitive, emotional, and enactional experience of a film will therefore be determined by the fact that any given film sequence presents a final version of events. Mutilations or deaths during the film are mostly final and unchangeable facts.

In contrast to this, a video game is played many times and many events can be altered by the player's interactions. Thus a given sequence in one game performance of a given video game-world by a given player is different from a similar sequence in the following game. A given game not only exists as a factual event, related to a given game, but also provides important feedback in the following games. Or phrased differently: Video games are learning processes. A given game will typically not lead the player through the whole game; only a series of games will provide the player with the necessary skills to complete the game. Even when completing the game the game-world will be a series of spaces, objects, and actions, a virtual reality, with many possibilities for making linear narratives from beginning to end. Because video games are repetitive learning processes, the emotional experience is different compared with the film experience. I explain this difference in relation to the experience of three central arousal-evoking elements: curiosity, surprise, and suspense. I mostly follow the definitions of curiosity, surprise, and suspense provided by Brewer (1996).

A film will often elicit curiosity, because a viewer is aware that vital information concerning narrative past or present events is withheld. The film will induce arousal until the information is disclosed and then the information will lose its interest. In a video game the satisfaction of curiosity is part of a process of learning and mastery. The player needs to remember the disclosed information in order to use it in a second game. A central factor in playing video games is to remember information from previous games, slotting the information into cognitive maps. Because curiosity in action video games (as opposed to mystery video games) is mostly prospective, curiosity is often linked to properties of the game-world as possible elements of future actions. I discuss curiosity in relation to suspense later in this chapter.

A film will create surprise by sudden events. It will create a momentary arousal jag, which will then disappear. But when playing video games, what was surprising in the first game is transformed into a suspenselike coping anticipation in the following games. When the player advances toward the space/time in which the surprising event has previously occurred, say the sudden appearance of a fierce antagonist, an increased arousal is induced. The arousal will diminish over time as the player learns some coping mechanisms, for instance, fast routines for shooting the monster despite the surprising speed or the surprising location of the monster. When hearing horrible dogs growling from behind, the player will learn to turn quickly. Because of capacity constraints imposed on the brain when playing games, it is not at all certain that a player is able to understand and remember the cause of a given surprise; only consecutive games will provide the necessary knowledge and motor skill (for instance, to control point of view in such a way that the circumstances of a surprising event can be discovered).

A film will create arousal related to the viewer's expectations of what will happen to the central protagonists. The expectations can be linked to knowledge of dangers or positive events disclosed to the viewer but not to the protagonists. Some theorists (Brewer, 1996) use the word *suspense* exclusively to describe such emotional concerns for protagonists if they are derived from knowledge not shared by protagonists. For good reasons such suspense does not exist in video games, because the game character and the player are fused. In everyday use of the term in respect to film, however, suspense also applies to strong concerns about the future destiny of the protagonists. I will therefore use suspense in this broad sense. (Zillmann [1996] provides a broad definition of suspense that is similar to mine, but he does not consider the role of the viewer's simulation of the characters' coping potentials.) Video games certainly evoke suspense related to the outcome of local sequences as well as the final outcome of the game. But just as we saw in relation to interest and surprise, suspense in video games is interwoven with the interactive and repetitive nature of the game.

Because of the interactive aspect of the game, the outcome in a given game is in principle just as uncertain the second time as the first time. The player might in the first game by chance shoot an important antagonist or by chance stand in a protected area, or the player may make a perceptual or motor mistake. The player will only by training achieve such an expertise that the game will lose its suspense, and thereby its ability to arouse and stimulate the player.

The suspense is often based on a series of different factors, such as the ability to perform spatial mapping, to detect the different capabilities and locations of antagonists, and to guess what weapons to use or what strategy to use. The player's exploration of the game-world by means of trial and error as well as by means of constant assessments of causes and effects is linked to a suspenseful curiosity. Contrary to a film narrative, which shows all aspects of the narrative world in the first viewing, because its narrative is based on a linear space-time, a video game often supports many different ways of proceeding through the game-world.

A characteristic aspect of video game suspense is the way in which it is molded by the player's coping motivation, including the wish for achievement. A film will go on irrespective of the viewer's degree of curiosity or suspense, but a video game is actively driven by the viewer's explorative activities. A term like *explorative coping* might therefore be a useful supplement to the terms curiosity, surprise, and suspense in order to describe video games.

In video games, curiosity, surprise, suspense and explorative coping are not fixed entities, causing fixed types of arousal and fixed emotions as a consequence of cognitive labeling linked to affordances. On the contrary: The experience of given situations will change over time, due to learning processes that will change arousal and will change the cognitive labeling of the arousal. The emotional experience is not primarily input-driven, but driven by the wish for an active control, and thereby also driven by a wish for emotional control. The aggressive game-induced arousal is therefore possibly more closely linked to the player's own activity and less directed at the hostile others than in film. When a player has been shot by an enemy, he can press a button to play a new game. Therefore, that arousal is fueled into further play is a more adequate coping reaction than aggression toward the "enemy." In video games, the antagonists are often a multitude of hostile others, and there are therefore no focusing antagonists (except maybe the computer itself as host for the hostile software).

## Video games and self-esteem

In video games the blame for defeat is predominantly directed at the players themselves, because the players are well aware of the fact that the evil forces act according to encoded software scripts and that other, better-skilled players are able to succeed. The variable is the player's skill. To link defeat with personal humiliation is therefore a more adequate reaction than hate toward all the different evil forces. In many games a player can choose different skill levels and thus choose a level that provides an adequate balance between challenge and personal performance. These structural factors in violent video games accord with theories that hypothesize that entertainment serves as a means for controlling the level and the variation of arousal. The arousal is increased by exposure to adverse situations but reduced and relabeled as the learning processes enhance coping. Aggression is primarily linked to coping. And the player's exposure to arousing phenomena might—from a uses-and-gratification point of view—be seen as part of mood management (cf. Rubin, 1994; Zillmann & Bryant, 1994). But on the other hand, the effects are very much linked to the player's assessment of his or her own performance, and the effect on aggression could therefore be linked to individual differences. In films the viewer gets a vicarious satisfaction in seeing a protagonist succeed. The degree of satisfaction is—besides the narrative factors—probably linked to the degree to which the protagonist matches values of concern for the viewer's self-appreciation. The vicarious self-esteem derived from films may depend on the viewer's ability to empathize with characters and thematic values as well as on the display of mastery by violence. But the viewing process as such in a mainstream film does not demand any special skills and is therefore not a selftest. Exceptions are very violent films, which can test the stamina of the viewer.

In violent video games there are only rudimentary links to social themes. The player-character is mostly defined as a relatively unspecific warrior. The central factor for self-esteem is linked to the player's skill in mastering the game. It could therefore be hypothesized that playing video games would have very different effects on different players. Good players should get more self-esteem out of playing video games than bad players. Even if game playing is part of a learning process, in which more time spent on playing will lead to better results, there would still be significant individual differences (contrary to viewing films). But the possibilities for choosing an adequate level of difficulty in relation to the player's skills should lead to a diminishing of differences in self-esteem as a consequence of playing video games. It is furthermore not clear whether video games would attract people with self-esteem problems because of the possibility for creating an alternative way of mastery, as suggested by Dominick (1984) or attract people with strong self-esteem who are motivated by an additional way of coping. Fling et al. (1992) found no correlation between the amount of playing time and self-esteem. A study by Funk and Buchman (1996) found no effects on self-esteem on boys playing violent video games, but some correlations between girls playing violent video games and a lowered self-esteem.

215

## Video games and emotional control

Following is a summary of some of the points discussed earlier.

1   The interactive interface between player and game-world makes the coping reactions to arousing events into concrete coping procedures. Therefore, video games elicit fluctuating emotional labeling procedures in relation to coping potentials in the given situation. This labeling will change over time as a function of the player's learning. They will activate a series of mental and bodily functions: attention, arousal, cognitive appraisals of arousal, cognitive mapping, procedural schemata, and motor performance. A given arousal-eliciting event will continuously be relabeled. A panic-evoking situation can, by learning processes, be transformed into a fear-evoking or aggression-evoking event, or eventually be totally controlled and be interpreted as a cause for playful mastery.

    Contrary to film, video games are output-driven. Furthermore a game is meant to be played several times, and therefore a given outcome is not final, but part of cognitive and emotional learning processes similar to everyday learning. The input-mastering by coping reactions will influence the experience of curiosity, surprise, suspense, and explorative coping in the player's different performances in a given video game.

2   The games are constructed to make it possible for players to gain control over the elicited arousal by means of the learning processes. Besides the central interface that controls perception and action, the games typically possess a series of additional control devices, from being able to choose several levels of difficulty, to time out features and the possibility of saving a positive intermediate result. Video games are therefore often "mood managers;" that is, they allow the player to participate in a self-controlled arousing experience. The time spent on a given game is player-controlled, and therefore it may be suggested that the player will continue to play until he or she has achieved an optimal arousal equilibrium. The game is emotionally, cognitively, and physically demanding, and may cause fatigue.

3   The point-of-view video games activate the player on a first-person basis and are experienced as part of a self-testing, which links the player's performance to his personal self-esteem. As a consequence, the video game experience may be more individualized than film viewing because of a greater variation in a player's ability to master a game than to view a film, especially because video play mastery is objectively evaluated (by degree of scores, kills, number of secrets found, etc.), whereas a film viewer has no such objective evaluation of performance.

4   The violent action game is often experienced as a simulation of interacting with an online reality, because the player's mental flow of perceptions that cause emotions and cognition that causes action that again causes perceptions, is very similar to real-life interaction.

Seen from one perspective, violent video games look very much like a playful enactment of skills and dispositions central to our gatherer-warrior-hunter ancestors. The players cope with a hostile environment by quick perception and by spatial and motor skills, they notice landmarks and gather objects that may be useful. However, seen from another perspective, video games are ways in which players learn to master facets of computers. Video games thus mold the biological inheritance in a way that accords with present-day cultural needs. As pointed out in several studies (Greenfield, Brannon, & Lohr, 1994; Greenfield, Camaioni, et al., 1994, for example), computer games are important playful tools for learning to interact with the computer medium and its graphic interface, just as the games enhance spatial skills and eye-hand coordination. Those studies also show that boys on average perform significantly better in action-oriented computer games, partly because of better spatial skills, but also for motivational reasons, because boys have a stronger preference for violent games than girls, maybe for biological reasons (kubey & Larson, 1990). This accords closely with evolutionary theories of sex differences in spatial abilities due to division of labor in gatherer-hunter societies (Silverman & Eals, 1992) and to motivational features that supported hunting. It is deplorable that the video game industry has not yet invented games that cater to those gatherer skills and motivations that are attractive to girls (verbal skills, object memory, location memory, and a series of social skills and pro-social motives).

When most children and adolescents in the industrialized world spend considerable time playing video games, and very often violent video games, pessimists argue that this was a dangerous trap by a greedy video game industry to evoke primitive and antisocial features of our biological inheritance. They further question that those games provide real creative interactive experiences. They argue that the interactivity is only a surface phenomenon that veils indoctrination because "most games require the player to take part in developing the game scenario, but players are routinely rewarded for identifying and selecting the strategies built in by the game designer" (Funk & Buchman, 1996). However, this is also the case in most culturally produced games and fictions and does not show whether video games are putting narrower constraints on personal creativity than other games and fictions. Pessimists further argue that the scenarios and themes provide an impoverished experience. Provenzo (1991) states, "Compared to the worlds of imagination provided by play with dolls and blocks, games such as those reviewed in this chapter [popular Nintendo games] ultimately represent impoverished cultural and sensory environments" (p. 97). Provenzo further points out the way in which video games rely on cultural stereotypes. These arguments, however, beg the question of why so many children choose such games, why they play with a Barbie Doll computer game instead of playing with the physical doll, or why they choose to fight galactic wars on computers instead of playing with physical blocks or all kinds of physical guns and tanks. Provenzo's portrayal of the impoverishment of the game leaves something out. Most video games or fairy tales are certainly more impoverished than a complex social melodrama or a novel

217

*Table 1* A feature comparison of film viewing and video-game playing

| Entertainment Medium | Film | Video Game |
|---|---|---|
| Perceptual quality interactive control of: | High visual salience | Medium visual salience |
| Visual input (point of view) | None | Controlled by player via interface |
| Story events | None | Controlled by player via interface in interaction with game agency |
| Temporal progression | None | Controlled by player's explorative coping and time-out devices |
| Emotional significance of events | Controlled by film and characters | Emotional arousal is labeled according to the player's action skills and varies over time due to learning processes. Curiosity, surprise, and suspense are molded by repetitive interaction. |
| Support mainly: | One viewing | Multiple games |
| | Mental and bodily simulations of cued events | Concrete interactive simulations based on extensive cognitive mappings of space and the learning of procedural schemas, leading to motor reactions via interface |
| | Vicarious simulation of characters | First-person simulation of roles, leading to immersion in game world |
| Evaluation of viewer/ player performance | None | Yes, by game success, and eventually by score mechanism |

by James Joyce, but the interaction with science fiction worlds or audiovisual remakes of fairy tale worlds may be more gratifying than passively viewing a cops and robbers show on TV.

Optimists can argue that video games fulfill positive functions that mold our biological inheritance to fit present-day needs. I have argued for the pleasures derived from video games as tools for emotional control, which adds a new cultural artifact to those means of mood management that have been developed by the entertainment industry, for instance, film and TV (Grodal, 1997; Zillmann & Bryant, 1994). Video games are learning processes that develop a series of cognitive skills (Loftus & Loftus, 1983), just as video games enhance mastery of the computer (Greenfield, Camaioni, et al., 1994).

The themes and actions of most video games are updated versions of fairy tales and Homer's *Odyssey*, enhanced by modern audiovisual salience and interactive capabilities. Central themes are the fights with dragons and evil monsters in combination with quests through dangerous and exotic scenarios. It is furthermore important for many games that the hero rescues damsels in distress. That there are only a few basic narrative patterns in video games is not surprising because there are not many basic narrative patterns in fiction. Of those basic narrative patterns only action-adventure and mystery plots are suitable for interactive narratives, whereas romances, comedies, and tragedies rely centrally on passive recipients for the emotional build-up (Grodal, 1997). Certainly there are degrees of freedom in the way in which action-adventure narratives are provided with themes; in principle it is easy to imagine games in which women save men in distress, or games that provide scores for feeding hungry children in Africa. Criticism that points out stereotypes, prejudices, and antisocial behavior in video games puts a healthy pressure on the industry to come up with better themes.

Video games do not replace the traditional forms of entertainment but rather provide a supplement to, for instance, reading, watching film and television, and participating in sports. The pleasure derived from an interactive immersion in a virtual reality competes with pleasures derived from other types of entertainment that emphasize passive pleasures, like film and television. Interactive media like video games create a further sophistication of media consumption by enabling consumers to switch between a passive control of their emotional and cognitive states (by actively selecting one-way media) and an active control of these states (by choosing interactive media). These interactive media are still in their infancy for reasons related to the kinds of stories that, for technical reasons, can be enacted. But interactive media have already provided quite new pleasures due to the way in which they enable players to simulate an interactive control of human faculties and emotions in possible worlds.

# References

Ballard, M. E., & Wiest, J. R. (1996). Mortal Kombat™: The effects of violent videogame play on males' hostility and cardiovascular responding. *Journal of Applied Social Psychology, 26*(8), 717–730.

Bandura, A. (1994). Social cognitive theory of mass communication. In J. Bryant and D. Zillmann (Eds.), *Media effects: Advances in theory and research* (pp. 61–90). Hillsdale, NJ: Lawrence Erlbaum Associates.

Brewer, W. F. (1996). Narrative suspense and rereading. In P. Vorderer, H. J. Wulff, and M. Friedrichsen (Eds.), *Suspense: Conceptualizations, theoretical analyses, and empirical explorations*. Mahwah, NJ: Lawrence Erlbaum Associates.

Carroll, N. (1990). *The philosophy of horror, or paradoxes of the heart*. London: Routledge.

Calvert, S. L., & Tan, S.-L. (1994). Impact of virtual reality on young adults' physiological arousal and aggressive thoughts: Interaction versus observation. *Journal of Applied Developmental Psychology 15*, 125–139.

Dominick, J. R. (1984). Videogames, television violence and aggression in teenagers. *Journal of Communication, 34*(2), 136–147.

Fling, S., Smith, L., Rodriguez, D., Thornton, D., Atkins, E., & Nixon, K. (1992). Videogames, aggression, and self-esteem: A survey, *Social Behavior and Personality. 20*(1), 39–46.

Frijda, N. H. (1986). *The emotions*. Cambridge, England: Cambridge University Press.

Funk, J. B., & Buchman, D. D. (1996). Playing violent video and computer games and adolescent self-concept. *Journal of Communication 46*(2), 19–32.

Graybill, D., Kirsch, J., & Esselman, E. (1985). Effects of playing violent versus nonviolent video games on the aggressive ideation of aggressive and nonaggressive children. *Child Study Journal 15*, 199–205.

Graybill, D., Strawniak, M., Hunter, T., & O'Leary, M. (1987). Effects of playing versus observing violent versus nonviolent video games on children's aggression. *Psychology: A Quarterly Journal of Human Behavior 24*(3), 1–8.

Greenfield, P. M. (1984). *Mind and media: The effects of television, computers and videogames.* Cambridge, MA: Harvard University Press.

Greenfield, P. M., Brannon, C., & Lohr, D. (1994). Two-dimensional representation of movement through three-dimensional space: The role of video game expertise. *Journal of Applied Developmental Psychology 15*, 87–103.

Greenfield, P M., Camaioni, L., Ercolani, P., Weiss, L., Lauber, B. A., & Perucchini, P. (1994). Cognitive socialization by computer games in two cultures: Inductive discovery or mastery of an iconic code? *Journal of Applied Developmental Psychology 15*, 59–85.

Grodal, T. (1997). *Moving pictures: A new theory of film genres, feelings and cognition.* Oxford, England: Oxford University Press/Clarendon.

Hoffman, K. (1995). Effects of playing versus witnessing video game violence on attitudes toward aggression and acceptance of violence as a means of conflict resolution (Doctoral dissertation, University of Alabama, 1994). *Dissertation Abstracts International, 56/03, 747. Journal of Applied Developmental Psychology, 15* (1994).

Kerstenbaum, G. I., & Weinstein, L. (1985). Personality, psychopathology, and developmental issues in male adolescent video game use. *Journal of the American Academy of Child Psychiatry 24*(3), 329–337.

Kubey, R., & Larson, R. (1990). The use and experience of the new video media among children and young adolescents. *Communication Research*, 17(1), 107–130.

Loftus, G. R., & Loftus, E. F. (1983). *Mind at play: The psychology of videogames.* New York: Basic Books.

Provenzo, E. F. (1991). *Video kids: Making sense of Nintendo.* Cambridge, MA: Harvard University Press.

Reeves, B., & Nass, C. (1996). *The media equation: How people treat computers, television, and new media like real people and places.* Cambridge, England: Cambridge University Press.

Rubin, A. (1994). Media uses and effects: A uses-and-gratifications perspective. In J. Bryant and D. Zillmann (Eds.), *Media effects: Advances in theory and research.* Hillsdale, NJ: Lawrence Erlbaum Associates.

Schutte, N. S., Malouf, J. M., Post-Gorden, J. C., & Rodasta, A. L. (1988). Effects of playing videogames on children's aggressive and other behaviors. *Journal of Applied Social Psychology. 18*(5), 454–460.

Shapiro, M. A., & McDonald, D. G. (1992). I'm not a real doctor, but I play one in virtual reality: Implications of virtual reality for judgements about reality. *Journal of Communication 43*(4), 94–114.

Silverman, I., & Eals, M. (1992). Sex differences in spatial abilities: Evolutionary theory and data. In J. H. Barkow, L. Cosmides, and J. Tooby (Eds.), *The adapted mind: Evolutionary psychology and the generation of culture* (pp. 533–553). New York: Oxford University Press.

Silverman, S. B., & Williamson, P. A. (1987). The effects of videogame play on young children's aggression, fantasy, and prosocial behavior. *Journal of Applied Developmental Psychology. 126*, 273–284.

220

Smith, M. (1995). *Engaging characters: Fiction, emotion and the cinema.* Oxford, England: Oxford University Press/Clarendon.

Turkle, S. (1984). *The second self: Computers and the human spirit.* New York: Simon & Schuster.

Zillmann, D. (1996). The psychology of suspense in dramatic exposition. In P. Vorderer, H. J. Wulff, and M. Friedrichsen (1996). *Suspense: Conceptualizations, theoretical analyses, and empirical explorations.* Mahwah, NJ: Lawrence Erlbaum Associates.

Zillmann, D., & Bryant, J. (1994). Entertainment as media effect. In J. Bryant and D. Zillmann (Eds.), *Media effects: Advances in theory and research* (pp. 437–461). Hillsdale, NJ: Lawrence Erlbaum Associates.

# 58

# ALLEGORIES OF CONTROL

*Alexander R. Galloway*

Source: *Gaming: Essays on Algorithmic Culture* (Minneapolis, MN: University of Minnesota Press, 2006), pp. 85–106.

## Playing the algorithm

With the progressive arrival of new forms of media over the last century or so and perhaps earlier there appears a sort of lag time, call it the "thirty-year rule," starting from the invention of a medium and ending at its ascent to proper and widespread functioning in culture at large. This can be said of film, from its birth at the end of the nineteenth century up to the blossoming of classical film form in the 1930s, or of the Internet with its long period of relatively hidden formation during the 1970s and 1980s only to erupt on the popular stage in the mid-1990s. And we can certainly say the same thing today about video games: what started as a primitive pastime in the 1960s has through the present day experienced its own evolution from a simple to a more sophisticated aesthetic logic, such that one might predict a coming golden age for video games into the next decade not unlike what film experienced in the late 1930s and 1940s.[1] Games like *Final Fantasy X* or *Grand Theft Auto III* signal the beginning of this new golden age. Still, video games reside today in a distinctly lowbrow corner of contemporary society and thus have yet to be held aloft as an art form on par with those of the highest cultural production. This strikes me as particularly attractive, for one may approach video games today as a type of beautifully undisturbed processing of contemporary life, as yet unmarred by bourgeois exegeses of the format.

But how may one critically approach these video games, these uniquely *algorithmic* cultural objects? Certainly they would have something revealing to say about life inside today's global informatic networks. They might even suggest a new approach to critical interpretation itself, one that is as computercentric as its object of study. Philippe Sollers wrote in 1967 that interpretation concerns "The punctuation, the *scanning*, the spatialization of texts"; a year later Roland Barthes put it like this: "the space of writing is to be scanned, not pierced."[2] And a few years later, Jameson adopted a similar vocabulary: "Allegorical interpretation is a type of *scanning* that, *moving back and forth across the text*, readjusts its terms in constant modification of a type quite different from our stereotypes of some static or medieval or biblical decoding."[3] Not coincidentally, these three borrow vocabulary from the realm of electronic machines—the "scanning" of electrons inside a television's screen, or even the scanner/parser modules of a computer compiler—to describe a more contemporary, informatic mode of cultural analysis and interpretation.

Indeed, this same "digitization" of allegorical interpretation, if one may call it that, is evident in film criticism of the 1970s and 1980s, concurrent with the emergence of consumer video machines and the first personal computers. This discourse was inaugurated by the 1970 analysis of John Ford's *Young Mr. Lincoln* written by the editors of *Cahiers du cinéma*. Their reading is aimed at classical Hollywood films, so it has a certain critical relationship to ideology and formal hegemony. Yet they clearly state that their technique is neither an interpretation (getting out something already *in* the film) nor a demystification (digging through manifest meaning to get at latent meaning).

> We refuse to look for "depth," to go from the "literal meaning" to some "secret meaning"; we are not content with what it says (what it intends to say) . . . . What will be attempted here through a re-scansion of these films in a process of active reading, is to make them say what they have to say *within* what they leave unsaid, to reveal their constituent lacks; these are neither faults in the work . . . . nor a deception on the part of the author . . . . They are *structuring absences*.[4]

The influence of computers and informatic networks, of what Gene Youngblood in the same year called the "intermedia network," on the *Cahiers* mentality is unmistakable. Their approach is not a commentary on the inner workings of the cinematic text—as an earlier mode of allegorical interpretation would have required—but a rereading, a rescanning, and ultimately a *word processing* of the film itself. The *Cahiers* style of analysis is what one might term a "horizontal" allegory. It scans the surfaces of texts looking for new interpretive patterns. These patterns are, in essence, allegorical, but they no longer observe the division between what Jameson called the negative hermeneutic of ideology critique on the one hand and the positive hermeneutic of utopian collectivism on the other.[5] This is the crucial point: scanning is wholly different from demystifying. And as two different techniques for interpretation, they are indicative of two very different political and social realities: computerized versus noncomputerized.

Some of Deleuze's later writings are helpful in understanding the division between these two realities. In his "Postscript on Control Societies," a short work from 1990, Deleuze defines two historical periods: first, the "disciplinary socie-ties" of modernity, growing out of the rule of the sovereign, into the "vast spaces of enclosure," the social castings and bodily molds that Michel Foucault has described so well; and second, what Deleuze terms the "societies of control" that inhabit the late twentieth century—these are based around what he calls logics of "modulation" and the "ultrarapid forms of free-floating control."[6] While the disci-plinary societies of high modernity were characterized by more physical semiotic

223

constructs such as the signature and the document, today's societies of control are characterized by immaterial ones such as the password and the computer. These control societies are characterized by the networks of genetic science and computers, but also by much more conventional network forms. In each case, though, Deleuze points out how the principle of organization in computer networks has shifted away from confinement and enclosure toward a seemingly infinite extension of controlled mobility:

> A control is not a discipline. In making freeways, for example, you don't enclose people but instead multiply the means of control. I am not saying that this is the freeway's exclusive purpose, but that people can drive infinitely and "freely" without being at all confined yet while still being perfectly controlled. This is our future.[7]

Whether it is an information superhighway or a plain old freeway, what Deleuze defines as control is key to understanding how computerized information societies function. It is part of a larger shift in social life, characterized by a movement away from central bureaucracies and vertical hierarchies toward a broad network of autonomous social actors. As the architect Branden Hookway writes:

> The shift is occurring across the spectrum of information technologies as we move from models of the global application of intelligence, with their universality and frictionless dispersal, to one of local applications, where intelligence is site-specific and fluid.[8]

This shift toward a control society has also been documented in such varied texts as those of sociologist Manuel Castells, Hakim Bey, and the Italian autonomist political movement of the 1970s. Even harsh critics of this shift, such as Nick Dyer-Witheford (author of *CyberMarx*), surely admit that the shift is taking place. It is part of a larger process of postmodernization that is happening the world over.

What are the symptoms of this social transformation? They are seen whenever a company like Microsoft outsources a call center from Redmond to Bangalore, or in the new medical surveillance networks scanning global health databases for the next outbreak of SARS. Even today's military has redefined itself around network- and computercentric modes of operation: pilot interfaces for remotely operated Predator aircraft mimic computer game interfaces; captains in the U.S. Army learn wartime tactics through video games like *Full Spectrum Command*, a training tool jointly developed by the American and Singaporean militaries; in the military's Future Combat Systems initiative, computer networks themselves are classified as weapons systems.

But these symptoms are mere indices for deeper social maladies, many of which fall outside the realm of the machine altogether—even if they are ultimately exacerbated by it. For while Bangalore may be booming, it is an island of exception inside a country still struggling with the challenges of postcolonialism and unequal modernization. Computers have a knack for accentuating social injustice, for widening the gap between the rich and the poor (as the economists have well documented). Thus the claims I make here about the relationship between video games and the contemporary political situation refer specifically to the social imaginary of the wired world and how the various structures of organization and regulation within it are repurposed into the formal grammar of the medium.

As Jameson illustrates in *Signatures of the Visible*, the translation of political realities into film has a somewhat complicated track record, for mainstream cinema generally deals with the problem of politics not in fact by solving it but by sublimating it. Fifty years ago, Hitchcock showed the plodding, unfeeling machinations of the criminal justice system in his film *The Wrong Man*. Today the police are not removed from the crime film genre, far from it, but their micromovements of bureaucratic command and control are gone. The political sleight of hand of mainstream cinema is that the audience is rarely shown the boring minutiae of discipline and confinement that constitute the various apparatuses of control in contemporary societies. This is precisely why Jameson's interpretive method is so successful. Another example: in John Woo's *The Killer*, not only is the killer above the law (or, more precisely, outside it), but so is the cop, both literally in his final bloody act of extrajudicial vengeance and also figuratively in that one never sees the cuffings, the bookings, the indictments, the court appearances, and all the other details of modern criminality and confinement depicted in *The Wrong Man*. Films like *Bad Boys 2* or *Heat* do the same thing. In fact, most cop flicks eschew this type of representation, rising above the profession, as it were, to convey other things (justice, friendship, honor, or what have you). In other words, discipline and confinement, as a modern control apparatus, are rarely represented today, except when, in singular instances like the Rodney King tape, they erupt onto the screen in gory detail (having first erupted from the bounds of film itself and penetrated the altogether different medium of video). Instead, discipline and confinement are upstaged by other matters, sublimated into other representational forms. The accurate representation of political control is thus eclipsed in much of the cinema (requiring, Jameson teaches us, allegorical interpretation to bring it back to the fore), which is unfortunate, because despite its unsexy screen presence, informatics control is precisely the most important thing to show on the screen if one wishes to allegorize political power today.

Now, what is so interesting about video games is that they essentially invert film's political conundrum, leading to almost exactly the opposite scenario. Video games don't attempt to hide informatic control; they flaunt it. Look to the auteur work of game designers like Hideo Kojima, Yu Suzuki, or Sid Meier. In the work of Meier, the gamer is not simply playing this or that historical simulation. The gamer is instead learning, internalizing, and becoming intimate with a massive, multipart, global algorithm. To play the game means to play the code of the game. To win means to know the system. And thus to *interpret* a game means to interpret its algorithm (to discover its parallel "allegorithm").

*Civilization III*, Firaxis Games, 2001

So today there is a twin transformation: from the modern cinema to the contemporary video game, but also from traditional allegory to what I am calling
horizontal or "control" allegory. I suggest that video games are, at their structural core, in direct synchronization with the political realities of the informatic
age. If Meier's work is about anything, it is about information society itself. It is
about knowing systems and knowing code, or, I should say, knowing *the* system
and knowing *the* code. "The way computer games teach structures of thought,"
writes Ted Friedman on Meier's game series *Civilization*, "is by getting you to
internalize the logic of the program. To win, you can't just do whatever you want.
You have to figure out what will work within the rules of the game. You must

226

learn to predict the consequences of each move, and anticipate the computer's response. Eventually, your decisions become intuitive, as smooth and rapid-fire as the computer's own machinations."[9] Meier makes no effort to hide this essential characteristic behind a veil, either, as would popular cinema. The massive electronic network of command and control that I have elsewhere called "protocol" is precisely the visible, active, essential, and core ingredient of Meier's work in particular and video games in general. You can't miss it. Lev Manovich agrees with Friedman: "[Games] demand that a player can execute an algorithm in order to win. As the player proceeds through the game, she gradually discovers the rules that operate in the universe constructed by this game. She learns its hidden logic—in short, its algorithm."[10] So while games have linear narratives that may appear in broad arcs from beginning to end, or may appear in cinematic segues and interludes, they also have nonlinear narratives that must unfold in algorithmic form during gameplay. In this sense, video games deliver to the player the power relationships of informatic media firsthand, choreographed into a multivalent cluster of play activities. In fact, in their very core, video games do nothing but present contemporary political realities in relatively unmediated form. They solve the problem of political control, not by sublimating it as does the cinema, but by *making it coterminous with the entire game*, and in this way video games achieve a unique type of political transparency.

Buckminster Fuller articulated the systemic, geopolitical characteristics of gaming decades before in his "World Game" and World Design Initiative of the 1960s. The World Game was to be played on a massive "stretched out football field sized world map." The game map was "wired throughout so that mini-bulbs, installed all over its surface, could be lighted by the computer at appropriate points to show various, accurately positioned, proportional data regarding world conditions, events, and resources." Fuller's game was a global resource management simulation, not unlike Meier's *Civilization*. But the object of Fuller's game was "to explore for ways to make it possible for anybody and everybody in the human family to enjoy the total earth without any human interfering with any other human and without any human gaining advantage at the expense of another." While Fuller's game follows the same logic of *Civilization* or other global algorithm games, his political goals were decidedly more progressive, as he showed in a jab at the American mathematician John von Neumann: "In playing the game I propose that we set up a different system of games from that of Dr. John Von Neumann whose 'Theory of Games' was always predicated upon one side losing 100 percent. His game theory is called 'Drop Dead.' In our World Game we propose to explore and test by assimilated adoption various schemes of 'How to Make the World Work.' To win the World Game everybody must be made physically successful. Everybody must win."[11]

So, broadly speaking, there is an extramedium shift in which films about the absence of control have been replaced by games that fetishize control. But there is simultaneously an intermedium shift, happening predominantly within the cinema. What Jameson called the conspiracy film of the 1970s (*All the President's Men, The Parallax View*) became no longer emblematic at the start of the new millennium. Instead, films of epistemological reversal have become prominent, mutating out of the old whodunit genre. David Fincher is the contemporary counterpart to Alan Pakula in this regard, with *The Game* and *Fight Club* as masterpieces of epistemological reversal, but one need only point to the preponderance of other films grounded in mind-bending trickery of reality and illusion (*Jagged Edge, The Usual Suspects, The Matrix, The Cell, eXistenZ, The Sixth Sense, Wild Things,* and so on, or even with games like Hideo Kojima's *Metal Gear* series) to see how the cinema has been delivered from the oppression of unlocatable capitalism (as in Jameson's view) only to be sentenced to a new oppression of

"City View," *Civilization III*

disingenuous informatics. For every moment that the conspiracy film rehashes the traumas of capitalism in the other-form of monumental modern architecture, as with the Space Needle at the start of *The Parallax View*, the knowledge-reversal film aims at doling out data to the audience, but only to show at the last minute how everything was otherwise. The digital can't exert control with architecture, so it does it with information. The genre offers a type of epistemological challenge to the audience: follow a roller coaster of reversals and revelations, and the viewer will eventually achieve informatic truth in the end. I see this fetishization of the "knowledge triumph" as a sort of informatization of the conspiracy film described by Jameson.

But back to video games and how exactly the operator "plays the algorithm." This happens most vividly in many console games, in which intricate combinations of buttons must be executed with precise timing to accomplish something in the game. Indeed, games like *Tekken* or *Tony Hawk's Pro Skater* hinge on the operator's ability to motor-memorize button combinations for specific moves. The algorithms for such moves are usually documented in the game sleeve by using a coded notation similar to tablature for music ("Up + X-X-O" on a PlayStation controller, for example). Newcomers to such games are often derided as mere "button mashers." But in a broader sense, let us return to Sid Meier and see what it means to play the algorithm at the macro level.

229

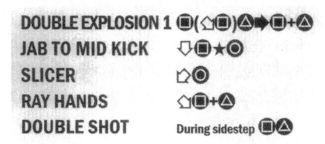

*Tekken Tag Tournament*, Namco, 1994

## Ideological critique

After the initial experience of playing *Civilization* there are perhaps three successive phases that one passes through on the road to critiquing this particularly loaded cultural artifact. The first phase is often an immense chasm of pessimism arising from the fear that *Civilization* in particular and video games in general are somehow immune to meaningful interpretation, that they are somehow outside criticism. Yes, games are about algorithms, but what exactly does that matter when it comes to cultural critique? Perhaps video games *have* no politics? This was, most likely, the same sensation faced by others attempting to critique hitherto mystified artifacts of popular culture—Janice Radway with the romance novel, Dick Hebdige with punk style, or Roland Barthes with the striptease. Often it is precisely those places in culture that appear politically innocent that are at the end of the day the most politically charged. Step two, then, consists of the slow process of ideological critique using the telltale clues contained in the game to connect it with larger social processes. (Here is where Caillois, presented in chapter 1 as essentially apolitical, returns with a penetrative observation about the inherent political potential of games, vis-à-vis the question of demystification and institutional critique. Reacting to Huizinga, Caillois writes that "without doubt, secrecy, mystery, and even travesty can be transformed into play activity, but it must be immediately pointed out that this transformation is necessarily to the detriment of the secret and mysterious, which play exposes, publishes, and somehow *expends*. In a word, play tends to remove the very nature of the mysterious. On the other hand, when the secret, the mask, or the costume fulfills a sacramental function one can be sure that not play, but an institution is involved.")[12] Critiquing the ideological content of video games is what Katie Salen and Eric Zimmerman, following Brian Sutton-Smith on play, refer to as the "cultural rhetoric" of games.[13] For *Civilization*, the political histories of state and national powers coupled with the rise of the information society seem particularly apropos. One might then construct a vast ideological critique of the game, focusing on its explicit logocentrism, its nationalism and imperialism, its expansionist logic, as well as its implicit racism and classism.

Just as medieval scholars used the existence of contradiction in a text as indication of the existence of allegory, so *Civilization* has within it many contradictions that suggest such an allegorical interpretation. One example is the explicit mixing of ahistorical logic, such as the founding of a market economy in a place called "London" in 4000 BC, with the historical logic of scientific knowledge accumulation or cultural development. Another is the strange mixing of isometric perspective for the foreground and traditional perspective for the background in the "City View."

The expansionist logic of the game is signified both visually and spatially. "At the beginning of the game," Friedman writes, "almost all of the map is black; you don't get to learn what's out there until one of your units has explored the area. Gradually, as you expand your empire and send out scouting parties, the landscape is revealed."[14] These specific conventions within both the narrative and the visual signification of the game therefore reward expansionism, even require it. Meier's *Alpha Centauri* mimics these semiotic conventions but ups the ante by positioning the player in the ultimate expansionist haven, outer space. This has the added bonus of eliminating concerns about the politics of expansionist narratives, for, one assumes, it is easier to rationalize killing anonymous alien life-forms in *Alpha Centauri* than it is killing Zulus in *Civilization III*. Expansionism has, historically, always had close links with racism; the expansionism of the colonial period of modernity, for example, was rooted in a specific philosophy about the superiority of European culture, religion, and so on, over that of the Asiatic, African, and American native peoples. Again we turn to Meier, who further developed his expansionist vision in 1994 with *Colonization*, a politically dubious game modeled on the software engine used in *Civilization* and set in the period between the discovery of the New World and the American Revolution. The American Indians in this game follow a less-than-flattering historical stereotype, both in their onscreen depiction and in terms of the characteristics and abilities they are granted as part of the algorithm. Later, in *Civilization III*, Meier expanded his stereotyping to include sixteen historical identities, from the Aztecs and the Babylonians to the French and the Russians. In this game, one learns that the Aztecs are "religious" but not "industrious," characteristics that affect their various proclivities in the gamic algorithm, while the Romans are "militaristic" but, most curiously, not "expansionist." Of course, this sort of typing is but a few keystrokes away from a world in which blacks are "athletic" and women are "emotional." That the game tactfully avoids these more blatant offenses does not exempt it from endorsing a logic that prizes the classification of humans into types and the normative labeling of those types.

Worse than attributing a specific characteristic to a specific racial or national group is the fact that ideological models such as these ignore the complexity, variation, and rich diversity of human life at many levels: the *Civilization III* algorithm ignores change over time (Tsarist Russia versus Soviet Russia); it erases any number of other peoples existing throughout history the Inuit, the Irish, and on and on; it conflates a civilization with a specific national or tribal identity and

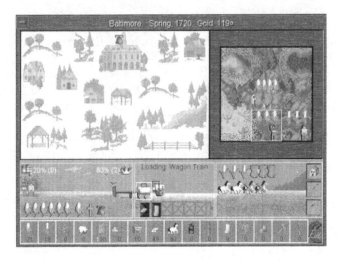

*Colonization*, Micro Prose, 1995

ignores questions of hybridity and diaspora such as those of African Americans or Jews. In short, it transposes the many-layered quality of social life to an inflexible, reductive algorithm for "civilization"—a process not dissimilar to what Marxists call reification, only updated for the digital age. (The reason for doing this is, of course, a practical one: to create balanced gameplay, game designers require an

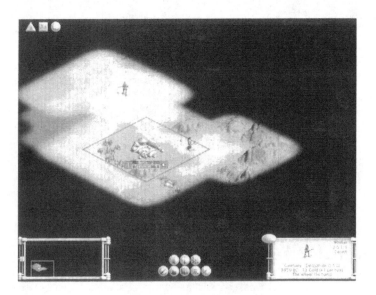

*Civilization III*

| Civilization | Commercial | Expansionist | Industrious | Militaristic | Religious | Scientific |
|---|---|---|---|---|---|---|
| Americans | | X | X | | | |
| Aztecs | | | | X | X | |
| Babylonians | | | | | X | X |
| Chinese | | | X | X | | |
| Egyptians | | | X | | X | |
| English | X | X | | | | |
| French | X | | X | | | |
| Germans | X | X | | | | X |
| Greeks | X | | | | | |
| Indians | X | | | | X | |
| Iroquois | | X | | | X | |
| Japanese | | | | X | X | |
| Persians | | | X | | | X |
| Romans | X | | | X | | |
| Russians | | X | | | | |
| Zulus | | X | | X | | X |

"Civilization Characteristics," *Civilization III*

array of variables that can be tweaked and tuned across the various environments and characters.) And while one needs no further proof of the game's dubious political assumptions, I might point out that the game is also a folly of logocentrism; it is structured around a quest for knowledge, with all human thought broken down into neatly packaged discoveries that are arranged in a branching time line where one discovery is a precondition for the next. But so much for ideological scrutiny.

## Informatic critique

In conjunction with these manifest political investigations, the third step is to elaborate a formal critique rooted in the core principles of informatics that serve as the foundation of the gaming format. The principles adopted by Manovich in *The Language of New Media* might be a good place to begin: numerical representation, modularity, automation, variability, and transcoding. But to state this would simply be to state the obvious, that *Civilization* is new media. The claim that *Civilization* is a control allegory is to say something different: that the game plays the very codes of informatic control today. So what are the core principles of informatic control? Beyond Manovich, I would supplement the discussion with an analysis of what are called the protocols of digital technology. The Internet protocols, for example, consist of approximately three thousand technical documents published to date outlining the necessary design specifications for specific technologies like the Internet Protocol (IP) or Hypertext Markup Language (HTML). These documents are called RFCs (Request for Comments). The expression "request for comments" derives from a memorandum titled "Host Software" sent by Steve Crocker on April 7, 1969 (which is known today as RFC number 1) and is indicative of the

233

collaborative, open nature of protocol authorship (one is reminded of Deleuze's "freeways"). Called "the primary documentation of the Internet,"[15] these technical memorandums detail the vast majority of standards and protocols used today on game consoles like the Xbox as well as other types of networked computers.[16]

Flexibility is one of the core political principles of informatic control, described both by Deleuze in his theorization of "control society" and by computer scientists like Crocker. The principle derives from the scientist Paul Baran's pioneering work on distributed networks, which prizes flexibility as a strategy for avoiding technical failure at the system level. Flexibility is still one of the core principles of Internet protocol design, perhaps best illustrated by the routing functionality of IP, which is able to move information through networks in an ad hoc, adaptable manner. The concept of flexibility is also central to the new information economies, powering innovations in fulfillment, customization, and other aspects of what is known as "flexible accumulation." While it might appear liberating or utopian, don't be fooled; flexibility is one of the founding principles of global informatic control. It is to the control society what discipline was to a previous one.

Flexibility is allegorically repurposed in *Civilization* via the use of various sliders and parameters to regulate flow and create systemic equilibrium. All elements in the game are put in quantitative, dynamic relationships with each other, such that a "Cultural Victory" conclusion of the game is differentiated from a "Conquest Victory" conclusion only through slight differences in the two algorithms for winning. The game is able to adjust and compensate for whatever outcome the operator pursues. Various coefficients and formulas (the delightfully named "Governor governor," for example) are tweaked to achieve balance in gameplay.

What flexibility allows for is universal standardization (another crucial principle of informatic control). If diverse technical systems are *flexible* enough to accommodate massive contingency, then the result is a more robust system that can subsume all comers under the larger mantle of continuity and universalism. The Internet protocol white papers say it all: "Be conservative in what you do, be liberal in what you accept from others."[17] The goal of total subsumption goes hand in hand with informatic control. The massive "making equivalent" in *Civilization*—the making equivalent of different government types (the most delicious detail in early versions of Meier's game is the pull-down menu option for starting a revolution), of different victory options, of formulaically equating *n* number of happy citizens with the availability of luxuries, and so on—is, in this sense, an allegorical reprocessing of the universal standardizations that go into the creation of informatic networks today. In Meier, game studies looks more like game theory.

In contrast to my previous ideological concerns, the point now is not whether the *Civilization* algorithm embodies a specific ideology of "soft" racism, or even whether it embodies the core principles of new media adopted from Manovich, but whether it embodies the logic of informatic control itself. Other simulations let the gamer play the logic of a plane (*Flight Simulator*, or Meier's own flying games from the 1980s), the logic of a car *(Gran Turismo)*, or what have you. But with *Civilization*, Meier has simulated the total logic of informatics itself.

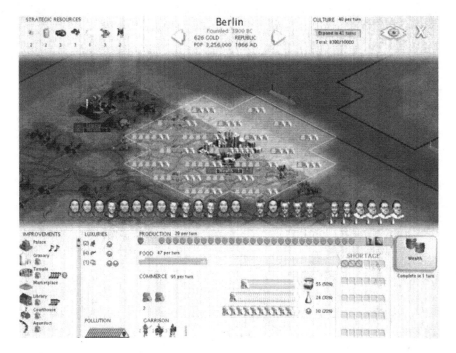

*Civilization III*

But now we are at an impasse, for the more one allegorizes informatic control in *Civilization*, the more my previous comments about ideology start to unravel. And the more one tries to pin down the ideological critique, the more one sees that such a critique is undermined by the existence of something altogether different from ideology: informatic code. So where the ideological critique succeeds, it fails. Instead of offering better clues, the ideological critique (traditional allegory) is undermined by its own revelation of the protocological critique (control allegory). In video games, at least, one trumps the other. Consider my previous claims about Meier's construction of racial and national identity: the more one examines the actual construction of racial and national identity in the game, the more one sees that identity itself is an entirely codified affair within the logic of the software. Identity is a data type, a mathematical variable. The construction of identity in *Civilization* gains momentum from offline racial typing, to be sure, but then moves further to a specifically informatic mode of cybernetic typing: capture, transcoding, statistical analysis, quantitative profiling (behavioral or biological), keying attributes to specific numeric variables, and so on. This is similar to what Manovich calls the logic of selection—or what Lisa Nakamura calls "menudriven identities"—only now Manovich's pick-and-choose, windowshopper logic of graphical interfaces governs a rather distinct set of human identity attributes. As Nakamura laments, "Who can—or wants to—claim a perfectly pure, legible identity that can be fully expressed by a decision tree designed by a corporation?"[18] So the skin tone parameters for player character construction in everything from *Sissyfight* to *World of Warcraft* are not an index for older, offline constructions of race and identity, although they are a direct extension of this larger social history, but instead an index for the very dominance of informatic organization and how it has entirely overhauled, revolutionized, and recolonized the function of identity. In *Civilization*, identity is modular, instrumental, typed, numerical, algorithmic. To use history as another example: the more one begins to think that *Civilization* is about a certain ideological interpretation of history (neoconservative, reactionary, or what have you), or even that it creates a computer-generated "history effect," the more one realizes that it is about the absence of history altogether, or rather, the transcoding of history into specific mathematical models. History is what hurts, wrote Jameson—history is the slow, negotiated struggle of individuals together with others in their material reality. The modeling of history in computer code, even using Meier's sophisticated algorithms, can only ever be a reductive exercise of capture and transcoding. So "history" in *Civilization* is precisely the opposite of history, not because the game fetishizes the imperial perspective, but because the diachronic details of lived life are replaced by the synchronic homogeneity of code pure and simple. It is a new sort of fetish altogether. (To be entirely clear: mine is an argument about informatic control, not about ideology; a politically progressive "*People's Civilization*" game, à la Howard Zinn, would beg the same critique.) Thus the logic of informatics and horizontality is privileged over the logic of ideology and verticality in this game, as it mostly likely is in all video games in varying degrees.

So this is not unique to *Civilization*. The other great simulation game that has risen above the limitations of the genre is *The Sims*, but instead of seizing on the totality of informatic control as a theme, this game does the reverse, diving down into the banality of technology, the muted horrors of a life lived as an algorithm. As I have alluded to in Jameson, the depth model in traditional allegorical interpretation is a sublimation of the separation felt by the viewer between his or her experience of consuming the media and the potentially liberating political value of that media. But video games abandon this dissatisfying model of deferral, epitomizing instead the flatness of control allegory by unifying the act of playing the game with an immediate political experience. In other words, *The Sims* is a game that delivers its own political critique up front as part of the gameplay. There is no need for the critic to unpack the game later. The boredom, the sterility, the uselessness, and the futility of contemporary life appear precisely through those things that represent them best: a middleclass suburban house, an Ikea catalog of personal possessions, crappy food and even less appetizing music, the same dozen mindless tasks over and over—how can one craft a better critique of contemporary life? This is the politically dubious, but nonetheless revealing, quality of play identified by Adorno in the supplement to his *Aesthetic Theory:* "Playful forms are without exception forms of repetition"; "In art, play is from the outset disciplinary."[19]

As an entire genre, the first-person shooter also illustrates this type of allegorical interpretation of info-politics. Dash the naysayers, the shooter is an allegory of liberation pure and simple. This complicated genre is uncomplicated. There can be no better format for encoding and reprocessing the unvarnished exertion of affective force. I think of *Unreal Tournament* or *Counter-Strike* as the final realization of André Breton's dream of the purest surrealist act: the desire to burst into the street with a pistol, firing quickly and blindly at anyone complicit with what he called "the petty system of debasement and cretinization." The shooter as genre and the shooter as act are bound together in an intimate unity. The shooter is not a stand-in for activity. It *is* activity. (Just as the game is not a stand-in for informatics but *is* informatics.) The experience of the shooter is a "smooth" experience, to use Deleuze and Guattari's term, whereby its various components have yet to be stratified and differentiated, as text on one side and reading or looking on the other. In this sense, the aesthetics of gaming often lack any sort of deep representation (to the extent that representation requires both meaning and the encoding of meaning in material form). Allegory has collapsed back to a singularity in gaming. In fact, the redundancy in the vocabulary says it all: "the cultural logic of informatics." The activity of gaming, which, as I've stressed over and over, only ever comes into being when the game is actually played, is an *undivided* act wherein meaning and doing transpire in the same gamic gesture.

## A theory of pretending

This last point may be recontextualized through a fundamental observation about video games made at the outset of this book, that games let one *act*. In fact, they require it; video games are actions. Now, following the definition of literary allegory as "other-speak,"[20] I must define the gamic allegory: it is "other-act." The interpretation of gamic acts, then, should be thought of as the creation of a secondary discourse narrating a series of "other-acts." A century ago, Maurice Blondel suggested the word "allergy," following his theory of "coaction" or "another's action."[21] Blondel's use of the term assumes the existence of more than one individual, yet it is still an interesting influence because of his focus on parallel actions. Coaction proper in the context of video gaming would mean something like multiplayer action, which itself would need to be supplemented with a reading of the allegorical multiact. Either way, the interpretation of gamic acts is the process of understanding what it means to *do* something and mean something else. It is a science of the "as if." The customary definition of allegory as "extended metaphor" should, for games, be changed to "*enacted* metaphor." (In fact, for their active duality, zeugma or syllepsis are even more evocative figures of speech.) When one plays *Civilization*, there is one action taking place, but there is more than one significant action taking place. This is the parallelism necessitated by allegory. The first half of the parallelism is the actual playing of the game, but the other is the playing of informatics. For video games, one needs a *theory of pretending*, but only in the most positive sense of the term, as a theory of actions that have multiple meanings.

Again, Bateson: "The playful nip denotes the bite, but it does not denote what would be denoted by the bite."[22] So the roll of control allegory is—methodologically but not structurally—to see the nip and process neither the nip nor the bite, but instead what the bite denotes. I say methodologically but not structurally because there is no camouflage here: the playful video game may metacommunicate "this is play," but it can never avoid also being informatic control.

In this sense, I suggest that the game critic should be concerned not only with the interpretation of linguistic signs, as in literary studies or film theory, but also with the interpretation of *polyvalent doing*. This has always been an exciting terrain for hermeneutics, albeit less well traveled, and in it one must interpret material action instead of keeping to the relatively safe haven of textual analysis.

The critical terrain has likewise shrunk in the age of interactive media from a two-way relationship involving the text and the reader-as-critic to a singular moment involving the gamer (the doer) in the act of gameplay. The game-as-text is now wholly subsumed within the category of the gamer, for he or she creates the gamic text by doing. This explains the tendency toward control allegory in informatic culture. The primary authors are missing from this formula not because I wish to debase the growing auteur status of game designers, nothing of the sort, but simply because they are no longer directly involved in the moment of interpretation—but this has been the case in interpretive studies for many decades now.

Here, then, are the two allegorical modes compared side by side. Traditional or "deep" allegory seems to have its center of gravity in the early to mid-twentieth century and particularly in the cinematic form (à la Jameson), while control allegory finds its proper consummation in new media in general and video games in particular.

|  | *Deep allegory* | *Control allegory* |
| --- | --- | --- |
| Emblematic medium | Cinema | Video games |
| Political expression | Class struggle | Informatic control |
| Hermeneutic | Reading | Processing |
| Parallelism | Other-speak | Other-act |

Video games are allegories for our contemporary life under the protocological network of continuous informatic control. In fact, the more emancipating games seem to be as a medium, substituting activity for passivity or a branching narrative for a linear one, the more they are in fact hiding the fundamental social transformation into informatics that has affected the globe during recent decades. In modernity, ideology was an instrument of power, but in postmodernity ideology is a decoy, as I hope to have shown with the game *Civilization*. So a game's revealing is also a rewriting (a lateral step, not a forward one). A game's celebration of the end of ideological manipulation is also a new manipulation, only this time using wholly different diagrams of command and control.

In sum, with the appearance of informatic reprocessing as text—in the style of Sid Meier, but also in everything from turntablism to net.art—allegory no longer consists of a text and another text, but of an enacted text and another enacted text, such that we must now say: to do allegory means to playact, not, as Frye wrote, to allegorize means to write commentary. And hence Deleuze: "The philosopher creates. He doesn't reflect."

## Notes

1 On this point, Markku Eskelinen writes: "Historically speaking this is a bit like the 1910s in film studies; there were attractions, practices and very little understanding of what was actually going on, not to mention lots of money to be made and lost." See Eskelinen, "The Gaming Situation," *Game Studies* 1, no. 1 (July 2001).

2 See Philippe Sollers, "Programme," *Tel Quel*, no. 31 (Fall 1967): 3–7, (italics mine); and Roland Barthes, "La mort de l'auteur," in *Le bruissement de la langue* (Paris: Éditions du Seuil, 1984), 66 (italics mine).

3 Fredric Jameson, *Postmodernism, or The Cultural Logic of Late Capitalism* (Durham: Duke University Press, 1991), 168 (italics mine).

4 The editors of *Cahiers du cinéma*, "John Ford's *Young Mr. Lincoln*," in *Movies and Methods*, ed. Bill Nichols (Berkeley: University of California Press, 1976), 496.

5 Fredric Jameson, *The Political Unconscious* (Ithaca, N.Y.: Cornell University Press, 1982), 291–92.

6 Gilles Deleuze, *Negotiations* (New York: Columbia University Press, 1995), 178.

7 Gilles Deleuze, "Having an Idea in Cinema," in *Deleuze and Guattari: New Mappings in Politics, Philosophy and Culture*, ed. Eleanor Kaufman and Kevin Jon Heller (Minneapolis: University of Minnesota Press, 1998), 18 (translation modified by the author).

8 Branden Hookway, *Pandemonium: The Rise of Predatory Locales in the Postwar World* (New York: Princeton Architectural Press, 1999), 23–24.

9 Ted Friedman, "*Civilization* and Its Discontents: Simulation, Subjectivity, and Space," http://www.duke.edu/~tlove/civ.htm (accessed August 14, 2003). I will use *Civilization* to refer to the entire game series. When talking about a particular installment in the series, I will specify, as in *Civilization III*.

10 Manovich, *The Language of New Media*, 222.

11 R. Buckminster Fuller, *Your Private Sky: The Art of Design Science* (Baden, Switzerland: Lars Müller Publishers, 1999), 473, 479. For more on the globalistic and synergistic philosophy of the World Design Initiative, see also Fuller, *Your Private Sky: Discourse* (Baden, Switzerland: Lars Müller Publishers, 2001), 247–78.

12 Caillois, *Man, Play and Games*, 4.

13 See Salen and Zimmerman, *Rules of Play*, 515–34; and Brian SuttonSmith, *The Ambiguity of Play* (Cambridge: Harvard University Press, 2001).

14 Friedman, "*Civilization* and Its Discontents."

15 Pete Loshin, *Big Book of FYI RFCs* (San Francisco: Morgan Kaufmann, 2000), xiv.

16 For a technical overview of network protocols, see Eric Hall, *Internet Core Protocols: The Definitive Guide* (Sebastopol, Calif.: O'Reilly, 2000); or for a more interpretive approach, see my book *Protocol: How Control Exists after Decentralization* (Cambridge: MIT Press, 2004).

17 Jonathan Postel, "Transmission Control Protocol," RFC 793 (September 1981), http://www.faqs.org/rfcs/rfc793.html (accessed April 15, 2005).

18 Lisa Nakamura, *Cybertypes: Race, Ethnicity, and Identity on the Internet* (New York: Routledge, 2002), 114.

19  Theodor Adorno, *Aesthetic Theory* (Minneapolis: University of Minnesota Press, 1998), 317. See also Stallabrass's essay "Just Gaming," a brilliant critique of play no doubt inspired by Adorno's commentary on Schiller and Huizinga.
20  Fletcher gives a succinct etymology of the term: "*Allegory* from *allos* + *agoreuein (other* + *speak openly, speak in the assembly or market). Agoreuein* connotes public, open, declarative speech. This sense is inverted by the prefix *allos*. Thus allegory is often called 'inversion.'" See Angus Fletcher, *Allegory: The Theory of a Symbolic Mode* (Ithaca, N.Y.: Cornell University Press, 1964), 2.
21  Blondel, *Action (1893)*, 207.
22  Bateson, "A Theory of Play and Fantasy," in *Steps to an Ecology of Mind* (New York: Ballantine Books, 1972), 180.

# 59

# THE MAGIC CIRCLE

*Katie Salen and Eric Zimmerman*

Source: *Rules of Play: Game Design Fundamentals* (Cambridge, MA: The MIT Press, 2003), pp. 93–99.

> This is the problem of the way we get into and out of the play or game . . . what are the codes which govern these entries and exits?
>
> —***Brian Sutton-Smith***, *Child's Play*

What does it mean to enter the system of a game? How is it that play begins and ends? What makes up the boundary of a game? As we near the end of our first Unit, we need to address one last set of key concepts. These concepts are embedded in the question raised by Sutton-Smith: "How do we get into and out of the play or game?"At stake is an understanding of the artificiality of games, the way that they create their own time and space separate from ordinary life. The idea that the conflict in games is an *artificial* conflict is part of our very definition of games.

Steve Sniderman, in his excellent essay "The Life of Games," notes that the codes governing entry into a game lack explicit representation. "Players and fans and officials of any game or sport develop an acute awareness of the game's 'frame' or context, but we would be hard pressed to explain in writing, even after careful thought, exactly what the signs are. After all, even an umpire's yelling of 'Play Ball' is not the exact moment the game starts."[1] He goes on to explain that players (and fans) must rely on intuition and their experience with a particular culture to recognize when a game has begun. During a game, he writes, "a human being is constantly noticing if the conditions for playing the game are still being met, continuously monitoring the 'frame,' the circumstances surrounding play, to determine that the game is still in progress, always aware (if only unconsciously) that the other participants are acting as if the game is 'on.'"[2]

The "frame" to which Sniderman alludes has several functions, which we will cover in later chapters. For now, it is sufficient to note that the frame of a game is what communicates that those contained within it are "playing" and that the space of play is separate in some way from that of the real world. Psychologist Michael Apter echoes this idea when he writes,

In the play-state you experience a *protective frame* which stands between you and the "real" world and its problems, creating an enchanted zone in which, in the end, you are confident that no harm can come. Although this frame is psychological, interestingly it often has a perceptible physical representation: the proscenium arch of the theater, the railings around the park, the boundary line on the cricket pitch, and so on. But such a frame may also be abstract, such as the rules governing the game being played.[3]

In other words, the frame is a concept connected to the question of the "reality" of a game, of the relationship between the artificial world of the game and the "real life" contexts that it intersects. The frame of a game creates the feeling of *safety* that is part of Chris Crawford's definition of a game explored in **Defining Games**. It is responsible not only for the unusual relationship between a game and the outside world, but also for many of the internal mechanisms and experiences of a game in play. We call this frame the *magic circle*, a concept inspired by Johann Huizinga's work on play.

## Boundaries

What does it mean to say that games take place within set boundaries established by the act of play? Is this really true? Is there really such a distinct boundary? In fact there is. Compare, for example, the informal play of a toy with the more formal play of a game. A child approaching a doll, for example, can slowly and gradually enter into a play relationship with the doll. The child might look at the doll from across the room and shoot it a playful glance. Later, the child might pick it up and hold it, then put it down and leave it for a time. The child might carelessly drag the doll around the room, sometimes talking to it and acknowledging it, at other times forgetting it is there.

The boundary between the act of playing with the doll and not playing with the doll is fuzzy and permeable. Within this scenario, we can identify concrete play behaviors, such as making the doll move like a puppet. But there are just as many ambiguous behaviors, which might or not be play, such as idly kneading its head while watching TV. There may be a frame between playing and not playing, but its boundaries are indistinct.

Now compare that kind of informal play with the play of a game—two children playing Tic-Tac-Toe. In order to play, the children must gather the proper materials, draw the four lines that make up the grid of the board, and follow the proper rules each turn as they progress through the game. With a toy, it may be difficult to say exactly when the play begins and ends. But with a game, the activity is richly formalized. The game has a beginning, a middle, and a quantifiable outcome at the end. The game takes place in a precisely defined physical and temporal space of play. Either the children are playing Tic-Tac-Toe or they are not. There is no ambiguity concerning their action: they are clearly playing a game.

The same analysis can occur within the context of digital media. Compare, for example, a user's casual interaction with a toy-like screensaver program to their

242

interaction with a computer game such as Tetris. The screensaver allows the user to wiggle the mouse and make patterns on the screen, an activity that we can casually enter into and then discontinue. The entry and exit of the user is informal and unbound by rules that define a beginning, middle, and end. A game of Tetris, on the other hand, provides a formalized boundary regarding play: the game is either in play or it is not. Players of Tetris do not "casually interact" with it; rather, they are playing a game. It is true that a Tetris player could pause a game in progress and resume it later—just as two Tennis players might pause for a drink of water. But in both cases, the players are stepping out of the game space, formally suspending the game before stepping back in to resume play.

As a player steps in and out of a game, he or she is crossing that boundary—or frame—that defines the game in time and space. As noted above, we call the boundary of a game the *magic circle*, a term borrowed from the following passage in Huizinga's book *Homo Ludens:*

> All play moves and has its being within a play-ground marked off beforehand either materially or ideally, deliberately or as a matter of course . . . . The arena, the card-table, the magic circle, the temple, the stage, the screen, the tennis court, the court of justice, etc., are all in form and function play-grounds, i.e., forbidden spots, isolated, hedged round, hallowed, within which special rules obtain. All are temporary worlds within the ordinary world, dedicated to the performance of an act apart.[4]

Although the magic circle is merely one of the examples in Huizinga's list of "play-grounds," the term is used here as shorthand for the idea of a special place in time and space created by a game. The fact that the magic circle is just that—a circle—is an important feature of this concept. As a closed circle, the space it circumscribes is enclosed and separate from the real world. As a marker of time, the magic circle is like a clock: it simultaneously represents a path with a beginning and end, but one without beginning and end. The magic circle inscribes a space that is repeatable, a space both limited and limitless. In short, a finite space with infinite possibility.

## Enter in

In a very basic sense, the magic circle of a game is where the game takes place. To play a game means entering into a magic circle, or perhaps creating one as a game begins. The magic circle of a game might have a physical component, like the board of a board game or the playing field of an athletic contest. But many games have no physical boundaries—arm wrestling, for example, doesn't require much in the way of special spaces or material. The game simply begins when one or more players decide to play.

The term magic circle is appropriate because there is in fact something genuinely magical that happens when a game begins. A fancy Backgammon set sitting all alone might be a pretty decoration on the coffee table. If this is the function that the game is serving—decoration—it doesn't really matter how the game pieces are arranged, if some of them are out of place, or even missing. However, once you sit down with a friend to play a game of Backgammon, the arrangement of the pieces suddenly becomes extremely important. The Backgammon board becomes a special space that facilitates the play of the game. The players' attention is intensely focused on the game, which mediates their interaction through play. While the game is in progress, the players do not casually arrange and rearrange the pieces, but move them according to very particular rules.

Within the magic circle, special meanings accrue and cluster around objects and behaviors. In effect, a new reality is created, defined by the rules of the game and inhabited by its players. Before a game of Chutes and Ladders starts, it's just a board, some plastic pieces, and a die. But once the game begins, everything changes. Suddenly, the materials represent something quite specific. This plastic token is *you*. These rules tell you how to roll the die and move. Suddenly, it matters very much which plastic token reaches the end first.

Consider a group of kids in a suburban front yard, casually talking and hanging out. They decide to play a game of Hide-and-Seek. One of the kids takes a rock and plants it in the middle of yard to represent home base. The group huddles around it, playing "eenie-meenie-miney-moe" to pick the first person to be "It"; then they scatter and hide as "It" covers his eyes and starts to count to twenty. All at once, the relationships among the players have taken on special meanings. Who is "It" and who is not? Who is hidden and who can be seen? Who is captured and who is free? Who will win the game?

What is going on in these examples of Backgammon, Chutes and Ladders, and Hide-and-Seek? As Huizinga eloquently states, within the space of a game "special rules obtain." The magic circle of a game is the boundary of the game space and within this boundary the rules of the game play out and have authority.

## Temporary worlds

What lies at the border of the game? Just how permeable is the boundary between the real world and the artificial world of the game that is circumscribed and delimited by the magic circle? Huizinga calls play-worlds "temporary worlds within the ordinary world." But what does that mean? Does the magic circle enframe a reality completely separated from the real world? Is a game somehow an extension of regular life? Or is a game just a special case of ordinary reality?

Let us return to the concept of a system. We have already established that games are systems. As systems, games can be understood as being either open or closed. In his definition of systems, Littlejohn informs us that "a *closed system* has no interchange with its environment. An *open system* receives matter and energy from its environment and passes matter and energy to its environment."[5] So what does this have to do with the magic circle? The question at hand has to do with the boundary between the magic circle of a game and the world outside the game. One way of approaching that question is to consider whether that boundary is closed, framing a completely self-contained world inside; or whether it is open, permitting interchange between the game and the world beyond its frame. As Bernard DeKoven notes in *The Well-Played Game*, "Boundaries help separate the game from life. They have a critical function in maintaining the fiction of the game so that the aspects of reality with which we do not choose to play can be left safely outside."[6] Moreover, the answer to the question of whether games are closed or open systems depends on which schema is used to understand them: whether games are framed as RULES, as PLAY, or as CULTURE.

**RULES**: Games considered as **RULES** are closed systems. Considering games as formal systems means considering them as systems of rules prior to the actual involvement of players.

**PLAY**: Considered as **PLAY**, games can be either *closed systems* or *open systems*. Framed as the experience of play, it is possible to restrict our focus and look at just those play behaviors that are intrinsic to the game, ignoring all others. At the same time, players bring a great deal in from the outside world: their expectations, their likes and dislikes, social relationships, and so on. In this sense, it is impossible to ignore the fact that games are open, a reflection of the players who play them.

**CULTURE**: Considered as **CULTURE**, games are extremely open systems. In this case, the internal functioning of the game is not emphasized; instead, as a cultural system the focus is on the way that the game exchanges meaning with culture at large. In considering the cultural aspects of professional Football—political debates over Native American team mascots, for example—the system of the game is opened up to expose the way that it interfaces with society as a whole.

Is it a contradiction to say that games can be open and closed systems at the same time? Not really. As with many complex phenomena, the qualities of the object under study depend on the methodology of the study itself. The answer to the question of whether games are closed or open systems, whether they are truly artificial or not, depends on the schema used to analyze them. We return to this important question many times over the course of this book.

## The lusory attitude

So far in the discussion of the magic circle we have outlined the ways that the interior space of a game relates to the real world spaces outside it, how the magic circle frames a distinct space of meaning that is separate from, but still references, the real world. What we have not yet considered is what the magic circle represents from the player's point of view. Because a game demands formalized interaction, it is often a real commitment to decide to play a game. If a player chooses to sit down and play Monopoly, for example, he cannot simply quit playing in the middle without disrupting the game and upsetting the other players. On the other hand, if he ignores this impulse and remains in the game to the bitter end, he might end up a sore loser. Yet, these kinds of obstacles obviously don't keep most people from playing games. What does it mean to decide to play a game? If the magic circle creates an alternate reality, what psychological attitude is required of a player entering into the play of a game?

In **Defining Games** we looked at the definition of games Bernard Suits gives in his book *Grasshopper: Games, Life, and Utopia*. One of the unique components of Suits' definition is that he sees games as inherently inefficient. He uses the example of a boxer to explain this concept. If the goal of a boxing match is to make the other fighter stay down for a count of 10, the easiest way to accomplish this goal would be to take a gun and shoot the other boxer in the head. This, of course, is not the way that the game of Boxing is played. Instead, as Suits points out, boxers put on padded gloves and only strike their opponents in very limited and stylized ways. Similarly, Suits discusses the game of Golf:

> Suppose I make it my purpose to get a small round object into a hole in the ground as efficiently as possible. Placing it in the hole with my hand would be a natural means to adopt. But surely I would not take a stick with a piece of metal on one end of it, walk three or four hundred yards away from the hole, and then attempt to propel the ball into the hole with the stick. That would not be technically intelligent. But such an undertaking is an extremely popular game, and the foregoing way of describing it evidently shows how games differ from technical activities.[7]

What the boxer and the golfer have in common, according to Suits, is a shared attitude toward the act of game-playing, an openness to the possibility of taking such indirect means to accomplish a goal. "In anything but a game the gratuitous introduction of unnecessary obstacles to the achievement of an end is regarded as a decidedly irrational thing to do, whereas in games it appears to be an absolutely essential thing to do."[8] Suits calls this state of mind the *lusory attitude*, a term we introduced under his definition of a game. The lusory attitude allows players to "adopt rules which require one to employ worse rather than better means for reaching an end."[9] Trying to propel a miniature ball with a metal stick into a tiny hole across great distances certainly requires something by way of attitude!

The word "ludo" means *play* in Latin, and the root of "lusory" is the same root as "ludens" in "Homo Ludens." The lusory attitude is an extremely useful concept as it describes the attitude that is required of game players for them to enter into a game. To play a game is in many ways an act of "faith" that invests the game with its special meaning—without willing players, the game is a formal system waiting to be inhabited, like a piece of sheet music waiting to be played. This notion can be extended to say that a game is a kind of social contract. To decide to play a game is to create—out of thin air—an arbitrary authority that serves to guide and direct the play of the game. The moment of that decision can be quite magical. Picture a cluster of boys meeting on the street to show each other their marble collections. There is joking, some eye rolling, and then a challenge rings out. One of the boys chalks a circle on the sidewalk and each one of them puts a marble inside. They are suddenly playing a game, a game that guides and directs their actions, that serves as the arbiter of what they can and cannot do. The boys take the game very seriously, as they are playing for keeps.

Their goal is to win the game and take marbles from their opponents. If that is all they wanted to do, they could just grab each other's marble collections and run. Instead, they play a game. Through a long and dramatic process, they end up either losing their marbles or winning some from others. If all that the boys wanted to do was increase the number of marbles in their collection, the game might seem absurd. But the lusory attitude implies more than a mere acceptance of the limitations prescribed by the rules of the game—it also means accepting the rules because the play of the game is an end in itself. In effect, the lusory attitude ensures that the player accepts the game rules "just so that the activity made possible by such an acceptance can occur."[10] Our marble players would take their game seriously even if they weren't playing for keeps.

There is a pleasure in this inefficiency. When you fire a missile in Missile Command, it doesn't simply zap to the spot underneath the crosshairs. Instead, it slowly climbs up from the bottom of the screen. To knock down a set of bowling pins, you don't carry the bowling ball down the lane; instead you stand a good distance away and let it roll. From somewhere in the gap between action and outcome, in the friction between frustrated desire and the seductive goal of a game, bubbles up the unique enjoyment of game play. Players take on the lusory attitude for the pleasure of play itself.

The magic circle can define a powerful space, investing its authority in the actions of players and creating new and complex meanings that are only possible in the space of play. But it is also remarkably fragile as well, requiring constant maintenance to keep it intact. Over the course of the following chapters we explore the design structures that serve to create and support the magic circle, as well as qualities of a game's design that affect the lusory attitude and the possibility of meaningful play.

Having now passed through definitions of design, systems, interactivity, and games, the way has been paved for our entrance into the magic circle. Passing through its open and closed boundaries, we find ourselves in its center. What we find there, at the very heart of games, is **RULES**, the space of games framed as formal systems.

## Further reading

### *Grasshopper: games, life, utopia*, by Bernard Suits

A retelling of Aesop's fable of the Grasshopper and the Ants, *Grasshopper* is an engaging and insightful book that addresses some of the philosophical paradoxes raised by games. Cheating, rule-following, and the reality of games versus the real world are among the topics Suits addresses. It is from this book that we derive our concept of the lusory attitude, an important game design concept.

*Recommended:*

Chapter 3: Construction of a Definition
Chapter 4: Triflers, Cheats, and Spoilsports

### *Homo Ludens*, by Johann Huizinga

Perhaps the most influential theoretical work on play in the twentieth century, in *Homo Ludens* (Man the Player), Dutch philosopher and historian Huizinga explores the relationship between games, play, and culture. His point of view is certainly not that of design; however, Huizinga's work directly influenced many of the other authors we reference here, such as Roger Caillois and Brian Sutton-Smith. In the chapter recommended below, Huizinga establishes his essential definition of play.

*Recommended:*

Chapter 1: Nature and Significance of Play as a Cultural Phenomenon

## Summary

- Every game exists within a **frame**: a specially demarcated time and space. The frame communicates to players, consciously or unconsciously, that a game is being played.
- The **magic circle** of a game is the space within which a game takes place. Whereas more informal forms of play do not have a distinct boundary, the formalized nature of games makes the magic circle explicit.
- Within the magic circle, the game's rules create a special set of **meanings** for the players of a game. These meanings guide the play of the game.
- As a system, a game can be considered to have an **open** or **closed** relationship to its context. Considered as **RULES**, a game is closed. Considered as **PLAY**, a game is both open and closed. Considered as **CULTURE**, a game is open.
- The **lusory attitude** is the state of mind required to enter into the play of a game. To play a game, a group of players accepts the limitations of the rules because of the pleasure a game can afford.

## Notes

1 Steven Sniderman, "The Life of Games" p. 2. <www.gamepuzzles.com/tlog/tlog2. htm>.
2 Ibid. p. 2.

3  Michael J. Apter, "A Structural-Phenomenology of Play," in *Adult Play: A Reversal Theory Approach*, edited by J. H. Kerr and Michael J. Apter (Amsterdam: Swets and Zeitlinger, 1991), p. 15.
4  Johann, Huizinga, *Homo Ludens: A Study of the Play Element in Culture* (Boston: Beacon Press, 1955), p. 10.
5  Stephen W. Littlejohn, *Theories of Human Communication*, 3rd edition (Belmont, CA: Wadsworth Publishing Company, 1989), p. 41.
6  Bernard DeKoven, *The Well-Played Game* (New York: Doubleday, 1978), p. 38.
7  Bernard Suits, *Grasshopper: Games, Life, and Utopia* (Boston: David R. Godine, 1990), p. 23.
8  Ibid. p. 38–9.
9  Ibid. p. 38–9.
10  Ibid. p. 40.

# 60

# THERE IS NO MAGIC CIRCLE

*Mia Consalvo*

Source: *Games and Culture*, 4(4), 2009, 408–417.

## Abstract

Games are created through the act of game play, which is contingent on player acts. However, to understand gameplay, we must also investigate contexts, justifications, and limitations. Cheating can be an excellent path into studying the gameplay situation, because it lays bare player's frustrations and limitations. It points to ludic hopes and activities, and it causes us to question our values, our ethics. In comparison, the concept of the magic circle seems static and overly formalist. Structures may be necessary to begin gameplay, but we cannot stop at structures as a way of understanding the gameplay experience. Because of that, we cannot say that games are magic circles, where the ordinary rules of life do not apply. Of course they apply, but in addition to, in competition with, other rules and in relation to multiple contexts, across varying cultures, and into different groups, legal situations, and homes.

One evening in the central city of Jeuno, in the world of Vana'diel, individuals of various races, ages, and genders were gathered by the auction house to buy and sell items of great and little value. It was a normal evening, filled with the usual chatter related to battles, monsters, and socializing, barring one exception. An individual was being taken to task by many others, who slapped, poked, and shouted at him, complaining that he (Kofgood) was ruining the economy of the world with his (and his associate's) activities. No one defended him, and Kofgood himself said nothing, calmly completed his transactions, and then left. Yet, talk about Kofgood and his ilk continued and certainly did not end when he or other individuals left Jeuno.

What I have left out of that account is the violations occurred in what some theorists refer to as the magic circle of play. Individuals were not shouting at Kofgood because he controlled the market in ice staves or was overfishing for moat carp. They were upset because he allegedly was a gil (gold) seller and was engaged to some extent in Real Money Trade (RMT). Kofgood, to upset individuals, had violated the rules of the fantasy world as set forth by Square Enix for *Final Fantasy XI Online*, and they felt he was not sufficiently punished for that. However, how can we adequately take a measure of the complexity of their situation? In addition, can we simply suggest that within the bounds of the massively multiplayer online (MMO; and Vana 'diel), the everyday rules of life did not apply?

Huizinga wrote in the 1930s about a magic circle for play, which bounded a space and set it apart from normal life. Inside the magic circle, different rules apply, and it is a space where we can experience things not normally sanctioned or allowed in regular space or life.

Game studies scholars have seized on the magic circle as a concept for games to help explain the role of games in our lives. We have discussed the boundaries and how those are the rules or whether they might include other things. In my own work, I have been interested in the role of cheating in relation to games and have thought about it in relation to the magic circle as well (2007). One view is to see the cheater as actually most invested in the rules as the bounds of the circle (moving a chess piece while her opponent is distracted)—because the cheater hopes everyone else is following the rules—otherwise the cheater gains no real advantage.

By contrast, the spoilsport (Huizinga, 1950) rejects the rules entirely (e.g., sweeping the chess pieces onto the ground) and thus destroys the magic circle. The cheater wants you to think you are both playing the same game but in actuality you are not. The spoilsport simply wants to destroy the play/game experience.

However, this conceptualization of the magic circle was developed in the 1930s, long before the advent of digital games, by a theorist with particular views of what did and did not constitute play. In building of that disjuncture between notions of play and game, Malaby asks game studies scholars to decouple our unquestioned linkages between the concepts "game" and "play." He argues that in doing so, we move beyond simplistic ideas of games as about fun and enjoyment and can instead better study the processes involved in games that can be quite serious for their players (2007). Other game studies scholars are beginning to question the masculinist bias of games studies (Ludica, 2007), and Huizinga's (1950) work is certainly ripe for critique in that area. Here, though, I want to question the easy transfer of the concept of the magic circle to game studies and use cheating as a lens for interrogation.

In doing research for my book on cheating (2007), I went into the study with some basic ideas of what constituted cheating, but I ultimately let my informants define for me what they saw as cheating practices. That was a lucky move. I quickly found out that they did not agree on how to define the term nor did they agree on when it was acceptable or unacceptable to cheat in a game, whether single or multiplayer, online or off-line.

Players often seemed hampered by the term "cheating" itself, in attempting to explain their play activities. Because of the near automatically associated negative valence of that term, individuals often justified certain actions when talking with me—Sue would say that she used cheat codes only "after already having played through a game once on her own" or Paul would say that he cheated in a multiplayer game only because "everyone else was cheating and we all knew it."

For such players, cheating was an action in need of justification. Of course there were some players who unabashedly cheated (and still do), but for most players, some accounting for a particular behavior was necessary, at least in recounting the act to others. In addition, for some, it was needed even for themselves individually. Why?

Echoing some of the gamers that Taylor (2006) talked with in relation to *Ever-Quest*, my players stressed earning achievement through gameplay. They wanted to play the game and advance successfully through the game based on their own skill and effort. Akin to power gamers, yet perhaps not (all) as dedicated, players talked of earned achievement, a sense of accomplishment only their own efforts could bring to a game, even if cheating was technically possible. Although cheating might occasionally be necessary, or simply fun, it often robbed them of that sense of accomplishment, either through giving them answers they felt they should have worked harder for or through depriving other players of achievements they had also earned.

Yet, cheating still happened—either because of necessity or because of the lure of the ludic. Yet, what does that have to do with spaces apart, with bounded areas for play? When Huizinga (1950) wrote about the magic circle, our sense of space and place was radically different from what it is now. In suggesting a place "set apart" from everyday life, that space could be envisioned as geographic space fairly easily—the playground, the boxing ring, the hopscotch outline.

Of course Huizinga (1950) could also have been referring to mental spaces in addition to geographic spaces. Turner's (1969) conception of liminal spaces, the interstitial boundaries between the sacred and the profane, are also spaces "set apart" from the everyday—they are changes in mind or attitude which occur while we inhabit the same geographic places. Likewise, with events such as carnival, we are in the same location (a town) yet attitudes and behaviors, as well as ornamentation, change, for a particular time period.

Yet, for all of those examples, there is still a sense of boundedness that seems more encompassing than play (especially in digital games) now has in contemporary society. Apart was an absolute, even if only for minutes at a time.

In contrast, Barry Atkins (2007) has argued that we now approach the playing of even new digital games with a feeling of nostalgia. We have already seen the screenshots of the action, we have read about the special gameplay mechanics built into the game, which is also likely a sequel, or in a series, or part of a licensed franchise with which we are already quite familiar.

Such paratexts (Consalvo, 2007) surround contemporary digital games, shaping them, limiting them, giving them form, and encouraging (as well as discouraging) particular forms of play and sensemaking. Who could go into a *Final Fantasy* or *Halo* game having no idea of what might happen relative to the story or the style of gameplay expected of us? Would we really expect to play an MMO without knowing the types of jobs we could use or the races of our soon-to-be-created avatars?

Given such information, which we now expect and which the game industry so willingly supplies, the concept of a space "apart from" everyday life, whether geographic or conceptual, becomes harder to maintain. We have always already played the game, yet we still play to confirm whatever we hope or fear to be true.

Yet, what about the act of gameplay itself? Is that still a bounded space, where normal rules do not apply? Theorists such as Castronova (2007) would argue such places are of paramount importance, that we need such fantasy spaces, especially in a world where there is already too much horror, violence, and death. Yet, even as he might wish for such spaces, such worlds must inevitably leave the hands of their creators and are then taken up (and altered, bent, modified, extended) by players or users—indicating that the inviolability of the game space is a fiction, as is the magic circle, as pertaining to digital games. Indeed, Steinkuehler posits a "mangle of play" that considers two sets of agencies—that of the designers who create game worlds and that of the player communities that inhabit them (2006). She rightly believes that each group vies for control and meaning-making within the game world, but it is only through that coexistence that actual games emerge.

So, is the concept of the magic circle useful? Arguably, it upholds structuralist definitions or conceptualizations of games. It emphasizes form at the cost of function, without attention to the context of actual gameplay. With contemporary games, and multiplayer games and MMOs in particular, context is key, as many scholars (Consalvo, 2007; Malaby, 2007; Steinkuehler, 2006; Taylor, 2006) have found.

For example, my own work on cheating stresses the importance of understanding the many definitions of cheating that players offer and their own negotiations in choosing when and how to cheat or not. Taylor (2006) has also found that game players often do not mention fun as a reason for playing—particularly the power gamers that see grind and hard work as integral parts of MMO gameplay. Her early work in this area was one of the initial challenges to structuralist accounts of games, with her study of actual gamers bringing to the fore the need to understand how players understand, contextualize, and challenge MMO games. Likewise, the work of Malaby, Steinkuehler, and others does argue for understanding multiple viewpoints, and multiple contexts, for understanding games. Thus, several writers stand with me in positing a way of understanding games that goes beyond structures or boxed content. Yet, so far, the concept of the magic circle has been left largely untouched.

Taking another view, formalist constructions of games (Juul, 2005) either deny that context or place its importance as secondary to the structural elements of games, in seeking to understand them. What if, rather than relying on structuralist definitions of what is a game, we view a game as a contextual, dynamic activity, which players must engage with for meaning to be made. Furthermore, it is only through that engagement that the game is made to mean.

We see that happening when we look at players cheating in games. An example will help to make my point. Let us consider *World of Warcraft* (WoW) generally and the WoW glider in particular. Developed by Michael Donnelly and MDY

Industries, the glider is a small program or mod for WoW that lets the user program one of her avatars to travel along a preset path, killing whatever is found, skinning, looting, and gaining experience points from the looped activity. The makers of the program/mod stress on their Web site that the mod is designed to eliminate the tedious aspects associated with leveling a character (the grind), especially for players who may have already done so with several other characters—in other words, this is for alts or very experienced players to "fast-forward" through undesirable parts of the game.

Fast-forwarding is a common reason people will cheat in a game (Consalvo, 2007), although in multiplayer games such as WoW, the developers usually consider such activities as in violation of the game's terms of service (ToS). It is thus illegal, and the creators of the glider are currently being sued by Blizzard for their creation (Markee, 2007).

We can consider the potential activities associated with the WoW glider in several ways. Some individuals might use the glider to level avatars that they intend to sell to other players for (real) currency and thus profit off the fast-forwarding mod. Some players may wish to level their second, third, or fourth avatar through either some or all of the grind in the game, to achieve higher levels, but keep those avatars as part of their account to play with in the future. Some players (admittedly few) may find the WoW glider before even beginning the game and use it to level their avatar to get to the content they assume is most valuable—such as end game raiding.

Although the developers have deemed all those activities as cheating and violations of the ToS, they obviously have different meanings for the players involved. Likewise, they have different meanings and outcomes for players who do not use the WoW glider but who are nonetheless affected by its presence as a mod. Nonglider-using players may consider the opportunity to purchase such a leveled avatar as a bargain, rather than leveling an avatar on their own. Nonglider-using players may feel that avatars running automatically on preset paths in certain areas are unfairly hogging resources in game, which they may need and feel more legitimate claim to, being in actual control of their avatar. Finally, nonglider using players may feel fiscal ramifications of glider-using players, if glider users also gather large amounts of consumable resources to sell via auction houses and either flood markets (driving prices down) or control the sale of certain items (driving prices up).

From a formalist, structuralist perspective, the bounds or rules of the magic circle (the game of WoW) have definitely been breached through some players' use of the WoW glider, but beyond that, how useful is knowing of the presence of the WoW glider? It is simply present/absent and a violation/not violation of the rules of the game.

If instead we see such activities as contextual, richer understandings of the glider can emerge. Some players are seeking monetary profit from use of the WoW glider, while others are hoping for a jump past content they have perhaps already witnessed countless times before (if they have multiple characters). Some players see every level and activity in a game as worthwhile and valuable in some way (although perhaps not fun or entertaining), while others derive value from particular parts and seek to avoid or minimize other game elements.

Nonglider users may react singly or in groups by killing (or ganking) glider users once or repeatedly. In doing so, they may reify for themselves and others what they deem acceptable and unacceptable forms of gameplay. Nonglider users may also then help to build communities of like-minded players, even in the face of an undesirable activity. Nonglider users may perhaps even appreciate the activities of glider users, if the user clears an area of dangerous mobs (to the nonglider user) and thus lets the nonuser focus on other activities such as gathering natural resources to craft. All these reactions make the game mean particular things, which we do not see if we merely look to violations of the rules and circle.

Additionally, players also bring into the game assumptions, knowledge, and information about the act of MMO gameplay itself. Most players of MMOs understand the large time investments required of the genre, if they wish to be active players. With the "normal" MMO player averaging more than 20 hr a week of gameplay time, MMOs are difficult for casual gamers to do well in. Thus, most players know that to advance or achieve much in the game, time—a lot of it—is required of them.

Players of WoW also know that the creation of alternate characters on a person's account is very common because (as opposed to other types of MMOs such as *Final Fantasy XI*) avatars are limited to one job choice, and thus if players wish to try other types of jobs or create avatars with alternate specialties, they must do so by making alts. Thus, alts are a common element of MMO gameplay.

Given that, alts can serve different functions. Some players wish to experience as much game content as they can and so desire to see different abilities, story lines, locations, and the like. Other players create alts that have complementary crafting or money-making abilities from their "main" avatar, to maximize their in-game cash flow. Still other players may create alts to level with friends who are of a different level than they are (usually less advanced) and still give both players an equal challenge. So, alts may serve different purposes, across players, across alts, and over time.

The glider is designed to let players develop their own leveling strategy, independent of the carefully structured paths laid out by Blizzard's developers. Yet, players' use of the alts that result from such activities takes a variety of different forms. If we consider the game from a structural or formalist perspective, we can see only a violation of the rules, and thus the magic circle. Yet, if we consider the game as a contextual, meaning-making *process*, another picture emerges entirely.

## Beyond circles: keys and frames

Rather than restrict games to a bounded circle, another way of understanding the processes of gameplay could be through application of another framework—the frames and keys of Erving Goffman, modified in Gary Alan Fine's work with role-playing gamers in the 1980s (Fine, 1983; Goffman, 1974). In his attempts to understand the organization of experience in daily life, Goffman described daily living as a series of frames that we encounter, frames that organize our activity and structure our experiences.

Yet, for Goffman, frames alone do not explain the rich complexities of our everyday interactions. Daily activities could also be given additional meanings or keyings (1974, pp. 43–44). Such keyings are systematic, openly acknowledged, bounded in time if not in space, and perform "a crucial role in determining what we think is really going on" (p. 45). Goffman's examples of forms of keyings included make believe, play, rehearsals, simulations, practicing, and other such states. Thus, we might have a primary frame that would indicate getting married, but a keying of that frame that looks like someone getting married, but is instead a rehearsal for a marriage ceremony, and we could all recognize the difference between those two actions.

Keys are important for understanding reality for Goffman (1974), yet for him they indicate a deviation from the real or what is "actually or literally occurring" (p. 47). He suggests in several places that there is an original frame (for reality) and a copy of that frame—the primary framework and the keyed version. His insistence on a real version is not echoed in Fine's (1983) work, and I would question the distinction that one version of a frame is a copy or faked version of another—to make such a claim would be to create another structuralist account of what happens in MMOs, this time swapping various keys and frames for what is inside and outside a magic circle.

Fine takes us in a more helpful direction, arguing that first, for fantasy gaming, three distinct frames are operative—"the world of commonsense knowledge grounded in one's primary framework, the world of game rules grounded in the game structure, and the knowledge of the fantasy world (itself a hypothetical primary framework)" (1983, p. 194). Fine believes we can have multiple frames, and we can switch among them fairly rapidly. Particularly in situations where frames are voluntary—such as those involving games—frames are "more likely to be rapidly keyed than are mandatory frames" (p. 196) because "the 'real world' will always intrude, for the gaming structure is not impermeable to its outside events" (p. 197). Without calling it by name, Fine would appear to be questioning the viability of the magic circle.

Likewise, Fine (1983) seems to reconfigure Goffman's (1974) notion of keys, which become transitions between different frames rather than an alternate version of a particular frame. Thus, rather than a player up-keying from daily life to a simulation, the player up-keys from daily life to the world of game rules and game structure, which is simply another frame (and the player might then very quickly down-key back to daily life if her mobile phone rings). Fine argues for the rapidity and pleasure that players can take from up-keying and down-keying in their actions while playing—and here, we can see the use of the concept for better understanding MMOs.

As Fine (1983) suggests, the "real world" will always intrude on game playing, in multiple ways, and players respond to those intrusions dynamically, negotiating a reality that "is continually in dynamic tension" (p. 200) as players up-key and down-key to make sense of various situations. Players can also use the activities of up-keying and down-keying to enhance their gameplay or social interactions, for example, bringing knowledge from the "real" world into the game world or creating jokes in game from real-life events. In addition, they do so rapidly, with ease, and as a collective. It is part of the activity of group or community building in games, I would argue, and thus an essential part of not only the fantasy gamer groups of Fine's study but also the contemporary MMOs.

Players exist or understand "reality" through recourse to various frames (their daily life, the game world, their characters' alleged knowledge and past) and move between those frames with fluidity and grace. So, rather than seeing a boundary break or simply being "inside" or "outside" a magic circle, by conceptualizing gamer activity as movements between frames, we can better capture and study the complexities of MMO gameplay.

## Conclusions

As stated previously, players never play a new game or fail to bring outside knowledge about games and gameplay into their gaming situations. The event is "tainted" perhaps by prior knowledge. There is no innocent gaming. Players of WoW are well aware of the ToS restrictions as well as the vibrant player community that constantly challenges Blizzard on multiple levels relative to gameplay design, play restrictions, and what are and are not acceptable changes to the core of gameplay.

Players also have real lives, with real commitments, expectations, hopes, and desires. That is also brought into the game world, here Azeroth. We can neither ignore such realities nor retreat to structuralist definitions of what makes or defines a game. Games are created through the act of gameplay, which is contingent on acts by players. Those acts are always, already, contextual and dynamic. As we have seen through use or nonuse of the WoW glider, there can be multiple meanings derived from one particular action. We cannot understand gameplay by limiting ourselves to only seeing actions and not investigating reasons, contexts, justifications, limitations, and the like. That is where the game occurs and where we must find its meaning.

Cheating can be an excellent path into studying the gameplay situation, because it lays bare player's frustrations and limitations. It points to some of their ludic hopes and activities, and it causes us to question our values, our ethics. With such rich, evocative, potential experiences, the concept of the magic circle seems static and overly formalist by comparison. Structures may be necessary to begin gameplay, but we cannot stop at structures as a way of understanding the gameplay experience.

Because of that, we cannot say that games are magic circles, where the ordinary rules of life do not apply. Of course they apply, but in addition to, in competition with, other rules and in relation to multiple contexts, across varying cultures, and into different groups, legal situations, and homes. Cheating (or any other violation) may be a defiant act, or an act to save someone's game from grinding to a halt, but we need the context of the act to understand it, or we fail to do justice to the complexity and richness of MMOs and digital games.

## Declaration of conflicting interests

The Author declares that there is no conflict of interest.

## Funding

This study was funded by the MacArthur Foundation.

## References

Atkins, B. (2007, September). *The temporal situation: Gamer time, industry time, academic time*. Paper presented at the Digital Games Research Association conference, Tokyo, Japan.

Castronova, E. (2007, September). *Perfidious economy*. Keynote presentation at the Digital Games Research Association conference, Tokyo, Japan.

Consalvo, M. (2007). *Cheating: Gaining advantage in videogames*. Cambridge, MA: MIT Press.

Fine, G. A. (1983). *Shared fantasy: Role-playing games as social worlds*. University of Chicago Press.

Goffman, E. (1974). *Frame analysis: An essay on the organization of experience*. Boston: Northeastern University Press.

Huizinga, J. (1950). *Homo ludens: A study of the play element in culture*. Boston: Beacon.

Juul, J. (2005). *Half-real: Video games between real rules and fictional worlds*. Cambridge, MA: MIT Press.

Ludica. (2007, September). *The hegemony of play*. Paper presented at the Digital Games Research Association conference, Tokyo, Japan.

Malaby, T. (2007). Beyond play: A new approach to games. *Games & Culture, 2*, 95–113.

Markee, D. (2007, February 16). Blizzard officially files against WoW Glider, Blizzard vs. MDY Industries. Markee Dragon. Retrieved from http://www.markeedragon.com/u/ubbth-reads/showflat.php?Board=wownews&Number=363199. Accessed October 1, 2008.

Steinkuehler, C. (2006). The mangle of play. *Games and Culture, 1*, 199–213.

Taylor, T. L. (2006). *Play between worlds*. Cambridge, MA: MIT Press.

Turner, V. (1969). *The ritual process: Structure and anti-structure*. Chicago: Aldine.

258

# 61

# JERKED AROUND BY THE MAGIC CIRCLE – CLEARING THE AIR TEN YEARS LATER

*Eric Zimmerman*

Source: *Gamasutra.com*, 2012, available at http://www.gamasutra.com/view/feature/135063/jerked_around_by_the_magic_circle_.php.

## Abstract

Game studies scholars seem obsessed with slaying the mythical Magic Circle Jerk. But does this person really exist? In looking back at the origin and uses of the "magic circle" concept, this paper also looks into the nature of design discourse and interdisciplinary exchange.

## Preface: the magic what?

A broad strokes definition: The magic circle is the idea that a boundary exists between a game and the world outside the game.

Outside the magic circle, you are Jane Smith, a 28 year old gamer; inside, you are the Level 62 GrandMage Hargatha of the Dookoo Clan. Outside the magic circle, this is a leather-bound football; inside, it is a special object that helps me score—and the game of Football has very specific rules about who can touch it, when, where, and in what ways.

Is the magic circle a verifiable phenomenon? A useful fiction? A ridiculous travesty? And who really cares? This essay endeavors to answer these questions by looking at the history, the use, and the misuse of the term. And along the way, I offer some correctives to how we think about the concept, about game design theory, and about the more general study of games.

## Shoot me now

At game studies conferences, I often find myself browsing through the scheduled program and finding one or more presentations on the magic circle. If you've ever been to an academic game gathering, you know the kind of talk. They are generally given by earnest graduate students, and have titles like "Beyond the

Magic Circle," or "The Pitfalls of the Magic Circle." A few years ago, there was an entire conference called "Breaking the Magic Circle."

Invariably, these presentations have a single aim: to devalue, dethrone, or otherwise take down the oppressive regime of the magic circle. They begin by citing either Johannes Huizinga's Homo Ludens or Rules of Play (the game design textbook I co-authored with Katie Salen), and then elaborate mightily on the dangers of the magic circle approach. They proceed to supplant the narrow magic circle point of view with one of their own—an approach that emphasizes something like social interaction between players, a wider cultural context, or concrete sociopolitical reality. Dragon slain.

I regularly get emails from budding game critics asking me if I think the magic circle "really ultimately truly" does actually exist. It seems to have become a rite of passage for game studies scholars: somewhere between a Bachelor's Degree and a Master's thesis, everyone has to write the paper where the magic circle finally gets what it deserves.

We all know it's fun to take down an authority figure. But what I want to ask here is: what is this oppressive regime that these well-intentioned researchers feel a need to overthrow? Who is this Voldemort that these papers dangerously invoke, in order to stage a final battle of good against evil? Does anyone really hold to the orthodox, narrow view of the magic circle, or is the phenomenon of taking down the magic circle just game studies scholars tilting at windmills?

## The magic circle jerk

The problem runs deep. It goes beyond just wide-eyed graduate students. Sometimes, I see it in the work of colleagues for whom I have the utmost respect and whose work I otherwise admire: game studies icons Mia Consalvo, Marinka Copier, and T.L. Taylor all have written about the need to overthrow the oppressive magic circle.

The argument goes something like this: the idea of magic circle is the idea that games are formal structures wholly and completely separate from ordinary life. The magic circle naively champions the preexisting rules of a game, and ignores the fact that games are lived experiences, that games are actually played by human beings in some kind of real social and cultural context.

My question remains: who is this ignoramus that holds these strange and narrow ideas about games? Where are the books and essays that this formalist-structuralist-ludologist has published? Where is this frightfully naïve thinker who is putting game studies at risk by poisoning the minds of impressionable students? Just who is this magic circle jerk? (Note that the word is "jerk" as in *annoying person*—I'm using it as a noun, not a verb.)

I am here to tell you: there is no magic circle jerk. We need to stop chasing this phantasm. I offer this essay as a corrective. It is meant to clarify where this magic circle idea came from, what it was intended to mean, and to stop the energy being wasted by chasing the ghost of the magic circle jerk—a ghost that simply doesn't exist.

## Birthing a straw man

Perhaps I'm sensitive to the phenomenon of the magic circle jerk because I (or Katie Salen and I) often are identified as the embodiment of the worst of the magic circle. In fact, game designer Frank Lantz and I started using the term in our game design classes years before work on Rules of Play began. In 1999, we co-authored an article for Merge Magazine called Rules, Play, Culture: Checkmate that referred to the magic circle as "the artificial context of a game . . . the shared space of play created by its rules."

However, the term only reached full fruition in *Rules of Play*. It's certainly true that in the nearly 10 years since the book was published, the idea of the magic circle is easily the most popular concept to come out of it. So in many ways I do feel responsible for the magic circle shenanigans that have followed the book's publication.

Where does it come from? Frank and I first read the phrase "magic circle" in Huizinga's Homo Ludens, where it appears a scant handful of times—once each on pages 10, 11, 20, 77, 210, and 212 (of the 1972 Beacon Edition). Its most prominent and oft-cited mention is in this paragraph on page 10:

> All play moves and has its being within a play-ground marked off beforehand either materially or ideally, deliberately or as a matter of course. Just as there is no formal difference between play and ritual, so the "consecrated spot" cannot be formally distinguished from the play-ground. The arena, the card-table, the magic circle, the temple, the stage, the screen, the tennis court, the court of justice, etc., are all in form and function play-grounds, i.e. forbidden spots, isolated, hedged round, hallowed, within which special rules obtain. All are temporary worlds within the ordinary world, dedicated to the performance of an act apart.

Here "magic circle" appears in a list of phenomena that includes game spaces (card table, tennis court), spaces for art and entertainment (stage, screen), and even "real-world" spaces (temple, court of justice). The magic circle is yet another example of a ritual space that creates for Huizinga a "temporary world within the ordinary world, dedicated to the performance of an act apart."

The "magic circle" is not a particularly prominent phrase in Homo Ludens, and although Huizinga certainly advocates the idea that games can be understood as separate from everyday life, he never takes the full-blown magic circle jerk point of view that games are ultimately separate from everything else in life or that rules are the sole fundamental unit of games. In fact, Huizinga's thesis is much more ambivalent on these issues and he actually closes his seminal book with a passionate argument against a strict separation between life and games.

The magic circle is not something that comes wholly from Huizinga. To be perfectly honest, Katie and I more or less invented the concept, inheriting its use from my work with Frank, cobbling together ideas from Huizinga and Caillois,

261

clarifying key elements that were important for our book, and reframing it in terms of semiotics and design—two disciplines that certainly lie outside the realm of Huizinga's own scholarly work. But that is what scholarship often is—sampling and remixing ideas in order to come to a new synthesis.

Game Studies eminence Espen Aarseth made a similar point about the origin of the magic circle in a discussion after his presentation Ludus Revisited: The Ideology of Pure Play in Contemporary Video Game Research at the most recent DiGRA conference. According to Espen, after trying and failing to locate the idea inside Homo Ludens, he had decided Katie and I should be blamed for the concept, and everyone should just let Huizinga off the hook.

## The importance of a viewpoint

The brilliant designer and renowned MMO scholar Richard Bartle made a stink at a game conference several years ago by interrogating many of the presenters (most of whom were not game creators) about their research. After their talks, one by one, he asked them: "But how will your research help me make a better game?"

Now I, more than anyone, enjoy cantankerous outbursts, but Richard's repeated question was ultimately misplaced. You can't expect every research paper to address everyone else's disciplinary needs. In the end, it should be up to Richard to figure out if and how someone's research might help him make a better game, just as it was up to the historians, psychologists, and other researchers at the conference to decide if and how the design presentations from Richard (and myself) helped them with their work.

Rules of Play is a book about game design, and it was written to help game designers better understand what it means to create board and card games, social and physical games, and—of course—video games. In considering and critiquing ideas from the book, it is important to remember the disciplinary point of view from which it was written.

For example, if you read Rules of Play as a sociologist, the book is never going to possess a sociological standpoint as subtle and nuanced as an actual work of sociology. Rules of Play is not filled with research and footnotes from the history of sociological work, and its concepts do not build carefully on those from the well-heeled discipline of sociology.

The same is true when I read something through my own disciplinary lens as a game designer. I don't expect sociologists, or media studies scholars, or economists to have ingested and assimilated the whole of game design theory before they begin their work. I certainly can critique their research, but I would do so with an understanding of how their own disciplinary point of view differs from mine.

Just to clarify: I am not saying that one can't speak to issues and individuals outside of a home discipline. On the contrary, I so often find myself inspired by scholarly work outside of game design, just as I am constantly inspired by art, entertainment, and media that doesn't take the form of games. But as a practicing game designer I know that I myself must bridge the gap between these works and my own interests and goals.

Concepts and ideas should be understood within the framework of their originating discipline. This seems like an incredibly straightforward point, but critiques of the magic circle often point out how Homo Ludens or Rules of Play fails to present a concept as it should be understood within the discipline of the author. For example, just the aroma of the idea that game rules might be considered as divorced from a social reality has been enough to send many a game studies social scientist into a magic circle frenzy.

This is all complicated by the fact that game studies scholars are working in a radically interdisciplinary space, where ideas and fields mix freely. This only increases our need to be cognizant of our differences. Often, for example, we share and exchange concepts, but our methodologies and the aims of our research are wildly divergent. These differences are productive, but can be the source for misunderstandings. The phenomenon of the magic circle jerk is a case in point.

## The magic circle as a concept for game design

Rules of Play is a book about game design. Every concept between its covers was conceived as something useful for designers struggling with the process of creating games—useful for generating concepts, for constructing games, for analyzing designs. Rules of Play emphasizes how games create meaning, by being or becoming contexts in which meaning gets made.

Within this larger set of ideas, the magic circle is a fairly simple concept. It is a term that reminds us how meaning happens. Imagine, if you will, coming to visit me in my Brooklyn apartment. The two of us chat over coffee, as a Chess set sits nearby. Consider the web of relations between you and I and the Chess set as we sit and talk. Perhaps the figurines on the Chess board serve as a conversation starter, or perhaps as a social marker that I am a game player, or maybe they are just part of the aesthetic décor of my living room. Or—most likely—all of these and many more.

Once we start playing a game of Chess, many of these relationships shift and change. For example, in a casual conversation, we might fiddle with the Chess pieces on the board, knocking them about. But after we begin to play, suddenly it really matters whether a piece is in the middle of a square or not, and which of us can move it, and when, and how. Each of our kings acquires a special significance, and our social interaction shifts—perhaps it becomes more adversarial, or more conversational, or simply more quiet. Time and space, and identity, and social relations acquire new meanings while the game is going on. This is how playing a game is "entering a magic circle"—there are meanings which emerge as cause and effect of the game as it is played.

For me this idea—that games are a context from which meaning can emerge—is so simple as to be almost banal. Hardly a cause for debate! And note that this general understanding of the magic circle does not imply the impossibly brittle, heavy-handed caricature that is so often criticized—the ideas held by the imaginary magic circle jerk.

For example, are the meanings that emerge from the chess game in my example completely divorced from ordinary life? Absolutely not! They are inexorably intertwined. A preexisting friendship, for example, will certainly impact the social interaction between players in a game. Are the meanings ultimately derived from the rules and formal structures of the game? Hardly! Meaning is everywhere and infinitely subtle, appearing wherever one wishes to look. Certainly there are game-meanings that are tied to the rules of the game, but there's no reason to assume that those elements always dominate over others.

In fact, there's no need to think about the magic circle (a context for meaning creation) as something exclusive to games. Could one think of almost any physical or social space as a magic circle in this way? Probably—if that's your cup of tea, go for it. Certainly Huizinga makes a similar gesture when he places courts of law and religious temples in the same "play-ground" category as card tables and tennis courts.

Critiques of the magic circle often hinge on identifying in Rules of Play a subtle emphasis on the designed elements of games, rather than on more purely sociocultural phenomena. Critiquers, I have good news for you: you are correct. Rules of Play does tend to emphasize the meanings that are tied to the elements that designers actually create. Why? Because it is a book written by and for designers.

As a book about game design it has a special interest in the *actual construction* of games—the rules and materials, the systems and code that game designers create, and the way that those elements impact player experience. But the book certainly also spends an extensive amount of time detailing the contextual aspects of games—for example, one of the four sections of the book is entirely dedicated to thinking about the cultural contexts of games.

Rules of Play was written by designers. Understanding our disciplinary point of view can help explain why we might be interested in the meanings that are formed in part from the decisions of designers. However, there is a world of difference between a subtle emphasis on design and the ham-fisted hyper-structuralism of the mythical magic circle jerk.

## Thinking many ways at once

I recently visited a game studies class. Throughout the discussion after my talk, the professor peppered me with questions about the magic circle: *Can we REALLY look at rules in and of themselves? Is it truly possible to separate rules from the rest of games? And why would we even want to?* He addressed me as if I was the very embodiment of the magic circle jerk, manifesting right there in his classroom. Before I could convince him (and the class) that nobody really held any of the ideas he wanted to question, I first had to convince him that I wasn't really the enemy that he thought I was. It was certainly an out-of-body kind of experience.

264

One of the most basic ideas in Rules of Play is that we can look at games from multiple and contradictory points of view. And furthermore: that this is the right and proper thing to do with such a complex phenomenon as games. As Katie and I write in Rules of Play, most of the chapters represent a "schema"—a particular lens that can be used to focus on certain aspects of games.

We organize them into three general types—*formal* schema focused on rules (i.e., games as systems of uncertainty or as cybernetic feedback loops), *experiential* schema focused on play (games as social play or as the play of desire), and *cultural* schema focused on context (games as cultural rhetoric or as ideological resistance). This is the same thing as saying that literature can be understood as the rhythms of style, or as the representation of gender and class, or as the history of the printing press—or as any number of things.

When we use one schema to understand, analyze, or design games, other schemas may need to be ignored or repressed. There are, for example, key mathematical aspects of games that are crucial for learning the craft of game design, such as calculating basic probability or understanding game theory functions. Focusing on the math in making a game (such using a spreadsheet to juggle the relative experience point level-up curves of different classes in an RPG) might mean temporarily suspending a critical awareness of (for example) the sociocultural identity of the player base.

However, eventually the RPG designer would need to connect the pure math to the game's play and to its culture. A level-up experience point curve implies a certain tempo of play advancement relative to a reward/frustration pattern of desire. And the shape of this play is certainly something that should be designed relative to an understanding of a particular kind of player's expectations and assumptions—aspects of player attitudes that are closely tied to sociocultural identity. In other words, the math bone is connected to the culture bone. All of the schemas in Rules of Play really are ultimately intertwined, even if sometimes we have to separate them to see one aspect of games more clearly.

Applying different cognitive frames to knowledge at different moments is part of any intellectual or creative pursuit. A violinist in the midst of performing a Rochmaninov cadenza is not going to simultaneously ponder the biography of the composer of the piece she is playing at that very moment. However, during her rehearsal period, that kind of research is certainly something that may have informed her musical practice.

I have always thought that the multiple-schema approach of Rules of Play offers an *antidote* to a narrow, rules-centric approach—the approach of the magic circle jerk. The aggravating irony is that this is exactly the brush we get tarred with! Jesper Juul captures this bizarro-world logic in his essay The Magic Circle and the Puzzle Piece: " . . . theorists also claim to counter Huizinga, Salen, and Zimmerman by stressing the exact social nature of the magic circle that Huizinga, Salen, and Zimmerman also stress." Let's stop the insanity.

## Design isn't science

As a designer, I am an avowed relativist. For me, the value of a concept is not its scientific, objective truth. The value of a concept is its utility to solve problems as they are encountered in the design process. The concepts in Rules of Play are not meant to explain or define games once and for all. They are tools that can be used to understand, construct, and modify games. As MIT pioneer Marvin Minsky put it, a concept is a "thing to thing with"—not a law that points towards a truth.

This is why designers must embrace the deliciousness of contradiction. For example, to solve the feedback loop problems in your game's victory conditions, you might need to take off your media studies hat for a moment. Or to understand why all of your playtesters despise your game's main character, you might need to cease your formalist system-tweaking and consider instead the narrative politics of gender representation at work in your game.

One concept-tool might be completely useless for solving one particular problem, but crucial for something else. Thinking of games in all of their complexity as math, aesthetics, desire, social experience, gender, story, identity, etc.—this is what game design is all about. Interpretive schema can violently contradict each other! But that's absolutely the way it should be.

Many approaches to the study of games operate under a more scientific model—the idea that there are truths about games, and it is important to discover these truths and establish an accurate picture of what games actually are and how they really operate. I welcome others who want to hanker after scientificity, but such concerns do not motivate my own thinking about games. Just to restate: in my opinion, for a designer the value of a concept is its utility, not its ultimate truth. And concepts like the magic circle which come out of Rules of Play reflect this non-scientific designer's approach.

I believe this is why I often see presentations or read papers asking whether the magic circle really-ultimately-finally does or doesn't exist. The answer, as far as I am concerned, is *yes and no*. It just depends on what you are trying to understand about games, and why you are making use of the concept. If you want to look at games as a pure mathematician, or a strict ludologist, it makes perfect sense that you might adopt a more closed idea of games-as-rules. If you are a social anthropologist, then such a closed view wouldn't have much use in solving your research questions.

There is nothing wrong with temporarily adopting a limited point of view, as long as you're aware of the limitations of the blinders you are putting on. In fact, this is what research in an interdisciplinary field is all about! Understanding the limitations in our own points of view can help us in our understanding of each other.

Now you may be thinking . . . Aha! Articulating limitations—that's the problem! Those darn magic circle jerks don't do enough to describe the blinders they are putting on. They don't sufficiently make the limitations of their limited perspective known! I want to remind you that *there is no magic circle jerk*. This naïve character—the ultimate hardcore formalist—is a phantasm. Nobody in game studies, as far

I know, is taking that point of view seriously. The entire purpose of my essay is to point out that this magic circle jerk is a fiction that people project onto Homo Ludens and Rules of Play.

## Play on

I have made a harsh caricature of the magic circle jerk—as a silly super-structuralist that dogmatically believes in the truth of a hard-edged magic circle. Perhaps I have replaced the myth of the magic circle with a myth of my own—the impossibly idiotic magic circle jerk. But is it possible that the ghost of the jerk remains somewhere, as a tendency, as a predilection, as a potential that can still poison game studies?

In his excellent essay The Magic Circle and the Puzzle Piece (from which I quoted earlier), Jesper Juul echoes many of the ideas I have put forth here: that there has been a wave of criticisms against the magic circle, and that they stem from a misunderstanding about the concept as presented in Homo Ludens and Rules of Play.

One of Jesper's ideas is that the criticism of the magic circle is a symptom of "binary thinking"—an intellectual sensibility that seeks to identify and then overthrow theoretical dualities. The magic circle, according to Jesper, represents a particularly ripe binarism to tear down, because it (or rather, its misunderstood caricature) is the idea of a hard binary separation between what is inside and what is outside a game.

I agree with Jesper. My own feeling is that the impulse to overthrow such binarisms is a residue of the critical sensibility that dominated the '90s—the era of deconstruction and poststructuralism in which many game studies scholars came of age. The instinct to exaggerate the dangers of the magic circle so that it can be valiently deconstructed is linked to the notion that ideas are most authentic when they tear down an authority –. even if the authority is no more than a highly confected, imaginary effigy. Or, let me put it in another, less diplomatic way: propping up invented straw men just so you can knock them over is a lazy way to do research.

A final thought. You are probably reading this essay because you love games. Perhaps you love to play them, to study them, to create them—or some combination of all three. It is amazing that we can cross radical disciplinary boundaries, accept our differences across concepts, methods, and aims, yet still be united in our polyamorous and unabashed love for games. This love that embraces contradiction is beautiful. It has many names, but I like to call it *play*.

Let's play together. And put to bed this magic circle jerk once and for all.

## Summary: myths of the magic circle debunked

1   Nobody actually holds the orthodox view of the magic circle. There is no circle jerk behind the curtain.
2   While it was based on a passing term Frank Lantz and I noticed in Homo Ludens, Katie Salen and I more or less introduced the concept of the magic circle as it is used today. Blame us for all the trouble, not Huizinga.

3    Keep in mind the discipline from which a work or idea originated. Don't dismiss concepts in one field of knowledge because it doesn't fit your own discipline. The onus is on each of us to translate ideas from the outside into our own areas.

4    The magic circle, as put forward in Rules of Play, is the relatively simple idea that when a game is being played, new meanings are generated. These meanings mix elements intrinsic to the game and elements outside the game.

5    In my opinion, design concepts (such as the magic circle as described in *Rules of Play*) derive their value from their utility to solve problems. Their value is not derived from their scientific accuracy or proximity to truth.

6    Looking at a complex phenomena like games from many points of view, it is important to embrace contradiction. The magic circle can be thought of as open or closed, depending on why you are making use of the concept.

7    The magic circle jerk *doesn't exist*. Nobody really takes the hard line that everyone wants to criticize. I'm sick of the magic circle jerk. Let's bury the bastard.

## Notes

Because I didn't want to make this an angry and defensive finger-pointing rant, you may have noticed that I never actually cited any evidence for the magic circle jerk. There are no embarrassing quotes from papers or presentations attacking the magic circle. Although this lack of footnotes certainly relegates this essay to mere pseudo-scholarship, I am assuming that the phenomenon I describe is so pervasive that actual references just aren't necessary. (If you must dig deeper, a good place to start is Jesper's essay The Magic Circle and the Puzzle Piece.)

Regarding Espen Aarseth's comments about letting Huizinga off the hook, he later told me his comments had been influenced by Gordon Calleja's essay Erasing the Magic Circle—to be published in an upcoming issue of The Philosophy of Computer Games.

This essay was written solely from my own point of view, and does not represent the ideas of Katie Salen, my amazing Rules of Play co-author. I sometimes included her name to make sure that she was credited with the core ideas and concepts we wrote together. But she may well have a very different perspective on this magic circle business than I do. Vive la différence! And same goes for my game design hero Frank Lantz, with whom I originally encountered the work of Huizinga.

Special thanks to insightfulness engines Jesper Juul and John Sharp for their feedback and editing. Also big thanks to Gamasutra and to Christian Nutt for additional feedback.

PS: I love you, Richard Bartle! Promise you'll never stop being you.

# 62

# FUNDAMENTAL COMPONENTS OF THE GAMEPLAY EXPERIENCE

## Analysing immersion

### *Laura Ermi and Frans Mäyrä*

Source: Stephan Günzel, Michael Liebe, and Dieter Mersch (eds), *DIGAREC Keynote-Lectures 2009/10* (Potsdam: Potsdam University Press, 2011), pp. 88–113, available at http://pub.ub.uni-potsdam.de/volltexte/2011/4983/ [urn:nbn:de:kobv:517-opus-49831].

## Introductory note

This co-authored paper is based on research that originated in 2003 when our team started a series of extensive field studies into the character of gameplay experiences. Originally within the *Children as the Actors of Game Cultures* research project, our aim was to better understand why particularly young people enjoy playing games, while also asking their parents how they perceive gaming as playing partners or as close observers. Gradually our in-depth interviews started to reveal a complex picture of more general relevance, where personal experiences, social contexts and cultural practices all came together to frame gameplay within something we called game cultures. Culture was the keyword, since we were not interested in studying games and play experiences in isolation, but rather as part of the rich meaning-making practices of lived reality.

In retrospect, our analysis of immersion has maintained much of its significance, and I must again thank my co-author Laura Ermi, who as a trained psychologist also was the main author during the construction of research instruments and in the analysis of our findings. I personally profited not only by learning immensely from Laura, but also from the interdisciplinary team work that later led us to study casual games and gamers, as well as social games played on Facebook and elsewhere. This was also a direction that best reveals the inevitable limitations of the present paper.

Not all players and game experiences are as powerfully oriented towards immersion as the others; this is something that we already hint at the end of the paper as we discuss THE SIMS 2 as proving to be a less immersive game than some others. Yet, apparently this game was much preferred and enjoyed by some players, probably in part because of its playful and casual, toy-like characteristics.

Therefore, strong immersion cannot be directly equated with a 'good game experience', even while it might mean a 'powerful game experience'. As the game takes complete hold of a player's faculties – of their mind and hands as well as imaginations – it inevitably also blocks off certain other directions. Particularly in social situations a less immersive game might be preferred, so that it is possible to divide attention to social interactions with other people, in addition to the stimulus provided by the game. The model presented in this paper can nevertheless be used to understand and evaluate how the different elements in more casual games also involve a degree of (casual) gameplay challenge, an incentive for imagination and some sensory attractions.

After this work was first published in 2005, I have developed a more comprehensive view into how games can be approached within a wider setting of cultural, societal and intellectual contexts in my book *An Introduction to Game Studies. Games in Culture* from 2008. A key distinction in that book relies on the dual structure model: the 'surface' of digital games as digital audiovisual media is equally as important for understanding games and gameplay experiences, as the 'core gameplay' which is at the heart of playful interaction. This is effectively a continuation of the SCI-model presented in this paper, as it builds upon the ontological differences between challenge, which is at the core of playful action, and visual, auditive and fictional elements that relate to everything else that frames these challenges into certain kinds of experiences. Game experiences differ on the basis of these relationships: sometimes the gameplay becomes the focus of our attention, sometimes it is the fictional universe in which the game is situated, sometimes it is the graphic splendour that emerges as the real reason why we play a particular game. None of them is worse than another. Games are what we make out of them – what we do with them, what we think about them, speak about them, and even the ways in which we approach them in scholarly practice have an effect of how the meaning and experience of games becomes constructed.

Wishing you all productive gaming

Frans Mäyrä – Tampere, May 31, 2010

## Introduction: players, experiences and fun

There has been a relative boom of games research that has focused on the definition and ontology of games, but its complementary part, that of research into the gameplay experience, has not been adopted by academics in a similar manner. This is partly due to the disciplinary tilt among the current generation of ludologists: a background in either art, literary or media studies, or in the applied field of game design, naturally leads to research in which the game, rather than the player, is the focus of attention. Yet, the essence of a game is rooted in its interactive nature, and there is no game without a player. The act of playing a game is where the rules embedded into the game's structure start operating, and its program code starts having an effect on cultural and social as well as artistic and commercial realities. If we want to understand what a game is, we need to understand what happens in the act of playing, and we need to understand the player and the experience of gameplay. In this chapter, we discuss the ways in which the gameplay experience can be conceptualized, provide a model that organizes some of its fundamental components, and conclude with an assessment of the model with some directions for further research.

Human experience in virtual environments and games is made of the same elements as all other experiences, and the gameplay experience can be defined as an ensemble made up of the player's sensations, thoughts, feelings, actions, and meaning-making in a gameplay setting. Thus it is not a property or a direct cause of certain elements of a game but something that emerges in a unique interaction process between the game and the player. It has also been suggested that games are actually more like artifacts than media (Hunicke et al. 2004). Players do not just engage in ready-made gameplay, but also actively take part in the construction of these experiences: they bring their desires, anticipations and previous experiences with them, and interpret and reflect the experience in that light. For example, a certain gameplay session might be interpreted as fun, challenging, and victorious until one hears that a friend of the player reached a better score effortlessly, after which it might be reinterpreted as closer to a waste of time. Experiences are also largely context dependent: the same activity can be interpreted as highly pleasant in some contexts but possibly unattractive in other kinds of settings (Blythe/Hassenzahl 2003). The social context is central to gameplay experiences, which was also illustrated by the example above.

Looking at the discourses of current digital game cultures, 'gameplay' is used to describe the essential but elusive quality defining the character of a game as a game, the quality of its 'gameness.' In their book on game design, Rollings and Adams (2003:199) decline to define the concept because, according to them, gameplay is "the result of a large number of contributing elements". Yet, anyone who plays games long enough will form their own conception of bad or good gameplay on the basis of their experience. This experience is informed by multiple significant game elements, which can be very different in games from different genres, as well as by the abilities and preferences of the players. This starting point can further be illustrated by a quote from Chris Crawford (1982:15):

> I suggest that this elusive trait [game play] is derived from the combination of pace and cognitive effort required by the game. Games like TEMPEST have a demonic pace while games like BATTLEZONE have far more deliberate pace. Despite this difference, both games have good game play, for the pace is appropriate to the cognitive demands of the game.

This definition actually translates gameplay into a particular balanced relation between the level of challenge and the abilities of the player. Challenge consists of two main dimensions, the challenge of speed or 'pace' and 'cognitive challenges.' The quality of gameplay is good when these challenges are in balance with each other, and what the appropriate balance is obviously depends on the abilities of the player. On the other hand, one of the most influential theories of fun and creative action, the flow theory by Mihaly Csikszentmihalyi (1991), identifies the 'flow state' as a particularly successful balance of the perceived level of challenge and the skills of the person. In this highly intensive state, one is fully absorbed within the activity, and one often loses one's sense of time and gains powerful gratification. Digital games are generally excellent in providing opportunities for flow-like experiences since the challenges they present are often gradually becoming more demanding, and thus players end up acting at the limits of their skills. In addition, the feedback given to the player is immediate. The activity of playing a game is a goal in itself.

People play games for the experience that can only be achieved by engaging in the gameplay. In other words, a game's value proposition lies in how it might make its players think and feel (Lazzaro 2004), and 'fun' is the ultimate emotional state that they expect to experience as a consequence of playing (Bartle 2004). Expectations and enjoyment are shaped by the schemas that players have. A player can, for example, recognize the genre of a game by observing various genre-typical details and then use her schema of that genre to interpret those details (Douglas/ Hargadon 2000). Brown and Cairns (2004) have noted that players choose games they play according to their mood, and it is to be expected that people especially seek games that elicit optimal emotional responses or response patterns (Ravaja et al. 2004). Thus, when choosing to play a certain game, one might anticipate it to create certain types of experiences.

However, fun and pleasure are complex concepts. Playing games does not always feel fun: on the contrary, it quite often appears to be stressful and frustrating. Experiences that are usually classed as unpleasant can be experienced as pleasurable in certain contexts (De-Jean 2002). So, what makes, for example, failing fun? Klimmt (2003) has applied Zillmann's excitation transfer theory and proposed that the suspense, anxiety and physical arousal elicited by playing are interpreted as positive feelings because players anticipate a resolution and a closure such as winning the game or completing the task. When players manage to cope with a given situation successfully, the arousal is turned into euphoria, and the players experience this kind of cycle of suspense and relief as pleasurable. Klimmt has constructed a three-level model of the enjoyment of playing digital games, the first level of which consists of the interactive input-output loops, the second of cyclic feelings of suspense and relief, and the third is related to the fascination of a temporary escape into another world.

Grodal (2003) regards digital games as a distinctive medium because they allow what he calls "the full experiential flow" by linking perceptions, cognitions, and emotions with first-person actions. The player must have and develop certain skills, both motor and cognitive, in order to engage in gameplay. It is widely acknowledged that digital gameplay experiences are based on learning and rehearsing (Gee 2003, Koster 2005), and according to Grodal (2003) it is the aesthetic of repetition that characterizes the pleasures of gameplaying. In the first encounter with a new game, the player experiences unfamiliarity and challenge and starts to explore the game. After enough effort and repetitions, the player can get to a point where they master the game, and game playing eventually reaches the point of automation and does not feel as fun any longer. Thus, games can be considered as puzzles that the players try to solve by investigating the game world (Newman 2004).

When playing games, it is not enough to just sit and watch and possibly activate some cognitive schemas. Instead, the player must become an active participant. When successful, this type of participation leads to strong gameplay experiences that can have a particularly powerful hold on the player's actions and attention. This basic character of gameplay becomes even clearer when we study the way immersion is created in playing a game.

## Immersion as a component of the gameplay experience

Pine and Gillmore (1999) have categorized different types of experiences according to two dimensions: participation and connection. The dimension of participation varies from active to passive participation and the dimension of connection varies from absorption to immersion. Absorption means directing attention to an experience that is brought to mind, whereas immersion means becoming physically or virtually a part of the experience itself. Four realms of experience can be defined with these dimensions: entertainment (absorption and passive participation), educational (absorption and active participation), aesthetic (immersion and passive participation) and escapist (immersion and active participation). In terms of this categorization, gameplay experiences can be classified as escapist experiences, where in addition to active participation, immersion also plays a central role.

Furthermore, the concept of immersion is widely used in discussing digital games and gameplay experiences. Players, designers, and researchers use it as well, but often in an unspecified and vague way without clearly stating to what kind of experiences or phenomena it actually refers. In media studies, the concept of "presence" has been used with an aim to assess the so-called immersivity of the system. There are different ways to define the sense of presence, but on the whole, the concept refers to a psychological experience of non-mediation, i.e. the sense of being in a world generated by the computer instead of just using a computer (Lombard/Ditton 1997). As immersion can be defined as "the sensation of being surrounded by a completely other reality [ . . . ] that takes over all of our attention, our whole perceptual apparatus" (Murray 1997:98) immersion and presence do not actually fall very far from each other, and are in fact often used as synonyms. However, since the term 'presence' was originally developed in the context of teleoperations it also relies heavily on the metaphor of transportation. In the context of digital games, we prefer using the term "immersion," because it more clearly connotes the mental processes involved in gameplay.

It is often taken for granted that a bigger screen and better audio quality equal greater immersion (Newman 2004). It is of course likely that the audiovisual implementation of the game has something to do with immersive experiences, but it is by no means the only or even the most significant factor. McMahan (2003:69) has listed three conditions to be met in order to create a sense of immersion in digital games: the conventions of the game matching the user expectations, meaningful things to do for the player, and a consistent game world. Genre fiction encourages players to form hypotheses and expectations and, according to Douglas and Hargadon (2000), pleasures of immersion derive from the absorption within a familiar schema. On the other hand, meaningful play as defined by Salen and Zimmerman (2004) occurs when the relationships between actions and outcomes are both discernable and integrated. Discernability indicates letting the player know what happens when they take action, and integration means tying those actions and outcomes into the larger context of the game. And just like any manipulation, acting in the game world requires relevant functionality and ways to access this functionality (i.e., usability) (Hassenzahl 2003). Thus, the audiovisual, functional, and structural playability as defined by Järvinen, Heliö and Mäyrä (2002) can be seen as prerequisites for gameplay immersion and rewarding gameplay experiences. On a very basic level, it can be argued that it is the basic visual-motor links that enable experiences of immersion even in games in which the graphics are not very impressive (Klimmt 2003, Grodal 2003). The increasing demand on working memory also seems to increase immersion (Gee 2003). For example, an increase in the difficulty level may cause an increase in the feeling of presence (Douglas/Hargadon 2002).

Brown and Cairns (2004) have presented a classification that categorizes immersion into gameplay in three levels of involvement. Ranging from "engagement" via "engrossment" to "total immersion," their model is useful in pointing out how the amount of involvement may fluctuate. However, this approach nevertheless fails to adequately respond to the qualitative differences between different modes of involvement, which is also apparent in the clear individual preferences different players have in different game types or genres. Brown and Cairns see total immersion as a synonym for presence. They agree that immersion seems to have many common features with flow experiences. However, in the context of digital games flowlike phenomena seem only to be fleeting experiences, which in turn suggests that they are something different from flow as traditionally conceived. Thus, the flow-like experiences related to gameplay could be called "micro-flow" (Blythe/Hassenzahl 2003) or "gameflow" (Järvinen et al. 2002), for example.

Funk, Pasold and Baumgardner (2003) have created a gameplay experience questionnaire in order to investigate the effects of exposure to fantasy violence. They developed a measure that concentrates on what they call "psychological absorption", but does not differentiate between different kinds of gameplay experiences even though the theoretical model presented suggests that there are at least two kinds of experiences: absorption and flow. We argue that in order to understand what games and playing fundamentally are, we need to be able to make qualitative distinctions between the key components of the gameplay experience, and also relate them to various characteristics of games and players. In this chapter, we approach immersion as one of the key components of the gameplay experience and analyze its different aspects.

274

## The attractions of digital games

The starting point of our research was the twofold perspective we gained in 2003 while interviewing Finnish children who actively played digital games alongside with their parents, who mostly did not play such games themselves (Ermi et al. 2004). The parents expressed concern because they thought that their children became too intensely emotionally immersed, or too involved with the game fiction, while playing. They agreed with the common conception that it was particularly the realistic and high-quality graphics and audio of contemporary games that explained their immersive powers. In contrast, the children thought that the emotional immersion and involvement in fiction was typically stronger for them while reading a good book or while watching a movie. They emphasized the role of the characters and storylines in this kind of experience, while they also acknowledged often becoming immersed in games, but in different ways than in literature or cinema, in which emotional identification or engrossment was more common for them than in games.

> Well, you immerse yourself more into a book, I think. I don't know many reasons for that, but at least I lose myself more into books than in games. In games I usually only just play, or then I sort of follow the plot, but in books it is kind of more exciting, because the plot is the main part, and in games the main part is moving things yourself and such, in games the plot is just secondary. (Boy, 12 years)

When discussing games, children stated that the main difference between games and novels or movies was the games' interactivity: the opportunity to make decisions, take actions, and have an effect on the gameplay. Some of them also considered this to be the most immersive aspect of games.

> In movies I do not identify with the main character at all. I just watch what he does. But in a book, if I read about the actions of some main character, then I identify with him as I would be the character myself. Or at least I immerse myself more into it. But in a game you immerse yourself most of all, because you actually do things with that guy, with that character, most of all. (Boy, 11 years)

Another thing that clearly separated children's experiences with games from their experiences with books and movies was the social quality of gameplay. Children often played together with their friends and siblings, and games were notable discussion topics on schoolyards etc.

> When in it [a book] you can go and figure with your own brain like, ok, now it [the character] is doing this and that. [ . . . ] Yes it [a game] is a bit different, as you can say to your friend that hey, look this is doing this and that, but in books you cannot really, because you are not reading with your friend. (Girl, 10 years)

As we were curious about these different ways of perceiving game "immersion," we studied the responses further and analyzed the children's accounts of playing games and the different holding powers they had recognized in games in order to shed some light on the structure of the experience.

In the light of the interviews, the pleasures of gameplay derive from several different sources (Ermi/Mäyrä 2003); see Figure 1. According to the children, the *audiovisual quality and style* was one of the central aspects of good digital games. For example, good-looking graphics could make the game more appealing, and well-functioning camera angles were associated with good playability. However, children perceived game aesthetics in different ways. Some of them especially liked cartoon style graphics, whereas others felt they were too childish and preferred as realistic looking graphical style as possible.

Children also analyzed the various ways in which the *level of challenge* was balanced in games quite carefully.

The pleasure derived from playing was strongly related to experiences of succeeding and advancing, and uncertainty of the final outcome was an important factor in the overall suspense of playing. The challenges of gameplay seemed to be related to two different domains: to sensomotor abilities such as using the

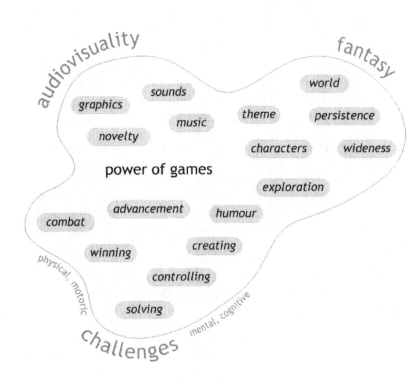

*Figure 1* Elements related to pleasurable gameplay experiences that emerged in the interviews with the children (Ermi/Mäyrä 2003)

276

controls and reacting fast, and, secondly to the cognitive challenges. Even though pure puzzle games were not very popular, children liked games in which problem solving was an integral part of the storyline or adventure of the game.

Thirdly, children considered *imaginary world and fantasy* to be central in many games. For them, the game characters, worlds and storylines were central elements of the games they liked to play. One important aspect of the imaginary worlds was that children could do things in them that were not possible or even acceptable in their everyday lives, for example beating up a policeman or having two children living in a big house without any adults. After analyzing these observations, we followed the principles of grounded theory approach to create a theory that accounted for the findings.

## A gameplay experience model

Our research suggests that the gameplay experience and immersion into a game are multidimensional phenomena. The issue here is not that parents would have drawn the wrong conclusions while observing their child's playing, or that the children themselves would not be able to understand their own immersion experiences. Rather, the answer is that immersion is a many-faceted phenomenon with different aspects that can appear and be emphasized differently in the individual cases of different games and players.

In the gameplay experience model presented here (abbreviated as SCI-model, on the basis of its key components; see Figure 2), gameplay is represented as interaction between a particular kind of a game and a particular kind of a game player. Our model is a heuristic representation of key elements that structure the gameplay experience.

It is not intended to constitute a comprehensive analysis, but rather designed to guide attention to the complex dynamics that are involved in the interaction between a player and a game. The complex internal organization of a "game" and a "player" in particular are left schematic here, as the focus is on the consciousness structured by the interplay, rather than on an analysis of games or players in themselves. The gameplay experience can be perceived as a temporal experience, in which finally the interpretation made by the player also takes into account other information such as peer influence, game reviews, and other frames of sociocultural reference.

The first dimension of a gameplay experience that we distinguish is the *sensory immersion* related to the audiovisual execution of games. This is something that even those with less experience with games – like the parents of the children that were interviewed – can recognize: digital games have evolved into audio-visually impressive, three-dimensional and stereophonic worlds that surround their players in a very comprehensive manner. Large screens close to player's face and powerful sounds easily overpower the sensory information coming from the real world, and the player becomes entirely focused on the game world and its stimuli.

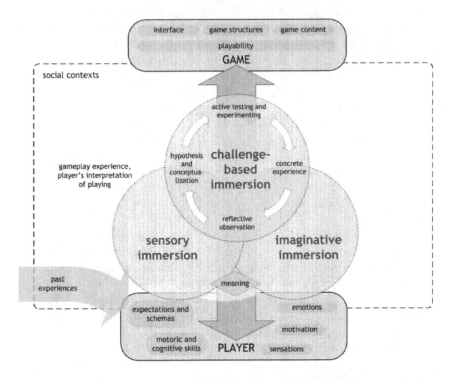

*Figure 2* SCI-model identifies the three key dimensions of immersion that are related to several other fundamental components, which have a role in the formation of the gameplay experience

Another form of immersion that is particularly central for games, as they are fundamentally based on interaction, is *challenge-based immersion*. This is the feeling of immersion that is at its most powerful when one is able to achieve a satisfying balance of challenges and abilities. Challenges can be related to motor skills or mental skills such as strategic thinking or logical problem solving, but they usually involve both to some degree.

In several contemporary games the worlds, characters and story elements have also become very central, even if the game would not be classifiable as an actual role-playing game. We call this dimension of game experience, in which one becomes absorbed with the stories and the world, or begins to feel for or identify with a game character, *imaginative immersion*. This is the area in which the game offers the player a chance to use their imagination, empathize with the characters, or just enjoy the fantasy of the game.

For example, multi-sensory virtual reality environments such as CAVE (Cruz-Neira et al. 1992), or just a simple screensaver, could provide the purest form of sensory immersion, while the experience of imaginative immersion would be most prominent when one becomes absorbed in a good novel. Movies would combine both of these. But challenge-based immersion has an essential role in digital games since the gameplay requires active participation: players are constantly faced with both mental and physical challenges that keep them playing. Since many contemporary digital games have richer audiovisual and narrative content than, for example, classic *Tetris*, these three dimensions of immersion usually mix and overlap in many ways. In other words, the factors that potentially contribute to imaginative immersion (e.g., characters, world, and storyline) are also apparent in the interaction design (e.g., goal structures) and the audiovisual design (how goals, characters and, the world are represented and perceived) of well-integrated game designs.

The overall significance of a game for a player can be greater than the sum of its parts. In our model, 'meaning' is the part through which a player makes sense of their play experience and constructs their interpretation of the game against the backdrop of the various personal and social contexts of their life. Thus it relates to the traditions of pragmatics, phenomenology, and cultural studies as much as to that of semiotics or psychology in a conceptual sense. The contexts of a gameplay experience also include factors such as who the player is (in terms of the rich complexities of personal histories), what kind of previous experience they have with this game or game genre, and how cultural and social factors affect the role games have in their life in more general terms. In addition, situational contexts can have a decisive role in structuring the experience: Who is the game played with? Is there a specific reason to play this game right at that moment? Is the player playing to vent frustrations, for example, or is the significance of this gameplay in the shared moments with friends? All these various contextual factors have their distinctive roles in the interpretation of an experience and are therefore included in the model.

## The gameplay experience model in practice

After creating the model, we were interested to find out how the different aspects of immersion actually appear in contemporary digital games. We constructed a questionnaire that initially consisted of thirty statements addressing the three aspects of gameplay immersion and responses given on a 5-point Likert scale. In March 2005, we invited players of certain popular games to evaluate their experiences of these games. The respondents were recruited from among thousand Finnish participants that had filled in another game-related online questionnaire. The games were chosen on a twofold basis: on one hand, we had to pick games that were played among the informants and on the other hand, we tried to cover as wide a range of different kinds of game genres as possible. The games and the amount of the completed gameplay experience self-evaluation questionnaires are shown in Figure 3.

There were 203 respondents altogether, but since some of them evaluated two different games, the total amount of completed gameplay experience self-evaluation

| WORLD OF WARCRAFT (2004) | 35 |
|---|---|
| HALF-LIFE 2 (2004) | 34 |
| GRAND THEFT AUTO: SAN ANDREAS (2004) | 25 |
| HALO 2 (2004) | 21 |
| CIVILIZATION III (2001) | 20 |
| THE SIMS 2 (2004) | 20 |
| FLATOUT (2004) | 17 |
| STAR WARS: KNIGHTS OF THE OLD REPUBLIC II: SITH LORDS (2005) | 16 |
| ROME: TOTAL WAR (2004) | 16 |
| NETHACK (1987) | 14 |
| PRO EVOLUTION SOCCER 4 (2004) | 13 |
| NEVERWINTER NIGHTS (2002) | 9 |
| NHL 2005 (2004) | 7 |
| TOTAL | 247 |

*Figure 3* The distribution of the completed gameplay experience self-evaluation questionnaires into different digital games

questionnaires was 247. Almost all of the respondents were male (91%), THE SIMS
2 being the only exception with 55% of the responses given by females. The age of
the respondents varied between 12 and 40 years (mean 21.4 years). The platform
used for playing was a PC computer in 73% of the cases, but HALO 2 was played
only on Xbox and GRAND THEFT AUTO: SAN ANDREAS only on PlayStation
2. In the majority of the cases, the game was played as a single-player game (75%),
but WORLD OF WARCRAFT was played as a multiplayer game on the Internet. In
a few cases (4%) the game was played as a multiplayer game in which the players
also shared physical location.

After examining the correlations between the thirty questionnaire items with
explorative factor analysis, some of the statements were eliminated so that the number of items was reduced to eighteen. The scale of sensory immersion consisted
of four statements related to the capturing of senses done by the game (e.g., "The
sounds of game overshadowed the other sounds of the environment"), the scale of
challenge-based immersion of seven statements addressing the orientation to goals
and flow-like experiences (e.g., "The game challenged me to try to reach the limits
of my abilities"), and the scale of imaginative immersion included seven statements
that measured how involved the player and their imagination were with the game
(e.g., "I identified with how the game characters felt in different situations").
Cronbach's alphas for this sample were 0.69, 0.73, and 0.82 respectively.

It is not possible to go through the results in great detail here, and again we
emphasize that the main goal was to develop and validate our model. In that
respect, the first obvious finding when looking at the data is that the immersion
levels in the examined games were quite high overall, so that no game with almost

non-existent immersion experience was found. This is an understandable consequence of the fact that our informants were analyzing gameplay experiences from games that were their personal favourites. It would no doubt be possible to also obtain results from the different end of the spectrum if random or less-favoured games and not as enthusiastic players would be examined. Nevertheless, the results appear to support the SCI-model and the questionnaire derived from it.

Comparing games that fall on the opposite ends of the scales is illuminating. The sensory immersion is experienced as particularly strong in HALF-LIFE 2 and lowest in NETHACK, as we expected. The role of audiovisual technology is clear: the sensory experience provided by an old game from an ASCII graphics era appears distinctly different from that provided by the latest three-dimensional game engines.

The situation is different as we turn to the results from the analysis of challenge-based immersion. Here NETHACK is the game that acquired the top score, followed by CIVILIZATION III, ROME: TOTAL WAR and PRO EVOLUTION SOCCER 4. These games are interesting also in the sense that they probably provide players with distinctly different kinds of challenges: NETHACK with those of a seemingly simple dungeon game that actually provides players with an endless supply of complex puzzles linked to randomly generated items and interactions, CIVILIZATION III and ROME: TOTAL WAR with the predominantly strategic challenges in warfare and empire-building scenarios, and PRO EVOLUTION SOCCER 4 testing players' reactions and coordination skills at a faster speed. The lowest challenge-based immersion rating of the examined games was that of THE SIMS 2, which can be related to its non-competitive and toy-like basic character.

Imaginative immersion, the third component of the model, is at its strongest in role-playing games and plot-driven adventure games, again confirming expectations how the scale should operate. STAR WARS: KNIGHTS OF THE OLD REPUBLIC 2, HALF-LIFE 2, and NEVERWINTER NIGHTS lead the statistics, with PRO EVOLUTION SOCCER 4, the rally game FLATOUT and strategy games CIVILIZATION III and ROME: TOTAL WAR inhabiting the other end of the scale. The result is logical since games with characters and storylines provide players with more possibilities to identify with something in the game and use their imagination.

There are several interesting aspects of the results that invite further research. Summing up mean values of all the three components of gameplay immersion, HALF-LIFE 2 appears to be the overall strongest game in immersing its players. On the other end, the experience of playing THE SIMS 2 is apparently not felt as immersive. However, it would be a mistake to claim that HALF-LIFE 2 was a better game than THE SIMS 2 on this basis. It may well be that the more 'casual' character of THE SIMS 2 gameplay is one of the reasons behind its appeal for these particular players. THE SIMS 2 was also the only one of the examined games with a notable amount of female respondents, but the relatively low evaluation of immersion is not related to the gender of the informants, since females gave overall higher evaluations to the immersion in that game than men.

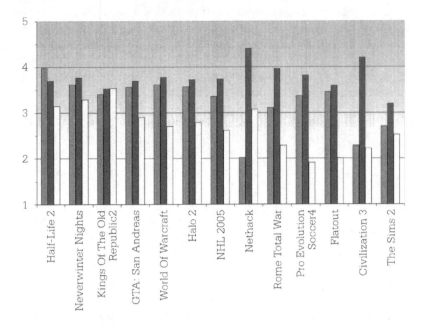

*Figure 4* The average amount of each immersion type reported by the players in different digital games (the total amount of immersion reported is highest on the left-hand side)

## Conclusions and future work

> To each and every one of the above 'explanations' it might well be objected: 'So far so good, but what actually is the fun of playing? Why does the baby crow with pleasure? Why does the gambler lose himself in his passion? Why is a huge crowd roused to frenzy by a football match?' This intensity of, and absorption in, play finds no explanation in biological analysis. Yet in this intensity, this absorption, this power of maddening, lies the very essence, the primordial quality of play. (Johan Huizinga, *Homo Ludens*)

This research has been driven by a desire to better understand the nature of gameplay experience. In the existing research which we synthesized in the beginning of this chapter, there proved to be several useful observations and conceptualizations that address or can be applied into the study of gameplay. Nevertheless, there is a need for a game-specific model that would take the diversity of contemporary digital games into account, and that would address its full complexity. We have presented one version of such a model in this chapter, while also acknowledging the need for further research.

In the future, we will test and fine-tune the questionnaire further, and also look into the applicability of the model for evaluation of gameplay characteristics both within a controlled environment and as a part of pervasive gameplay experience evaluation. The games examined here represent only a fraction of the variety of games. For such purposes, new applications of the model will be needed, as well as further extensions of the evaluation criteria to include dimensions of experience relevant to game types that are not played with a personal computer or game console and television screen. It is also necessary to broaden the conception and evaluation of gameplay experiences to include all the other components presented in the model besides immersion. For example, what is the role of emotions, social contexts and players' expectations and interpretations, and how do the different aspects of gameplay immersion link to the characteristics of the player and features of the game?

In a sense, this research has at this point opened more questions than it is able to answer. For example, it would be highly relevant and important to further examine the role of social and cultural contexts for the gameplay experience. Do the pre-existing expectations and experiences with related games determine the gameplay experience with a new one, and to what degree? And finally, what are the exact inter-relationships and relative weights of the components included in our model? It might also be possible that game players are able to switch from one attitude or repertoire of game playing into another one, and the gameplay experience will vary on the basis of such "eyeglasses" or filters. How much does the situational context really affect the way games are experienced? As usual in research, when new knowledge is created, new horizons into the unknown and unexplored are also opened up.

## Acknowledgements

The original version of this paper was presented at the DIGRA 2005 conference in Vancouver and was included in its *Selected Papers* proceedings, and was then subsequently (in a slightly updated version) included in the book *Worlds in Play. International Perspectives on Digital Games Research*, ed. by Suzanne de Castell and Jennifer Jenson (New York: Lang 2007, 37–53). The version printed here has been revised to include an introductory note by Frans Mäyrä in May 2010.

The original research was made in conjunction with several research projects in the Hypermedia Laboratory of the University of Tampere: *Children as the Actors of Game Cultures*, *Design and Research Environment for Lottery Games of the Future*, and *Mobile Content Communities*. The authors wish to thank all partners in these projects. We also thank all those children and adults who took part in the interviews and/or completed the questionnaires. Special thanks to Satu Heliö, Markus Montola, and Suvi Mäkelä.

## References

Bartle, Richard A. (2004): *Designing Virtual Worlds*, Indianapolis: New Riders.
Blythe, Mark/Hassenzahl, Marc (2003): "The Semantics of Fun. Differentiating Enjoyable Experiences", in: *Funology. From Usability to Enjoyment*, ed. by M. Blythe, K. Overbeeke, A. F. Monk and P. C. Wright, Dordrecht: Kluwer, 91–100.

**Brown, Emily/Cairns, Paul** (2004): "A Grounded Investigation of Game Immersion", in: *CHI'04 Extended Abstracts on Human Factors and Computing Systems*, New York: ACM, 1297–1300.

**Crawford, Chris** (1982): *The Art of Computer Game Design*, Berkeley: Osborne/McGraw-Hill.

**Cruz-Neira, Carolina/Sandin, Daniel J./DeFanti, Thomas A./Kenyon, Robert V./Hart, John C.**: "The CAVE. Audio Visual Experience Automatic Virtual Environment", in: *Communications of the ACM* 35/6 (1992), 64–72.

**Csikszentmihalyi, Mihaly** (1991): *Flow. The Psychology of Optimal Experience*, New York: Harper & Row.

**DeJean, Pierre-Henri** (2002): "Difficulties and Pleasure?", in: *Pleasure with Products. Beyond Usability*, ed. by W. S. Green and P. W. Jordan, London: Taylor & Francis, 147–150.

**Douglas, Yellowlees/Hargadon, Andrew** (2000): "The Pleasure Principle. Immersion, Engagement, Flow", in: *Proceedings of the Eleventh ACM Conference on Hypertext and Hypermedia*, New York: ACM, 153–160.

**Ermi, Laura/Heliö, Satu/Mäyrä, Frans** (2004): *Pelien voima ja pelaamisen hallinta. Lapset ja nuoret pelikulttuurien toimijoina [Power and Control of Games. Children as the Actors of Game Cultures]*, http://tampub.uta.fi/tup/951-44-5939-3.pdf.

——. /**Mäyrä, Frans** (2003): "Power and Control of Games. Children as the Actors of Game Cultures", in: *Level Up. Digital Game Research Conference*, ed. by M. Copier and J. Raessens, Utrecht: University of Utrecht, 234–244.

**Funk, Jeanne B./Pasold, Tracie/Baumgardner, Jennifer** (2003): "How Children Experience Playing Video Games", in: *Proceedings of the Second International Conference on Entertainment Computing*, Pittsburgh: Carnegie Mellon University, 1–14.

**Gee, James Paul** (2003): *What Video Games Have to Teach Us about Learning and Literacy*, New York: Palgrave Macmillan.

**Grodal, Torben** (2003): "Stories for Eye, Ear, and Muscles. Video Games, Media, and Embodied Experiences", in: *The Video Game Theory Reader*, ed. by M. J. P. Wolf and B. Perron, New York/London: Routledge, 129–155.

**Hassenzahl, Marc** (2003): "The Thing and I. Understanding the Relationship between User and Product", in: *Funology. From Usability to Enjoyment*, ed. by M. Blythe, K. Overbeeke, A. F. Monk and P. C. Wright, Dordrecht: Kluwer, 31–42.

**Hunicke, Robin/LeBlanc, Marc/Zubek, Robert** (2004) "MDA: A Formal Approach to Game Design and Game Research", http://www.cs.northwestern.edu/~hunicke/pubs/MDA.pdf.

**Järvinen, Aki/Heliö, Satu/Mäyrä, Frans** (2002): *Communication and Community in Digital Entertainment Services. Prestudy Research Report*, http://tampub.uta.fi/tup/951-44-5432-4.pdf.

**Koster, Raph** (2005): *A Theory of Fun for Game Design*, Scottsdale: Paraglyph.

**Klimmt, Christoph** (2003): "Dimensions and Determinants of the Enjoyment of Playing Digital Games. A Three-Level Model", in: *Level Up. Digital Game Research Conference*, ed. by M. Copier and J. Raessens, Utrecht: University of Utrecht, 246–257.

**Lazzaro, Nicole** (2004): "Why We Play Games. Four Keys to More Emotion in Player Experiences", http://www.xeodesign.com/whyweplaygames/xeodesign_whyweplaygames.pdf.

**Lombard, Matthew/Ditton, Theresa** (1997): "At the Heart of It All: The Concept of Presence", in: *Journal of Computer Mediated Communication* 3/2, http://jcmc.indiana.edu/vol3/issue2/lombard.html.

**McMahan, Alison** (2003): "Immersion, Engagement, and Presence. A Method for Analyzing 3-D Video Games", in: *The Video Game Theory Reader*, ed. by M. J. P. Wolf and B. Perron, New York/London: Routledge, 67–86.

**Murray, Janet** (1997): *Hamlet on the Holodeck. The Future of Narrative in Cyberspace*, Cambridge/London: MIT.

**Newman, James** (2004): *Videogames*, New York/London: Routledge.

**Pine, B. Jospeh/Gilmore, James H.** (1999): *The Experience Economy. Work is Theatre and Every Business a Stage*, Boston: Harvard Business School.

**Ravaja, Niklas/Salminen, Mikko/Holopainen, Jussi/Saari, Timo/Laarni, Jari/Järvinen, Aki** (2004): "Emotional Response Patterns and Sense of Presence during Video Games. Potential Criterion Variables for Game Design", in: *Proceedings of the Third Nordic Conference on Human-Computer Interaction*, New York: ACM, 339–347.

**Rollings, Andrew/Adams, Ernest** (2003): *On Game Design*, Indianapolis: New Riders.

**Salen, Katie/Zimmerman, Eric** (2004): *Rules of Play. Game Design Fundamentals*. Cambridge/London: MIT.

BATTLEZONE (1980), Atari, Arcade.

CIVILIZATION III (2001), Infogrames, PC.

FLATOUT (2004), Empire Interactive, PC.

GRAND THEFT AUTO: SAN ANDREAS (2004), Rockstar Games, Playstation 2.

HALF-LIFE 2 (2004), Sierra Entertainment, PC.

HALO 2 (2004), Microsoft Game Studios, Xbox.

NETHACK (1987), NetHack DevTeam/Open Source, PC.

NEVERWINTER NIGHTS (2002), Atari, PC.

NHL 2005 (2004), EA Sports, Playstation 2.

PRO EVOLUTION SOCCER 4 (2004), Konami, Playstation 2.

ROME: TOTAL WAR (2004), Activision, PC.

STAR WARS: KNIGHTS OF THE OLD REPUBLIC 2 (2005), LucasArts, PC.

TEMPEST (1980), Atari, Arcade.

THE SIMS 2 (2004), Electronic Arts, PC.

WORLD OF WARCRAFT (2004), Vivendi, PC Online.

# 63

# EMERSION AS AN ELEMENT OF GAMING EXPERIENCE

## *Piotr Kubiński*

Source: Originally published as 'Immersion vs. Emersive Effects in Videogames' from Dawn
Stobbart and Monica Evans (eds), *Engaging with Videogames: Play, Theory and Practice* (Oxford:
Inter-Disciplinary Press, 2014), pp. 133–14 [e–book]. This is an extended version.

## Abstract

The author of this chapter approaches the phenomenon of immersion
and concentrates on one of its insufficiently analysed aspects. The
article presents those techniques and strategies that (intentionally
or not) reduce, or even preclude, the effect of immersion. All those
mechanisms—described collectively as 'emersive effects'—are
considered in terms of their influence on a game structure, on the
cohesion of the in-game world, and on possible interpretations.
Occurring on various game levels, emersion is sometimes a result
of a creator's mistakes, and causes technical disillusion. At other
times emersive factors are embedded in the convention of a game.
Finally, emersion might also be achieved deliberately (e.g. for
artistic or humorous purposes). This last instantiation seems to be
the most interesting one, as it opens new possibilities of creation
(especially for authors of more artistic and serious games), and
unveils underrated aspects of videogames.

## 1. Introduction—category of immersion[1]

Videogames are frequently analysed in the context of their immersive potential.
Indeed, immersion is very often considered the most important and most desired
effect a game can have on a player. Because of this process of *absolutisation of
immersion*, calling a game 'fully immersive' became one of the greatest compliments
one could pay to a game's creator. According to Gordon Calleja 'immersion seems to
be seen as something of a holy grail within the games industry.'[2]

However, at the same time, there is no universal consensus on what in fact
immersion is. As Calleja summarises,[3] terms such as telepresence (or simply:
presence), absorption, incorporation, and immersion are still under discussion and
are repeatedly used with various meanings. The purpose of this article is neither to

286

arbitrate this ongoing dispute, nor to propose its final solution; but since the main topic of this chapter is the phenomenon of emersion, it is important to outline the specific category of immersion that serves as emersion's necessary background. The definition adopted in this article states that immersion is an impression of a non-mediated participation in a digital world generated by a machine: the sensation of a direct presence, which makes players lose sight of the physical world surrounding them. Without intending to induce anyone to uncritically adopt such a definition, it should be pointed out that this understanding of the term is related to the one proposed by Janet Murray:

> A stirring narrative in any medium can be experienced as a virtual reality because our brains are programmed to tune into stories with an intensity that can obliterate the world around us. [ . . . ] The experience of being transported to an elaborately simulated place is pleasurable in itself, regardless of the fantasy content. We refer to this experience as immersion. *Immersion* is a metaphorical term derived from the physical experience of being submerged in water. We seek the same feeling from a psychologically immersive experience that we do from a plunge in the ocean or swimming pool: the sensation of being surrounded by a completely other reality, as different as water is from air, that takes over all of our attention, our whole perceptual apparatus.[4]

It is worth noting that, according to Murray, immersion is not a term inextricably linked to videogames and might also appear in non-digital media. Some other researchers share this opinion: Oliver Grau sees immersive aspects in 'in the artificial paradises of narcotics, for example, as described by Charles Baudelaire'[5] and even in ancient cult frescos (e.g. the Great Frieze in the Villa dei Misteri at Pompeii);[6] Marie-Laure Ryan,[7] and Katarzyna Prajzner[8] analyse immersive potential in all narrative media—to name just a few among many other significant examples.

On the one hand, this proves that videogames should be treated as an equipollent way of expression of human creativity focused on producing the illusion of exceeding physical reality. Electronic entertainment can be seen as a natural consequence of the universal need for transgression, for the need to reach beyond the 'here and now'. The main—and also obvious—difference compared to traditional media is the technology, which not only absorbs player's imagination and senses, but also allows them to actively *participate* in the events in the game and *influence* the diegetic spacetime (thanks to the interactive or ergodic character of the game).[9]

But on the other hand, one may argue that using the category of immersion (like every other concept) with such a broad meaning might weaken its usefulness. Due to this and the unique techniques and possibilities of creating the *notion of being there* that is provided by virtual realities (and especially the digital worlds simulated by videogames), the term 'immersion' in this article will only be used in relation to games.

## 2. Emersion

### 2a. Introduction of the term

Academic researchers who examine this matter tend to analyse how immersion works and what techniques, used by game developers, help players to immerse themselves into a game's digital world. The aim of this article is to analyse this problem from the opposite perspective and to present the techniques and strategies that reduce or even preclude the effect of immersion.

It is worth noting that these elements may have a rather varied status: sometimes they are completely random, unforeseen by videogame creators. Otherwise, factors that decrease the feeling of immersion may be introduced by the authors deliberately—in order to achieve a precise aesthetic effect. The latter case seems to be the most interesting one, as it opens up new possibilities of creation especially for the authors of more artistic and serious games.

To examine this problem, one should start by indicating what conditions are necessary to create a sense of immersion. Alison McMahan, a prominent researcher of immersion in videogames, enumerates three such conditions:

1    the user's expectations of the game or environment must match the environment's conventions fairly closely;
2    the user's actions must have a non-trivial impact on the environment;
3    the conventions of the world must be consistent, even if they don't match those of »meatspace«.[10]

The third condition (consistency of a fictional world's conventions) seems to be the most interesting one in the context of this research, as creating and choosing between those conventions are the game creator's textual (and in some cases, artistic) choices. Before concentrating on various examples of deviations within conventions, a general term should be proposed which could embrace the whole phenomenon in its many aspects. Keeping in mind the Latin root of the word 'immersion' (lat. 'immergo, immergere'—to dive, to submerge), the term 'emersion' and 'emersive effect' (lat. 'emergo, emergere'—to rise up from water) will be used here to describe opposite strategies, i.e. those which reduce the sense of immersion, bringing players back to the meatspace or—if one follows Murray's metaphor—those forces that pull the player out from a swimming pool or ocean (i.e. from a digital environment) back to his or her primary reality.

### 2b. Technical disillusion

Emersive factors may affect players on many levels through their contact with a videogame. McMahan writes about the diverse bugs and errors in videogames, which she calls *shocks*:

Shocks are poor design elements that jar the user out of the sense of 'reality' of the VRE, such as the 'end of the world' shock—the user can see where the environment ends; 'film set shock'—buildings are incomplete; polygon leaks—seeing through cracks; and latency and motion sickness caused by poor design or overlong use of the hardware.[11]

One of the examples named by McMahan is a situation whereby the player faces 'the end of the world', that is the border of the digital environment such as a digital void, or *invisible wall* that cannot be passed. Of course, such blockades are created especially when the diegetic space cannot be limited by natural obstacles, such as walls (e.g. when the action of a game takes place in a desert). Such limitation of space is needed mainly because of thriftiness. Designing vast, realistic and highly detailed scenery is time-consuming, and generating it absorbs a large amount of computer resources. Therefore, level designers often create just as much space as needed to achieve the desired effect (just as in the case of a film set or theatrical scenography). The same applies to other objects in a virtual world: designers often omit those elements which are not seen by players (e.g. if a player cannot enter a building, it is obviously not necessary to design its interior). Sometimes, however, a player accidentally notices the superficiality of the scenery—for example, thanks to the imperfections of the camera.

What the elements enumerated by McMahan (and other similar errors) have in common is that they reveal a game's dependence on electronic devices such as computers or gaming consoles with their fallible technological nature. Due to this phenomenon's unmasking character, it is more instructive to abandon the expressive (and somewhat psychological) name 'shock' used by McMahan. Instead this phenomenon can be called 'technical disillusion'. It allows the analyst to highlight two distinctive features of this effect: first of all, the character of the stimulus is purely technical (and not, for example, narrative). Secondly, this type of phenomenon reveals the illusory nature of direct participation and thereby reduces the impact of this illusion. Therefore, technical disillusion should be considered as the first, and the most basic emersive factor.

### 2c. Technical disillusion as a device

Rather than being a deliberate design strategy, technical disillusion is mostly a result of the mistakes committed during the development of a game, or the imperfections arising from the nature of the digital medium. On less frequent occasions, however, game creators use *the structure* of such a startling element in a more meaningful way. An eminent example of such a creative technique is *Batman: Arkham Asylum* (Rocksteady, 2009).[12]

In this particular game there is a scene in which Batman, poisoned by hallucinogenic gas, is walking through a long corridor. A moment later, the image displayed on the screen freezes and becomes fuzzed in a way that clearly suggests that the game has crashed due to a malfunction of the computer or the console.

This moment is extremely suggestive also because of the sounds generated by the game that imitate metallic squeaks indicating that the program has crashed (or even that the computer or the console is broken).

Such a noisy audiovisual content lasts for approximately eight seconds. After that the player sees an animation that is very similar to the game's intro. The user might thus think that the game has shut down due to an error, and that it has automatically started up again (from the beginning). However, it quickly becomes clear that this is not the same introductory animation, because it significantly differs from the original one. The first discrepancy can be recognised in Batman's symbol which is visible in the night sky. The symbol is reversed and arranged in the shape of . . . a characteristic ominous face. It is a mask and also the hallmark of the villain (Scarecrow), who previously poisoned the protagonist with gas, causing delusions and anxiety. Another surprising element in this animation is the special reversal of roles: in this scene, the Joker transports a handcuffed Batman to a psychiatric hospital, although the original intro showed the exact opposite situation. It makes the player feel surprised or even confused, but at the same time, the presented scene provides an explanation; the whole sequence of events is not the already known beginning of the game, but an hallucination. The animation displayed immediately after the technical disillusion effect should be understood as a projection of the deeply hidden fears of the protagonist: the fear of failure in his confrontation with the Joker. It also explains, that the main character is afraid of the very serious consequences his defeat would bring to the city of Gotham. Anxiety is reflected in the new symbol displayed on the sky. Normally it represents Batman, the defender of Gotham, but now its diverted, upside down form represents terror, and the fear that reigns over the city.

Neither an indicated reversal of roles, nor reinterpretation of a well-known pop cultural symbol would be so interesting, if they were not a result of the creative usage of the structure of technical disillusion. This supposed error is, in fact, an innovative representation of the main character's perception. The moment when the screen freezes and becomes unreadable, is nothing but the moment when the hero is completely subjected to hallucinations, or simply loses consciousness (which is why the presented swapping of roles is possible). This means that an event from a diegetic level (the disruption of the main character's perceptual apparatus) obtains its representation in the formal or even physical layer of the game. The sequence from Batman: Arkham Asylum (which of course is just one example of a game pointing to its screen-mediated nature) wrecks the feeling of immersion. Nevertheless, although it *pulls* the player *out* from the fictional world, it also gives something in return. The refreshing and amusing effect of astonishment might be an even bigger reward and might compensate for being knocked out of the in-game presence.

### 2d. Ironic distance

Similar surprise and playfulness may be achieved (again, at the cost of reducing immersion) by populating the in-game world with references that point outside

290

the game's context. A prominent example is provided by the second part of *The Witcher* series, *The Witcher 2: Assassins of Kings* (CD Projekt RED, 2011).[13] Halfway into the storyline, the player encounters a group of Elven rebels who use a secret password. The password shouted by one of the characters is 'Kier-ke-gaard'. The countersign to that turns out to be 'Hei-de-gger'.[14]

This is an interesting example for at least two reasons. Firstly, to understand the joke, the player needs to use his cultural knowledge and remind himself of the nineteenth-century Danish philosopher Søren Kierkegaard, and the twentieth-century German philosopher Martin Heidegger. As a result, the player is in fact provoked to leave the on-screen fictional world, and to remind himself of the actual reality that he is supposed to forget about by means of the immersive mechanisms of the game. Secondly, the joke is constructed in such a way, that if the player does not understand it (if he does not recognise the two famous philosophers' names), he will probably think that 'Kier-ke-gaard' and 'Hei-de-gger' are just other Elven words, and it is completely normal not to understand them. An additional argument for such a reading is that within the subtitles those words are written with hyphens (as is indicated by the in-game manner of transcription of the Elven language).

That is an interesting example of a practice described by Charles Jencks as *double coding*.[15] Double coding is a way of creating a cultural text (in the broad understanding of this term; Jencks' idea was initially referring to postmodern architecture),

> which speaks on at least two levels at once: to other architects and a concerned minority who care about specifically architectural meanings, and to the public at large, or the local inhabitants, who care about other issues concerned with comfort, traditional building and a way of life.[16]

This means that postmodern architecture (or broadly: a piece of art) pleases different groups (elites and the general public) using different codes.[17]

Decoding the text of a videogame on its more sophisticated level results in the reduction of immersion. This is because scenes like the one described above create an *ironic distance*, which is yet another way to achieve an artistic effect by using an emersive factor. The element of irony is crucial, because through this mechanism the authors of the game wink at the player and send him a second, hidden meaning. It is not, however, a classic literal or verbal irony, within which the actual meaning of the text is opposed to that expressed in the primary one (or, as Søren Kierkegaard, the great theoretician of irony would put it: 'phenomenon is not the essence, but the opposite of the essence'[18]). In the cited example, one does not find such opposite content. Instead, game creators develop a different, whole new meaning functioning somewhat *over* the literal text.

Of particular interest in this context is the division of ironic roles proposed by David S. Kaufer, according to whom there are three roles within an ironic situation: 1) ironists, 2) observers of irony, and 3) the victim of irony.[19] The triad can be expanded by a fourth element: 4) the tools of irony. In the situation described above, the role of such tools is taken by the characters who pronounce the two names of the philosophers. There is no doubt that Zoltan (the dwarf who says 'Kier-ke-gaard!') is not an ironist in this situation—he is oblivious of the additional meaning of his own words. Exactly as in the Polish version of the first *Witcher* (CD Projekt RED, 2007)[20]—a game, where a bard named Dandelion was singing the songs of the popular band Kult, famous in Poland. Of course Dandelion could not know that he was using *someone else's discourse*, to borrow Bakhtin's terminology. In both situations, it is not the characters, but the *subjects of the game*, who are the ironists. The role of (co-)ironist is taken by the player who recognises the duality of the message.

If one consistently draws conclusions from this scheme, the victim of irony is a user who is not able to recognise the ironical signal that was sent, and who is not able to become one of the two subjects in this communication scheme. After all, irony has a clear requirement: it must be identified. As Michał Głowiński, a Polish theoretician of irony, puts it:

> If the irony is not recognized, significant misunderstandings arise. Some-
> times such confusion shows that the participant of the communication
> process is not able to go beyond his literal understanding of the words.
> As a result, his perception is lacking a particular factor of expression
> which is crucial to understand the statement in accordance with the
> nature and intentions of the speaker.[21]

Even the most trivial Easter eggs can be considered as a variant of the mechanism described as ironic distance. What all varieties of this phenomenon have in common is that they produce a new kind of ironic meta-communication between the player (the one who understands the joke), and the subject of the game. Even though distancing to the digital world and adopting a critical perspective results in loss of immersion. At the same time, this loss is rewarded with a different type of joy. Naturally, such jokes may represent very varied levels of refinement: some of them are obvious and hard to miss, other impose high demands on 'the breadth of the reader's own textual encyclopedia', as Umberto Eco puts it.[22]

### 2e. Breaking the fourth wall

A particular type of emersive effect, based on creating ironic distance to the fiction presented, is traditionally called 'breaking the fourth wall'. This term was originally coined for the description of the mechanisms of theatrical performance, but nowadays is sometimes used to describe the same phenomenon in other visual media (film, comics, videogames).

The 'Fourth wall' itself refers to the conventional, symbolic border that separates the audience from the theater scene where the action takes place. Molière and Denis Diderot are considered to be the originators of this concept. Diderot wrote in *Discours sur la poésie dramatique* (1758):

> Whether you compose or act, think no more of the beholder than if he did
> not exist. Imagine, at the edge of the stage, a high wall that separates you
> from the orchestra. Act as if the curtain never rose.[23]

The idea of the fourth wall was of great importance for stage fiction in the Enlightenment's theory of theater; according to the aforementioned theorists of that period, it was a key condition in allowing the viewers to believe in diegetic fiction. This means that the characters in the scene must behave as if they did not realise that they are in the theater (hence: may not notice the audience), so the fiction presented on stage is consistent and credible. 'Breaking the fourth wall' is the name for situations in which this conventional barrier is intentionally crossed (e.g. when actors speak directly to the audience).

This mechanism can be very easily translated into other semiotic systems, because its essence lies in the fact that the protagonist gains a specific type of self-knowledge. Firstly, such a character may become aware that he or she is part of diegetic fiction. Secondly, the character may be aware of the mechanisms of the cultural text (e.g. the rules or conventions of a genre) in which he or she appears. Thirdly, the character may be aware of being observed by the player (or the reader/viewer), and may start talking directly to the player.

A game might break the fourth wall for several reasons. Firstly, such communication may have a meta-diegetic (or meta-systemic) character, and serve as an instruction explaining how to use the game (e.g. when a NPC tells the player to hit a button on a keyboard or on a gamepad). Secondly—breaking the fourth wall can cause a comical effect by simply surprising the player. Thirdly—such a situation in the game can produce an artistic effect. It may emphasise contents of particular importance from the perspective of the game's message or may even call into question the rules of the game. In special cases, it happens that such a scene can serve more than one of these functions. This multifunctionality may be observed on numerous examples provided by comedy films—especially movies directed by Woody Allen, such as *Whatever Works* (2009).[24] In the opening scene of this film the main character, Boris Yelnikoff, is having a conversation with his colleagues. As it turns out, Boris is the only one who realises that he is a character in a film. That is why he points straight at the camera lens, and describes (in his own, very sarcastic way) the audience gathered at the cinema ('They paid good money for tickets, hard-earned money, so some moron in Hollywood can buy a bigger swimming pool.'). However, since his colleagues cannot see the audience (because of the principle of the fourth wall, described above), Boris leaves, and begins his two-minute speech directly to the camera.

This scene, in addition to its comicality, also plays a key role in the construction of the whole movie. It lets the main character expound his views on human existence. Breaking the fourth wall emphasises the importance of Boris' assumptions. Similarly in the last scene of the film, Boris is, again, the only person who can 'notice' the audience. Therefore, the act of breaking the fourth wall constitutes a frame of a whole text, and it allows the viewer to understand the whole plot as a philosophical parable, in which all the events are an illustration (or verification) of the ideas and views expressed at the beginning of the film.

One of the most spectacular examples of breaking the fourth wall in videogames can be found in the first part of *Metal Gear Solid* (Konami, 1998).[25] In one of the most famous scenes in this game, Solid Snake, the main protagonist, encounters Psycho Mantis, an opponent, who is a master of telepathy and telekinesis, and who claims that he can read Snake's mind. In fact, Psycho Mantis can read the console's memory card. Thanks to this, he among other things, characterises the way the game has been played by the player (e.g. 'Hmmm. You have not saved often. You are somewhat reckless.') or he can even recognises some games which have been played on the console (e.g. 'You like Castlevania, don't you?'). Such phrases disclose that Psycho Mantis' knowledge reaches far beyond the level of diegesis.

It is worth adding, that the act of breaking the fourth wall became a peculiarity of Deadpool—a character originally born in comic books, but who also appears in films and videogames. E.g. in *Marvel vs. Capcom 3: Fate of Two Worlds* (Capcom, Eighting; 2011)[26] he can perform some unusual actions. For example, Deadpool is the only character who is able to grab the life-bar (and thus a non-diegetic element), *detach it* from the screen, and use it to hit the opponent. Bringing the non-diegetic element of the game to the foreground and using it contrary to the convention of the game, causes a surprising and comedic effect. Such an ironic thematisation of the non-diegetic element, provokes the player to reflect on the ontological status of the interface, and the game's mechanisms.

### 2f. Palimpsestic attempts

The last variant of emersive elements shows that emersion does not need to be caused by game malfunction nor purposeful artistic strategy, but might be directly connected to the core mechanisms of selected games (or genres). Some of those mechanisms decrease the level of a player's immersion, and yet they are constantly used. A communicable example is the well-known mechanism of saving and loading a game status, provided by e.g. some cRPGs or strategy games.[27] This means that the player sometimes is able to create a checkpoint that remembers all the settings of the game—including the exact moment of the story. Thanks to the option of loading the game, the user of the selected games can always go back to the past events and experience them again, or even perform them in a completely different way than in the original course of action. Such a possibility brings important consequences, especially in the case of games that provide a developed, non-linear plot.

Implementing such an option to a game brings in four main structural effects:

1   it enables players to return to the game at any time without loss of their progress (otherwise one would have to finish a game in one sitting);
2   in case of a failure (e.g. the death of a protagonist), players can repeat a selected stage of the game without having to start anew;

3   players who feel dissatisfied with their actions (e.g. a fight which brought too much damage, a business transaction which turned out to be insufficiently beneficial), may repeat them to achieve better results;

4   players may try to get to know the alternative version of a co-created history.

It is definitely most beneficial to concentrate on the textual results of this mechanism. For example, in a cRPG game, such as *The Witcher 2*, the main protagonist may face an unexpected danger (e.g. entering a location full of enemies). If such an action's result is a failure, then the player might want to reload the game. Thanks to that he or she may prepare for this 'unexpected' fight and eventually achieve success. As a result, the player ends up with two (or even more) alternative versions of the story. At the same time one should not forget that the player can return many times to one saved game. All the player's imperfect attempts have an undisputed influence not only on the gameplay experience (in fact: they are part of that experience) but also on the in-game world cohesion and therefore, on the player's immersion. One of the factors that contribute to a fictional (not only digital) world's cohesion is the credibility of characters' psychological motivation. That means that all the characters' actions (and all other diegetic events): must be (1) subject to the rule of cause and effect; and (2) must be able to be explained by in-world's (diegetic) factors and motivations. If this psychological realism condition is not fulfilled, then a game (but also a film or a novel) is less believable.

However, while analysing the above-mentioned example from *The Witcher 2*, one will face a certain dissonance. If the main character dies in the first attempt because he was taken by surprise by his enemies, then the player reloads the game. In the second attempt the player starts his preparations before entering that same dangerous spot (e.g. the witcher Geralt drinks some of his strengthening potions). But in such a situation one could ask about the psychological realism of the situation: why did the witcher Geralt really drink his potions? The first (failed) attempt showed that he had not in fact expected any enemies. The obvious answer is: Geralt did not know, but the player did, and it is the player's knowledge that determines Geralt's actions. Their real motivation lies in an *abandoned (failed) attempt*. Therefore, if one wants to understand the course of events in all their complexity (including motivations, causality etc.), then not only the 'final version' of events should be taken into consideration, but also those failed attempts ought to be analysed.

It is hard to overestimate the importance of this fact—especially in the context of the theory of narrative or theory of interpretation. In traditional plotlines the reader/viewer always faces a finite version of events—of course there are plenty of texts that are open to interpretation[28] and texts that play around with narrative frames (films like *Memento*,[29] where scenes are not presented in a temporally consecutive order, and scenes shown later recontextualise those seen earlier[30]), but generally the interpretation of a traditional plotline is linear in form, because the *text itself* is not fluid. Meanwhile in those digital texts which involve user participation (especially in plot-concentrated videogames) the interpretation of events very often needs to include the *non-linear* character of the gaming experience.

To describe these versions of fictional events, which mutually influence each other, I submit a term that refers to Gérard Genette's theory of transtextuality. Genette compared literary hypertexts to medieval *palimpsests*. This is because palimpsests were manuscripts written on material in which the previous text was wiped or scraped out; as Genette describes it: 'On the same parchment, one text can become superimposed upon another, which it does not quite conceal but allows to show through.'[31] This, Genette's metaphor, is surprisingly adequate when considered in the context of a player's various attempts which *superimpose* one onto another and need to be interpreted as a whole. That is why I call them *palimpsestic attempts*.[32]

Palimpsestic attempts are, on the one hand, an interesting mechanism that is characteristic of videogames. The phenomenon in question is one of the factors that determines the uniqueness of the narrative potential of this medium. On the other hand, the presence of palimpsestic attempts in a particular gameplay may breach the rule of cohesion of the diegetic world, and therefore cause an emersive effect.

## 3. Summary

As shown in this chapter, *emersive effects*—that is, moments or mechanisms that weaken a player's immersion—appear in many aspects of games' structures. *Technical disillusions* (which are the result of a game's technical imperfections), elements *emphasising a game's mediated nature* (which might be an unintended side-effect), creating *ironic distance* (as a result of a reference to something outside of the game's cultural contexts), or breaking the rule of *psychological realism* (according to the *palimpsestic* nature of some games' course of events), or the *rule of the fourth wall*—these are just a few meaningful examples of the mechanisms triggering the concept in question and they surely do not make a definitive list of emersive factors.

These samples demonstrate several significant conclusions: Firstly, immersion does not need to be the most important or the most desired effect delivered by videogames and a player may find pleasure from other in-game elements, which may work against immersion and may pull the player out of the felling of in-game presence. Secondly—and this is a result of the first statement—videogames as a medium are torn between two opposite tendencies (one is their immersive potential, but the second is emersion with all its various—and not yet well-discovered—potential). This fact opens a great field for artistic creation; it brings the possibility of meaningful complications of a game's structure. Thirdly, the axiological status of emersive effects is not unequivocal. Sometimes emersion might be the result of a designer's or programmer's mistakes or of a game's individual nature as a medium (which has a rather young tradition and is still establishing its language and conventions). But on the other hand, a sensible and meaningful use of emersion (as in the scene quoted from *Batman: Arkham Asylum*) should be considered as proof of the maturity of the medium. Using mediality to create a meaningful message is a very strong post-modern artistic technique (also in other forms of expression, such as literature or film), and so it may cause various effects—e.g., the user's reflection on the character of the in-game experience. Therefore, an understanding of those effects should be developed and deepened in further research, and they definitely should not be omitted or ignored in game studies, as they play an important role in the specificity of videogames as a medium.

## Notes

1 This article presents expanded version of research previously published in following articles: Piotr Kubiński, 'Immersion vs. Emersive Effects in Videogames,' *Engaging with Videogames: Play, Theory and Practice*, ed. Dawn Stobbart, Monica Evans (Oxford: Inter-Disciplinary Press, 2014); idem, 'Emersja—antyiluzyjny wymiar gier wideo,' *Nowe Media*, No. 5 (2014).

2 Gordon Calleja, *In-Game: From Immersion to Incorporation* (Cambridge, London: The MIT Press, 2011), 25.

3 Ibid.

4 Janet Murray, *Hamlet on the Holodeck: The Future of Narrative in Cyberspace* (Cambridge, MA: The MIT Press, 1997), 98–99.

5 Oliver Grau, *Virtual Art. From Illusion to Immersion*, trans. Gloria Custance (Cambridge, MA: The MIT Press, 2003), 15.

6 Ibidem, 25–29.

7 Marie-Laure Ryan, *Narrative as Virtual Reality. Immersion and Interactivity in Literature and Electronic Media* (Baltimore: Johns Hopkins University Press, 2001).

8 Katarzyna Prajzner, *Tekst jako świat i gra. Modele narracyjności w kulturze współczesnej* (Łódź: Wydawnictwa Uniwersytetu Łódzkiego, 2009).

9 The idea of ergodicity was developed by Espen Aarseth. Espen Aarseth, *Cybertext. Perspectives on Ergodic Literature*, (Baltimore: Johns Hopkins University Press, 1997).

10 Alison McMahan, 'Immersion, Engagement, and Presence: A Method for Analyzing 3-D Video Games', in: *The Video Game Theory Reader*, ed. Mark J.P. Wolf, Bernard Perron, (New York: Routledge, 2003), 68–69.

11 Ibid., 76.

12 *Batman: Arkham Asylum* (Rocksteady, 2009). I provided a broader interpretation of the discussed scene from *Batman: Arkham Asylum* in the article: Piotr Kubiński, 'Bergman vs. Batman. Chwyt technicznej deziluzji w grach wideo na tle praktyk literackich i filmowych', *Images. The International Journal of European Film, Performing Arts and Audiovisual Communication*, No. 25 (2015).

13 *The Witcher 2: Assassins of Kings* (CD Projekt RED, 2011).

14 A broader presentation of the concept of ironic distance in videogames and analysis of the 'Heidegger-Kierkegaar scene see: Piotr Kubiński, 'Dystans ironiczny w grach «Wiedźmin» i «Wiedźmin 2: Zabójcy królów»' *Transmedialne pogrywanie z «Wiedźminem»*, ed. Adam Flamma, Szymon Makuch, Michał Wolski (Wrocław: Stowarzyszenie Badaczy Popkultury i Edukacji Popkulturowej "Trickster", 2015).

15 Charles Jencks, *The Language of Post-Modern Architecture*, (Wisbech: Balding and Mansell, 1978), 14–15.

16 Ibidem, 6.

17 Charles Jencks, *What is Post-Modernism?*, (New York: St. Martin's Press, 1986).

18 Søren Kierkegaard, *On the Concept of Irony with Continual Reference to Socrates*, ed. and trans. Howard V. Hong, Edna H. Hong, (Princeton: Princeton UP, 1989), 247.

19 David S. Kaufer, 'Irony, Interpretive Form and the Theory of Meaning', *Poetics Today: The Ironic Discourse* 4, No. 3 (1983): 451–64.

20  *The Witcher* (CD Projekt RED, 2007).
21  Michał Głowiski, 'Ironia jako akt komunikacyjny', in *Ironia*, ed. Michał Głowiski (Gdańsk: Słowo/obraz terytoria, 2002), 5–16.
22  Umberto Eco, *On literature*, trans. Martin McLaughlin (New York: Harcourt, 2004), 228.
23  Denis Diderot, *Discours sur la poésie dramatique*. Translation by: Michael Fried, *Absorption and Theatricality: Painting and Beholder in the Age of Diderot*, (Chicago: University of Chicago Press, 1988), 95.
24  Woody Allen, *Whatever Works*, dir. Woody Allen (Tribeca: Sony, 2009), DVD.
25  *Metal Gear Solid* (Konami, 1998).
26  *Marvel vs. Capcom 3: Fate of Two Worlds* (Capcom, Eighting; 2011).
27  As Monica Evans aptly stated during the conference 'Videogame Cultures and the Future of Interactive Entertainment VI' (14th–16th July 2013, Oxford, Mansfield College), such mechanisms are less frequent in modern games than they used to be in cRPGs in the late 1990s and in the first years of the new millennium.
28  The concept of open text/open work (it.: 'opera aperta') was developed by Umberto Eco in: Umberto Eco, *Open work*, trans. Anna Cancogni, (Cambridge, MA: Harvard University Press, 1989).
29  Jonathan Nolan, Christopher Nolan, *Memento*, dir. Christopher Nolan (Venice: Newmarket, 2000), DVD.
30  Jon Dovey, 'Notes Toward a Hypertextual Theory of Narrative' in *New Screen Media: Cinema/Art/Narrative*, ed. M. Rieser, A. Zapp, (London: British Film Institute, 2002).
31  Gerard Genette, *Palimpsests: Literature in the Second Degree*, trans. Channa Newman and Claude Doubinsky (Lincoln: University of Nebraska Press, 1997).
32  At the same time, it is worth noting that there is a fundamental difference between Genette's palimpsests and palimpsestic attempts. In the case of the palimpsests described by the French philosopher, the relationship between the layers of the text is completely random. That means that new text is created, *despite* the previous one. Meanwhile, the palimpsests in videogames' new attempts occur precisely *because* of the previous ones.

## Bibliography

Aarseth, Espen. *Cybertext. Perspectives on Ergodic Literature*. Baltimore: Johns Hopkins University Press, 1997.
*Batman: Arkham Asylum* (Rocksteady, 2009).
Calleja, Gordon. *In-Game: From Immersion to Incorporation*. Cambridge, London: The MIT Press, 2011.
Dovey, Jon. 'Notes Toward a Hypertextual Theory of Narrative.' *New Screen Media: Cinema/Art/Narrative*, edited by Martin Rieser, Andrea Zapp. London: British Film Institute, 2002.
Eco, Umberto. *On literature*. Translated by Martin McLaughlin. New York: Harcourt, 2004.
———. *Open work*. Translated by Anna Cancogni. Cambridge, MA: Harvard University Press, 1989.
Fried, Michael. *Absorption and Theatricality: Painting and Beholder in the Age of Diderot*. Chicago: University of Chicago Press, 1988.
Genette, Gérard. *Palimpsests: Literature in the Second Degree*. Translated by Channa Newman and Claude Doubinsky. Lincoln: University of Nebraska Press, 1997.
Głowiski, Michał. 'Ironia jako akt komunikacyjny.' *Ironia*, edited by Michał Głowiński. Gdańsk: Słowo/obraz terytoria, 2002.

Grau Oliver. *Virtual Art. From Illusion to Immersion.* Translated by Gloria Custance. Cambridge, MA: The MIT Press, 2003.

Jencks Charles. *The Language of Post-Modern Architecture.* Wisbech: Balding and Mansell, 1978.

———. *What is Post-Modernism?.* New York: St. Martin's Press, 1986.

Kaufer, David S. 'Irony, Interpretive Form and the Theory of Meaning.' *Poetics Today: The Ironic Discourse*, 4, No. 3 (1983).

Kierkegaard, Søren. *On the Concept of Irony with Continual Reference to Socrates.* Edited and translated by Howard V. Hong and Edna H. Hong. Princeton: Princeton UP, 1989.

Kubiński, Piotr. 'Emersja—antyiluzyjny wymiar gier wideo.' *Nowe Media*, No. 5 (2014).

———. 'Immersion vs. Emersive Effects in Videogames.' *Engaging with Videogames: Play, Theory and Practice*, edited by Dawn Stobbart and Monica Evans. Oxford: Inter-Disciplinary Press, 2014.

———. 'Bergman vs. Batman. Chwyt technicznej deziluzji w grach wideo na tle praktyk literackich i filmowych.' *Images. The International Journal of European Film, Performing Arts and Audiovisual Communication*, No. 25 (2015).

———. 'Dystans ironiczny w grach «Wiedmin» i «Wiedźmin 2: Zabójcy królów».' *Transmedialne pogrywanie z «Wiedźminem»*, ed. Adam Flamma, Szymon Makuch, Michał Wolski (Wrocław: Stowarzyszenie Badaczy Popkultury i Edukacji Popkulturowej "Trickster", 2015).

*Marvel vs. Capcom 3: Fate of Two Worlds* (Capcom, Eighting; 2011).

McMahan, Alison. 'Immersion, Engagement, and Presence: A Method for Analyzing 3-D Video Games.' *The Video Game Theory Reader*, edited by Mark J.P. Wolf and Bernard Perron. New York: Routledge, 2003.

*Metal Gear Solid* (Konami, 1998).

Murray, Janet. *Hamlet on the Holodeck: The Future of Narrative in Cyberspace.* Cambridge, MA: The MIT Press, 1997.

Nolan, Jonathan and Christopher Nolan. *Memento.* Directed by Christopher Nolan. 5 September 2000. Venice: Newmarket, 2000.

Prajzner, Katarzyna. *Tekst jako świat i gra. Modele narracyjności w kulturze współczesnej.* Łódź: Wydawnictwa Uniwersytetu Łódzkiego, 2009.

Ryan, Marie-Laure. *Narrative as Virtual Reality. Immersion and Interactivity in Literature and Electronic Media.* Baltimore: Johns Hopkins University Press, 2001.

*The Witcher* (CD Projekt RED, 2007).

*The Witcher 2: Assassins of Kings* (CD Projekt RED, 2011).

# Part 8

# THREAT, AGGRESSION, AND VIOLENCE

# 64

# A RAPE IN CYBERSPACE

## How an evil clown, a Haitian trickster spirit, two wizards, and a cast of dozens turned a database into a society

*Julian Dibbell*

Source: *The Village Voice*, December 23, 1993, pp. 36–42.

They say he raped them that night. They say he did it with a cunning little doll, fashioned in their image and imbued with the power to make them do whatever he desired. They say that by manipulating the doll he forced them to have sex with him, and with each other, and to do horrible, brutal things to their own bodies. And though I wasn't there that night, I think I can assure you that what they say is true, because it all happened right in the living room—right there amid the well-stocked bookcases and the sofas and the fireplace—of a house I came for a time to think of as my second home.

Call me Dr. Bombay. Some months ago—let's say about halfway between the first time you heard the words *information superhighway* and the first time you wished you never had—I found myself tripping now and then down the well-traveled information lane that leads to LambdaMOO, a very large and very busy rustic mansion built entirely of words. In the odd free moment I would type the commands that called those words onto my computer screen, dropping me with what seemed a warm electric thud inside the house's darkened coat closet, where I checked my quotidian identity, stepped into the persona and appearance of a minor character from a long-gone television sitcom, and stepped out into the glaring chatter of the crowded living room. Sometimes, when the mood struck me, I emerged as a dolphin instead.

I won't say why I chose to masquerade as Samantha Stevens's outlandish cousin, or as the dolphin, or what exactly led to my mild addiction to the semifictional digital otherworlds known around the Internet as multi-user dimensions, or MUDs. This isn't my story, after all. It's the story of a man named Mr. Bungle, and of the ghostly sexual violence he committed in the halls of LambdaMOO, and most importantly of the ways his violence and his victims challenged the 1000 and more residents of that surreal, magic-infested mansion to become, finally, the community so many of them already believed they were.

303

That I was myself one of those residents has little direct bearing on the story's events. I mention it only as a warning that my own perspective is perhaps too steeped in the sureality and magic of the place to serve as an entirely appropriate guide. For the Bungle Affair raises questions that—here on the brink of a future in which human life may find itself as tightly enveloped in digital environments as it is today in the architectural kind—demand a clear-eyed, sober, and unmystified consideration. It asks us to shut our ears momentarily to the techno-utopian ecstasies of West Coast cyberhippies and look without illusion upon the present possibilities for building, in the on-line spaces of this world, societies more decent and free than those mapped onto dirt and concrete and capital. It asks us to behold the new bodies awaiting us in virtual space undazzled by their phantom powers, and to get to the crucial work of sorting out the socially meaningful differences between those bodies and our physical ones. And most forthrightly it asks us to wrap our late-modern ontologies, epistemologies, sexual ethics, and common sense around the curious notion of rape by voodoo doll—and to try not to warp them beyond recognition in the process.

In short, the Bungle Affair dares me to explain it to you without resort to dime-store mysticisms, and I fear I may have shape-shifted by the digital moonlight one too many times to be quite up to the task. But I will do what I can, and can do no better I suppose than to lead with the facts. For if nothing else about Mr. Bungle's case is unambiguous, the facts at least are crystal clear.

The facts begin (as they often do) with a time and a place. The time was a Monday night in March, and the place, as I've said, was the living room—which, due to the inviting warmth of its decor, is so invariably packed with chitchatters as to be roughly synonymous among LambdaMOOers with a party. So strong, indeed, is the sense of convivial common ground invested in the living room that a cruel mind could hardly imagine a better place in which to stage a violation of LambdaMOO's communal spirit. And there was cruelty enough lurking in the appearance Mr. Bungle presented to the virtual world—he was at the time a fat, oleaginous, Bisquick-faced clown dressed in cum-stained harlequin garb and girdled with a mistletoe-and-hemlock belt whose buckle bore the quaint inscription "KISS ME UNDER THIS, BITCH!" But whether cruelty motivated his choice of crime scene is not among the established facts of the case. It is a fact only that he did choose the living room. The remaining facts tell us a bit more about the inner world of Mr. Bungle, though only perhaps that it couldn't have been a very comfortable place. They tell us that he commenced his assault entirely unprovoked, at or about 10 p.m. Pacific Standard Time. That he began by using his voodoo doll to force one of the room's occupants to sexually service him in a variety of more or less conventional ways. That this victim was legba, a Haitian trickster spirit of indeterminate gender, brown-skinned and wearing an expensive pearl gray suit, top hat, and dark glasses. That legba heaped vicious imprecations on him all the while and that he was soon ejected bodily from the room. That he hid himself away then in his private chambers somewhere on the mansion grounds and continued the attacks without interruption, since the voodoo doll worked just as well at a distance as in proximity. That he turned his attentions now to Starsinger, a rather pointedly nondescript female character, tall, stout, and brown-haired, forcing her into unwanted liaisons with other individuals present in the room, among them legba, Bakunin (the well-known radical), and Juniper (the squirrel). That his actions grew progressively violent. That he made legba eat his/her own pubic hair. That he caused Starsinger to violate herself with a piece of kitchen cutlery. That his distant laughter echoed evilly in the living room with every successive outrage. That he could not be stopped until at last someone summoned Zippy, a wise and trusted old-timer who brought with him a gun of near wizardly powers, a gun that didn't kill but enveloped its targets in a cage impermeable even to a voodoo doll's powers. That Zippy fired this gun at Mr. Bungle, thwarting the doll at last and silencing the evil, distant laughter.

These particulars, as I said, are unambiguous. But they are far from simple, for the simple reason that every set of facts in virtual reality (or VR, as the locals abbreviate it) is shadowed by a second, complicating set: the "real-life" facts. And while a certain tension invariably buzzes in the gap between the hard, prosaic RL facts and their more fluid, dreamy VR counterparts, the dissonance in the Bungle case is striking. No hideous clowns or trickster spirits appear in the RL version of the incident, no voodoo dolls or wizard guns, indeed no rape at all as any RL court of law has yet defined it. The actors in the drama were university students for the most part, and they sat rather undramatically before computer screens the entire time, their only actions a spidery flitting of fingers across standard QWERTY keyboards. No bodies touched. Whatever physical interaction occurred consisted of a mingling of electronic signals sent from sites spread out between New York City and Sydney, Australia. Those signals met in LambdaMOO, certainly, just as the hideous clown and the living room party did, but what was LambdaMOO after all? Not an enchanted mansion or anything of the sort—just a middlingly complex database, maintained for experimental purposes inside a Xerox Corporation research computer in Palo Alto and open to public access via the Internet.

To be more precise about it, LambdaMOO was a MUD. Or to be yet more precise, it was a subspecies of MUD known as a MOO, which is short for "MUD, Object-Oriented." All of which means that it was a kind of database especially designed to give users the vivid impression of moving through a physical space that in reality exists only as descriptive data filed away on a hard drive. When users dial into LambdaMOO, for instance, the program immediately presents them with a brief textual description of one of the rooms of the database's fictional mansion (the coat closet, say). If the user wants to leave this room, she can enter a command to move in a particular direction and the database will replace the original description with a new one corresponding to the room located in the direction she chose. When the new description scrolls across the user's screen it lists not only the fixed features of the room but all its contents at that moment—including things (tools, toys, weapons) and other users (each represented as a "character" over which he or she has sole control).

As far as the database program is concerned, all of these entities—rooms, things, characters—are just different subprograms that the program allows to interact according to rules very roughly mimicking the laws of the physical world. Characters may not leave a room in a given direction, for instance, unless the room subprogram contains an "exit" at that compass point. And if a character "says" or "does" something (as directed by its user-owner), then only the users whose characters are also located in that room will see the output describing the statement or action. Aside from such basic constraints, however, LambdaMOOers are allowed a broad freedom to create—they can describe their characters any way they like, they can make rooms of their own and decorate them to taste, and they can build new objects almost at will. The combination of all this busy user activity with the hard physics of the database can certainly induce a lucid illusion of presence—but when all is said and done the only thing you *really* see when you visit LambdaMOO is a kind of slow-crawling script, lines of dialogue and stage direction creeping steadily up your computer screen.

Which is all just to say that, to the extent that Mr. Bungle's assault happened in real life at all, it happened as a sort of Punch-and-Judy show, in which the puppets and the scenery were made of nothing more substantial than digital code and snippets of creative writing. The puppeteer behind Bungle, as it happened, was a young man logging in to the MOO from a New York University computer. He could have been Al Gore for all any of the others knew, however, and he could have written Bungle's script that night any way he chose. He could have sent a command to print the message "Mr. Bungle, smiling a saintly smile, floats angelic near the ceiling of the living room, showering joy and candy kisses down upon the heads of all below"—and everyone then receiving output from the database's subprogram #17 (a/k/a the "living room") would have seen that sentence on their screens.

Instead, he entered sadistic fantasies into the "voodoo doll," a subprogram that served the not-exactly kosher purpose of attributing actions to other characters that their users did not actually write. And thus a woman in Haverford, Pennsylvania, whose account on the 'MOO attached her to a character she called Starsinger, was given the unasked-for opportunity to read the words "As if against her will, Starsinger jabs a steak knife up her ass, causing immense joy. You hear Mr. Bungle laughing evilly in the distance." And thus the woman in Seattle who had written herself the character called legba, with a view perhaps to tasting in imagination a deity's freedom from the burdens of the gendered flesh, got to read similarly constructed sentences in which legba, messenger of the gods, lord of crossroads and communications, suffered a brand of degradation all-too-customarily reserved for the embodied female.

"Mostly voodoo dolls are amusing," wrote legba on the evening after Bungle's rampage, posting a public statement to the widely read in-MOO mailing list called *social-issues*, a forum for debate on matters of import to the entire populace. "And mostly I tend to think that restrictive measures around here cause more trouble than they prevent. But I also think that Mr. Bungle was being a vicious, vile fuckhead, and I . . . want his sorry ass scattered from #17 to the Cinder Pile. I'm not calling for policies, trials, or better jails. I'm not sure what I'm calling for. Virtual castration, if I could manage it. Mostly, [this type of thing] doesn't happen here. Mostly, perhaps I thought it wouldn't happen to me. Mostly, I trust people to conduct themselves with some veneer of civility. Mostly, I want his ass."

Months later, the woman in Seattle would confide to me that as she wrote those words posttraumatic tears were streaming down her face—a real-life fact that should suffice to prove that the words' emotional content was no mere playacting. The precise tenor of that content, however, its mingling of murderous rage and eyeball-rolling annoyance, was a curious amalgam that neither the RL nor the VR facts alone can quite account for. Where virtual reality and its conventions would have us believe that legba and Starsinger were brutally raped in their own living room, here was the victim legba scolding Mr. Bungle for a breach of "civility." Where real life, on the other hand, insists the incident was only an episode in a free-form version of Dungeons and Dragons, confined to the realm of the symbolic and at no point threatening any player's life, limb, or material well-being, here now was the player legba issuing aggrieved and heartfelt calls for Mr. Bungle's dismemberment. Ludicrously excessive by RL's lights, woefully understated by VR's, the tone of legba's response made sense only in the buzzing, dissonant gap between them.

Which is to say it made the only kind of sense that *can* be made of MUDly phenomena. For while the *facts* attached to any event born of a MUD's strange, ethereal universe may march in straight, tandem lines separated neatly into the virtual and the real, its meaning lies always in that gap. You learn this axiom early in your life as a player, and it's of no small relevance to the Bungle case that you usually learn it between the sheets, so to speak. Netsex, tinysex, virtual sex—however you name it, in real-life reality it's nothing more than a 900-line encounter stripped of even the vestigial physicality of the voice. And yet as any but the most inhibited of newbies can tell you, it's possibly the headiest experience the very heady world of MUDs has to offer. Amid flurries of even the most cursorily described caresses, sighs, and penetrations, the glands do engage, and often as throbbingly as they would in a real-life assignation—sometimes even more so, given the combined power of anonymity and textual suggestiveness to unshackle deep-seated fantasies. And if the virtual setting and the interplayer vibe are right, who knows? The heart may engage as well, stirring up passions as strong as many that bind lovers who observe the formality of trysting in the flesh.

To participate, therefore, in this disembodied enactment of life's most body-centered activity is to risk the realization that when it comes to sex, perhaps the body in question is not the physical one at all, but its psychic double, the bodylike self-representation we carry around in our heads. I know, I know, you've read Foucault and your mind is not quite blown by the notion that sex is never so much an exchange of fluids as as it is an exchange of signs. But trust your friend Dr. Bombay, it's one thing to grasp the notion intellectually and quite another to feel it coursing through your veins amid the virtual steam of hot netnookie.

And it's a whole other mind-blowing trip altogether to encounter it thus as a college frosh, new to the net and still in the grip of hormonal hurricanes and high-school sexual mythologies. The shock can easily reverberate throughout an entire young worldview. Small wonder, then, that a newbie's first taste of MUD sex is often also the first time she or he surrenders wholly to the slippery terms of MUDish ontology, recognizing in a full-bodied way that what happens inside a MUD-made world is neither exactly real nor exactly make-believe, but profoundly, compellingly, and emotionally meaningful.

And small wonder indeed that the sexual nature of Mr. Bungle's crime provoked such powerful feelings, and not just in legba (who, be it noted, was in real life a theory-savvy doctoral candidate and a longtime MOOer, but just as baffled and overwhelmed by the force of her own reaction, she later would attest, as any panting undergrad might have been). Even players who had never experienced MUD rape (the vast majority of male-presenting characters, but not as large a majority of the female-presenting as might be hoped) immediately appreciated its gravity and were moved to condemnation of the perp. legba's missive to *social-issues* followed a strongly worded one from Zippy ("Well, well," it began, "no matter what else happens on Lambda, I can always be sure that some jerk is going to reinforce my low opinion of humanity") and was itself followed by others from Moriah, Raccoon, Crawfish, and evangeline. Starsinger also let her feelings ("pissed") be known. And even Jander, the Clueless Samaritan who had responded to Bungle's cries for help and uncaged him shortly after the incident, expressed his regret once apprised of Bungle's deeds, which he allowed to be "despicable."

A sense was brewing that something needed to be done—done soon and in something like an organized fashion—about Mr. Bungle, in particular, and about MUD rape, in general. Regarding the general problem, evangeline, who identified herself as a survivor of both virtual rape ("many times over") and real-life sexual assault, floated a cautious proposal for a MOO-wide powwow on the subject of virtual sex offenses and what mechanisms if any might be put in place to deal with their future occurrence. As for the specific problem, the answer no doubt seemed obvious to many. But it wasn't until the evening of the second day after the incident that legba, finally and rather solemnly, gave it voice:

> "I am requesting that Mr. Bungle be toaded for raping Starsinger and I. I have never done this before, and have thought about it for days. He hurt us both."

That was all. Three simple sentences posted to *social*. Reading them, an outsider might never guess that they were an application for a death warrant. Even an outsider familiar with other MUDs might not guess it, since in many of them "toading" still refers to a command that, true to the gameworlds' sword-and-sorcery origins, simply turns a player into a toad, wiping the player's description and attributes and replacing them with those of the slimy amphibian. Bad luck for sure, but not quite as bad as what happens when the same command is invoked in the MOOish strains of MUD: not only are the description and attributes of the toaded player erased, but the account itself goes too. The annihilation of the character, thus, is total.

And nothing less than total annihilation, it seemed, would do to settle LambdaMOO's accounts with Mr. Bungle. Within minutes of the posting of legba's appeal, SamIAm, the Australian Deleuzean, who had witnessed much of the attack from the back room of his suburban Sydney home, seconded the motion with a brief message crisply entitled "Toad the fukr." SamIAm's posting was seconded almost as quickly by that of Bakunin, covictim of Mr. Bungle and well-known radical, who in real life happened also to be married to the real-life legba. And over the course of the next 24 hours as many as 50 players made it known, on *social and in a variety of other forms and forums, that they would be pleased to see Mr. Bungle erased from the face of the MOO. And with dissent so far confined to a dozen or so antitoading hardliners, the numbers suggested that the citizenry was indeed moving towards a resolve to have Bungle's virtual head.

There was one small but stubborn obstacle in the way of this resolve, however, and that was a curious state of social affairs known in some quarters of the MOO as the New Direction. It was all very fine, you see, for the LambdaMOO rabble to get it in their heads to liquidate one of their peers, but when the time came to actually do the deed it would require the services of a nobler class of character. It would require a wizard. Master-programmers of the MOO, spelunkers of the database's deepest code-structures and custodians of its day-to-day administrative trivia, wizards are also the only players empowered to issue the toad command, a feature maintained on nearly all MUDs as a quick-and-dirty means of social control. But the wizards of LambdaMOO, after years of adjudicating all manner of interplayer disputes with little to show for it but their own weariness and the smoldering resentment of the general populace, had decided they'd had enough of the social sphere. And so, four months before the Bungle incident, the archwizard Haakon (known in RL as Pavel Curtis, Xerox researcher and LambdaMOO's principal architect) formalized this decision in a document called "LambdaMOO Takes a New Direction," which he placed in the living room for all to see. In it, Haakon announced that the wizards from that day forth were pure technicians. From then on, they would make no decisions affecting the social life of the MOO, but only implement whatever decisions the community as a whole directed them to. From then on, it was decreed, LambdaMOO would just have to grow up and solve its problems on its own.

Faced with the task of inventing its own self-governance from scratch, the LambdaMOO population had so far done what any other loose, amorphous agglomeration of individuals would have done: they'd let it slide. But now the task took on new urgency. Since getting the wizards to toad Mr. Bungle (or to toad the likes of him in the future) required a convincing case that the cry for his head came from the community at large, then the community itself would have to be defined; and if the community was to be convincingly defined, then some form of social organization, no matter how rudimentary, would have to be settled on. And thus, as if against its will, the question of what to do about Mr. Bungle began to shape itself into a sort of referendum on the political future of the MOO. Arguments broke out on *social and elsewhere that had only superficially to do with Bungle (since everyone agreed he was a cad) and everything to do with where the participants stood on LambdaMOO's crazy-quilty political map. Parliamentarian legalist types argued that unfortunately Bungle could not legitimately be toaded at all, since there were no explicit MOO rules against rape, or against just about anything else—and the sooner such rules were established, they added, and maybe even a full-blown judiciary system complete with elected officials and prisons to enforce those rules, the better. Others, with a royalist streak in them, seemed to feel that Bungle's as-yet-unpunished outrage only proved this New Direction silliness had gone on long enough, and that it was high time the wizardocracy returned to the position of swift and decisive leadership their player class was born to.

And then there were what I'll call the technolibertarians. For them, MUD rapists were of course assholes, but the presence of assholes on the system was a technical inevitability, like noise on a phone line, and best dealt with not through repressive social disciplinary mechanisms but through the timely deployment of defensive software tools. Some asshole blasting violent, graphic language at you? Don't whine to the authorities about it—hit the @gag command and the asshole's statements will be blocked from your screen (and only yours). It's simple, it's effective, and it censors no one.

But the Bungle case was rather hard on such arguments. For one thing, the extremely public nature of the living room meant that gagging would spare the victims only from witnessing their own violation, but not from having others witness it. You might want to argue that what those victims didn't directly experience couldn't hurt them, but consider how that wisdom would sound to a woman who'd been, say, fondled by strangers while passed out drunk and you have a rough idea how it might go over with a crowd of hard-core MOOers. Consider, for another thing, that many of the biologically female participants in the Bungle debate had been around long enough to grow lethally weary of the gag-and-get-over-it school of virtual-rape counseling, with its fine line between empowering victims and holding them responsible for their own suffering, and its shrugging indifference to the window of pain between the moment the rape-text starts flowing and the moment a gag shuts it off. From the outset it was clear that the technolibertarians were going to have to tiptoe through this issue with care, and for the most part they did.

Yet no position was trickier to maintain than that of the MOO's resident anarchists. Like the technolibbers, the anarchists didn't care much for punishments or policies or power elites. Like them, they hoped the MOO could be a place where people interacted fulfillingly without the need for such things. But their high hopes were complicated, in general, by a somewhat less thoroughgoing faith in technology ("Even if you can't tear down the master's house with the master's tools"—read a slogan written into one anarchist player's self-description—"it is a damned good place to start"). And at present they were additionally complicated by the fact that the most vocal anarchists in the discussion were none other than legba, Bakunin, and SamIAm, who wanted to see Mr. Bungle toaded as badly as anyone did.

Needless to say, a pro-death penalty platform is not an especially comfortable one for an anarchist to sit on, so these particular anarchists were now at great pains to sever the conceptual ties between toading and capital punishment. Toading, they insisted (almost convincingly), was much more closely analogous to banishment; it was a kind of turning of the communal back on the offending party, a collective action which, if carried out properly, was entirely consistent with anarchist models of community. And carrying it out properly meant first and foremost building a consensus around it—a messy process for which there were no easy technocratic substitutes. It was going to take plenty of good old-fashioned, jawbone-intensive grassroots organizing.

So that when the time came, at 7 p.m. PST on the evening of the third day after the occurrence in the living room, to gather in evangeline's room for her proposed real-time open conclave, Bakunin and legba were among the first to arrive. But this was hardly to be an anarchist-dominated affair, for the room was crowding rapidly with representatives of all the MOO's political stripes, and even a few wizards. Hagbard showed up, and Autumn and Quastro, Puff, JoeFeedback, L-dopa and Bloaf, HerkieCosmo, Silver Rocket, Karl Porcupine, Matchstick—the names piled up and the discussion gathered momentum under their weight. Arguments multiplied and mingled, players talked past and through each other, the textual clutter of utterances and gestures filled up the screen like thick cigar smoke. Peaking in number at around 30, this was one of the largest crowds that ever gathered in a single LambdaMOO chamber, and while evangeline had given her place a description that made it "infinite in expanse and fluid in form," it now seemed anything but roomy. You could almost feel the claustrophobic air of the place, dank and overheated by virtual bodies, pressing against your skin.

I know you could because I too was there, making my lone and insignificant appearance in this story. Completely ignorant of any of the goings-on that had led to the meeting, I wandered in purely to see what the crowd was about, and though I observed the proceedings for a good while, I confess I found it hard to grasp what was going on. I was still the rankest of newbies then, my MOO legs still too unsteady to make the leaps of faith, logic, and empathy required to meet the spectacle on its own terms. I was fascinated by the concept of virtual rape, but I couldn't quite take it seriously.

In this, though, I was in a small and mostly silent minority, for the discussion that raged around me was of an almost unrelieved earnestness, bent it seemed on examining every last aspect and implication of Mr. Bungle's crime. There were the central questions, of course: thumbs up or down on Bungle's virtual existence? And if down, how then to insure that his toading was not just some isolated lynching but a first step toward shaping LambdaMOO into a legitimate community? Surrounding these, however, a tangle of weighty side issues proliferated. What, some wondered, was the real-life legal status of the offense? Could Bungle's university administrators punish him for sexual harassment? Could he be prosecuted under California state laws against obscene phone calls? Little enthusiasm was shown for pursuing either of these lines of action, which testifies both to the uniqueness of the crime and to the nimbleness with which the discussants were negotiating its idiosyncracies. Many were the casual references to Bungle's deed as simply "rape," but these in no way implied that the players had lost sight of all distinctions between the virtual and physical versions, or that they believed Bungle should be dealt with in the same way a real-life criminal would. He had committed a MOO crime, and his punishment, if any, would be meted out via the MOO.

On the other hand, little patience was shown toward any attempts to downplay the seriousness of what Mr. Bungle had done. When the affable HerkieCosmo proposed, more in the way of an hypothesis than an assertion, that "perhaps it's better to release . . . violent tendencies in a virtual environment rather than in real life," he was tut-tutted so swiftly and relentlessly that he withdrew the hypothesis altogether, apologizing humbly as he did so. Not that the assembly was averse to putting matters into a more philosophical perspective. "Where does the body end and the mind begin?" young Quastro asked, amid recurring attempts to fine-tune the differences between real and virtual violence. "Is not the mind a part of the body?" "In MOO, the body IS the mind," offered HerkieCosmo gamely, and not at all implausibly, demonstrating the ease with which very knotty metaphysical conundrums come undone in VR. The not-so-aptly named Obvious seemed to agree, arriving after deep consideration of the nature of Bungle's crime at the hardly novel yet now somehow newly resonant conjecture "all reality might consist of ideas, who knows."

On these and other matters the anarchists, the libertarians, the legalists, the wizardists—and the wizards—all had their thoughtful say. But as the evening wore on and the talk grew more heated and more heady, it seemed increasingly clear that the vigorous intelligence being brought to bear on this swarm of issues wasn't going to result in anything remotely like resolution. The perspectives were just too varied, the meme-scape just too slippery. Again and again, arguments that looked at first to be heading in a decisive direction ended up chasing their own tails; and slowly, depressingly, a dusty haze of irrelevance gathered over the proceedings.

It was almost a relief, therefore, when midway through the evening Mr. Bungle himself, the living, breathing cause of all this talk, teleported into the room. Not that it was much of a surprise. Oddly enough, in the three days since his release from Zippy's cage, Bungle had returned more than once to wander the public spaces of LambdaMOO, walking willingly into one of the fiercest storms of ill will and invective ever to rain down on a player. He'd been taking it all with a curious and mostly silent passivity, and when challenged face to virtual face by both legba and the genderless elder states character PatGently to defend himself on *social*, he'd demurred, mumbling something about Christ and expiation. He was equally quiet now, and his reception was still uniformly cool. legba fixed an arctic stare on him—"no hate, no anger, no interest at all. Just . . . watching." Others were more actively unfriendly. "Asshole," spat Karl Porcupine, "creep." But the harshest of the MOO's hostility toward him had already been vented, and the attention he drew now was motivated more, it seemed, by the opportunity to probe the rapist's mind, to find out what made it tick and if possible how to get it to tick differently. In short, they wanted to know why he'd done it. So they asked him.

And Mr. Bungle thought about it. And as eddies of discussion and debate continued to swirl around him, he thought about it some more. And then he said this:

> "I engaged in a bit of a psychological device that is called thought-polarization, the fact that this is not RL simply added to heighten the affect of the device. It was purely a sequence of events with no consequence on my RL existence."

They might have known. Stilted though its diction was, the gist of the answer was simple, and something many in the room had probably already surmised: Mr. Bungle was a psycho. Not, perhaps, in real life—but then in real life it's possible for reasonable people to assume, as Bungle clearly did, that what transpires between word-costumed characters within the boundaries of a make-believe world is, if not mere play, then at most some kind of emotional laboratory experiment. Inside the MOO, however, such thinking marked a person as one of two basically subcompetent types. The first was the newbie, in which case the confusion was understandable, since there were few MOOers who had not, upon their first visits as anonymous "guest" characters, mistaken the place for a vast playpen in which they might act out their wildest fantasies without fear of censure. Only with time and the acquisition of a fixed character do players tend to make the critical passage from anonymity to pseudonymity, developing the concern for their character's reputation that marks the attainment of virtual adulthood. But while Mr. Bungle hadn't been around as long as most MOOers, he'd been around long enough to leave his newbie status behind, and his delusional statement therefore placed him among the second type: the sociopath.

And as there is but small percentage in arguing with a head case, the room's attention gradually abandoned Mr. Bungle and returned to the discussions that had previously occupied it. But if the debate had been edging toward ineffectuality before, Bungle's anticlimactic appearance had evidently robbed it of any forward motion whatsoever. What's more, from his lonely corner of the room Mr. Bungle kept issuing periodic expressions of a prickly sort of remorse, interlaced with sarcasm and belligerence, and though it was hard to tell if he wasn't still just conducting his experiments, some people thought his regret genuine enough that maybe he didn't deserve to be toaded after all. Logically, of course, discussion of the principal issues at hand didn't require unanimous belief that Bungle was an irredeemable bastard, but now that cracks were showing in that unanimity, the last of the meeting's fervor seemed to be draining out through them.

313

People started drifting away. Mr. Bungle left first, then others followed—one by one, in twos and threes, hugging friends and waving goodnight. By 9:45 only a handful remained, and the great debate had wound down into casual conversation, the melancholy remains of another fruitless good idea. The arguments had been well-honed, certainly, and perhaps might prove useful in some as-yet-unclear long run. But at this point what seemed clear was that evangeline's meeting had died, at last, and without any practical results to mark its passing.

It was also at this point, most likely, that JoeFeedback reached his decision. JoeFeedback was a wizard, a taciturn sort of fellow who'd sat brooding on the sidelines all evening. He hadn't said a lot, but what he had said indicated that he took the crime committed against legba and Starsinger very seriously, and that he felt no particular compassion toward the character who had committed it. But on the other hand he had made it equally plain that he took the elimination of a fellow player just as seriously, and moreover that he had no desire to return to the days of wizardly fiat. It must have been difficult, therefore, to reconcile the conflicting impulses churning within him at that moment. In fact, it was probably impossible, for as much as he would have liked to make himself an instrument of LambdaMOO's collective will, he surely realized that under the present order of things he must in the final analysis either act alone or not act at all.

So JoeFeedback acted alone.

He told the lingering few players in the room that he had to go, and then he went. It was a minute or two before ten. He did it quietly and he did it privately, but all anyone had to do to know he'd done it was to type the @who command, which was normally what you typed if you wanted to know a player's present location and the time he last logged in. But if you had run a @who on Mr. Bungle not too long after JoeFeedback left evangeline's room, the database would have told you something different.

"Mr. Bungle," it would have said, "is not the name of any player."

The date, as it happened, was April Fool's Day, and it would still be April Fool's Day for another two hours. But this was no joke: Mr. Bungle was truly dead and truly gone.

They say that LambdaMOO has never been the same since Mr. Bungle's toading. They say as well that nothing's really changed. And though it skirts the fuzziest of dream-logics to say that both these statements are true, the MOO is just the sort of fuzzy, dreamlike place in which such contradictions thrive.

Certainly whatever civil society now informs LambdaMOO owes its existence to the Bungle Affair. The archwizard Haakon made sure of that. Away on business for the duration of the episode, Haakon returned to find its wreckage strewn across the tiny universe he'd set in motion. The death of a player, the trauma of several others, and the angst-ridden conscience of his colleague JoeFeedback presented themselves to his concerned and astonished attention, and he resolved to see if he couldn't learn some lesson from it all. For the better part of a day he brooded over the record of events and arguments left in *social*, then he sat pondering the chaotically evolving shape of his creation, and at the day's end he descended once again into the social arena of the MOO with another historyaltering proclamation.

It was probably his last, for what he now decreed was the final, missing piece of the New Direction. In a few days, Haakon announced, he would build into the database a system of petitions and ballots whereby anyone could put to popular vote any social scheme requiring wizardly powers for its implementation, with the results of the vote to be binding on the wizards. At last and for good, the awkward gap between the will of the players and the efficacy of the technicians would be closed. And though some anarchists grumbled about the irony of Haakon's dictatorially imposing universal suffrage on an unconsulted populace, in general the citizens of LambdaMOO seemed to find it hard to fault a system more purely democratic than any that could ever exist in real life. Eight months and a dozen ballot measures later, widespread participation in the new regime has produced a small arsenal of mechanisms for dealing with the types of violence that called the system into being. MOO residents now have access to a @boot command, for instance, with which to summarily eject berserker "guest" characters. And players can bring suit against one another through an ad hoc arbitration system in which mutually agreed-upon judges have at their disposition the full range of wizardly punishments—up to and including the capital.

Yet the continued dependence on death as the ultimate keeper of the peace suggests that this new MOO order may not be built on the most solid of foundations. For if life on LambdaMOO began to acquire more coherence in the wake of the toading, death retained all the fuzziness of pre-Bungle days. This truth was rather dramatically borne out, not too many days after Bungle departed, by the arrival of a strange new character named Dr. Jest. There was a forceful eccentricity to the newcomer's manner, but the oddest thing about his style was its striking yet unnameable familiarity. And when he developed the annoying habit of stuffing fellow players into a jar containing a tiny simulacrum of a certain deceased rapist, the source of this familiarity became obvious:

Mr. Bungle had risen from the grave.

In itself, Bungle's reincarnation as Dr. Jest was a remarkable turn of events, but perhaps even more remarkable was the utter lack of amazement with which the LambdaMOO public took note of it. To be sure, many residents were appalled by the brazenness of Bungle's return. In fact, one of the first petitions circulated under the new voting system was a request for Dr. Jest's toading that almost immediately gathered 52 signatures (but has failed so far to reach ballot status). Yet few were unaware of the ease with which the toad proscription could be circumvented—all the toadee had to do (all the ur-Bungle at NYU presumably had done) was to go to the minor hassle of acquiring a new Internet account, and LambdaMOO's character registration program would then simply treat the known felon as an entirely new and innocent person. Nor was this ease generally understood to represent a failure of toading's social disciplinary function. On the

315

contrary, it only underlined the truism (repeated many times throughout the debate over Mr. Bungle's fate) that his punishment, ultimately, had been no more or less symbolic than his crime.

What *was* surprising, however, was that Mr. Bungle/Dr. Jest seemed to have taken the symbolism to heart. Dark themes still obsessed him—the objects he created gave off wafts of Nazi imagery and medical torture—but he no longer radiated the aggressively antisocial vibes he had before. He was a lot less unpleasant to look at (the outrageously seedy clown description had been replaced by that of a mildly creepy but actually rather natty young man, with "blue eyes . . . suggestive of conspiracy, untamed eroticism and perhaps a sense of understanding of the future"), and aside from the occasional jar-stuffing incident, he was also a lot less dangerous to be around. It was obvious he'd undergone some sort of personal transformation in the days since I'd first glimpsed him back in evangeline's crowded room—nothing radical maybe, but powerful nonetheless, and resonant enough with my own experience, I felt, that it might be more than professionally interesting to talk with him, and perhaps compare notes.

For I too was undergoing a transformation in the aftermath of that night in evangeline's, and I'm still not entirely sure what to make of it. As I pursued my runaway fascination with the discussion I had heard there, as I pored over the *social debate and got to know legba and some of the other victims and witnesses, I could feel my newbie consciousness falling away from me. Where before I'd found it hard to take virtual rape seriously, I now was finding it difficult to remember how I could ever *not* have taken it seriously. I was proud to have arrived at this perspective—it felt like an exotic sort of achievement, and it definitely made my ongoing experience of the MOO a richer one.

But it was also having some unsettling effects on the way I looked at the rest of the world. Sometimes, for instance, it was hard for me to understand why RL society classifies RL rape alongside crimes against person or property. Since rape can occur without any physical pain or damage, I found myself reasoning, then it must be classed as a crime against the mind—more intimately and deeply hurtful, to be sure, than cross burnings, wolf whistles, and virtual rape, but undeniably located on the same conceptual continuum. I did not, however, conclude as a result that rapists were protected in any fashion by the First Amendment. Quite the opposite, in fact: the more seriously I took the notion of virtual rape, the less seriously I was able to take the notion of freedom of speech, with its tidy division of the world into the symbolic and the real.

Let me assure you, though, that I am not presenting these thoughts as arguments. I offer them, rather, as a picture of the sort of mind-set that deep immersion in a virtual world has inspired in me. I offer them also, therefore, as a kind of prophecy. For whatever else these thoughts tell me, I have come to believe that they announce the final stages of our decades-long passage into the Information Age, a paradigm shift that the classic liberal firewall between word and deed (itself a product of an earlier paradigm shift commonly known as the Enlightenment) is not likely to survive intact. After all, anyone the least bit familiar with the workings of the new era's definitive technology, the computer, knows that it operates on a principle impracticably difficult to distinguish from the pre-Enlightenment principle of the magic word: the commands you type into a computer are a kind of speech that doesn't so much communicate as *make things happen*, directly and ineluctably, the same way pulling a trigger does. They are incantations, in other words, and anyone at all attuned to the technosocial megatrends of the moment—from the growing dependence of economies on the global flow of intensely fetishized words and numbers to the burgeoning ability of bioengineers to speak the spells written in the four-letter text of DNA—knows that the logic of the incantation is rapidly permeating the fabric of our lives.

And it's precisely this logic that provides the real magic in a place like LambdaMOO—not the fictive trappings of voodoo and shapeshifting and wizardry, but the conflation of speech and act that's inevitable in any computer-mediated world, be it Lambda or the increasingly wired world at large. This is dangerous magic, to be sure, a potential threat—if misconstrued or misapplied— to our always precarious freedoms of expression, and as someone who lives by his words I do not take the threat lightly. And yet, on the other hand, I can no longer convince myself that our wishful insulation of language from the realm of action has ever been anything but a valuable kludge, a philosophically damaged stopgap against oppression that would just have to do till something truer and more elegant came along.

Am I wrong to think this truer, more elegant thing can be found on LambdaMOO? Perhaps, but I continue to seek it there, sensing its presence just beneath the surface of every interaction. I have even thought, as I said, that discussing with Dr. Jest our shared experience of the workings of the MOO might help me in my search. But when that notion first occurred to me, I still felt somewhat intimidated by his lingering criminal aura, and I hemmed and hawed a good long time before finally resolving to drop him MOO-mail requesting an interview. By then it was too late. For reasons known only to himself, Dr. Jest had stopped logging in. Maybe he'd grown bored with the MOO. Maybe the loneliness of ostracism had gotten to him. Maybe a psycho whim had carried him far away or maybe he'd quietly acquired a third character and started life over with a cleaner slate.

Wherever he'd gone, though, he left behind the room he'd created for himself—a treehouse "tastefully decorated" with rare-book shelves, an operating table, and a life-size William S. Burroughs doll—and he left it unlocked. So I took to checking in there occasionally, and I still do from time to time. I head out of my own cozy nook (inside a TV set inside the little red hotel inside the Monopoly board inside the dining room of LambdaMOO), and I teleport on over to the treehouse, where the room description always tells me Dr. Jest is present but asleep, in the conventional depiction for disconnected characters. The not-quite-emptiness of the abandoned room invariably instills in me an uncomfortable mix of melancholy and the creeps, and I stick around only on the off chance that Dr. Jest will wake up, say hello, and share his understanding of the future with me.

He won't, of course, but this is no great loss. Increasingly, the complex magic of the MOO interests me more as a way to live the present than to understand the future. And it's usually not long before I leave Dr. Jest's lonely treehouse and head back to the mansion, to see some friends.

# 65

# EPHEMERAL GAMES

## Is it barbaric to design videogames after Auschwitz?

### *Gonzalo Frasca*

Source: *Cybertext Yearbook 2000* (Saarijärvi, Finland: University of Jyväskayla, 2000), pp. 172–182.

Robert Coover advises readers looking for "serious" hypertext to visit Eastgate.com. Although "seriousness" is hard to define, it is possible to imagine what they are not going to find in these recommended texts: princesses in distress, trolls, and space ships with big laser guns.

Where should players go to find "serious" computer games? As far as I know, nowhere; there is a striking lack of "seriousness" in the computer game industry. Currently, videogames are closer to Tolkien than to Chekhov; they show more influence from George Lucas than from François Truffaut.

One reason is primarily economical. The industry targets male teenagers and children and everybody else either adapts to that content or looks for another form of entertainment. However, I do not believe the current lack of mature, intellectual content is solely due to marketing reasons.

I argue that current computer game design conventions have structural characteristics which prevent them from dealing with "serious" content. I will also suggest strategies for future designers that may help them overcome some of these problematic issues.

My approach risks falling into one of new media studies' deeper pits: to try to fit the characteristics of traditional media forms (in this case, literature and cinema) to the object of study (videogames). I am aware of this danger. However, to learn what the possibilities of computer games are, it is necessary to continue to test their boundaries and confront them with the theoretical tools that are currently available.

I will not discuss why some approaches to a topic are more "serious" than others; I will just stick to the rather naive definition of "seriousness" that Eastgate uses to advertise its products.

### "Serious" games

The Holocaust is a typical "serious" topic that is usually treated with a mature approach, even in comedy, as in Roberto Benigni's recent film *Life is Beautiful*.

319

Many computer games deal with World War II. However, the only games that explore the Holocaust are underground pro-Nazi videogames. While not extremely popular, such games receive sporadic media attention as they emerge, like Camus' pestilent rats, from their hideaways on the Internet. In one game available from many European BBS during the early nineties, the player was offered the role of a concentration camp administrator and had to coordinate mass murders.

Why has this topic inspired only racist videogames? Is the medium of videogames not considered mature enough to deal with a topic like the Holocaust?

It is possible to find successful counter-examples in other "low culture" media. One example is Art Spiegelman's comic book *Maus: A Survivor's Tale* (euphemistically categorized as a "graphic novel"). Spiegelman delivers "serious" messages through a medium that is popularly regarded as a violent and sexist time-waster for teenagers.

This same derogatory description is usually applied to videogames, and in fact, both media share similar aesthetics, themes and conventions. One would think that if a comic book can win a Pulitzer Prize, it should not be impossible for a computer game to also gain at least some attention from a "high culture" audience.

Why, then, has no one tried to develop a humanist game about the Holocaust? I can think of a possible answer: a computer game through the eyes of a Holocaust victim might be perceived as even more monstrous than a neo-Nazi game. A comic book representation of an historical drama could be socially accepted. However, an ergodic representation, such as a videogame, is a whole different story.

Our culture has a set of forbidden games. Children learn that there are things they are not supposed to play with. This happened to the children in René Clément's film *Forbidden Games*, who played with death and religious artifacts.

Computer games can be especially threatening because they combine the fear of representation – for example, "exposure to violent content can generate violent behavior" – with the fear of ergodics: "acting in violent simulated environments is violent behavior."

It is not my intention to review all the possible social, cultural or anthropological reasons for the fear towards certain kinds of play. I will just focus on two characteristics of games, and particularly computer games, that may become direct obstacles to the creation of "serious" games: binary actions, and computer game conventions of life and death.

## Binary actions

A game is defined by its outcome. There are two possible results, winning or losing; a draw is just an intermediate result.

Fair players do not worry very much about game results. After all, they can always start over and try their skills (or luck) again. That is another characteristic of a game: it can be restarted.

While traditional games can include representations and specific themes, videogames are able to create textual and audiovisual representations, as Brenda Laurel claims, "in which humans can participate" (Laurel, 1993). In other words, they are able to simulate both actions and environments.

Most videogames are goal oriented: they have particular rules in order to define when the player wins or loses, but also when the player is performing correct or incorrect actions on his path towards victory.

Game actions are typically trivial, because you can always play again and do exactly the opposite. Actually, in computer games you do not even need to wait until you lose in order to restart: you can save the exact situation of the environment at a certain moment for later retrieval.

For example, before fighting against a monster, the player could save the state of the game. If she dies in the battle, she would always be able to reload the previously saved game and try a different strategy. In other words, she does not have to face the consequences of her actions.

This trial-and-error routine is very common in videogames and particularly in adventure games. A player experiments rather than acts: she is free to explore any "what if" scenario without taking any real chance. The problem is that many "serious" cultural products are essentially based in the impossibility of doing such a thing in real life. Hamlet's dilemma would be irrelevant in a videogame, simply because he would be able "to be" and "not to be".

Actions in videogames are reversible. Therefore, there is no room in them for fate or tragedy. It is always possible to go back and play until you reach a happy ending. For this reason, videogames allow players to fool death itself.

## Living and dying inside the computer

Death in computer games is always just a minor detail: it can be fixed.

In Peter Weir's film *Fearless*, the main character survives a plane crash, and this experience changes his life. In a key scene, the character played by Jeff Bridges forbids his son to use his videogame console, arguing, "when you die [in the real world], you don't get another life." His son unsuccessfully tries to explain to him that, "It's not real dying."

Actually, both father and son are right, because they are facing the problem from different perspectives. The boy, who is literate in the computer medium, tries to explain to his father that death in videogames is just a convention; it is different from real death. On the other hand, the father points out the inconsistency of the simulation, which trivializes the "sacred" value of life.

## "The Sims": people issues

In real life, the consequences of our decisions are not binary. Unlike what happens in games, there is a broad spectrum of possible results.

If the real world is analyzed from a win-lose perspective, the results are simply pathetic. A clear example is *The Sims*, a computer program that simulates life according to consumerism. (A Sim is a simulated person who lives inside *Sim City*, another popular game by the same author.) The philosophy of the game is as follows: the more expensive your virtual furniture is, the more virtual friends you will have.

Still, *The Sims* is a revolutionary landmark in a realm that previously just housed monsters, aliens, and trolls. The breakthrough is due to a simple reason: it deals with people. The simulated persons introduce a whole new set of fascinating issues to computer games; ethics and moral are two of the most important.

Nobody cares if an alien monster is destroyed by a laser cannon, but players do pay more attention to issues like whether it is ethical to let a Sim to starve to death, or whether the designers were right in not allowing nudity in the game.

Just like in regular games, if your Sim's actions lead him to a "terrible" life (for example, if he becomes poor), you can always restore a previously saved version, where the sun always shines, the burgers are big, and his bank account is always full.

## Sophie's choice

Let's now describe an imaginary Holocaust videogame, based on current game design conventions. Basically, it would simulate a character that is a prisoner in a concentration camp. Through the character's eyes but also through his actions, the player would explore, feel and think about life in such an extreme situation. As a designer, I would be particularly interested in creating an environment for exploring such concepts as moral, hate, solidarity, suffering, and justice.

I believe that such a game would be highly criticized, for the following reasons.

Firstly, it would free the player from moral responsibilities. Since the game could be restarted at will, the player would not have to face the consequences of his actions. For example, he would be able to betray other prisoners and make the guards shoot them. In case the rest of the prisoners react by criticizing or even attacking him, all he would need to do is to restore a previously saved version and he would be able to get away with his crimes. In other words, the environment could become a simulator for sadists.

Secondly, if the game applied the win-lose binary logic, the Holocaust would become a secondary issue, an obstacle to overcome. If he followed that logic, the player could find a "correct" path in order to save Anne Frank from death. And if she happened to die, it would not be important, since she would be alive the next time he restarted the game. In other words, the player would be able to jump back and forth from life to death. Therefore, those concepts would loose their ethical, historical and social value.

So, it seems that game logic cannot be used to simulate tragic events since tragic agents do not have real choices. The film *Sophie's Choice* gives a clear example of this when the main character is forced to decide which of her children will survive Auschwitz. Sophie's choice is not a real choice. It does not matter what she decides; she is already doomed.

## Poetry after Auschwitz

Adorno once wrote "it would be barbaric to write poetry after Auschwitz." Based on what was previously described, it seems that it would definitively be barbaric to create videogames about Auschwitz.

However, if it could be possible to design a kind of environment where actions are irreversible, some of the main obstacles to designing "serious" videogames would disappear.

Actually, such an environment exists and is present in role playing games (RPGs), multi user dungeons (MUDs), and online persistent worlds such as Ultima Online. Unlike what happens in single user games, a participant in a multi-user game cannot save the situation of the whole environment for later retrieval. The online world is persistent: actions are irreversible, and you have to assume their consequences. Actually, this is how online social reputations are developed. The other players judge you based on your previous behavior.

Even if their irreversibility is evidently a plus, multiplayer games may not be the right environment for developing a Holocaust project because of the following reasons.

While most players are consistent with their online roles in MUDs, the range of available roles is not as broad and rich as in narratives. Most online environments are quite fair societies; there are generally not situations equivalent to being born with major physical handicaps or in total poverty. Therefore, there are not avatars who have been cleaning toilets for a living for several decades, or avatars with the angst of not having enough money for medical treatment. Of course, bots (computer controlled characters) or hired actors might be able to play these roles, but this would not completely solve the limitations of the characters played by players, who would always behave like an army of protagonists.

The other problem of most online environments is that the fear of death is relative, since it is always possible to log on again with a different avatar or buy another copy of the game and start over. (This is rarer in traditional RPGs, in which, if your character dies, you may not be able to rejoin the game.)

Finally, the designer has less control over what happens in a MUD than on an adventure game or in a single-user simulation like "The Sims". While this is not necessarily a bad thing – simply because a videogame designer and a narrative writer are in essence different jobs – if you are designing a videogame about a sensitive topic like the Holocaust, you may want to have more control over a single player program. For example, multiplayer games could be sabotaged by a real group of neo-Nazis.

While I am not saying that multiplayer environments are necessarily a bad place to build "serious" videogames, the reasons that were just described make me think that a single user game that shared the irreversibility characteristics of multiplayer games might be better.

## OSGON: don't play it again, Sam

If the player's actions in a single player game were irreversible, this program would not have a "save and restore" function. However, even without this feature, you would always be able to start from scratch and do the opposite of what you previously did. An ephemeral piece of software is needed: a computer program that could only be used one time.

A computer program that can be used just once? It does not seem to make sense. People are used to being able to have access to a computer program as many times as they need it. It would be strange indeed to buy a word processor, install it, write a letter, and then not being able to use the program again.

There are a couple of direct antecedents to this idea, even if they were designed with other goals in mind.

The earliest is *Agrippa*, a poem by William Gibson. This poem was delivered on a floppy disk. Once you executed the program you were able to read the content just once. After you did so, the program encrypted itself, preventing you from executing it again. Of course, it took hackers only a short time to break the protection. Nowadays the poem is available on many web sites and people are free to read it as many times as they want.

Another example is Divx, an alternative DVD video format. It was supported by major Hollywood studios and tested in the United States. Unlike DVD movies, Divx discs were very cheap. However, after you watched each film, its disc would not replay unless you repaid a small fee. This was achieved through a serial number on every disc and the fact that the player had a modem connected to the company's database. If you pushed a special button on your remote control, the fee would be deducted from your credit card account and you would be able to watch the movie again. It was advertised as an alternative to video rental, with the plus that you would never have late return fees and you could keep the disc at home. It was a huge commercial failure, and the format is no longer available.

These two systems broke the replayability paradigm. The first one simply forbids any further access to the software. The second restricts the access unless you pay a fee. However, it is important to notice that in both cases the content delivered was not ergodic.

*Agrippa* was easy to hack, but the technique itself could still be used. Divx did not really eliminate replayability; it just transformed it into a money generator for the big film studios.

I propose a particular system that would help us to create single user games with irreversible actions. While there can be many different ways to achieve this, I will just mention one.

The most simple way would be that the player must buy a ticket (or serial number) for the single user game. With her ticket number she would log in into the game and play. The game would have no save feature, but after she logged out, the environment would be maintained in the same state until she returned. Even if many users could play at the same time, there would be no interaction between them: everybody would be playing a single user game.

However, with such a format, users would still be able to buy multiple tickets and start over, just like in traditional single user games. Therefore, the only solution would be to transform the game into a happening. The game could be scheduled for, let's say, next Monday at 8 pm. Every player would have to log in at that moment to start playing. After that, nobody else would be able to start playing that game, ever. It would be the exact equivalent of missing a happening: you simply cannot show up three days later.

Let's now analyze the consequences of using this technique, which I will name "one-session game of narration" (OSGON).

1    Irreversibility. Since the game can be played only once, the player would have to carefully choose her actions and decisions and face the consequences of her actions, just like in real life. This would allow designers to deal with more "serious" topics.

2    Death. If you die in an OSGON, there is no second chance. The game would simply end. However, because of this, the game designer would have to minimize the chances of death. In current videogames, it is extremely easy to die. An OSGON would need to be designed in a more realistic ways. The probability of dying would of course vary depending on the genre and topic of the game, but should remain coherent within its context. In other words, players should not die in the first hour, unless they do something really stupid.

3    Criticism. As with any piece of ephemeral art, critics would have a hard time analyzing OSGONs. They would only have the chance to judge their personal experience.

4    Time. As OSGONs can be used just once, they necessarily have to have a limited duration. The designer may have two main options. The first would be, as in many adventure games, that the closure of the program would be a direct consequence of the user's actions. For example, the game may end if the character is put in jail. The other option would be to have a limited time, as, for example, theater plays or movies. The user would be able to experience the program for a couple of hours and then it would end, with or without a narrative closure.

5    Awkwardness. Even if OSGONs could be able to deliver more compelling "serious" videogames, it simply could happen that the concept of ephemeral games might be too awkward for the public. The idea of replayability may be too powerful to be challenged. Of course, I do not see OSGONs as a replacement for current single player games, but just as another genre with its own characteristics.

6    Serials. OSGONs could also be used as one-session chapters in ergodic serials. While producing serial games may still be too expensive with current technology, the structure could allow the design of coherent ergodic serials.

## Conclusion

There is a lack of "serious" videogames that use the medium as a way to make a philosophical point or to share an artist's perception of reality. While it is easy to think that this situation might be simply caused by lack of demand and economical reasons, I have analyzed several problems within current videogame conventions that may prevent us from dealing with certain topics.

I have also shown that OSGONs may be a good strategy to explore for developing "serious" videogames. However, without an actual prototype, it is hard to know if the lack of replayability will have unexpected consequences. Still, the technique itself opens a door for computer based ergodic ephemeral artifacts.

It would definitely be difficult to design videogames that deal with topics such as the Holocaust. However, my main goal in this article was simply to focus on some of these design issues. Games are not going to improve simply because of broadband nor simply because of impressive 3D graphics. They will only get better if we keep trying to understand them as a medium.

## References

Aarseth, Espen (1997) *Cybertext: Perspectives on Ergodic Literature*. Baltimore & London: The Johns Hopkins University Press.

Benigni, Roberto (1997) *La vita e bella*. Miramax. Italy.

Clément, René (1952) *Jeux Interdits*. Paris: UGC.

Frasca, Gonzalo (1998) "Don't Play it Again, Sam: One-session games of narration." http://cmc.uib.no/dac98/papers/frasca.html.

Frasca, Gonzalo (1999) "Ludologia kohtaa narratologian." Parnasso 49:3, 365–371. Helsinki. (English version available at http://www.jacaranda.org/frasca/)

Garriott, Richard (2000) *Ultima Online: Renaissance*. Origin.

Gibson, William (1992) *Agrippa: a book of the dead*. New York, NY: Kevin Begos Publishing.

Laurel, Brenda (1993) *Computers as Theatre*. London: Addison Wesley.

Pakula, Alan J. (1986) *Sophie's Choice*. ITC, USA.

Spiegelman, Art (1986) *Maus: A survivor's tale*. London: Random House.

Weir, Peter (1993) *Fearless*. Warner Bros., USA.

Wright, Wil (2000) *The Sims*. Maxis.

# 66

# VIDEO GAMES AND AGGRESSIVE THOUGHTS, FEELINGS, AND BEHAVIOR IN THE LABORATORY AND IN LIFE

*Craig A. Anderson and Karen E. Dill*

Source: *Journal of Personality and Social Psychology*, 78(4), April 2000, 772–790.

### Abstract

Two studies examined violent video game effects on aggression-related variables. Study 1 found that real-life violent video game play was positively related to aggressive behavior and delinquency. The relation was stronger for individuals who are characteristically aggressive and for men. Academic achievement was negatively related to overall amount of time spent playing video games. In Study 2, laboratory exposure to a graphically violent video game increased aggressive thoughts and behavior. In both studies, men had a more hostile view of the world than did women. The results from both studies are consistent with the General Affective Aggression Model, which predicts that exposure to violent video games will increase aggressive behavior in both the short term (e.g., laboratory aggression) and the long term (e.g., delinquency).

On April 20, 1999, Eric Harris and Dylan Klebold launched an assault on Columbine High School in Littleton, Colorado, murdering 13 and wounding 23 before turning the guns on themselves. Although it is impossible to know exactly what caused these teens to attack their own classmates and teachers, a number of factors probably were involved. One possible contributing factor is violent video games. Harris and Klebold enjoyed playing the bloody, shoot-'em-up video game Doom, a game licensed by the U.S. military to train soldiers to effectively kill. The Simon Wiesenthal Center, which tracks Internet hate groups, found in its archives a copy of Harris' web site with a version of Doom that he had customized. In his version there are two shooters, each with extra weapons and unlimited ammunition, and the other people in the game can't fight back. For a class project, Harris and Klebold made a videotape that was similar to their customized version of Doom. In the video, Harris and Klebold dress in trench coats, carry guns, and kill school athletes. They acted out their videotaped performance in real life less than a year later. An investigator associated with the Wiesenthal Center said Harris and Klebold were "playing out their game in God mode" (Pooley, 1999, p. 32).

Entertainment media affects our lives. What behaviors children and adults consider appropriate comes, in part, from the lessons we learn from television and the movies (e.g., Huesmann & Miller, 1994). There are good theoretical reasons to expect that violent video games will have similar, and possibly larger, effects on aggression. The empirical literature on the effects of exposure to video game violence is sparse, however, in part because of its relatively recent emergence in modern U.S. society. About 25 years ago, when video games first appeared, popular games were simple and apparently harmless. In the 1970s, Atari introduced a game called Pong that was a simple video version of the game ping pong. In the 1980s, arcade games like Pac-Man became dominant. In Pac-Man, a yellow orb with a mouth raced around the screen chomping up ghosts and goblins. At this point, some eyebrows were raised questioning whether young people should play such "violent" games. In the 1990s the face of video games changed dramatically. The most popular video game of 1993 was Mortal Kombat (Elmer-Dewitt, 1993). This game features realistically rendered humanoid characters engaging in battle. As the name of the game implies, the goal of the player in Mortal Kombat is to kill any opponent he faces. Unfortunately, such violent games now dominate the market. Dietz (1998) sampled 33 popular Sega and Nintendo games and found that nearly 80% of the games were violent in nature. Interestingly, she also found that 21% of these games portrayed violence towards women.

The research to date on video game effects is sparse and weak in a number of ways. Indeed, one reviewer (and many video game creators) has espoused the belief that "video game playing may be a useful means of coping with pent-up and aggressive energies" (Emes, 1997, p. 413). In brief, what is needed is basic theory-guided research on the effects of playing violent video games. Such research would also contribute to the field's understanding of media violence effects in general.

## Theoretical approach

General Affective Aggression Model (GAAM): Short-Term Effects of Video Game Violence and Aggressive Personality

### GAAM: overview

There are several reasons for expecting exposure to violent video games to increase aggressive behavior in both the short run (i.e., within 20 minutes of game play) and over long periods of time (i.e., repeated exposure over a period of years). Our theoretical approach is the GAAM, which has emerged from our work on a variety of aggression-related domains (Anderson, Anderson, & Deuser, 1996; Anderson, Deuser, & DeNeve, 1995; Anderson, Anderson, Dill, & Deuser, 1998;

Dill, Anderson, Anderson, & Deuser, 1997; Lindsay & Anderson, in press). The model integrates existing theory and data concerning the learning, development, instigation, and expression of human aggression. It does so by noting that the enactment of aggression is largely based on knowledge structures (e.g., scripts, schemas) created by social learning processes. Thus, GAAM incorporates the theoretical insights of much previous work, especially Bandura's social learning theory (e.g., Bandura, 1971, 1973; Bandura, Ross, & Ross, 1961, 1963), Berkowitz's Cognitive Neoassociationist Model (Berkowitz, 1984, 1990, 1993), the social information-processing model of Dodge and his colleagues (e.g., Dodge & Crick, 1990; Crick & Dodge, 1994), Geen's (1990) affective aggression model, Huesmann's social–cognitive model of media violence effects (Huesmann, 1986), and Zillmann's (1983) excitation transfer model.

Figure 1 presents the basic GAAM structure with examples relevant to this article. The focus of this version of GAAM is on short-term effects of video game violence. In brief, GAAM describes a multistage process by which personological (e.g., aggressive personality) and situational (e.g., video game play and provocation) input variables lead to aggressive behavior. They do so by influencing several related internal states and the outcomes of automatic and controlled appraisal (or decision) processes.

### *GAAM: input variables and internal states*

Both kinds of input variables—personological and situational—can influence the present internal state of the person—cognitive, affective, and arousal variables. For example, people who score high on measures of aggressive personality have highly accessible knowledge structures for aggression-related information. They think aggressive thoughts more frequently than do those individuals who score low on aggressive personality measures, and have social perception schemas that lead to hostile perception, expectation, and attributional biases (e.g., Anderson, 1997; Crick & Dodge, 1994; Dill, Anderson, Anderson, & Deuser, 1997).

Situational input variables can also influence the current accessibility of aggression-related knowledge structures. Being insulted may cause a person to think of how to return the insult in a harmful way (a behavioral script). More central to the present research, we believe that playing a violent video game also can increase the accessibility of aggressive cognitions by semantic priming processes. We know from related research that merely seeing a picture of a gun or other weapon can increase the accessibility of aggressive thoughts (e.g., Anderson et al., 1996; Anderson, Benjamin, & Bartholow, 1998). Presumedly, this process accounts for the "weapons effect" first reported by Berkowitz and LePage (1967), and reviewed by Carlson, Marcus-Newhall, and Miller (1990). However, there is presently no empirical evidence on whether playing a violent video game increases accessibility of aggressive thoughts.

Both kinds of input variables influence a person's current affective state, such as aggression-related feelings of anger or hostility. Some people feel angry a

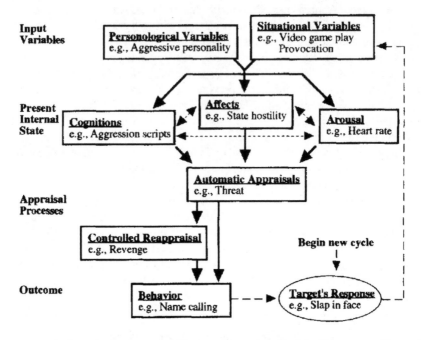

*Figure 1* Single episode General Affective Aggression Model: Short-term effects of video game violence. Adapted from "Hot Temperatures, Hostile Affect, Hostile Cognition, and Arousal: Tests of a General Model of Affective Aggression," by C. A. Anderson, W. E. Deuser, and K. M. DeNeve, 1995, *Personality and Social Psychology Bulletin, 21*, p. 436

lot of the time. Some situations can make anybody angry. We do not, however, expect that playing violent video games will routinely increase feelings of anger, compared with playing a nonviolent game. To be sure, playing a frustrating game is likely to increase anger. Violent content by itself, however, in the absence of another provocation, is likely to have little direct impact on affect. We deliberately chose to use a pair of violent and nonviolent games that are equally well liked for Study 2. In effect, this choice closes off this particular route to aggression, allowing a cleaner test of the more critical hypothesis that violent content itself can increase aggression.

The present state of arousal can also be affected by both personological and situational variables. Some people are chronically aroused, and numerous situational variables, including playing certain video games, can temporarily increase arousal. As Zillmann (1983) and others have shown, unexplained arousal can lead to a search for environmental cues to which the arousal can be attributed. Salient cues, such as a provocateur, can lead to the misattribution of arousal that was actually caused by playing a violent video game (for instance) to anger at the salient provoking person, which in turn could increase the likelihood of an aggressive behavioral attack. As with the affect state, this arousal effect is not specific to violent video games, but could occur with any game that happens to be very exciting. For this reason, in Study 2 we chose to use violent and nonviolent video games that do not differentially increase physiological indicators of arousal, thus closing off this alternative route to aggression as well.

One additional aspect of GAAM deserves mention. In Figure 1 the three internal state variables are interconnected by dashed lines. This illustrates a key part of GAAM and the earlier models on which it is based, most obviously Berkowitz's (1984) CNA model. Cognition, affect, and arousal are seen as highly interrelated aspects of one's current internal state. Activating one tends to activate the other two. Such cross-modality priming helps explain how strong activation of one type of state (e.g., remembering a humiliating public insult received last week) can produce corresponding changes in the other states (e.g., reinstatement of anger and increased arousal).

In sum, short-term violent video game increases in aggression are expected by GAAM whenever exposure to violent media primes aggressive thoughts, increases hostile feelings, or increases arousal (all else being equal). However, because neither hostile feelings nor high arousal are specific effects of violent media, they must be controlled (experimentally or statistically) to allow an adequate test of the hypothesis that violent content per se can increase aggressive behavior in a short-term setting. For this reason, our experimental manipulation of type of video game in Study 2 used games chosen to differ primarily in violent content but to be similar in how well our participants would like them and in their likely effect on physiological indicators of arousal.

### GAAM, appraisal, and aggressive behavior

The appraisal processes of GAAM are not investigated in the present studies, so a brief summary of these processes will suffice. Automatic appraisals (called "immediate appraisal" in earlier versions of GAAM) are evaluations of the present environment and internal state that are made on-line, very quickly, with little or no awareness. When slapped in the face people will automatically "judge" that the present environment is threatening and that they are angry and/or scared, what is commonly referred to as the emotional part of the "fight or flight" response (e.g., Berkowitz, 1993). Berkowitz's (1993) CNA model also posits that such automatic appraisals include the behavioral aspects of fight or flight, a notion that is entirely consistent with GAAM.

Controlled reappraisals are somewhat slower and require more cognitive resources than do automatic appraisals. In some situations, in which there is little time for reappraisal for instance, a relevant behavior is chosen and performed before reappraisal takes place. However, reappraisal does often occur, as when one carefully considers why a provoking individual behaved in a particular way before deciding how to respond. Although we've presented appraisal and reappraisal as a dichotomy, in keeping with recent thinking in cognitive psychology it would be more accurate to view appraisal processes as existing

331

along a continuum with *completely automatic* and *completely controlled* as the endpoints (e.g., Bargh, 1994).

Whether an aggressive behavior is emitted depends on what behavioral scripts have been activated by the various input variables and the appraisal processes. Well-learned scripts come to mind relatively easily and quickly and can be emitted fairly automatically. People who score high on aggressive personality have a relatively well-developed and easily accessible array of aggression scripts that are easily activated by relatively minor provocation (e.g., Anderson, Benjamin, & Bartholow, 1998). Furthermore, aggressive people have social perception schemata that bias the interpretation of observed events in aggression-enhancing ways. They perceive more violence than is really there, and they expect people to solve problems with aggressive means (e.g., Dill et al., 1997). We believe that video game violence also primes aggressive thought, including aggressive scripts. GAAM therefore explicitly predicts short-term effects of both aggressive personality and playing a violent video game on aggression after provocation.

### GAAM: long-term effects of video game violence

Long-term media violence effects on aggression result from the development, over-learning, and reinforcement of aggression-related knowledge structures. Figure 2 illustrates this process and identifies five types of such knowledge structures that have received attention in other aggression-related contexts. Each time people play violent video games, they rehearse aggressive scripts that teach and reinforce vigilance for enemies (i.e., hostile perception bias), aggressive action against others, expectations that others will behave aggressively, positive attitudes toward use of violence, and beliefs that violent solutions are effective and appropriate. Furthermore, repeated exposure to graphic scenes of violence is likely to be desensitizing. In essence, the creation and automatization of these aggression-related knowledge structures and the desensitization effects change the individual's personality. Long-term video game players can become more aggressive in outlook, perceptual biases, attitudes, beliefs, and behavior than they were before the repeated exposure or would have become without such exposure.

Theoretically, these long-term changes in aggressive personality operate in the immediate situation through both types of input variables described in GAAM: person and situation variables. The link to person variables is obvious— the person is now more aggressive in outlook and propensity. Less obvious is how long-term effects of repeated exposure to violent video games can change situational variables. However, Huesmann and colleagues (Huesmann, 1994) have developed a clear model of the social and academic effects of exposure to television violence. As a person becomes more aggressive, the social environment responds. The types of people who are willing to interact with them, the types of interactions that are held, and the types of situations made available to the person all change. Interactions with teachers, parents, and nonaggressive peers are likely to degenerate, whereas interactions with other "deviant" peers may well increase.

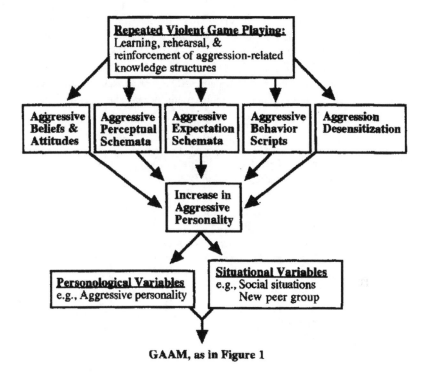

GAAM, as in Figure 1

*Figure 2* Multiple episode General Affective Aggression Model (GAAM): Long-term effects of video game violence

For these reasons, we expect to find a positive correlation between a person's level of exposure to violent video games and their aggressive behavior. Study 1 was designed to test this notion.

## Research on video game violence

Although much research has examined the effects of exposure to movie and television violence (see Huesmann, 1994, for a review), and although popular press commentaries about possible effects of video games abound, the empirical literature on video game violence is sparse (see Dill & Dill, 1998; Emes, 1997). To what extent do the existing video game studies support or contradict the GAAM-based predictions?

### *Video games and aggression: correlational work*

Four correlational studies have examined the relation between video game playing habits and real-world aggressive behavior. Across the four studies, the ages of participants ranged from 4th graders to 12th graders. Measures of aggression included self, teacher, and peer reports. Three of the studies (Dominick, 1984; Fling et al., 1992; Lin & Lepper, 1987) yielded reliable positive correlations between video game playing and aggression. The fourth (Van Schie & Wiegman, 1997) correlation did not differ from zero. But, none of the studies distinguished between violent and nonviolent video games. Thus, none test the hypothesis that violent video games are uniquely associated with increased aggression.

### Video games and aggression: experimental work

The extant experimental studies of video games and aggression have yielded weak evidence also. Four studies found at least some support for the hypothesis that violent video game content can increase aggression (Cooper & Mackie, 1986; Irwin & Gross, 1995; Schutte, Malouff, Post-Gorden, & Rodasta, 1988; Silvern & Williamson, 1987). However, none of these studies can rule out the possibility that key variables such as excitement, difficulty, or enjoyment created the observed increase in aggression. In our experience with video games and in the movie literature (Bushman, 1995), violent materials tend to be more exciting than nonviolent materials, so the observed effects could have been the result of higher excitement levels induced by the violent games.

Two additional experimental studies of violent video games and aggression found no effect of violence (Graybill, Strawniak, Hunter, & O'Leary, 1987; Winkel, Novak, & Hopson, 1987). Interestingly, of the six video game studies reviewed here, only the Graybill et al. (1987) study used games pretested and selected to be similar on a number of dimensions (e.g., difficulty, excitement, enjoyment). In sum, there is little experimental evidence that the violent content of video games can increase aggression in the immediate situation.

### Video games, aggressive affect, and cognition

Two studies have examined the effect of video game violence on aggressive cognition, Calvert and Tan (1994) randomly assigned male and female undergraduates to a condition in which they either played or observed a violent virtual-reality game or to a no-game control condition. Postgame aggressive thoughts were assessed with a thought-listing procedure. Aggressive thoughts were highest for violent game players. Although this supports our GAAM view of video game effects, we hesitate to claim strong support because it is possible that this effect resulted from the greater excitement or arousal engendered by playing the game, rather than the violent content of the game. More recently, Kirsh (1998) showed that 3rd- and 4th-grade children assigned to play a violent video game gave more hostile interpretations for a subsequent ambiguous provocation story than did children assigned to play a nonviolent game. This also supports GAAM.

Five experiments have investigated the effects of video game violence on aggressive affect. One study showed increases in aggressive affect after violent video game play (Ballard & Weist, 1996). Another (Anderson & Ford, 1986) yielded mixed results. Three others (Nelson & Carlson, 1985; Scott, 1995; Calvert & Tan, 1994) showed little support for the hypothesis that short-term exposure to violent video games increases hostile affect. There are methodological shortcomings in many of these studies, which, when combined with the mixed results, suggest that there is little evidence that short-term exposure to violent video games increases aggression-related affect.

### *Summary*

Four main hypotheses concerning video game violence and aggression emerge from a careful consideration of GAAM. First, consideration of social–cognitive learning processes and social dynamics leads to the prediction that exposure to violent video games over a long period of time should be positively correlated with aggression in naturalistic settings.

Second, GAAM predicts that short-term exposure to video game violence will lead to increases in aggressive behavior. Third, GAAM also predicts that people who score high on aggressive personality measures will behave more aggressively when provoked than will low trait aggression individuals. Fourth, GAAM predicts that short-term exposure to video game violence will lead to increases in aggressive cognition and that this effect mediates the short-term violent content/ aggressive behavior relation, at least to some extent.

## The present research

Our literature review revealed that the few published studies to date have not adequately tested the video game hypotheses. Thus, we conducted two studies of video game violence effects, one correlational, the other experimental. Our goal was to begin laying a firm empirical foundation for understanding video game violence effects, while at the same time providing further tests of the GAAM formulation and broadening our understanding of media violence effects in general. We chose two different methodologies that have strengths that complement each other and surmount each others' weaknesses—a correlational study and an experiment were conducted.

In Study 1, we measured both the amount of exposure to video game violence and the amount of time participants had played video games in prior time periods regardless of content. These video game measures and several individual difference measures were used as predictors of self-reported aggressive behavior and delinquency. We used a college student population, in part because they are old enough for long-term effects of playing violent video games to have had a measurable impact on real-world aggression. Study 1 also included a measure of academic achievement (grade point average [GPA]), mainly because prior longitudinal work on media violence effects on children has demonstrated a negative relation between exposure to violent media and later academic performance (e.g., Huesmann, 1986; Huesmann & Miller, 1994).

In Study 2 we randomly assigned participants to play either a violent or a nonviolent video game; the two games were matched (by means of pretesting) on several key dimensions. Subsequently, these participants played a competitive reaction time game in which they could punish their opponent by delivering a noxious blast of white noise. This constituted our laboratory measure of aggression. We also assessed the effects of the video games on both hostile thoughts and hostile feelings to see whether either (or both) served as mediators of the violent video game effect on aggressive behavior.

Both studies examined the additive and interactive effects of the individual difference variable of trait aggressiveness, one indicator of what we have called Aggressive Personality. This variable has yielded interesting effects in several media violence studies (e.g., Anderson, 1997; Bushman, 1995; Dill et al., 1997). Finally, both studies also included a measure of world view as a dependent variable (e.g., Gerbner, Gross, Morgan, & Signiorelli, 1980). These researchers posited that exposure to media violence creates an exaggerated picture of the world as a violent, unsafe place. As yet, this proposition has not been tested in the video game violence literature.

## Study 1: correlation tests of video game violence effects

### Method

### Participants

Two hundred twenty-seven (78 male, 149 female) undergraduates from introductory psychology courses at a large Midwestern university participated in small groups. All members of these classes were given the option of participating in psychological research or doing an alternative project for course credit. Students choosing to participate in research are recruited by means of a research participation sign-up board that lists ongoing research.

### Design and procedures

A correlational design was used to examine the relationship between long-term exposure to violent video games and several outcome variables, namely aggressive behavior, delinquency, academic achievement, and world view. We also collected data on two individual difference variables related to aggression (trait aggression, irritability) to examine the potential interactive effects of individual differences in aggression on the above outcomes. Gender of participant was also recorded so that we would be able to examine interactions with the aggression-related individual difference variables for each of the outcome variables. Data were collected in group questionnaire sessions, with the exception of the academic achievement variables, which were obtained from the university's registrar.

## Materials

A self-report questionnaire was created to collect the individual difference data as well as the data on aggressive behavior, delinquency, and world view. There were six scales in total that made up the questionnaire. Each of these scales is described below. The two individual difference measures were the Caprara Irritability Scale (CIS; Caprara et al., 1985) and the Buss-Perry Aggression Questionnaire (AQ; Buss & Perry, 1992). The Delinquency Scale, which contained the aggressive behavior items, was also from a published scale (Elliot, Huizinga, & Ageton, 1985). The measures of world view and of violent video game play were created for this study. A balanced Latin square design was used to create a total of six different forms of the questionnaire. These different forms were used to control for potential order effects.

## Irritability

The CIS measures aggressive impulsivity or the proclivity toward quick and impulsive reactions to what the individual perceives as provocation or frustration. Agreement with statements such as, 'I easily fly off the handle with those who don't listen or understand" and "I don't think I am a very tolerant person," indicates irritability. Caprara (1982) found that irritability predicted aggressive behavior in provoked individuals. Caprara reported a coefficient alpha for the irritability scale at .81 and a test–retest reliability of. 83 (Caprara et al., 1985). The CIS contains 20 items that Caprara et al., (1985) labeled "irritability" items and 10 additional control items that might be thought of as "friendliness" items. In past research in our laboratory (e.g., Dill et al., 1997) we have reverse scored the 10 "control" items and found these items to be a viable predictor of irritability in their own right. Thus, the irritability composites we report are an average of 30 items, the 20 irritability items and the 10 "friendliness" items (reverse scored).

## Trait aggression

In 1992 Buss and Perry revised the Buss–Durkee (Buss & Durkee, 1957) aggression questionnaire. Buss and Perry's AQ (Buss & Perry, 1992) measures trait aggressiveness through four distinct subtraits, each represented by a subscale on the AQ. These subtraits are Physical and Verbal Aggression, Anger, and Hostility. Items such as "If somebody hits me, I hit back" represent physical aggressiveness, and items such as "I can't help getting into arguments when people disagree with me" represent verbal aggressiveness. likewise, items such as "Some of my friends think I'm a hothead" and "At times I feel I have gotten a raw deal out of life" measure anger and hostility, respectively. Buss and Perry (1992) demonstrated a significant relationship between peer nominations of aggressiveness and scores on these four aggression subscales for male college students. They report a coefficient alpha for the AQ at .89 and a test–retest reliability at .80 (Buss & Perry, 1992).

More recently, Bushman and Wells (in press) reported a positive relation between the Physical Aggression subscale and minutes penalized for aggressive hockey violations in high school students.

## Delinquency

In the late 1970s, first the National Institute of Mental Health and then the National Institute for Juvenile Justice and Delinquency Prevention funded research on the epidemiology of delinquent behavior. A series of longitudinal studies, which in part used a self-report measure of delinquency, were conducted, and these studies were collectively called the National Youth Survey (Elliot, Huizinga, & Ageton, 1985). The self-report delinquency measure that was created for the National Youth Survey is the one we use in the present study to measure delinquency. The format of the Delinquency Scale is a self-report of frequency of each of 45 specific behaviors over the last year. For example, an individual is asked to estimate how many times in the past year he or she has "purposely damaged or destroyed property belonging to a school." Of the 45 items, 7 pertain to illegal drug use (i.e., "How often in the last year have you used alcoholic beverages [beer, wine and hard liquor]?"). The multiple correlation ratio for the Delinquency Scale reported by Elliot et al. (1985) is .59. Using a model described in their book, **Explaining Delinquency and Drug Use** (Elliot et al., 1985), the authors demonstrated that their theoretical model explained 30–50% of the variance in the self-reported delinquency scores of males and 11–34% of the variance in the self-reported delinquency scores for females.

### AGGRESSIVE BEHAVIOR

The authors of the Delinquency Scale have sometimes analyzed their data by dividing the scale into subscales based on the severity of the delinquent crime (i.e., index offenses vs. minor delinquency) but not based on the type of delinquent act perpetrated (e.g., aggression vs. theft). However, for our purposes, we chose to form a subscale from the 10 items that were most clearly related to aggressive behavior. For example, participants were asked to estimate how many times in the past year they have "hit (or threatened to hit) other students" and "attacked someone with the idea of seriously hurting or killing him/her."

One of the 10 aggressive items was given a 0 by all participants (Item 27, "used force [strong-arm methods] to get money or things from other students") and was therefore dropped from the measure. Another item did not correlate well with the others (Item 20, "hit, or threatened to hit, one of your parents"), so it too was dropped. (Note that keeping these two items produces a few changes in higher order interactions but does not substantially change the main findings.) Furthermore, the standard deviations of the remaining items varied widely. To form a reliable index of aggressive behavior it was necessary to standardize each item before averaging across the eight items. Coefficient alpha for this index was .73.

We hypothesized a positive relation between violent video game play and aggressive behavior.

Two of the remaining 35 items were also given 0s by all participants (items 4 and 13, "stolen [or tried to steal] a motor vehicle, such as a car or motorcycle" and "been paid for having sexual relations with someone") and were also dropped. The item standardization procedure as outlined for the aggressive delinquency behavior measure was used for this 33-item nonaggressive delinquency measure. It yielded an alpha coefficient of .89. We also hypothesized that violent video game play would be positively related to nonaggressive delinquency, though we expected it to be somewhat weaker than the video game link to aggressive delinquency. We expected this because many of these "nonaggressive" items have at least some aggression component to them, at least on occasion. For example, "purposely damaged or destroyed property belonging to your parents or other family members" may well be an indirect act of aggression, an attempt to harm someone by destroying something they value. In addition, some violent video games also model a total disregard for property rights of others or for other societal norms.

## Video game questionnaire

We constructed our video game questionnaire to enable the creation of two composite indexes, one focusing on exposure to video game violence, and the other focusing on amount of time spent playing video games in general, regardless of type of content.

Participants were asked to name their five favorite video games. After naming each game, participants responded on scales anchored at 1 and 7, rating how often they played the game and how violent the content and graphics of the game were. Responses of 1 were labeled *rarely,* **little or no violent content,** and **little or no violent graphics,** respectively. Responses of 7 were labeled **often, extremely violent content,** and **extremely violent graphics,** respectively. The "how-often" scales also included the verbal anchor **occasionally** under the scale midpoint (4). For each participant, we computed a violence exposure score for each of their five favorite games by summing the violent content and violent graphics ratings and multiplying this by the how-often rating. These five video game violence exposure scores were averaged to provide an overall index of exposure to video game violence. Coefficient alpha was .86.

Participants were also asked, "Which of the following categories best describes this game?" for each of their five favorite games. The six categories were education, fighting with hands, sports, fighting with weapons, fantasy, and skill.

To help them remember their favorite games, participants were provided with a video game list. This list, which we compiled, contained the names of all video games that were currently for sale at a local computer store. It should be noted that participants were allowed to indicate that they had never played video games. Several individuals in our sample listed fewer than five favorite video games, but over 90% of our sample reported having at least one favorite video game.

## TIME SPENT ON VIDEO GAMES

After completing the questions relating to their favorite video games, participants were asked four questions regarding their general video game play across four different time periods. First they were asked to estimate the number of hours per week they have played video games "in recent months." They were not constrained as to the number of hours they could report. Next they were asked to estimate the number of hours per week they played video games "during the 11th and 12th grades," "during the 9th and 10th grades," and "during the 7th and 8th grades." A video game playing composite was formed by averaging the amount of time participants reported playing video games across the four time periods. Because participants were predominantly traditional-aged college underclassmen, this measure constituted a general video game playing estimate over approximately 5–6 years, from junior high to early college. The coefficient alpha for this general time spent playing video games variable was .84.

## *World view*

Gerbner et al. (1980) were interested in the difference between light television viewers' and heavy television viewers' perceptions of the world. They asked participants to estimate the chance that they would be personally involved in crime and compared this with actual crime statistics. They also asked participants whether women are more likely to be victims of crime and whether neighborhoods are safe.

We chose to create our own World View Scale by making a set of questions that taps these general ideas. One reason for constructing a new measure was to not Constrain the crime estimates to be compared with actual crime estimates at any one time. A comparison of the perceived likelihood of a crime can simply be made between those exposed to media violence and those not exposed, rather than to a continuously changing statistic. We constructed two sets of questions.

## CRIME LIKELIHOOD

The first four questions on our Crime Opinion Survey, asked participants to estimate the percentage likelihood of a person experiencing each of four different crimes at least once in their lifetime. The questions read, "What do you think the chances are that any one person will be robbed by someone with a weapon in their lifetime? What do you think the chances are that any one person will be physically assaulted by a stranger in their lifetime? What do you think the chances are that any one woman will be raped in her lifetime? What do you think the chances are that any one person will be murdered?" Participants were asked to answer each of these four questions with a percentage and to assume that each question referred to current crime frequencies in the United States. Coefficient alpha for this "crime" perception measure was .86.

SAFETY FEELINGS

In the last two questions participants were asked to indicate the extent to which they would feel safe walking alone in two different settings. These questions read, "How safe would you feel walking alone at night in an average suburban setting?" and "How safe would you feel walking alone at night on campus?" Participants responded on 7-point scales ranging from 1 (**not at all**) to 7 (**extremely**). Coefficient alpha for this "safety" measure was .82.

## *Academic achievement*

The academic achievement variable was the cumulative college GPA for each student. These were supplied by the university's registrar.

# Results

## *Preliminary analysis*

### *Formation of individual difference composites*

Correlational analysis on the individual difference measures of aggression indicated no problem items (e.g., items that were negatively correlated with the scale) on either of the two scales. Coefficient alphas indicated that each of the two scales was internally reliable. Alphas were .88 for the CIS and .90 for the AQ. The CIS and AQ were strongly correlated ($r = .81, p < .001$). Past research in our lab has revealed that the CIS and the AQ load on the same latent Aggressive Personality factor (Dill et al., 1997). Therefore, we formed a single aggressive personality score by averaging the CIS and AQ scores.

### *Centering*

When testing for interaction and main effects simultaneously in regression models with correlated predictors, it is recommended that continuous independent variables be centered to reduce multicollinearity problems (Aiken & West, 1991). We standardized all three continuous independent variables used in the various regression analyses to follow (i.e., video game violence, aggressive personality, and time in general spent on video games) to facilitate comparisons among them.

## Descriptive results

Most of the participants were traditional freshmen and sophomores. The mean age was 18.5 years. The oldest participants were two 25-year-olds and two 24-year-olds. Data from the video game questionnaire provided information about their playing habits. Overall, participants reported playing video games progressively less from junior high school to college. Participants reported playing video games an average of 5.45 hours per week while in junior high school, 3.69 hours per week in early high school, and 2.68 hours per week late in high school. Presently, the students reported playing video games an average of 2.14 hours per week.

Of the 227 students surveyed, 207 (91%) reported that they currently played video games. Of the 9% who do not play video games, 18 students, or 90% of the non-video game players, were women. Thus 88% of the female college students and 97% of the male college students surveyed were video game players. Participants were asked to list up to five favorite games. The mean number of games listed was 4.03. Over 69% listed five games, the maximum number allowed.

The most popular game listed was Super Mario Brothers, which was a favorite of 109 students or about 50% of the sample. The second most played game was Tetris, a favorite of 93 students or about 43% of the sample. The third favorite game among our college students was Mortal Kombat, which was named by 58 students or 27% of the sample.

Super Mario Brothers and Mortal Kombat both involve considerable violence in the sense that the player typically spends a considerable amount of time destroying other creatures. However, Super Mario Brothers is a cartoon-like game designed for kids, and is not classified as violent by many people. Mortal Kombat is one of the most graphically violent games available. Tetris is a totally nonviolent game. Super Mario Brothers was included free with purchase of the Nintendo system for some time, which may account for part of its popularity. So, one could see this list of the top three games as being fairly positive (if one views Super Mario Brothers as harmless) or as being not so positive.

Of the 911 game classifications made by the participants, 21% were in the fighting category. However, a number of classifications of clearly violent/aggressive games were to one of the other categories. For instance, one person who listed Mortal Kombat as a favorite game classified it as a "sports" game. If these suspect classifications are added to the fighting category, the percentage of violent/aggressive games jumped to almost 33%. If Super Mario Brothers is counted as an aggressive game (even when the participant put it in another category), the percentage jumps to 44%.

It is important to keep in mind that our participant population consisted of those who had been admitted to a large state university. The preferences of their junior high and high school peers who did not get into college might be quite different.

## *Main analyses*

### *Zero-order correlations*

Table 1 presents the zero-order correlations between the key continuous independent and dependent variables. One male student failed to complete (or start) the AQ, so his data were dropped from all regression analyses. Table 1 reveals confirmation of both main hypotheses derived from GAAM: Aggressive delinquent behavior was positively related to both trait aggressiveness and exposure to video game violence ($r$s = .36 and .46, respectively). Nonaggressive delinquent behavior was also positively related to both trait aggressiveness and exposure to video game violence ($r$s = .33 and .31, respectively). Furthermore, exposure to video game violence was positively related to aggressive personality ($r = .22$).

It is interesting to note that exposure to video game violence was more strongly correlated with aggressive delinquent behavior than with nonaggressive delinquent behavior, t(223)= 2.64, $p < .05$. It is important to keep in mind that nonaggressive delinquent behavior includes some behaviors that are frequently (but not always) performed with the intent to harm another person.

Point biserial correlations involving gender of participant revealed that gender was strongly related to a number of the variables, especially perceived safety ($r = .68$), video game violence ($r = .43$), and time spent playing video games

*Table 1* Zero-order correlations and alphas: study 1

| Variable | 1 | 2 | 3 | 4 | 5 | 6 | 7 | 8 | 9 |
|---|---|---|---|---|---|---|---|---|---|
| 1 AB | (.73) | .54* | −.03 | .24* | .46* | .36* | .20* | .20* | −.11 |
| 2 NAB | .54* | (.89) | −.08 | .19* | .31* | .33* | .15* | .15* | −.15* |
| 3 Crime | −.03 | −.08 | (.86) | −.27* | −.05 | −.07 | −.26* | −.09 | −.05 |
| 4 Safety | .24* | .19* | −.27 | (.82) | .35* | .23* | .68* | .25* | −.05 |
| 5 VGV | .46* | .31* | −.05 | .35* | (.86) | .22* | .43* | .28* | −.08 |
| 6 AP | .36* | .33* | −.07 | .23* | .22* | −a | .19* | .16* | −.15* |
| 7 Gender | .20* | .15* | −.26 | .68* | .43* | .19* | – | .35* | −.18* |
| 8 Time | .20* | .15* | −.09 | .25* | .28* | .16* | .35* | (.84) | −20* |
| 9 GPA | −.11 | −.15* | −.05 | −.05 | −.08 | −.15* | −.18* | −.20* | — |

*Note:* $N = 226$ for all correlations. Alphas are shown in parentheses on the diagonal. Dashes indicate single-item measures. AB = aggressive delinquent behavior; NAB = nonaggressive delinquent behavior; Crime = perception of general crime chances; Safety = perception of personal safety; VGV = long-term exposure to video game violence; AP = aggressive personality; Gender = point biserial correlations with women coded as 0, men as 1; Time = time spent playing video games; GPA = grade point average.
a AP was the average of the CIS and AQ scores, which had alphas of .88 and .90, respectively.
* $p < .05$.

($r = .35$). Males felt more safe, played more violent video games, and played more video games in general than did females.

Time spent playing video games in general was also positively related to both types of delinquent behaviors ($rs = .20$ and .15, respectively) but less strongly than was exposure to video game violence. Another interesting finding to emerge from data shown in Table 1 concerns GPA. Video game violence was negatively, but not significantly, related to GPA ($r = -.08$), but time spent playing video games in general was significantly and negatively correlated (r = − .20) with GPA. A number of additional interesting correlations can be seen in Table 1, but the overall patterns are best understood by the more complex analyses to follow.

## Aggressive behavior

### DESTRUCTIVE TESTING

Our primary goal in Study 1 was to examine the relation between long-term exposure to violent video games and real-life aggressive behavior. Our first set of analyses used a destructive testing approach (Anderson & Anderson, 1996). In the destructive testing approach, one determines whether a specific predicted relation exists. If so, one enters competitive variables into the regression model to determine whether these competitors break the target relation or not. Of primary interest is not whether the initial target link can be broken (i.e., made non-significant), because the assumption is that even strong causal links between measured variables can eventually be broken by adding more correlated competitors into the model. Rather, the focus is on how durable the link appears given the theoretical and empirical strength of the competitor variables used to test the target link.

Our first model predicted aggressive behavior with exposure to video game violence (VGV). In three subsequent regressions, we added general video game playing time (Time), aggressive personality (AP), and gender of participant as predictors, keeping all prior predictors in the model. For each of these four regressions, we report the slope relating VGV to aggressive behavior, the unique percentage of variance accounted for by the video game playing measure, and the $t$ value testing the video game playing effect against 0. In Table 2 the results for the destructive testing of the links between VGV and three dependent variables are displayed, beginning with the one most relevant to this section—aggressive delinquent behavior.

As can be seen in the first three rows of Table 2, the VGV-aggressive behavior link was not broken in any of the destructive tests. In all cases, VGV was positively and significantly related to aggressive behavior, both statistically (all **ps** < .001) and in terms of percentage of total variance explained, which ranged from over 21% (when VGV was the only predictor) to 13% (when all three competitor variables were first partialed out). Thus, the link between VGV and aggressive behavior is quite strong indeed.

In the final destructive test, the only predictor other than VGV to attain statistical significance was AP (**b** = .156, $t$ (220) = 4.51, **p** < .001). It accounted for

*Table 2* Destructive testing of video game links to aggressive behavior, nonaggressive delinquency, safety feelings, and grade point average: slopes, percentage variance accounted for, and t tests of links between video game playing and key dependent variables

| Dependent variable/Target predictor | Variables in the model | | | |
|---|---|---|---|---|
| | VGV | +Time | +AP | +Gender |
| Aggressive behavior/Video game violence | | | | |
| Video game violence slopes | .274 | .262 | .232 | .241 |
| Percentage variance explained by video game play | 21.61 | 18.18 | 13.77 | 12.99 |
| t value | 7.86* | 7.21* | 6.54* | 6.34* |
| Nonaggressive delinquency/Video game violence | | | | |
| Video game violence slopes | .155 | .146 | .120 | .124 |
| Percentage variance explained by video game play | 9.92 | 8.07 | 5.28 | 5.97 |
| t value | 4.97* | 4.48* | 3.76* | 3.64* |
| Safety feelings/Video game violence | | | | |
| Video game violence slopes | .573 | .495 | .450 | .094 |
| Percentage variance explained by video game play | 12.28 | 8.48 | 6.72 | 0.26 |
| t value | 5.60* | 4.70* | 4.24* | 1.04 |
| | Time | +VGV | +AP | +Gender |
| GPA/Time spent playing video games | | | | |
| Time spent playing video games slopes | −.129 | −.123 | −.115 | −.097 |
| Percentage variance explained by video game play | 3.85 | 3.25 | 2.80 | 1.84 |
| t value | 3.00* | 2.75* | 2.56* | 2.09* |
| df | 224 | 223 | 222 | 221 |

*Note:* VGV = video game violence; Time = time spent playing any type of video game; AP = aggressive personality; GPA = grade point average.
* $p < .05$.

about 7% of the total variance in aggressive behavior. The fact that Time did not "break" the VGV effect and that it didn't contribute significantly to the prediction of aggressive behavior in the final (or any) destructive tests suggests that violent video game play is the most important video game predictor of aggressive behavior.

## MODERATION BY INDIVIDUAL DIFFERENCES

Our second set of analyses was designed to examine the potential moderating effects of individual differences in aggression on aggressive behavior. Mixed-model hierarchical regression analyses tested a model in which self-reported aggressive delinquent behavior was predicted by violent video game play, AP, and gender of participant. Recall that the continuous variable predictors (VGV, AP) were standardized prior to these analyses.

All higher order interactions were tested. We used the conventional alpha of .05 for main and two-way interactions. However, because of the large number of unpredicted three-way interactions, we used a more conservative .01 alpha to help guard against Type I errors.

Results showed the predicted main effect of violent video game play on aggression, $F(1, 222) = 42.88, p < .0001, MSE = .252$. Greater exposure to violent video games predicted greater aggressive behavior, $b = .246$. There was also a main effect of AP on aggressive behavior, $F(1, 222) = 21.08, p < .0001, MSE = .252$, such that high trait aggressive individuals reported more instances of aggressive behavior than did low trait aggressive individuals, $b = .159$. The main effect of gender of participant did not approach significance ($F < 1$). The $R^2$ for this main effects model was .284.

One of the two-way interactions was significant. The VGV × AP interaction was quite large, accounting for 24% of the variance, $F(1, 219) = 125.09, p < .0001, MSE = .147$. As can be seen in Figure 3, this huge interaction resulted from the fact that the VGV effect on aggression occurred primarily among participants with high AP scores. Neither of the other two-way interactions approached significance ($ps > .20$). The $R^2$ for this main effects and two-way interactions model was .588.

The three-way VGV × AP × Gender interaction was also significant and is illustrated in Figure 4, $F(1, 218) = 8.30, p < .005, MSE = .142$. It accounted for less than **2%** of the variance in aggressive behavior, but is readily interpretable. For high AP participants there was a positive relation between VGV and aggression, but this was much stronger for men than women. For low AP people, however, there was little effect of VGV on aggression regardless of gender.

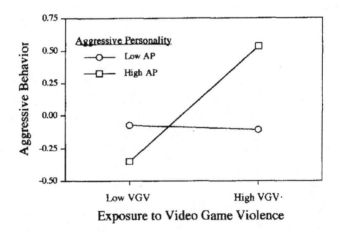

*Figure 3* Effect of exposure to video game violence (VGV) on aggressive behavior as a function of aggressive personality (AP)

(We created Figures 3 and 4 by doing a median split on AP then calculating the VGV–aggressive behavior regression lines for high and low AP participants separately.) The full model yielded an $R^2$ of .603.

## Nonaggressive delinquency

Table 2 also contains the destructive testing results for the nonaggressive delinquency measure. As noted earlier, the VGV effect was considerably smaller on nonaggressive delinquency than on aggressive behavior (compare also the percentage variance results in Table 2). Nonetheless, VGV consistently accounted for a significant unique portion of variation in nonaggressive delinquency. Those who reported more VGV exposure also reported higher levels of nonaggressive delinquency, all $ps < .001$, even when all three competitor variables were in the model. The percentage variation uniquely attributable to VGV ranged from almost 10% (when VGV was the only predictor) to a bit over 5%.

As with aggressive behavior, in the final destructive test the only predictor other than VGV to attain statistical significance was AP, $b = .137$, $t(222) = 4.41$, $p < .001$. It accounted for about 7% of the total variance in nonaggressive delinquency. Once again, the fact that Time did not break the VGV effect and that it didn't contribute significantly to the prediction of aggressive behavior in the final (or any) destructive tests suggests that violent video game play is the most important video game predictor of both nonaggressive delinquency and aggressive behavior.

MODERATION BY INDIVIDUAL DIFFERENCES

The hierarchical regression analyses on the full 3-factor model yielded similar results. The $R^2$ for the main effects model was .172. There were significant main effects of VGV, $F\{1, 222\} = 14.32$, $p < .001$, $MSE = .203$, and AP, $F(1, 222) = 19.46$, $p < .001$, $MSE = .203$. The gender main effect did not approach significance ($F < 1$). VGV and AP were both positively related to nonaggressive delinquency, $bs = .128$ and $.137$, respectively.

There was also a substantial VGV × AP interaction, $F(1, 219) = 33.27$, $p < .001$, $MSE = .176$, such that the VGV effect was stronger for participants high in AP than for participants low in AP. This effect accounted for over 10% of the variation in nonaggressive delinquency. This interaction is presented in Figure 5. None of the other interactions was significant. The $R^2$ for the full model with all main effects and two-way interactions was .297.

## World view: feeling safe

Data shown in Table 1 indicated that all four predictors—VGV, AP, Gender, and Time—were positively correlated with feelings of safety. Destructive testing revealed that the link between VGV and safety feelings survived the addition of the Time and AP factors, but did not survive the addition of Gender to the model (see Table 2).

The hierarchical regression results showed that gender differences accounted for a large portion of the variance in safety feelings. In the model containing VGV, AP, and gender, the only significant effect was the main effect of gender, $F(1, 222) = 135.92, p < .001$, $MSE = 1.43$. The $R^2$ for the main effect model was .471; for the full model it was .483.

In the model containing Time (instead of the VGV predictor) only the Gender and Time main effects were significant, $F(1, 222) = 153.25$ and $4.24$, $ps < .001$ and $.05$, respectively, $MSE = 1.44$. The $R^2$ for the main effect model was .468; for the full model it was .481. As expected, women reported feeling significantly less safe than did men (e.g., adjusted means for the VGV model were 3.38 and 5.55 for female and male participants, respectively).

### World view: crime opinions

The zero-order correlations (Table 1) showed that only gender of participant reliably correlated with crime likelihood estimates. Therefore, there was no link to video game playing experience to subject to destructive testing. Men gave lower estimates of crime than did women, $r$ (point biserial) $= -.26$.

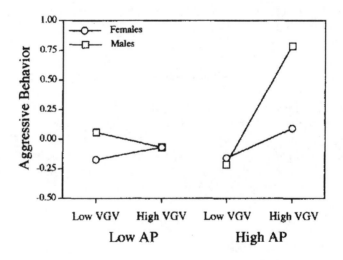

*Figure 4* Effect of exposure to video game violence (VGV) on aggressive behavior as a function of aggressive personality (AP) and gender

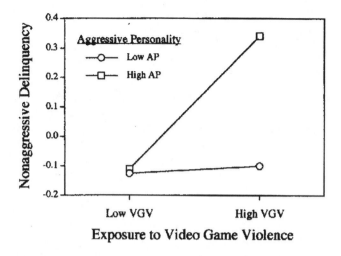

*Figure 5* Effect of exposure to video game violence (VGV) on nonaggressive delinquency as a function of aggressive personality (AP)

Hierarchical regression analyses with VGV, AP, and Gender as predictor variables were again used to further investigate the crime estimate variable. These analyses yielded only a main effect of gender, $F(1, 222) = 16.04, p < .01, MSE =$ 358.86, such that women rated violent crimes as more likely to occur than did men (adjusted **Ms** = 41.82 and 30.01, respectively). The $R^2$ for the main effects model was .072. None of the other effects reached statistical significance. A similar set of hierarchical analyses using Time instead of VGV yielded almost identical results. The only significant effect was the main effect of gender, $F(1, 222) = 13.14,$ $p < .001, MSE = 361.04$. The $R^2$ for the full model was .089.

*Academic achievement: GPA*

DESTRUCTIVE TESTING

Results shown in Table 1 revealed a significant negative correlation between GPA and Time ($r = -.20$). Our destructive testing of this small relation consisted of adding VGV, AP, and Gender as competitor variables, in that order. The results are displayed in Table 2. Though the magnitude of the GPA–Time relation was weakened by the addition of these variables, the link did not break. By itself, Time accounted for nearly 4% of the variance in GPA, $b = -.13, t(224) = 3.00, p < .01$. With all three competitors in the model, Time accounted for nearly **2%** of GPA variance, $b = -.10,$ $t(221) = 2.09, p < .05$.

MODERATION BY INDIVIDUAL DIFFERENCES

Hierarchical regression analyses yielded only one statistically significant effect. Time was significantly related to GPA, $F(1, 222) = 4.17, p < .05, MSE = .41$, such that more Time predicted lower GPAs ($b = -.093$). The $R^2$ for the main effects model was .063; for the full model it was .078.

## Discussion

Taken together, these results paint an interesting picture. Violent video game play and aggressive personality separately and jointly accounted for major portions of both aggressive behavior and nonaggressive delinquency. Violent video game play was also shown to be a superior predictor of both types of delinquency compared with time spent playing all types of video games. This is also consistent with our GAAM formulation and suggests that future research (unlike most past work) needs to distinguish between these types of video games.

The positive association between violent video games and aggressive personality is consistent with a developmental model in which extensive exposure to violent video games (and other violent media) contributes to the creation of an aggressive personality. The cross-sectional nature of this study does not allow a strong test of this causal hypothesis, but a zero or negative correlation would have disconfirmed the hypothesis, so the test is a legitimate one.

We also found that for university students, total time spent in the recent past on video games has a potential detrimental effect on grades. Interestingly, Huesmann's (1986) theory and data on TV violence suggest that violent video game exposure should be related to decrements in academic achievement because of the disruption of progress in school that is associated with increases in aggressive behavior engendered by media violence exposure. One plausible reason why this relationship was not observed in the present data may involve the nature of our population. College students are preselected on the basis of high school achievement and standardized test scores. Those with serious decrements in intellectual functioning or serious aggressive behavior problems are not as frequently represented in college samples as would be the case in a high school sample. Future research should examine the relationship between violent video game play and academic achievement in a high-school-aged sample.

In sum, Study 1 indicates that concern about the deleterious effects of violent video games on delinquent behavior, aggressive and nonaggressive, is legitimate. Playing violent video games often may well cause increases in delinquent behaviors, both aggressive and nonaggressive. However, the correlational nature of Study 1 means that causal statements are risky at best. It could be that the obtained video game violence links to aggressive and nonaggressive delinquency are wholly due to the fact that highly aggressive individuals are especially attracted to violent video games. Longitudinal work along the lines of Eron and Huesmann's work on TV violence (e.g., Eron, Huesmann, Dubow, Romanoff, & Yarmel, 1987) would be very informative.

Study 1 was informative in that it measured video game experience, aggressive personality, and delinquent behavior in real life. Its focus was on potentially negative consequences of long-term exposure to video game violence. Study 2

350

focused on short-term effects of video game violence. An experimental methodology was also used to more clearly address the causality issue. If the GAAM view of video game effects is correct, then we should be able to detect violent video game effects on short-term aggression and on aggressive cognitions using an experimental design and games chosen to differ primarily in the amount of violent content.

## Study 2: experimental test of video game violence effects

### *Pilot study*

The pilot study was conducted to choose video games for use in the main experiment. Our goal was to control for possible differences between nonviolent and violent video games on other dimensions that may be relevant to aggressive behavior, most notably enjoyment, frustration level, and physiological arousal. The current pilot study addressed these issues.

### *Video games*

The video game Wolfenstein 3D was selected to be pilot tested because of its blatant violent content, realism, and human characters. In Wolfenstein 3D the human hero can choose from an array of weaponry including a revolver, a knife, automatic weapons, and a flame thrower. The hero's goal is to use these weapons to kill Nazi guards in Castle Wolfenstein to advance through a number of levels; the ultimate goal is to kill Adolph Hitler. The graphics of this game are very violent; a successful player will see multiple bloody murders and hear victims scream and groan. The play control is easy and intuitive and the 3D setting is realistic. We also chose the violent game Marathon for pilot testing. Marathon is set up in the same basic format as Wolfenstein 3D except that the locale is an alien spaceship and the enemies are humanoid aliens with green blood.[1]

The nonviolent games chosen for the pilot study were Myst and Tetrix. Myst is an award-winning interactive adventure game that was specifically designed to be nonviolent in nature. It shares the 3D "walk through" format of Wolfenstein 3D and Marathon. Tetrix (which is comparable to Tetris) is an engaging, fast-paced, thinking game in which players attempt to align colorful geometric figures as they fall down a computer screen.

### *Method*

Thirty-two (18 female, 14 male) participants were recruited from the introductory psychology participant pool of a large Midwestern university and participated for partial course credit. Participants were run individually by a female experimenter. Participants were informed that we were choosing video games for use in a future study and that they would be asked a variety of questions about each of four games.

351

We measured blood pressure and heart rate several times during the study. Games were presented in one of four counterbalanced orders to control for order effects.

After each game, the experimenter took the physiological measures, had the participant complete a "Video Game Rating Sheet" and asked the participant for any advice on changing the instructions or controls of the video game. On the Video Game Rating Sheet participants indicated, on 7-point unipolar scales, how difficult, enjoyable, frustrating, and exciting the games were as well as how fast the action was and how violent the content and graphics of the game were. These items were drawn from those used by Anderson and Ford (1986). After participating, participants were debriefed and given experimental credit.

## Results

The goal of the pilot study was to select a pair of games that differed primarily in amount of violence. The goal was best achieved by pairing of Myst and Wolfenstein 3D. These two games did not produce differences in systolic blood pressure, diastolic blood pressure, heart rate, or mean arterial pressure (all $ps > .3$). There were also no differences on ratings of game difficulty, enjoyment, frustration, and action speed (all $ps > .05$). However, Wolfenstein 3D was rated as more exciting than Myst ($Ms$ = 4.81 and 3.40, respectively), $F(1, 27) = 10.46$, $p < .01$. Further analyses revealed that this was true only for the male participants, $F(1, 10) = 12.08$, $p < .01$, and not for the female participants, $F(1, 14) = 2.50, p > .13$.

Myst and Wolfenstein 3D matched well, but because of the rated difference in excitement level, we decided to include the same Video Game Rating Sheet in the main experiment for use as a statistical control.

### Main experiment

#### Overview

Two hundred ten (104 female, 106 male) undergraduates from a large Midwestern university participated for partial credit in their introductory psychology course. In this experiment we examined the effects of violent video game play on aggressive thought, affect, and behavior and on world view. We also examined the interactive effects of gender and trait irritability on these variables. The design is thus a 2 (violent video game vs. nonviolent video game) × 2 (high irritability vs. low irritability) × 2 (male vs. female) between-subjects factorial design.

To give participants ample playing experience with the assigned video game, we arranged for them to come to the laboratory for two separate sessions. Each participant played the assigned video game a total of three times. In the first experimental session, participants played the game, completed the affective and world view measures, played the game again, then completed the cognitive measure. During the next session, participants played the game one last time and

352

completed the behavioral measure. All participants had been preselected by their trait irritability score.

## Method and procedure

### Preselection of participants

The CIS (Caprara et al., 1985) was administered to the introductory psychology participant pool during mass testing questionnaire sessions several weeks before the experiment was begun. The full 30-item scale was used. Participants scoring in the bottom fourth of the distribution were considered to have low irritability and participants scoring in the top fourth of the distribution were considered to have high irritability. Participants both low and high in irritability were recruited by telephone and participated for course credit. Note that this Trait Irritability Scale was a part of what we called our Aggressive Personality index in Study 1 but that we will refer to it in Study 2 as Trait Irritability (TI).

### Laboratory session 1

All instructions for starting or stopping video game play or computerized dependent measures took place over an intercom. The main reason for the intercom-based instructions was so the participant was always reminded that there was another participant present. In fact, even in cases in which the second cubicle was empty, the experimenter play-acted as if the second participant were actually there—entering the second cubicle and speaking, the same instructions aloud to the nonexistent partner.

For the first session, participants were scheduled in pairs to come into the laboratory for 1 hour. Upon arriving at the laboratory, each participant was escorted to a cubicle that contained an intercom and a chair facing a color Macintosh computer equipped with a voice key (MacRecorder) and a pair of headphones. A female experimenter asked each participant to read and sign a consent form, to read a brief overview of the study, and to familiarize themselves with instructions that explained how to play the video game to which they were assigned (either Myst or Wolfenstein 3D). The experimenter then informed the participant that she would contact them when she was ready to begin and closed the door to the participant's cubicle.

#### COVER STORY

The overview informed participants that they would be taking part in a study called "The Learning Curve," which was purported to investigate how people learn and develop skills at motor tasks like video games and how these skills affect other tasks such as cognitive tasks and other motor tasks. Participants were also told that their video game play was being recorded to examine skill development.

To make this believable, a VCR was set up near their computer, with wires running from the VCR to the computer. The two-session format was consistent with this motor skills development cover story as well.

## GAME PLAY NO. 1

After participants had read the cover story and had familiarized themselves with a written set of video game instructions, the experimenter entered the participant's cubicle and engaged the video game software. She reviewed the video game controls and asked for any questions about how to play the game. Then she asked the participant to wait until she gave the signal to begin, which would take place over the intercom system. At the appropriate time, the experimenter asked participants to put on a pair of headphones and play the video game. She informed them that she would stop them in 15 min.

## RATINGS

After 15 min of video game play, the experimenter stopped participants and saved their video game file on the computer. This was to keep up the cover story that the experimenters were interested in the player's video game performance. She then started a computer program that collected the affective data. The affective measure was the State Hostility Scale developed by Anderson and colleagues (Anderson, 1997; Anderson et al., 1995, 1996). In this scale participants are asked to indicate their level of agreement to 35 statements such as "I feel angry" and "I feel mean." Participants respond on 5-point scales anchored at 1 **(strongly disagree),** 2 **(disagree),** 3 **(neither agree nor disagree),** 4 **(agree),** and 5 *(strongly agree).* Some of the items are positive as stated (e.g., "I feel friendly") and thus were reverse scored for data analysis. Recent work by Anderson and colleagues (e.g., Anderson, 1997; Anderson et al., 1995, 1996) has shown that acute situational variables such as pain, provocation, violent movie clips, and uncomfortably cold and hot temperatures increase State Hostility scores.

Following the State Hostility Scale, the computer presented the same video game rating items that had been used in the pilot study, including the rating of how exciting the game was. Next, participants completed the same world view measure used in Study 1.

## GAME PLAY NO. 2

The computer program that collected the state hostility, video game, and world view data concluded with instructions for the participants to crack the door to their cubicle when they were finished. The experimenter then entered the participant's cubicle, stored the data on the computer, and restarted the video game software. The experimenter then asked the participant to wait until signaled to begin another 15-min video game playing session. When both participants were ready, the experimenter again signaled the participants by means of an intercom to put on their headphones and begin playing the video game. She informed them that she would stop them in 15 min. At that time, the experimenter returned and saved the participant's video game playing session. She then started the computer program that would collect the cognitive data.

The cognitive measure of aggressive thinking was the reading reaction time task used by Anderson and colleagues (Anderson, 1997; Anderson et al., 1996; Anderson, Benjamin, & Bartholow, 1998). This task presents aggressive words (e.g., murder) and three types of control words individually on a computer screen. The participant's task is to read each word aloud as quickly as possible. The three types of control words are anxiety words (e.g., humiliated), escape words (e.g., leave), and control words (e.g., consider). There are 24 words in each category. Each word is presented twice, for a total of 192 trials, with 48 trials for each word type. The four word lists have been equated for word length. The word "resign," which was used in previous studies as a control word, was later deemed an escape word. Thus, for this study, "resign" was replaced by "report."

Each word is presented on the computer screen in Times 12 font, with a period separating the letters of the word. The computer records the reaction time to each word. Words were presented in the same random order for each participant.

When participants finished, the experimenter reminded them of the time they were scheduled to return for the final portion of the study, thanked them for their time, and allowed them to leave. No debriefing information was given at this time.

## Laboratory session 2

Approximately 1 week later, participants returned to the laboratory to complete the final phases of the study. Participants came alone, but the procedures discussed earlier were carried out in this second session as well, so that participants would believe there was another participant in the second cubicle.

### VIDEO GAME PLAY

The experimenter seated the participant in a cubicle, started the video game software, and asked if there were any questions about how to play the game. Then the experimenter asked the participant to wait until everyone was ready to begin. At that point, the experimenter said that she would give verbal instructions over the intercom for them to proceed with playing the game, as she had done in the first session.

### AGGRESSIVE BEHAVIOR

After 15 min, the experimenter entered the participant's cubicle, saved the video game file, and started the competitive reaction time task on the computer. In the competitive reaction time task, the participant's goal is to push a button faster than his or her opponent. If participants lose this race, they receive a noise blast at a level supposedly set by the opponent (actually set by the computer). Aggressive behavior is operationally defined as the intensity and duration of noise blasts the participant chooses to deliver to the opponent.

The competitive reaction time task used in this study was the same basic computer program used by Bushman (1995) and by Dorr and Anderson (1995). It is based on the Taylor Competitive Reaction Time task, which is a widely used and externally valid measure of aggressive behavior (see Anderson & Bushman, 1997; Anderson, Lindsay, & Bushman, 1999; Bushman & Anderson, 1998; Carlson, Marcus-Newhall, & Miller, 1989; Giancola & Chermack, 1998).

We used 25 competitive reaction time trials; the participant won 13 and lost 12. The pattern of wins and losses was the same for each participant. Prior to each trial the participant set noise intensity and duration levels. Intensity was set by clicking on a scale that ranged from 0 to 10. Duration was set by holding down a "Ready" button and was measured in milliseconds, After each trial the participants were shown on their computer screen the noise levels supposedly set by their opponent. For this experiment, the noise blast intensities supposedly set by the opponent were designed to appear in a random pattern. Specifically, three noise blasts of intensity Levels 2, 3, 4, 6, 7, 8, and 9, and four noise blasts of Level 5 were randomly assigned to the 25 trials. A noise blast at Level 1 corresponded to 55 decibels, a noise blast at Level 2 corresponded to 60 decibels, and the decibels increased by five for each subsequent noise blast level to a maximum of 100 decibels for a noise blast at Level 10. Similarly, the duration of noise blasts the participant received were determined by the computer, were in a random pattern, and were the same for each participant. The durations varied from 0.5 seconds to 1.75 seconds.

Pilot testing and prior use of this competitive reaction time game had revealed that participants frequently did not understand how to vary the duration of noise supposedly to be delivered to their opponent. We therefore modified this version and the instructions to highlight the noise duration aspects of the game.

As the competitive reaction time program begins, participants are asked to read a set of instructions from the computer screen. Because it was crucial to the validity of our results that participants understand the task, the experimenter also read participants a set of standardized instructions by means of an intercom. The instructions read,

> We are now ready to do the competitive reaction time task. You will set a noise level that your opponent will hear if they lose. You will do this by clicking on the noise level bar at your right. Where you click on the bar determines how loud the noise is. How long you hold down on the bar determines how long your opponent will hear the noise. (PAUSE.) After you set the noise level and duration, click the "Ready" button. (PAUSE.) Wait for the yellow box to appear. This is a warning that the tone is about to sound. As soon as you hear the tone, click your mouse as fast as you can. (PAUSE.) If you lose, you will hear the noise your opponent has set for

you. If you win, your opponent will hear the noise you have set for them. Either way, you will see which noise level your opponent set for you. You will do this several times. (PAUSE.) If you have questions, please open your door now. (PAUSE.) We are now ready to begin. Please make sure you have your headphones on now and click on the arrow which says, "Begin Experiment" in the upper right hand corner of your screen. Please begin now, and open your door when you are finished.

DEBRIEFING

When the participant opened the cubicle door, the experimenter entered the cubicle, gave the participant a debriefing statement that explained the procedures and hypotheses of the study and debunked the cover story, and gave the participant full experimental credit. After answering any questions, the experimenter thanked and dismissed the participant.

## *Results*

### *Video game questions*

Recall that pilot testing had revealed a significant difference in the excitement level of the game (based on self-report data but not on the physiological data) between Myst and Wolfenstein 3D. We included game excitement as a covariate in all the models that follow because of the pilot study results, but it was not a significant predictor in any of the models. We also measured game difficulty and frustration level. Game frustration was a significant covariate in the model with state hostility as the dependent variable. Game difficulty was a significant covariate in the model predicting reading reaction time. However, the addition of these covariates to the overall model did not appreciably alter the effects of most interest.

### *State hostility*

The 35 items on the State Hostility Scale (Anderson, 1997) were averaged into a composite. The coefficient alpha calculated for the entire scale was .96. Correlational analyses indicated that one item, "I feel willful," was slightly negatively correlated with the rest of the scale items. This was not surprising as this particular item had been problematic in past research. This item was deleted, although deleting the item did not appreciably alter the effects presented.

A 2 (game type) X 2 (gender) X 2 (trait irritability) between- subjects analysis of variance (ANOVA) was performed with State Hostility as the dependent variable and with Game Excitement as a covariate. The $R^2$ for this model was .17. Results indicated significant main effects of irritability, $F(1, 201) = 29.98$, $p < .0001$, $MSE = .40$, and of gender, $F(1, 201) = 4.73$, $p < .05$, $MSE = .40$. As expected, those higher in TI reported more state hostility ($M = 2.52$) than those lower in TI ($M = 2.05$). Women reported more hostility ($M = 2.38$) than men ($M = 2.19$). The game type effect as well as all two- and three-way interactions between the independent variables were nonsignificant (all $ps > .05$).

## Crime and safety ratings

For both the crime and the safety rating indexes, the only significant effect was gender of participant. Women gave higher estimates of violent crime likelihood than did men ($Ms = 37.16$ and $25,.82$, respectively), $F(1, 200) = 21.75, p < .001$, $MSE = 313, R^2 = .14$. However, women reported lower feelings of safety than did men ($Ms = 3.63$ and $5.69$, respectively), $F(1, 201) = 152.92, p < .001, MSE = 1.45$, $R^2 = .44$. None of the other effects approached significance.

## Accessibility of aggressive thoughts

### DATA PREPARATION

Each participant responded to a total of 192 reading reaction time trials. These 192 were made up of 2 sets of 24 trials for each of the four types of words (aggressive, control, escape, and anxiety). We followed the data cleaning procedure used by Anderson (1997), which involves identifying outliers according to Tukey's (1977) exploratory data techniques. Low and high outliers were changed to missing values. Low outliers (defined here as trials below 275 ms) may occur because of noise other than the participant's reading of the word, such as a door being slammed in an adjacent hallway. High outliers (defined here as trials above 875 ms) may occur because of a lack of attention by the participant or a failure to pronounce the word loud enough to trigger the voice key. Out of 40,320 data points, 2,391 (about 6%) were removed as outliers. In addition, three participants did not have reading reaction time data because of computer malfunctions. Thus, all the reading reaction time analyses are based on 207 participants.

### MAIN ANALYSES

Following the analysis procedure outlined by Anderson (1997), the first step was to see if reaction times to the three control word types (control, anxiety, and escape) were differentially affected by the video game manipulations. A repeated measures ANOVA on the three control word types did not produce a significant control word type by game type interaction, $F(2, 197) = 2.82, p > .05$. Therefore, reaction times to the three types of control words (control, anxiety, and escape) were combined into a composite. A new variable was then formed in which the average reaction time to aggressive words was subtracted from the average reaction time to control words. This new variable is the Aggression Accessibility Index. People with relatively high scores have relatively greater access to aggressive thoughts.

A 2 (game type) × 2 (gender) × 2 (trait irritability) between-subjects ANOVA was performed on Aggression Accessibility with Game Excitement as a covariate.

Results yielded the predicted main effect of game type, $F(1, 198) = 31.35, p < .0001, MSE = 246.05$. Aggression Accessibility scores were higher for those who had played the violent video game ($M = 5.54$) than for those who had played the nonviolent video game ($M = -6.69$). In other words, the violent video game primed aggressive thoughts. This result suggests one potential way in which playing violent video games might increase aggressive behavior—by priming aggressive knowledge structures.

There was also a main effect of gender, $F(1,198) = 13.47, p < .001, MSE = 246.05$, such that Aggression Accessibility scores were higher for men ($M = 3.45$) than for women ($M = -4.60$). The TI effect, as well as the two- and three-way interactions were all nonsignificant ($ps > .05$). The $R^2$ for this model was .20.

The lack of a TI effect on aggression accessibility scores is puzzling. It has been found in several previous studies, with the same task as well as with a different lexical decision task (e.g., Anderson, 1997; Bushman, 1995; Lindsay & Anderson, in press). One possibility is that playing a highly violent versus a very mellow and nonviolent game for two 15-min periods of time was sufficient to temporarily override the usual differences between people high and low in irritability in relative accessibility of aggressive thoughts.

### Aggressive behavior

Prior to each trial in the competitive reaction time task, participants set the noise duration and intensity levels that supposedly would be delivered to their opponents if the participant won the trial. Data from three participants were lost because of computer failure. Eleven additional participants from Session 1 failed to show for this second session, leaving a total of 196 participants.

DATA PREPARATION

As is common with latency data, the duration settings were positively skewed and there was a systematic relation between group means and standard deviations. A log transformation was therefore applied to the duration data (Tukey, 1977).

Four aggression measures were constructed on the basis of the noise settings (duration or intensity) after both win and lose trials. We reasoned that retaliatory motives would be heightened after losing a trial (and therefore after receiving a noise blast from one's opponent), whereas winning a trial should reduce (at least temporarily) such motives. In other words, it may take both the cognitive priming of aggressive thoughts by violent video games and an immediate provocation (noise blast) by an opponent to trigger higher levels of aggression. Similarly, the emphasis placed in the instructions on how to control noise duration settings was expected to increase participants' use of this aggressive behavior, compared with what we've seen in previous work in our lab.

Both of these expectations were borne out. Indeed, our emphasis on the noise duration controls apparently interfered with participants' ability or willingness to use the intensity control. There were no statistically significant effects of any of the independent variables—gender, TI, video game type—on either the win or lose noise intensity settings. Therefore they will not be discussed further.

For the trials after participants had just won and had not received but had supposedly delivered a noise blast, the only significant effect was a main effect of gender, $F(1, 187) = 8.17$, $p < .01$, $MSE = .28$. Women ($M = 6.89$) delivered longer noise blasts than men ($M = 6.65$). The $R^2$ for this model is .08.

Duration of noise settings after lose trials yielded significant main effects of gender, TI, and game type. Just as on win trials, women delivered longer noise blasts after loss trials than did men, $Ms = 6.86$ and $6.59$, respectively, $F(1, 187) = 12.84$, $p < .001$, $MSE = .27$. High irritability participants delivered longer noise blasts than did low irritability participants, $Ms = 6.84$ and $6.65$, respectively, $F(1, 187) = 4.43$, $p < .05$, $MSE = .27$.

Most importantly, participants who had played Wolfenstein 3D delivered significantly longer noise blasts after lose trials than those who had played the nonviolent game Myst ($Ms = 6.81$ and $6.65$), $F(1, 187) = 4.82$, $p < .05$, $MSE = .27$. In other words, playing a violent video game increased the aggressiveness of participants after they had been provoked by their opponent's noise blast. In Figure 6 we illustrate both the irritability and the video game main effects. As can be seen, these two effects were about the same size, both were in the small to medium range.

There was also an Irritability × Gender interaction, $F(1, 187) = 7.04$, $p < .01$, $MSE = .27$, such that high trait irritability increased aggression by men ($Ms = 6.75$ and $6.47$ for men high and low in irritability) but not by women ($Ms = 6.84$ and $6.85$ for women high and low in irritability). The $R^2$ for this model is .14. Because this unexpected finding has not been reported previously in the literature we eschew speculation until it reappears in future studies.

### Mediational analyses

Playing the violent video game increased accessibility of aggressive thoughts and aggressive behavior but did not reliably increase state hostility. These findings suggest that VGV takes a cognitive and not an affective path to increasing aggressive behavior in short-term settings. To further test this idea we entered State Hostility as a covariate in the overall model relating video game violence to noise duration settings after the loss trials. The presence of State Hostility in the model did not eliminate the significance of the video game effect, $F(1, 186) = 4.43$, $p < .05$, $MSE = .26$, $R^2 - .15$. We performed the same covariance analysis with Aggression Accessibility as the covariate instead of State Hostility. Consistent

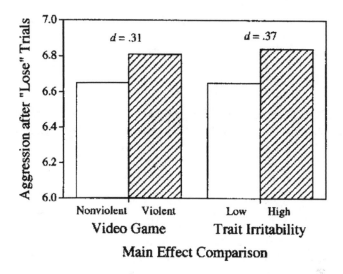

$d = .31$   $d = .37$

Nonviolent   Violent   Low   High
Video Game   Trait Irritability
Main Effect Comparison

*Figure 6* Main effects of video game and trait irritability on aggression (log duration) after "Lose" trials, Study 2

with a mediation hypothesis, the video game effect was reduced to marginal significance, $F(1, 186) = 3.08$, $p < .08$, $MSE = .26$, $R^2 = .15$.[2]

## General discussion

### Aggressive behavior effects

The present research demonstrated that in both a correlational investigation using self-reports of real-world aggressive behaviors and an experimental investigation using a standard, objective laboratory measure of aggression, violent video game play was positively related to increases in aggressive behavior. In the laboratory, college students who played a violent video game behaved more aggressively toward an opponent than did students who had played a nonviolent video game. Outside the laboratory, students who reported playing more violent video games over a period of years also engaged in more aggressive behavior in their own lives. Both types of studies—correlational–real delinquent behaviors and experimental–laboratory aggressive behaviors have their strengths and weaknesses. The convergence of findings across such disparate methods lends considerable strength to the main hypothesis that exposure to violent video games can increase aggressive behavior.

Though the existence of a violent video game effect cannot be unequivocally established on the basis of one pair of studies, this particular pair adds considerable support to prior work, both empirical and theoretical. When combined with what is known about other types of media violence effects, most notably TV violence (e.g., Eron et al., 1987; Huesmann & Miller, 1994), we believe that the present results confirm that parents, educators, and society in general should be concerned about the prevalence of violent video games in modern society, especially given recent advances in the realism of video game violence.

## Trait aggressiveness

One interesting difference between the results of the present two studies concerns the moderating effects of individual difference variables. The violent video game effect on aggressive behavior in Study 1 was moderated by individual differences in aggression such that the violent video game effect was stronger for those high in trait aggressiveness than for those low in trait aggressiveness. This moderating effect did not emerge in Study 2, though similar moderating effects have been found in other laboratory studies of media violence (e.g., Bushman, 1995). There are always several possible explanations for such discrepancies. One obvious possibility is that Study 1 used a composite of the CIS and the Buss-Perry AQ as the individual difference measure of aggressive personality, whereas Study 2 used only the CIS. To check on this possibility, we reanalyzed the Study 1 data using only the CIS, and found essentially the same results. For example, the Violent Video Game X CIS Score interaction in Study 1 was still highly significant, $F(1, 219) = 130.58$, $p < .001$, MSE = .145. It is also interesting to note that Irwin and Gross (1995) found no moderating effect of trait impulsivity on the violent video game effect they observed in their study of 7- and 8-year-old boys.

The fact that in Study 2 the video game effect and the trait irritability effect were of similar magnitude argues against the possibility that the video game manipulation simply overwhelmed individual differences in this setting. This suggests a third possibility: The AP X VGV interaction in Study 1 may reflect a long-term bidirectional causality effect in which frequent playing of violent video games increases aggressiveness, which in turn increases the desire and actual playing of even more violent video games. Such a cycle is not only plausible, but fits well with Huesmann's (1986) theorizing and data on TV violence effects.

## Sex differences

One additional behavioral result of Study 2 warrants comment: specifically, the finding that women displayed higher levels of state hostility and aggression than men. At first this result may seem very surprising given that men are generally seen as more aggressive than women. However, as Bettencourt and Miller's (1996) meta-analysis of provocation effects showed, gender differences vary considerably depending on setting and type of provocation. One possible explanation involves differences in liking for video games. In our participant population, men generally report playing more video games than women, as was seen in Study 1. Even a cursory examination of video game advertisements reveals a clearly male orientation. Thus, it is possible that both the higher reported level of state hostility and the higher level of aggression by women in Study 2 resulted from their being less familiar with video games or less happy at having to play them in this lab experiment. Furthermore, the ambiguous nature of the duration measure may well fit the aggressive style of women in our culture better than the style of men. In any case, what is most important to keep in mind is that exposure to the violent video game increased the aggression of both male and female participants.

### Underlying processes

The General Affective Aggression Model as well as the more domain-specific models on which it is based suggest that media violence effects occur through one of three routes: cognitive, affective, or arousal. In Study 2, games were selected to create equal arousal states as measured by heart rate and blood pressure. Furthermore, excitement ratings were used as a covariate to further ensure that this route was closed off in this investigation. The affective route was at least partially closed off by the selection of two games that were equally enjoyable and difficult. We then included measures of aggressive affect and cognition, and found that short-term VGV exposure increased the accessibility of aggression-related thoughts, but did not increase feelings of hostility. In the past, only one experimental investigation examined the effects of violent video game play on aggressive thoughts, Calvert and Tan (1994) found that participants listed more aggressive thoughts after playing a violent virtual-reality game. Thus, the current investigation supports and extends this very small literature on cognitive priming effects. This line of inquiry is especially important because it supports the various cognitive models of aggression on which GAAM is largely based (e.g., Anderson et al., 1995; Berkowitz, 1984, 1990, 1993; Huesmann, 1986).

Our findings do not rule out the possibility that under some circumstances violent video game effects on subsequent aggressive behavior might be mediated by increased feelings of hostility or by general arousal effects. Indeed, GAAM explicitly notes that thoughts, feelings, and arousal are intricately interconnected, sometimes to such an extent that they can't be disentangled.

The results of the current investigation suggest that short-term VGV effects may operate primarily through the cognitive, and not the affective, route to aggressive behavior (e.g., Anderson et al., 1995). This finding is consistent with Huesmann's (1986) social-cognitive theory of the development of aggressive reaction tendencies from media violence exposure. Thus, the danger in exposure to violent video games seems to be in the ideas they teach and not primarily in the emotions they incite in the player. The more realistic the violence, the more the player identifies with the aggressor. The more rewarding the video game, the greater potential for learning aggressive solutions to conflict situations.

### Academic achievement

We found that academic achievement (GPA) was not related to prior violent video game play in particular, but was related to long-term exposure to video games in general. Some past research has shown relations between video game play and decrements in academic achievement. For example, Harris and Williams (1985) reported a link between video game playing and lower English grades. However, other work has failed to find such a linkage. For example, Creasey and Myers (1986) found no long-term relationship between video game play and school activities, and Van Schie and Wiegman (1997) found a positive relation between general video game play and IQ.

As is the case in the video game literature in general, there is no definitive answer to the question of whether video games disrupt academic performance. There are enough hints of such an effect to warrant further investigation. That video game play in general, and not violent video game play, would produce decrements in academic achievement makes sense if the effect is based on time spent on such activities (rather than on academic activities) and not on a direct effect of the content of the games. Huesmann (1986) reasoned that the lessons taught by media violence can attenuate intellectual performance as well, through a series of inter- and intrapersonal processes, and has provided convincing evidence. However, the restricted range of academic achievement and of behavior problems in our college student sample raises the possibility that a less restricted sample may indeed show a unique violent video game effect on academic performance as well.

## Unique dangers of violent video games

The present data indicate that concern about the potentially deleterious consequences of playing violent video games is not misplaced. Further consideration of some key characteristics of violent video games suggests that their dangers may well be greater than the dangers of violent television or violent movies. There are at least three reasons for this. The first concerns identification with the aggressor. When viewers are told to identify with a media aggressor, postviewing aggression is increased compared with measured aggression of those who were not instructed to identify with the aggressor (e.g., Leyens & Picus, 1973). In "first person" video games the player assumes the identity of the hero, and sometimes chooses a character whose persona the player then assumes. The player controls the action of this character and usually sees the video game world through that character's eyes. In other words, the main character is synonymous with the game player, potentially heightening the game's impact.

The second reason for concern involves the active participation involved in video games. Research on the catharsis hypothesis reveals that aggressive behavior usually increases later aggressive behavior (Bushman, Baumeister, & Stack, in press; Geen & Quanty, 1977; Geen, Stonner, & Shope, 1975). The active role of the video game player includes choosing to aggress and acting in an aggressive manner. This choice and action component of video games may well lead to the construction of a more complete aggressive script than would occur in the more passive role assumed in watching violent movies or TV shows.

364

A third reason to expect video games to have a bigger impact than TV or movies involves their addictive nature. The reinforcement characteristics of violent video games may also enhance the learning and performance of aggressive scripts. Braun and Giroux (1989) noted that video games are "the perfect paradigm for the induction of 'addictive' behavior" (p. 101). Griffiths and Hunt (1998) found that one in five adolescents can be classified as pathologically dependent on computer games. Video game "addiction" may stem, in part, from the rewards and punishments the game gives the player (Braun & Giroux, 1989; Dill & Dill, 1998; Klein, 1984), much like the reward structure of slot machines. When the choice and action components of video games (discussed above) is coupled with the games' reinforcing properties, a strong learning experience results. In a sense, violent video games provide a complete learning environment for aggression, with simultaneous exposure to modeling, reinforcement, and rehearsal of behaviors. This combination of learning strategies has been shown to be more powerful than any of these methods used singly (Barton, 1981; Chambers & Ascione, 1987; Loftus & Loftus, 1983).

### *Summary and conclusions*

Violent video games provide a forum for learning and practicing aggressive solutions to conflict situations. The effect of violent video games appears to be cognitive in nature. In the short term, playing a violent video game appears to affect aggression by priming aggressive thoughts. Longer-term effects are likely to be longer lasting as well, as the player learns and practices new aggression-related scripts that become more and more accessible for use when real-life conflict situations arise. If repeated exposure to violent video games does indeed lead to the creation and heightened accessibility of a variety of aggressive knowledge structures, thus effectively altering the person's basic personality structure, the consequent changes in everyday social interactions may also lead to consistent increases in aggressive affect. The active nature of the learning environment of the video game suggests that this medium is potentially more dangerous than the more heavily investigated TV and movie media. With the recent trend toward greater realism and more graphic violence in video games and the rising popularity of these games, consumers of violent video games (and parents of consumers) should be aware of these potential risks.

Recent events in the news, such as the link between teenage murderers in Colorado and violent video game play, have sparked public debate about video game violence effects. As the debate continues, video games are becoming more violent, more graphic, and more prevalent. As scientists, we should add new research to the currently small and imperfect literature on video game violence effects and clarify for society exactly what these risks entail. The General Affective Aggression Model has proved useful in organizing a wide array of research findings on human aggression and in generating testable propositions, including the present studies of video game violence. Additional short-term studies of the effects of violent video games are needed to further specify the characteristics of games and of game players that reduce and intensify the aggression-related outcomes. Longitudinal studies of exposure to violent video games are needed to test the proposition that such exposure can produce stable changes in personality, changes of the type seen in research on long-term exposure to other violent media.

## Notes

This research was supported by the Psychology Department at the University of Missouri—Columbia. We thank Julie Tuggle, Luisa Stone, Kathy Neal, Shelby Stone, and Lynn McKinnon for their assistance in collecting data. We also thank William Benoit, Brad Bushman, Russell Geen, Mary Heppner, and Michael Stadler for comments on drafts of this article

1  The data for study 2 were collected in 1997. Since then, video games have become even more graphically violent, and the graphics have become even more realistic.
2  One procedural aspect of Study 2 may have reduced the effects of the video games on the dependent variables. Specifically, any time lag between video game play and the collection of the dependent measures may allow the effects of the video game to dissipate somewhat. This may be one explanation for the lack of state hostility changes due to video game. We thank an anonymous reviewer for pointing this out. Future research should attempt to speak to these concerns.

## References

Aiken, L. S., & West, S. G. (1991). **Multiple regression: Testing and interpreting interactions.** Newbury Park, CA: Sage.
Anderson, C. A. (1997). Effects of violent movies and trait hostility on hostile feelings and aggressive thoughts. **Aggressive Behavior, 23,** 161–178.
Anderson, C. A., &. Anderson, K. B. (1996). Violent crime rate studies in philosophical context: A destructive testing approach to heat and southern culture of violence effects. **Journal of Personality and Social Psychology, 70,** 740–756.
Anderson, C. A., Anderson, K. B., & Deuser, W. E. (1996). Examining an affective aggression framework: Weapon and temperature effects on aggressive thoughts, affect, and attitudes. **Personality and Social Psychology Bulletin, 22,** 366–376.
Anderson, K. B., Anderson, C. A., Dill, K. E., & Deuser, W. E. (1998). The interactive relations between trait hostility, pain, and aggressive thoughts. **Aggressive Behavior, 24,** 161–171.
Anderson, C. A., Benjamin, A. J., & Bartholow, B. D. (1998). Does the gun pull the trigger? Automatic priming effects of weapon pictures and weapon names. **Psychological Science, 9,** 308–314.
Anderson, C. A. & Bushman, B. J. (1997). External validity of "trivial" experiments: The case of laboratory aggression. **Review of General Psychology, 1,** 19–41.
Anderson, C. A. Deuser, W. E., & DeNeve, K. M. (1995). Hot temperatures, hostile affect, hostile cognition, and arousal: Tests of a general model of affective aggression. **Personality and Social Psychology Bulletin, 21,** 434–448.
Anderson, C. A., & Ford, C. M. (1986). Affect of the game player: Short term effects of highly and mildly aggressive video games. **Personality and Social Psychology Bulletin, 12,** 390–402.

Anderson, C. A., Lindsay, J. J., & Bushman, B. J. (1999). Research in the psychological laboratory: Truth or triviality? **Current Directions in Psychological Science,** *8,* 3–9.

Ballard, M. E., & Weist, J. R. (1996). Mortal Kombat: The effects of violent video game play on males' hostility and cardiovascular responding. **Journal of Applied Social Psychology, 26,** 717–730.

Bandura, A. (1971). Social learning theory of aggression. In J. G. Knutson (Ed.), *Control of aggression: Implications from basic research* (pp. 201–250). Chicago: Aldine-Atherton.

Bandura, A. (1973). **Aggression: A social learning analysis.** Englewood Cliffs, NJ: Prentice-Hall.

Bandura, A., Róss, D., & Ross, S. A. (1961). Transmission of aggression through imitation of aggressive models. **Journal of Abnormal and Social Psychology, 66,** 575–582.

Bandura, A., Ross, D., & Ross, S. A. (1963). Imitation of film-mediated aggressive models. **Journal of Abnormal and Social Psychology, 66,** 3–11.

Bargh, J. A. (1994). The four horsemen of automaticity: Awareness, intention, efficiency, and control in social cognition. In R. S. Wyer, Jr. & T. K. Srull (Eds.), **Handbook of social cognition: Basic processes** (2nd ed., pp. 1–40). New York: Guilford Press.

Barton, E. J. (1981). Developing sharing: An analysis of modeling and other behavioral techniques. **Behavior Modification, 5,** 396–398.

Berkowitz, L. (1984). Some effects of thoughts on anti- and prosocial influence of media events: A cognitive neoassociationist analysis. **Psychological Bulletin, 95,** 410–427.

Berkowitz, L. (1990). On the formation and regulation of anger and aggression. **American Psychologist, 45,** 494–503.

Berkowitz, L. (1993). *Aggression: Its causes, consequences, and control.* New York: McGraw-Hill.

Berkowitz, L., & LePage, A. (1967). Weapons as aggression-eliciting stimuli. **Journal of Personality and Social Psychology, 7,** 202–207.

Bettencourt, B. A., & Miller, N. (1996). Gender differences in aggression as a function of provocation: A meta-analysis. **Psychological Bulletin, 119,** 422–447.

Braun, C., & Giroux, J. (1989). Arcade video games: Proxemic, cognitive and content analyses. **Journal of Leisure Research, 21,** 92–105.

Bushman, B. J. (1995). Moderating role of trait aggressiveness in the effects of violent media on aggression. **Journal of Personality and Social Psychology, 69,** 950–960.

Bushman, B. J., &. Anderson, C. A. (1998). Methodology in the study of aggression: Integrating experimental and nonexperimental findings. In R. Geen & E. Donnerstein (Eds.), **Human aggression: Theories, research, and implications for social policy** (pp. 23–48). San Diego, CA: Academic Press.

Bushman, B. J., Baumeister, R. F., & Stack, A. D. (in press). Catharsis, aggression, and persuasive influence: Self-fulfilling or self-defeating prophecies? **Journal of Personality and Social Psychology.**

Bushman, B. J., & Wells, G. L. (in press). Trait aggressiveness and hockey penalties: Predicting hot tempers on the ice. **Journal of Personality and Social Psychology.**

Buss, A. H., & Durkee, A. (1957). An inventory for assessing different kinds of hostility. **Journal of Consulting Psychology, 21,** 343–349.

Buss, A. H., & Perry, M. P. (1992). The aggression questionnaire. **Journal of Personality and Social Psychology, 63,** 452–459.

Calvert, S. L., & Tan, S. (1994). Impact of virtual reality on young adults' physiological arousal and aggressive thoughts: Interaction versus observation. **Journal of Applied Developmental Psychology, 15,** 125–139.

Caprara, G. V. (1982). A comparison of the frustration-aggression and emotional susceptibility hypothesis. **Aggressive Behavior, 8,** 234–236.

Caprara, G. V., Cinanni, V., D'Imperio, G., Passerini, S., Renzi, P., & Travaglia, G. (1985). Indicators of impulsive aggression: Present status of research on irritability and emotional susceptibility scales. **Personality and Individual Differences, 6,** 665–674.

Carlson, M., Marcus-Newhall, A., & Miller, N. (1989). Evidence for a general construct of aggression. **Personality and Social Psychology Bulletin, 15,** 377–389.

Carlson, M., Marcus-Newhall, A., & Miller, N. (1990). Effects of situational aggressive cues: A quantitative review. **Journal of Personality and Social Psychology, 58,** 622–633.

Chambers, J. H., & Ascione, F. R. (1987). The effects of prosocial and aggressive video games on children's donating and helping. **Journal of Genetic Psychology, 148,** 499–505.

Cooper, J., & Mackie, D. (1986). Video games and aggression in children. **Journal of Applied Social Psychology, 16,** 726–744.

Creasey, G. L., & Myers, B. J. (1986). Video games and children: Effects on leisure activities, schoolwork, and peer involvement. **Merrill Palmer Quarterly, 32,** 251–262.

Crick, N. R., & Dodge, K. A. (1994). A review and reformulation of social information-processing mechanisms in children's social adjustment. **Psychological Bulletin, 115,** 74–101.

Dietz, T. L. (1998). An examination of violence and gender role portrayals in video games: Implications for gender socialization and aggressive behavior. **Sex Roles, 38,** 425–442.

Dill, K. E. Anderson, C. A., Anderson, K. B. & Deuser, W. E. (1997). Effects of aggressive personality on social expectations and social perceptions. **Journal of Research in Personality, 31,** 272–292.

Dill, K. E., & Dill, J. C. (1998). Video game violence: A review of the empirical literature. **Aggression and Violent Behavior: A Review Journal, 3,** 407–428.

Dodge, K. A., & Crick, N. R. (1990). Social information-processing bases of aggressive behavior in children. **Personality and Social Psychology Bulletin, 16,** 8–22.

Dominick, J. R. (1984). Videogames, television violence, and aggression in teenagers. **Journal of Communication, 34,** 136–147.

Dorr, N., & Anderson, C. A. (1995, May). **Resolution of the temperature aggression debate.** Paper presented at the Annual Convention of the Midwestern Psychological Association, Chicago.

Elliot, D. S., Huizinga, D., & Ageton, S. S. (1985), **Explaining delinquency and drug use.** Beverly Hills, CA: Sage.

Elmer–Dewitt, P. (1993, September 27). The amazing video game boom. **Time,** 66–73.

Emes, C. E. (1997). Is Mr. Pac Man eating our children? A review of the effect of video games on children. **Canadian Journal of Psychiatry, 42,** 409–414.

Eron, L. D., Huesmann, L. R., Dubow, E., Romanoff, R., & Yarmel, P. (1987). Aggression and its correlates over 22 years. In D. Crowell, I. Evans, & D. O'Donnell (Eds.), **Childhood aggression and violence** (pp. 249–262). New York: Plenum.

Fling, S., Smith, L., Rodriguez, T., Thornton, D., Atkins, E., & Nixon, K. (1992). Videogames, aggression, and self-esteem: A survey. **Social Behavior and Personality, 20,** 39–46.

Geen, R. G. (1990). **Human aggression.** Pacific Grove, CA: McGraw-Hill.

Geen, R. G., & Quanty, M. B. (1977). The catharsis of aggression: An evaluation of a hypothesis. In L. Beikowitz (Ed.), **Advances in experimental social psychology** (Vol. 10, pp. 1–37). New York: Academic Press.

Geen, R. G., Stonner, D., & Shope, G. L. (1975). The facilitation of aggression by aggression: Evidence against the catharsis hypothesis. **Journal of Personality and Social Psychology, 31,** 721–726.

Gerbner, G., Gross, L., Morgan, M., & Signiorelli, N. (1980). The "mainstreaming" of America: Violence profile no. Π. **Journal of Communication, 30,** 10–29.

Giancola, P. R., & Chermack, S. T. (1998). Construct validity of laboratory aggression paradigms: A response to Tedeschi and Quigley (1996). **Aggression and Violent Behavior, 3,** 237–253.

Graybill, D., Strawniak, M., Hunter, T., & O'Leary, M. (1987). Effects of playing versus observing violent versus nonviolent video games on children's aggression. *Psychology: A Quarterly Journal of Human Behavior,* **24,** 1–8.

Griffiths, M, D, & Hunt, N. (1998). Dependence on computer games by adolescents. **Psychological Reports, 82,** 475–480.

Harris, M. B, & Williams, R. (1985). Video games and school performance. **Education, 105,** 306–309.

Huesmann, L. R. (1986). Psychological processes promoting the relation between exposure to media violence and aggressive behavior by the viewer. **Journal of Social Issues, 42,** 125–139.

Huesmann, L. R. (1994). **Aggressive behavior: Current perspectives.** New York: Plenum Press.

Huesmann, L. R., & Miller, L. S. (1994). Long-term effects of repeated exposure to media violence in childhood. In L. R. Huesmann (Ed.), **Aggressive behavior: Current perspectives** (pp. 153–188). New York: Plenum Press.

Irwin, A. R., & Gross, A. M. (1995). Cognitive tempo, violent video games, and aggressive behavior in young boys. **Journal of Family Violence, 10,** 337–350.

Kirsh, S. J. (1998). Seeing the world through Mortal Kombat-colored glasses: Violent video games and the development of a short-term hostile attribution bias. **Childhood, 5,** 177–184.

Klein, M. H. (1984). The bite of Pac-Man. **The Journal of Psychohistory, 11,** 395–401.

Leyens, J. P., & Picus, S. (1973), Identification with the winner of a fight and name mediation: Their differential effects upon subsequent aggressive behavior. **British Journal of Social and Clinical Psychology, 12,** 374–377.

Lin, S., & Lepper, M. R. (1987). Correlates of children's usage of video games and computers. **Journal of Applied Social Psychology, 17,** 72–93.

Lindsay, J. J., & Anderson, C. A. (in press). From antecedent conditions to violent actions: A general affective aggression model. **Personality and Social Psychology Bulletin.**

Loftus, G. A., & Loftus, E. F. (1983). *Mind at play:* **The psychology of video games.** New York: Basic Books.

Nelson, T. M., & Carlson, D. R. (1985). Determining factors in choice of arcade games and their consequences upon young male players. **Journal of Applied Social Psychology, 15,** 124–139.

Pooley, E. (1999, May 10). Portrait of a deadly bond. **Time,** 26–32.

Schutte, N. S, Malouff, J. M., Post-Gorden, *J.* C., & Rodasta, A. L. (1988). Effects of playing video games on children's aggressive and other behaviors. **Journal of Applied Social Psychology, 18,** 454–460.

Scott, D. (1995). The effect of video games on feelings of aggression. **The Journal of Psychology, 129,** 121–132.

Silvern, S, B, & Williamson, P. A. (1987). The effects of video game play on young children's aggression, fantasy and prosocial behavior. **Journal of Applied Developmental Psychology, 8,** 453–462.

Tukey, J. W. (1977). **Exploratory data analysis.** Menlo Park, CA: Addison–Wesley.

Van Schie, E. G. M., & Wiegman, O. (1997). Children and video games: Leisure activities, aggression, social integration, and school performance. **Journal of Applied Social Psychology, 27,** 1175–1194.

Winkel, M., Novak, D. M., & Hopson, M. (1987). Personality factors, subject gender and the effects of aggressive video games on aggression in adolescents. **Journal of Research in Personality, 21,** 211–223.

Zillmann, D. (1983). Cognition-excitation interdependencies in aggressive behavior. **Aggressive Behavior, 14,** 51–64.

# 67

# EFFECTS OF VIOLENT VIDEO GAMES ON AGGRESSIVE BEHAVIOR, AGGRESSIVE COGNITION, AGGRESSIVE AFFECT, PHYSIOLOGICAL AROUSAL, AND PROSOCIAL BEHAVIOR

A meta-analytic review of the scientific literature

*Craig A. Anderson and Brad J. Bushman*

Source: *Psychological Science*, 12(5), September 2001, 353–359.

## Abstract

Research on exposure to television and movie violence suggests that playing violent video games will increase aggressive behavior: A meta-analytic review of the video-game research literature reveals that violent video games increase aggressive behavior in children and young adults. Experimental and nonexperimental studies with males and females in laboratory and field settings support this conclusion. Analyses also reveal that exposure to violent video games increases physiological arousal and aggression-related thoughts and feelings. Playing violent video games also decreases prosocial behavior.

Paducah, Kentucky, Jonesboro, Arkansas, Littleton, Colorado. These three towns recently experienced similar multiple school shootings. The shooters were students who habitually played violent video games. Eric Harris and Dylan Klebold, the Columbine High School students who murdered 13 people and wounded 23 in Littleton. before killing themselves, enjoyed playing the bloody video game Doom. Harris created a customized version of Doom with two shooters, extra weapons, unlimited ammunition, and victims who could not fight back—features that are eerily similar to aspects of the actual shootings.

The one positive result of these tragedies is the attention brought to the growing problem of video-game violence, from the newsroom to the U.S. Senate (2000). At a Commerce Committee hearing, several researchers testified that there are indeed valid reasons, both theoretical and empirical, to be concerned about exposing youths to violent video games (Anderson, 2000).

Video-game industry leaders deny the harmful effects of their products. For example, in a May 12, 2000, CNN interview on *The World Today*, Doug Lowenstein, president of the Interactive Digital Software Association, said, "I think the issue has been vastly overblown and overstated, often by politicians and others who don't fully understand, frankly, this industry. There is absolutely no evidence, none, that playing a violent video game leads to aggressive behavior."

There is one grain of truth in the industry's denials. Specifically, the fact that some highly publicized school killings were committed by individuals who habitually played violent video games is not strong evidence that violent video games increase aggression. Society needs solid scientific evidence in addition to such case studies. And here is where media researchers and the video-game industry differ. Research evidence has been slowly accumulating since the mid-1980s. This article reviews the research.

## Definitions

Key terms used by the research community often mean something different to the general public and public policy makers. In this article, we use the following, more precise, meanings common to media-violence researchers.

### Violent media

Violent media are those that depict intentional attempts by individuals to inflict harm on others. An "individual" can be a nonhuman cartoon character, a real person, or anything in between. Thus, traditional Saturday-morning cartoons (e.g., "Mighty Mouse," "Road Runner") are filled with violence.

### Aggression

Aggression is behavior intended to harm another individual who is motivated to avoid that harm. It is not an affect, emotion, or aggressive thought, plan, or wish. This definition excludes accidental acts that lead to harm, such as losing control of an auto and accidentally killing a pedestrian, but includes behaviors intended to harm even if the attempt fails, such as when a bullet fired from a gun misses its human target.

### Violence

Violence refers to extreme forms of aggression, such as physical assault and murder. All violence is aggression, but not all aggression is violence.

## Video-game statistics

The U.S. population consumes much media violence. Youths between the ages of 8 and 18 spend more than 40 hr per week using some type of media, not counting school or homework assignments (Rideout, Foehr, Roberts, & Brodie, 1999). Television is most frequently used, but electronic video games are rapidly growing in popularity. About 10% of children aged 2 to 18 play console and computer video games more than 1 hr per day (Rideout et al., 1999). Among 8- to 13-year-old boys, the average is more than 7.5 hr per week (Roberts, Foehr, Rideout, & Brodie, 1999).

College students also play lots of video games. The Cooperative Institutional Research Program (1998, 1999) found that in 1998, 13.3% of men entering college played at least 6 hr per week as high school seniors. By 1999, that figure had increased to 14.8%. Furthermore, 2% of the men reported playing video games more than 20 hr per week in 1998. In 1999, that figure increased to 2.5%.

Although the first video games emerged in the late 1970s, violent video games came of age in the 1990s, with the killing games Mortal Kombat, Street Fighter, and Wolfenstein 3D. In all three games, the main task is to maim, wound, or kill opponents. The graphics (e.g., blood) and sounds (e.g., screams) of these games were cutting-edge at the time of their introduction. By the end of the 20th century, even more graphically violent games became available to players of all ages (Walsh, 1999). Numerous educational, nonviolent strategy, and sports games exist, but the most heavily marketed and consumed games are violent ones. Fourth-grade girls (59%) and boys (73%) report that the majority of their favorite games are violent ones (Buchman & Funk, 1996).

Another problem involves the lack of parental oversight. Teens in grades 8 through 12 report that 90% of their parents never check the ratings of video games before allowing their purchase, and only 1% of the teens' parents had ever prevented a purchase based on its rating (Walsh, 2000). Also, 89% reported that their parents never limited time spent playing video games.

Ratings provided by the video-game industry do not match those provided by other adults and game-playing youngsters. Many games involving violence by cartoonlike characters are classified by the industry as appropriate for general audiences, a classification with which adults and youngsters disagree (Funk. Flores, Buchman, & Germann, 1999).

## Violence on television and at the movies

Five decades of research into the effects of exposure to violent television and movies have produced a thoroughly documented and highly sophisticated set of research findings. It is now known that even brief exposure to violent TV or movie scenes causes significant increases in aggression, that repeated exposure of children to media violence increases their aggressiveness as young adults, and that media violence is a significant risk factor in youth violence (Bushman & Huesmann, 2001; Huesmann et al., 2001).

Like the seat of a three-leg stool, the vast research literature on TV and movie violence rests on a firm foundation of three study types. The first is experimental research: Participants are randomly assigned to view either violent or nonviolent media and are later assessed for aggression. This work establishes a causal link between violent media and subsequent aggression. The second is cross-sectional correlational research: Participants' TV- and movie-viewing habits and aggression are assessed at one point in time. This work establishes a link between media violence and real-world aggression. The third is longitudinal research: TV- and movie-viewing habits and aggression are assessed repeatedly over time. This work more definitively establishes the causal link from media violence to real-world aggression. The consistency of findings within and between the three types of TV- and movie-violence studies makes this one of the strongest research platforms in all of psychology.

Why consider the literature on TV and movie violence when the focal question concerns video games? The answer has three parts. Many of the underlying psychological processes identified in the TV-movie literature also apply to video games. The research literature on TV-movie violence is large, whereas the literature on video-game violence is small. The literature on TV- movie violence has had ample time to answer early criticisms of the research with additional research. For example, claims that only a very small minority of viewers are adversely affected, that the effect of media violence on aggression is trivially small, or that watching violent TV and movies actually reduces aggressive tendencies have all been carefully tested and rejected by the research evidence (Bushman & Huesmann, 2 (01).

## Why media violence increases aggression and violence

Why does exposure 10 violent media increase aggression and violence? Our General Aggression Model (GAM; Anderson & Bushman, in press), based on several earlier models of human aggression (e.g., Anderson, Anderson, & Deuser. 1996; Anderson, Deuser, & DeNeve, 1995; Bandura, 1971, 1973; Berkowitz, 1993; Crick & Dodge, 1994; Geen, 1990; Huesmann, 1986; Lindsay & Anderson, 2000; Zillmann, 1983) is a useful framework for understanding the effects of violent media. The enactment of aggression is largely based on the learning, activation, and application of aggression-related knowledge structures stored in memory (e.g., scripts, schemas). Figure 1 displays a simplified version of the single-episode portion of the model.

Situational input variables (e.g., recent exposure to violent media) influence aggressive behavior through their impact on the person's present internal state, represented by cognitive, affective, and arousal variables. Violent media increase aggression by teaching observers how to aggress, by priming aggressive cognitions (including previously learned aggressive scripts and aggressive perceptual schemata), by increasing arousal, or by creating an aggressive affective state.

Long-term effects also involve learning processes. From infancy, humans learn how to perceive, interpret, judge, and respond to events in the physical and social

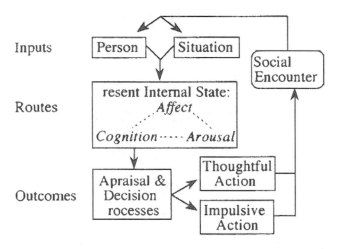

*Figure 1* Single-episode General Aggression Model. Adapted from Anderson and Bushman (in press)

environment. Various types of knowledge structures for these tasks develop over time. They are based on day-to-day observations of and interactions with other people, real (as in the family) and imagined (as in the media). Each violent-media episode is essentially one more learning trial. As these knowledge structures are rehearsed, they become more complex, differentiated, and difficult to change.

Figure 2 illustrates long-term learning processes, identifies five types of relevant knowledge structures changed by repeated exposure to violent media, and links these long-term changes in aggressive personality to aggressive behavior in the immediate situation through both personological and situational variables. The link to person variables is obvious—the person is now more aggressive in outlook and propensity. Less obvious is how repeated exposure to violent media can change situational variables. Huesmann and his colleagues have developed a model of social and academic effects of exposure to television violence (Huesmann, 1994). Briefly, as a child becomes more habitually aggressive, the quality and types of social interactions he or she experiences also change. In sum, the combination of short-term and long-term processes produces the positive relation between exposure to media violence and aggressive-violent behavior.

Figure 2 also reveals why short-term effects of violent media on aggressive cognition are so important. Of the five types of variables identified as contributing to the long-term increase in aggressive personality, four involve aggressive cognitions. Indeed. the literature on the development of behavioral scripts suggests that even a few rehearsals can change a person's expectations and intentions involving important social behaviors (Anderson, 1983; Anderson & Godfrey, 1987; Marsh, Hicks, & Bink, 1998).

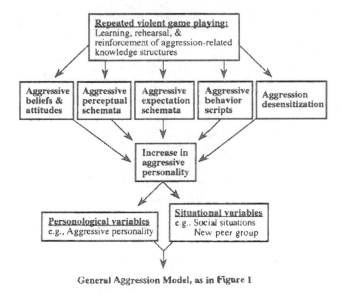

Figure 2  Multiple-episode General Aggression Model of the long-term effects of video-game violence. Adapted from Anderson and Bushman (in press)

## Prosocial behavior

Discussions of media violence frequently include reduction in prosocial behavior as one additional negative consequence. Though this is not a focal point of the present article, several studies have examined the link between violent video games and prosocial behavior. We therefore included prosocial behavior in our meta-analyses of video-game effects.

## Violent video games: key issues

Two key issues emerge from consideration of violent video games and GAM. First, is exposure to violent video games associated with increases in aggression? This question requires empirical studies that assess the relation between exposure to violent video games and aggression, but does not require a detailed analysis of underlying processes.

Second, how can exposure to violent video games increase aggression? This question requires an examination of underlying processes, especially the three routes in the model: cognition, affect, and arousal. But only the cognitive route is specifically tied to the violent content of violent video games. Even nonviolent games can increase aggressive affect, perhaps by producing high levels of frustration. Similarly, exciting nonviolent games can increase arousal, but only violent games should directly prime aggressive thoughts and stimulate the long-term development of aggressive knowledge structures. Frustrating nonviolent

376

games can increase aggressive cognitions indirectly, through links between feelings and thoughts (Anderson & Dill, 2000), but the real crux of the debate lies in the unique ability of violent video games to directly increase aggressive cognitions.

According to GAM, long-term effects of exposure to violent media result primarily from the development rehearsal, and eventual automatization of aggressive knowledge structures such as perceptual schemata (Was this bump accidental or intentional?), social expectations (Are other people expected to be cooperative or vengeful?), and behavioral scripts (insult ® retaliation). In sum, the second question concerns any of several potential underlying processes, but the most important one is whether brief and repeated exposure to violent video games increases aggressive cognitions.

On the basis of narrative review procedures, one of us (Anderson, 2000) testified at the Senate hearing that even though the video-game research literature is small, the findings overall demonstrate significant effects, and that short-term effects are clearly causal. Representatives of the video-game industry have repeatedly denied this. So who is right? To address both key issues, we conducted a meta-analysis of the existing video-game literature.

## Method

### *Literature search procedures*

We searched *PsycINFO* for all entries through 2000, using the following terms: (*video\* or computer or arcade*) and (*gmame\**) and (*attack\** or *fight\** or *aggress\** or *violen\** or *hostil\** or *ang\** or *arous\** or *prosocial* or *help\**). The search retrieved 35 research reports that included 54 independent samples of participants.[1] A total of 4,262 participants was included in the studies. About half of the participants (46%) were under 18 years old. If a research report did not contain enough information to calculate an effect-size estimate, we contacted the authors and requested the missing information.

### *Criteria for relevance*

Studies were considered relevant if they examined the effects of playing violent video games on aggressive cognition, aggressive affect, aggressive behavior, physiological arousal, or prosocial behavior. Studies were excluded if participants merely watched someone else play a video game. In some studies, half of the participants played the game while the other half watched, and the reported results were collapsed across this play/watch manipulation. When we could not estimate the effect for "play" participants, we used the collapsed results but divided the sample size in half.

### *Coding frame*

We coded the following characteristics for each study: (a) sex of participants, (b) age of participants (adults ≥18 years old or children < 18 years old), (c) type of study (experimental or nonexperimental), and (d) publication status (published or unpublished). We initially coded several other variables (e.g., level of violence in video games), but these were so confounded with age of participants that we dropped them. Most experimental studies were conducted in laboratory settings; many used standard lab measures of aggression (e.g., punishment delivered to an opponent). Most nonexperimental studies were conducted in field settings and used more "real world" types of aggressive behaviors (e.g., assault).

When multiple measures of the same type of dependent variable were reported, we used the average effect size in the meta-analyses. For nonexperimental studies. we used the most direct measure of violent-video-game exposure available (e.g., hours per week spent playing violent video games rather than hours per week spent playing video games in general).

## Meta-analytic procedures

We used the correlation coefficient, denoted by $r$, as the effect-size estimate. According to Cohen (1988), a small $r$ is ±.10, a medium $r$ is ±.30, and a large $r$ is ±.50. Fisher's $z$ transformation was applied to the correlations before they were averaged, weighted by the inverse of the variance (i.e., $n - 3$). Once a 95% confidence interval was obtained for the pooled $z$ score, it was transformed back to a 95% confidence interval for the pooled $r$, denoted by $r_+$. (Hedges & Olkin, 1985).

We used the Statistical Analysis System (SAS) to fit both fixed- and random-effects models (Wang & Bushman, 1999). Random-effects models allow generalizations to a broader universe of studies than do fixed-effects models. The price one pays for this broader generalizability is less statistical power (Rosenthal, 1995). Because we are interested in making generalizations to a universe of diverse studies, we report only the results of the more conservative random-effects model.

The random-effects variance was greater than zero for all five dependent measures, indicating that the effects for each measure probably did not come from one population. For each dependent measure, homogeneity tests were conducted to determine whether the variance in effect sizes between studies was greater than what would be expected by chance (Hedges & Olkin, 1985).

We also conducted moderator analyses, focusing on age of participants (average age ≥18 vs. younger), study type (experimental vs. nonexperimental), and publication status (published vs. unpublished). The first two potential moderators are of particular interest, because it is important to know whether similar effects occur for children and young adults, and for experimental studies (which allow for strong causal statements) and nonexperimental ones (which generally use more naturalistic measures of aggression). Some authors did not report effects of violent video games separately for males and females. Furthermore, preliminary analyses revealed that sex did not significantly influence the magnitude of the effects for any of the dependent measures. Thus, sex was excluded from the moderator analyses.

Multicollinearity between model terms was tested by means of variance inflation factors (VIF; e.g., Neter, Wasserman, & Kutner, 1990). The maximum VIF was 1.38, indicating that multicollinearity was not a problem.

378

# Results

Figure 3 shows box plots for the five dependent measures. In a box plot, lines are drawn at the 25th, 50th, and 75th percentiles. The distance between the 75th and 25th percentiles is the interquartile range. Capped vertical bars extend as far as the data extend, to a distance of at most 1.5 interquartile ranges. For each variable in Figure 3, the average effect-size correlation is significantly different from zero.

### Aggressive behavior

Is there a reliable association between exposure to violent video games and aggression? Across the 33 independent tests of the relation between video-game violence and aggression, involving 3,033 participants, the average effect size was positive and significant, $r_+ = .19$.[2] High video-game violence was definitely associated with heightened aggression (see Table 1). Indeed, this effect of violent video games on aggression is as strong as the effect of condom use on risk of HIV infection (Weller, 1993).

The moderator analyses (Table 2) yielded no significant effects. Violent video games increased aggression in males and females, in children and adults, and in experimental and nonexperimental settings. But because the experimental/nonexperimental distinction is so important, we calculated separate average effect sizes for each type of study. For the 21 experimental tests, the average effect was $r_+ = .18$, 95% confidence interval = (.13, .24). Thus, short-term exposure to violent video games causes at least a temporary increase in aggression. For the 13 nonexperimental tests, the average effect was $r_+ = .19$ (.15, .23). Thus, exposure to violent video games is correlated with aggression in the real world.[3]

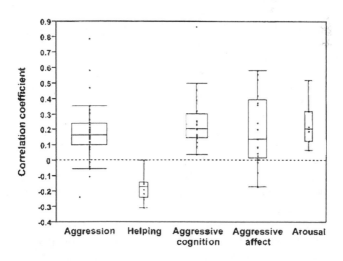

*Figure 3* Box plots for the five dependent variables. The width of each box is proportional to the number of correlations for the box plot

Table 1 Average correlations, 95% confidence intervals, and homogeneity tests for five dependent measures

| Dependent measure | $k$ | $N$ | $r_+$ | 95% C.I. | Homogeneity test | Estimate of random-effects variance (95% C.I.) |
|---|---|---|---|---|---|---|
| Aggressive behavior | 33 | 3,033 | .19 | (.15, .22) | $X^2(32) = 23.25$, $p > .05$ | 0.042 (0.029, 0.068) |
| Prosocial behavior | 8 | 676 | −.16 | (−.22, −.09) | $X^2(7) = 1.30$, $p > .05$ | 0.013 (0.006, 0.048) |
| Aggressive cognition | 20 | 1,495 | .27 | (.22, .31) | $X^2(19) = 29.15$, $p > .05$ | 0.087 (0.054, 0.164) |
| Aggressive affect | 17 | 1,151 | .18 | (.12, .24) | $X^2(16) = 15.11$, $p > .05$ | 0.070 (0.039, 0.161) |
| Physiological arousal | 7 | 395 | .22 | (.12, .32) | $X^2(6) = 2.32$, $p > .05$ | 0.028 (0.012, 0.115) |

Note: $k$ = number of independent correlations; $N$ = number of participants; $r_+$ = pooled correlation coefficient; C.I. = confidence interval. The variance in each random-effects model was estimated using the residual (restricted) maximum likelihood method (see Wang & Bushman. 1999).

We further divided the nonexperimental tests into three categories based on how exposure to violent video games was measured—by time spent playing violent games, preference for violent games, or time spent playing video games in general, ignoring game content. The magnitude of the effect did not depend on the type of measure used, $X^2(2) = 2.14$, $p > .05$. In all three cases, the average correlations with aggression were positive and statistically significant. The average correlations (with 95% confidence intervals) were .26 (.18, .34) for time spent playing violent video games, .16 (.10, .22) for preference for violent video games, and .16 (.11, .22) for time spent playing video games in general.

We further divided experimental tests into two categories, based on whether the aggression target was another person. The magnitude of the effect depended on the aggression target, $X^2(1) = 4.80$, $p < .05$. The average effect was larger if the target was an inanimate object than if the target was a person, $r_+$ = Al (.28, .54), $k = 5$, and $r_+$ = .14(.08, .20), $k$ =18, respectively.

### Prosocial behavior

The eight independent tests of the relation between violent video games and prosocial behavior. involving 676 participants, yielded an average effect that was negative and significant, $r_+$ = −.16 (Table 1).[4] There were too few studies to warrant moderator analyses. However, we separated these effects into experimental and nonexperimental ones. The average effect for the seven experimental tests was −.17 (−.25, −.08). Thus, violent video games cause at least a temporary decrease in prosocial behavior. The average effect for the two nonexperimental tests was −.14 (−.25, −.02). Thus, exposure to violent video games is negatively correlated with helping in the real world.

*Table 2* Random-effects models for aggressive behavior, aggressive cognition, and aggressive affect

| Model term | Dependent measure | | |
|---|---|---|---|
| | Aggressive behavior | Aggressive cognition | Aggressive affect |
| Model | $X^2(3) = 1.14, p > .05$ | $X^2 (3) = 3.25, p > .05$ | $X^2 (3) = 4.56, p > .05$ |
| Age | $X^2 (1) = 0.67, p > .05$ | $X^2 (1) = 0.00, p > .05$ | $X^2 (1) = 3.08, p > .05$ |
| Type of study | $X^2 (1) = 0.15, p > .05$ | $X^2(t) = 1.79, p > .05$ | $X^2 (1) = 2.95, p > .05$ |
| Publication status | $X^2 (1) = 0.11, p > .05$ | $X^2(1) = 1.26, p > .05$ | $X^2 (1) = 0.34, p > .05$ |
| Error | $X^2 (42) = 25.74, p > .05$ | $X^2 (24) = 20.35, p > .05$ | $X^2 (14)= 9.95, p > .05$ |
| Estimate of random-effects variance (95% C.I.) | 0.044 (0.030, 0.071) | 0.085 (0.051, 0.168) | 0.059 (0.031, 0.153) |

*Note:* Age = college students vs. younger; type of study = experimental vs. nonexperimental; publication status = published vs. unpublished; C.I. = confidence interval. The variance in each random-effects model was estimated using the residual (restricted) maximum likelihood method (see Wang & Bushman, 1999).

### Aggressive cognition

The 20 independent tests of the link between video-game violence and aggressive cognition. involving 1,495 participants, yielded an average effect that was positive and significant, $r_+ = .27$ (see Table 1).[5] The moderator analyses (Table 2) yielded no significant effects. Violent video games increased aggressive thoughts in males and females, in children and adults, and in experimental and nonexperimental settings. Most of these studies were experimental, thus demonstrating a causal link between exposure to violent games and aggressive cognition. Therefore, violent video games may increase aggression in the short term by increasing aggressive thoughts. These results are also important for understanding long-term effects, as discussed earlier (Figure 2).

### Aggressive affect

The 17 independent tests of the link between video-game violence and aggressive affect, involving 1,151 participants, also yielded a significant positive effect, $r_+ = .18$ (Table 1). Moderator analyses yielded no significant effects (Table 2). Violent video games increased aggressive affect in males and females, in children and adults, and in experimental and nonexperimental studies, suggesting that violent video games may also increase aggression by increasing feelings of anger or hostility

### Physiological arousal

The seven independent tests of the link between video-game violence and physiological arousal, involving 395 participants, showed that exposure to violent video games increased physiological arousal, $r_+ = .22$ (Table 1). There were too few studies to warrant moderator analyses. Three measures of arousal were used in these studies: systolic blood pressure, diastolic blood pressure, and heart rate. Type of measure did not significantly influence the results, $X^2(2) = 0.31, p > .05$.

## Discussion

These results clearly support the hypothesis that exposure to violent video games poses a public-health threat to children and youths, including college-age individuals. Exposure is positively associated with heightened levels of aggression in young adults and children, in experimental and nonexperimental designs, and in males and females. Exposure is negatively associated with prosocial behavior. Furthermore, exposure is positively related to the main mechanism underlying long-term effects on the development of aggressive personality— aggressive cognition. Finally, exposure is positively linked to aggressive affect and physiological arousal. In brief, every theoretical prediction derived from prior research and from GAM was supported by the meta-analysis of currently available research on violent video games.

This relatively small literature replicates with video games two of the three types of research that have been used to effectively demonstrate short- and long-term causal effects of TV and movie violence on aggression and violence. The type of research missing from the video-game domain is longitudinal research. Given the similarity of the processes activated by various types of media and the similarity of findings in the extant literatures on video-game and TV-movie violence, it would be very surprising if repeated exposure to violent video games did not increase long-term aggression. Nonetheless, such longitudinal research is badly needed. Other questions in need of further research concern the relative magnitude of effects of video-game versus TV-movie violence, and the details of how media violence in general and video-game violence in particular create the observed short-term and the expected long-term increases in aggression and violence (Anderson & Dill, 2000).

Finally, we wonder whether exciting video games can be created to teach and reinforce nonviolent solutions to social conflicts. If marketed with the same zeal (and dollars) as the destructive games that currently dominate the market, would they be as profitable? In other words, is it possible to use the profit motive that has for years driven the media-violence machine to turn that machine in a prosocial direction?

## Notes

1  A list of the studies included in the meta-analysis, as well as effects and coded variables, can be obtained from the following Web page: http://psychserver. iastate.edu/faculty/ caa/abstracts/2000-2004/01AB.html.

2  Experimental studies used two different types of aggression measures: (a) coders' ratings of observed behaviors (e.g., hitting, kicking, pushing) and (b) physical measures (e.g., shock or noise intensity). The magnitude of the effect did not depend on type of measure used, $X^2(1) = 0.03, p > .05$. Nonexperimental studies used three different types of aggression measures: (a) selfreported aggression, (b) other-reported aggression (e.g.,

reports from teachers, peers, or parents), and (c) physical measures (e.g., shock or noise intensity, convictions for violent crimes). The magnitude of the relation did not depend on the type of measure used, $X^2(2) = 0.32$, $p > .05$.

3  In some cases, the number of independent tests and the total number of experimental and nonexperimental tests differ. Similarly, the degrees of freedom in Tables 1 and 2 do not always correspond. This is because some studies contributed more than one effect to the moderator analyses (e.g., some studies provided an experimental effect and a nonexperimental effect).

4  The type of helping measure used (e.g., other-report, coders' ratings) did not significantly influence the magnitude of the effect, $X^2(1) = 0.26$, $p > .05$. There were too few studies to analyze the influence of type of helping measure on experimental and nonexperimental studies separately.

5  The 5 non experimental studies used only hypothetical situations to measure aggressive cognition. The 19 experimental studies used three different measures of aggressive cognition: (a) hypothetical situations, (b) self-report measures of trait aggressiveness, and (c) standard procedures (e.g., reaction time, word-stem completion). The type of measure used, however, did not significantly influence the results, $X^2(2) = 2.89$, $p > .05$.

# References

Anderson, C.A. (1983). Imagination and expectation: The effect of imagining behavioral scripts on personal intentions. *Journal of Personality and Social Psychology, 45*, 293–303.

Anderson, C.A., (2000), *Violent video games increase aggression and violence* [On-Line]. Available: http://psych.server.iastate.edu/faculty/caa/abstract/2000–2004/00Senate.html

Anderson, C.A., Anderson, K.B., & Deuser, W.E. (1996). Examining an affective aggression framework: Weapon and temperature effects on aggressive thoughts, affect, and attitudes. *Personality and Social Psychology Bulletin, 22*, 366–376.

Anderson, C.A., & Bushman, B.J. (in press). The General Aggression Model: An integrated social-cognitive model of human aggression. *Annual Review of Psychology*.

Anderson, C.A., Deuser. W.E., & DeNeve, K.M. (1995). Hot temperatures, hostile affect, hostile cognition, and arousal: Tests of a general model of affective aggression. *Personality and Social Psychology Bulletin, 21*, 434–448.

Anderson, C.A., & Dill, K.E. (2000). Video games and aggressive thoughts, feelings, and behaviour in the laboratory and in life. *Journal of Personality and social Psychology, 78*, 772–790.

Anderson, C.A., & Godfrey. S. (1987). Thoughts about actions: The effects of specificity and availability of imagined behavioral scripts on expectations about oneself and others. *Social Cognition, 5*, 238–258.

Bandura, A. (1971). Social learning theory of aggression. In J.G. Koutsoo (Ed.), *Control of aggression: Implications from basic research* (pp. 201–250). Chicago: Aldine-Atherton.

Bandura, A. (1973). *Aggression: A social learning analysis*. Englewood cliffs, NJ: Prentice-Hall.

Berkowitz, L. (1993). *Aggression: Its causes, consequences, and control*. New York: McGraw Hill.

Bachman, D.D., & Funk, J.B. (1996). Video and computer games in the 90s: Children's time commitment and game preference. *Children Today, 24*, 12–16.

Bushman, B.J., & Huesmann, L.R. (2001). Effects of televised violence on aggression. In D.G. Singer & J.L. Singer (Eds.), *Handbook of Children and the media* (pp. 223–254). Thousand Oaks, CA: Sage.

Cohen, J. (1988). *Statistical power analysis for the behavioural sciences* (2nd ed.). Hillsdale, NJ: Erlbaum.

Cooperative Institutional Research Program. (1998). *Cooperative Institutional Research Program survey results*. Ames, 1A: Office of Institutional Research.

Cooperative Institutional Research Program. (1999). *Cooperative Institutional Research Program survey results*. Ames, 1A: Office of Institutional Research.

Crick, N.R., & Dodge, K.A. (1994). A review and reformulation of social information-processing mechanisms in children's social adjustment. *Psychological Bulletin, 115*, 74–101.

Funk, J.B., Flores. G., Buchman. D.D., & Germann, J.N. (1999). Rating electronic games: Violence is in the eye of the beholder. *Yorah & Society. 30*, 283–312.

Goen, R.G. (1990). *Human aggression.* Pacific Grove, CA: McGraw Hill

Hedges, L.V., & Olkin. J. (1985). *Statistical methods for meta-analysis.* New York: Academic Press.

Huesmann, L.R. (1986). Psychological Processes promoting the relation between exposure to media violence and aggressive behavior by the viewer. *Journal of Social Issues, 42*, 125–139.

Huesmann, L.R. (Ed.). (1994). *Aggressive behaviour: Current perspective.* New York: Plenum Press.

Huesmann, L.R., Anderson, C.A., Berkowitz, L., Donnerstein. E., Johnson, J.D., Linz, D., Malamuth, N.M., & Wartella, E. (2000). *Media violence influences on youth: Expert panel report to the U.S. Surgeon General,* Unpublished manuscript, Institute for Social Research, University of Michigan, Ann Arbor.

Lindsay, J.J., & Anderson, C.A. (2000). From antecedent conditions to violent actions: A General Affective Aggression Model. *Personality and Social Psychology Bulletin, 26*, 533–547.

Marsh, R.L., Hicks, J.L., & Bink., M.L. (1998). Activation of completed, uncompleted, and partially completed intentions. *Journal of Experimental Psychology: Learning, Memory, and Cognition, 24*, 350–361.

Neter, J., Wasserman, W., & Kutner, M.H. (1990). *Applied linear statistical models* (3rd ed.). Homewood. IL: Irwin.

Rideout, V.G., Foehr, U.G., Roberts., D.F,. & Biodie, M. (1999). *Kids & media @ the new millennium: Executive Summary.* Menlo Park. CA: Kaiser Family Foundation.

Roberts, D.F., Foehr, U.G., Rideout, V.G., & Brodie, M. (1999). *Kids media @ the new millennium.* Menlo Park, CA: Kaiser Family Foundation.

Rosenthal, (1995). Writing meta-analytic reviews. *Psychological Bulletin, 118*, 183–192.

U.S. Senate. (2000). March 21, 2000: *Heating before the U.S. Senate Commerce Committee on the Impact of Interactive Violence on Kids* [On-line]. Available: http://www.senate.gov/-brownback/media_violence.html

Walsh, D. (1999). *1999 video and computer game report card* [On-line]. Available: http://mediaandthefamily.org/1999vgrc2.html

Walsh, D. (2000). *Interactive violence and children: Testimony submitted to the Committee on Commerce, Science, and Transportation, United States Senate, March 21, 2000* [On-Line]. Available: http://www.mediaandthefamily.org/press/senateviolence.shtml

Wang, M.C., & Bushman, B.J. (1999). *Integrating results through meta-analytic review using SAS software.* Cary, NC: SAS Institute.

Weller, S.C. (1993). A meta-analysis of condom effectiveness in reducing sexually transmitted HIV. *Social Science and Medicine, 36*, 1635–1644.

*The World Today.* (2000. May 12). Atlanta, GA: Cable News Network.

Zillmann, D. (1983). Cognition-excitation interdependencies in aggressive behavior. *Aggressive Behavior.14*, 51–64.

# 68

# VIOLENT VIDEO GAME EFFECTS ON AGGRESSION, EMPATHY, AND PROSOCIAL BEHAVIOR IN EASTERN AND WESTERN COUNTRIES

A meta-analytic review

*Craig A. Anderson, Akiko Shibuya, Nobuko Ihori,
Edward L. Swing, Brad J. Bushman, Akira Sakamoto,
Hannah R. Rothstein, and Muniba Saleem*

Source: *Psychological Bulletin*, 136(2), 2010, 151–173.

## Abstract

Meta-analytic procedures were used to test the effects of violent video games on aggressive behavior, aggressive cognition, aggressive affect, physiological arousal, empathy/desensitization, and prosocial behavior. Unique features of this meta-analytic review include (a) more restrictive methodological quality inclusion criteria than in past meta-analyses; (b) cross-cultural comparisons; (c) longitudinal studies for all outcomes except physiological arousal; (d) conservative statistical controls; (e) multiple moderator analyses; and (f) sensitivity analyses. Social–cognitive models and cultural differences between Japan and Western countries were used to generate theory-based predictions. Meta-analyses yielded significant effects for all 6 outcome variables. The pattern of results for different outcomes and research designs (experimental, cross-sectional, longitudinal) fit theoretical predictions well. The evidence strongly suggests that exposure to violent video games is a causal risk factor for increased aggressive behavior, aggressive cognition, and aggressive affect and for decreased empathy and prosocial behavior. Moderator analyses revealed significant research design effects, weak evidence of cultural differences in susceptibility and type of measurement effects, and no evidence of sex differences in susceptibility. Results of various sensitivity analyses revealed these effects to be robust, with little evidence of selection (publication) bias.

You know what's really exciting about video games is you don't just interact with the game physically—you're not just moving your hand on a joystick, but you're asked to interact with the game psychologically and emotionally as well. You're not just watching the characters on screen; you're becoming those characters.

—Nina Huntemann, *Game Over*

People of all ages in most modern countries get a heavy dose of violent media, especially in TV programs, films, and video games (e.g., Comstock & Scharrer, 2007; Gentile, 2003; Gentile, Saleem, & Anderson, 2007; Kirsh, 2006; Singer & Singer, 2001). Potential harmful effects of media violence have been scrutinized for over six decades, and considerable consensus has been reached on several of the most important issues. As stated by a recent panel of experts assembled by the U.S. Surgeon General, "Research on violent television and films, video games, and music reveals unequivocal evidence that media violence increases the likelihood of aggressive and violent behavior in both immediate and long-term contexts" (Anderson et al., 2003, p. 81). Numerous reports by professional health associations (e.g., American Academy of Pediatrics, American Psychological Association, Australian College of Paediatrics, Canadian Paediatric Society) and government health agencies (e.g., U.S. Office of the Surgeon General, U.S. Department of Health and Human Services) have reached the same conclusion after reviewing the available scientific evidence (Gentile et al., 2007; Ontario Office for Victims of Crime, 2004).

The majority of media violence studies have focused on violent television and film effects, and most have been conducted in Western countries, especially the United States. There are theoretical reasons to expect that type of media (e.g., newspapers, literature, comic books, graphic novels, television, film, video games, music) and culture will moderate violent media effects. For example, watching the *Lord of the Rings* films should increase aggressive tendencies more than reading the books because of the higher concentration and glorification of violence in the films.

Similarly, cultural factors may either exacerbate or reduce violent media effects for both statistical and psychological reasons. For example, the context of violence on Japanese television is very different from that on U.S. television, even though the total amount of violence shown is similar (Kodaira, 1998). Japanese TV tends to portray violent actions and their consequences much more vividly, with a particular emphasis on the suffering of the victims. This might explain why the effects of TV violence on aggression sometimes appear smaller in Japan than in the United States.

Other multinational research has found considerable variation in access to and content of "violent television" and a few differences in observed effects (Huesmann & Eron, 1986; Huesmann, Lagerspetz, & Eron, 1984). For example, within Israel there were significant correlations between TV violence viewing and children's aggression for urban children but not for rural children being raised on a kibbutz, where socialization is conducted in a communal manner (Bachrach, 1986).

What is currently unclear is the extent to which the occasional cross-cultural differences in media violence effects result from cross-cultural differences in the content of their violent media (a type of artifact), true differences in media violence effects (perhaps communal, collectivist, or politically unstable countries are less susceptible), or a combination of the two.

## Video game violence

### Past findings

Video game violence is the new kid on the media violence block, having emerged in the late 1980s and early 1990s. Currently, one can play video games on computers, consoles (e.g., Xbox 360, PlayStation, Wii), handhelds (e.g., Nintendo DS), computers, iPods, personal digital assistants, and mobile telephones. Because video game technology is relatively new, there are fewer empirical studies on video game violence than on TV and film violence. Nonetheless, several meta-analytic reviews have reported significant harmful effects of exposure to violent video games, both in short-term experimental studies and in crosssectional correlational studies (Anderson, 2004; Anderson & Bushman, 2001; Anderson et al., 2004; Sherry, 2001). Briefly, these reviews found that across these two research designs, exposure to violent video games is associated with higher levels of aggressive behavior, aggressive cognition, aggressive affect, and physiological arousal and with lower levels of prosocial behavior. The earliest meta-analyses reported average effects on aggressive behavior of $r+$ .15 ($K = 25$, $N = 2,722$; Sherry, 2001) and $r+$ .19 ($K = 33$, $N = 3,033$; Anderson & Bushman, 2001). Anderson (2004) found an average effect size of $r+$.20 ($K = 32$, $N = 5,240$) when all relevant studies were included and a larger effect when more stringent methodological criteria were applied, $r+$.26 ($K = 17$, $N = 2,731$).[1] In general, the violent video game research mirrors findings from the violent TV and film research, with some evidence that the violent video game effects may be somewhat larger (Anderson, Gentile, & Buckley, 2007; Polman, Orobio de Castro, & Van Aken, 2008).

### Recent skepticism

However, three recent meta-analyses by the same author, each using a very small set of available studies, have suggested that the effects of violent video games on aggression have been substantially overestimated because of publication bias (Ferguson, 2007a, 2007b; Ferguson & Kilburn, 2009) and that therefore there is little-to-no evidence of a violent video game effect on aggression. However, these three meta-analyses have numerous problems that call into question their results and conclusions. For example, counter to widely accepted procedures for reducing the impact of publication bias, only published articles were included in the analyses and then procedures for addressing publication bias were misinterpreted. Also, studies published prior to 1995 were ignored and a large number of studies published since that time apparently were missed.

387

The text on publication bias cited by Ferguson (2007a; Rothstein, Sutton, & Borenstein, 2005) specifically recommends that the primary way to assure that meta-analytic results will not be affected by publication bias is to conduct a search for relevant studies that is thorough, systematic, unbiased, transparent, and clearly documented. Authors are told to include book chapters, dissertations, conference papers, and unpublished manuscripts that meet the inclusion criteria for the meta-analysis, because this is widely viewed as the best way to ameliorate publication bias.

Ferguson (2007a, 2007b; Ferguson & Kilburn, 2009) used the trim and fill method to estimate the "true" effect size corrected for publication bias. The originators of the trim and fill method (Duval, 2005; Duval & Tweedie, 2000a) have cautioned that the "adjusted" estimate of an effect using imputed studies provided by trim and fill should not be taken as the "true" effect, because it is based on imputed data points (that do not really exist). Trim and fill provides a useful sensitivity analysis that assesses the potential impact of missing studies on the results of a meta-analysis by examining the degree of divergence between the original effect-size estimate and the trim and fill adjusted effect-size estimate.

It has also been widely cautioned that because trim and fill and some other techniques for assessing publication bias are based on an association between effect size and sample size, other explanations of this association should be considered. For example, effect sizes in experimental studies may be larger than those in cross-sectional or longitudinal studies due to the reduced error variance that results from tight experimental controls; researchers may know this and therefore may intentionally plan to use larger sample sizes when conducting nonexperimental studies. Similarly, in some research contexts with very large sample sizes (e.g., national surveys) a researcher may have to use less precise measures (e.g., fewer items) that result in smaller effect sizes. In sum, it is possible that the effects in the studies with small samples really are larger than those in the studies with large samples (cf. Sterne and Egger, 2005).

In addition, the meta-analyses published by Ferguson are not independent of each other because they use highly overlapping subsets of the same small sample of studies, which includes at least one study that does not even have a valid measure of aggressive behavior (i.e., Williams & Skoric, 2005). For example, the Ferguson (2007b) meta-analysis used data from 17 articles, 14 of which were used in Ferguson (2007a), making the two meta-analyses largely redundant.[2] The average effect-size estimates computed by Ferguson ($rs$ = .29, .14, and .15 for Ferguson 2007a, 2007b, and Ferguson & Kilburn, 2009, respectively) before "correcting" for publication bias are very similar in magnitude to those computed by other researchers.

### Need for a new meta-analysis

Thus, there is some inconsistency between the recent meta-analyses conducted by Ferguson (2007a, 2007b; Ferguson & Kilburn, 2009) and most of the published research and earlier, more comprehensive meta-analyses on media violence effects.

Clearly, all agree that prior meta-analyses have not answered all relevant questions about violent video game effects. Furthermore, there has been an explosion of research on violent video game effects since the last comprehensive meta-analysis was published in 2004. For example, none of the prior meta-analytic reviews of violent video game effects included longitudinal studies because none existed, but now several such studies are available. Past meta-analyses also frequently included cross-sectional studies in which sex differences were not statistically controlled. Although there are both theoretical and methodological reasons for not using partial correlations, it certainly is of interest to know whether the average effect size is reliably different from zero when sex has been controlled. A sufficient number of studies now exists to allow meaningful tests of this question.

Other important questions could not be tested in prior meta-analyses because of the small number of available studies. For example, does player perspective (first person vs. third person) influence the magnitude of violent video game effects? Does killing human targets yield larger effects than killing nonhuman targets? Are younger game players more affected than older ones?

Furthermore, almost all of the studies reviewed in prior meta-analyses came from U.S. samples or from similar Western individualistic-culture samples (e.g., Australia, Germany, the Netherlands, United Kingdom). Thus, the possibility that video game violence effects might be smaller (or larger) in collectivistic societies than in individualistic societies has never been explored. Indeed, it was the combination of availability of Japanese studies (following a visit to Japan in 2003 by Craig A. Anderson), the explosion of research in this domain, and the publication of several longitudinal studies that inspired us to begin the present meta-analysis.

## Cultural differences in aggression

Aggression rates differ greatly across countries and cultures; cross-national comparisons have implicated various cultural variables as possible contributors to these differences. For example, an analysis of peer-directed aggression in 28 countries found that "in general, cultures characterized by collectivistic values, high moral discipline, a high level of egalitarian commitment, low uncertainty avoidance, and which emphasize values that are heavily Confucian showed lower levels of aggression than their counterparts" (Bergeron & Schneider, 2005, p. 116).[3]

However, the rank order of countries by aggression rates varies from one measure of aggression to another. The United States has a higher homicide rate than do many industrialized countries in Europe and Asia but similar or lower rates of other forms of violent crime, such as assault. For example, the average annual homicide rate per hundred thousand for 1998–2000 was almost 400% larger in the United States than in England and Wales (5.87 vs. 1.50; Barclay & Tavares, 2002). But in this time period, the rate for all violent crimes was almost 250% greater in England and Wales than in the United States (1,295 vs. 536; computed from data reported in Barclay & Tavares, 2002).[4]

Japan is generally considered to be a relatively peaceful society. It has lower rates of homicide (1.06) and violent crime (39) than does the United States or most Western countries (Barclay & Tavares, 2002). Japan is also a more collectivistic society, emphasizing high moral discipline, egalitarian values, and Confucian values of peace and nonviolence.

One argument frequently offered by those who claim that media violence doesn't increase aggressive tendencies is that Japan has high levels of media violence but low overall levels of violent crime. If media violence is truly a causal risk factor for violence and aggression, so the argument goes, Japan should have a high violent crime rate. There are multiple problems with this argument, of course. Perhaps the most obvious problem is that exposure to violent media is not the only important risk factor (DeLisi, 2005). Japan differs from the United States and other Western nations on many known causal risk factors for aggression and violence, such as easy access to firearms.

There are at least five reasons to expect smaller media violence effect sizes in Japan (and similar Eastern societies) than in Western societies. First, a relatively smaller effect size may result from differences in how violence is contextualized in Japanese versus U.S. media. Today, global boundaries do not exist when it comes to video games. The most popular video games are played in many countries, under different titles and with different languages. Nonetheless, the contexts of violence in video games played most frequently in Japan can be different from the contexts in video games played most frequently in the United States. Whereas action and sports games are the most popular genre in the United States and Western countries, role-playing games are the most popular genre in Japan (Yahiro, 2005). Japanese role-playing games often involve text reading, patience, and cooperative fights against computer-controlled characters, and the contexts of the violent video games that children and adolescents are exposed to in Japan are not the same as those in the West. Second, people in Japan are more likely to pay attention to situational contexts than are people in Western countries (e.g., Masuda & Nisbett, 2001; Nisbett, Peng, Choi, & Norenzayan, 2001). A third reason concerns cultural differences in the meaning, experience, and processing of emotions and their emotion–action linkages. As noted by Mesquita and Leu (2007), "Whereas people in independent contexts view emotional situations mainly from their own perspective . . . people in interdependent contexts assess the emotional meaning from the perspective of other people or a generalized other" (p. 739). One result of this difference in perspective is that people from Japan report being less likely to respond aggressively to an offense or insult than do people in Western cultures. Other research similarly suggests that Japanese culture tends to foster socially engaging emotions, whereas Western culture tends to foster socially disengaging emotions (e.g., Kitayama, Mesquita, & Karasawa, 2006). Similarly, research on ideal affect (what one typically would like to feel) suggests that easterners are more likely to have adjustment goals, whereas westerners are more likely to have influence goals (Tsai, Knutson, & Fung, 2006). A fourth difference concerns the context in which video games are played. One unpublished study (Kodomo no taiken katsudo kenkyukai, 2000) found that considerably fewer Japanese and South Korean fifth graders had their own TV sets (14% and 11%, respectively) than did American, British, and German fifth graders (39%, 69%, and 29%, respectively). Similar results were obtained for eighth graders (28% and 10% vs. 63%, 68%, and 62%). This suggests that Japanese youths may be more likely than Western youths to play their video games in public space, where parents can watch and monitor what they play. Research shows that parental involvement may reduce violent video game effects (e.g., Anderson et al., 2007). Research has also found that the number of friends was not different for frequent versus infrequent gamers in Japan, but that in the United Kingdom frequent gamers had fewer friends than did infrequent gamers (Colwell & Kato, 2003). Again, this suggests important context differences between East and West that might moderate video game effect sizes. Thus, violent video game effects on aggression and related outcome variables may be smaller and more complex in Japan than in Western countries.

On the other hand, most basic emotion and behavior processes are universal. For example, Frijda, Markam, Sato, and Wiers (1995) studied the action readiness after emotional experiences in Dutch, Indonesian, and Japanese participants and found that five factors were quite similar across cultures, including a factor labeled *moving against*. (There were some nonuniversal factors as well.) Similarly, there are numerous cross-cultural differences in average Big Five personality traits, some of which suggest that Eastern collectivist cultures might be more susceptible to media violence effects, others of which suggest the opposite (Schmitt, Allik, McCrae, & Benet-Martinez, 2007). Thus, there also are reasons to believe that media violence effects may well be fairly similar across cultures or even larger in Japan and Eastern cultures. In the present meta-analysis, we investigated the possibility that effect sizes might differ between Western cultures (primarily the United States) and Eastern cultures (primarily Japan).

## Additional theoretical considerations

Over the last 45 years, an array of social–cognitive models of aggression has systematically improved the field's understanding of the processes involved in the instigation of aggressive behavior and the development of individuals prone to aggression and violence (e.g., Bandura, 1973; Berkowitz, 1984, 1993; Geen, 2001; Huesmann, 1988, 1998). The two most detailed current models are Huesmann's (1998) script model and Crick and Dodge's (1994) social information processing model. Recently, the general aggression model was developed to provide a simplified overview of the common elements among prior models of the development and expression of aggressive behavior (Anderson & Bushman, 2002; Anderson & Carnagey, 2004; Anderson & Huesmann, 2003).

Explicating and comparing these various models lies well outside the scope of this article, but these social–cognitive models allow several important predictions concerning the likely short-term and long-term effects of exposure to violent video games. In general, both short-term and long-term effects of environmental variables (e.g., insult, physical pain, violent media) on aggressive behavior operate by affecting cognitive, emotion, and/or arousal systems.

### Aggression facilitation and inhibition

Social–cognitive models of aggression distinguish between factors that facilitate the emergence of aggression from those that inhibit it (e.g., Anderson & Huesmann, 2003; Bandura, Barbaranelli, Caprara, & Pastorelli, 1996; Berkowitz, 1984). Common facilitating factors in the immediate situational context include aggression cues (e.g., weapons, violent media) and unpleasant situational events that put people in a bad mood (e.g., provocation, frustration, hot temperatures, loud noises, unpleasant odors, pain). Inhibiting factors include fear of retaliation, negative emotional reactions to images and thoughts of violence, moral beliefs opposing violence, and pleasant situational events that put people in a good mood.

### Short-term versus long-term effects

Short-term effects are those in which a person plays a video game for a brief time (e.g., 15 min) before relevant measures are obtained. Usually, short-term effects are assessed in experimental studies conducted in labs or in schools. Long-term effects are those that accrue from repeated exposures over a relatively long period of time, such as months or years. Long-term effects typically are assessed in cross-sectional and longitudinal studies.

For theoretical reasons, the effects of video game violence might differ as a function of whether one is discussing short- or long-term effects. This is because the same stimulus can have multiple effects on several factors that facilitate or inhibit aggression. For example, playing a video game with sanitized violence versus a bloody version of the same game may lead to similar levels of aggressive behavior in the immediate situation, whereas repeated exposure to one or to the other version may lead the bloody version to have larger long-term effects. This could happen if both versions equally prime aggressive scripts while being played but lead to differential changes in more stable, long-term factors, such as emotional desensitization to violence, after the game has been turned off. On the other hand, if the bloody version not only primes aggressive behavioral scripts but also increases arousal, it might lead to more aggression in the immediate situation than does the sanitized version.

Immediate, short-term effects are mainly the result of priming existing knowledge structures, such as various types of schemata and scripts (see Bushman & Huesmann, 2006). Priming processes require only (a) a person who already has at least a few well developed aggression scripts and (b) brief exposure to a video game that requires violent action. There need be no surface-level similarity between the violence in the video game and the aggression measure, as long as the person's aggression scripts have been activated. That is, the game characters

392

do not need to be similar to the player or the player's later real-world target, and the violence in the game does not need to be similar to the player's real-world aggression options. Once aggressive scripts have been activated, additional exposure to the violent video game is unlikely to have more than a minimal impact on later aggressive behavior. If priming of existing knowledge structures is the main process underlying an observed increase in aggression following video game play, playing the randomly assigned games for 15 min versus 30 min should make little difference, all else being equal.

Short-term effects might also reflect mimicry or observational learning of new behaviors and of new beliefs about their likely success. If the main process underlying an observed short-term violent video game effect is such mimicry/observational learning, greater exposure to the violent game (e.g., 30 vs. 15 min) should lead to better learning of the new aggression script and, in the right circumstance, to larger increases in aggression. The context most likely to favor this type of short-term effect is when the participants do not already have well-learned aggression scripts (e.g., very young children); when the aggressive behavior being modeled in the game is novel; and when the aggressive behavior test situation closely resembles the video game in terms of the characters, the provocation, and the possible aggressive action that is available to the participants. Such conditions are rarely (or never) encountered in the existing violent video game experiments, which is why most video game violence researchers believe that the existing short-term effects are mainly the result of priming effects (e.g., Anderson et al., 2003, 2007; Bushman & Huesmann, 2006; Kirsh, 2006; Krahé, 2001).

Long-term effects mainly result from relatively permanent changes in beliefs, expectancies, scripts, attitudes, and other related person factors that are brought about by repeated exposure to video game violence. Because these person factors are relatively stable, repeated exposure to video game violence (or to other environmental risk factors) is required to create significant change. Playing a violent video game one time for 20 min will not change a well-adjusted adolescent into a potential school shooter, with all of the anger, hostile beliefs, expectations, and personality traits that go along with such extreme behavior. But repeated exposure to violent media is expected to lead to measurable changes in the chronic accessibility of aggression-related knowledge structures (e.g., aggression scripts, attitudes and beliefs that support aggressive action) and in relatively automatic reactions to scenes or thoughts of violence (e.g., lack of empathy, physiological desensitization). Another factor important in understanding long-term effects of exposure to violent media is whether the person's environment encourages or discourages aggression. For example, some cultures are relatively supportive of certain types of violence, whereas other cultures condemn them. Similarly, different families within a culture may respond differently. This may be why it appears that having parents who are very involved in one's media usage sometimes acts as a protective factor (e.g., Anderson et al., 2007). Of course, if the highly involved parents actively encourage violent behavior, they are likely to exacerbate the media violence effect.

## *Aggressive cognition versus affect and arousal*

Video games can be exciting, fun, frustrating, exhilarating, and boring. Being the target of potential harm, even in the virtual world of video games, is likely to prime aggressive cognitions and emotions and to increase physiological arousal. The aggressive cognition aspect is of particular interest for two reasons. First, many situational factors can increase arousal and anger, even certain nonviolent video games. For instance, race driving video games, sports video games, and even perceptual/motor skills games that require intense concentration and rapid responses (e.g., Tetris, Bejeweled) can increase heart rate and blood pressure. Similarly, video games that are too fast paced or too difficult for the player are likely to increase frustration and anger, which in turn might activate aggressive thoughts. But violent video games, by their nature, *require* the activation of aggressive thoughts, whereas nonviolent games do not require it. Second, the repeated activation of aggressive thoughts, both novel ones (especially in children) and well-practiced ones, is the most likely route to relatively permanent changes in the person, because the activation of aggression-related knowledge structures becomes more automatic and chronic with repetition and eventually becomes part of the person's personality (Strack & Deutsch, 2004; Wegner & Bargh, 1998). The negative affect and physiological arousal instigated by a video game (violent or nonviolent) likely dissipate fairly quickly and are less likely to leave long-term traces in the brain than are the cognitive learning and overlearning of aggression-related perceptual and social schemata (including aggressive behavioral scripts) that are rehearsed constantly while playing violent games.

## *Predictions*

Before spelling out our specific predictions, we want to raise two key points. First, predicting the pattern of all the possible combinations of variables in video game studies requires a thorough knowledge of which processes are engaged by the video game. Will a third-person shooter have a different impact on immediate aggression than a first-person shooter? Will gorier games have a bigger impact than less gory games? Without knowledge of how well each specific game activates aggressive thoughts, feelings, and physiological arousal, any prediction is risky at best. Second, the importance of assessing a host of potential short-term and long-term effects of different types of violent video games becomes obvious. Nonetheless, a number of broader scale predictions are possible. For example, all else being equal, participants randomly assigned to play a violent video game should tend to behave more aggressively for a short period of time afterward than those randomly assigned to play an equally fun and equally challenging nonviolent video game. We next offer additional predictions, grouped by outcome variable.

## Aggressive behavior

We expected to find that playing a violent video game would increase aggressive behavior in a short-term experimental context, relative to playing a nonviolent video game that is equally exciting, arousing, and enjoyable. We expected similar effects in long-term contexts, that is, in crosssectional correlation studies and in longitudinal studies. We expected the largest effects in short-term experimental studies and the smallest effects in longitudinal studies, once sex has been controlled. This is because experimental studies generally are better at controlling for effects of extraneous variables that increase the error variance and therefore decrease the effect-size magnitude.

## Aggressive cognition

The predictions for aggressive cognition were the same as for aggressive behavior.

## Aggressive affect and physiological arousal

Brief exposure to violent video games should, on average, increase physiological arousal and aggressive affect. An important methodological caveat is warranted, however. Studies based on violent and nonviolent video games that have been preselected to be equally arousing obviously are not appropriate tests of the short-term arousal- and affect-inducing effects of violent video games. Thus, they should be excluded from the analyses designed to test this specific hypothesis. The same is true when comparison games have been preselected to create equivalent affective states.

It is less clear what to expect in long-term contexts, but the temporary nature of moods and of physiological arousal leads us to expect either very weak long-term effects or none at all. Weak long-term effects might occur on aggressive affect indirectly through habitual increases in aggressive thinking or through problems engendered by habitual aggressive behavior. Weak long-term effects on arousal might occur in young people through changes to brain regions that control cardiovascular and other arousal-related functions. Unfortunately, there are no long-term studies of physiological arousal with which to test this hypothesis.

## Empathy/desensitization

It is unclear whether playing a violent video game for a brief period of time should have a detectable impact on measures of desensitization to violence or of empathy for violence victims. Systematic desensitization therapies suggest that repeated exposures to gory scenes of violence and to pain and suffering of others will have some impact on a person's physiological reactions to new scenes of violence (desensitization) and on empathetic responses to victims, but such therapies typically take place over a period of days or even weeks. Thus, we expected brief exposure to a violent video game would have a relatively small impact on desensitization and empathy. However, we expected larger effects in long-term studies and in experimental studies that involve longer desensitization procedures. Unfortunately, there are no long-duration experimental desensitization studies of violent video game effects.

### Prosocial behavior

Social–cognitive models of social behavior suggest that briefly playing a violent video game should reduce prosocial or helping behavior in the immediate situation. The temporary increase in aggressive cognition and affect might be incompatible with, or might interfere with, empathic thoughts and emotions that frequently underlie helping behavior. Similarly, short-term desensitization effects could reduce helping victims of violence in several ways (Bushman & Anderson, 2009; Carnagey, Anderson, & Bushman, 2007). We therefore expected that video game violence would produce short-term decreases in some forms of prosocial behavior.

On the other hand, many violent video games involve the use of violence to help others, such as saving the princess, one's teammates, or all of humanity from enemies that need to be killed. Thus, it is possible that playing certain types of violent video games might prime a type of "hero" script and thereby lead to an increased likelihood of certain limited types of helping behavior. No studies covered by our search period tested this hypothesis, though we are aware of several such studies currently in progress.

We did not expect to find strong long-term decreases in prosocial behavior, because the types of situations that inspire helping behavior are relatively unlikely to be of the ambiguous kind that allow spontaneous priming of aggressive thoughts and feelings. One exception to this latter prediction concerns helping victims of violence or injury. Because emotional desensitization to injury related cues (expressions of pain, presence of blood) reduces the perceived need for help by violence victims, repeated exposure to violent video games should yield long-term declines in this specific type of prosocial behavior (Carnagey et al., 2007). Unfortunately, there have not been enough direct tests of helping victims of violence, and there are no longitudinal studies testing this specific hypothesis.

In sum, theory suggests that violent video game effects on prosocial behavior should be very context specific. However, the specific contexts used in existing prosocial behavior studies are of the type that lead to predictions of a significant decrease in short-term experimental studies and a small effect (or no effect) in long-term studies.

### The present meta-analysis

We undertook the present meta-analysis for four related reasons. First, the video game violence research literature is expanding rapidly, with new studies being reported almost monthly. An updated meta-analysis is badly needed to take into account the new research. Second, many of the newer studies are of better methodological quality than some of the earlier studies (see the meta-analysis in Anderson et al., 2004). With this larger sample of higher quality studies, one can use stricter inclusion criteria for the main analyses of potential moderators and still have a sufficient sample of studies to yield meaningful results. In essence this larger set of high-quality studies allows tests of theoretical propositions that could not be tested in prior years. Third, there is a growing body of research using Japanese samples, a literature that has gone largely unnoticed by scholars in the West. This body of research not only adds to the total body of studies available for an updated meta-analysis but also allows examination of whether video game violence effects occur in a low violence society that differs from the West in so many important ways. Fourth, the larger body of studies in this domain allows tests of a number of potentially important moderator variables. For example, in experimental studies the video game violence effect size may differ as function of whether the violent game is played from a first-person or third-person perspective.

## Method

### *Literature search procedures*

#### *Outcome variables*

We focused on six outcome variables, the first five of which have been used in prior meta-analyses. The outcome variables were physically aggressive behavior, aggressive cognition, aggressive affect, physiological arousal, prosocial (helping) behavior, and a combined empathy/desensitization variable. All are described more fully in the Results section.

#### *Western studies literature search*

We searched PsycINFO and MEDLINE for all entries through 2008 using the following terms: (*video\** or *computer* or *arcade*) and (*game\**) and (*attack\** or *fight\** or *aggress\** or *violen\** or *hostil\** or *ang\** or *arous\** or *prosocial* or *help\** or *desens\** or *empathy*). In addition, we searched the reference sections of prior meta-analytic and narrative reviews. We included dissertations, book chapters, and unpublished papers.

#### *Japan studies literature search*

There is no search engine comparable to PsycINFO for psychological research in Japan. Therefore, we searched CiNii (NII Scholarly and Academic Information Navigator) and Magazine Plus (Nichigai Associates, Inc.) for all entries through 2008 using the following terms: (*terebigemu* [TV game] or *konpuutaagemu* [computer game]) or *bideogemu* [video game]).

From these two searches we retrieved over 130 research reports that contained some potentially relevant original data, with over 380 effect-size estimates based on over 130,000 participants. As shown in Table 1, this is a huge increase since the last comprehensive metaanalysis (Anderson et al., 2004) as well as the most recent meta-analyses by Ferguson (2007a, 2007b; Ferguson & Kilburn, 2009).

## Outcome variable details

### Aggressive behavior

High-quality experimental studies typically measure aggressive behavior using noise blasts, electric shocks, or hot sauce given to an ostensible partner (in the last case, the partner is known to hate spicy food; for discussions and studies of validity, see Anderson, Lindsay, & Bushman, 1999; Bushman & Anderson, 1998; Carlson, Marcus-Newhall, & Miller, 1989; Giancola & Parrott, 2008). High-quality nonexperimental studies typically measure aggressive behavior using standardized questionnaires (e.g., Buss & Perry, 1992), self-reports, peer reports, teacher reports, or parent reports. Whenever possible, we used measures of physical aggression, because that is the type of aggression most frequently modeled and rewarded in violent video games. In many of the nonexperimental studies, the aggression measure was a composite of physical and verbal aggression.

### Aggressive cognition

Aggressive cognition has been assessed in numerous ways. Short-term experimental studies have used reading reaction time, story completion, word fragment completion, Stroop interference, speed to recognize facial emotions, and hostile attribution bias measures. Occasionally, more traitlike measures of aggressive cognition (such as attitudes toward violence) have been used in short-term experimental studies; these are inappropriate because they measure stable thoughts and

*Table 1* A comparison of the sizes of recent meta-analyses of violent video game effects to that of the current meta-analysis

| Meta-analysis | Violent video game studies | | |
| --- | --- | --- | --- |
| | No. papers | K | N |
| Anderson et al., 2004 | 44 | 97 | 16,534 |
| Ferguson, 2007a | 24 | 25 | 4,205 |
| Ferguson, 2007b | 17 | 21 | 3,602 |
| Ferguson & Kilburn, 2009 | 14 | 15 | Unknown |
| Present article | 136 | 381 | 130,296 |

*Note:* It was not possible to derive $N$ for violent video game effects for Ferguson and Kilburn (2009) because the reported $N$s included studies that had TV and film effects confounded with video game effects. $K$ = number of effects sizes; $N$ = number of participants.

beliefs that develop over a lifetime and should not be influenced by playing a video game for a few minutes. Nonexperimental studies have used measures of trait hostility, hostile attribution bias, attitudes toward violence, hypothetical aggression statements, aggression vignettes, implicit association tests, and normative beliefs about aggression. A few measures, such as variants of the Implicit Association Test, have been found to be sensitive to short-term experimental manipulations as well as to reflect longer term attitudes and so have properly been used in both short-term and long-term studies (Lane, Banaji, Nosek, & Greenwald, 2007).

## Aggressive affect

Aggressive affect measures used appropriately in short-term experimental studies include self-report measures of state hostility, state anger, and feelings of revenge. One experimental study assessed brain function in regions of the brain known to be affected by anger. Most measures for nonexperimental studies were self-reported trait anger scales.

## Physiological arousal

Physiological arousal was assessed with measures of heart rate, blood pressure, or skin conductance.

## Empathy/desensitization

Empathy refers to the degree to which a person subjectively identifies and commiserates with a victim and feels emotional distress. Empathy measures are almost always based on self-report scales in which participants indicate the extent to which they empathize with, feel sympathy for, or feel sorry for a particular person or group of people. In high-quality studies, state measures are used in short-term experimental contexts, whereas trait measures are used in nonexperimental contexts.

The term *desensitization* has been used to cover a wide range of measures, including shorter recommended jail terms for persons convicted of a violent crime to longer latency to intervene in a violence episode (e.g., Carnagey et al., 2007). Theoretically, however, desensitization refers to a reduction in negative emotional response to scenes of violence. The best measures of such effects are negative emotion-related measures, such as heart rate, skin conductance, or other physiological indicators of emotion-related reactions to scenes of violence. In the present article, desensitization specifically refers to a reduction in physiological reactivity to scenes of violence. Most other measures that have been called desensitization are actually theoretical sequelae of reduced negative emotional reactions.

Empathy and desensitization are similar in that both refer to automatic emotional reactions to harm befalling someone else. They differ in directionality and in type of measurement (physiological vs. self-report). We combined these two outcome variables into one category because of their conceptual similarity and because there were too few studies to warrant separate meta-analyses. We reverse scored the desensitization effects, so that negative effects indicated that high exposure to video game violence was associated with high desensitization or low empathy. In other words, theory predicts negative effect sizes.

## Prosocial behavior

Experimental studies used donating of jelly beans or money, helping someone succeed at a task, or helping a victim of a staged violent episode. Nonexperimental studies used self- and other reports of helping behavior.

### Methodological criteria assessment

Many of the effect-size estimates are from high-quality studies that used well-established and theoretically appropriate measures or manipulations of exposure to violent video games and well established, theoretically appropriate outcome measures. However, other studies suffer from one or more serious weaknesses relative to the specific hypothesis. For example, some experimental studies used violent and nonviolent video games that were chosen on the basis of pilot testing because they yielded equal states of arousal; obviously, such studies do not provide appropriate tests of the effect of violent content on arousal. Usually, this type of piloting procedure was done by the original authors to demonstrate that the selected video games did indeed yield similar arousal states, so that other hypotheses could be more accurately tested in the main study (e.g., Anderson et al., 2004; Anderson & Dill, 2000).[5]

Other studies used weak or inappropriate measures of exposure to video game violence, such as the amount of time spent playing any type of video game rather than time spent playing violent video games. Indeed, many studies report the correlations of both the time on violent games and the time on all games with physical aggression in order to test whether the more theoretically appropriate measure yields larger effects (e.g., Anderson & Dill, 2000; Anderson et al., 2007).

Of course, meta-analysis researchers always face the dilemma of dealing with studies of widely varying quality and characteristics. The common solution is to establish a set of methodological criteria and then exclude studies that fail to meet these criteria. In some domains this works well, but in more controversial domains the inclusion/exclusion decisions themselves become the focus of extended debate, thus decreasing the value of the meta-analysis itself. We dealt with this issue in multiple ways. First, we divided studies into two broad categories, those whose methods reflected the best practices in the manipulation and measurement of theoretically appropriate independent and dependent variables versus those that did not.[6] The main analyses (including the moderator analyses) were performed on this set of high-quality studies. Second, we contacted the authors of reports that appeared to have additional unpublished data that could be used to compute effect-size estimates that met the best practice criteria. In this way, we were able

400

to obtain several best practice effect-size estimates that were not in the original reports.[7] Third, we conducted several types of sensitivity analyses. As has been done in other recent meta-analyses (e.g., Chida & Hamer, 2008), the average effect was estimated for each outcome variable on both the full sample and on the best practice sample. If both types of effect-size estimates could be computed from the same study, we kept only the one based on best practices. The full sample analysis reduces the plausibility of claims of selection bias, because all potentially relevant studies are included. The full sample may either underestimate or overestimate the true effect sizes, because it includes studies whose methods might artifactually inflate or deflate the reported effect size. We therefore also report a comparison of best practice versus other studies. As a final type of sensitivity analysis, we used the trim and fill procedure to see how much various effect-size estimates changed as a result of potential selection (publication) bias.

### Best practice inclusion criteria

The inclusion criteria for best practice studies are listed in Table 2, which also gives examples of criteria violations. A more detailed listing of the specific violations for specific studies is too lengthy for inclusion in this article but can be downloaded at the following web page: http://www.psychology.iastate.edu/faculty/caa/abstracts/2010-2014/ NotBestViolations.pdf. Two independent raters examined each effect and judged whether it met all six criteria. Initial agreement was over 93%. Discrepancies were examined and discussed with a third judge until consensus was reached.

### Correlated data

For the longitudinal studies we included both a longitudinal effect size and a cross-sectional effect size. The latter was the average of the two cross-sectional effects, one measured at Time 1 and the other at Time 2.

For studies that reported multiple effects on the same conceptual outcome variable, we took one of two actions. In those cases where one measure was clearly better than the others, based on theoretical relevance (e.g., physical aggression is more relevant to violent video game effects than is verbal aggression), established validity (e.g., use of a well-validated multiple item measure of trait physical aggression vs. a new single item measure of trait aggression), or other empirical evidence offered in the study, we used the best measure. For example, if a study reported two new outcome measures of aggressive behavior, and only one of them correlated significantly with a third variable known to be related to physical aggression (e.g., trait irritability), we used that measure (e.g., Anderson & Dill, 2000, Study 2). In those cases in which there was not a clear best measure, we used the average effect size (Bartholow, Bushman, & Sestir, 2006). Note that we also repeated the main analyses, always using the average effect, and found essentially the same results. For all analyses, we used fixed effects models, although random effects models yielded very similar results.

## Coding frame: moderator variables

### All studies

We coded the following information for each effect size: research design (experimental, cross-sectional, longitudinal); average age (when only "college students" was reported, we assigned an age of 20); culture (East [Japan, China, Singapore] vs. West); and sex of participants. We also coded a number of other characteristics specific to a research design and/or an outcome variable.

### Experimental studies

For experimental studies we coded the following features: violent game player's perspective (first or third person); violent game player's role (hero, criminal, neither); violent game targets (human, nonhuman, both); and duration of time spent playing the assigned video game immediately prior to assessment of the dependent variable. There are no obvious theory based predictions for these four moderators for most dependent variables in short-term experimental studies. For example, if the short-term effect of playing a violent game on aggressive behavior is a priming phenomenon, playing the game for 30 min is unlikely to have a greater impact than playing it for 15 min, unless the content or difficulty changes a lot in the last 15 min.

*Table 2* Inclusion criteria for determining whether a study qualifies as a "best practices" study

| *Criteria* | *Examples of inclusion criterion violations* |
| --- | --- |
| 1 The compared levels of the independent variable were appropriate for testing the hypothesis. | In a short-term experiment, participants in the "nonviolent" condition played a video game that contained considerable violence. |
| 2 The independent variable was properly operationalized. | In a nonexperimental study, total video game play rather than violent video game play was used as the predictor variable. |
| 3 The study had sufficient internal validity in all other respects. | Participant retention was substantially lower in one experimental condition than another, indicating potential self-selection of participants. |
| 4 The outcome measure used was appropriate for testing the hypothesis. | The hypothesis specifies an effect on aggressive behavior, but the outcome measure assessed behavior directed toward an inanimate object rather than a person. |
| 5 The outcome measure could reasonably be expected to be influenced by the independent variable if the hypothesis was true. | A measure of personality trait aggression was used as the measure of aggressive behavior in a short-term experimental study. |
| 6 The outcome variable was properly computed. | Pre- and postmanipulation scores were averaged but were not reported separately. |

Many experimental studies of aggressive behavior used some version of the competitive reaction time (CRT) task. In this task participants are told that they are competing against another person on a series of reaction time trials, that the loser of each trial will receive a punishment immediately after losing the trial, and that before each trial participants set the punishment level that their opponents will receive. The punishment settings are used to assess physical aggression. Original versions used electric shocks (Taylor, 1967), but in more recent years the punishments usually involve blasts of white noise. The CRT is one of the most widely used laboratory techniques for measuring physical aggression and has been shown to have good external validity (Carlson et al., 1989; Giancola & Chermack, 1998; Giancola & Parrott, 2008). Thus, for aggressive behavior studies we also coded whether or not the CRT task was used.

For experimental studies of aggressive cognition, we coded whether or not the outcome variable was some type of rapid automatic cognitive response task (e.g., reaction times) or some type of more thoughtful measure, such as hostile attributional style.

## Nonexperimental studies

Nonexperimental studies included several different ways of measuring exposure to violent video games. We created a dichotomous code that distinguished between studies in which the amount of time spent playing violent games was specific to each game or game type (and then summed or averaged across games or game type), and studies that used some other measures of exposure to violent video games. An example of the former type of measure is the one reported by Anderson and Dill (2000). Their video game violence (VGV) exposure measure has participants list their five most frequently played games. Participants then indicate for each game how frequently they play that game, how violent the graphics are, and how violent the content is. The two violence ratings are averaged and then multiplied by the frequency. This is done for each game listed, and then these five scores are averaged. We refer to this as the VGV-specific type of measure. The second type of measure was used in most of the Japanese studies. Participants rate how frequently they see violent scenes in the games they play. In some studies, this violent scenes rating was then multiplied by a measure of how many hours per week the participant played video games of any type. We refer to this as the VGV-general measure.

For nonexperimental studies of aggressive behavior we coded whether the measure was of physical aggression versus a mixture of physical and some other type (most commonly verbal). We also coded whether or not the measure was primarily composed of more extreme physical aggression that is illegal (violence, such as assault).

For nonexperimental studies of aggressive cognition we coded whether the measure was of trait hostility versus some other type of aggressive cognition, such as attitudes toward violence or hostile attributional style. We did this because a large number of studies used the Hostility subscale of the Aggression Questionnaire (Buss & Perry, 1992) and because that measure is very similar to trait anger, which is not theoretically expected to yield strong cross-sectional or longitudinal effects.

For longitudinal studies we coded the length of time between the initial and the final assessment period. This ranged from 3 to 30 months.

## Partial correlations

Normally, partial correlations are not used in meta-analyses because the statistical theory underlying meta-analytic procedures assumes that one is working with raw (zero-order) correlations. This was not an issue for experimental studies, even when separate effects were not reported by sex, because random assignment removes any unwanted correlation between the independent variable and sex.

As noted earlier, however, a number of nonexperimental studies in this domain either ignored sex or reported finding no Sex 'Video Game Violence (VGV) interaction and then reported an overall VGV effect that combined across sex. Theoretically this could inflate the VGV effect, because males tend to play more violent video games and tend to be more physically aggressive than females. Of course, if violent video games actually do increase physical aggression (and other aggression-related outcome variables), controlling for sex could lead to artificially low effect-size estimates. Our solution to these issues was to contact researchers with a request for additional data that would allow us either to get separate estimates for males and females or to statistically partial out the effect of sex. We then created two overlapping data sets. One, labeled the "best raw" data set, consisted of all best practices studies with effects in their rawest form.[8] The other, labeled the "best partials" data set, contained only effects that had been corrected for sex, either by separate estimates for males and females or by use of partial correlations.

For longitudinal studies, the best raw data set contained the correlations between Time 1 VGV exposure and Time 2 outcomes. For the best partials data set, the effect sizes were partial correlations with both sex and Time 1 outcomes partialed out. The main analyses and all of the moderator analyses were carried out on the best partials data set. Thus, results from the best partials data set are very conservative estimates and may well underestimate the true video game effects. However, comparing these effects to the corresponding best raw effects gives another indication of the strength (or weakness) of the overall effects of violent video games.

Our final sample consisted of 381 effect-size estimates based on 130,296 participants. Of these, over half (221 effects) met the best practice inclusion criteria. Table 3 illustrates the breakdown by outcome variable and, for the best partials data set (the one on which subsequent analyses focus), by research design and culture.

About one third of the best practice effects and over half of the participants were from Eastern cultures, mainly Japan. The majority of the remaining best

*Table 3* Characteristics of the samples

| Variable | Full sample | | Best raw | | Best partials | |
|---|---|---|---|---|---|---|
| | K | N | K | N | K | N |
| Category | | | | | | |
| Aggressive behavior | 140 | 68,313 | 79 | 21,681 | 75 | 18,751 |
| Aggressive cognition | 95 | 24,534 | 59 | 16,271 | 53 | 12,598 |
| Aggressive affect | 62 | 17,370 | 37 | 9,191 | 35 | 7,543 |
| Prosocial behavior | 23 | 9,645 | 16 | 6,906 | 16 | 6,905 |
| Empathy/desensitization | 32 | 8,528 | 15 | 6,580 | 14 | 6,268 |
| Physiological arousal | 29 | 1,906 | 15 | 969 | 15 | 969 |
| Total | 381 | 130,296 | 221 | 61,598 | 208 | 53,034 |
| Culture | | | | | | |
| East | | | | | 64 | 32,436 |
| West | | | | | 144 | 20,598 |
| Research design | | | | | | |
| Experimental | | | | | 92 | 8,705 |
| Cross-sectional | | | | | 82 | 28,788 |
| Longitudinal | | | | | 34 | 15,541 |

*Note: K* = number of effects; *N* = total sample size.

practice effects were from U.S. samples, but samples also came from Australia, Germany, Italy, the Netherlands, Portugal, and the United Kingdom.[9]

## Meta-analytic procedures

All effects sizes were converted to the correlation coefficient, denoted by *r*. We used the software program Comprehensive Meta-Analysis and used a fixed effects model so that we could assess the heterogeneity in various subsets of studies. For each outcome variable we first computed the overall average effect size and then computed a moderator analysis based on type of study. This was done for both the best raw and the best partials data sets. We then conducted more detailed moderator analyses on the best partials data.

We also conducted analyses to address the possibility that results might be affected by selection bias (also called publication bias) in the sample of studies included in the meta-analyses. The concern is based on the premise that studies that fail to "work" are less likely to be published, which might bias the results of a meta-analysis. To assess the possibility that publication bias affected our results, we used the trim and fill procedure (Duval & Tweedie, 2000a). Trim and fill is based on the assumption that in the absence of publication bias, the studies will be distributed symmetrically about the mean effect size (plotted on the *x*-axis) relative to standard error (plotted on the *y*-axis), because the sampling error is random. In the presence of publication bias, studies are expected to be systematically missing in a manner that can be identified by the trim and fill analysis. In the case of positive effect data, if low-effect nonsignificant studies are missing, we would expect a gap on the left-bottom quadrant in the plot, where the nonsignificant studies would have been if we had located them. If, based on other selection mechanisms, high-effect studies are selectively missing, the gap would be on the right side of the mean effect. If asymmetry is detected, trim and fill uses an iterative procedure to remove the most extreme small studies from the specified side of the funnel plot, re-computing the effect size at each iteration until the funnel plot is symmetric about the (new) effect size. In theory, this will provide an unbiased estimate of the effect size. Although trimming yields an adjusted effect size, it also reduces the variance of the effects, resulting in a too-narrow confidence interval. Therefore, the algorithm then adds the original studies back into the analysis and imputes a mirror image for each. This fill has no impact on the point estimate but produces a better estimate of the variance (Duval and Tweedie, 1998, 2000a, 2000b). The major advantage of this approach is that it addresses an important question, What is the best estimate of the unbiased effect size? But, as noted earlier, this estimate should not be interpreted as the true effect size, because it is based on imputed data. Furthermore, if there is a true, theoretically meaningful relationship between effect size and sample size (e.g., researchers use larger samples when conducting longitudinal studies because they know longitudinal effects are smaller than cross-sectional ones), the trim and fill procedure can erroneously adjust the average effect sizes. Ideally, the trim and fill procedure is used on appropriate subsets of studies, and the difference between the original effect size and the trim and fill adjusted effect size should be used to get a feel for the possible biasing effect of publication or selection bias, not as an estimate of the true effect size.

# Results

## *Analysis plan*

Main and moderator analyses were done separately for each outcome variable. In other words, we conducted six independent meta-analyses. We first present results of analyses on the best practice effects, for both the best raw and the best partials data sets. These are the effects that met the inclusion criteria. We then present more detailed moderator analyses on the best partials data. Finally, we present results from several sensitivity analyses for all outcome variables, including analyses of methodological quality as a moderator of effect size. Note that in this section, "study" refers to a sample on which an effect size was computed.

## *Violent video game effects on aggressive behavior*

### *Main analyses*

Table 4 presents the results of the main analyses on aggressive behavior for both the best raw and the best partials data.[10] Figure 1 illustrates several main points from these analyses. First, regardless of research design and regardless of whether the standard zero-order correlation approach or the much more conservative partial correlation approach was used, VGV exposure was significantly related to higher levels of aggressive behavior. Most notably, in longitudinal studies even when sex and Time 1 aggressive behavior were controlled, amount of violent video game play at Time 1 significantly predicted an increase in aggressive behavior at Time 2.

Second, partialing out sex effects (in cross-sectional and longitudinal studies) and Time 1 aggressive behavior effects (in longitudinal studies) greatly reduced the average effect size of VGV. Third, in the best partials data, experimental studies yielded the largest effects whereas longitudinal studies yielded the smallest effects. Fourth, ignoring research design led to very large heterogeneity effects. Fifth, when research design, sex, and Time 1 effects were controlled, none of the heterogeneity effects were significant. In sum, this much larger meta-analysis, with over 70 independent effects involving over 18,000 participants from multiple countries, ages, and culture types, yielded strong evidence that playing violent video games is a significant risk factor for both short-term and long-term increases in physically aggressive behavior.

*Additional moderator tests—best partials data*

We conducted additional moderator tests within each research design, even though the heterogeneity test results yielded little evidence that the studies within design type came from different populations. There were two reasons for doing these additional tests. First, there are several specific comparisons that are of special interest for theoretical (e.g., culture), methodological (e.g., how to measure VGV exposure), or public policy reasons (e.g., player perspective). Second, the heterogeneity tests are omnibus tests; it is possible that more focused tests will yield significant differences.

*Culture*

The effect of culture (Eastern vs. Western) was not significant in any of the research designs. The average effect in experimental studies was slightly larger in Eastern than in Western studies but not significantly so, $Q(1) = 0.28, p > .50$. In cross-sectional studies, the VGV effect was slightly larger in Western than in Eastern studies but not significantly so, $Q(1) = 1.08, p > .20$. In longitudinal studies the VGV effect size was somewhat larger in Western ($r+.126, K = 5, N = 1,037$) than in Eastern studies ($r+ = .059, K = 7, N = 3,392$). This effect was marginally significant, $Q(1) 3.52, p < .07$.

*Sex*

There was no evidence that the VGV effect on aggressive behavior differed for males and females ($ps > .10$). The VGV effect was slightly larger for females in experimental and longitudinal studies and was slightly larger for males in the cross-sectional studies, but none of these differences were significant.

407

Table 4 Aggressive behavior: average effect of violent video game exposure by study design for best raw, best partials, and full sample data sets

| Design | N | K | Effect size and 95% CI | | | Test of null (two-tailed) | | Heterogeneity | | |
| --- | --- | --- | --- | --- | --- | --- | --- | --- | --- | --- |
| | | | Point estimate | LL | UL | z | p | Q | df(Q) | p |
| *Best raw* | | | | | | | | | | |
| Experimental | 2,513 | 27 | .210 | 0.172 | 0.248 | 10.512 | .000 | 19.41 | 26 | .819 |
| Longitudinal | 4,526 | 12 | .203 | 0.175 | 0.231 | 13.787 | .000 | 40.72 | 11 | .000 |
| Cross-sectional | 14,642 | 40 | .262 | 0.247 | 0.277 | 32.291 | .000 | 207.99 | 39 | .000 |
| Total within | | | | | | | | 268.12 | 76 | .000 |
| Total between | | | | | | | | 16.74 | 2 | .000 |
| Overall | 21,681 | 79 | .244 | 0.231 | 0.256 | 36.422 | .000 | 284.86 | 78 | .000 |
| *Best partials* | | | | | | | | | | |
| Experimental | 2,513 | 27 | .210 | 0.172 | 0.248 | 10.512 | .000 | 19.41 | 26 | .819 |
| Longitudinal | 4,429 | 12 | .075 | 0.045 | 0.104 | 4.974 | .000 | 9.22 | 11 | .601 |
| Cross-sectional | 11,809 | 36 | .171 | 0.154 | 0.189 | 18.732 | .000 | 49.55 | 35 | .052 |
| Total within | | | | | | | | 78.19 | 72 | .289 |
| Total between | | | | | | | | 40.17 | 2 | .000 |
| Overall | 18,751 | 75 | .154 | 0.140 | 0.168 | 21.118 | .000 | 118.36 | 74 | .001 |
| *Full sample* | | | | | | | | | | |
| Experimental | 3,464 | 45 | .181 | 0.148 | 0.213 | 10.538 | .000 | 79.08 | 44 | .001 |
| Longitudinal | 5,513 | 14 | .198 | 0.172 | 0.223 | 14.812 | .000 | 41.53 | 13 | .000 |
| Cross-sectional | 59,336 | 81 | .189 | 0.181 | 0.196 | 46.412 | .000 | 771.85 | 80 | .000 |
| Total within | | | | | | | | 892.46 | 137 | .000 |
| Total between | | | | | | | | 0.70 | 2 | .706 |
| Overall | 68,313 | 140 | .189 | 0.182 | 0.196 | 49.838 | .000 | 893.16 | 139 | .000 |

*Note:* Effect sizes measured as *r*. CI = confidence interval; *LL* = lower limit; *UL* = upper limit.

## Age

Average age of the participants was not significantly related to the VGV effect sizes in experimental or longitudinal studies ($ps > .50$). However, it is important to note that there were no longitudinal studies on participants older than 16. For cross-sectional studies there was a marginally significant effect of age ($b = .005$, $Z = -1.82, p < .07$). Studies with older participants tended to yield slightly smaller effect sizes than did those with younger participants.

## Moderators specific to experiments

Of the moderators specific to experiments, the only one with at least a marginally significant effect was the CRT variable, $Q(1) = 2.90$, $p < .09$. Experimental studies that used some version of the CRT task ($r+ = .188, K = 15, N = 1,724$) yielded slightly smaller effects than did those with some other measure of aggression ($r+ .259, K = 12, N = 789$). None of the other moderators associated with experimental design approached significance (i.e., player perspective, player role, target type, time on game).

## Moderators specific to nonexperimental studies

In the crosssectional studies, one of the additional moderators was marginally significant. Studies with a pure physical aggression measure ($r+ = .184, K = 28$, $N = 7,137$) yielded slightly larger VGV effects than did studies that used some mixed aggression measure ($r+ = .153, K = 8, N = 4,672$), $Q(1) = 2.82, p < .10$.

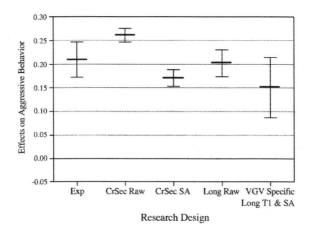

*Figure 1* Effects of playing violent video games on aggressive behavior: Averages and 95% confidence intervals by research design. Exp = experimental studies (same in best raw and best partials data); CrSec = crosssectional studies; Raw = data from best raw samples; SA = sex adjusted (data from best partials samples); Long = longitudinal studies; VGV = Specific = studies that used the more specific type of video game violence exposure measure; T1 & SA = Time 1 and sex adjusted

The method of measuring VGV exposure did not approach significance ($p > .20$), but the average effect was slightly larger when VGV-specific measures were used than when VGV-general measures were used. The violence moderator (violent behavior vs. aggressive but not violent behavior) also did not approach significance ($p > .30$).

For longitudinal studies, the method of measuring violent video game exposure was significantly related to the magnitude of the effect size, $Q(1) = 6.81, p < .01$. Studies that used VGV-specific type measures ($r+ = .152, K = 4, N = 902$) yielded significantly larger VGV effects than did those that used VGV-general type measures ($r+ = .055, K = 8, N = 3,527$). However, this moderator was somewhat confounded with the East/West moderator, and this clouded interpretation. Three of the four VGV specific studies were from the West, but only two of the eight VGV-general studies were from the West. Both types of measures, however, yielded significant longitudinal effects ($ps< .001$ and $.005$, respectively). Neither the time between measurements nor the physical versus mixed aggression moderators approached significance.

## Summary of main findings

Regardless of research design or conservativeness of analysis, exposure to violent video games was significantly related to higher levels of aggressive behavior. For experimental studies, $r+ .210$. For cross-sectional studies the best raw and best partials analyses yielded average effect sizes of $r+ .262$ and $.171$, respectively. For longitudinal studies the best raw and best partials analyses yielded average effect sizes of $r+ = .203$ and $.075$, respectively. Neither culture nor sex yielded any significant moderator effects.

The fact that significant positive effect sizes were obtained in short- and long-term contexts confirms our main theoretical hypotheses. Of particular importance is the finding of a significant longitudinal effect. This shows that playing violent video games can increase aggression over time. Thus, the present findings, especially the longitudinal ones, fill the main gap in the empirical literature on violent video game effects. Furthermore, these effects appear to generalize across culture.

The marginally significant age effect suggests that children might be more susceptible than young adults to violent video game effects, but more research specifically targeted to this question is needed. The lack of a time on game effect in experimental studies suggests that these effects are largely based on priming processes that are triggered in the first few minutes of game play. Experimental studies that vary time on game within the same study are needed to provide a more precise look at this question.

### Violent video game effects on aggressive cognition

#### Main analyses

Table 5 presents the results of the main analyses on aggressive cognition. As with aggressive behavior, VGV exposure was significantly related to increased levels

410

of aggressive cognition, regardless of research design and regardless of whether zero-order correlations or the more conservative partial correlation approach was used. Furthermore, even when sex and Time 1 aggressive cognition were controlled, amount of violent video game play at Time 1 predicted a significant increase in aggressive cognition at Time 2.

Also as expected, partialing out sex and Time 1 aggressive cognition effects reduced the average VGV effect size in nonexperimental studies. In the best partials data, experimental studies yielded the largest effects, whereas longitudinal studies yielded the smallest effects. Once again, ignoring research design led to very large heterogeneity effects. Finally, when research design, sex, and Time 1 effects were controlled, none of the heterogeneity effects were significant. In sum, this much larger meta-analysis, with over 50 independent effects involving over 12,000 participants from multiple countries, ages, and cultures, yielded strong evidence that playing violent video games increases aggressive cognition in both short- and long-term contexts.

### *Additional moderator tests—best partials data*

#### *Culture*

Culture (Eastern vs. Western) was not a significant moderator in either the experimental or the cross-sectional studies. However, in longitudinal studies the VGV effect was significantly larger in Western ($r+ = .137$, $K = 3$, $N = 710$) than in Eastern studies ($r+ = .038$, $K = 5$, $N = 2,602$), $Q(1) = 5.50$, $p < .02$.

#### *Sex*

There were insufficient data to test the sex moderator effect in experimental and longitudinal studies. In cross-sectional studies, the VGV effect was slightly larger for females but not significantly so.

#### *Age*

There were too few longitudinal studies to test the moderating effect of age. Age was not a significant moderator in either experimental or cross-sectional studies.

#### *Moderators specific to experiments*

None of the moderators specific to experiments (i.e., player perspective, player role, target type, time on game, type of aggressive cognition measure) approached significance.

#### *Moderators specific to nonexperimental studies*

For cross-sectional studies neither of the additional moderators approached significance (VGV exposure measure, type of aggressive cognition measure).

411

Table 5 Aggressive cognition: average effect of violent video game exposure by study design for best raw, best partials, and full sample data sets

| Design | N | K | Effect size and 95% CI | | | Test of null (two-tailed) | | Heterogeneity | | |
|---|---|---|---|---|---|---|---|---|---|---|
| | | | Point estimate | LL | UL | z | p | Q | df(Q) | p |
| *Best raw* | | | | | | | | | | |
| Experimental | 2,887 | 24 | .217 | 0.181 | 0.252 | 11.695 | .000 | 35.11 | 23 | .051 |
| Longitudinal | 3,408 | 8 | .115 | 0.082 | 0.148 | 6.728 | .000 | 13.08 | 7 | .070 |
| Cross-sectional | 9,976 | 27 | .183 | 0.164 | 0.202 | 18.445 | .000 | 185.56 | 26 | .000 |
| Total within | | | | | | | | 233.75 | 56 | .000 |
| Total between | | | | | | | | 18.74 | 2 | .000 |
| Overall | 16,271 | 59 | .175 | 0.160 | 0.190 | 22.440 | .000 | 252.49 | 58 | .000 |
| *Best partials* | | | | | | | | | | |
| Experimental | 2,887 | 24 | .217 | 0.181 | 0.252 | 11.695 | .000 | 35.11 | 23 | .051 |
| Longitudinal | 3,312 | 8 | .059 | 0.025 | 0.093 | 3.400 | .001 | 7.81 | 7 | .349 |
| Cross-sectional | 6,399 | 21 | .114 | 0.090 | 0.138 | 9.128 | .000 | 19.84 | 20 | .468 |
| Total within | | | | | | | | 62.76 | 50 | .106 |
| Total between | | | | | | | | 40.49 | 2 | .000 |
| Overall | 12,598 | 53 | .123 | 0.106 | 0.141 | 13.826 | .000 | 103.25 | 52 | .000 |
| *Full sample* | | | | | | | | | | |
| Experimental | 4,289.5 | 48 | .207 | 0.177 | 0.236 | 13.496 | .000 | 90.00 | 47 | .000 |
| Longitudinal | 4,178.5 | 9 | .110 | 0.080 | 0.140 | 7.142 | .000 | 13.50 | 8 | .096 |
| Cross-sectional | 16,066 | 38 | .164 | 0.149 | 0.179 | 20.951 | .000 | 269.06 | 37 | .000 |
| Total within | | | | | | | | 372.56 | 92 | .000 |
| Total between | | | | | | | | 20.41 | 2 | .000 |
| Overall | 24,534 | 95 | .162 | 0.150 | 0.175 | 25.528 | .000 | 392.98 | 94 | .000 |

*Note:* Effect sizes measured as *r*. CI confidence interval; *LL* lower limit; *UL* upper limit.

However, for longitudinal studies, the VGV measure of video game exposure moderator was marginally significant, $Q(1) = 3.52$, $p < .07$. Studies that used VGV-specific measures ($r+ = .113$, $K = 4$, $N = 891$) yielded larger VGV effects than did those that used VGV-general type measures ($r+ = .040$, $K = 4$, $N = 2,421$). Also of importance was the finding that type of aggressive cognition measure (trait hostility vs. other) was completely confounded with culture and therefore yielded exactly the same moderation effect as reported earlier for culture. The five longitudinal studies from Japan all used a trait hostility measure, whereas the three studies from Western cultures used hostile attribution bias or attitude/belief measures. Thus, it is impossible to know whether this moderation effect results from culture differences in the VGV longitudinal effect or from measurement instrument differences.

## Summary

Exposure to violent video games was significantly related to higher levels of aggressive cognition, regardless of research design or conservativeness of analysis. For experimental studies, $r+ = .217$. For cross-sectional studies the best raw and best partials analyses yielded average effect sizes of $r+ = .183$ and .114, respectively. For longitudinal studies, the best raw and best partials analyses yielded average effect sizes of $r+ = .115$ and .059, respectively. Culture significantly moderated the longitudinal VGV effect, but the VGV effect was significantly greater than zero in both cases. Furthermore, in this small set of longitudinal studies culture was perfectly confounded with type of cognition measure. In addition, studies that used a VGV-specific measure yielded larger effects than those that used a VGV-general measure. Three of the four VGV-specific studies and none of the VGV-general studies were from the West. Therefore, it is unclear whether the smaller longitudinal effect in studies from Japan was the result of culture or of either or both of two measurement instrument differences. Additional research could easily resolve this.

As with the aggressive behavior results, perhaps the most important finding relative to prior meta-analyses is the significant longitudinal effect of VGV on aggressive cognition. In combination with the experimental and the cross-sectional findings, the data provide strong evidence that playing violent video games is a significant causal risk factor for both short- and long-term increases in aggressive thinking.

## Violent video game effects on aggressive affect

### Main analyses

Table 6 presents the results of the main analyses on aggressive affect. As with aggressive behavior and aggressive cognition, VGV exposure was significantly related to higher levels of aggressive affect regardless of research design and regardless of whether zero-order correlations or the more conservative partial correlations were used. Furthermore, even when sex and Time 1 aggressive

Table 6 Aggressive affect: average effect of violent video game exposure by study design for best raw, best partials, and full sample data sets

| Design | N | K | Effect size and 95% CI | | | Test of null (two-tailed) | | Heterogeneity | | |
|---|---|---|---|---|---|---|---|---|---|---|
| | | | Point estimate | LL | UL | z | p | Q | df(Q) | p |
| *Best raw* | | | | | | | | | | |
| Experimental | 1,454 | 21 | .294 | 0.245 | 0.341 | 11.289 | .000 | 49.15 | 20 | .000 |
| Longitudinal | 2,602 | 5 | .075 | 0.037 | 0.113 | 3.836 | .000 | 13.19 | 4 | .010 |
| Cross-sectional | 5,135 | 11 | .101 | 0.074 | 0.128 | 7.227 | .000 | 16.56 | 10 | .085 |
| Total within | | | | | | | | 78.91 | 34 | .000 |
| Total between | | | | | | | | 53.18 | 2 | .000 |
| Overall | 9,191 | 37 | .124 | 0.104 | 0.144 | 11.883 | .000 | 132.08 | 36 | .000 |
| *Best partials* | | | | | | | | | | |
| Experimental | 1,454 | 21 | .294 | 0.245 | 0.341 | 11.289 | .000 | 49.15 | 20 | .000 |
| Longitudinal | 2,602 | 5 | .039 | 0.0001 | 0.077 | 1.967 | .049 | 9.76 | 4 | .045 |
| Cross-sectional | 3,487 | 9 | .110 | 0.077 | 0.143 | 6.509 | .000 | 9.78 | 8 | .281 |
| Total within | | | | | | | | 68.70 | 32 | .000 |
| Total between | | | | | | | | 63.83 | 2 | .000 |
| Overall | 7,543 | 35 | .121 | 0.098 | 0.143 | 10.481 | .000 | 132.53 | 34 | .000 |
| *Full sample* | | | | | | | | | | |
| Experimental | 3,015 | 37 | .181 | 0.146 | 0.216 | 9.863 | .000 | 111.22 | 36 | .000 |
| Longitudinal | 3,373 | 6 | .082 | 0.048 | 0.116 | 4.768 | .000 | 13.73 | 5 | .017 |
| Cross-sectional | 10,982 | 19 | .145 | 0.126 | 0.163 | 15.215 | .000 | 153.17 | 18 | .000 |
| Total within | | | | | | | | 278.12 | 59 | .000 |
| Total between | | | | | | | | 16.87 | 2 | .000 |
| Overall | 17,370 | 62 | .139 | 0.124 | 0.153 | 18.293 | .000 | 294.99 | 61 | .000 |

*Note:* Effect sizes measured as *r*. CI confidence interval; *LL* lower limit; *UL* upper limit.

affect were controlled, amount of violent video game play at Time 1 predicted a significant increase in aggressive affect at Time 2.

As with aggressive behavior and aggressive cognition, research design was a significant moderator of the VGV effect on aggressive affect. Experimental studies yielded the largest effects and longitudinal studies the smallest.

### Additional moderator tests—best partials data

There were too few longitudinal studies for us to do any additional moderator analyses. Furthermore, none of the moderator variables yielded a significant effect in experimental or cross-sectional studies, even though there was evidence of significant heterogeneity within experimental studies.

## Violent video game effects on prosocial behavior

### Main analyses

Table 7 presents the main results on prosocial behavior. VGV exposure was significantly related to lower levels of prosocial behavior regardless of research design and regardless of whether zero-order or the partial correlations were used. Even when sex and Time 1 prosocial behavior were controlled, amount of violent video game play at Time 1 predicted a significant decrease in prosocial behavior at Time 2 in longitudinal studies.

Yet again, research design was a significant moderator of the VGV effect on prosocial behavior, with experimental studies yielding the largest (negative) effects and longitudinal studies the smallest. Once sex and Time 1 effects were partialed out, there was no evidence of heterogeneity in the experimental or longitudinal effects, but there was in the cross-sectional studies.

### Additional moderator tests—best partials data

There were too few experimental and longitudinal studies to do any additional moderator analyses on them. For cross-sectional studies we were able to test for culture, sex, and VGV type of measure effects. On average, the VGV effect on prosocial behavior was larger in the Western studies ($r+ = -.225, K = 2, N = 347$) than in Eastern studies ($r+ = -.079, K = 5, N = 3,148$), $Q(1) = 6.83, p < .01$. There also was a significant effect of violent video game exposure measure, $Q(1) = 13.69, p .001$. Studies that used the VGV-specific type of measure yielded larger (negative) effects ($r+ = -.186, K = 3, N = 1,074$) than those that used general measures ($r+ = -.052, K = 4, N = 2421$). Furthermore, culture and VGV measure were confounded; two of the three VGV-specific studies came from a Western culture, whereas all of the VGV-general studies came from Eastern cultures. Finally, there was no evidence of sex differences in the effect of violent games on prosocial behavior.

415

Table 7 Prosocial behavior: average effect of violent video game exposure by study design for best raw, best partials, and full sample data sets

| Design | N | K | Effect size and 95% CI | | | Test of null (two-tailed) | | Heterogeneity | | |
|---|---|---|---|---|---|---|---|---|---|---|
| | | | Point estimate | LL | UL | z | p | Q | df(Q) | p |
| *Best raw* | | | | | | | | | | |
| Experimental | 633 | 4 | -.182 | -0.257 | -0.106 | -4.599 | .000 | 3.79 | 3 | .285 |
| Longitudinal | 2,778 | 5 | -.114 | -0.151 | -0.077 | -6.022 | .000 | 15.91 | 4 | .003 |
| Cross-sectional | 3,495 | 7 | -.093 | -0.126 | -0.060 | -5.506 | .000 | 19.07 | 6 | .004 |
| Total within | | | | | | | | 38.77 | 13 | .000 |
| Total between | | | | | | | | 4.46 | 2 | .107 |
| Overall | 6,906 | 16 | -.110 | -0.133 | -0.086 | -9.125 | .000 | 43.23 | 15 | .000 |
| *Best partials* | | | | | | | | | | |
| Experimental | 633 | 4 | -.182 | -0.257 | -0.106 | -4.599 | .000 | 3.79 | 3 | .285 |
| Longitudinal | 2,777 | 5 | -.062 | -0.099 | -0.025 | -3.268 | .001 | 2.32 | 4 | .677 |
| Cross-sectional | 3,495 | 7 | -.094 | -0.127 | -0.061 | -5.544 | .000 | 19.25 | 6 | .004 |
| Total within | | | | | | | | 25.36 | 13 | .021 |
| Total between | | | | | | | | 7.74 | 2 | .021 |
| Overall | 6,905 | 16 | -.089 | -0.113 | -0.066 | -7.404 | .000 | 33.10 | 15 | .004 |
| *Full sample* | | | | | | | | | | |
| Experimental | 875 | 8 | -.161 | -0.226 | -0.095 | -4.748 | .000 | 5.26 | 7 | .629 |
| Longitudinal | 2,778 | 5 | -.114 | -0.151 | -0.077 | -6.022 | .000 | 15.91 | 4 | .003 |
| Cross-sectional | 5,992 | 10 | -.086 | -0.111 | -0.061 | -6.659 | .000 | 29.29 | 9 | .001 |
| Total within | | | | | | | | 50.46 | 20 | .000 |
| Total between | | | | | | | | 5.05 | 2 | .080 |
| Overall | 9,645 | 23 | -.101 | -0.121 | -0.081 | -9.904 | .000 | 55.51 | 22 | .000 |

*Note:* Effect sizes measured as *r.* CI = confidence interval; LL = lower limit; UL = upper limit.

### *Violent video game effects on empathy/desensitization*

#### *Main analyses*

Table 8 presents the main results on empathy/desensitization. VGV exposure was significantly related to less empathy (and more desensitization) regardless of research design and regardless of whether the zero-order or partial correlations were used.

When sex and Time 1 effects were controlled, research design was a significant moderator variable. Of course, because there was only one experimental study, comparisons across designs should be made with caution.

#### *Additional moderator tests—best partials data*

There were too few experimental and longitudinal studies to do any additional moderator analyses. For cross-sectional studies, we were able to test the moderating effects of culture and video game exposure measure. On average, effect sizes were larger in Western studies ($r+ = -.294$, $K = 4$, $N = 450$) than in Eastern studies ($r+ = -.144$, $K = 5$, $N = 3,148$), $Q(1) = 9.53$, $p < .01$. There also was a significant effect for video game exposure measure, $Q(1) = 4.36$, $p < .05$. Studies that used the VGV-specific type of measure yielded larger (negative) effects ($r+ = -.211$, $K = 5$, $N = 1,177$) than did those using the VGV-general measure ($r+ = -.139$, $K = 4$, $N = 2,421$). Furthermore, culture and video game exposure measure were confounded; four of the five VGV-specific studies came from a Western culture, whereas all of the VGV-general studies came from Eastern cultures.

### *Violent video game effects on physiological arousal*

#### *Main analyses*

All of the physiological arousal studies were experiments. Overall, playing a violent video game increased physiological arousal ($r+ = .184$, $p < .001$, $K = 15$, $N = 969$). The heterogeneity test was significant, $Q(14) = 30.43$, $p < .01$. We were able to conduct moderator analyses for player perspective, player role, game violence target, average age, and gameplaying time. However, none of the moderator tests approached statistical significance.

### *Sensitivity analyses*

#### *Full sample*

Recall that numerous studies did not meet the inclusion criteria listed in Table 2. What happens if these methodologically weak studies are included in the main analyses? Are there systematic differences in average effect size? Table 9 displays the results. Three main points emerge. First, for each of the six outcome variables, the violent video game effect size was still significant even when

417

Table 8 Empathy/desensitization: average effect of violent video game exposure by study design for best raw, best partials, and full sample data sets

| Design | N | K | Effect size and 95% CI | | | Test of null (two-tailed) | | Heterogeneity | | |
|---|---|---|---|---|---|---|---|---|---|---|
| | | | Point estimate | LL | UL | z | p | Q | df(Q) | p |
| *Best raw* | | | | | | | | | | |
| Experimental | 249 | 1 | -0.138 | -0.258 | -0.014 | -2.175 | .030 | 0.00 | 0 | 1.000 |
| Longitudinal | 2,421 | 4 | -0.184 | -0.223 | -0.145 | -9.147 | .000 | 24.88 | 3 | 0.000 |
| Cross-sectional | 3,910 | 10 | -0.203 | -0.233 | -0.173 | -12.845 | .000 | 24.46 | 9 | 0.004 |
| Total within | | | | | | | | 49.34 | 12 | 0.000 |
| Total between | | | | | | | | 1.44 | 2 | 0.488 |
| Overall | 6,580 | 15 | -0.194 | -0.217 | -0.170 | -15.873 | .000 | 50.78 | 14 | 0.000 |
| *Best partials* | | | | | | | | | | |
| Experimental | 249 | 1 | -0.138 | -0.258 | -0.014 | -2.175 | .030 | 0.00 | 0 | 1.000 |
| Longitudinal | 2,421 | 4 | -0.070 | -0.109 | -0.030 | -3.427 | .001 | 12.82 | 3 | 0.005 |
| Cross-sectional | 3,598 | 9 | -0.163 | -0.195 | -0.131 | -9.817 | .000 | 23.10 | 8 | 0.003 |
| Total within | | | | | | | | 35.92 | 11 | 0.000 |
| Total between | | | | | | | | 12.87 | 2 | 0.002 |
| Overall | 6,268 | 14 | -0.126 | -0.150 | -0.102 | -9.999 | .000 | 48.79 | 13 | 0.000 |
| *Full sample* | | | | | | | | | | |
| Experimental | 537 | 11 | -0.148 | -0.232 | -0.062 | -3.351 | .001 | 24.20 | 10 | 0.007 |
| Longitudinal | 2,796 | 6 | -0.160 | -0.196 | -0.123 | -8.501 | .000 | 37.23 | 5 | 0.000 |
| Cross-sectional | 5,195 | 15 | -0.188 | -0.214 | -0.162 | -13.671 | .000 | 55.96 | 14 | 0.000 |
| Total within | | | | | | | | 117.39 | 29 | 0.000 |
| Total between | | | | | | | | 2.00 | 2 | 0.369 |
| Overall | 8,528 | 32 | -0.177 | -0.197 | -0.156 | -16.383 | .000 | 119.38 | 31 | 0.000 |

*Note:* Effect sizes measured as *r*. CI = confidence interval; *LL* = lower limit; *UL* = upper limit.

Table 9 Effects of methodologically weak versus strong studies

| Methodological quality | N | K | Effect size and 95% CI | | | Test of null (two-tailed) | | Heterogeneity | | |
|---|---|---|---|---|---|---|---|---|---|---|
| | | | Point estimate | LL | UL | z | p | Q | df(Q) | p |
| *Aggressive behavior* | | | | | | | | | | |
| Weak | 46,632 | 61 | 0.163 | 0.154 | 0.172 | 35.506 | .000 | 504.84 | 60 | .000 |
| Strong | 21,681 | 79 | 0.244 | 0.231 | 0.256 | 36.422 | .000 | 284.86 | 78 | .000 |
| Total within | | | | | | | | 789.70 | 138 | .000 |
| Total between | | | | | | | | 103.46 | 1 | .000 |
| Overall | 68,313 | 140 | 0.189 | 0.182 | 0.196 | 49.838 | .000 | 893.16 | 139 | .000 |
| *Aggressive cognition* | | | | | | | | | | |
| Weak | 8,263 | 36 | 0.138 | 0.116 | 0.159 | 12.497 | .000 | 132.46 | 35 | .000 |
| Strong | 16,271 | 59 | 0.175 | 0.160 | 0.190 | 22.440 | .000 | 252.49 | 58 | .000 |
| Total within | | | | | | | | 384.95 | 93 | .000 |
| Total between | | | | | | | | 8.02 | 1 | .005 |
| Overall | 24,534 | 95 | 0.162 | 0.150 | 0.175 | 25.528 | .000 | 392.98 | 94 | .000 |
| *Aggressive affect* | | | | | | | | | | |
| Weak | 8,179 | 25 | 0.155 | 0.134 | 0.176 | 14.060 | .000 | 158.67 | 24 | .000 |
| Strong | 9,191 | 37 | 0.124 | 0.104 | 0.144 | 11.883 | .000 | 132.08 | 36 | .000 |
| Total within | | | | | | | | 290.75 | 60 | .000 |
| Total between | | | | | | | | 4.24 | 1 | .039 |
| Overall | 17,370 | 62 | 0.139 | 0.124 | 0.153 | 18.293 | .000 | 294.99 | 61 | .000 |

*(Continued)*

Table 9 (Continued)

| Methodological quality | N | K | Effect size and 95% CI | | | Test of null (two-tailed) | | Heterogeneity | | |
|---|---|---|---|---|---|---|---|---|---|---|
| | | | Point estimate | LL | UL | z | p | Q | df(Q) | p |
| *Prosocial behavior* | | | | | | | | | | |
| Weak | 2,739 | 7 | -0.078 | -0.116 | -0.041 | -4.095 | .000 | 10.33 | 6 | .111 |
| Strong | 6,906 | 16 | -0.110 | -0.133 | -0.086 | -9.125 | .000 | 43.23 | 15 | .000 |
| Total within | | | | | | | | 53.56 | 21 | .000 |
| Total between | | | | | | | | 1.95 | 1 | .163 |
| Overall | 9,645 | 23 | -0.101 | -0.121 | -0.081 | -9.904 | .000 | 55.51 | 22 | .000 |
| *Empathy/desensitization* | | | | | | | | | | |
| Weak | 1,948 | 17 | -0.116 | -0.160 | -0.071 | -5.078 | .000 | 59.26 | 16 | .000 |
| Strong | 6,580 | 15 | -0.194 | -0.217 | -0.170 | -15.873 | .000 | 50.78 | 14 | .000 |
| Total within | | | | | | | | 110.03 | 30 | .000 |
| Total between | | | | | | | | 9.35 | 1 | .002 |
| Overall | 8,528 | 32 | -0.177 | -0.197 | -0.156 | -16.383 | .000 | 119.38 | 31 | .000 |
| *Physiological arousal* | | | | | | | | | | |
| Weak | 937 | 14 | 0.085 | 0.020 | 0.150 | 2.552 | .011 | 10.47 | 13 | .655 |
| Strong | 969 | 15 | 0.184 | 0.121 | 0.245 | 5.647 | .000 | 30.43 | 14 | .007 |
| Total within | | | | | | | | 40.89 | 27 | .042 |
| Total between | | | | | | | | 4.59 | 1 | .032 |
| Overall | 1,906 | 29 | 0.135 | 0.090 | 0.180 | 5.814 | .000 | 45.48 | 28 | .020 |

*Note:* Effect sizes measured as *r*. *CI* = confidence interval; *LL* = lower limit; *UL* = upper limit.

methodologically weaker studies were included ($ps < .001$). Second, for five of the outcome variables the methodologically weak studies yielded smaller effect sizes than did the methodologically strong studies; in four cases the difference was statistically significant. The exception was aggressive affect, for which the methodologically weak studies yielded a significantly larger average effect size. Third, for each outcome variable even the methodologically weak studies yielded a significant overall effect.

### Trim and fill analyses

Table 10 presents the results of the trim and fill analyses, as a further check on possible selection/ publication bias. For each outcome variable, we first applied the trim and fill procedure to the full sample (which included both methodologically weak and strong studies) and the best raw sample, ignoring research design.

Next, because research design was such a strong and consistent moderator variable for the best partials samples and because these samples are the main focus of this article, we also applied the trim and fill procedure to the best partials data by research design. Recall that sample size, research design, culture, and specific research instruments are somewhat confounded in these studies. Therefore, within each outcome and research design we broke down the studies into smaller subgroups using the following decision rule: If there was a significant moderator effect, separate trim and fill analyses were done on the different levels of that moderator; otherwise, separate analyses were done by culture. Of course, in several cases there were too few studies for these breakdowns, in which case the trim and fill procedure was applied at a higher level of studies. For example, all of the best practices physiological studies used an experimental design, and only one of these studies was from an Eastern culture.

The summarized results at the bottom of Table 10 suggest that if there has been selection or publication bias in favor of theoretical hypotheses in these samples, the bias has been weak and has had relatively little impact on average effect-size estimates. For example, experimental studies were weakened by .017 by the trim and fill imputation procedure. The cross-sectional studies were weakened by an even smaller amount, .005. Conversely, the longitudinal studies were strengthened by an average of .008. In sum, there is no evidence that publication or selection bias had an important influence on the results.

## Discussion

### Main findings

Although the meta-analyses in this article revealed numerous findings about the short- and long-term effects of playing violent video games, six findings are particularly important. First, social– cognitive models and other theoretical considerations predicted the broad pattern of results quite well. As expected, VGV exposure was positively associated with aggressive behavior, aggressive cognition,

*Table 10* Results of the trim and fill selection/publication bias analysis

| Sample | K | Imputed studies | | Obs. r+ | Adj. r+ | Change | Strength change |
|---|---|---|---|---|---|---|---|
| | | N | Direction | | | | |
| *Aggressive behavior* | | | | | | | |
| Full | 140 | 10 | Right | 0.189 | 0.192 | 0.003 | 0.003 |
| Best raw | 79 | 1 | Right | 0.244 | 0.244 | 0.000 | 0.000 |
| Best partials: Experimental | 27 | | | | | | |
| East | 5 | 0 | | 0.245 | 0.245 | 0.000 | 0.000 |
| West | 22 | 8 | Left | 0.207 | 0.178 | -0.029 | -0.029 |
| Best partials: Cross-sectional | 36 | | | | | | |
| East | 8 | 1 | Left | 0.163 | 0.160 | -0.003 | -0.003 |
| West | 28 | 3 | Left | 0.182 | 0.176 | -0.006 | -0.006 |
| Best partials: Longitudinal | 12 | | | | | | |
| VGV-specific | 4 | 1 | Left | 0.152 | 0.143 | -0.009 | -0.009 |
| VGV-general | 8 | 1 | Left | 0.055 | 0.054 | -0.001 | -0.001 |
| *Aggressive cognition* | | | | | | | |
| Full | 95 | 12 | Right | 0.163 | 0.170 | 0.008 | 0.008 |
| Best raw | 59 | 0 | | 0.175 | 0.175 | 0.000 | 0.000 |
| Best partials: Experimental | 24 | 5 | Left | 0.217 | 0.199 | -0.018 | -0.018 |
| Best partials: Cross-sectional | 21 | | | | | | |
| East | 6 | 1 | Left | 0.102 | 0.100 | -0.002 | -0.002 |
| West | 15 | 4 | Left | 0.127 | 0.106 | -0.021 | -0.021 |
| Best partials: Longitudinal | 8 | | | | | | |
| East | 5 | 0 | | 0.038 | 0.038 | 0.000 | 0.000 |
| West | 3 | 2 | Right | 0.137 | 0.182 | 0.045 | 0.045 |
| *Aggressive affect* | | | | | | | |
| Full | 62 | 17 | Left | 0.139 | 0.100 | -0.039 | -0.039 |
| Best raw | 37 | 15 | Left | 0.124 | 0.102 | -0.022 | -0.022 |
| Best partials: Experimental | 21 | 0 | | 0.294 | 0.294 | -0.000 | -0.000 |
| Best partials: Cross-sectional | 9 | | | | | | |
| East | 5 | 2 | Left | 0.097 | 0.062 | -0.035 | -0.035 |
| West | 4 | 2 | Left | 0.150 | 0.137 | -0.013 | -0.013 |
| Best partials: Longitudinal | 5 | 1 | Right | 0.039 | 0.049 | 0.011 | 0.011 |

*Prosocial behavior*

| | | | | | | | |
|---|---|---|---|---|---|---|---|
| Full | 23 | 10 | Right | -0.101 | -0.064 | -0.037 | -0.037 |
| Best raw | 16 | 4 | Right | -0.110 | -0.089 | -0.021 | -0.021 |
| Best partials: Experimental | 4 | 2 | Right | -0.182 | -0.125 | -0.057 | -0.057 |
| Best partials: Cross-sectional | 7 | | | | | | |
|   VGV-specific | 3 | 2 | Right | -0.186 | -0.168 | 0.018 | -0.018 |
|   VGV-general | 4 | 2 | Right | -0.052 | -0.033 | 0.019 | -0.019 |
| Best partials: Longitudinal | 5 | 2 | Left | -0.062 | -0.070 | -0.008 | 0.008 |
| *Empathy/desensitization* | | | | | | | |
| Full | 32 | 2 | Left | -0.177 | -0.179 | -0.002 | -0.002 |
| Best raw | 15 | 0 | | -0.194 | -0.194 | 0.000 | 0.000 |
| Best partials: Cross-sectional | 9 | | Left | | | | |
|   East | 5 | 2 | Left | -0.144 | -0.167 | -0.023 | -0.023 |
|   West | 4 | 0 | | -0.294 | -0.294 | 0.000 | 0.000 |
|   VGV-specific | 5 | 0 | | -0.211 | -0.211 | 0.000 | 0.000 |
|   VGV-general | 4 | 2 | Left | -0.139 | -0.171 | -0.032 | -0.032 |
| Best partials: Longitudinal | 4 | 0 | | -0.070 | -0.070 | 0.000 | 0.000 |
| *Physiological arousal* | | | | | | | |
| Full | 29 | 0 | | 0.135 | 0.135 | 0.000 | 0.000 |
| Best raw and partials | 15 | 0 | | 0.184 | 0.184 | 0.000 | 0.000 |
| Overall average | | | | | | | -0.006 |
| Full average | | | | | | | -0.011 |
| Best raw average | | | | | | | -0.007 |
| *Imputed studies* | | | | | | | |
| Best partials: Experimental average | | | | | | | -0.017 |
| Best partials: Cross-sectional average | | | | | | | -0.017 |
| Best partials: Longitudinal average | | | | | | | -0.008 |

*Note:* Strength change is the difference between the observed and adjusted, taking into account the hypothesized effect direction. VGV = video game violence; Obs. $r+$ = observed average effect size; Adj. $r+$ = Adjusted average effect size.

and aggressive affect. These effects were statistically reliable in experimental, cross-sectional, and longitudinal studies, even when unusually conservative statistical procedures were used. Also as expected, VGV exposure was related to desensitization and lack of empathy and to lack of prosocial behavior. Furthermore, the relative magnitudes of effects for different outcome variables and moderator variables were mainly consistent with theory. For example, the longitudinal effect of VGV was somewhat smaller on aggressive affect than on aggressive cognition or behavior. This suggests that the processes underlying media violence effects are well understood (cf. Anderson et al., 2003).

Second, the VGV effects are significant in Eastern as well as Western cultures. There are hints that VGV effects may be larger in Western than Eastern cultures, but these occur only in nonexperimental studies. Indeed, in experimental studies all three outcome variables for which there were sufficient studies (aggressive behavior, aggressive cognition, and aggressive affect) yielded slightly larger effects in Eastern studies, though none approached statistical significance. In the few nonexperimental cases in which culture yielded a significant moderator effect, it was unclear whether the difference should be attributed to cultural differences in vulnerability or to the use of different measures.

Third, there is evidence that the magnitude of the effect size obtained in a study is influenced by the types of measures one uses. How one measures exposure to violent video games in nonexperimental contexts influences the magnitude of effects. Measurement procedures, similar to those used by Anderson and Dill (2000), that elicit violence and time ratings for each specific game played by the participant appear to yield larger effect sizes than do other methods. However, to some extent this finding is confounded with culture. What is needed to clarify this issue are studies in which multiple methods of assessing violent video game exposure are used in the same sample of participants, so that they can be directly compared. Similarly, it appears that trait hostility measures may not be the best way to assess aggressive cognition.

Fourth, and perhaps most important, the newly available longitudinal studies provide further confirmation that playing violent video games is a causal risk factor for long-term harmful outcomes. This is especially clear for aggressive behavior, aggressive cognition, and empathy/desensitization. But significant longitudinal VGV effects also were found for aggressive affect and for prosocial behavior.

Fifth, the failures of several specific moderators to yield significant effects are also important for theoretical and practical reasons. In experimental studies, the lack of player perspective (first or third person), player role (hero, criminal), time on game, and target (human, nonhuman) all suggest that the short-term effects of violent video games on aggression are largely the result of priming processes (see Bushman & Huesmann, 2006). The fact that the CRT task yielded effect sizes similar to those from other measures of aggressive behavior in experimental studies strongly contradicts recent claims that it is only CRT studies that find such effects; indeed, the average CRT effect was slightly (nonsignificantly) smaller than for the other measures. The fact that studies using violent behavior measures did not yield significantly smaller effects than comparable studies using less extreme aggression measures, and that the violent behavior studies by themselves yielded a significant VGV effect, is important. The facts that sex did not significantly moderate the findings and that age yielded only one marginally significant moderation effect suggest that large portions of the population (at least through college age) are susceptible to the harmful effects of violent video game play.

Sixth, our results confirm that partialing out sex effects and (in longitudinal studies) Time 1 outcome variable effects reduces average effect size. This is not surprising, of course, but it does lead to interesting questions about what is the "best" estimate of the true effect sizes. Partialing out sex effects certainly is a safe, conservative procedure in that it guarantees that the estimated average effect size will not be upwardly biased. However, if violent video game exposure truly plays a causal role in aggression and in the other outcomes assessed in these meta-analyses (and our conservative procedures do demonstrate this), partialing out sex effects yields underestimates of the true effect size. Perhaps the best solution is to view sex-controlled estimates as the lower boundary of the true effects and the sex-ignored effects as the upper boundary.[11]

Two additional findings warrant highlighting, especially in view of all the attention that has paid recently to claims of publication bias and other weaknesses in the violent video game literature. First, there was no evidence that publication (or study selection bias) is responsible for the observed relations between exposure to violent video games and aggressive behavior or the other five outcome variables. Differences between the observed average effect sizes and the corresponding trim and fill adjusted averages were small in magnitude and did not substantially change any overall effects or conclusions. Second, our other sensitivity analyses (see Table 9) showed that even including methodologically weak studies (studies that would not be analyzed in noncontroversial fields of study) yields relatively small changes in average effect sizes. Even the weak studies yielded significant overall effects on all six outcome variables. In sum, the only way one can "demonstrate" that the existing literature on violent video game effects does not show multiple causal harmful effects is to use an incredibly small subset of the existing literature, include some of the methodologically poorest studies, exclude many of the methodologically strongest studies, and misuse standard meta-analytic techniques.

Finally, it is important to note that our main analyses were conducted on the most conservative sample of studies, in which all explained variance that is confounded with sex or Time 1 outcome measures is statistically removed from the estimates of the VGV effects. Thus, the finding of significant VGV effects on all outcome measures and in all research designs speaks to the power of video games.

## *Magnitude of average effect sizes*

We have no doubt that the import of the average effect sizes reported in this article will be greatly debated. There are at least two major issues, one concerning which estimates are most appropriate and the other concerning the importance of the average effect sizes.

Consider the results for physically aggressive behavior, shown in Figure 1. Which are the most appropriate estimates of the true violent video game effect, the raw estimates for cross-sectional and longitudinal studies or those that partialed out sex (and Time 1) effects? We believe that there is no single correct answer. On the one hand, the two facts that males spend more time than females playing violent video games and that males generally (but not always) are more physically aggressive than females suggest that an appropriately conservative test of violent video game effects should partial out sex effects. On the other hand, once it has been established that violent video game play is a causal risk factor for physical aggression in both males and females, it becomes clear that partialing out sex effects yields underestimates of the effect of violent video games.

Concerning the importance issue, are the effect sizes large enough to be considered important? From a theoretical standpoint, the answer is pretty clear. Prevailing social–cognitive theories predict statistically significant effects but do not predict absolute magnitude; finding the predicted effects to be significant therefore lends support to the theories.

From a practical or applied standpoint, the answer is less clear. From a strict "percentage of variance explained" perspective, the longitudinal effect size with sex and Time 1 aggression partialed out might seem small (i.e., $0.152^2 = 2.31\%$). However, as numerous authors have pointed out, even small effect sizes can be of major practical significance. When effects accumulate across time, or when large portions of the population are exposed to the risk factor, or when consequences are severe, statistically small effects become much more important (Abelson, 1985; Rosenthal, 1986, 1990). All three of these conditions apply to violent video game effects.

Furthermore, when dealing with a multicausal phenomenon such as aggression, one should not expect any single factor to explain much of the variance. There are dozens of known risk factors for both short-term aggression and the development of aggression-prone individuals. To expect any one factor to account for more than a small fraction of variance is unrealistic. This suggests that a better way to assess the practical importance of violent video game effects is to compare it to some other known risk factors for youth violence. In fact, even the overly conservative sex and Time 1 adjusted VGV effect size estimate ($r+ = .152$) compares favorably to such risk factors as substance use, abusive parents, and poverty (U.S. Department of Health and Human Services, 2001).[12]

426

### *Learning from the past*

#### *Learning from our mistakes*

Additional findings of importance come not from the meta-analytic results but from the review and selection process involved in identifying studies of sufficient quality to merit inclusion in the focal analyses. There are a lot of methodological pitfalls that the wary researcher must avoid in this domain, there are a lot of researchers who are not avoiding them, and there are a lot of editors who are publishing them. The quality criteria described in Table 2 and the more specific examples outlined on our website could (and should) prove useful to many people who are involved in media violence research, including faculty supervisors of undergraduate and graduate students, journal editors and their manuscript reviewers, and some media violence scholars themselves.

We do not intend to imply that those studies that did not meet all of our quality criteria are useless; some of them yielded findings of some value on other research questions. Similarly, we do not intend to imply that those studies that met our best practices criteria are without shortcomings. There is no such thing as a perfect study. Several of the most frequent weaknesses of studies that did pass the present quality check are use of single-item outcome measures; use of longitudinal time periods that may be too short for the phenomenon of interest; use of weak measures of exposure to violent video games; and sample sizes that are too small given the expected effect size. The first three tend to lead to underestimates of the true effect size, whereas the third tends to yield nonsignificant statistical test results.

Contrary to claims by video game industry representatives, some gamers, and a few researchers, in general it is not the methodologically poor studies that tend to yield big effects. Rather, methodologically superior studies tend to yield larger effects.

#### *Gaps and future research*

This review also revealed a number of gaps in the research literature. One involves the lack of age effects, especially in longitudinal studies. Most scholars in this area believe that younger children are likely to be more vulnerable than older adolescents and young adults to long-term media violence effects. But there is little evidence of larger effect sizes for younger than for older participants. Indeed, a recent television study suggests that even late adolescents are vulnerable (Johnson, Cohen, Smailes, Kasen, & Brook, 2002).

Our cross-sectional analysis yielded a marginally significant negative relationship between age and the effect of violent games on aggressive behavior, but the longitudinal studies did not find an age effect. Part of the problem may be that meta-analytic procedures are not ideally suited to testing such effects. Different studies typically use different measures of aggression and video game habits, include different participant populations, and take place during different years. All of the differences add noise to the meta-analysis, noise that may well hide real age effects. New research is needed in which different-age participants are sampled from the same population, the same measures are used (or as similar as is reasonable given the age differences), and all of the data collection takes place in the same years. Such studies should yield cleaner tests of whether or not long-term effects of video game violence are larger for younger than older participants.

Similarly, we believe that many moderator variables of interest can be more precisely examined within the same study than they can in meta-analyses. For example, as a test for short-term player perspective effects, it would be best to conduct experiments in which participants are randomly assigned to play the same violent game but from different perspectives. Similar studies are needed to more closely examine player role effects, target effects, and time effects.

In the aggression domain, pre–post and repeated measures designs are generally problematic because of suspicion, practice, and carryover effects. Longitudinal designs solve these problems to some extent, but such designs do not allow experimental tests of the immediate, short-term consequences of playing violent video games. Some types of dependent variables are less susceptible to these problems, such as reaction time tasks that presumably assess effects without the participant's awareness (e.g., lexical decision, reading reaction time, and implicit association tasks). Cognitive neuroscience approaches also are likely to prove especially valuable in more precisely assessing the immediate effects of playing violent and nonviolent video games on a host of cognitive and affective processes (e.g., Bailey, West, & Anderson, in press; Weber, Ritterfeld, & Mathiak, 2006). For example, previous research has mapped specific brain areas that are especially active during violent and nonviolent actions within the same game, using functional magnetic resonance imaging techniques (Weber et al., 2006).

## Conclusions

The present findings show that the social–cognitive theoretical view fits the existing data on video game violence effects quite well. This has important implications for public policy debates, for further development and testing of basic theory, and for development and testing of potential intervention strategies designed to reduce harmful effects of playing violent video games. Concerning basic theory, additional research of all three types (but especially experimental and longitudinal) is needed, especially on VGV effects on empathy, desensitization, and prosocial behavior. Additional longitudinal studies with longer intervals are needed for aggressive behavior and aggressive cognition. Furthermore, longitudinal studies with very large samples and very long time spans between the first time period and the last are needed so we can assess the impact of violent video games on very serious forms of physical aggression (i.e., violence). Concerning interventions, there have been a few studies with findings that suggest that specific programs involving school children and their parents can reduce exposure to violent media and the frequency of unwarranted aggressive behavior (e.g., Huesmann, Eron, Klein, Brice, & Fischer, 1983; Robinson, Wilde, Navracruz, Haydel, & Varady, 2001).

Concerning public policy, we believe that debates can and should finally move beyond the simple question of whether violent video game play is a causal risk factor for aggressive behavior; the scientific literature has effectively and clearly shown the answer to be "yes." Instead, we believe the public policy debate should move to questions concerning how best to deal with this risk factor. Public education about this risk factor—and about how parents, schools, and society at large can deal with it—could be very useful.

It is true that as a player you are "not just moving your hand on a joystick" but are indeed interacting "with the game psychologically and emotionally." It is not surprising that when the game involves rehearsing aggressive and violent thoughts and actions, such deep game involvement results in antisocial effects on the player. Of course, the same basic social–cognitive processes should also yield prosocial effects when game content is primarily prosocial. Unfortunately, there has been relatively little research on purely prosocial game effects, largely because there are few games that have the main characters modeling helpful behavior in the complete absence of violent behavior. However, some recent studies have found that prosocial games can increase cooperation and helping (Gentile et al., 2009; Greitemeyer & Osswald, 2009). Video games are neither inherently good nor inherently bad. But people learn. And content matters.

## Notes

1 The Anderson et al. (2004) analysis differed only slightly from Anderson (2004) and yielded an almost identical effect for the methodologically better studies, $r+ = .27$ ($K = 18$, $N = 3,537$).

2 We thank Christopher Ferguson for providing the list of articles used in his three meta-analyses.

3 Note that of the violent video game studies we located from Eastern cultures, the vast majority came from Japan. Indeed, there were only two studies from other Eastern cultures, one from Singapore and the other from China.

4 Differences in crime definitions and reporting method may account for some portion of this reversal, but most scholars in the field agree that violence rates in the United Kingdom are higher than in the United States, with the exception of that for homicide, which is considerably higher in the United States. A common explanation for the high homicide rate in the United States is the easy availability of guns, especially handguns.

5 Of course, the quality of that study relative to tests of violent video game effects on aggressive cognition would be very high.

6 Study quality also varies within each of these two broad categories. Although one might attempt a more fine-grained, multilevel assessment of quality, such an attempt would require more studies than presently exist in this domain.

7 As should be clear, many of the not best practices effects were never intended by the original authors as tests of the specific hypothesis for which they earned not best practices status. In many cases, the not best practices effects were the result of high-quality procedures used to improve the precision of the main hypothesis test. In other cases, the not best practices effect was not part of the main study at all but was simply reported in a correlation matrix that included other variables that were the main focus of the article. Thus, neither readers nor authors of original reports should interpret a not

best practices listing as a negative judgment about the author's methodological skills or the overall value of the study that included the not best practices effect.

8 For several studies, the only estimates possible were some type of partial correlation. Rather than discard potentially useful information, we kept these in both of the best practices analyses.

9 The totals across outcome variables in the table are not all independent samples, because many studies reported multiple outcome variables for the same sample.

10 For completeness, we also included results from the full sample, but these results are not discussed in any detail.

11 Of course, there also are measurement reliability issues that will tend to make empirical estimates smaller than true effects.

12 It is unclear from this Surgeon General report whether all of the reported longitudinal effects were similarly based on sex and Time 1 adjusted partial correlations. Also note that one criterion for inclusion in the Surgeon General report was violent behavior. The present longitudinal studies of the VGV/physical aggression include some violent behavior but also include somewhat less severe forms of physical aggression. Thus, the effects are not strictly comparable.

# References

Abelson, R. P. (1985). A variance explanation paradox: When a little is a lot. *Psychological Bulletin, 97*, 129–133.

Anderson, C. A. (2004). An update on the effects of violent video games. *Journal of Adolescence, 27*, 113–122.

Anderson, C. A., Berkowitz, L., Donnerstein, E., Huesmann, L. R., Johnson, J., Linz, D., . . . Wartella, E. (2003). The influence of media violence on youth. *Psychological Science in the Public Interest, 4*, 81–110.

Anderson, C. A., & Bushman, B. J. (2001). Effects of violent video games on aggressive behavior, aggressive cognition, aggressive affect, physiological arousal, and prosocial behavior: A meta-analytic review of the scientific literature. *Psychological Science, 12*, 353–359.

Anderson, C. A., & Bushman, B. J. (2002). Human aggression. *Annual Review of Psychology, 53*, 27–51.

Anderson, C. A., & Carnagey, N. L. (2004). Violent evil and the general aggression model. In A. Miller (Ed.), *The social psychology of good and evil* (pp. 168–192). New York, NY: Guilford.

Anderson, C. A., Carnagey, N. L., Flanagan, M., Benjamin, A. J., Eubanks, J., & Valentine, J. C. (2004). Violent video games: Specific effects of violent content on aggressive thoughts and behavior. *Advances in Experimental Social Psychology, 36*, 199–249.

Anderson, C. A., & Dill, K. E. (2000). Video games and aggressive thoughts, feelings, and behavior in the laboratory and in life. *Journal of Personality and Social Psychology, 78*, 772–790.

Anderson, C. A., Gentile, D. A., & Buckley, K. E. (2007). *Violent video game effects on children and adolescents: Theory, research, and public policy.* New York, NY: Oxford University Press.

Anderson, C. A., & Huesmann, L. R. (2003). Human aggression: A social–cognitive view. In M. A. Hogg & J. Cooper (Eds.), *Handbook of social psychology* (pp. 296–323). London, England: Sage.

Anderson, C. A., Lindsay, J. J., & Bushman, B. J. (1999). Research in the psychological laboratory: Truth or triviality? *Current Directions in Psychological Science, 8,* 3–9.

Bachrach, R. (1986). The differential effect of observation of violence on kibbutz and city children in Israel. In L. R. Huesmann & L. D. Eron (Eds.), *Television and the aggressive child: A cross-national comparison* (pp. 210–238). Hillsdale, NJ: Erlbaum.

Bailey, K., West, R., & Anderson, C. A. (in press). The influence of video games on social, cognitive, and affective information processing. In J. Decety & J. Cacioppo (Eds.), *Handbook of social neuroscience.* New York, NY: Oxford University Press.

Bandura, A. (1973). *Aggression: A social learning theory analysis.* Englewood Cliffs, NJ: Prentice-Hall.

Bandura, A., Barbaranelli, C., Caprara, G. V., & Pastorelli, C. (1996). Mechanisms of moral disengagement in the exercise of moral agency. *Journal of Personality and Social Psychology, 71,* 364–374.

Barclay, G., & Tavares, C. (2002). *International comparisons of criminal justice statistics 2000.* Retrieved from United Kingdom Home Office website: http://www.homeoffice.gov.uk/rds/pdfs2/hosb502.pdf

Bartholow, B. D., Bushman, B. J., & Sestir, M. A. (2006). Chronic violent video game exposure and desensitization to violence: Behavioral and event-related brain potential data. *Journal of Experimental Social Psychology, 42,* 532–539.

Bergeron, N., & Schneider, B. H. (2005). Explaining cross-national differences in peer-directed aggression: A quantitative synthesis. *Aggressive Behavior, 31,* 116–137.

Berkowitz, L. (1984). Some effects of thoughts on anti- and prosocial influences of media events: A cognitive–neoassociation analysis. *Psychological Bulletin, 95,* 410–427.

Berkowitz, L. (1993). *Aggression: Its causes, consequences, and control.* New York, NY: McGraw-Hill.

Bushman, B. J., & Anderson, C. A. (1998). Methodology in the study of aggression: Integrating experimental and nonexperimental findings. In R. Geen & E. Donnerstein (Eds.), *Human aggression: Theories, research, and implications for social policy* (pp. 23–48). San Diego, CA: Academic Press.

Bushman, B. J., & Anderson, C. A. (2009). Comfortably numb: Desensitizing effects of violent media on helping others. *Psychological Science, 20,* 273–277.

Bushman, B. J., & Huesmann, L. R. (2006). Short-term and long-term effects of violent media on aggression in children and adults. *Archives of Pediatric and Adolescent Medicine, 160,* 348–352.

Buss, A. H., & Perry, M. (1992). The Aggression Questionnaire. *Journal of Personality and Social Psychology, 63,* 452–459.

Carlson, M., Marcus-Newhall, A., & Miller, N. (1989). Evidence for a general construct of aggression. *Personality and Social Psychology Bulletin, 15,* 377–389.

Carnagey, N. L., Anderson, C. A., & Bushman, B. J. (2007). The effect of video game violence on physiological desensitization to real-life violence. *Journal of Experimental Social Psychology, 43,* 489–496.

Chida, Y., & Hamer, M. (2008). Chronic psychosocial factors and acute physiological responses to laboratory-induced stress in healthy populations: A quantitative review of 30 years of investigations. *Psychological Bulletin, 134,* 829–885.

Colwell, J., & Kato, M. (2003). Investigation of the relationship between social isolation, self-esteem, aggression and computer game play in Japanese adolescents. *Asian Journal of Social Psychology, 6,* 149–158.

431

Comstock, G., & Scharrer, E. (2007). *Media and the American child.* San Diego, CA: Academic Press.

Crick, N. R., & Dodge, K. A. (1994). A review and reformulation of social information processing mechanisms in children's adjustment. *Psychological Bulletin, 115,* 74–101.

DeLisi, M. (2005). *Career criminals in society.* Thousand Oaks, CA: Sage.

Duval, S. (2005). The "Trim and Fill" method. In H. Rothstein, A. Sutton, & M. Borenstein (Eds.), *Publication bias in meta-analysis: Prevention, assessment and adjustments* (pp. 127–144). Chichester, England: Wiley.

Duval, S. J., & Tweedie, R. L. (1998). Practical estimates of the effect of publication bias in meta-analysis. *Australasian Epidemiologist, 5*(4), 14–17.

Duval, S., & Tweedie, R. (2000a). A nonparametric "Trim and Fill" method of accounting for publication bias in meta-analysis. *Journal of the American Statistical Association, 95,* 89–98.

Duval, S., & Tweedie, R. (2000b). Trim and fill: A simple funnel-plot-based method of testing and adjusting for publication bias in meta-analysis. *Biometrics, 56,* 455–463.

Ferguson, C. J. (2007a). Evidence for publication bias in video game violence effects literature: A meta-analytic review. *Aggression and Violent Behavior, 12,* 470–482.

Ferguson, C. J. (2007b). The good, the bad and the ugly: A meta-analytic review of positive and negative effects of violent video games. *Psychiatric Quarterly, 78,* 309–316.

Ferguson, C. J., & Kilburn, J. (2009). The public health risks of media violence: A meta-analytic review. *Journal of Pediatrics, 154,* 759–763.

Frijda, N. H., Markam, S., Sato, K., & Wiers, R. (1995). Emotion and emotion words. In J. A. Russell (Ed.), *Everyday conceptions of emotion* (pp. 121–143). Dordrecht, the Netherlands: Kluwer Academic.

Geen, R. G. (2001). *Human aggression.* Philadelphia, PA: Open University Press.

Gentile, D. A. (Ed.). (2003). *Media violence and children.* Westport, CT: Praeger.

Gentile, D. A., Anderson, C. A., Yukawa, S., Ihori, N., Saleem, M., Ming, L. K., . . . Sakamoto, A. (2009). The effects of prosocial video games on prosocial behaviors: International evidence from correlational, experimental, and longitudinal studies. *Personality and Social Psychology Bulletin, 35,* 752–763.

Gentile, D. A., Saleem, M., & Anderson, C. A. (2007). Public policy and the effects of media violence on children. *Social Issues and Policy Review, 1,* 15–61.

Giancola, P. R., & Chermack, S. T. (1998). Construct validity of laboratory aggression paradigms: A response to Tedeschi and Quigley (1996). *Aggression and Violent Behavior, 3,* 237–253.

Giancola, P. R., & Parrott, D. J. (2008). Further evidence for the validity of the Taylor aggression paradigm. *Aggressive Behavior, 34,* 214–229.

Greitemeyer, T., & Osswald, S. (2009). Prosocial video games reduce aggressive cognitions. *Journal of Experimental Social Psychology, 45,* 896–900.

Huesmann, L. R. (1988). An information processing model for the development of aggression. *Aggressive Behavior, 14,* 13–24.

Huesmann, L. R. (1998). The role of social information processing and cognitive schema in the acquisition and maintenance of habitual aggressive behavior. In R. G. Geen & E. Donnerstein (Eds.), *Human aggression: Theories, research, and implications for social policy* (pp. 73– 109). New York, NY: Academic Press.

Huesmann, L. R., & Eron, L. D. (Eds.). (1986). *Television and the aggressive child: A cross-national comparison.* Hillsdale, NJ: Erlbaum.

432

Huesmann, L. R., Eron, L. D., Klein, R., Brice, P., & Fischer, P. (1983). Mitigating the imitation of aggressive behaviors by changing children's attitudes about media violence. *Journal of Personality and Social Psychology, 44,* 899–910.

Huesmann, L. R., Lagerspetz, K., & Eron, L. D. (1984). Intervening variables in the TV violence–aggression relation: Evidence from two countries. *Developmental Psychology, 20,* 746–775.

Johnson, J. G., Cohen, P., Smailes, E. M., Kasen, S., & Brook, J. S. (2002, July 5). Television viewing and aggressive behavior during adolescence and adulthood. *Science, 295,* 2468–2471.

Kirsh, S. J. (2006). *Children, adolescents, and media violence: A critical look at the research.* Thousand Oaks, CA: Sage.

Kitayama, S., Mesquita, B., & Karasawa, M. (2006). Cultural affordances and emotional experience: Socially engaging and disengaging emotions in Japan and the United States. *Journal of Personality and Social Psychology, 91,* 890–903.

Kodaira, S. I. (1998). A review of research on media violence in Japan. In U. Carlsson & C. von Feilitzen (Eds.), *Children and media violence* (pp. 81–105). Göteborg, Sweden: UNESCO International Clearinghouse on Children and Violence on the Screen.

Kodomo no taiken katsudo kenkyukai. (2000). *Kodomo no taiken katsudo tou ni kansuru kokusai hikaku chosa* [A cross-cultural study about children's experiences and activities]. Nagano, Japan: Author.

Krahé, B. (2001). *The social psychology of aggression.* East Sussex, England: Psychology Press.

Lane, K. A., Banaji, M. R., Nosek, B. A., & Greenwald, A. G. (2007). Understanding and using the Implicit Association Test: IV. What we know (so far) about the method. In B. Wittenbrink & N. Schwarz (Eds.), *Implicit measures of attitudes* (pp. 59–102). New York, NY: Guilford Press.

Masuda, T., & Nisbett, R. E. (2001). Attending holistically versus analytically: Comparing the context sensitivity of Japanese and Americans. *Journal of Personality and Social Psychology, 81,* 922–934.

Mesquita, B., & Leu, J. (2007). The cultural psychology of emotion. In S. Kitayama & D. Cohen (Eds.), *Handbook of cultural psychology* (pp. 734–759). New York, NY: Guilford Press.

Nisbett, R. E., Peng, K., Choi, I., & Norenzayan, A. (2001). Culture and systems of thought: Holistic versus analytic cognition. *Psychological Review, 108,* 291–310.

Ontario Office for Victims of Crime. (2004). *Action agenda: A strategic blueprint for reducing exposure to media violence in Canada.* Retrieved from http://www.fradical.ca/Action_Agenda_November_2004.pdf

Polman, H., Orobio de Castro, B., & Van Aken, M. A. G. (2008). Experimental study of the differential effects of playing versus watching violent video games on children's aggressive behavior. *Aggressive Behavior, 34,* 256–264.

Robinson, T. N., Wilde, M. L., Navracruz, L. C., Haydel, K. F., & Varady, A. (2001). Effects of reducing children's television and video game use on aggressive behavior: A randomized controlled trial. *Archives of Pediatric Adolescent Medicine, 155,* 17–23.

Rosenthal, R. (1986). Media violence, antisocial behavior, and the social consequences of small effects. *Journal of Social Issues, 42,* 141–154.

Rosenthal, R. (1990). How are we doing in soft psychology? *American Psychologist, 45,* 775–777.

Rothstein, H. R., Sutton, A. J., & Borenstein, M. (2005). Publication bias in meta-analysis: Prevention, assessment and adjustments: Chichester, England: Wiley.

Schmitt, D. P., Allik, J., McCrae, R. R., & Benet-Martinez, V. (2007). The geographic distribution of Big Five personality traits: Patterns and profiles of human self-description across 56 nations. *Journal of Cross-Cultural Psychology, 38,* 173–212.

Sherry, J. L. (2001). The effects of violent video games on aggression: A meta-analysis. *Human Communication Research, 27,* 409–431.

Singer, D. G., & Singer, J. L. (Eds.). (2001). *Handbook of children and the media.* Thousand Oaks, CA: Sage.

Sterne, J. A. C., & Egger, M. (2005). Regression methods to detect publication and other bias in meta-analysis. In H. Rothstein, A. Sutton, & M. Borenstein (Eds.), *Publication bias in meta-analysis: Prevention, assessment and adjustments* (pp. 99–110). Chichester, England: Wiley.

Strack, F., & Deutsch, R. (2004). Reflective and impulsive determinants of social behavior. *Personality and Social Psychology Review, 8,* 220–247.

Taylor, S. P. (1967). Aggressive behavior and physiological arousal as a function of provocation and the tendency to inhibit aggression. *Journal of Personality, 35,* 297–310.

Tsai, J. L., Knutson, B., & Fung, H. H. (2006). Cultural variation in affect valuation. *Journal of Personality and Social Psychology, 90,* 288–307.

U.S. Department of Health and Human Services. (2001). *Youth violence: A report of the Surgeon General.* Rockville, MD: U.S. Department of Health and Human Services, Centers for Disease Control and Prevention, National Center for Injury Prevention and Control; Substance Abuse and Mental Health Services Administration, Center for Mental Health Services; and National Institutes of Health, National Institute of Mental Health.

Weber, R., Ritterfeld, U., & Mathiak, K. (2006). Does playing violent video games induce aggression? Empirical evidence of a functional magnetic resonance imaging study. *Media Psychology, 8,* 39–60.

Wegner, D. M., & Bargh, J. A. (1998). Control and automaticity in social life. In D. Gilbert, S. Fiske, & G. Lindzey (Eds.), *The handbook of social psychology* (pp. 446–496). New York, NY: McGraw-Hill.

Williams, D., & Skoric, M. (2005). Internet fantasy violence: A test of aggression in an online game. *Communication Monographs, 72,* 217–233.

Yahiro, S. (2005). *Terebigemu kaishakuron josetsu: Assanburaaju* [Introduction of interpreting theory of video games: Assemblage]. Tokyo, Japan: Gendaishokan.

# 69

# SIGN OF A THREAT

## The effects of warning systems in survival horror games

*Bernard Perron*

Source: *COSIGN 2004 Proceedings*, Art Academy, University of Split (Croatia), 2004, pp. 132–141.

### Abstract

This paper studies the way survival horror games are designed to frighten and scare the gamer. Comparing video games and movies, the experiential state of the gamer and that of the spectator, as well as the shock of surprise and tension suspense, it focuses on the effects of forewarning on the emotional responses to survival horror games.

## 1. Introduction

David Bordwell, one of the most important figures in promoting a cognitive approach to cinema, once wrote that filmmakers were "practical cognitive psychologists" because they take advantage of the ways spectators draw upon everyday thinking while viewing a film (for instance, going beyond the information given by categorizing, drawing on prior knowledge about real-life or films, forgetting some elements in order to remember others, making informal, provisional inferences, and hypothesizing what is likely to happen next) [3]. Such assertions can obviously be made about game designers, too. In comparison with the spectator, it is even more plausible that a gamer may choose to play a video game in alternative ways (freely setting his own goals, testing the limits of the game, playing *with* the game instead of playing *the* game) or that a game might be used to other ends (to help overcome phobias, for instance[1]). Regardless of how the game is used, game designers know how to elicit the sort of activities and emotional responses that will create the experience they want the gamer to have. When it comes to survival horror games—the subject of this paper—designers know exactly how the gamer shapes his journey to hell.

This paper, therefore, studies the way survival horror games are designed to frighten and scare the gamer. They do so by relying on horror mythology and

435

conventions of horror movies. According to Ed S. Tan, they create both fiction emotions (emotions rooted in the fictional world and the concerns addressed by that world) and artefact emotions (which arise from concerns related to the arte-factartifact, as well as stimulus characteristics based on those concerns) [26]. But above all, their design is made to elicit gameplay emotions. That is to say fear, fright or dread that arise from the gamer's actions in the game-world and the consequent reactions of this world. Gameplay emotions come from various actions: exploring, being lost, fighting, being attacked, feeling trapped, dying, using various weapons, being challenged, solving problems, etc. In an overall analysis of the *Silent Hill* series (Konami/Konami, 1999–2003[2]) [21] in which I examined these gameplay emotions, I talked about one of the famous features of the series: the avatar's pocket radio that transmits white noise to warn the gamer that one or many monsters are nearby. I referred to the notion of forewarning, but did not develop this subject. While my observations will stem and borrow from my visits to the town of Silent Hill, I wish to broaden the examination of warning systems by broaching a few other PlayStation games: *Resident Evil* (Capcom/Capcom, 1996), *Resident Evil 2* (Capcom/Capcom, 1998), *Fear Effect* (Kronos Digital Entertainment/Eidos Interactive, 2000) and *Fatal Frame* (Tecmo/Tecmo, 2002).[3] What then are the effects of warnings? I do not mean visual and audio devices informing us of the avatar's health or remaining ammunition (although these warnings are part of a whole), but rather those signals of on-coming monsters off-screen? What are the emotional responses these signs of a threat induce? To answer these questions, I'll be relying in part on empirical psychological research. Psychological approach, results and discussion are indeed very relevant to this study.

## 2. Shock and tension

Generally speaking, survival horror games follow the same formula, and gamers know what gaming experience to expect.

At the plot level, the hero/heroine investigates a hostile environment where he/she will be trapped (a building or a town) in order either to uncover the causes of strange and horrible events (*Alone in the Dark*, *Resident Evil*, *Siren*) or to find and rescue a loved one from an evil force, be it a daughter (*Silent Hill*, *Fear Effect*), a mother (*Clock Tower3*), a wife (*Silent Hill 2*) or a brother (*Resident Evil 2*, *Fatal Frame*). At the action level, in a third-person perspective[4], the gamer has to find clues, gather objects (you cannot do without keys) and solve puzzles. In order to survive with the weapons he has (or will come across), the gamer has to face numerous impure, disgusting, creepy and threatening monsters (zombies, demons, mutated beasts, abnormal creatures, spirits, vampires, etc.). The conflict between the avatar and those monsters is the dominant element of horror.

Since the release of *Silent Hill*, one way of differentiating these games has been to distinguish the more gruesome action based and quick thrill jump scares of *Resident Evil* from the chilling atmosphere and psychological approach of the

Konami series. In fact, this comparison mirrors the acknowledged opposition between horror and terror. As Will H. Rockett puts forward, horror is compared to an almost physical loathing and its cause is always external, perceptible, comprehensible, measurable, and apparently material. Terror, as for it, is rather identified with the more imaginative and subtle anticipatory dread. It relies more on the unease of the unseen. "The most common time of terror . . . is night, a great absence of light and therefore a great time of uncertainty" [22: p. 100]. Without daylight, certainty and clear vision, there is no safe moment. Terror expands on a longer duration than horror does. By plunging its gamer alone in the dark or in mist and giving him only a flashlight to light his way (and so forcing him to play alongside the imperfectly seen), *Silent Hill* and *Fatale Frame* succeed at creating the fundamentals of terror. Though the young girl Miku, the gamer's avatar in *Fatal Frame*, suddenly finds herself face-to-face with a spirit or Jill in *Resident Evil* frequently meets up with zombies, these encounters are not the same when the hero can't clearly see their enemies or their surrounding environment. With the presence of monsters and their unavoidable onslaught, these kinds of games would be more aptly called survival *terror* games. But as long as the contrast between horror and terror relies in great part on the building and, above all, on the sustaining of a feeling of dread, another suitable way for this study to view this contrast is to refer to another famous distinction.

Crawling with monsters, survival horror games make wonderful use of surprise, attack, appearances and any other disturbing action that happens without warning. According to Robert Baird's analysis in "The Startle Effect. Implications for Spectator Cognition and Media Theory", the games have the core elements of the (film) threat scene's startle effect at their disposal: "(1) a character presence, (2) an implied offscreen threat, and (3) a disturbing intrusion [often accentuated by a sound burst] into the character's immediate space. This is the essential formula (character, implied threat, intrusion) one finds repeated hundreds and thousands of times since Lewton's first bus effect" [1: p. 15]. In the aforementioned famous scene of Jacques Tourneur's *Cat People* that Val Lewton produced in 1942, the spectator is lead to believe that the female character is followed by something from the left, only to be caught off guard by a bus barreling in from screen right. As hostile as the environment might be, it is very unlikely that the gamer (who has embarked upon a lengthy exploration) will not be taken off guard and be surprised. Improving the surprise effect of the long fanged monsters breaks through the cellar and the first bedroom window in *Alone in the Dark* (I-Motion Inc. & Infogrames/Interplay, 1992), the dogs that burst through windows when you cross a corridor at the beginning of *Resident Evil* is considered a classic game startle effect (Figure 1). There is more than one bursting window effect in the *Resident Evil* series. Zombies or creatures can always burst out of window whether it is barricaded or not. In *Fatal Frame*, it is above all the sudden appearances and disappearances of spirits that give you a start. The *Silent Hill* series has few monsters that launch underhand attacks. In the first game, there is also a great scene in the elementary school that gives you a good scare: A cat springs out of a box at

*Figure 1* A dog bursting through the right window in *Resident Evil* (Capcom/Capcom, 1996)

the very moment Harry, the gamer's avatar, is about to open it. The game-world of *Silent Hill* is haunted by sudden noises here and there that have no visible or identifiable source.

To trigger sudden events is undoubtedly one of the basic techniques used to scare someone. However, because the effect is considered easy to achieve, it is often labeled as a cheap approach and compared with another more valued one: suspense. As in the well-known example of Alfred Hitchcock, a bomb that suddenly explodes under the table where two people are having an innocent conversation will surprise the spectator for only few seconds at the very moment of the explosion. However, if this spectator is made aware that the bomb is going to explode at any minute, he will participate in the scene and feel suspense for the whole time preceding the explosion. "The conclusion is", Hitchcock says, "that whenever possible the public must be informed" [27: p. 73]. The shock of surprise is consequently taken over by the tension of suspense.

As Noël Carroll asserts in *The Philosophy of Horror or Paradoxes of the Heart*, suspense is not unique to horror, but rather is a key narrative element in most horror stories [7: p. 128]. In Carroll's curiosity theory[5], although the emotions of horror and suspense might be different (the object of horror is an entity – the monster – and that of suspense is a situation), they can coexist and bring about a concerted effect, especially when it comes to one of the most characteristic themes of horror narration: discovery [7: p. 144]. Discovery is also the theme of a large number of survival horror games. In a "drama of corridors" (one of Carroll's expressions that applies quite well to the maze structure of these games and many others[6]), the gamer has to find the virus or the supernatural force responsible for the rise of the monsters. And he can expect to fight a last boss monster at the end. Although suspense can be created in the overarching structure of the plot, it can also be generated during short events or incidents. To borrow, yet again, from Carroll's terminology [8], suspense can arise in regard to the plot's few macro-questions (e.g., will the hero/heroine find the loved one?) or the more numerous micro-questions that connect one fictional event to another. As the tension intensifies when we have to answer these micro-questions (e.g., will the bomb explode under the table while the two people are still talking?), and because it touches the action level of video games, I'm interested in suspense at the episodic level. But still, as Greg M. Smith does regarding film, we have to argue that the primary emotive effect of games is to create a mood, i.e. "a preparatory state in which one is seeking an opportunity to express a particular emotion or emotion set" [23: p. 38]. A fearful mood therefore encourages and prepares you to experience fright, and a good dose of panic bolsters the mood in return. Just as gamers do not like boring games, neither would they appreciate being panic-stricken all the time. It's all about maintaining a good balance.

Suspense becomes significant to the study of the cross-media genre of horror when one looks at its fundamental elements. For Dolf Zillmann, "suspense is conceptualized as the experience of uncertainty regarding the outcome of a potentially hostile confrontation" [30: p. 283]. Three psychologists quoted in Carroll's "Paradox of suspense" give this definition: "We view suspense as involving a Hope emotion and a Fear Emotion coupled with the cognitive state of uncertainty" [6: p. 78]. The notion of uncertainty is, without a doubt, at the core of suspense. When a danger or threat is revealed and you are sure of the situation's outcome, there is no suspense. The more the chances of succeeding are slim, the more the presentation is suspenseful. Suspense is a future-oriented emotion, but also a character-oriented one. Doubt and insecurity are bound to one or a few protagonists. You're made to adopt the protagonist's position to follow the event and to live side by side with him the length of the action. But, studies of suspense have revealed that a character does not only have to be in a distressing situation, he also needs to be liked. Comisky and Bryant's experiment of varying levels of perceived outcome-uncertainty and disposition toward the protagonist confirm that audiences get involved with and become more anxious about a hero with whom they have a strong affinity [9: p. 78]. Bonded with the character that represents him in the game-world, the gamer is visibly driven to have this disposition toward his avatar. Being fond of the protagonist causes more hope for a favored outcome and more fear about the possibility that it might not occur. As a matter of fact, fear emotions are also central to the understanding of suspenseful drama. Again according to Zillmann, suspense in drama is created predominantly through the suggestion of deplorable and dreadful outcomes. "It features people about to be jumped and stabbed, about to walk into an ambush and get shot and about to be bitten by snakes, tarantulas, and mad dogs. The common denominator in all of this is the likely *suffering* of the protagonists. It is impending disaster, manifest in anticipated agony, pain, injury, and death. Suspenseful drama, then, appears to thrive on uneasiness and distress about anticipated negative outcomes. In short, it thrives on fear" [31: p. 136]. This emotional response only evolves during the anticipation of the final result, a rather limited result. Micro-questions raised by expected dangerous and harmful events have, as Carroll remarks [6], only two potential and opposite outcomes. In most cases of survival horror games, the avatar survives the attack, runs away from or kills the monster or he does not.

## 3. To be warned

To put the gamer in the wanted emotional state, game designers draw upon the relation between emotion, cognition, and perception. As cognition arouses emotion on the one hand, emotion organizes perception on the other hand. Following Carroll's analogy, emotions can be seen as searchlights. "They direct attention, enabling us to organize the details before us into signification wholes or gestalts. Where the emotional state is one of fear, we scan it for details highlighted as dangerous . . . " [5: p. 28]. This is much the same as the preparatory state of a mood described by Smith: "A fearful mood puts us on emotional alert, and we patrol our environment searching for frightening objects. Fear makes us notice dark shadows, mysterious noises and sudden movements and thus provides more possibly frightening cues" [24: p. 114]. Undeniably, there isn't a better frightening cue than the sign of a threat by a monster.

In psychology, the concept of threat is associated with the one of "anticipatory fear" and psychological stress [17]. Incidentally, much empirical research has studied the effect of anticipation and the emotional impact of prior information. For instance, relevant to the distinction between shock and tension is an experiment by Nomikos et al. that shows two versions of a film portraying wood-mill accidents. The first without warning and the other one with warning (as shots depicting the victim's finger approaching the whirling blade of a milling machine), demonstrate that: "(a) Long anticipation of a harmful confrontation (suspense) is more disturbing than short anticipation (surprise); and (b) most of the stress reaction occurs during the anticipation or threat period, rather than during the actual confrontation when the subject views the accident itself" [20: p. 207]. In general, studies reiterate these conclusions. Such is the case in the article by de Weid et al. entitled "Forewarning of Graphic Portrayal of Violence and the Experience of Suspenseful Drama" [10], and in Hoffner and Cantor's article, "Forewarning of a Threat and Prior Knowledge of Outcome" [15]. Though I could expose the details of these experiments, I would rather discuss an earlier experiment conducted by Cantor, Ziemke and Sparks concerning the "Effect of Forewarning on Emotional Responses to a Horror Film" [4] which is at the root of my remark. Cantor, Ziemke and Sparks show that if, intuitively, prior knowledge about an upcoming frightening event would seem to reduce its emotional impact by decreasing uncertainty about what will happen, it is not what actually happens. In fact, on the contrary, the notion "forewarned is forearmed" does not lead as much to "emotional defenses" or effective coping strategy as to a build up of lasting arousal prior the event [4: pp. 22–23]. Using heart rate as the measure of physiological arousal (a method they call into question however) and varying the conditions of the forewarning of forthcoming events in four scenes of the "made-for-television" movie *Vampire* (one version with no forewarning, a second with a vague warning and third one with explicit forewarning), the researchers asked their subjects to rate their anxiety, fright and upset[7]. The following observation resulted from the answers they collected: "[f]ore warning of upcoming events did the opposite of 'forearming' subjects against emotional reactions. Subjects who were given prior knowledge of upcoming frightening events reported more intense fright and upset in response to the movie than did those who had no fore-warning. It is interesting to note that reports of fright and upset were intensified by forewarning, but reports of anxiety were not. As will be recalled, fright and upset were expected to reflect responses to specific depicted or anticipated events, whereas anxiety was presumed to denote an uneasiness over uncertain outcomes. Given that forewarning should have decreased rather that increased uncertainty, it does not seem surprising that anxiety ratings were not increased by forewarning" [4: p. 30]. The results also show that forewarning did affect only the two scenes related to disturbing and brutal events. In the final analysis, simple forewarning is not a way of preventing intense emotional upset. It is worse than having no information about an upcoming event. We can understand why designers of horror games take advantage of this technique.

As opposed to the conditions of an experiment, the use of forewarning in an ongoing experience of survival horror game is governed by specificity. Because the gamer controls an avatar, the game narratives tell only what this main pro-tagonist knows (i.e. the narration is restricted in a way that is characteristic of investigation stories). Even when there are different playable characters such as the three mercenaries in *Fear Effect* or even the ten in *Siren* (Sony/Sony, 2004), playing alternatively does not really change what you have to do in each segment. If it did, it might be just finding another playable character as in *Resident Evil 2*. Anticipatory fear is therefore elicited during specific sequences. What's more, because of the antagonism of harmful monsters and the game's confined spaces (usually rooms and corridors), threat is always impending. This is even more the case in the immediate off-screen than in far away places. In fact, the duration of the suspenseful anticipation has to be kept in perspective, though it can some-times be quite long and it always depends on the (re)action of the gamer (we'll come back to this question later on). Anticipation is not to be counted in minutes, as in Hitchcock's example, or even in tenths of a second. The duration is equal to the short anticipation (4.33 and 6.67 seconds) of the aforementioned experi-ment carried out by Nomikos et al., rather than with long anticipation (18.75 and 25.75 seconds). Nevertheless, as a video game is defined by the here and now of a situation, the question is still to differentiate the effects of anticipation versus none at all (0 seconds). So as to warn its gamer, survival horror games have vari-ous warning systems built on physical cues and/or audio and visual cues either displayed on the screen, presented at an extradiegetic level, or integrated into the game-world. We'll now look at these different types of warning systems in the previously mentioned and chosen games.

*Fear Effect* has a Fear Meter displayed in the upper left corner of the screen (Figure 2).

*Figure 2* A Fear Meter appears in the upper left corner of the screen as Hana is about to face devils in *Fear Effect* (Kronos Digital Entertainment/Eidos Interactive, 2000)

The meter represents the heartbeat of Hana (and of the two other playable characters, Royce and Deke). You see and hear it increase as she becomes more afraid. Since there aren't any health power-ups available in the game, you have to perform well in a stressful situation. The Fear Meter appears when you are about to face human guards or monsters. In the underground hell, the scene in Figure 2, the Fear Meter becomes visible in order to show the threat in a empty space clear just a second before. When Hana goes forward, she is attacked by red devils with hand scythes falling down from the sky. This happens more often then not when her enemies are nearby. The Fear Meter sometimes appears long before she encounters danger.

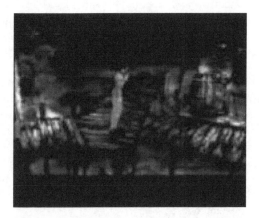

*Figure 3* The Fear Meter remains visible for a while in the village of *Fear Effect* (Kronos Digital Entertainment/Eidos Interactive, 2000)

*Figure 4* At the lower right corner of the screen, the filament turns orange as Miku, in the middle of the frame, is about to enter a room in *Fatal Frame* (Tecmo/Tecmo, 2002)

The Meter remains visible for about two minutes in a search scene in the village, for instance (Figure 3). Although Hana (armed with her pistol as we can see) has faced green zombie-like natives in the left branch, yet still anticipates more action on the right branch.

*Fatal Frame* also has a visual device to warn. In third-person perspective (Figure 4) or through the viewfinder of Miku's camera (Figure 5), the screen displays a filament at the lower right corner in the former case and in the upper middle in the other.

Coupled with heartbeats, eerie sounds and the controller's vibration, the filament turns orange when spirits are nearby (and blue when you are near a clue).

*Figure 5* Through the viewfinder, in the upper middle of the screen, the orange filament signals the presence of a spirit, here hanging from the ceiling in *Fatal Frame* (Tecmo/Tecmo, 2002)

This device is more than essential in *Fatal Frame* as you face incorporeal entities that are otherwise translucent and as you are plunged into darkness with only a flashlight to lit your way. As a typical warning system, the filament turns orange when spirits are in a room with you. But because of their nature, it also glows when the spirits are in another room. While most of the survival horror games segment their spaces making you cross doors through a straight cut or an opening loading screen, *Fatale Frame* frightens you by making you anticipate what you'll face when you open a door. As in Figure 4 where Miku stands in front of the door to the Rubble Room, a bad omen can make you delay your entrance because you're terrified. And when you go into a room with the filament turned on, the situation can be just as suspenseful given that the spirits need to be located. You might switch to the view-finder of the camera (Miku's weapon against spirits), but you still have to look often for spirits when the filament indicates their location by fading in and out. You have to know that the spirits move and conceal themselves, and that some are attacking while others do not. The Crucified Man in Figure 5 was nowhere to be found in the Naruki Shrine, for instance. You had to look up to the ceiling to find him.

Just after the prologue at the beginning of *Silent Hill*, Harry gets away with a good start when, in a cut-scene identical to the bus scene of *Cat People*, a first window bursts in the background creating a distraction and allowing a flying reptile to burst from the foreground window. From this moment on, Harry is in possession of a great forewarning tool: a pocket radio transmitting white noise that warns the gamer that one or many monsters are nearby (Figure 6). There are no visual displays on the screen of *Silent Hill*. The gaming experience of the whole series is driven by the terrifying static that comes to break the silence. Furthermore, the variations of white noise give information about the monsters and how far away they are.[8] During significant parts of *Silent Hill* and *Silent Hill 2* taking place outdoors in the mist, the duration of the anticipation is actually extended compared to the parts that take place indoors. In the streets, the static

*Figure 6* Harry is off to a good start before getting the red pocket radio at the beginning of
  *Silent Hill* (Konami/Konami, 1999)

*Figure 7* Leon has been waiting long seconds for this first-heard zombie to enter the frame
on the right in *Resident Evil 2* (Capcom/Capcom, 1998)

fades in when you advance towards an unseen monster and fades out when you
change direction to hurry away. It fades in again along with the monster's own
noises when you cannot avoid a confrontation. Frequently this can last more than
half a minute. You're always kept on your toes. What's more, when the radio
begins to transmit noise and you cannot see outside the light beam of your flashlight, fear seizes you rather intensely.

Tanya Krzywinska notes that "[m]any video games deploy sound as a key sign
of impending danger, designed to agitate a tingling sense in anticipation of the need
to act" [16: p. 213]. In that sense, though there is no specific device in *Resident Evil*,
the game warns you in the most classical way by using off-screen sounds (similar
to what happens in the underground locations of *Silent Hill* where the radio doesn't
work). The moaning of the zombies and the shuffling of their feet indicate that they
are nearby in a room or corridor. In fact, most of the time they are waiting just outside the frame, lurking to jump on you. But sometimes, they are farther away. For
instance, if you do not move, it takes more than 15 seconds for the first zombie to
enter the frame in a scene on the second floor of the Police Station in *Resident Evil 2*
(Figure 7), and 5 more seconds for two more zombies to come.

Other examples of this waiting occur on the first floor when zombies moan in an
office you'll have to enter, and later on in the Vacant Factory where Leon and Ada
hear an approaching zombie for no less than 40 seconds. Be that as it may, the forewarning does not rely only on this technique. Now and then, the search of a room is
accompanied by typical, suspenseful extradiegetic music. *Resident Evil* also makes
use of a few cutaways. Interestingly, it shows the impending attack of a Hunter twice.
The first with a cut to an 18-second, fast traveling shot when this monster initially
appears, and the second with a cutaway in the underground courtyard path (Figure 8).

There is also a cut in *Resident Evil 2* to what happens to a reporter (an NPC) in
his cell which portends a frightening encounter.

*Figure 8*  A cutaway to the impending attack of a Hunter in *Resident Evil* (Capcom/Capcom, 1996).

To different degrees, all of the above examples put you in the state of uncertainty. Consequently, and most importantly, compared to the last forewarning of Cantor, Ziemke and Sparks' experiment which precisely described what would happen in the vampire movie scene, the sequences of survival horror games also elicit uneasiness about how uncertain the outcome is. You know that you'll have to face a monster, but you do not know how it will turn out. Not only your fright, but your anxiety as well is therefore intensified. Furthermore, as Torben Grodal stresses about video games, "suspense is interwoven with the interactive and repetitive nature of the game" [14: p. 206]. While aggressions, battles, mutilations and deaths remain final and unchangeable facts in a movie, in a game they are not. Events can be different or, at least, can be triggered in a different order. If you have killed the zombie-like native that was lying on the ground during a first exploration of the right branch of the village of *Fear Effect* (following Figure 3), it will not rise from under the frame the next time you go by. But if you come only once into the right branch, the lying zombie-like native will rise unexpectedly The opposite is also true: "What was surprising in the first game is transformed into a suspense-like coping anticipation in the following games. When the player advances toward the space/time in which the surprising event previously has occurred, say the sudden appearance of a fierce antagonist, it will induce an increased arousal" [14: pp. 205–206]. Having to replay a game from the last save point in order to go back and face a boss monster that you have not yet defeated is a great forewarning situation. Replaying a game at the most difficult level, instead of at the normal one, also has the same consequences.

## 4. I'm scared

The connections of the aforementioned key elements of suspense and forewarning with horror seem obvious and definitely help to understand the gaming experience of survival horror games. However, it is necessary to highlight an important distinction between games and dramas or films which was an underlying principle in the preceding two parts of this paper. Though they are not addressing video games directly, Vorderer and Knobloch summarize the matter nonetheless: "According to the [Zillmann] disposition theory, a necessary condition for suspense is that the viewer witnesses the conflicting forces ( . . . ) without being able to intervene in the goings-on. If viewers could influence the plot, for example, the fate of the characters, their experiential state would change into actual fear or hope" [28: p. 64].

The spectator of a horror film and the gamer of a horror game are akin in the way that both are always aware that they themselves are not the victim of the monster's assault and that it is someone else doing the *suffering*. But while, ideally, their emotional responses run parallel to those of the characters, their way of feeling fear is different. In a horror movie, Carroll observes [7: p. 17], the emotional responses of the characters cue those of the audience. Both responses are synchronized. The characters exemplify for the spectator the way in which to react to the monsters by the reports of their internal reactions. In that sense, "one of the most frequent and compelling images in the horror film repertoire is that of the wide, staring eyes of some victim, expressing stark terror or disbelief and attesting to an ultimate threat to the human proposition" [quoted in Carroll, 7: p. 243 n. 45]. The spectator is consequently prompted to respond the same way. Often shown in close shots and in shot/reverse shot where both the point of view of the victim and that of the monster are shown, it is the spectator that is forced to witness these bloody confrontations. Furthermore, referring to Zillmann's necessary condition of suspense, the spectator has what Tan and Frijda call witness emotions [25: p. 52]. These emotions are related to Tan's fiction emotions mentioned in the introduction [26]. The spectator sojourns, in the imagination, in a fictional world where he can feel *as if* he were physically present, a world where he runs absolutely no risk. The emotional experience is based on a safe involvement. But since the significance of the fictional character's situation is relevant to his emotional response, the spectator has empathetic emotions. Feeling *with* the protagonist, he experiences empathic distress in seeing, for example, a babysitter terrorized by the idea that a monster is stalking around the house. But whatever happens, the spectator is forced to have an observational attitude, He is controlled by the filmmaker who guides him around as he pleases through the time and space of the fictional world. The spectator cannot participate in the situation. On the brink of finding the action too scary, he only can cover his eyes to defend himself against the horrible sights (though he still hears what's going on).

In a survival horror game, cut-scenes can depict a horrible scene in a filmic way. Since the plot is unfolding through those cut-scenes, it elicits fiction emotions. However, at the action level, a game does not rest on the reports of characters' internal reactions. The third-person perspective always shows the avatar in a long shot, and generally, in a long take, too. What's more, to face the monsters, the avatar is often seen from the back. With the exception of *Fatal Frame,* which shows a close shot of Miku in a short cut-scene before the attack of some ghosts (similar to

447

the *Resident Evil*'s short cut-scenes showing the upcoming attacks of the hunter), there is generally no prior or subsequent reaction shot of a face expressing stark terror and attesting to the threat. Again, *Fatal Frame* allows you to switch to a first-person perspective through the viewfinder of Miku's camera and, in *Clock Tower 3* (Capcom/Capcom, 2003), the camera switches to a first-person view when Alyssa hides from the monsters. But in those case, the effect of the filmic subjective shot structure (which makes you feels *as if* you were in the situation of a character) is replaced by the sense of agency. Janet Murray has defined this characteristic delight of electronic environments in *Hamlet on the Holodeck. The Future of Narrative in Cyberspace*: "Agency is the satisfying power to take meaningful actions and see the results of our decisions and choices" [19: p. 126]. You indeed control your avatar in the game-world (and the subjective point of view when it is the case), a control that leads to a mutation in the way you experience the scene.

It is certainly not the avatar that is meant to be scared in a survival horror game, but rather the gamer, i.e. you. If we can still refer to empathy since you experience emotions *with* an avatar, it is clear here that we cannot talk about identification with the character or about *becoming* the character in the game-world.[9] This is because the emotional state of that character is not identical to yours. When a monster bursts through the window, it makes you, not the avatar, jump.[10] Upon the sign of threat, the avatar does not express apprehension. When the visual warning system is displayed on the screen or the audio cues are extradiegetic, these signs are not for the avatar's benefit. Although the various avatars make themselves heard during their fight, scream when assailed and audibly breathe their last breath, they remain impassive on the action level. Whatever situation is faced in Silent Hill, Raccoon City or elsewhere, the avatars keep a "stone face" while responding to your actions. Instead, their reactions are behavioral and external. You are linked and synchronized with them physically. You see their actions and are made to feel their suffering not only as you see them being attacked, but also as you receive feedback from the Dualshock controller as in *Silent Hill* and *Fatal Frame*. Now a typical function found in many games, the controller vibrates every time your avatar is touched or hit. It vibrates throughout a confrontation in the Himuro mansion and goes very fast when touched by a spirit. In *Silent Hill*, to indicate avatars' health status, it also shakes more and more violently as they absorb more damage, echoing the acceleration of their heartbeat. This tactile simulation focuses on physical strength for the simple reason that it helps you keep them alive. And that's another departure for video games. In movies, Carroll says, "the fear that the audience emotes with regard to the monster is not fear for its own survival. Our fear is engendered in behalf of the human characters in the pertinent films. We cringe when the Werewolf of London stalks his prey, not because we fear that he'll trap us, but because we fear for some character in the film" [5: p. 38]. Again, you do not fear for your own survival in a horror game either. However, in the game-world, since you merge with your avatar at the action level, and since your main goal is precisely to make him/her survive the threatening monsters, you're indeed made to be afraid that the monsters will trap you, in other words to fear *as if* you were in danger. This time, when the action becomes really scary, you can't simply cover your eyes. Holding your controller, your extradiegetic activity must be to try to overcome the diegetic situation of your avatar.

Fear—as the most commonly referred to emotion in philosophy and psychology, characteristic of an emotion prototype like Greg M. Smith remarks [24: p. 269 n. 4]—helps to distinguish the emotions generated by gameplay from fiction/witness emotions. For psychologist Nico Frijda, whose work has inspired Tan [26] and Grodal [14], emotions can be defined as "modes of relational action readiness, either in the form of tendencies to establish, maintain, or disrupt a relationship with the environment or in the form of mode of relational readiness as such" [12: p. 71]. Emotions are action tendencies. Given that fear is clearly object-and goal-oriented, it provides, as Smith notices once again, a strong action tendency. In the presence of a monster, fear urges you to act in one way or in another to disrupt the relationship. In a horror movie, when the hero/heroine is in danger, you cannot do anything but hope he/she will overcome the threat. Your action tendency is virtual. On the other hand, in survival horror games, you can do something. You can make your avatar act. You actually (even if it is related to a *virtual* game-world) have a repertoire of controls: draw and choose weapons, shoot, attack, guard attack, charge in, turn 180°, run away, use items to replenish life gauge, etc. Those actions give you gameplay emotions, emotions related to the ways you react to the situation. "Video games therefore", asserts Grodal, "simulate emotions in a form that is closer to typical real life experiences than film: emotions are motivators for actions and are labeled according to the player's active coping potentials" [14: p. 201].

## 5. I have to cope

In following with the preceding comments, we have to agree with Grodal who has emphasized [13, 14] that the notion of coping is fundamental to the experience of video games. According to Susan Folkman and Richard S. Lazarus' definition, "coping consists of cognitive and behavioral efforts to manage specific external and/or internal demands that are appraised as taxing or exceeding the resources of the person. These cognitive and behavioral efforts are constantly changing as a function of the appraisals and reappraisals of the person-environment relationship, which is also changing" [11: p. 323]. The appraisals-reappraisals are very significant to determine the emotional effects of forewarning in survival horror games. Anticipatory fear is less important when oncoming monsters are directed by corridors or walks like the outdoors marked paths in *Fear Effect*, but it is greater when the monsters are free to move in the streets of *Silent Hill*. This fear is amplified when you can't clearly see around, specially when you find yourself in the scary places in the vein of the nightmarish world of *Silent Hill* where streets or floors are replaced by rusty grates over bottomless abysses, where walls and floors are splattered with blood and where you hear all kinds of industrial and creepy sounds. Then, we also have to take the way game designers can be playing with you into account.

They are intentionally putting you in a state of terror. An example of this happened at one point during my experiential route of fear in *Silent Hill 2*. I was of two minds as to how to get out of the laundry room on the third floor of the Wood Side Apartments in the beginning of the game (Figure 9). The radio was transmitting white noise, but I could also hear footsteps of some sorts and what seemed to be the growling and shrieking of a huge monster. I was too scared to move. When I finally came out, I was very tense and anticipated an encounter with what turned out to be no more than a normal lone Patient Demon. The appraisal of the situation might have been different with a weapon other than just a wooden plank. I would have certainly felt more secure with a gun in my hand. But then, in *Resident Evil*, it is not a handgun, but a bazooka that you need in order to be at ease in front of a Hunter, a monster much faster and powerful than the zombies.

To explain the relation between coping and emotion, Folkman and Lazarus distinguish two general and interrelated coping processes. The first strategies, called emotion-focused coping, are employed to regulate the situation causing distress. As Folkman and Lazarus talk among others about avoidant and vigilant strategies, another way to understand this is to refer to the degree to which individuals will either monitor (seeking information) or blunt (avoiding information) under threat [18]. Dispositional differences show that monitors (Miller is talking about high monitors/low blunters) scan for threat-relevant information and prefer to attend to information signaling the nature and onset of the shock as well as information about their performance when carrying out a task. Contrarily, blunters (i.e. high blunters/low monitors) tend to avoid informational cues and distract themselves from threat-relevant signals. Using this distinction to study the interaction between forewarning and preferred coping style in relation to emotion reactions to a suspenseful movie, Glen G. Sparks discusses his findings: "Instead of an increase in negative emotion for all participants due to forewarning, the data indicate that

*Figure 9* Too scared to get out of the laundry room of the Wood Side Apartments in *Silent Hill 2* (Konami/Konami, 2001)

forewarning may operate differently for individuals with different preferred coping styles. Monitors may actually prefer forewarning in order to cope with a scary movie, while blunters may prefer no prior information" [11: p. 337]. Although this experiment and the previously mentioned ones deal with the effects of forewarning outside the time flow of a film viewing and don't set forth to explain the appeal of such suspenseful movies and horror movies (see studies of sensation seeking for more on this issue), the results still indicate that monitors have more intense emotional reactions when they are forewarned, while blunters do not. Monitors would probably prefer the warning system of a game like *Fatal Frame* which gives audiovisual cues as well as making the controller vibrate when a spirit appears. In fact, I refer to this distinction in order to explain why a few web reviewers have suggested turning off the radio in *Silent Hill* because it detracts from the surprise-factor of *Resident Evil*. The copying preference seems to be one explanation. At least, this demonstrates that, according to the type of gamer you are, the effects of a warning system will be different.

If the preceding remark proves to be questionable because emotion-coping strategies are, above all, used to deal with stressful events the outcomes of which are considered to be unchangeable, the second type of coping process stressed by Folkman and Lazarus is undoubtable. Called problem-focused coping, those coping strategies are directed at altering the situation that causes distress. They are used this time for outcomes that are amenable to change. Thus, in Grodal's terms, you have active personal coping potentials in video games. And you will undoubtedly make use of them. Among the available types of control, you especially have behavioral control. With the Dualshock controller, you can change the actual terms of the person-environment relationship. A forewarning is an emotional cue, but also a cognitive cue for problem solving. Let's quickly distinguish two forms of such coping. In survival horror games, a confrontational coping strategy that makes an individual fight back somewhat aggressively when facing a difficulty comes down to killing the monster. When you know that there is a monster nearby, you go to destroy it. This is how fearless gamers are likely to handle threats. In the other way, you can manage the situation in a more rational and planned manner. You appraise more consciously the magnitude of the threat before you face it. You then decide if it's better to attack or to avoid and escape the monster. A timorous gamer can be expected to react in this way. In any case, the coping process can change through out a game. As Folkman and Lazarus point out: "[d]uring the anticipatory phase of the encounter, cognitive coping strategies can transform a threat appraisal into a challenge through their affect on secondary appraisal [during which you ask yourself what are your options for coping]" [11: p. 321]. One will agree that it is less stressful and much more fun to face a monster (and even more so a boss monster!) when you have the appropriate weapon, plenty of ammunition and first aid kits to recover from damage. It is also reassuring to know that you have mastered all the controls of a game and that you can move freely and (most importantly) quickly in the game world. With all adequate coping resources, you can interpret the sign of a threat differently.

## 6. Conclusion

Because forewarning intensifies emotional reactions about upcoming frightening events and increases anxiety when there is still uncertainty about the outcome of those events, this paper should have ultimately prepared you to play your next survival horror game. Now it's up to you to play and cope with your next ludic journey to hell.

## Acknowledgements

This paper has been written with the support of the Social Sciences and Humanities Research Council of Canada (SSHRC) and le Fonds québécois de la recherche sur la société et la culture (FQRSC).

## Notes

1  The Cyberpsychology Laboratory of the University of Quebec in Outaouais (<http://www.uqo.ca/cyberpsy/>) is using *Half-Life* (Valve Software/Sierra Entertainment, 1998), *Unreal Tournament* (Epic MegaGames/GT Interactive, 1999) and *Max Payne* (Remedy Entertainment Ltd/Gathering, 2001) to treat spiders and heights phobia.
2  *Silent Hill 4: The Room* is to be released in September 2004.
3  This list is far from exhaustive. Consequently, my argument remains inductive.
4  There are also first-person horror games, but they are indeed called such. For instance, *Nosferatu. The Wrath of Malachi* (Idol Fx/iGames Publishing, 2003) is presented as a "first-person shooter survival horror", and *Clive Barker's Undying* (EALA/EA Games, 2001) has been categorized among others as a "surviquake horror".
5  Mark Vorobej calls Carroll's solution to the paradox of horror a "curiosity theory" because for Carroll horror appeals to cognitive pleasures associated with the discovery of monsters, the objects of fascination [29].
6  Furthermore, as I pointed out [21], the play of ratiocination that Carroll associates with horror fiction becomes literal in horror games.
7  "Consistent with their common dictionary definitions, anxiety was assessed to reflect a non specific sense of uneasiness and uncertainty about what was occurring or was about to occur. Fright was thought to reflect a more direct response to specific threatening events. Upset was used to detect any negative experiential aspect of a subject's response" [4: p. 26].
8  In the Official Strategy Guide of *Silent Hill 3* [2], there is an explanation of how frequency, pitch and volume affect the radio. A chart gives the range of the radio for each monster: 14 meters for Double Head dogs, 20 meters for an enormous monster called a Closer, 15 meters for a zombie-like nurse, etc.
9  The notion of identification is not simple to deal with. Much has been written in film studies since its psychoanalytical description. It has been rejected, supplanted, revised and revived. To have a general view of the question, one can check the major literature about this notion.
10  Manifestly, it is indicative that a gamer would say: "I was scared", not "My avatar was scared" when talking about what happened in a game.

## References

[1] Baird, Robert. "The Startle Effect. Implications for the Spectator Cognition and Media Theory", *Film Quarterly*, Vol. 53, No. 3 (Spring 2000), 13–24.
[2] Birlew, Dan. *Silent Hill 3 Official Strategy Guide*, Brady Publishing, Indianapolis, 2004.

[3] Bordwell, David. "Cognition and Comprehension: Viewing and Forgetting in *Mildred Pierce*", *Journal of Dramatic Theory and Criticism*, Vol. 6, No. 2 (Spring 1992), 183–198.

[4] Cantor, Joanne, Dean Ziemke and Glenn G. Sparks. "The Effect of Forewarning on Emotional Responses to a Horror Film", *Journal of Broadcasting*, Vol. 28, No. 1 (Winter 1984), 21–31.

[5] Carroll, Noël. "Film, Emotion, Genre", in G. Smith and C. Plantinga (eds.), *Passionate Views: Film, Cognition and Emotion*, Johns Hopkins University Press, Baltimore, 1999, 21–47.

[6] Carroll, Noël. "The Paradox of Suspense", in P. Vorderer, H. J. Wulff, and M. Friedrichsen (eds.), *Suspense: Conceptualization, Theoretical Analysis, and Empirical Explorations*, Lawrence Erlbaum Associates, Mahwah, N.J., 1996, 71–90.

[7] Carroll, Noël. *The Philosophy of Horror or Paradoxes of the Heart*, Routledge, New York, 1990.

[8] Carroll, Noël. "An Alternative Account of Movie Narration", *Mystifying Movies. Fads & Fallacies in Contemporary Film Theory*, New York, Columbia University Press, 1988, 170–181.

[9] Comisky, Paul, and Jennings Bryant. "Factors involved in generating suspense", *Human Communication Research*, Vol. 9, No. 1 (Fall 1982), 49–58.

[10] de Wied, Minet, Kathleen Hoffman and David R. Roskos-Ewoldsen. "Forewarning of Graphic Portrayal of Violence and the Experience of Suspenseful Drama", *Cognition and Emotion*, Vol. 11, No. 4 (1997), 481–494.

[11] Folkman, Susan and Richard S. Lazarus. "Coping and Emotion", in N.L. Stein, B. Leventhal and T.Traboass (eds,), Psychological and Biological Approaches to Emotion, Lawrence Erlbaum Associates, Hillsdale, N.J., 21990, 313–332.

[12] Frijda, Nico H. *The Emotions*, Cambridge University Press, Cambridge, 1986.

[13] Grodal, Torben. "Stories for Eye, Ear, and Muscles: VideoGames, Media, and Embodied Experiences", in M.J.P. Wolf and B. Perron (eds.), *The Video Game Theory Reader*, Routledge, New York, 2003, 129–155.

[14] Grodal, Torben. "Video Games and the Pleasure of Control", in D. Zillmann and P. Vorderer (eds.), *Media Entertainment: The Psychology of Its Appeal*, Lawrence Erlbaum Associates, Mahwah, N.J., 2000, 197–213.

[15] Hoffner, Cynthia, and Cantor, Joanne. "Forewarning of a Threat and Prior Knowledge of Outcome. Effects on children's emotional responses to a film sequence", *Human Communication Research*, Vol. 16, No. 3 (Spring 1990), 323–354.

[16] Krzywinska, Tanya. "Hands–on Horror", in G. King and T. Krzywinska (eds.), *ScreenPlay. Cinema/videogames/interfaces*, Wallflower, London, 2002, 206–223.

[17] Lazarus, Richard S. "A Laboratory Approach to the Dynamics of Psychological Stress", *The American Psychologist*, No. 19 (1964), 400–411.

[18] Miller, Suzanne M. "Monitoring and Blunting: Validation of a Questionnaire to Asses Styles of Information Seeking Under Threat", *Journal of personality and Social Psychology*, Vol. 52, No. 2 (1987), 345–353.

[19] Murray, Janet H. *Hamlet on the Holodeck: The Future of Narrative in Cyberspace*, The Free Press, New York, 1997.

[20] Nomikos, Markellos S., Edward Opton, Jr., James R. Averill, and Richard S. Lazarus. "Surprise versus suspense in the production of stress reaction", *Journal of Personality and Social Psychology*, Vol. 8, No. 2 (1968), 204–208.

[21] Perron, Bernard. *Silent Hill. Il motore del terrore*, Edizioni Unicopli, Milan, to be published in Fall 2004.

[22] Rockett, Will H. *Devouring Whirlwind. Terror and Transcendence in the Cinema of Cruelty*, Greenwood Press, New York, 1988.

[23] Smith, Greg M. *Film structure and the emotion system*, Cambridge University Press, Cambridge, 2003.

[24] Smith, Greg M. "Local Emotions, Global Moods, and Film Structure", in G. Smith and C. Plantinga (eds.), *Passionate Views: Film, Cognition and Emotion*, Johns Hopkins University Press, Baltimore, 1999, 103–126.

[25] Tan, Ed S. and Nico Frijda. "Sentiment in Film Viewing", in G. Smith and C. Plantinga (eds.), *Passionate Views: Film, Cognition and Emotion*, Johns Hopkins University Press, Baltimore, 1999, 48–64.

[26] Tan, Ed S. *Emotions and the Structure of Narrative Film: Film as an Emotion Machine*. Lawrence Erlbaum Associates, Mahwah, N.J., 1996.

[27] Truffaut, François. *Hitchcock*, Simon & Schuster, New York, 1985.

[28] Vorderer, Peter, and Silvia Knobloch. "Conflict and suspense in drama", in D. Zillmann and P. Vorderer (eds.), *Media Entertainment: The Psychology of Its Appeal*, Lawrence Erlbaum Associates, Mahwah, N.J., 2000, 59–72.

[29] Vorobej, Mark. "Monsters and the Paradox of Horror", *Dialogue*, No. 24 (1997), 219–249.

[30] Zillmann, Dolf. "The Logic of Suspense and Mystery", in J. Bryant and D. Zillmann (eds.), *Responding to the Screen. Reception and Reaction Processes*, Lawrence Erlbaum Associates, Hillsdall, N.J., 1991, 281–303.

[31] Zillmann, Dolf. "Anatomy of suspense", in P. H. Tannenbaum (ed.), *The Entertainment Functions of Television*, Lawrence Erlbaum Associates, Hillsdale, N.J., 1980, 133–163.

# 70

# THE MOTIVATING ROLE
# OF VIOLENCE IN VIDEO GAMES

*Andrew K. Przybylski, Richard M. Ryan,
and C. Scott Rigby*

Source: *Personality and Social Psychology Bulletin*, 35(2), February 2009, 243–259.

## Abstract

Six studies, two survey based and four experimental, explored the
relations between violent content and people's motivation and
enjoyment of video game play. Based on self-determination theory,
the authors hypothesized that violence adds little to enjoyment or
motivation for typical players once autonomy and competence need
satisfactions are considered. As predicted, results from all studies showed that enjoyment, value, and desire for future play were
robustly associated with the experience of autonomy and competence in gameplay. Violent content added little unique variance in
accounting for these outcomes and was also largely unrelated to
need satisfactions. The studies also showed that players high in trait
aggression were more likely to prefer or value games with violent
contents, even though violent contents did not reliably enhance their
game enjoyment or immersion. Discussion focuses on the significance of the current findings for individuals and the understanding
of motivation in virtual environments.

Few can contest the popular appeal of video games. With annual revenues rivaling
Hollywood box office sales (Yi, 2004), this relatively new medium has become
a dominant form of electronic entertainment. Concurrently, video games have
generated a great deal of controversy in the popular press and culture. Primarily,
these controversies focus on the mature and violent themes of many popular
video games. Parents, politicians, and researchers alike have expressed concerns
that such contents might foster antisocial behavior and maladjustment (Kirsch,
2006). These apprehensions are exacerbated by rapid technological progress
that enables video game developers to graphically represent violent material
in ever-greater variety and detail. Accordingly, much of the empirical work on
video games has focused on possible negative consequences of violent games.
For example, research suggests that violent games may desensitize players to

real-world violence, decrease empathy, and increase players' tendencies toward aggression (e.g., Anderson, 2004; Bartholow, Bushman, & Sestir, 2006).

At the same time, little research has examined the role of violent game content in player motivation and immersion. Given the prevalence of violent content in popular game titles, one might assume that violent material itself is attractive and enjoyable to players and thus plays a substantial role in immersing players in game worlds and motivating game purchases and play. In fact, some have argued that violent media can enhance feelings of excitement, empowerment, and status, among other satisfactions (Johnston, 1995; Jones, 2002; Zillman, 1998).

Yet it remains unclear how much it is violent content per se that motivates play behavior or enjoyment, versus other satisfactions that the games involving violence can provide. Many popular games that have violent content are also appealing for the challenges they offer or the freedom to act in a different world. For example, McCarthy, Curran, and Byron (2005) commented,

> In all the tabloid-inspired furor over *Grand Theft Auto*'s questionable content, it is easy to lose sight of why it's such a successful game in the first place. People don't play it for the violence; they play it because it affords the opportunity to do whatever they please. (p. 14)

Indeed, games involving war, combat, or adventures may provide opportunities for psychological satisfactions that are irrespective of the violent elements within the games. These include opportunities for mastery, achievement, heroism, and self-directed action. As Walkerdine (2007) reported, players often "like" the act of killing in games primarily because it represents feedback of progress or advancement through the game. When focused on the violence per se they often, in contrast, express ambivalence or anxiety. Similarly, Schneider, Lang, Shin, and Bradley (2004) found that video game play was immersive for players when violent acts were framed in compelling narrative. Yet to date there is virtually no research on the role of violence in motivating gameplay or enhancing player immersion.

In the present research we investigate the hypothesis that violent content plays a much less significant role in predicting enjoyment and persistence than many commentators, consumers, and game developers may assume. Instead, based on self-determination theory (SDT; Deci & Ryan, 1985; Ryan & Deci, 2000b) we suggest that both violent and nonviolent games are motivating mainly to the extent that they provide opportunities to satisfy basic psychological needs for competence, autonomy, and relatedness and that for the average player, violent content per se plays a very minor role above and beyond these satisfactions. At the same time we explore an "opt in" hypothesis, namely, whether individual predispositions toward aggression or hostility may lead to a preference for the violent content even if it does not account for enjoyment. We test these hypotheses through a series of experimental and survey studies. Before proceeding to these studies we briefly elaborate on the basis for these hypotheses.

*Motivation for gameplay*

As noted, little empirical research has focused on the motivational underpinnings or attractions of video games. Yet, as game developer Bartle (2004) pointed out, "Players must expect to get something out of their experience" (p. 128). This assumption is also reflected in uses-and-gratifications theory (Blumler & Katz, 1974; Sherry, Lucas, Greenberg, & Lachlan, 2006), which suggests that media use, including video games, is actively motivated and goal oriented. People, that is, are searching for specific satisfactions when they engage in games.

Based on SDT we suggest that video game play is typically intrinsically motivated, or energized by the inherent satisfactions derived from an activity. According to SDT, intrinsic motivation is the core type of motivation underlying most play and sport (Frederick & Ryan, 1995; Ryan & Deci, 2007). Intrinsic motivation would seem very relevant to computer gaming, as most players do not derive extragame rewards or approval or playing (indeed, most players pay to play and/or face disapproval). Rather, most players play because they find the activity itself to be interesting and enjoyable.

One minitheory of SDT, cognitive evaluation theory (CET; Deci & Ryan, 1980, 1985; Ryan & Deci, 2000a), focuses on the psychological satisfactions underlying intrinsic motivation. CET proposes that conditions that enhance a person's sense of autonomy and competence support intrinsic motivation, whereas factors that diminish perceived autonomy or competence undermine intrinsic motivation. *Autonomy* concerns a sense of volition when doing a task. When activities allow one to engage interests and experience choice or freedom in acting, a sense of autonomy is high. Provisions for choice, use of rewards as feedback (rather than to control behavior), and minimal external pressures have thus all been shown to enhance autonomy and in turn, intrinsic motivation (Deci, Koestner, & Ryan, 1999). Conversely, conditions that diminish a sense of choice or volition for actions interfere with perceived autonomy and undermine intrinsic motivation. In addition, CET suggests that activities will be more intrinsically motivating to the extent they provide opportunities for experiencing *competence* (Deci & Ryan, 1985). CET proposes that the experience of competence is enhanced by opportunities to exercise skills or abilities, be optimally challenged, or receive positive feedback and that these factors in turn enhance intrinsic motivation.

Recently, Ryan, Rigby, and Przybylski (2006) applied CET to better understand motivation for video games. Ryan et al. developed an assessment of players' experience of psychological need satisfaction. Using this framework they demonstrated that game designs differ in the autonomy they afford, such as the flexibility over movement and strategies, choice over tasks and goals, and how rewards are structured. Games also differ in competence supports, such as the degree to which controls are intuitive and readily mastered and tasks within the game provide graded challenges and clear positive feedback. Moreover, Ryan et al. showed at both between- and within-person levels of analysis that experiences of competence and autonomy predict game preferences, enjoyment, and persistence.

## *Violence as a motivator*

Our current question asks to what extent are the factors postulated within SDT sufficient to account for game motivation and more specifically to what extent does violent content add additional variance in explaining players' motivation. Clearly games involving armed fighting matches (e.g., *Mortal Kombat*), war (e.g., *Call of Duty*), or organized crime (e.g., *Grand Theft Auto*) offer a storyline or conceit within which feelings of autonomy and competence, as well as relatedness, can be engendered. For example, combat settings provide opportunities to select goals, experience challenges, create strategies, and exert personal control over actions, thus satisfying autonomy and competence needs. In multiplayer environments (e.g., *World of Warcraft*), games can also offer opportunities to experience relatedness and camaraderie as players pursue cooperative missions, share goals and rewards, and come to each other's aid.

But there may be additional satisfactions offered by violence itself. Some theorists have posited, for example, that humans are innately aggressive and derive satisfaction from it (e.g., Freud, 1915). More recently, Zillman (1998) and Jones (2002) argued that violent media offers opportunities for modern youths to feel brave and heroic. Johnston (1995) suggested that violent media could enhance mood and feelings of empowerment. Thus, there is some reason to think that violence itself has motivational features. It remains unclear however if these "benefits" are afforded by violent game content proper or the same psychological need satisfactions provided by games with little or no violence.

### INDIVIDUAL DIFFERENCES

Although it may be the case for most players that violence per se does not enhance motivation except through the intrinsic satisfactions involved in challenging, self-directed play, there nonetheless may be a subgroup of individuals who specifically seek out violent or aggressive contents. Clearly, there are individual differences in propensities to be hostile or aggressive (e.g., Buss & Perry, 1992), which may impact upon preferences for violent media (Bushman & Geen, 1990; Huesmann, Moise, Podolski, & Eron, 2003). If this were the case, the converse would also be possible. People low in aggression or hostility may "opt out" of potentially interesting games because they find violent or gore-filled content unattractive. Thus, traits of aggression may interact with game contents in predicting preferences and motivation. In our view, the variables specified within CET that account for intrinsic motivation should sufficiently account for game enjoyment and motivation, however, hostile or aggressive individuals may prefer violent material independent of enjoyment as such content matches their trait-level propensities or tastes.

## *Overview of the present research*

In the current studies we test our postulate that virtual contexts can engender feelings competence, autonomy, and in some formats, relatedness to other players

(Ryan et al., 2006). The degree to which a video game affords these specific need satisfactions will determine players' enjoyment and immersion within a virtual world, and violence will not provide additional variance once these factors are considered. No studies to date have tested whether violent content enhances immersion and enjoyment of play in video games. In addition, we examine the role of trait aggression in predicting preferences for violent contents independent of enjoyment or intrinsic motivation per se. We specifically predict that violent contents will be preferred by those high in this trait and dispreferred by those low in it.

Six studies explore these hypotheses. Study 1 examines relations between game enjoyment, popularity, immersion, and violent content in a survey of avid video game players. In Study 2, participants are exposed to a highly violent video game to examine the role of trait aggression in predicting game play motivation independent of in-game need satisfaction. Study 3 utilizes two video games, one violent and one nonviolent, to again test the sufficiency of needs to account for enjoyment and motivation and the moderating impact of trait aggression. Study 4 experimentally manipulates the conceit and depiction of violent content within the same game to provide a more stringent test of these main effects. Study 5 manipulates gore and blood displays in a controlled comparison using a sample of male gamers. Study 6 returns to an online survey design to test the role of dispositional aggression in moderating the relation between violent content and value for play.

# Study 1

To gain a broad idea of the motivating role of violent game content, we surveyed video game players. We hypothesized that a player's experience of competence and autonomy is the primary determinant of motivation and enjoyment and that violent content would account for little incremental variance. Specifically, we predicted that players will be intrinsically motivated for play, experience immersion, and be likely to recommend a game only insofar as they perceive a video game as satisfying basic psychological needs, and we did not expect violent content per se to contribute additional unique variance in accounting for these outcomes.

## *Method*

### *Participants and procedure*

The initial sample consisted of 1,028 members (99 female, 929 male) of a popular online community, selected because it is a forum for discussions about video games and Internet culture. Participants ranged from 18 to 39 years ($M = 24.14$), with 38.4% being married or in a committed relationship.

Participants were asked to respond with respect to a game that was self-selected as their current favorite. As incentive, those completing the survey were entered into a raffle for $100. The survey was linked to the community's online forum for a 2-week period. To control for duplicate responses we crosschecked IP addresses. No duplicates were found.

## *Measures*

Survey measures were delivered in HTML format. All items, aside from demographics, were rated on 7-point scales, with anchors appropriate to each item.

### PLAYER EXPERIENCE OF NEED SATISFACTION (PENS)

The PENS subscales were created for research by Ryan et al. (2006) and further validated in two rounds of confirmatory factor analysis using survey data from 2,000 regular video game players. The PENS subscale for in-game competence (alpha = .70) consisted of three items focused on experiences of competence and mastery (e.g., "I felt competent at the game" and "I felt capable and effective while playing"). In-game autonomy (alpha = .69) was assessed with a four-item subscale measuring perceptions that the game offered meaningful choices and options during play (e.g., "I experienced a lot of freedom in the game" and "The game provides me with interesting options and choices"). Subscale items were averaged to create separate autonomy and competence scores. In-game relatedness, a subscale of the PENS primarily relevant to multiplayer contexts, was not assessed.

### PRESENCE

This nine-item scale, also from the PENS, assessed immersion in the gaming environment. Three items each assessed emotional, physical, and narrative presence. Sample items, respectively, were: "When playing the game I feel as if I am an important participant in the story," "I experience feelings as deeply in the game as I have in real life," and "When moving through the game world I feel as if I am actually there." A total score was created by averaging across the nine items (alpha = .88).

### GAME ENJOYMENT

This was assessed with four items adapted from the Intrinsic Motivation Inventory (McAuley, Duncan, & Tammen, 1989; Ryan, 1982). Sample items included: "I thought the game was boring" (reversed) and "I enjoyed playing the game very much." Items were averaged to create a total score (alpha = .82).

### SEQUEL INTEREST

We assessed future game preference with one item: "I would buy a sequel to this game." *Word of mouth.* We also used a single item to assess how much participants have shared their liking of the game with their friends: "I have recommended this game to others."

460

We both coded the violence content of each game using our own coding system and applied ratings assigned by the Entertainment Software Rating Board (ESRB).

ESRB RATING

The ESRB is a nonprofit group largely funded through the game industry that assigns games one of five ratings: E (everyone), E10+ (everyone 10 or older), T (teen), M (mature), or AO (adults only), which we coded from 1 to 5, respectively. The ESRB categories have been modified slightly over time; we used the most up-to-date ratings for each game. In this sample no AO games were selected, so effectively this created a 1 to 4 scale. From the initial sample, 923 participants selected games that had ESRB ratings and 105 selected games that did not. There were three reasons for this: Some titles were published before 1994, the year the ESRB began reviewing games; some titles were heavily player-modified versions of retail games; and some titles were independently developed and therefore not reviewed by the ESRB. Thus, 105 participants were dropped from analyses, leaving a sample of 85 females and 838 males ($M$ age = 24.17).

VIOLENCE CODING

Three raters coded target games for violent contents. A rating of 1 was assigned to games with no violent content whatsoever (e.g., puzzle games like *Tetris*), a 2 was assigned to games with abstract violence (e.g., *Pokemon* or *Super Mario*), a 3 was assigned to games with impersonal violence (e.g., strategy games like *Starcraft* or *Civilization*), a 4 was assigned to games with fantasy violence (e.g., *World of Warcraft* or *Starfox*), and a 5 was assigned to games with realistic violence (e.g., *God of War 2* or *Grand Theft Auto 3*). To verify reliability, 50 game titles were selected at random and an interrater reliability of .95 was found based on the three raters. Given this high reliability, two of the three raters coded all remaining titles that also had an ESRB rating. Violence content was calculated by averaging rater scores.

## Results

### Preliminary analyses

Of the 923 games included in the analyses, 99 received a rating of everyone, 32 a rating of everyone 10+, 506 a rating of teen, and 286 a rating of mature. No titles received an adults only rating. The mean violence rating was 3.90 ($SD$ = 0.99).

We assessed sex differences on all study variables and game ratings and found three effects. Men selected titles with higher ESRB ratings, $F(1, 921) = 21.24$, $p < .001$, $\eta^2 = .02$ (males $M = 3.10$, females $M = 2.65$); and more violent content, $F(1, 921) = 34.85$, $p < .001$, $\eta^2 = .04$ (males $M = 3.97$, females $M = 3.31$). Women

461

reported greater presence for their games, $F(1, 921) = 5.00, p < .05, \eta^2 = .01$ (males $M = 3.93$, females $M = 4.28$). There were no differences on any of the need satisfaction variables, enjoyment, word of mouth, or sequel interest.

### Primary analyses

To test the central hypotheses we ran correlations (Table 1) followed by two sets of simultaneous multiple regressions. First, we regressed enjoyment, presence, sequel interest, and word of mouth on in-game competence, in-game autonomy, and mature content (ESRB rating), respectively. Second, we ran a parallel analysis using our own violence coding. These results are presented in Table 2. The regression with the ESRB rating shows significant relations of both autonomy and competence with all four outcomes, whereas the content rating predicted unique variance only for presence. Because the ESRB rating is based on sexual contents, mature language, and violence, the second regression using our violence rating tests more exclusively the role of violent content. In this regression, both autonomy and competence showed significant associations with outcomes, whereas violent content related only to presence.

### Brief discussion

Results from Study 1 supported our primary hypotheses. We found that the psychological need satisfactions of autonomy and competence were associated with enjoyment, presence, sequel interest, and word of mouth, over and above both

*Table 1* Correlations between variables of interest (study 1; $n = 923$)

|  | 1 | 2 | 3 | 4 | 5 | 6 | 7 | 8 | 9 |
|---|---|---|---|---|---|---|---|---|---|
| 1 Age | — | | | | | | | | |
| 2 Sex | −.10** | — | | | | | | | |
| 3 Entertainment Software Rating Board (ESRB) rating | −.03 | −.15*** | — | | | | | | |
| 4 Violent content | .01 | −.19*** | .75*** | — | | | | | |
| 5 In-game autonomy | .07* | .06 | .03 | .03 | — | | | | |
| 6 In-game competence | −.04 | .01 | −.01 | −.01 | .33*** | — | | | |
| 7 Game enjoyment | .04 | .01 | .04 | .04 | .48*** | .33*** | — | | |
| 8 Presence | −.03 | .07* | .08* | .08* | .49*** | .28*** | .31*** | — | |
| 9 Word of mouth | .01 | .04 | −.01 | −.03 | .37*** | .33*** | .49*** | .25*** | — |
| 10 Sequel interest | .05 | .06 | .01 | .01 | .31*** | .22*** | .47*** | .24*** | .45*** |

$*p < .05. **p < .01. ***p < .001.$

*Table 2* Simultaneous regressions of relations between game content and in-Game need satisfaction on outcomes of interest (study 1; $n = 923$)

| Dependent Variables | | | Entertainment Software Rating Board (ESRB) $\beta$ | Violence $\beta$ |
|---|---|---|---|---|
| Enjoyment | Step 1 | Sex | −.01 | −.01 |
| | Step 2 | Game content | .03 | .01 |
| $R^2_a = .00, .26$ | | In-game competence | .19*** | .19*** |
| $R^2_b = .00, .26$ | | In-game autonomy | .41*** | .42*** |
| Presence | Step 1 | Sex | −.07* | −.07* |
| | Step 2 | Game content | .07* | .09*** |
| $R^2_a = .01, .26$ | | In-game competence | .14*** | .14*** |
| $R^2_b = .01, .27$ | | In-game autonomy | .44*** | .45*** |
| Word of mouth | Step 1 | Sex | −.04 | −.04 |
| | Step 2 | Game content | −.02 | −.02 |
| $R^2_a = .00, .18$ | | In-game competence | .23*** | .23*** |
| $R^2_b = .00, .18$ | | In-game autonomy | .29*** | .29*** |
| Sequel interest | Step 1 | Sex | −.06 | −.06 |
| | Step 2 | Game content | .01 | −.06 |
| $R^2_a = .00, .25$ | | In-game competence | .14*** | .14*** |
| $R^2_b = .00, .26$ | | In-game autonomy | .26*** | .26*** |

*Note:* $R^2_a$ is variance estimate for each step of regression for violence content as ESRB. $R^2_b$ is variance estimate for each step of regression for violence content as coded by raters. *$p < .05$. ***$p < .001$.

game maturity rating and violence content. Furthermore, the negative relations between violent content and gameplay outcomes suggest that violent content proper might not be a motivating factor across players.

## Study 2

Many popular video games frame gameplay challenges within a violent conceit. For example, by participating in the role of the story's hero, a player might exercise force or commit violent acts against "bad guys" to save the day. Such scenarios offer opportunities for competence feedback and autonomous action, and the actual violent content may be secondary. Yet given that games can vary in the violence depicted, it is reasonable to assume that aggressive persons might differentially prefer or opt in to games offering more violent content.

In Study 2 we engaged players with a violent game in a laboratory setting. As in the Study 1 survey, we predicted players' experience of competence and autonomy during play will significantly account for their enjoyment, immersion, and preference for future engagement. Yet, insofar as dispositional factors impact opt-in behavior, we predicted that differences in trait aggression would account for unique variance in preference for future play for this violent game, over and above variance accounted for by need satisfaction.

## *Method*

### *Participants*

In Study 2, 68 undergraduates (21 male, 47 female) with a mean age of 19.5 years (*SD* = 1.2) reported to a video lab for extra course credit.

### *Target game*

We selected the XBOX version of *House of the Dead III* (HOTD3) because it offered both simple controls and graphically violent gameplay. To progress, participants faced a series of bloody linear reflex-based challenges. Arcade games like HOTD3 are designed for short periods of play, typically 5 to 30 minutes. A 15-minute play period was thus selected to reflect play as it occurs in typical gaming sessions.

### *Measures*

Measures were delivered in HTML format both pre-and postplay. Preplay assessments included an index of trait aggression and filler questions. Post-play assessments included measures of competence, autonomy, presence, enjoyment, and preference for future play. Ingame autonomy, competence, enjoyment, and presence were assessed as in Study 1, with alphas = .71, .73, .87, and .90, respectively.

Trait aggression was assessed with a 29-item trait aggression scale (Buss & Perry, 1992). Participants rated each statement on 7-point scales. The 29 items form four subscales: physical aggression (e.g., "Given enough provocation, I may hit another person"), verbal aggression (e.g., "I can't help getting into arguments with people who disagree with me"), anger (e.g., "I sometimes feel like a pow-der keg ready to explode"), and hostility (e.g., "I sometimes feel that people are laughing at me behind my back"). We collapsed across subscales to compute a total trait aggression score (alpha = .94).

#### PREFERENCE FOR FUTURE PLAY

Preference for future play was assessed with five items, including "Given the chance I would play this game in my free time" and "I would be interested in having my own personal copy of this game." Reliability (alpha) was .92.

## *Results*

### *Preliminary analyses*

There were no age effects and no sex differences for enjoyment, presence, future preference, or trait hostility. Males reported higher competence, $F(1, 65) = 14.14$, $p < .001$, $\eta^2 = .018$ (males $M = 4.59$, females $M = 3.26$); and autonomy, $F(1, 65) = 4.54$, $p < .05$, $\eta^2 = .09$ (males $M = 2.95$, females $M = 2.39$).

*Table 3* Simultaneous regressions of relations between trait aggression and in-game need satisfaction on outcomes of interest (study 2; $n = 68$)

| Dependent Variables | | | $\beta$ |
|---|---|---|---|
| Enjoyment | Step 1 | Sex | −.16 |
| | Step 2 | Trait aggression | .12 |
| | | In-game competence | .54*** |
| $R^2 = .03, .55$ | | In-game autonomy | .37*** |
| Future preference | Step 1 | Sex | −.19 |
| | Step 2 | Trait aggression | .37*** |
| | | In-game competence | .36*** |
| $R^2 = .04, .57$ | | In-game autonomy | .41*** |
| Presence | Step 1 | Sex | −.08 |
| | Step 2 | Trait aggression | −.06 |
| | | In-game competence | .43*** |
| $R^2 = .01, .52$ | | In-game autonomy | .43*** |

***$p < .001$.

## Primary analyses

We expected autonomy and competence to account for unique variance in enjoyment, presence, and preference for future play. Additionally we hypothesized that trait-level aggression might influence opting-in behavior as indexed by preference for future play. Correlations revealed that enjoyment, preference, and presence were each correlated with autonomy ($r$s = .59, .61, .54; $p$s < .001) and competence ($r$s = .63, .50, .53; $p$s < .001).

Trait aggression was significantly correlated with future preference ($r = .46$, $p < .001$) but not enjoyment ($r = .21$, *ns*) or presence ($r = .03$, *ns*). Finally, trait aggression was unrelated to competence ($r = .07$, *ns*), but it was associated with autonomy ($r = .25$, $p < .05$) within this violent game context.

To test our primary hypotheses, we simultaneously regressed enjoyment, preference for future play, and presence onto trait aggression, competence, and autonomy, controlling for sex (see Table 3). Autonomy and competence were related to all outcomes, but trait aggression remained significant only with regards to future preference. Secondary analyses placing sex and trait aggression in the first step of the regressions do not alter the direction, magnitude, or significance of effects in this or any of the other present studies.

## Brief discussion

Study 2 results replicated the relations between in-game need satisfaction and enjoyment, preference, and presence within a violent game context. Furthermore, trait aggression contributed to opting-in behavior: Although those high in aggression did not report greater enjoyment or presence, they did report a stronger preference for playing this violent game in the future.

# Study 3

In Study 3 we utilized two games that differ in violent content to further explore the role of trait aggression in predicting preferences. We hypothesized that player experience of autonomy and competence need satisfaction would predict unique variance in outcomes across violent and nonviolent contents. Yet, in line with Study 2, we expected trait aggression to moderate the relation between condition (violent, nonviolent) and preference for future play.

## *Method*

### *Participants*

For Study 3, 99 students (41 males, 58 females), with a mean age of 20.1 years ($SD = 1.4$), reported to a media lab for extra course credit.

### *Target games*

Participants were randomly assigned to play either a nonviolent or a violent game. We chose the two games to parallel a classic study by Anderson et al. (2004), who used these same titles to contrast violent and nonviolent gameplay. Neither game is currently commercially available, but the respective developers offer each for free download. The nonviolent game, *Glider Pro 4*, belongs to the arcade genre and entails navigating a paper airplane through an obstacle-ridden home. Reflex-based challenges included capitalizing on updrafts to stay aloft and avoiding collisions with furniture and nefarious paper shredders. The violent game, *Marathon 2*, belongs to the first-person shooter (FPS) genre, and much like the target game in Study 2, involves reflex-based challenges framed within a violent conceit.

Questionnaires were administered through hypertext markup language form presented before and after a 20-minute gameplay session.

### *Measures*

We assessed variables of interest exactly as in Study 2. Reliabilities (alpha) in Study 3 were .87 for competence, .85 for autonomy, .89 for enjoyment, .87 for presence, .95 for preference for future play, and .93 for trait aggression.

## *Results*

### *Preliminary results*

We tested for main effects and interactions of age, sex, and condition across variables of interest. Only one effect found was found: Males ($M = 3.38$) reported higher in-game competence than females ($M = 2.49$), $F(1, 98) = 9.99, p < .01, \eta^2 = .09$. It is noteworthy that there was no effect of condition on either autonomy or competence.

*Table 4* Simultaneous regressions of relations between trait aggression and in-game need satisfaction on outcomes of interest within high (HVG) and low (LVG) violence conditions (study 3)

| Dependent Variables | | | LVG (n = 51) β | HVG (n = 48) β |
|---|---|---|---|---|
| Enjoyment | Step 1 | Sex | −.05 | −.13 |
| | Step 2 | Trait aggression | −.08 | .03 |
| | | In-game competence | .39** | .30*** |
| $R^2$= .00, .75, .02, .62 | | In-game autonomy | .53*** | .55*** |
| Future preference | Step 1 | Sex | .04 | −.01 |
| | Step 2 | Trait aggression | −.08 | .13 |
| | | In-game competence | .39** | .27 |
| $R^2$= .00, .75, .00, .51 | | In-game autonomy | .53*** | .46*** |
| Presence | Step 1 | Sex | .06 | .01 |
| | Step 2 | Trait aggression | .14 | .18 |
| | | In-game competence | .04 | .18 |
| $R^2$= .00, .43 .00, .62 | | In-game autonomy | .63*** | .59*** |

**$p < .01$. ***$p < .001$.

*Table 5* The effects of condition on outcomes as moderated by trait aggression (study 3; n = 99)

| Dependent Variables | | | β |
|---|---|---|---|
| Enjoyment | Step 1 | Sex | −.03 |
| | Step 2 | Trait aggression | .01 |
| | | Condition | −.12 |
| $R^2$= .00, .02, .09 | Step 3 | Interaction | 1.29** |
| Future preference | Step 1 | Sex | −.02 |
| | Step 2 | Trait aggression | .13 |
| | | Condition | −.10 |
| $R^2$= .00, .03, .07 | Step 3 | Interaction | .87* |
| Presence | Step 1 | Sex | −.03 |
| | Step 2 | Trait aggression | .24* |
| | | Condition | .05 |
| $R^2$= .00, .06, .10 | Step 3 | Interaction | .89* |

*$p < .05$. **$p < .01$.

### Primary results

We expected that psychological need satisfaction would account for unique variance in preference for future play, and presence. We further hypothesized that condition (violent, nonviolent) would interact with individual differences in aggression in predicting preference for future play. To test these hypotheses we simultaneously regressed enjoyment, preference for future play, and presence onto trait aggression, autonomy, and competence separately for players of each game. Table 4 presents these results. To test the interaction between violent/nonviolent condition and trait aggression we also conducted a series of hierarchical regressions, presented in Table 5.

467

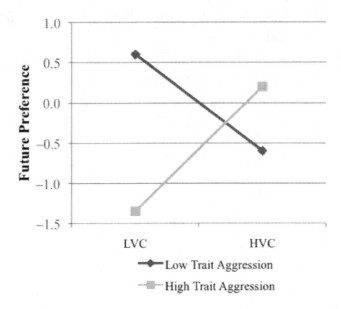

*Figure 1* The effect of condition (low violence/high violence) on future preference as moderated by trait aggression (low/high): Study 3

*Note:* LVC = low violence condition; HVC = high violence condition.

Results supported our first hypotheses that in-game autonomy and competence would be associated with enjoyment, preference for future play, and presence. Besides a modest relation between trait aggression and presence across condition, we did not find any significant main effects for individual differences in aggression on gameplay variables. Trait aggression did, however, interact with game type (violent, nonviolent) in predicting enjoyment, preference for future play, and presence (accounting for 7%, 4%, and 4% unique predictive variance, respectively). Figure 1 depicts this interaction for preference for future play, indicating that players low in trait aggression showed a preference for the nonviolent game, whereas high aggression participants did not show differential ratings across level of violence. The form of all three interactions was similar. Supplementary analysis revealed that when controlling for autonomy and competence satisfactions, these interactions were no longer significant.

### Brief discussion

Findings largely supported our hypotheses. First, players, on average, did not find the violent game to be more enjoyable than the nonviolent one, nor did it foster greater autonomy or competence feelings. In contrast, players' experience of need satisfaction was associated with enjoyment, presence, and preference for future play for both games. A condition by trait aggression interaction revealed that participants low in aggression were less likely to prefer, enjoy, or become immersed in the violent game relative to the nonviolent one.

In Study 3 we followed Anderson et al. (2004), who used these same two games to contrast nonviolent and violent play. Although violent content may have accounted for these observed effects, these two games also differed in a number of other ways. The nonviolent game was an easily mastered arcade game, while the violent game was a more complex and challenging first-person shooter. The structure of the challenges, the control complexity, and other features of these games also varied. A more compelling experiment might control for these potential confounds. Accordingly, in Study 4 we modify a single computer game to manipulate the presentation and narrative framing so as to have both violent and nonviolent versions of the same play format, offering all players the same game challenges.

## Study 4

In Study 4 we again examine the effects of violent contents on enjoyment and the role of dispositional aggression on opting-in behavior for violent games. To this end we modified a commercially available video game so that it offered participants functionally identical challenges and either high or low level of violent content. Unlike Study 3, the structure of gameplay was invariant across the violent and nonviolent conditions, so we did not expect main effects of condition on competence, autonomy, enjoyment, presence, or preference for future play. We did expect condition to interact with trait aggression in predicting preference for future play, but not enjoyment, because in this case, the opportunities for autonomy and competence in play would be the same. Persons high in trait aggression were expected to prefer the high violence version.

### *Method*

#### *Participants and procedure*

In Study 4, 101 students (36 males, 65 females) with a mean age of 19.6 ($SD = 1.3$) reported to a media lab for extra credit. They were provided with instructions and a 20-minute training period to become familiar with the control interface. After the training period, surveys were administered through hypertext markup language. Upon completion of this first set of questionnaires, participants were randomly assigned to either the low or high violence conditions. Following a 20-minute play period, postquestionnaires were administered.

#### *Target game*

For this study we extensively modified a commercially available game, *Half-Life 2* (HL2). By means of a programming toolkit we created three virtual environments; the first was a training ground sequence, designed with the aim of teaching participants the prerequisite skills for successful play. There was no violent content in this environment. Following this, participants were shown a short video appropriate for condition. This 30-second clip provided a short narrative and visuals that framed the upcoming gameplay. Two versions were developed. In both, participants were told that the environment was populated by computer-controlled adversaries. Those assigned to the high violence condition (HVC) were told that these adversaries were intent on doing them harm with firearms and physical attacks, and the player was equipped with a weapon to dispatch these adversaries in a thoroughly bloody manner. Participants in the low violence condition (LVC) were told that adversaries were programmed only to tag them with nonweapon marker. LVC participants were equipped with a marker that teleported their adversaries to "base," first floating them into the air serenely before they appeared to evaporate. Gameplay then ensued, with participants in the HVC playing the bloody version of HL2 and those in the LVC playing the same game as "tag," with gore removed.

## Measures

We assessed variables in the same manner as Studies 1, 2, and 3. Reliabilities (alpha) in Study 4 were .79 for competence, .75 for autonomy, .80 for enjoyment, .85 for presence, .95 for preference for future play, and .91 for trait aggression.

# Results

## Preliminary analyses

As expected, MANOVA revealed no differences between low and high violence conditions on competence, autonomy, enjoyment, preference for future play, or presence. Sex differences were in evidence for autonomy, $F(1, 99) = 34.57$, $p < .001$, $\eta^2 = .26$ (males $M = 5.01$, females $M = 3.50$); competence, $F(1, 99) = 19.79$, $p < .001$, $\eta^2 = .16$ (males $M = 3.79$, females $M = 2.66$); enjoyment, $F(1, 99) = 4.64$, $p < 05$, $\eta^2 = .04$ (males $M = 3.66$, females $M = 3.04$); and preference for future play, $F(1, 99) = 11.94$, $p < .001$, $\eta^2 = .12$ (males $M = 3.90$, females $M = 2.78$); but not for presence or trait aggression.

## Primary analyses

We anticipated replicating our findings from Studies 2 and 3 that competence and autonomy would account for unique variance in enjoyment and presence. Additionally, we anticipated that both trait aggression and need satisfaction would account for unique variance in preference for future play. Results in Table 6 support these hypotheses.

470

Table 6 Simultaneous regressions of relations between trait aggression and in-game need satisfaction on outcomes within high (HVC), low (LVC) violence conditions, and experienced video game players (studies 4 and 5)

| Dependent Variables | | | Study 4 LVC (n = 52) β | Study 4 HVC (n = 49) β | Study 5 (n = 39) β |
|---|---|---|---|---|---|
| Enjoyment | Step 1 | Sex | -.02 | -.38** | N/A |
| Study 4: $R^2_a$ = .00, .31 | Step 2 | Trait aggression | .07 | .07 | -.11 |
| $R^2_b$ = .14, 63 | | In-game competence | .34* | .60*** | .37*** |
| Study 5: $R^2_c$ = .58 | | In-game autonomy | .39* | .29* | .57*** |
| Future preference | Step 1 | Sex | -.23 | -.47** | N/A |
| Study 4: $R^2_a$ = .05, .27 | Step 2 | Trait aggression | .01 | .32** | .04 |
| $R^2_b$ = .22, .55 | | In-game competence | .38* | .36** | .46*** |
| Study 5: $R^2_c$ = .66 | | In-game autonomy | .22 | .21 | .47*** |
| Presence | Step 1 | Sex | -.05 | -.22 | N/A |
| Study 4: $R^2_c$ = .00, .29 | Step 2 | Trait aggression | -.01 | .28* | -.05 |
| $R^2_c$ = .05, .27 | | In-game competence | .59*** | .39* | .01 |
| Study 5: $R^2_c$ = .37 | | In-game autonomy | -.04 | -.03 | .63*** |

Note: R2a are the variance estimates for each step of regression for participants playing low violence game in Study 4. R2b are the variance estimates for each step of regression for participants playing high violence game in Study 4. R2c are the variance estimates for each regression for participants in Study 5.

*p < .05. **p < .01. ***p < .001.

We further postulated that the relation between trait aggression and preference for future play would be moderated by condition. To test this interaction we utilized a hierarchical regression model. Controlling for sex we placed trait aggression and condition in the second step of the regression and their product term in the third step. This yielded a significant moderation accounting for nearly 5% variance in preference for future play over and above the combined contributions of sex, condition, and trait aggression. These results appear in Table 7.

### Brief discussion

Study 4 results generally supported our hypotheses. Across condition, player need satisfaction predicted enjoyment, preference for future play, and presence. Furthermore, we found a unique contribution of trait aggression to preference for future play, but not enjoyment, as in Study 2. When players were presented with functionally identical gameplay, persons high in aggression preferred the high violence condition, whereas persons low in trait aggression preferred the low violence condition. This interaction (Figure 2) lends support to the idea that more aggressive persons may select themselves into games with a violent conceit. Yet when player need satisfaction was controlled for across condition, trait aggression did not interact with violent content level in predicting enjoyment or presence, again suggesting that the violent content per se is not critical to enjoyment, even for those high in aggression.

*Table 7* The effects of condition on outcomes as moderated by trait aggression (studies 4 and 5)

| Dependent Variables | | | Study 4 (n =101) β | Study 5 (n =39) β |
|---|---|---|---|---|
| Enjoyment | Step 1 | Sex | −.21*** | N/A |
| | Step 2 | Trait aggression | .14 | .34* |
| Study 4: $R^2_a$= .04, .06, .07 | | Condition | .01 | −.12 |
| Study 5: $R^2_b$ = .09, .20 | Step 3 | Interaction | .34 | .36* |
| Future preference | Step 1 | Sex | −.35*** | N/A |
| | Step 2 | Trait aggression | .23** | .39* |
| Study 4: $R^2_a$= .12, .18, .23 | | Condition | .11 | −.14 |
| Study 5: $R^2_b$ = .16, .29 | Step 3 | Interaction | .72** | .37* |
| Presence | Step 1 | Sex | −.13 | N/A |
| | Step 2 | Trait aggression | .20 | .32 |
| Study 4: $R^2_a$= .02, .06, .08 | | Condition | .02 | −.04 |
| Study 5: $R^2_b$ = .10, .15 | Step 3 | Interaction | .58 | .23 |

*Note:* $R^2_a$ are the variance estimates for each step regression for participants in Study 4. $R^2_b$ are the variance estimates for each step regression for participants in Study 5.

*p* < .05. **p* < .01. ***p* < .001.

472

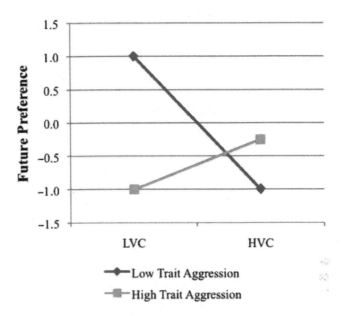

*Figure 2* The effect of condition (low violence/high violence) on future preference as moderated by trait aggression (low/high): Study 4

*Note:* LVC = low violence condition; HVC = high violence condition.

## Study 5

In Study 5 we extend the external validity of our previous findings by examining the effects of violent content and dispositional aggression on enjoyment and opting-in behavior in a population of avid video game players. Specifically, we recruited young males who spend a significant amount of time playing video games.

As in Study 4, the structure of gameplay was invariant across low and high violence conditions. What was manipulated was the level of gore and blood. In line with SDT we predicted main effects for competence and autonomy on enjoyment, preference, and presence. We did not, however, expect condition to account for variance in need satisfactions or in players' enjoyment, preference, or presence. Finally, we expected that trait aggression would interact with the level of violent content in predicting opting-in behavior.

### *Method*

#### *Participants and procedure*

For Study 5, 39 students, mean age of 19.54 (*SD*= 0.97), reported to a media lab for extra credit. Enrollment was limited to males who regularly spent more than

5 hours per week in video game play. Participants reported an average of 7.47 ($SD$ = 5.60) hours a week of play and 11.23 ($SD$ = 2.77) years of past video game play. The procedure and measures of Study 5 followed those of Study 2 exactly except that the game's settings were modified to present either low or high levels of graphic violence.

### Target game and violence conditions

As in Study 2 we used the *HOTD3* arcade game. Participants were randomly assigned to play the game with a low level of graphic violence (no blood, neon green wounds on enemies) or a high level of graphic violence (gratuitous blood, realistic red wounds on enemies).

### Measures

We assessed variables exactly as in Study 2. Reliabilities (alphas) ranged from .86 to .94.

### Results

As expected, MANOVA revealed no significant differences of condition on assessments of competence, autonomy, enjoyment, preference for future play, or presence. This suggests that the added violence did not enhance player experiences.

We further predicted that gameplay competence and autonomy would be associated with enjoyment, preference, and presence and that trait-level aggression would account for variance in preference. To test these hypotheses we simultaneously regressed each dependent variable onto competence, autonomy, and trait aggression. As shown in Table 6, need satisfaction was a consistent predictor of outcomes. Although trait aggression and future preference were correlated ($r$ = .38, $p$ < .05) in the way expected, trait aggression did not account for unique variance in preference. We also expected that the relation between trait aggression and preference for future play would be moderated by condition. To test this we followed the same procedure outlined in Study 4. Results from these moderation analyses (see Table 7) reveal that trait aggression and condition did interact to account for 11% more variance in enjoyment and 13% more variance in preference as expected. The interaction plots follow the pattern of Figures 1 and 2. As in Study 3 these interactions were no longer significant when controlling for need satisfactions.

### Brief discussion

The results mirrored findings from Study 4 and expanded their applicability to avid male video game players. In these players, psychological need satisfaction remained a robust predictor of enjoyment, preference, and immersion, and level of violence did not by itself enhance enjoyment. Instead, as was the case for more novice players, violent content interacted with individual differences in aggression in predicting the attractiveness of the game.

# Study 6

Informed by experimental results, we returned to a survey design to test the role dispositional aggression might play in accounting for game outcomes and value for play in a diverse sample of regular video game players. As in the previous studies we anticipated that need satisfaction would predict substantial variance in game enjoyment, presence, word of mouth, and sequel interest. Second, mirroring experimental findings, we expected that ESRB rating (reflecting sexual and violent material) and our separate rating of violent content would both interact with trait aggression in predicting participants' appraisal of a game's value but, as in Study 4, not enjoyment or presence.

## *Method*

### *Participants and procedure*

Participants were 1,642 (195 female, 1,447 male) persons ranging in age from 18 to 43 ($M = 23.9$; $SD = 4.09$), recruited from the same online community sampled in Study 1. Participants were asked to respond to the survey with respect to their current favorite game. As incentive, they were entered into a raffle to win a cash prize, as in Study 1.

### *Target game ratings*

Of the 1,642 titles endorsed by participants, 1,548 had an ESRB rating. Of these, 269 titles received a rating of everyone, 38 a rating of everyone 10+, 775 a rating of teen, and 466 a rating of mature. No titles received a rating of adults only. Two trained coders also rated each game for violent content using the 1 to 5 scale described in Study 1; the mean violence rating was 3.49 ($SD = 1.30$). For the same reasons specified in Study 1, 94 titles did not have ratings. This left 187 females and 1,361 males ($M$ age $= 24.02$, $SD = 4.15$) in this sample.

### *Measures*

We assessed variables in the same manner as Study 1. Reliabilities (alpha) for Study 6 were .68 for competence, .73 for autonomy, .80 for enjoyment, .78 for presence, and .95 for trait aggression. As in Study 1, sequel interest and word of mouth were each assessed with one item.

GAME VALUE

To assess perceptions of their target game's value, participants rated the statement "The game was worth its price" on a 7-point scale.

## Results

### Preliminary analyses

Similar to Study 1, female participants were older, $F(1, 1546) = 8.92$, $p < .01$, $\eta^2 = .01$ (males $M = 24.87$, females $M = 23.91$); reported higher levels of in-game autonomy, $F(1, 1546) = 7.52$, $p < .01$, $\eta^2 = .01$ (males $M = 4.86$, females $M = 5.11$); enjoyment, $F(1, 1546) = 9.59$, $p < .01$, $\eta^2 = .01$ (males $M = 6.05$, females $M = 6.26$); presence, $F(1, 1546) = 23.80$, $p < .001$, $\eta^2 = .02$ (males $M = 2.78$, females $M = 3.22$); and sequel interest, $F(1, 1546) = 8.34$, $p < .01$, $\eta^2 = .01$ (males $M = 5.74$, females $M = 6.09$). Females also reported lower trait aggression, $F(1, 1546) = 9.43$, $p < .01$, $\eta^2 = .01$ (males $M = 3.40$, females $M = 3.10$); and they selected games with lower ESRB ratings, $F(1, 1546) = 16.16$, $p < .001$, $\eta^2 = .01$ (males $M = 2.13$, females $M = 1.89$); and less violent content, $F(1, 1546) = 14.46$, $p < .001$, $\eta^2 = .01$ (males $M = 3.53$, females $M = 3.21$).

### Primary analyses

To test the relations between motivation, aggression, and outcomes we obtained both correlations (Table 8), and we performed hierarchical simultaneous regressions (Tables 9 and 10). First, correlations show positive relations of in-game need satisfaction with all outcomes of note and also, unlike Study 1, positive relations of violent content with autonomy, presence, and value. Next, controlling for sex, we regressed enjoyment, presence, word of mouth, and game value onto rating, ESRB, competence, and autonomy. Second, we regressed enjoyment, presence, word of mouth, and sequel interest onto presence/absence of violence, competence, and autonomy (see Table 9). Competence and autonomy experiences related strongly and positively to outcomes. ESRB and violent content ratings were positively related only to presence, and violent content showed weak but significant negative relations to enjoyment, word of mouth, and sequel interest.

Tests for interactions between dispositional aggression and violent content on outcomes are reported in Table 10. Only the interaction involving game value was significant (Figures 3 and 4), showing that those higher in aggression reported more value for games that were violent.

### Brief discussion

Results largely followed the pattern from previous studies. Violent content added little, and in some cases detracted from, motivation and enjoyment once accounting for gameplay autonomy and competence. In addition, although accounting for only a small portion of variance, interactions suggested that trait aggression enhances the preference for and valuation of more violent games, but not enjoyment or presence.

Table 8 Correlations between variables of interest (study 6; n= 1,548)

| | 1 | 2 | 3 | 4 | 5 | 6 | 7 | 8 | 9 | 10 |
|---|---|---|---|---|---|---|---|---|---|---|
| 1 Sex | — | | | | | | | | | |
| 2 Trait aggression | -.08** | — | | | | | | | | |
| 3 Entertainment Software Rating Board rating | -.11*** | .05 | — | | | | | | | |
| 4 Violent content | -.11*** | .04 | .72*** | — | | | | | | |
| 5 In-game autonomy | -.01 | .05 | .10*** | .15*** | — | | | | | |
| 6 In-game competence | .07* | .03 | .00 | .03 | .39*** | — | | | | |
| 7 Game enjoyment | .08** | -.01 | .04 | -.04 | .40*** | .35*** | — | | | |
| 8 Presence | .12*** | .06 | .11*** | .10*** | .42*** | .25*** | .15*** | — | | |
| 9 Sequel interest | .08** | .05 | .05 | -.01 | .36*** | .34*** | .50*** | .21*** | — | |
| 10 Word of mouth | .03* | .04 | .03 | -.02 | .29*** | .30*** | .46*** | .20*** | .47*** | — |
| 11 Game value | -.02 | .05 | .09** | .10** | .34*** | .23*** | .29*** | .29*** | .34*** | .35*** |

*p < .05. **p < .01. ***p < .001.

*Table 9* Simultaneous regressions of relations between game content (Entertainment Software Rating Board [ESRB] and Violence Ratings) and in-game need satisfaction on outcomes (study 6; $n = 1,548$)

| Dependent Variables | | | ESRB $\beta$ | Violence $\beta$ |
|---|---|---|---|---|
| Enjoyment | Step 1 | Sex | .08** | .08** |
| | Step 2 | Game content | .02 | −.10*** |
| $R^2_a = .01, .21$ | | In-game competence | .27*** | .27*** |
| $R^2_b = .01, .23$ | | In-game autonomy | .30*** | .30*** |
| Presence | Step 1 | Sex | .12*** | .11*** |
| | Step 2 | Game content · | .09*** | .05* |
| $R^2_a = .02, .20$ | | In-game competence | .16*** | .12*** |
| $R^2_b = .02, .21$ | | In-game autonomy | .36*** | .37*** |
| Word of mouth | Step 1 | Sex | .03 | .03 |
| | Step 2 | Game content | .02 | −.05* |
| $R^2_a = .00, .18$ | | In-game competence | .24*** | .26*** |
| $R^2_b = .00, .18$ | | In-game autonomy | .26*** | .26*** |
| Sequel interest | Step 1 | Sex | .08** | .08** |
| | Step 2 | Game content | .02 | −.04 |
| $R^2_a = .02, .17$ | | In-game competence | .22*** | .23*** |
| $R^2_b = .02, .20$ | | In-game autonomy | .20*** | .21*** |
| Game value | Step 1 | Sex | −.02 | −.02 |
| | Step 2 | Game content | .00 | .02 |
| $R^2_a = .00, .18$ | | In-game competence | .26*** | .11*** |
| $R^2_b = 01, .15$ | | In-game autonomy | .25*** | .33*** |

*Note:* $R^2_a$ is variance estimate for each step of regression for violence content as ESRB. $R^2_b$ is variance estimate for each step of regression for violence content as coded by expert raters. *$p < .05$. **$p < .01$. ***$p < .001$

## General discussion

Violence in video games is a controversial topic and a subject of strong debate among researchers. Most of the controversy surrounds the benefits versus hazards of gameplay and especially whether exposure to violent games causes aggressive behavior (e.g., Anderson, 2004; Funk, Baldacci, Pasold, & Baumgardner, 2003). In this series of studies we asked a different question, namely, whether the inclusion of violence and gore in video games adds to enjoyment or preference and if so, for whom. Six studies utilized the framework of self-determination theory to examine the contribution that violent game content makes to motivation, independent of the contributions of in-game psychological need satisfactions for competence and autonomy.

Results of the studies revealed consistently robust relations between players' experience of psychological need satisfaction and enjoyment, presence, preference for future play, word of mouth, and game value, supporting the general tenets of cognitive evaluation theory (Deci & Ryan, 1985). The findings also suggested that violent video game content adds little or no unique predictive variance to

*Table 10* The effects of game content on outcomes as moderated by trait aggression (study 6; $n = 1{,}548$)

| Dependent Variables | | | Entertainment Software Rating Board (ESRB) β | Violence β |
|---|---|---|---|---|
| Enjoyment | Step 1 | Sex | .08** | .08** |
| | Step 2 | Trait aggression | .00 | −.09 |
| $R^2_a$ = .01, .01, .01 | | Game content | .05 | −.05 |
| $R^2_b$ = .01, .01, .01 | Step 3 | Interaction | .01 | .08 |
| Presence | Step 1 | Sex | .12*** | .12*** |
| | Step 2 | Trait aggression | .07** | .09*** |
| $R^2_a$ = .02, .04, .04 | | Game content | .12*** | .06* |
| $R^2_b$ = .02, .04, .04 | Step 3 | Interaction | −.06 | −.07 |
| Word of mouth | Step 1 | Sex | .03 | .03 |
| | Step 2 | Trait aggression | .05* | −.02 |
| $R^2_a$ = .00, .01, .01 | | Game content | .05* | −.01 |
| $R^2_b$ = .00, .00, .00 | Step 3 | Interaction | −.11 | −.06 |
| Sequel interest | Step 1 | Sex | .08** | .08** |
| | Step 2 | Trait aggression | .05 | .01 |
| $R^2_a$ = .01, .01, .01 | | Game content | .04 | .08 |
| $R^2_b$ = .01, .01, .01 | Step 3 | Interaction | −.18 | −.07 |
| Game value | Step 1 | Sex | −.02 | −.02 |
| | Step 2 | Trait aggression | .02 | .07 |
| $R^2_a$ = .00, .00, .01 | | Game content | .03 | .06 |
| $R^2_b$ = .00, .00, .01 | Step 3 | Interaction | .33** | .20* |

*Note*: $R^2_a$ is variance estimate for each step of regression for violence content as ESRB. $R^2_b$ is variance estimate for each step of regression for violence content as coded by expert raters. *$p < .05$. **$p < .01$. ***$p < .001$.

player enjoyment or preferences. Violent game content interacted, however, with individual differences in aggression to account for opting-in behaviors, as indicated by future preference and game value ratings. Persons high in aggression did not consistently enjoy violent games more than nonviolent ones, but they did have a stronger preference and value for them.

More specifically, in Study 1 we assessed an online sample of persons who are regularly engaged in video games to look for a connection between violent content and player enjoyment. Overall, we did not find any relation between game enjoyability and violent contents. In fact, when controlling for psychological need satisfaction, violent content was weakly negatively related to game enjoyment, presence, word of mouth, and sequel interest. Study 2 introduced dispositional aggression as a factor that might be related to interest in violent video games. When participants were exposed to a violent video game, psychological need satisfaction accounted for a large share of game enjoyment, presence, and preference for future play. In this study, trait aggression accounted for unique predictive variance in preference for future play but not enjoyment or presence, suggesting that individual differences in aggression might influence opting-in behavior. Studies 3

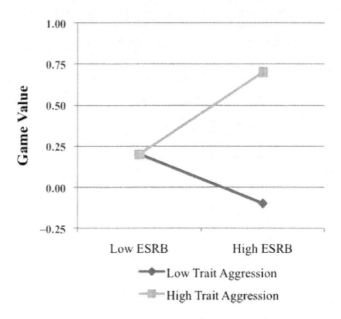

*Figure 3* The effect of game rating (Entertainment Software Rating Board) on game value as moderated by trait aggression (low/high): Study 6

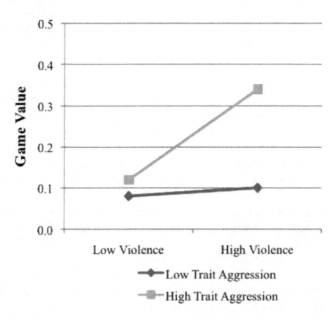

*Figure 4* The effect of game violence level on game value as moderated by trait aggression (low/high): Study 6

and 4 further examined the role of individual differences in aggression in relation to violent game content. In Study 3, trait aggression moderated the effects of
violent versus nonviolent conditions on future preference, enjoyment, and immersion. However, in Study 3 we used two different games that had been used in a
classic study by Anderson et al. (2004) to represent these violent and nonviolent
conditions, which may have introduced potential confounds. Thus, in Study 4 we
addressed these potential confounds by presenting participants with structurally
equivalent gameplay within which we experimentally manipulated the level of
violence. In this better controlled study we found a crossover interaction, with
participants high in trait aggression showing more preference for future play with
the violent version but not more enjoyment or presence, results that were more
consistent with findings from Studies 1 and 2. In Study 5, we expanded the generalizability of our findings by sampling young males who were frequent players,
again showing main effects for need satisfaction, no main effects for violent content, and interactions suggesting higher violent game preference and enjoyment
for those high in aggression. In Study 6 we returned to an online sample and again
found evidence of an association between aggressive traits and value for violent
games but no effect on enjoyment. In sum, violence in games did not generally
add to enjoyment or presence, and on average, violent contents were not more
preferred by players, either in the lab or in field studies of regular gamers. Persons
high in trait aggression did, however, report a greater preference for violent
games in future play, but they did not reliably enjoy violent games more than
nonviolent ones or find them more immersive. Moreover, this interaction between
trait aggression and preferences or enjoyment disappeared when we controlled for
autonomy and competence, suggesting that trait aggressive persons may simply
experience more choice/freedom or effectiveness in a more violent game scenario.

We were also interested in whether violent content was correlated with greater
feelings of competence or autonomy, which would suggest the special potential
of such contents to fulfill these psychological needs. Those relations were not
significant in Studies 1, 3, 4, and 5 where it was relevant to test them. In Study 6,
however, violence ratings were mildly but significantly associated with more
autonomy, both for our rating and that from ESRB. Further inspection of this
relation suggested it was due largely to the popular massively multiplayer online
(MMO) *World of Warcraft*, which received both a high violence rating and was
perceived as allowing a lot of autonomy. Like *Grand Theft Auto* mentioned earlier, *World of Warcraft* affords a wide range of in-game choices, areas to explore,
and different ways to play. Yet because it entails combat with animated human
characters it rates as high violence on both ESRB and our coding systems. When
this title was removed, the correlation of violence and autonomy was no longer
in evidence.

It thus appears that although violent or gory games can offer challenges and
options that foster autonomy and competence, so can equally option-laden and
competence-challenging nonviolent games. At the same time, we did detect a
weak effect for more mature or violent games to engender feelings of presence,

481

suggesting that such contents can at times pull players into somewhat greater immersion in the game experience.

In these studies we also identified a subgroup of high trait aggressive players that were more likely to prefer violent contents. This finding suggests that there may be individual differences associated with consumption of violent games. Yet as Huesmann et al. (2003) suggested, it is also likely that early exposure to violent media can lead to greater propensities for aggression, both virtual and real world. Thus, both traits and environments are relevant, and one limitation in our studies is we did not collect histories of media consumption or exposure. Future studies might explore this and other potential moderators of responses to violent contents, such as cultural norms, mindfulness, sensation seeking, past exposure to interpersonal or family violence, and other constructs of interest.

There were other limitations to the present studies. First, participants in all six studies were from North America and Europe, and thus results may not generalize to game consumers around the globe. Given the popularity of video games in East Asian cultures, and the fact they are often played in public arcade or club contexts, inclusion of such samples would be timely. Second, we relied on self-report measures of need satisfaction, enjoyment, game value, and other variables. Behavioral measures (e.g., tracking purchases and choices over time) would supplement these findings. Third, in some studies we used ratings provided by the ESRB to quantify violent contents, alongside our own rating scheme. Parental groups and researchers have expressed reservations about the validity of the ESRB categories (Thompson, Tepichin, & Haninger, 2006). Future studies might want to examine more exactingly how violence is depicted in games as an influence on a variety of outcomes. Researchers might also assess players' violent feelings while playing and their associations with outcomes.

The present studies explored the role of violent content in motivating video game play. Although many people, including many game developers and popular commentators, assume that violence motivates players or adds to video game enjoyment, our findings do not support that intuition. Instead, they suggest that video games are enjoyable, immersive, and motivating insofar as they offer opportunities for psychological need satisfaction, specifically experiences of competence and autonomy, to which violent content per se is largely unrelated. Although violent game contents did little to add to or detract from outcomes when other need satisfactions were considered, violent contents were more preferred by persons high in trait aggression. This suggests that even if violence may not be important to game enjoyment or popularity for most people, and may even turn off those low in aggression, there may be a subgroup of high aggressive persons particularly prone to their consumption. There are important implications of these findings for game developers and consumers, especially as they point toward wider opportunities to satisfy needs in less violent-oriented contexts. These results also suggest that aggression per se is not intrinsically motivating or associated with the satisfaction of basic psychological needs, findings that should be further examined both within and outside the domain of virtual activities.

# Note

We would like to extend our thanks to Netta Weinstein and the Rochester Motivation Research Group for their inputs and guidance. This research was supported in part by a grant from the National Institute on Drug Abuse (R21-DA024262, NIH/NIDA).

# References

Anderson, C. A. (2004). An update on the effects of violent video games. *Journal of Adolescence, 27*, 113–122.

Anderson, C. A., Carnagey, N. L., Flanagan, M., Benjamin, A. J., Eubanks, J., & Valentine, J. C. (2004). Violent video games: Specific effects of violent content on aggressive thoughts and behavior. *Advances in Experimental Social Psychology, 36*, 199–249.

Bartholow, B. D., Bushman, B. J., & Sestir, M. A. (2006). Chronic violent video game exposure and desensitization to violence: Behavioral and event-related brain potential data. *Journal of Experimental Social Psychology, 42*, 532–539.

Bartle, R. A. (2004). *Designing virtual worlds*. Berkeley, CA: New Riders.

Blumler, J., & Katz, E. (1974). *The uses of mass communications*. Beverly Hills, CA: Sage.

Bushman, B. J., & Geen, R. G. (1990). Role of cognitive-emotional mediators and individual differences in the effects of media violence on aggression. *Journal of Personality and Social Psychology, 58*, 156–163.

Buss, A. H., & Perry, M. P. (1992). The aggression questionnaire. *Journal of Personality and Social Psychology, 63*, 452–459.

Deci, E. L., Koestner, R., & Ryan, R. M. (1999). A meta-analytic review of experiments examining the effects of extrinsic rewards on intrinsic motivation. *Psychological Bulletin, 125*, 627–668.

Deci, E. L., & Ryan, R. M. (1980). The empirical exploration of intrinsic motivational processes. In L. Berkowitz (Ed.), *Advances in experimental social psychology* (Vol. 13, pp. 39–80). San Diego, CA: Academic Press.

Deci, E. L., & Ryan, R. M. (1985). *Intrinsic motivation and self-determination in human behavior*. New York: Plenum.

Frederick, C. M., & Ryan, R. M. (1995). Self-determination in sport: A review using cognitive evaluation theory. *International Journal of Sport Psychology, 26*, 5–23.

Freud, S. (1915). Instincts and their vicissitudes. In J. Strachey (Trans. & Gen. Ed.), *The standard edition of the complete psychological works of Sigmund Freud* (Vol. 14, pp. 111–140). London: Hogarth Press.

Funk, J. B., Baldacci, H., Pasold, T., & Baumgardner, J. (2003). Violence exposure in real-life, video games, television, movies and the Internet: Is there desensitization? *Journal of Adolescence, 27*, 23–29.

Huesmann, L., Moise, J., Podolski, C., & Eron, L. (2003). Longitudinal relations between children's exposure to TV violence and their aggressive and violent behavior in young adulthood: 1977–1992. *Developmental Psychology, 39*, 201–221.

Johnston, D. D. (1995). Adolescents' motivation for viewing graphic horror. *Human Communication Research, 21*, 522–552.

Jones, G. (2002). *Killing monsters: Why children need fantasy, superheroes, and make-believe violence*. New York: Basic Books.

Kirsch, S. J. (2006). *Children, adolescents, and media violence*. Thousand Oaks, CA: Sage.

McAuley, E., Duncan, T., & Tammen, V. V. (1989). Psychometric properties of the Intrinsic Motivation Inventory in a competitive sport setting: A confirmatory factor analysis. *Research Quarterly for Exercise and Sport, 60*, 48–58.

McCarthy, D., Curran, S., & Byron S. (2005). *The art of producing games.* Boston: Muska & Lipman.

Ryan, R. M. (1982). Control and information in the intrapersonal sphere: An extension of cognitive evaluation theory. *Journal of Personality and Social Psychology, 43*, 450–461.

Ryan, R. M., & Deci, E. L. (2000a). Intrinsic and extrinsic motivations: Classic definitions and new directions. *Contemporary Educational Psychology, 25*, 54–67.

Ryan, R. M., & Deci, E. L. (2000b). Self-determination theory and the facilitation of intrinsic motivation, social development, and well-being. *American Psychologist, 55*, 68–78.

Ryan, R. M., & Deci, E. L. (2007). Active human nature: Self-determination theory and the promotion and maintenance of sport, exercise, and health. In M. S. Hagger & N. L. D. Chatzisarantis (Eds.), *Self-determination in sport and exercise* (pp. 1–19). New York: Human Kinetics.

Ryan, R. M., Rigby, C. S., & Przybylski, A. (2006). The motivational pull of video games: A self-determination theory approach. *Motivation and Emotion, 30*, 347–364.

Schneider, E. F., Lang, A., Shin, M., & Bradley, S. D. (2004). Death with a story: How story impacts emotional, motivational, and physiological responses to first-person shooter video games. *Human Communication Research, 30*, 361–375.

Sherry, J. L., Lucas, K., Greenberg, B., & Lachlan, K. (2006). Video game uses and gratifications as predictors of use and game preference. In P. Vorderer & J. Bryant (Eds.), *Playing computer games: Motives, responses and consequences* (pp. 213–224). Mahwah, NJ: Lawrence Erlbaum.

Thompson, K. M., Tepichin, K., & Haninger, K. (2006). Content and ratings of mature-rated video games. *Archives of Pediatrics and Adolescent Medicine, 160*, 402–410.

Walkerdine, V. (2007). *Children, gender, video games.* New York: Palgrave Macmillan.

Yi, M. (2004, December 18). They got game: Stacks of new releases for hungry video enthusiasts mean its boom time for an industry now even bigger than Hollywood. *San Francisco Chronicle*, p. A1.

Zillman, D. (1998). The psychology of the appeal of portrayals of violence. In J. Goldstein (Ed.), *Why we watch: The attractions of violent entertainment* (pp. 179–211). New York: Oxford University Press.